FROM VINLAND TO MARS

ABOUT THE AUTHOR

RICHARD S. LEWIS, former editor of *The Bulletin of the Atomic Scientists*, has been science editor of the *Chicago Sun-Times* and city editor of the *Indianapolis Times*. One of the best-known science writers in the country, he is the author of numerous books, among them *The Other Child, A Continent for Science, Appointment on the Moon*, and *The Voyages of Apollo*, which was nominated for the National Book Award in science in 1974. His most recent book is *The Other Child Grows Up*.

FROM VINLAND TO MARS

A Thousand Years of Exploration

RICHARD S. LEWIS

QUADRANGLE BOOKS

Published by Quadrangle/ The New York Times Book Co.

Maps on pages 22 and 48–49 drawn by Kay Jambois. Maps on pages 27 and 34 reproduced by permission of Northwestern University Press from *Magellan's Voyage Around the World— Three Contemporary Accounts,* edited by Charles E. Nowell, Evanston, 1962. Map on pages 48–49 adapted from *So Noble a Captain* by Charles McKew Parr, copyright © 1953 by Charles McKew Parr, with permission of Thomas Y. Crowell Company, Inc. The fossil pictures on pages 104–105 reproduced courtesy of Dr. Edwin H. Colbert.

First Quadrangle paperback edition, 1978

Quadrangle Books are published by Quadrangle/The New York Times Book Co., Inc., Three Park Avenue, New York, N.Y. 10016.

Library of Congress Cataloging in Publication Data

Lewis, Richard S., 1916-
   From Vinland to Mars.

   Includes bibliographical references and index.
   1. Astronautics—History. 2. Planets—Exploration.
3. Discoveries (in geography) I. Title.
TL788.5.L48   629.4'09   76-9716
ISBN 0-8129-6297-4

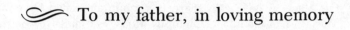 To my father, in loving memory

On Mars, as on Earth, there is a mountain called Olympus. The Martian mountain, Olympus Mons, is a massive volcano, the largest yet discovered in the solar system. In the Greek pantheon of the bronze age, Mount Olympus in Thessaly was the home of the gods. On Mars, Olympus II is also a symbol of man's search for genesis. The search has turned from myth and mysticism to science in the space age. But in all the ages of man, it has been, and is, the greatest adventure.

R.S.L.

CONTENTS

Introduction   xi

I RECONNAISSANCE OF THE EARTH

I. Vinland   3

985–1026   Eric the Red banished from Iceland. Leads colonists to Greenland. Leif finds Vinland the Good. Lumber and
mild winters attract colonists. Strife and murder break out.
Leif's half sister, Freydis, massacres the women. Indians attack. Norse attempts at settlement abandoned.

II. The Passage   25

1459–1580   Ptolemy's geography rediscovered and imitated.
Marco Polo finds Indian Ocean open. Portuguese sail around
Africa. Exclusive Portuguese empire arises in Indian Ocean.
Columbus seeks a competitive route to the Indies for Spain.
Magellan sets sail a generation later on a similar mission, finds
the "southwest passage." Vastness of the Pacific Ocean re-
vealed. Drake seeks the fabled southern continent, Terra
Australis Nondam Cognita, in one hemisphere, Northwest
Passage in the other. The world is encompassed.

III. Terra Australis   67

1768–1970   Cook sails under secret orders to find Southern
Continent. Also seeks Northwest Passage. Antarctica peninsula
sighted in 1820. Ross enters the great Pacific embayment of
the antarctic ice cap to locate the south magnetic pole. Wilkes
sights East Antarctica. Nature of the region called the most important geographic problem of the age. The heroic period of
antarctic exploration opens. Amundsen reaches the south pole;

Scott perishes. Scientific investigation begins. Antarctica becomes the key to geophysical problems. Reptile fossils prove continental drift.

II ANOTHER SEA

IV.   The Enterprise of the Moon   111

1932–1961   Dreams of interplanetary travel motivate early rocket development. The rocket becomes a stragetic weapon with the V-2. Russia leads in post-World War II development. Sputnik shocks America. A missile gap charged. NASA is created to centralize space activity. Yuri Gagarin orbits the Earth. Soviet space successes dim America's technological image, impel the Kennedy administration to take a bold step—a manned lunar landing.

V.   Genesis   155

1961–1968   Naval doctrine cited as a rationale for space power. Project Mercury begins. America's first true space rocket, the Saturn 1, is tested, opening the way to the Moon. NASA begins to overtake the Soviets in Project Gemini. Escalating costs of Project Apollo trigger national debate. New records set in Gemini. Soviets launch the Zond series of circumlunar flights. NASA accelerates pace to be first on the moon. *Apollo VIII* flies to lunar orbit. A new vision of Earth is revealed.

VI.   Victory and Retreat   195

1968–1972   The risks of *Apollo VIII*. Komarov perishes in Soyuz crash. Saturn 5 flight test reveals "pogo" problem. *Apollo IX* tests the lunar module in Earth orbit, and *Apollo X* tests it in Moon orbit. *Apollo XI*—the giant step. With the Moon race won, Washington cuts the space program. The fabulous space task group report. Landing in Oceanus Procellarum. *Apollo XIII* debacle. Fra Mauro and the golf ball experiment. Soviets keep cosmonauts in Earth orbit. Americans begin retreat from the Moon.

VII. Détente   234

1972–1975   A new era of space cooperation dawns. Skylab launched. Repairmen in orbit. New solar corona structure is seen. Astronauts photograph a comet in space. Man's adaptation to months in space is charted; trip to Mars appears physiologically feasible. Salyut, the Russian space station, flies. Europe to build Spacelab as prime Shuttle payload. The Shuttle takes shape, making Apollo obsolete. Détente in orbit—the Apollo-Soyuz Test Project.

III THE NEW WORLDS

VIII. The Search for Creation   287

1969–1975   The Apollonian period of lunar exploration raises new questions—about the Moon, Earth, and solar system. Glowing seas on a melted Moon. Catastrophic bombardment. The Jupiter connection. Mysterious magnetized rocks. The mountains and the rille. Imbrium dated. The most ancient rocks. Conflicting theories of origin persist. Where the moon fits in the solar system. Evidence of variable sun. Implications for Antarctica and Greenland. The next port of call.

IX. The Liquid Planet   317

1970–1975   The Grand Tour project. TOPS. Outer planet survey reduced to Pioneer-class spacecraft reconnaissance. *Pioneers X* and *XI* launched to Jupiter. Perils of the journey cited: the Asteroid Belt; the Jovian magnetosphere. Through the Asteroid Belt without a near-miss. Pioneer "zapped" by Jove's thunderbolts. Encounter with Jupiter. Maria seen on Ganymede. The Io flux tube. Nature of the Red Spot. A star that never made it.

X.   Viking   351

1964–1976   The peculiar history of Mars. Early conceptions of a dying civilization. Canals. *Mariner IV* finds a cratered landscape. Soviet Mars reconnaissance. American and Russian excursions to Venus. Nature of Venus and early speculations. Photos. *Mariner IX* in Mars orbit. A Martian ice age. *Mariner X* reconnoiters Venus and Mercury. The Mercurian synthesis of planetary evolution. Mars landers launched by USSR fail. The argon clue to a denser atmosphere. Rivers, streams, and ice caps. Water vapor discovered. Two Viking orbiters/landers launched. A Martian cactus? The search for life.

Notes   407

Index   427

INTRODUCTION

How do we account for the space age?

Is it the inevitable consequence of technoscientific evolution and development? Does it express some innate, biological compulsion driving man to seek his fate among the stars? Or is it an anomaly, an excursion, a digression from the main stream of human concerns, brought about by the politics of the Cold War?

In terms of chemical evolution, it can be said that man is, after all, descended from stars. Is he attempting to return to them in an effort to discern the processes of creation? It is a romantic thought. The reality is that we do not know how to reach any star beyond our own. The idea seems quite impossible. But then, so did the prospect of landing men on the Moon only a generation ago. We do not know what is impossible.

Having reported major events of the space age since it began, I believe that it can be defined reasonably as the modern extension of a process of exploration that began a thousand years ago with the Norse voyages to Greenland and to North America. The Age of Discovery in the late Renaissance, the reconnaissance of the planet that followed, polar exploration in the early part of this century, and space exploration in the last two decades—all are part of this continuum.

In each period—medieval, Renaissance, and modern—the Western view of the Earth and of man's relation to it has undergone change. Columbus and Magellan transformed the narrow, Ptolemaic horizon of the second century to its true, global dimension. Drake and Cook completed the reconnaissance of the world ocean. Polar exploration opened windows to climatic oscillations and the drift of continents. From the landings on the moon and the soundings of the planets emerge new concepts of the origin and evolution of the solar system.

Now, in the world of Olympus Two, science seeks to explain genesis in terms of chemical evolution, thus to perceive the past and forecast the future. The investigation is open ended. From Leifsbudir in Vinland, it has led men to Tranquility Base on the Moon and has sent electronic robots from Mercury to Jupiter and Saturn.

I have begun the narrative of this process in the year 985, the start of the Norse voyages to Greenland and eastern Canada. It is not sufficient simply to recall the details of these great adventures. I have sought to identify the evolutionary process each period of exploration and expansion appears to demonstrate.

The common denominator is intraspecific competition as the motivation: deadly competition among men and families for land, among nations for power and wealth. This is the force that drove the have-nots in medieval Scandinavia across uncharted seas, impelled Renaissance Europe to seek the wealth of the Indies and circumnavigate the planet, urged Amundsen and Scott on the tragic race to the geographic south pole, and launched Americans to the Moon. The persistence of this feature of human behavior may carry future generations to the stars. We cannot see the end; but looking back only a thousand years, we can examine the beginning.

 PART I

RECONNAISSANCE OF THE EARTH

CHAPTER I

VINLAND

The discovery of America by European people was not a single event. It was part of a groping, migratory process that surged westward, receded, and surged west again over a span of six centuries. In the beginning, the process operated blindly. Mariners on voyages of discovery did not know where they were going, and when they reached new lands they did not know where they were. When Christopher Columbus died in 1506, he still believed that the lands he had found for Spain were part of Asia. It was not until Amerigo Vespucci, sailing for Portugal, reported that the coast of Brazil was certainly part of a new continent that the name *America* began to appear on maps of the new lands and the concept of a New World was established.

This long, intermittent process of expansion began with the Norse voyages of the ninth, tenth, and eleventh centuries. Thousands of these seafaring people were driven westward by population pressure in Scandinavia. They steered their long, wooden ships with woolen sails into the North Atlantic along latitudes corresponding to those of their homes or ports in Norway to raid, invade, and settle. In those latitudes lie the North Atlantic islands: the Hebrides off Scotland, the Orkneys, the Shetlands, and the Faeroes. These were settled. A week's sail westward, with a fair wind, lay Iceland. Beyond, the east wind would drive the ship to Greenland in another four to seven days. From the Greenland settlements, it was neither a long nor arduous voyage to Newfoundland Island, where Leif Ericsson built the first European settlement in the New World circa 1002.

Iceland was the first stepping-stone across the Atlantic from Scandinavia. It was settled by Norwegians in the second half of the ninth century. Greenland was settled from Iceland late in the tenth century, and the place Leif called Vinland was settled in the first quarter of the eleventh.

Unless they are considered part of a long-term migratory process, the Norse discoveries of Greenland and eastern Canada appear to be irrelevant to the main European Age of Discovery that opened 500 years later with Columbus, the Cabots, and Magellan. Certainly, their influence seems to have been minimal—so faint, in fact, as to be subliminal.

After Norse sea power waned in the thirteenth and fourteenth centuries, Vinland faded from European consciousness as a geographical reality. It acquired an aura of legend. Greenland was gradually abandoned by Iceland and Norway. The weather grew colder as the centuries passed, sea communication withered away, and the settlements perished. By the end of the sixteenth century, there remained only shallow graves and crumbling ruins to mark the early European thrust to Greenland and America.

The apparent lack of connection between the eleventh- and fifteenth-century voyages of discovery testifies to the persistence of the exploration imperative in Western culture. Here are two independent exploratory surges, 500 years apart. The first was short-lived. In the main, it lacked sufficient technological development, organization, and support at home to sustain it. Norse supply lines were long and uncertain. Their tools were poor. Their weapons, except for steel blades, were scarcely more advanced than those of the Eskimos or Indians they encountered. The Norse system of penetrating an inhabited region by subduing or slaughtering the inhabitants failed in North America, where the invaders were greatly outnumbered by a determined foe.

Except for information obtained from recent, but meager, archaeological finds, our knowledge of this initial surge of Europeans to America is drawn from the sagas. There are two well-known records of these events—an Icelandic version known as the "Saga of Eric the Red" and a Greenlandic version, "Tale of the Greenlanders." As might be expected from stories handed down by word of mouth or related by professional storytellers (skalds), there is a considerable amount of disagreement between these sources.[1] *

Both are essentially family histories and pedigrees as well as narratives of events. Both are laced with digressions into the supernatural and fantasy, but the main pattern of the happenings they relate is clear enough. They leave no doubt that Norse expeditions from Greenland and Iceland planted settlements on the east coast of Canada, probably Newfoundland Island, but had to abandon them because of hostile pressure from the Skraelings, who were Indians, Eskimos, or both. Skraeling, the Norse term for the natives, is a term of contempt. It means ill-favored wretch, and that is the way the Norse regarded the people who barred their settlement in the New World a millennium ago.

During the Icelandic period of Norse expansion, the situation in the European world was described in the Icelandic "Landnamabok" ("Book of Settlements," circa 1250) as follows:

* Notes for each chapter begin on page 407.

When Iceland was discovered and settled from Norway [A.D. 860] Adrian was Pope in Rome and, after him, John, who was the fifth of that name in the Apostolic seat. Louis, son of Louis, was emperor north of the Alps and Leo, and Alexander, his son, over Byzantium.

Harald Fairhair was King of Norway; Eirik Eymundarson, King of Sweden and, Bjorn, his son; and Gorm the Old was King of Denmark. Alfred the Great was King of England and Edward, his son. Kjarval in Dublin and earl Sigurd, the Mighty, in Orkney.

Learned men state that from Stad in Norway it is seven days sail west to Horn in the east of Iceland; and from Snaefellsnes [Iceland] where the distance is shortest it is four days by sea west to Greenland. If one sails from Bergen [Norway] due west to Hvarf in Greenland, one's course will lie 70 miles or more south of Iceland.[2]

In medieval Scandinavia, population pressure was expressed in the form of competition for what arable land existed and for pasturage; there were blood feuds at home and Viking raids and incursions abroad. The feuds were settled for the most part by the payment of indemnities (weregelt) or by banishment of one party. Sometimes, a defeated contestant took to his heels or to his longship and went searching for a place where no one was looking for him. The "Book of Settlements" tells of a man named Naddod, a great Viking, who antagonized so many people in Norway that he went off to make a home for himself in the Faeroe Islands, "for the good reason that he knew nowhere else where he would be safe."

A homicidal feud was the stimulus that persuaded many a stout fellow to leave Norway for Iceland and Iceland for Greenland. That is the story of Eric Thorvaldsson, also known as Eric the Red, the colonizer of Greenland. From there his three sons, Leif, Thorvald, and Thorstein, and his illegitimate daughter, Freydis, attempted to colonize Newfoundland along with the Icelandic entrepreneur Thorfinn Karlsefni and his beautiful wife, Gudrid.

Social, technological, and climatological factors help us account for this westward surge. Before the coming of Christianity to Norway in A.D. 1000 under King Olaf Tryggvason, polygamy and concubinage were not uncommon in the country, especially among the lords and nobles of the realm. One consequence was that the landed gentry produced an oversupply of landless "second" sons; only the legitimate firstborn could inherit.

These young men found employment as warriors and sailors, as did their counterparts throughout Europe, and they provided a large reserve of battle-ax fodder for the raids, invasions, skirmishes, and wars of the time. Eventually, the young men who survived sought farmsteads or estates of their own, but where? There was no room for them in Norway (or in Denmark either, for that matter). And so they raided and invaded, muscling in on the territory of others where they could and leaving Scandinavian genes all over maritime Europe, the British Isles, and the lands around the Baltic.

It was cheaper and safer in the long run to go where there were no other inhabitants or where the local people were too weak to resist. In Iceland the

Norse found sparse settlements of Irish monks who had come there for peace and quiet and who promptly left when the newcomers moved in.

Norse shipbuilding technology was the most advanced in Europe a thousand years ago. No navy in the world could stand against a Viking flotilla. Scandinavian mariners developed two types of oceangoing ships—the famous longship, seventy-nine feet long with a beam of sixteen and one-half feet, and a smaller freight vessel called the *knarr*, which was fifty-four feet long with a beam of fourteen feet, nine inches.

Both types were clinker-built (the external planks overlapped). Shiplap construction persists not only in small boats but also in modern housing, where wood siding is used. Their keels were of oak, their planking of pine, and they were held together by linden pegs and iron bolts affixed to iron plates inside the hull. Caulked by tarred animal hair, they were exceptionally seaworthy and flexible. They were propelled by a huge, square, woolen sail strengthened by rope netting and by up to sixteen pairs of twenty-foot oars. Partly decked over, the *knarr* could carry a crew of thirty to thirty-five men, a sizable cargo, and several head of cattle. Both types were capable of crossing the ocean and sailing inland up shallow creeks and estuaries. The longship drew three and one-half feet of water. A replica of a longship found in 1880 at Gokstad, Norway, was sailed from Bergen to Newfoundland in 1893 by Magnus Andersen in twenty-eight days.[3]

The third factor favoring the westward migration was climate. After 800 years of cold winters—between 300 B.C. and 500 A.D., when the arctic ice pack came farther south in the North Atlantic than it does today—a warming trend appeared in the northern regions. It is sometimes referred to as the Little Climatic Optimum. The average annual temperature of the northern region rose two to three degrees. The ice virtually disappeared in the high oceanic latitudes. Spring came sooner, summer lasted longer, winter was less severe, and the storms were less frequent and ferocious.

The mild period began in the ninth century and lasted until the thirteenth. Large areas of meadow grass and scrub vegetation appeared on the west coast of Greenland as the glacier shrank back in the mountains. In maritime Canada, some areas, including Newfoundland Island, apparently were free of winter snow. The way was open for Viking ships, the world's best at that time, to cross the North Atlantic Ocean to the New World.

Part of this westward movement is chronicled in the "Saga of Eric the Red," so-called because he had red hair. As these accounts usually do, the "Saga" sets the stage with Eric's pedigree. It relates:

> There was a king named Olaf, who was known as Olaf the White. He was a son of King Ingjald, son of Helgi, son of Olaf, son of Gudrod, son of Halfdan Whiteleg, the Upplanders' king.
> Olaf went raiding in the west and conquered Dublin, Ireland along with the Dublin territory and made himself its king. He married Aud the Deep-Minded,

the daughter of Ketil Flatnose, son of Bjorn Buna, a man of rank from Norway; and the name of their son was Thorstein the Red.

Olaf fell in battle there in Ireland, after which Aud and Thorstein made their way to the Hebrides. . . . Thorstein became a warrior king and allied himself with earl Sigurd, the Mighty, son of Eystein the Rattler, and they conquered Caithness and Sutherland, Ross and Moray and more than half Scotland. Thorstein made himself king there, until the Scots betrayed him and he fell there in battle.

What does all this have to do with Eric the Red? It opens the scene (as Shakespeare does) and introduces the company, so to speak. The period is the second half of the ninth century, when the "Book of Settlements" tells us that Sigurd the Mighty ruled in the Orkneys and Alfred the Great was king of England. (It may sound strange to generations of American schoolchildren who know all about Columbus but little about the Norse voyages that preceded his to cast the discovery of America in the period between King Alfred and William the Conqueror, but that is when it was discovered the first time.)

These events took place before Eric was born. They characterize the political turbulence of the period in which an unstable and loosely knit Norse empire was beginning to expand across the North Atlantic Ocean. It was this pattern of events into which Eric was born and that would impel him and his sons to become colonizers.

After her son, Thorstein, was killed in Scotland, Aud, her daughter, Groa, and some of their kinsmen and retainers escaped from the Scots by secretly building a ship in the forest and sailing it to the Orkneys. There they lived in peace for awhile. Groa was married and had a daughter, Grelod, who grew up in the islands and married one Thorfinn Skullsplitter.

With daughter and granddaughter safely wed, Aud, who seems to represent the type of intelligent and resourceful Viking woman the sagas revere, set off in her ship to Iceland with twenty of her retainers—all free men—and wintered there with her brother, Bjorn. Among those who accompanied her was Vifil, a freed thrall, to whom Aud eventually gave some land. Vifil settled down, married, and had two sons, Thorgeir and Thorbjorn. And Thorbjorn begat a daughter named Gudrid, a beauty who was as intelligent, accomplished, and adventurous as her prototype, Aud the Deep-Minded.

Now this brings us to the time of Thorvald, the son of Asvald, son of Ulf Oxen-Thorir's son. Thorvald lived in Norway and had a son called Eric the Red, who was born circa 950. The "Saga" tells: "Both father and son left the Jaeder (in Norway) for Iceland because of some killings."

According to one chronology,[4] Eric and his father settled in the Hornstrandir area of Iceland in 963, which would make Eric only thirteen years old. Some time later, Thorvald died. Eric then married Thjodhild, daughter of Jorund Ulfsson and Thorbjorg Ship-Bosom. At the urging of Thjodhild and Thorbjorg Ship-Bosom, Eric left the unproductive Hornstrandir to settle in Haukadal. There his troubles began.

One day, Eric's thralls caused a landslide to fall on the farm of one Valthjof, whereupon Valthjof's kinsman Eyjolf Sauer killed the slaves. Eric responded to this indignity by killing Eyjolf Sauer. When Holmgang-Hrafn tried to interfere, Eric killed him, too. The kinsmen of Eyjolf took a dim view of the slayings, aroused the neighborhood against Eric, and forced him to leave Haukadal. Eric then moved his family to Oxney, where he established another home. The year was probably 977, when Leif was six years old. Eric's other sons, Thorstein and Thorvald, and daughter, Freydis, who was born out of wedlock, are not accounted for at this time.

Whether the social consequences of her birth deranged her personality or whether she was psychopathic, Freydis Ericsdottir is depicted in the sagas as a homicidal maniac. Her deeds make Salomé look like a camp fire girl.

Three years passed, and trouble came once more. During the winter (980–981),[5] Eric lent his dais beams to a neighbor named Thorgest. The beams were movable planks used as bed frames and beautifully carved. With the scarcity of wood in Iceland, they were extremely valuable. Then it happened that when Eric wanted the beams returned, Thorgest's men refused. Always the man of action, Eric broke into Thorgest's house and took the beams. Thorgest pursued Eric, and the two, with their retainers, came to blows. In the fight, two of Thorgest's sons were killed. A new feud was on.

From then on, the combatants kept large bodies of men under arms, threatening the peace and safety of the whole region. The feud came for judgment before the Thorsness Thing, the legislative assembly. Eric was banished from Iceland for three years.

Where to now? Thrown out of Norway, expelled from Iceland, Eric, now thirty years old, faced a grim future. Now, under the sentence of banishment, he was fair game for Thorgest, and he went into hiding until he could outfit his ship. As for his father and so many others, the ship was the means of escape from intolerable circumstances. There was only one way left to go: west. Eric told his friends he meant to search for a land that Gunnbjorn, son of Ulf the Crow, had sighted some fifty years before when he was storm-driven westward across the ocean. Should he find such a land, Eric promised, he would return at the end of his banishment term and tell his friends where it was.

In the summer of 981,[6] Eric and thirty crewmen set sail along the sixty-fifth parallel; in hardly more than seven days, they sighted the icebound east coast of Greenland. They turned south, rounded Cape Farewell at Greenland's southern tip, and sailed northward off the west coast. There, Eric and his men saw islands, fjords, and grassy hills rising all the way back to the great glacier. It was a land abounding in caribou, arctic fox, bear, walrus, seal, and, in the sea and streams flowing down the icy mountains, numberless fish. For land-hungry refugees, exiled from the world they knew, it was the promised land.

For the next three years Eric explored the coast, sailing northward along it

to Cape Burnil and crossing Davis Strait to the Cumberland Peninsula of
Baffin Island.[7]

He built a home at an inlet called Eiriksfjord at a place called Brattahlid
and laid the foundations for a colony that would thrive for 250 years, until
the Little Climatic Optimum ended and the fimbulwinter of another period
of cold filled the seas with ice and killed the livestock.

In the spring of 984, Eric and his men sailed back to Iceland. He called his
friends together at Breidafjord, where he described the new land he had discovered. Although there was some evidence that it had once been inhabited,
there were no human inhabitants there now, and the land was free, fair, and
open to all. He called it Greenland, the "Saga" relates, "for he argued that
men would be all the more drawn to go there if the land had an attractive
name."

Before long, Eric once more came to blows with Thorgest. The "Saga"
says that Eric got the worst of it, but the two antagonists finally managed to
patch up a peace. Eric wasn't staying in Iceland anyway, a factor that may
have promoted the settlement of the feud.

Eric began to recruit colonists. Icelandic farming never had been very
good, but it had been particularly miserable in the last quarter of the tenth
century. To make matters worse, the fish catch had fallen off. Trade with
Norway had declined, and many a farmer and fisherman were desperate. To
those who were having hard times, Eric loomed as a Norse Moses, leading
his friends to the promised land. Greenland! It was a name to conjure up
visions of broad meadows with deep, lush grass for grazing and spring
flowers.

Among the Icelanders who became sold on Greenland from Eric's description was Vifil's son, Thorbjorn, who had backed Eric in the feud with
Thorgest. Thorbjorn had a daughter named Gudrid, "the most beautiful of
her sex and in every respect a very superior woman," the "Saga" tells. One
day, a friend of the family, a man named Orm, came to Thorbjorn in the role
of a matchmaker, proposing a match between Gudrid and a dashing, young
merchant named Einar. There was only one hitch. Einar's father was a
manumitted thrall. Thorbjorn did not take kindly to the suggestion that his
daughter was only good enough to marry the son of a freed slave. It reflected
on Thorbjorn's status in the community, and he threw Orm out of his house.
In his indignation, Thorbjorn seemed to forget that he, too, was the son of a
manumitted thrall—Vifil.

Perhaps Thorbjorn's overreaction was prompted by the fact that his for-
tunes were failing, as were those of hundreds of farmers and owners of small
estates in Iceland. One spring day he invited his neighbors to a great feast,
and in the midst of the merrymaking he announced he was emigrating from
Iceland. He said he found himself in "straightened circumstances" and would
rather abandon his farm "than lose my honor and rather leave the country
than bring disgrace upon my family." He said: "I plan to fall back on the

promise of my friend, Eric the Red, which he made when we parted from each other in Breidafjord, and if things go as I would have them, I mean to go to Greenland this summer." [8] Thorbjorn sold his farm, bought a ship, and sailed with Gudrid and thirty retainers for Greenland. Whether he went with the first contingent of colonists or later is not clear.

The first contingent of Greenland settlers, their goods, and their livestock filled twenty-five ships, but only fourteen ships reached the southwest coast of Greenland, where Eric had staked out a colony, the Eastern Settlement. It was located in the region of present-day Julianehaab and Ivigtut.

Developing around Eric's homestead at Brattahlid, the settlement thrived. As more Icelanders arrived, a second colony, the Western Settlement, was started farther north, in the area of modern Godthaab.

From the original nucleus of 450 persons, the population of colonial Greenland rose to more than 3,000 by the end of the twelfth century. The Eastern Settlement had 190 farms, 12 parish churches, a cathedral at the town of Gardar, a monastery, and a nunnery.[9] The Western Settlement had 90 farms and 4 churches at the height of its development.

Eric's children grew up at Brattahlid. The three brothers—Leif, Thorvald, and Thorstein—were all accounted fine young men, but the sagas have no good to say of Eric's illegitimate daughter, Freydis. She married a man named Thorvald and "was very much the virago, while Thorvald was just a nobody. She married him for his money." [10]

One of the original colonists was Herjolf, an unsuccessful Icelandic farmer who had a son named Bjarni, "a most promising young man." [11] Bjarni did well in sea trade and became the owner of a fine ship, which he sailed between Norway and Iceland. Returning to Iceland from Norway in the summer of 986, Bjarni found that his father had gone off to Greenland with Eric and had sold the homestead. "I shall steer my ship to Greenland if you are prepared to go along with me," he told his crew.[12] "Our voyage will appear foolhardy since no one of us has entered the Greenland sea." Nevertheless, the crew agreed.

So it was that, seeking his father like the good son he was, Bjarni Herjolfsson set out for Greenland, was blown off course by storms, and accidentally discovered America. It was one of the most reluctant discoveries in the history of navigation. Bjarni's ship proceeded westward slowly for three days before losing sight of Iceland. Then, the following wind the ship's crew had enjoyed died down. A cold wind began to blow out of the north, bringing a dense, polar fog. For days, Bjarni and his crew ran before the wind, unable to see the sun or stars. When the sun broke through the clouds and mist at last, Bjarni took a sighting, but little good it did him. He did not know where Greenland might be; all he knew was its general direction from Iceland.

A day's sail brought the wayfarers to a strange coast. As it rose above the horizon, they saw a land of low hills richly forested with tall trees. The crewmen were excited and wanted to explore, but Bjarni was too cautious to risk his cargo-laden ship on a strange coast. The place obviously was not Greenland, which he had heard was icy and mountainous and deeply indented by fjords. So, leaving this land to the port of them, the sailors let their sheet turn toward the land and sailed northward. Although Bjarni did not know the whereabouts of Greenland, the elevation of the sun above the horizon at high noon told him he was fairly far south of Iceland and therefore south of Greenland. An educated guess is that Bjarni and his crew had seen southern Labrador.[13]

Two days later, they sighted another land. The crew asked Bjarni if this was Greenland. It was a flat country covered with forest. But Bjarni decided that it was no more Greenland than the first land, "for there are very big glaciers reported to be in Greenland." [14] Again, the crew asked permission to go ashore to look around. They pleaded that they had to replenish stores of water and wood. But Bjarni said no. "You lack for neither," he said, and he got some hard words for this from his crew.[15] This may also have been a part of Labrador, just south of the tenth-century tree line and present-day Nain.

Bjarni gave orders to hoist the sail and turn the prow of the ship away from this tempting land. For three more days they sailed northward, driven by a southwest wind until they sighted a third land. This one was high, mountainous, and glaciered. Again the crew asked to go ashore. Again Bjarni refused. He was sure this was not Greenland, and he said that the land looked good for nothing. Without lowering their sail, they coasted along the shore and found it was only an island—probably the southern extremity of Baffin Island near Resolution Island and Frobisher Bay.[16]

Now they sailed on for four more days, with a strong following wind—so strong that Bjarni had to warn the men not to crowd on too much sail. A fourth land loomed ahead on the misty sea. Was that Greenland? the crew demanded. It certainly appeared to be, Bjarni said, and they sailed straight for it.

Toward evening, they reached a cape, and there, on the beach, was a boat. Beyond was the farm and dwelling of none other than Bjarni's father, Herjolf. The cape was known ever after as Herjolfsness ("Herjolf's Cape"). At last Bjarni was reunited with his father and the crew was allowed to go ashore.

For the next dozen years, nothing came of those chance discoveries. Bjarni remained on the Greenland farm with his father. The hiatus appears to be curious indeed, unless we take into account the hardships the colonists faced in establishing themselves in a rough land.[17] Houses had to be built, mostly of sod and stone; pastures had to be laid out for livestock; and hunting and fishing grounds had to be found. The colony had little opportunity to draw supplies from Iceland or Norway; it had to be virtually self-sufficient. It is easy to conclude that little time or energy remained for further exploration. However, accounts of forested lands to the southwest might have stirred some interest, inasmuch as there was no timber in Greenland except what the colonists imported.

The next thing that happened, as the sagas are wont to say, was that Bjarni and Leif made voyages to Norway. The order of these voyages is not clear; but it is important, because the rationale for Leif's future activities depends on it. The sequence that makes sense is that Bjarni Herjolfsson left the farm at Herjolfsness and sailed to Norway circa 998. At that time, Olaf Tryggvason had subdued most of his rivals, and he held the throne of Norway. However, a powerful earl, Eric Hakonarson, controlled part of the country as the liege man of the king of Denmark. For political reasons not given, Bjarni became the retainer of the earl, and during his stay in Norway, he told all about his discoveries twelve years earlier. The tale aroused interest, and those who heard it thought that Bjarni had shown a conspicuous lack of enterprise in failing to explore the new lands, "and he won some reproach for this." [18]

Leif then sailed for Norway in the year 1000. En route, his ship was driven ashore at the Hebrides Islands, where the weather forced him and his crew to remain most of the summer. There, Leif had a love affair with a lady named Thorgunna, "a woman of good birth and Leif had an idea she saw farther into things than most." [19]

As Leif prepared to make sail for Norway, Thorgunna came to his ship and asked to go with him. Leif refused on the grounds that it was imprudent to carry off so high-born a lady with so many relatives when "we are too few for it." Thorgunna then informed Leif that she was pregnant. Having the gift of prophecy, which is not an uncommon trait among saga personnel, she said that the child would be a boy. When he was grown, she swore that she would send him to Greenland and might even go there herself. Leif gave her a gold ring, a cloak of Greenland wool, and a belt of walrus ivory. Years later, the boy, named Thorgils, did show up at Brattahlid, and Leif admitted paternity.

When he finally reached Norway, Leif, being the son of an important Greenlander, was accepted into the entourage of King Olaf. There, presumably, he heard of the exploits of his fellow Greenlander Bjarni.

King Olaf not only was a practicing Christian but also a proselytizer of first rank. He converted Leif and his crew to Christianity and ordered Leif to return to Greenland with priests and persuade the heathen there to embrace the Catholic faith. And this Leif did, bringing Christianity to Greenland about the same time it became the legal religion of Iceland. Later that year, King Olaf was killed in a sea fight at Svold, and one of his foes was Earl Eric Hakonarson.

When Leif landed at Eiriksfjord in Greenland, he was welcomed at Brattahlid with open arms. He preached Christianity throughout the settlement, but Eric took coldly to the idea of abandoning the Norse gods and heroes, some of whom, he was sure, had been reincarnated as polar bears. Eric's wife, Thjodhild, embraced Christianity at once and had a church built. After she had taken the new faith, Thjodhild no longer would sleep with Eric, "a circumstance which vexed him very much." [20]

Leif was stirred by the stories he had heard in Norway of Bjarni's discoveries, and he went to Herjolfsness to confer with him. The result of the visit was that Leif bought Bjarni's ship, rounded up a crew of thirty-five, and made ready to sail in search of the lands Bjarni had reported. He asked old Eric to join the expedition since, in spite of the fact that Eric had been expelled from Norway and Iceland, he was reputed to have that mystical quality called luck—without which no one got anywhere in the world of the sagas.

At first, Eric demurred, but then he yielded to his son's pleading. On the way to the ship, however, Eric's horse stumbled, and he fell off, injuring his foot in one version of this incident and cracking several ribs in another. Eric decided he was now too old to go sailing off into the unknown and returned to Brattahlid. Leif then set sail in the summer of 1002 on the first intentional expedition to find North America.

HELLULAND, MARKLAND, VINLAND

Leif and his men "lighted on that land first which Bjarni and his people had lighted on last." [21] It was the mountainous, glaciered scape that Bjarni had characterized as good for nothing. The cliffs came down almost to the pounding surf. What little beach there was was covered with big, flat stones, undoubtedly a deposit from the last (Wisconsin) ice age. Leif called the place Helluland, or land of the flat stones. It probably was the southern coast of Baffin Island. [22]

So far, the expedition was on course. Leif sailed on, and the next landfall was the coast where Bjarni had seen a forested plain. Leif and his men pulled up on the beach and explored inland briefly. They named it Markland ("Wooded Land") and then returned without dallying to their ship.

Markland was remarkable not only for its trees but also for a beach of white sand stretching mile after mile along an otherwise rockbound coast. The explorers called it the Furdustrand, or wonder strand. One might suppose that such a landmark still exists, and it does. Leif's Furdustrand extends for 40 miles north of Cape Porcupine, Labrador, and is up to 200 feet wide. [23]

Once more, the expedition sailed southward, veering to the west before a sharp, northeast wind. After several days (probably two), they sighted another coast and beached the ship. It was an island just north of a promontory of what appeared to be a mainland.

Leif and his men drank the dew that lay heavily on the coarse grass. It tasted sweet after the stale water they had on board ship. Returning to the ship, they sailed through a sound between the island and the promontory or cape. To the west, they found an attractive shore where a river flowed out of a lake into the surf. They eased the *knarr* into the shallows, and when it went aground they took the small boat, which was always towed by Norse vessels, and rowed to the beach.

They waited until the tide rose again and then they rowed back to the ship and brought her through the river and into the lake, where they anchored. Then they went ashore with their sheepskin and cowhide sleeping bags and built booths (lean-tos). It was a fair land, and after a few days they decided to spend the winter there.

The "Tale" goes: "There was no lack of salmon there in the river or lake, salmon bigger than they had ever seen before. The nature of the land was so choice, it seemed to them that none of the cattle would require fodder for the winter. No frost came during the winter and the grass was hardly withered. Day and night were of a more equal length there than in Greenland and Iceland. On the shortest day of winter, the sun was visible in the middle of the afternoon as well as at breakfast time." (That is, for three hours before and three hours after high noon.)

Leif was characterized as "big and strong, of striking appearance, shrewd, and, in every respect, a temperate and fair dealing man." He divided his men into two platoons, one to explore while the other remained in camp. He insisted that the exploring party always return by nightfall.

One evening, a man was missing when the exploring party returned. He was a German named Tyrkir who had lived with Leif's family for many years. Leif regarded Tyrkir as his foster father, so close had they been since Leif was a boy. Now Tyrkir had disappeared, and Leif was greatly disturbed.

Picking a dozen men, Leif set out to look for Tyrkir; but before they had gone far, they met the German hurrying toward them, bursting with excitement. The "Tale" relates:

> Leif could see at once that his foster father was in fine fettle. He was a man with a bulging forehead, rolling eyes and an insignificant, little face, short and not much to look at, but handy at all sorts of craft.
>
> "Why are you so late, foster-father?" Leif asked him, "and parted this way from your companions?"
>
> By way of a start, Tyrkir held forth a long while in German, rolling his eyes all ways and pulling faces. They had no notion what he was talking about. Then, after a while, he spoke in Norse. "I went no great way farther than you, yet I have a real novelty to report. I have found vines and grapes."
>
> "Is that the truth, foster-father?" Leif asked.
>
> "Of course, it's the truth!" Tyrkir replied. "I was born where wine and grapes are no rarity."
>
> They slept overnight. Then, in the morning, Leif made this announcement to his

crew: "We now have two jobs to get on with and on alternate days we must gather or cut vines and fell timber, so as to provide a cargo of such things for my ship."

When the spring came in the year 1003, they had filled the ship's cargo space. The "Tale" continues: "Leif gave the land a name in accordance with the good things they found in it, calling it Vinland, Wineland; after which they sailed out to sea and had a good wind till they sighted Greenland and the mountains under the glaciers."

Where was Vinland? Since the discovery of the ruins and artifacts of an apparent Norse settlement on the northern tip of Newfoundland Island in 1960–1964, there has been a growing consensus among scholars that it was the site of Leifsbudir ("Leif's Booths"), the first European settlement in America.

The land descriptions in the "Tale of the Greenlanders" correspond to Belle Isle, where they drank the sweet dew. The cape they rounded might have been Cape Bauld; the strait through which they sailed could have been the Strait of Belle Isle; and the description of the place where they first built booths and later more permanent dwellings fits the vicinity of the present-day hamlet of Anse-aux-Meadow ("Bay of the Meadow"). There the Norwegian explorer and archaeologist Helge Ingstad found the remnants of an eleventh-century settlement; some artifacts found in the ruins leave no doubt that it was Norse.[24] The main drawback to identifying this site as Vinland is that it lies too far north for grapes. Two allowances may be made. In the early eleventh century, during the Little Climatic Optimum, it might have been warm enough for grapes to grow in Newfoundland. The region seemed to be snow-free then in winter, and cattle could be left outside all winter long. Or, what Leif's expedition referred to as grapes might have been a variety of wild red currant, gooseberry, or mountain cranberry.

As the Leif Ericsson expedition approached Greenland, Leif sighted a wrecked ship on a reef. He pulled the *knarr* up close and sent Tyrkir ashore in the dinghy. Among the stranded party were Gudrid (Thorbjorn's daughter) and her husband, a man named Thorir Eastman. Leif took them off the reef along with their crew of fifteen men and put them up at Brattahlid for the winter. There, Thorir died, and Gudrid remained in the household. Some time later, Leif's brother, Thorstein, married her.

As a result of the rescue, Leif became known as Leif the Lucky, presumably because he not only gained merit by saving lives but wealth from salvaging the cargo. The rescue is a nexus in the two Vinland histories, which otherwise diverge considerably. In the "Tale of the Greenlanders," which I have cited, Leif sails home directly from Norway, looks up Bjarni Herjolfsson, buys his ship, and then sets sail for the new lands, which he names Helluland, Markland, and Vinland. But this voyage does not take place until fourteen years after Bjarni's accidental discoveries.

In the "Saga of Eric the Red," Leif is blown off course on his return from Norway and is storm-driven to "those lands whose existence he had not so much as dreamt of before." These were lands of self-sown wheat, grapes growing wild, and even maple trees. Some trees were so big that they could be used in house building.

Thus, it is Leif, not Bjarni, who discovers America accidentally circa 1001 in the "Saga," which omits any mention of Bjarni. Also unmentioned in the "Saga" is the identity of the principal castaways Leif rescued on his return from America—that is, Thorir and Gudrid.

The problem appears to be not so much which version to believe, but how to extract the most likely narrative from both. I find the "Tale of the Greenlanders" more coherent in spite of its contradictions. It provides a detailed description of Vinland, and the progression of voyages is clear, orderly, and reasonable. The "Saga of Eric the Red" appears to telescope the voyages of Bjarni and Leif. However, each version contains material missing from the other.

The "Tale of the Greenlanders," which some scholars believe is older,[25] elevates Leif's encounter with the New World from a happenstance to a planned expedition. Although the main thread of my narrative of the New World discoveries is recited in the "Tale," I believe that it can be reasonably supplemented with additional material from the "Saga" to synthesize a plausible history.

Leif's report of the bounties of Vinland—its wood, grapes, and even self-sown wheat, not to mention the mild climate and longer winter daylight—stirred considerable discussion around the hearth fires at Brattahlid during the long winter evenings. Leif's brother, Thorvald, was critical of the limited exploration Leif had allowed.

Of course, Leif's fraternal response was to advise Thorvald to go see for himself. Thorvald took Leif's advice, and Leif agreed to lend him a ship and the use of Leifsbudir, the camp in Vinland. But first, Leif and his men used the vessel to salvage the timber and other goods from the wreckage of Thorir Eastman's ship.

In the summer of 1004, Thorvald and thirty companions set sail for Vinland with oral sailing directions from Leif. These proved good enough to enable these skillful mariners to reach Vinland. However, if Leif's settlement was on the northward-pointing promontory of Newfoundland Island, as the evidence suggests, it would not have been difficult to find.

Thorvald's expedition wintered at Leifsbudir, eating a diet consisting mainly of fish. "It looked to them a beautiful and well-wooded land, the woods scarely any distance from the sea, with white sands and a great many islands and shallows. Nowhere did they come across habitation of man or beast, but on an island to the west found a wooden grain holder. They saw no other work of man." [26]

As autumn 1004 came, the men returned to Leifsbudir from weeks of exploration. The winter passed and then another summer of timber cutting and more reconnaissance. The second winter passed without notable incident, and the next summer (1006) Thorvald loaded the ship and set off northeastward along the coast. Before long, a storm blew up and drove the ship on shore so hard that the keel was broken on "a certain cape." They repaired the keel, and Thorvald called the cape Kjalarnes ("Keel-ness"). Sailing farther to the east, they entered a large fjord (Hamilton Inlet?) and moored the ship to a headland. Thorvald was pleased with the woodland beauty of the scene and announced that he would like to make his home there.

Returning to the ship from a brief look around, Thorvald and his men noticed three strange mounds on the sand. They walked to them and discovered that the mounds were skin boats, each with three men under it. Following the Viking visitation policy of striking first and asking questions later, they immediately attacked the natives, killing eight. One got away, and the wars between the Norse invaders and the natives they called the Skraelings began.

Looking around further, the expedition found additional mounds along the fjord, and Thorvald assumed they also were skin-boat huts. It appeared that the beautiful homestead he wanted to carve out of the wilderness was already occupied, in contrast to Greenland, which his father, Eric, had found uninhabited.

Wearied by the slaughter of the Skraelings, Thorvald and his men took a nap. They were awakened suddenly by a mysterious cry: "Rouse, ye, Thorvald, and all your company, if you would stay alive. Back to your ship with all your men and leave this land as fast as you can." The source of the cry was not identified, and the "Tale" suggests that it could have been attributed to a supernatural agency, as such warnings frequently were in the sagas, rather than to the sentry Thorvald should have posted.

At any rate, Thorvald and his men ran to their ship. They saw a "countless fleet" of little skin boats swarming toward them on the fjord. The Greenlanders rigged their shields on the ship's gunwales in time to fend off the volleys of arrows shot by the natives (Indians or Eskimos). When the attackers saw that their arrows were thunking harmlessly into the shield wall, they paddled away as fast as they could. Only Thorvald was hit. An arrow passed between the gunwale and a shield and entered his armpit, inflicting a fatal wound.

As he lay dying, Thorvald instructed his men to bury him on the headland he had picked for a homesite. "Maybe it was truth that came into my mouth, that I should dwell there awhile, for there you shall bury me and set crosses at my head and feet and call it Krossanes ["Cross-ness"] for ever more." [27]

Thorvald's men carried out his last wish and then sailed the ship back to Leifsbudir, where they spent the third and last winter of the expedition loading the ship with grapevines and timber. When they returned to Eiriksfjord in the spring of 1007 with news of Thorvald's death, Thorstein decided to sail to the headland and bring back his brother's body for burial in Greenland. He took twenty-five men and his wife, Gudrid, on the expedition that summer; but wild storms from the west and northwest drove the vessel far to the east, between Greenland and Iceland, and Thorstein was hard pressed to get back to Greenland.

That winter Thorstein died in an epidemic at Lysufjord in the Western Settlement, where he owned a half interest in a farm with another man named Thorstein, who called himself Thorstein the Black. The widow Gudrid then returned to Brattahlid.

About the summer of 1008, an Icelander named Thorfinn Karlsefni enters the tale. He sailed his ship to Greenland with a rich cargo and was warmly received at Brattahlid, where he was immediately attracted to Gudrid. At this point, in the "Tale of the Greenlanders," Eric is dead and his estate has passed to Leif, who is now the first citizen of Greenland. In the "Saga of Eric the Red," however, Eric is still alive. In the former version, Karlsefni appeals to Leif for Gudrid's hand, and in the latter, to Eric. No matter; consent was given, and Karlsefni and Gudrid were married that winter.

The "Tale of the Greenlanders" then tells:

> There was the same talk and to-do over the Vinland voyages as before and the people there, Gudrid as well as the rest, put strong pressure on Karlsefni to undertake an expedition. So his voyage was decided upon and he secured himself a ship's company of 60 men and five women. Karlsefni entered into this agreement with his shipmates, that they should receive equal shares of everything they made by way of profit. They took with them all sorts of livestock for it was their intention to colonize the country if they could manage it. Karlsefni asked Leif for his house in Vinland. He would lend the house, he said, but not give it.

The voyage to Leifsbudir circa 1009 was uneventful. On the beach, the colonists found a dead whale, which they cut up for food. Ashore the livestock thrived but proved difficult to manage. The winter was mild. In the spring, the Skraelings appeared. In the "Tale" they are woodland Indians, but in the "Saga," the description of their appearance tallies more closely with that of the Eskimo.

The natives apparently had never seen cattle, and when the bull began to bawl, they were terrified. They ran toward Karlsefni's house to take shelter from the bull, but Karlsefni's men kept them out. Neither party could understand the other, and the confusion could have started a battle, but eventually the natives calmed down, untied their bales, and produced furs for trading. The natives wanted the Norsemen's weapons in exchange, but Karlsefni refused to give up what little edge his men had in armament to the Skraelings and offered them milk instead. "The moment they saw the milk, that was the one thing they wanted to buy, nothing else." [28]

Karlsefni was delighted with the exchange of milk for sable and fox fur, a deal in the spirit of Peter Minuit's purchase of Manhattan Island for twenty-four dollars worth of trinkets 600 years later. After the natives departed, filled with milk, Karlsefni took the precaution of building a stockade around the settlement. Later in the year, Gudrid gave birth to a boy who was named Snorri, the first European child to be born in North America. When the second winter set in, the natives again appeared to barter skins for milk. This time all did not end peacefully. One of Karlsefni's housecarls caught a native trying to steal weapons and killed him on the spot. The rest ran away.

Karlscfni cxpcctcd that the Skraelings would be back in force. IIe deployed ten of his men in an open field between the forest and the lake and had the others move the cattle through the woods with the bulls in the lead so that they could be stampeded into the enemy. The "Tale" relates:

> The Skraelings advanced to the spot Karlsefni had fixed on for battle, battle was joined and many fell among the Skraelings' host. There was one big, fine looking man in the Skraeling host who, Karlsefni imagined, must be their chief. One of the Skraelings had picked up an axe, he stared at it for awhile, then swung it at a comrade of his and cut at him. He fell dead on the instant, whereupon the big man caught hold of the axe, stared at it for a while, then flung it as far out over the water as he could. After which they fled into the forest, each as best he might, and that was the end of the encounter.

ANOTHER VERSION

A different and more sensational account of this battle is recited in the "Saga of Eric the Red," in which Leif's half sister, Freydis, is depicted as a barebreasted, sword swinging valkyrie. In the Saga, the Karlsefni expedition consists of three ships and 160 men plus women. It takes place about twelve years later than the account in the "Tale."

First, Karlsefni and a partner, Snorri Thorbrandsson, decide to leave Iceland for Greenland with a cargo of trade goods. Two other Icelanders, Bjarni Grimolfsson and a partner, Thorhall Gamlason, think that's a good idea, and they go, too, in their own ship.

Both ships anchor in Eiriksfjord, and the four entrepreneurs are wined and dined by Eric at Brattahlid. That winter, Karlsefni marries Gudrid (who has been widowed, as in the "Tale," by Thorstein's death) and decides to go to Vinland after hearing about it from Leif. The other Icelanders want to go, too, and prepare their ship. Thorvald (who has been killed by Skraelings in the "Tale" but who is still alive in this version) and Freydis and her husband, Thorvard, join the expedition, acquiring the ship that Gudrid's father, Thorbjorn, used to emigrate to Greenland some years earlier.

Accompanying Thorvald, Freydis, and Thorvard is a strange character named Thorhall the Hunter, not to be confused with Thorhall Gamlason, the Icelander. Thorhall the Hunter is a big, dark, ogreish man, offensive in speech and manner, who for years had been Eric's hunting partner and part-time bailiff and who was considered an expert on "unsettled lands."

The flotilla first sails northward from Eiriksfjord in the Eastern Settlement to the Western Settlement, and then it turns south. Then the ships reach the lands that Karlsefni now calls Helluland, Markland, and Kjalarnes. Beyond the forty-mile Furdustrand, Karlsefni puts into shore and sends two Scot slaves, a man and woman given to Leif by King Olaf Tryggvason and lent to Karlsefni by Leif, to reconnoiter the land. The "Saga" describes the Scots as fleeter of foot than deer, wearing only sleeveless, one-piece garments fastened by a single loop between the legs. After three days, the two Scots return bearing grapes and self-sown wheat.

Then Karlsefni leads the expedition to a fjord. Off its mouth lies an island, and surrounding the island are strong currents. He calls it Straumsfjord ("Stream-fjord") and the island Straumsey. Birds are so thick on the island that a man cannot walk there without stepping on eggs.

The expedition builds a settlement there and prepares for a dismal winter, when everyone is short of food. Nearly everyone prays to God, except Thorhall the Hunter, who goes off by himself, stands on a cliff, and recites a poem to his patron, Thor. Soon, a whale of a type no one has ever seen before is cast up on the beach and eagerly cut up for rations. But when the men learn from Thorhall that it is Thor's doing, they refuse to accept the gift of a heathen god and toss the whale over a cliff. With this act of rejection, fish once more appear in the sea and streams, and there is food for all.

In the spring, Thorhall the Hunter decides to explore north via the Furdustrand and Kjalarnes to seek Vinland. Only nine men go with him; Thorvard and Freydis stay at Straumsfjord. The vessel Thorhall uses is presumably one of the small boats with a sail. It is blown out to sea and eventually wrecked on the coast of Ireland, where Thorhall is killed and his men are beaten.

Meanwhile, Karlsefni sails south from Straumsfjord on a "long journey" and enters an estuary he calls Hóp ("Landlocked Bay"). Here the landscape is quite similar to the "Tale's" description of Vinland. There are long shallows and a river flowing out of a lake and into the sea. Karlsefni and Bjarni have to wait for flood tide before they can move their ships over the shallows and anchor in the river or the lake. Hóp looks like the promised land, and there the expedition builds a settlement. The colonists find self-sown wheat in the lowlands and grapevines in the hills.

Then one morning the Skraelings appear in the estuary in little skin boats and stare in astonishment at the newcomers. They are described as "small [dark], ill-favored men. They had ugly hair on their heads. They had big eyes and were broad in the cheeks." After a short time, they paddle away.

The winter is quiet. As at Leifsbudir in the "Tale," the "Saga" reports that no snow falls and the cattle graze in the open. Then, when spring comes, a multitude of the skin boats return, so many that "the bay appeared sown with coals." The small, dark men are swinging staves "sunwise." Karlsefni interprets this as a peaceful gesture and orders a similar response by the display of a white shield. Then, both sides start brisk trading, the Indians (or Eskimos) exchanging furs for red cloth.

Suddenly the bull runs out of the cattle corral, bellowing loudly, and the natives, terrified, run away to their boats and paddle off. Three weeks later, they reappear "from the south like a streaming torrent." The natives jump ashore and attack the expedition, hurling stones from war slings and a huge ball that makes "a hideous noise" when it comes down in the Norse ranks and explodes (probably an inflated moose bladder).

Fearing his outnumbered men would be surrounded, Karlsefni orders a retreat to some rocks. This maneuver incenses Freydis, who is pregnant at the time, and she screams: "Why are you running from wretches like these? Such gallant lads as you! I thought for sure you would have knocked them on the head like cattle. Why, if I had a weapon, I think I could put up a better fight than any of you."

The men pay little attention to her, but Freydis keeps following them. However, she is slowed down by her pregnancy, and as she stumbles through the forest, the Skraelings come at her. Their mistake! She picks up the sword of a dead man named Thorbrand Snorrason, who has a flat stone sticking out of his head, and prepares to do battle. As the Skraelings close in, she pulls out her breasts from under her shift and slaps them with the flat of the sword, screaming a war chant. At this spectacle, "the Skraelings took fright and ran off to their boats and rowed away." Freydis had saved the day.

After this encounter, Karlsefni returns to Straumsfjord. On an excursion seeking Thorhall the Hunter, he and Thorvald encounter the mythical humanoid being known to medieval lore as the Uniped. The creature, who has only one foot, shoots an arrow that kills Thorvald.

The expedition spends its third and last winter at Straumsfjord, where "bitter quarelling" breaks out between the bachelors and the husbands over the wives. It is obviously time to go home, and the expedition sets sail for Greenland. En route, the Norsemen seize two Skraeling boys as captives and take them back to Greenland. Snorri, the child born to Gudrid during the first autumn of the expedition, is three years old by the time they reach Eiriksfjord.

Meanwhile, the Icelander Bjarni Grimolfsson is blown off course on the return voyage, and his worm-eaten ship founders. Only half of the crew can be saved in the small boat, and Bjarni gives up his place in the lifeboat to a youth he had promised to protect; and so he goes down with his ship. The "Saga" relates that the survivors reached Ireland.

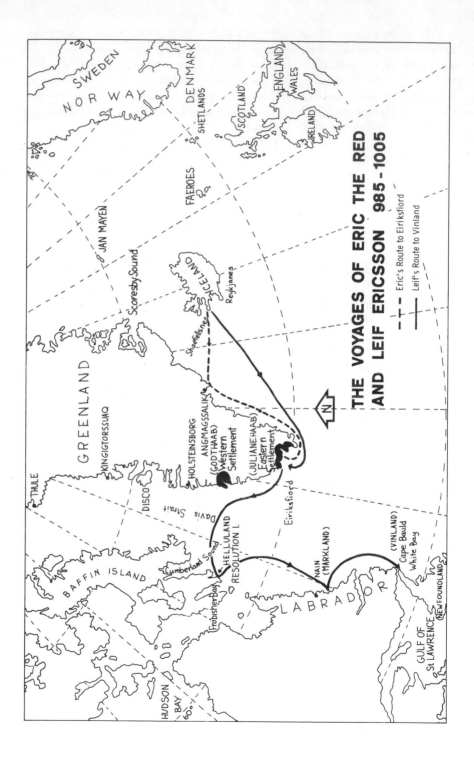

THE VOYAGES OF ERIC THE RED
AND LEIF ERICSSON 985 - 1005

– · – Eric's Route to Eiriksfjord
——— Leif's Route to Vinland

FREYDIS'S VOYAGE

Whichever version one prefers, both agree that Karlsefni's colonizing ambitions were discouraged by native hostility. The "Saga" says: "It now seemed plain . . . that though the quality of the land was admirable there would always be fear and strife dogging them there on account of those who already inhabited it."

He and Gudrid later sailed to Norway with a cargo of logs from Straumsfjord and Hóp (Vinland). After they sold it, they resettled in Iceland. Snorri became a man of substance and the ancestor of a distinguished line. When Karlsefni died, Gudrid made a pilgrimage to Rome and retired to a convent.

In Greenland, voyaging to Vinland was still considered an attractive and profitable enterprise. Returning to the "Tale of the Greenlanders," we are told that in the summer of 1012, a ship arrived in Greenland owned by two brothers, Helgi and Finnbogi, Icelandic traders. Naturally, they called at Leif's house, as visitors from overseas usually did. Freydis (who had not accompanied Karlsefni in this version) now desired to visit Vinland.

She had been living in a community called Gardar with her husband, Thorvard, but came to see the brothers to propose a joint Vinland expedition using Leifsbudir as a base. She and Thorvard would sail one ship there and the Icelanders would use the other, each with an equal force of thirty men plus women.

At the outset, Freydis double-crossed the brothers, concealing five extra men aboard her ship. The brothers arrived at Vinland before Freydis and stowed their gear in Leif's house, which Freydis had borrowed for the expedition. But when Freydis arrived, she angrily ordered them out, saying that Leif had lent the house to her, not to them. At this point, Helgi and Finnbogi discovered the extra men Freydis had recruited. "We are no match for you in wickedness, we brothers," said Helgi.

They moved out their possessions and built their own house near the lake. Freydis put her men to work cutting down trees for the timber cargo. During the long winter nights, attempts were made at games between the two groups; but the hostility between them deepened, and eventually, the "Tale" relates, "there was no coming or going between the houses."

Then early one dark winter morning, Freydis got out of bed, wrapped her husband's cloak around her, and walked barefooted across the grass to the house of the brothers. Finding the door ajar, she pushed it open and stood silently in the doorway. Finnbogi was awake and saw her standing there. "What do you want, Freydis?" he asked. "For you to come outside with me," said she. "I want to talk to you." Finnbogi came out, and they walked to a tree stump and sat down. "How are you liking things?" she asked, to start the conversation. "I think the country a good and fruitful one," he said, "but this cold wind blowing between us, I think that bad, for I swear there is no reason for it." "As you say," Freydis responded agreeably. "I think the same. But my business in coming to see you is that I should like to trade ships with you brothers, for you have a bigger one than mine and I want to get away from here." "I can meet you on that, if it will please you," said Finnbogi.

With that, they parted, and Finnbogi went back to bed. When Freydis returned to Leif's house, she climbed into bed with her cold feet, and at this, her husband, Thorvard, awoke and asked why she was so cold and wet. She answered angrily, "I have been to those brothers asking to buy their ship. I wanted a bigger one. But they took it so badly that they beat me, maltreated me—and you, wretch that you are, will avenge neither my shame nor your own! I can see now that I am not back home in Greenland, but [when I am] I shall separate from you unless you take vengeance for this."

Aroused by her pleadings and threats, Thorvard called up his men and seized the brothers and their sleeping crew. Each man was bound, and Freydis ordered each killed as he was marched out of the house. Five women were left. None of Thorvard's men would kill them. The "Tale" relates: "Hand me an axe," commanded Freydis. It was done, and "she turned upon the five women they had there and left them dead."

After the mass murder, Freydis warned her men that she would be the death of anyone who so much as mentioned it. The official story was to be that Helgi and Finnbogi had remained behind. In the spring, Freydis and Thorvard sailed the brothers' ship back to Greenland with its cargo of lumber and furs. Freydis paid off the crew handsomely. Nevertheless, some of them talked, and eventually the story of the slaughter reached Leif. Outraged, he had three of the crewmen tortured until they confessed and their confessions tallied.

Then he seized his half sister but admitted that he had not the heart to treat her as she deserved. "But I predict this of her and her husband," he said. "No offspring of theirs will come to much good." And such proved to be the case, the "Tale" assures us. "From then on, no one thought anything but ill of them."

With this crime, the Norse attempt to colonize eastern Canada in the eleventh century ended. Vinland faded from European consciousness until the colonial episode was hardly distinguishable from myth.

In 1347, the "Annals" report, "there came also a ship from Greenland, less in size than small Icelandic trading vessels. It came into the outer stream firth (on the west coast of Iceland). It was without an anchor. There were 17 men on board and they had sailed to Markland and had afterward been driven hither by storms at sea."

After that, nothing more was recorded about Vinland, and even Greenland began to fade from the European scene. When the English sea captain John Davis visited the west coast of Greenland in 1585, he found no Europeans there, only Eskimos.[29]

CHAPTER II

THE PASSAGE

During the four centuries between the voyages of Leif Ericsson and Christopher Columbus, the chief sources of knowledge about the Earth were the geography and cosmology of Claudius Ptolemaeus (Ptolemy) of Alexandria (circa 150 A.D.) and the travels of Marco Polo (circa 1254–1324).

Ptolemy, a Greek scientist residing in Alexandria, then the intellectual center of Mediterranean culture, was the most prolific compiler of classical Greek science in the ancient world. His cosmological system, following that of Hipparchus (second century B.C.), depicted the Earth as a sphere hanging stationary in the center of the universe. The sun, Moon, and stars revolved around the Earth in circular orbits and at uniform velocity. The Earth-centered cosmos of the Ptolemaic system became so deeply embedded in the world view of orthodox Christian theology in Europe that challenges to it in the Renaissance were judged heretical by the Holy Inquisition.

The intellectual revolution that freed Europeans from the astronomical and geographical misconceptions of Ptolemy began with the Polish astronomer Nicolaus Copernicus. His monumental treatise, "De revolutionibus orbium coelestium," presented a universe in which the Earth and other planets revolved around the sun. In view of the harsh repression of the Inquisition, his work was not published until he lay dying in 1543.

Giordano Bruno, a brilliant, nonconformist, Italian scholar, was convicted of heresy and burned at the stake by the Inquisition in Rome in 1591 for advocating the sun-centered theory of the solar system and for propounding aspects of relativity theory.

Galileo Galilei proved that Copernicus was right by observing the phases of Venus with a new invention, the telescope. But rather than risk Bruno's fate, the aging Galileo recanted Copernican theory on his knees before the Inquisition in Rome in 1633. By that time, however, the sun-centered universe had become established in intellectual circles beyond the Inquisition's reach.

Shaking off Ptolemy's geographical misconceptions of the Earth, however, took longer. With the telescope, it was possible to perceive the geometry of the solar system; to define the geography of the Earth required centuries of exploration.

Ptolemy's world map showed the Eurasian landmass joined on the east to a hypothetical southern continent called Terra Incognita. It was assumed to exist to balance the land mass on the north, otherwise the Earth would tip over. On the west, Terra Incognita was joined to Africa, thus enclosing the Indian Ocean. What lay beyond the Pillars of Hercules (the Straits of Gibraltar) was vague. The Atlantic Ocean was dotted with mythical islands, and beyond them lay the misty coast of Asia.

Ptolemy calculated the breadth of the known world as follows: *

> We have divided the inhabited regions into three large divisions—that part of the Earth which is inhabited by us is bounded on the east by the unknown land which borders on the Eastern races of Greater Asia, namely the Sinae and Seres, and on the south by the likewise unknown land which encloses the Indian Sea, which encompasses Ethiopia south of Libya, the country called Agisymba, and on the west by the unknown land encircling the Ethiopian Gulf of Libya and by the Western Ocean bordering on the westernmost parts of Africa and Europe and on the north by the continuous ocean called the Ducalydonian and Sarmatian, which encompasses the British islands and the northernmost parts of Europe, and by the unknown land bordering on the northernmost parts of Greater Asia, that is to say on Sarmatia and Scythia and Serica. The water moreover is much greater in extent than is the land. Wherefore the entire Earth consists of three continents, Asia, Africa and Europe . . . of the seas surrounded by land, the first in size is the Indian Sea, the second is Our Sea and third, the Hycanium or Caspian . . . the southern boundary of the inhabited Earth is defined by the parallel which is south of the equator by 16 degrees and 25 minutes. The most northern parallel is 63 degrees north of the equator and is called the parallel passing through the Island of Thule. Wherefore the breadth of the entire Earth which is as yet known to us is 79 degrees 25 minutes, or approximately 80 degrees, or 40,000 stadia, inasmuch as 1 degree measures 500 stadia, and the circuit of the whole Earth is 180,000 stadia. [1]

Assuming that Ptolemy's "stadium" equalled about 549 feet, or 0.104 miles, we see that his calculation of the breadth of the "known world" comes out to 4,160 miles. His "circuit of the whole Earth" amounts to 18,720 miles. That is 6,180 miles short of the equatorial circumference of about 24,900 miles. Ptolemy's estimate of the Earth's circumference persisted through the Middle Ages and the Renaissance, until the time of Magellan. It was to have a decisive influence on Spain's decision to launch Columbus and Magellan on their voyages of discovery.

The first big hole in the Ptolemaic idea of a closed Indian Ocean was punched by the merchandising expeditions of the Polo brothers, Niccolo and

* The length of the stadium in Ptolemy's time is ambiguous. Although Webster's Seventh New Collegiate Dictionary gives it as 607 to 738 feet, the measure apparently used by Eratosthenes was equal to 549.12 feet.

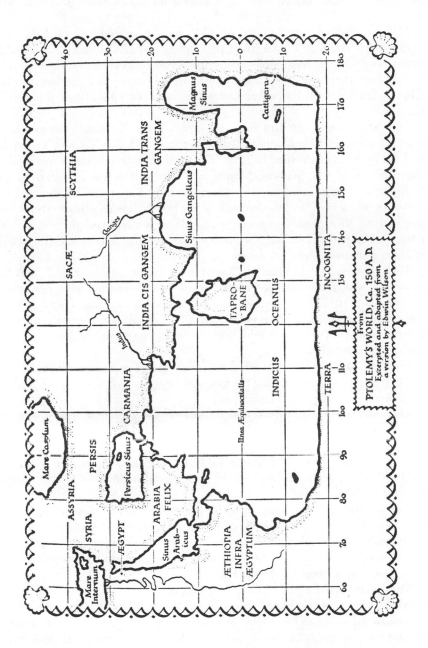

From
PTOLEMY'S WORLD, Ca. 150 A.D.
Excerpted and adapted from
a version by Edwin Wilson

Maffeo, and Niccolo's son, Marco, in the thirteenth century. They traveled overland to China before the Turks closed the route through the Middle East.

Marco was about twenty-one years old when he arrived with his father and uncle at the court of Kublai Khan in Peiping in 1275. A smart, personable young man, Marco was employed by the Khan on several business deals in central and northern China and in Southeast Asia and India. He learned that Chinese junks regularly sailed along the coast of China into the Indian Ocean.

After seventeen years in China, the Polos made the long journey home, crossing mountains and deserts, escorting one of Kublai's wives to Persia, and finally reaching Venice in 1295. The restless Marco became involved in the commercial war between Venice and Genoa. He was captured by the Genoese and imprisoned for two years. During that time, he dictated his memoirs to a scribe, and the account of his travels was an electric shock that touched off an explosive interest in east Asia. It described the wealth and power of the peoples of Asia, the Arab world, Japan, Sumatra and the islands of Indonesia, and even east Africa.

This remarkable document, "The Book of Ser Marco Polo," was occasionally exaggerated where it reported hearsay but remarkably perceptive where it reported direct observations and experiences of the Polos. It lifted the curtain in maritime Europe on the rich potential of Far Eastern markets—a source of human productivity only barely glimpsed by Europeans during the Crusades.

Further, Marco's story revealed the existence of a passage to India from the east coast of Asia. Finding the passage became one of the great goals of the fifteenth and sixteenth centuries.

The Polo report had a profound impact on the Ptolemaic concept of the world. On a commission from Prince Henry of Portugal, Fra Mauro, an Italian monk specializing in cartography, drew a world map in 1459 incorporating Polo's observations. It showed the Indonesian archipelago in some detail, with notes about the sources of spices, commodities of vital economic interest to all of Europe.

Fra Mauro's principal amendment to the Ptolemaic conception was the delineation of an open ocean south of Africa and Asia. This first demonstrated the possibility of reaching the East Indies by sea, an important, new idea in the fifteenth century, when the Republic of Venice held a monopoly on the spice trade by arrangement with Egypt.

The collapse of the Ptolemaic conception of a landlocked Indian Ocean removed a critical psychological impediment to discovery. Portugal developed the eastward route to the Indies around Africa and guarded it murderously against trespassers, with the "legal" sanction of papal rulings and agreements with Spain. The only route by which Spanish mercantile interests could reach the Indies and compete for the lucrative spice trade was from the west.

That alternative was the basis of Columbus's approach to Ferdinand and Isabella after King John II of Portugal turned him down in 1484. It was also the basis of Magellan's petition a generation later to their grandson, Charles I, after Portugal's King Emanuel I rejected Magellan's plan. Competition for the Indies trade that forced Spain and, later, England and France to seek a westward passage to the Far East was the mainspring of the Age of Discovery. Spices were the great objective. The term covered a number of products: condiments for seasoning and preserving meat, pharmaceuticals, dyes, perfumes, sugar, unguents, and cosmetics.[2]

Warehouse lists showed 288 different "spices," including eleven kinds of sugar, waxes and gums, even glue. Most of the pepper came from western India, but the best pepper came from Sumatra. Cinnamon was found only on the Island of Ceylon. Nutmegs were gathered on the islands of the Banda Sea, and cloves grew only in the Molucca Islands, most profusely on Ternate and Tidore.

At the height of the Mongol Empire, products of China and the Indies were carried in camel caravans across Asia to terminals in the Levant and Black Sea ports. They were transshipped to Western Europe by Italian merchants operating out of Constantinople or Tana in the Crimea.

In the fourteenth century, as Mongol power ebbed, the overland trail to Cathay was cut off by nomadic horse barbarians, themselves victims of drought conditions in central Asia. The only safe way to bring the goods to the West was by sea. Chinese merchants sailed their junks to the Moluccas to pick up cloves and to other Indonesian islands for nutmeg, and they delivered this produce to the Malay port of Malacca. From there, Moslem merchants shipped it across the Bay of Bengal to India. The cargoes were resold along with cinnamon from Ceylon and Indian pepper to Arab traders in the spice ports of Calicut, Cochin, and Goa on the Malabar coast.

From these ports, Arab *baghlas* (sailing vessels) hauled the spices to Persia, Arabia, and east Africa. They were transshipped through the Red Sea in coastwise vessels to Suez—the Red Sea port for Cairo—or to Ethiopia, where they were carried by armed caravans to Alexandria. Another route led through the Persian Gulf to Aleppo or to Constantinople. Italian ships then hauled the spices to Venice or Genoa. Venice had the Egyptian franchise to distribute spices from Alexandria and dominated the Levantine outlets as well.

So profitable was this trade that it was said that a merchant could lose five cargoes and still make an overall profit on the sixth. The German banking house of Fugger and the Italian house of Medici turned profits of 200 to 400 percent on cargoes they financed.[3]

The principal costs in sea transportation through the Indian Ocean and the Red Sea were the middleman profit and the tolls, duties, or tribute paid to sultans, rajahs, or sheiks at every transshipment port. In addition, piracy was rampant in those seas, and hijacking on land during transfer of cargoes was a constant threat.

If the spice trade was profitable under those conditions, it was easy to imagine how rich it might become if the middlemen, brokers, port shake-downs, and hijacking could be eliminated by direct transportation of the produce in well-armed European ships. The lure of big spice profits and rivalry to control this commerce in Europe stimulated the European exploration of the planet in the Age of Discovery. However, the stimulus reflects underlying factors: the economic drive of an expanding society seeking to finance its growth by trade and exploitation; advances in shipbuilding and navigation that made world trade possible; the rise of naval artillery and firearms that gave European ships of the fifteenth and sixteenth centuries naval superiority over Arab, Hindu, Malay, and Chinese vessels; and finally, a religious rationale—that these voyages of discovery were a means of converting the heathen to the Catholic faith.

Catalyzed by greed, these factors launched 400 years of discovery, exploitation, and colonization by Western society. Europeans expanded into the New World, and they completed the exploration of the Earth.

COLUMBUS

Because of its economic importance, then, the passage to the Indies by sea became the great maritime challenge of the Renaissance. Its promise of wealth and power, enhanced by Marco Polo's lurid accounts of the wonders and riches of the East, was a loadstone to sophisticated mariners and intellectuals who believed, just as the ancients had, that the world was round and the East could be reached by sailing west.

Indeed, this possibility was a principal object of study at the Institute of Geography, founded by Prince Henry of Portugal, third son of King John I and a grandson of an English lord, John of Gaunt, Duke of Lancaster. Henry the Navigator, as history calls him, was a geographer rather than a ship's pilot. He had the means to indulge his curiosity about the Earth by practical experiment. From 1418 until his death in 1460, he sent out expeditions about once a year to reconnoiter a sea route first to Guinea and the west coast of Africa and then around Africa to the east coast. If that could be done, he reasoned, it would be possible to sail all the way to India.

Like their Norse predecessors who island-hopped from Norway to Iceland to Greenland to Newfoundland, Portuguese mariners reached the Madeira

Islands in 1418, the Azores in 1427, and tried to occupy the Canary Islands in 1425 to exclude Spain from the African trade. By the Treaty of Alcocovas in 1480, however, Spain received title to the Canary Islands, whereas exclusive rights to Guinea, west Africa, and the Cape Verde Islands were ceded to Portugal.

Prince Henry's sea captains reached Cape Verde, on the shoulder of Africa, in 1445; they arrived at the Cape Verde Islands about a decade later. After Prince Henry's death, the tradition of maritime exploration he founded continued. Portuguese ships reached the Island of St. Thomas in the Gulf of Guinea in 1470 and the mouth of the Congo River in 1484.

Intent on developing a maritime and commercial empire in Africa and the Indian Ocean, King John II of Portugal was intrigued, but not impressed, by the scheme of a Genoese mariner, one Cristoforo Colombo, to reach the fabled island of Cipangu (Japan), Cathay, and the Indies by sailing due west across the Atlantic Ocean.

King John's Naval Advisory Commission, consisting of the most learned mathematicians and geographers of the age, reported that such a scheme was possible, but they did not accept it as feasible. The commission found Columbus' estimate of the transatlantic distance to Japan, the oriental land he expected to reach first, much too low.

Columbus had calculated the distance as 2,400 nautical miles, according to Samuel Eliot Morison.[4] A nautical mile is one minute of arc (sixty to the degree) and equals 6,076.115 feet, or 1,852 meters. It is about 15 percent longer than the English statute mile of 5,280 feet. Columbus's calculation was based on a sequence of errors, beginning with Ptolemy's estimate of the circumference of the Earth and Columbus's calculation of the width of a degree of longitude. His main mistake, of course, was the omission of North and South America and the Pacific Ocean in his estimate.

In the fifteenth century, no one knew the circumference of the earth with any precision, although some close estimates had been made in antiquity. An Alexandrian mathematician, Eratosthenes, in the third century B.C., applied elementary geometry to the problem of finding the circumference of the Earth and nearly got it right. He reasoned that if he could find the angular distance between two points on the surface whose overland distance was known, he could calculate the Earth's circumference, assuming that the earth was a sphere.

The two points Eratosthenes selected for the measurement were the Egyptian capital, Alexandria, and the inland city of Syene (Aswan), 5,000 stadia (about 520 miles) distant. The straight-line distance from Alexandria to the Tropic of Cancer is 520 miles. Thus, a stadium equals 549.12 feet (0.104 miles) on the basis of 5,000 stadia.

It was known that at noon on the day of the summer solstice, the sun did not cast a shadow at Syene, which is on the Tropic of Cancer. The sun was directly overhead. However, at that precise moment, the sun did cast a shadow at Alexandria, 520 miles to the north. The angle of the shadow was measured at seven degrees twelve minutes of arc, representing one-fiftieth of a circle. On this basis, the circumference of the Earth was calculated at fifty times 520 miles, or 26,000 miles. That is not far off the modern value of 24,902.4 statute miles, or 21,600 nautical miles, at the equator.

Once this number was known, the width of a degree of longitude at the equator could be ascertained as 1/360 of the circumference or, in modern terms, sixty nautical miles. The width decreases north and south of the equator, of course, as the meridians converge toward the poles.

In the fifteenth century, as in the eleventh, sailors could determine latitude by measuring the elevation of the sun or the North Star above the horizon, but longitude was another matter. Its measurement required a precise clock, which did not exist then. Longitude from a base point could be calculated by measuring the average speed of the ship (by dropping a piece of wood in the water at the bow and timing its passage to stern) if the equatorial width of a degree was known. But this required knowing the circumference of the Earth—and estimates varied considerably.

If Columbus had accepted Eratosthenes' value, his expedition might never have left Spain. The distance would have appeared much too great for the *naos* ("ships") and caravels of the time to cover without resupply of food and water. Morison tells us that Columbus calculated the width of a degree at the equator at forty-five miles, based on Arab estimates, thus reducing the size of the Earth by one-fourth.[5] He then calculated the distance across the Atlantic from Europe to Japan by subtracting the supposed extent of Europe and Asia from his reduced circumference figure.

According to Ptolemy, the Eurasian landmass began at Cape Saint Vincent at the southwest tip of Portugal and ended on the coast of China at a place called Cattigara. It was 180 degrees from Cape Saint Vincent to Cattigara, according to calculations based on Ptolemy. Although this was an overestimate, as Morison points out, Columbus preferred a calculation based on the more exaggerated estimate of Marinus of Tyre, a second-century mathematician, and of Marco Polo. According to these two sources, the "known world" stretched a total of 300 degrees eastward from the Canary Islands, Columbus's jumping-off place, to the Island of Cipangu. That left Cipangu, or Japan, only 60 degrees west of the Canaries across the Atlantic, an equatorial distance of 2,700 nautical miles, by Columbus's reckoning.

However, Columbus planned to cross the ocean on the twenty-eighth parallel, where he calculated the width of a degree of longitude as only 40 miles. Presto! The sea route from the Canaries to Japan was thus reduced to only 2,400 (nautical) miles, or about 750 leagues. That was a manageable distance for a well-provisioned fleet with an experienced crew, even though no landfall could be expected before reaching Japan. It was a significant shortcut to the Indies and the spice islands. Just across the Atlantic, according to this calculation, lay the wealth of the Indies. (The great circle distance from Europe to Japan is actually 10,600 nautical miles.)

It does not appear that the Norse voyages to Greenland and New-foundland in the eleventh century had any bearing at all on Columbus's theories. Morison suggests that Columbus had probably sailed to Iceland in his career but had not learned of the voyages of Leif Ericsson or Thorfinn Karlsefni. Instead, Columbus, like other mariners and geographers of the period, was fascinated by the legendary islands of the Atlantic. Off Ireland lay the fabled island of Hy Brasil; south of the Canaries might be found the Island of Antillia, supposedly settled by Portuguese refugees from the Moorish invasion in the tenth and eleventh centuries. These were utopian lands. On Antillia had risen the "Seven Cities," an urban myth that lasted long and died hard. At the end of the sixteenth century, Coronado was still looking for them in sunny Arizona.

In the archives of the Portuguese Institute of Navigation was a letter from Paolo Toscanelli, a Florentine geographer and physician, who was highly regarded as an authority on the far lands of the Earth. In 1474, he set forth that it was possible to sail from Portugal due west some 5,000 miles to Quin-say, the capital of the Chinese province of Mangi. This province was next to the province of Cathay, seat of the Grand Khan, according to Toscanelli. Morison said Toscanelli probably got his information from "The Book of Ser Marco Polo." However, Toscanelli added, there was another route to Japan and the Far East via the Island of Antillia. From there, it was only 2,000 miles to Cipangu, "most fertile in gold, pearls and precious stones," wrote Toscanelli.

The Toscanelli thesis showed that Portuguese maritime authorities were aware of a westward route or, at least, the possibility of one. But they were not impressed by Columbus's distance calculations, which they regarded as fantasies. Nevertheless, Columbus's enterprise of the Indies was not entirely disregarded. Although King John had little faith in it, he offered to commis-sion Columbus to make the voyage at his own expense. After a year of fruit-less petitioning for crown financing of the venture, Columbus gave up in 1485 and journeyed to Castile. There, however, Ferdinand and Isabella, who had united the kingdoms of Castile, Aragon, and León, were preoccupied by the project of pushing the Moors out of Granada, their last stronghold in Iberia.

During the seven years that Columbus waited for a royal decision in Spain, events in Portugal conspired to make his project of special interest to Spanish mercantile ambitions. Bartholomeu Diaz sailed around the stormy tip of South Africa in 1487 and entered the Indian Ocean, which Ptolemaic geography said was closed. Rounding the Cape of Good Hope opened up a vast eastern seaway to the east coast of Africa, India, the Malay peninsula, and the spice islands, known as the Moluccas, as well as to the wealth of

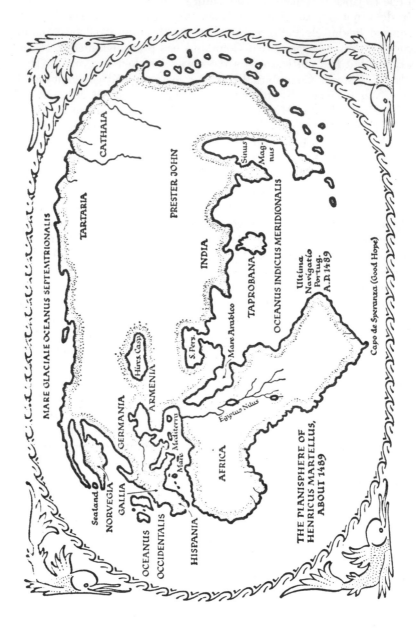

THE PLANISPHERE OF
HENRICUS MARTELLUS,
ABOUT 1489

MARE GLACIALE OCEANUS SEPTENTRIONALIS

TARTARIA

CATHAIA

PRESTER JOHN

Sinus Magnus

OCEANUS INDICUS MERIDIONALIS

INDIA

TAPROBANA

Ultima Navigatio Portug. A.D. 1489

Capo de Speranza (Good Hope)

Mare Arabico

S. Pers.

Hircs Casp

ARMENIA

GERMANIA

Mare Mediterm

Egyptus Nilus

AFRICA

Sealand

NORVEGIA

GALLIA

OCEANUS OCCIDENTALIS

HISPANIA

Cathay. It remained only for Vasco Da Gama to reach the city of Calicut on the Malabar coast of India in May 1498 to establish the Portuguese empire of the East Indies.

The Portuguese breakthrough into the Indian Ocean had the effect of closing the eastward route to the Indies to Spain. As Portugal thrust toward India, Columbus arrived in Seville with his plan to reach the Indies from the west. The learned men of Castile agreed that it might be possible but, like the Portuguese, questioned the plan's feasibility. No European had crossed the Atlantic in the latitude at which Columbus proposed to sail to Japan. The project was one of exceptionally high risk, especially to a monarchy nearly bankrupted by war.

Had it not been for last-minute mercantile pressure on Queen Isabella, persuading her to reconsider rejection of Columbus's plan and to recall the navigator after he had been dismissed from the royal presence, the enterprise that led to a New World for Europe might never have been launched—at least not by Spain.

Columbus's grand enterprise of the Indies left Palos, Spain, August 3, 1492. It consisted of ninety men in three ships. Columbus, who was promoted to Admiral of the Ocean Sea by the sovereigns, commanded the expedition from his flagship, *Santa Maria*. According to one reconstruction,[6] the vessel's deck was seventy-seven and one-half feet long; its keel was fifty-one and one-half feet long; its beam (width) was twenty-six feet, and its hold was twelve feet eight inches deep. The vessel drew six feet eleven inches of water and had a capacity of 105.9 tons. It was a type known as a *nao*, or ship.

The other two vessels were the type called caravels, somewhat smaller. The *Pinta* was seventy-three to seventy-five feet long, with a beam of twenty-five feet and a hold depth of eleven feet. It had a capacity of fifty-five to sixty tons, and it was commanded by Martin Alonso Pinzón. The other caravel was the *Nina*, of about sixty tons burden, commanded by Vicente Yáñez Pinzón. In spite of its diminutive name, the *Nina* was probably slightly larger than the *Pinta*.

Reaching the Canary Islands, the fleet put in for repairs to the *Pinta* and to top off provisions, water, and firewood. Anchors were lifted September 6, 1492, and the enterprise of the Indies sailed off into the unknown on the voyage that altered the shape of Western civilization more than any other.

For a month, Columbus sailed due west by his magnetic compass; however, according to Morison, because of an unsuspected variation, the fleet actually was veering to the southwest. By October 6, the vessels had covered more than the 750 leagues that Columbus had calculated as the distance between the Canaries and Japan. The crew became restless, began to mutter, and soon fell into a premutinous state of mind. Martin Alonso Pinzón pleaded with the admiral to head southwest, fearing the fleet had missed Japan. At this point, according to Morison, Columbus decided to make for China and then visit Japan on the return voyage. The little vessels were bobbing about hardly 350 miles east of the Bahamas.

On October 10, as the fleet was heading straight for the Bahamas only 200 miles away, the crew of the *Santa Maria* threatened to mutiny to force a return to Spain. Many of the sailors had never fully trusted Columbus's calculations. But Columbus was able to cool the men down by promising to turn back to Spain if land was not sighted in a few days. There was the further persuasion, as he scarcely needed to remind them, that the mutineers would surely be hanged if they seized the ship and returned to Spain.

Barely two days later, on the night of October 11, Columbus thought he saw a light. Others thought they saw it, too. Then on October 12, in the early morning darkness illuminated by a nearly full moon, Rodriga de Triano, the *Pinta*'s lookout, spied the shapes of distant hills and cried out, "Tierra! Tierra!" It was the coast of an island the natives called Guanahani and Columbus renamed San Salvador.

It was obviously not any of the Japanese islands. But persisting in the belief he was near them, Columbus pressed on in the Caribbean Sea until he sighted Cuba. He was certain it must be Japan. That hope faded when no sign of the golden-roofed palaces that were thought to be characteristic of that rich country appeared.

After his *Santa Maria* was wrecked Christmas Eve of 1492 on the north coast of Hispaniola, Columbus returned to Spain in the *Nina*, leaving thirty-nine men to build a base on Hispaniola (Santo Domingo). His discovery of the "Indies" was hailed in Castile as a triumph of the age, as indeed it was. In a few generations, it was to elevate Spain from a petty, impoverished kingdom to the most powerful empire in Europe.

The following October, Columbus sailed from Cádiz for Hispaniola with 1,200 colonists. On his second voyage, he found the Leeward Islands—Saint Kitts, the Virgin Islands, and Puerto Rico. On his third voyage, in 1498, the year that Da Gama reached India, he landed in Trinidad and sailed across the mouth of the Orinoco River, exploring the Gulf of Paria off the coast of Venezuela and still hoping to find Japan or China.

Maladministration in the colony at Hispaniola impelled the crown to send a political administrator, Francisco de Bobadilla. He placed Columbus under arrest on charges of illegal actions and shipped him back to Spain in chains. These were struck off by the sovereigns, and Columbus was restored to his post as admiral, but his star was fading.

He was able to collect four more ships and hire crews for a fourth effort to find the East Indies in 1502. The fleet reached Honduras, sailed along the coast of Central America to the Gulf of Darien, and explored its treacherous waters. Columbus was marooned for a time in Jamaica. He returned to Spain, exhausted and defeated. The Indies lay beyond his grasp. He found a New World instead, but he did not know it when he died in Valladolid in 1506 at the age of fifty-five, convinced that he had failed.

MAGELLAN

After Columbus came the deluge. Transatlantic traffic picked up with remarkable speed to the new lands in the west. By the end of the first decade of the sixteenth century, the conviction was growing in European intellectual circles that a New World had been found. Cipangu and Cathay must lie beyond it—how far, no man knew. The search for the westward passage was now focused on a way around or through the interposing lands.

In 1496, a Venetian merchant, John Cabot, obtained a royal charter and a small ship, the *Matthew*, from King Henry VII of England to seek in the north the passage that Columbus had failed to find in the south.

Departing Bristol May 20, 1497, Cabot and his eighteen-man crew made a fast trip across the North Atlantic in their fifty-ton vessel. They rediscovered the Island of Newfoundland, apparently sighting land on the island's northern tip, where Leif Ericsson had built his base nearly 500 years earlier.

Like Columbus, Cabot believed that he had reached the coast of Asia shown on the 1492 globe of Martin Behaim. That influential map maker also had amended Ptolemy's world map by opening a strait to the Indian Ocean between China and the Island of Ceylon.

In 1498, King John of Portugal sent Duarte Pacheco Pereira on a transatlantic mission to find lands in the west that Columbus had missed, such as Antillia or Hy Brasil. Pereira must have reached South America and possibly part of the coast of North America, for he reported the existence of a vast coastline extending over ninety-eight degrees of latitude from north to south.

Sailing for Spain in 1499, Alonso de Ojeda and Amerigo Vespucci found the mouth of the Amazon River. They coasted around the bulge of Brazil to Cape San Roque. The same year, Vicente Yanez Pinzón, who had captained the *Nina* on Columbus' first voyage, commanded a ship that explored the South American coast north of Cape San Roque. Also that year, Diego de Lepe followed the coast of Brazil from Cape San Roque to ten degrees south latitude.

In 1500, only eight years after Columbus had broken the trail, a Portuguese mariner, Pedro Álvares Cabral, with a fleet of thirteen ships, made a detour on a voyage to India and landed on the coast of Brazil. He formally took possession of it for Portugal and called it Tierra de Vera Cruz. Cabral then sailed the fleet eastward across the South Atlantic, around Africa, and into the Indian Ocean to India to establish a trading colony. Portugal thus acquired Brazil in passing, as it were. The same year, another Portuguese captain, Gaspar de Corte Real, sought the elusive passage to India in the north. He sailed first to Greenland and then, following the old Norse route, explored part of Labrador and Newfoundland.

Belief in a northwest passage was very old. Norse seafarers believed that it existed to the west of Greenland, leading to eastern lands. It was called, in Norse lore, the Ginnungagap.

Year by year voyages were launched, with England, France, and later Holland sending out ships to explore the new transatlantic lands. Perhaps the most effectively publicized of these expeditions was one made in 1502 by Amerigo Vespucci. He was a well-to-do citizen of Florence who lived for many years in Seville as an agent of the Medici banking house. On a mission for Portugal to determine the extent of the Brazilian coast, Vespucci sailed to forty-seven degrees south latitude and found the Río de la Plata, which he named the River Jordan.

Like Columbus, Vespucci kept a journal, in which he aired not only his experiences, but his opinions and observations. He was convinced that the great extent of unbroken coast he had seen was continental land. He was sure that it could not be Asia, because it was inhabited only by primitive people. It could be only a New World, unsuspected by Europeans before Columbus. That idea gained currency in Europe. Every new report confirmed it. It was expressed graphically in two maps of the "New World" drawn by a German cartographer, Martin Waldseemuller, who called the region Amerigo's Land, or America.[7]

Now the search for a westward sea route to the Indies became concentrated on locating a passage through America. There were two possibilities: Martin Behaim's suggestion of a strait between a southward-pointing Asian peninsula and Ceylon in the south, and the Norse Ginnungagap, the Northwest Passage, beyond Greenland.

Belief in the probability of a strait in the south was enhanced by the discovery of the Mar de Sur, or South Sea, by Vasco Núñez de Balboa in 1513 from a peak in the Isthmus of Darien. No one knew how big that sea might be, but the most learned geographers could speculate that it was nothing less than the Magnus Sinus of Ptolemy, the Great Bay of China. Whereupon the chief pilot of Spain, Juan Diaz de Solis, pressed the search for a strait to the South Sea in the big estuary of the Río de la Plata. Making a reconnaissance of the river in 1516, de Solis and a boatload of men were seized by cannibals, killed, and eaten. The surviving crew on shipboard sailed back to Spain with the grim tidings.

Spain's interest in finding the passage was whetted by the steady expansion of the Portuguese empire in the Indian Ocean during the first quarter of the sixteenth century. Portugal had gained control of the Indian Ocean from east Africa virtually to the Malay peninsula during that period. A fleet under Francisco de Almeida seized the east African port of Mombasa from its Moslem rulers and then set up a chain of forts on the Malabar (west) coast of India at Calicut and other ports. In 1509 Almeida clinched Portuguese control by destroying a combined Egyptian-Indian fleet in the Battle of Diu in the Arabian Sea.

One of Almeida's bright young men on this conquest was Fernao de

Magalhaese e Sousa, better known as Ferdinand Magellan. Born in 1480 in Portugal's only landlocked province, Trás os Montes, he became a page of Queen Leonora, wife of John II, and was entranced by the aura of seafaring adventure and great voyages that permeated the court. He was an excited teenager when da Gama returned in 1499 with the report that he had reached India by sea.

Magellan sailed with Almeida's fleet in 1505, taking part in the capture of Mombasa and the great sea battle. In 1511, he took part in the capture of the city of Malacca by Afonso de Albuquerque. The port, along with Goa on the Malabar coast of India, became a prime Portuguese stronghold. It controlled passage through the Straight of Malacca between Malaysia and Sumatra, and thus access to Indonesia. From Malacca, Albuquerque sent ships into Indonesian waters, where the Portuguese sought the richest of all sources of spice, the Moluccas.

In the second decade of the sixteenth century, the Moluccas became a focus of commercial rivalry between Portugal and Spain. But access to them was controlled by Portuguese warships patrolling African ports and the Indian Ocean. The eastward approach to the Moluccas around Africa was closed to Spanish ships. The westward route was open—if it could be found. This situation became established in what passed in that period for international law among the sea powers in the following way.

After Columbus returned to Spain from his first voyage, Ferdinand and Isabella petitioned Pope Alexander VI to confirm their claims to the lands that Columbus had found and to all other lands in that part of the world. Alexander VI was Rodrigo Borgia, prelate of Aragon, who sired famous children. Two of them were Lucrezia, the brilliant duchess of Ferrara, and Cesare, who rose to power in Italy by poisoning or strangling his political rivals.

In 1493, the Borgia pope issued a series of "bulls," or papal *pronunciamentos*, establishing a line of demarcation running from pole to pole 100 leagues west and south of the Azores. All new lands found to the west of that line (at 36 degrees west longitude by modern reckoning [8]) were assigned to Spain. Later, the pope extended the grant to include lands in the Indian Ocean, Portugal's private preserve.

King John of Portugal made it clear to Ferdinand and Isabella that he would not accept the decision of the Spanish priest in the secular matter of dividing up the world. Rather than fight a naval war, the Spanish sovereigns agreed to negotiate, and the result was the Treaty of Tordesillas, in 1494. It moved the line of demarcation farther west, 370 leagues west of the Cape Verde Islands (46 degrees 30 minutes west longitude [9]) and gave Spain a free hand west of the line and Portugal a free hand east of it. Portugal thus acquired Brazil, and Spain obtained the rest of Latin America.

At the outset, the treaty framers were thinking only of the western hemisphere. With the discovery of the Moluccas, however, the antipodal location of the line came into question. The Moluccas might well be in the Spanish sphere of influence that was considered to extend 180 degrees west of the meridian in the Atlantic.

This was not a question that could be settled scientifically then, inasmuch as the circumference of the Earth was still undetermined, and no reliable means existed for ascertaining longitude. However, Portugal persuaded Pope Leo X to issue a bull in 1514 granting it all lands that it might seize from heathen people in Africa, India, or any other region that might be reached by sailing east.[10]

So the search for the westward passage became more intense, leading to the European reconnaissance of the entire planet. This form of international rivalry for the riches of the Earth, so intense in the early sixteenth century, becomes the leitmotif of exploration and discovery for the ensuing 400 years, leading to the conquest of the poles and the landing on the moon.

The world stage is now set for the entrance of Magellan. But before he appears on the scene with another scheme for reaching the Indies by sailing west, it is advisable to introduce his wartime buddy, possibly his cousin, Francisco Serrao. Magellan and Serrao had campaigned together in the Indies and, on two occasions, Magellan had saved Serrao's life. Their association was to prove a major factor in the great voyage of Magellan, the first expedition to circumnavigate the Earth.

Serrao had been a member of an expedition that Albuquerque sent from Malacca in 1511 to explore Indonesia and establish trade with China. One of the expedition's goals was the spice islands. Storms and shipwreck prevented it from reaching the Moluccas, but one of its officers did. He was Serrao. With six men, Serrao made his way by native craft to the Mollucan island of Ternate after their ship was wrecked in the Lucipara Islands of the Banda Sea, south of the Moluccan chain. An adaptable man, Serrao settled down on the friendly island, won the confidence of its ruler, the Rajah Boleyse, and acquired property and a harem. When a Portuguese trading vessel finally reached the Moluccas in 1513, Serrao was an important man on the island.

He dispatched two letters by the ship. One was addressed to Portugal's king, Emanuel I, announcing that he, Serrao, had found the Moluccas and that he would serve the interests of Portugal there.[11] The other was addressed to Magellan. It advised his former shipmate and comrade-in-arms of the wealth of the islands and gave a description of their location, which turned out to be inaccurate.

Meanwhile, Magellan had been mustered out of Portuguese military service under a cloud of unsubstantiated charges, later dropped, that he had profiteered in the sale of captured livestock during a campaign in Morocco. Partly because of these charges and partly because of an earlier falling out with Albuquerque in the Indies, Magellan lost favor in the court of Emanuel I. Nevertheless, he appeared before the king with a proposal to sail to the Moluccas from the west. His arguments were similar to, but more specific than, those of Columbus, who had presented his enterprise to Emanuel's father, John II, a generation earlier.

Magellan's plan was straightforward enough. He would sail across the Atlantic to the great peninsula of Asia that was called America and turn south to seek the strait that would lead into Ptolemy's Magnus Sinus and the Indian Ocean. Having accomplished that, he believed he could speedily reach the Moluccas, saving thousands of miles of sea travel compared with the eastern route.[12]

Emanuel was cold to the idea. He regarded Magellan as an insubordinate and opportunist and rejected Magellan's theory that the westward route to the Indies was a shortcut. The king turned down the proposal peremptorily, giving Magellan the impression there would be no more commissions for him from Portugal.

Like Columbus, Magellan then went to Spain. Unlike Columbus, however, he had a partner in his venture, a nervous hypochondriac named Ruy Faleiro—astrologer, mathematician, and general scientist—who had invented a way of determining longitude, or so Magellan believed. Faleiro provided the intellectual backing for the venture, at least in its early stages.

Arriving in Seville in 1517, Magellan found an excited, expectant outlook toward exploration and discovery in contrast to the indifferent one that Columbus had encountered a generation earlier. Once the transatlantic trail had been blazed, the gold rush was on.

There was a new king in Spain. Isabella had died in 1504 and Ferdinand in 1516. Their only child, Joanna, was mentally ill, and this illness deepened with the sudden, mysterious death of her husband, Philip I, in 1506. Her father, Ferdinand, had ruled Castile for her as regent. When he died, Joanna was still locked up in the gloomy castle of Tordesillas, and her son, Charles, who had been reared in Flemish Ghent, was brought to Valladolid to ascend the throne of Castile and a united Spain at the age of seventeen.

Young Charles I was instantly one of the most powerful monarchs in Europe. From his father, he inherited the Netherlands, Flanders, and Luxembourg. He was heir to the German possessions of his paternal grandfather, Maximilian I, the Holy Roman Emperor. And he was elected to that office, defeating Henry VIII of England and Francis I of France, when Maximilian died in 1519.

From a political standpoint, the time was ripe for Spain to challenge the mercantile mastery of Portugal in the Indies. Columbus's effort had been short-circuited by the unexpected discovery of the New World. Its metes and bounds were unknown, but beyond it lay the real goal of Hispanic ambition in this period: Japan, China, and the Moluccas.

This is the prospect that Magellan hoped to lay before King Charles once he had established contact with the chain of functionaries that led to the throne room. Magellan impressed Spanish court officials as a practical adventurer—tough, experienced, and deeply religious. He was a short, stocky, swarthy man, who limped from a leg wound in Morocco.

There were other forces at work that launched Magellan on man's first orbit of the Earth. Relative to the opulent but static empires of the East, Renaissance Europe was a developing society. Economically, it required trade with the East; politically, it had to expand. Technologically, it could expand, because, like the Viking lands of the eleventh century, it had the means of doing so. These were advances in shipbuilding, navigation, and armament, enabling Europeans to exploit the undeveloped regions of the Earth and challenge the more developed but less aggressive ones for control of commerce.

The Iberian kingdoms sought the wealth of the Indies to finance their own development. But the real power behind the Age of Discovery was the money power. Although the great voyages were commissioned by kings and councils, they were financed by loans from moneylenders who, in the sixteenth century, were developing the practices and techniques that would elevate them to the status of international bankers.

In the time of Magellan, the leading international bankers were the House of Jakob Fugger, of Augsburg, and the House of Medici in Florence. The Medici interests were focused chiefly on North Africa and the Levant. Fugger capital moved into Iberia to fill the vacuum created by the expulsion of the Jews from Spain in 1492.

A detailed analysis of the interconnections of banking, political, and commercial interests in the voyages of discovery is given by the industrialist-historian Charles McKew Parr.[13] Almost from the start, according to Parr, Magellan's enterprise of the Moluccas was dominated by Fugger's Lisbon subsidiary, the House of de Haro, founded by the brothers Cristobal and Diego de Haro. In 1500, the family wealth of the Fuggers was 63 million florins, about $1 billion in purchasing power circa 1950.[14]

In Lisbon, the House of de Haro had financed two of the thirteen ships in Cabral's fleet. The brothers had built up a chain of warehouses in east Africa, India, and Malacca as part of their overseas trading organization. With Fugger funds, they acquired a fleet of fifteen *naos* ("ships") for the East Indies. The de Haros were probably the largest commercial shipowners in the world at that time.

A shorter route to the Indies than the one around Africa certainly appealed to them. They had sent expeditions of their own to seek the southwest passage. One vessel under the command of Christopher Jacques had reached the Río de la Plata. Parr explains that these excursions, along with others sent by King Emanuel, were classified operations. The secrecy that surrounds them seems to have caused detailed accounts of them to be lost from history.

At the instigation of the Medici, Emanuel I became concerned about the rising power of the de Haro brothers. It was rumored that they were converted Jews and, therefore, subject to extortion, imprisonment, or execution at the whim of the crown.

Whether or not the de Haros were of Jewish origin, Emanuel I dealt with them as though he believed they were. He instructed his agents in India to seize their cargoes. He ordered his warships to hijack de Haro ships off the coast of Africa.

When news of these seizures reached Lisbon, Diego de Haro and his brother, Cristobal, realized it was time to leave before they, themselves, were seized. Diego loaded the family treasure on a mule caravan and escaped across the Spanish border into Andalusia, while Cristobal and a squad of armed retainers fled on horseback to Seville. There, the de Haros had a silent partner, none other than Juan Rodriquez de Fonseca, the bishop of Burgos and director of the powerful Casa de Antillas, the Spanish overseas development and trading organization.

The de Haros now directed their money and talent against Portugal. They became intensely interested in developing a westward route to the Indies for Spain. Bishop Fonseca had been heavily involved in managing the later voyages of Columbus for the crown. He was a leading promoter of the westward passage. He had sent Vespucci and Ojeda to seek the southwest passage in 1497–1499—at the same time that Fugger loans to Henry VII of England financed John Cabot's voyage to find the northwest passage.

While Magellan was seeking royal support in Lisbon, Bishop Fonseca and Cristobal de Haro sought to reconnoiter the Río de la Plata farther, to complete Solis's unfinished reconnaissance. Fonseca picked a Portuguese mariner named Estevan Gomes to command an expedition. However, as Gomes began to collect a fleet, the bishop was advised that the expatriate mariner had been seen with Emanuel's emissaries and could not be trusted to represent Spanish interests in the enterprise. Bishop Fonseca's adviser in this matter was also an expatriate Portuguese mariner, Dioga Barbosa, who had married an Andalusian heiress and become governor of the castle of Seville. Fonseca began looking for another commander of the expedition. Barbosa recommended Magellan, an unemployed compatriot.

But de Haro was convinced that Gomes could be relied on to serve whoever was paying him. He persuaded Fonseca to reconsider. The bishop reluctantly agreed to reinstate Gomes, but on the condition that a Spanish co-commander be appointed to protect Spanish interests. The man he wanted for that post was his own natural son, Juan de Cartagena.

The bishop and the banker then presented their enterprise to the court. King Charles took a dislike to the hesitant, bumbling Gomes and refused to approve the project. The plan of Gomes was vague. It lacked the conviction of careful analysis. Fonseca and de Haro then took a longer look at Magellan. His proposal, backed by the most advanced geographical theory, appeared to be more promising. Faleiro, his partner, had made a favorable impression on those in Seville who were considered to be navigation experts. Now Diogo Barbosa—wealthy and influential—took Magellan in hand. He presented Magellan to Fonseca and to Juan de Aranda, the general manager of the Casa de Antillas. Preparations were made to present Magellan to the King's advisers and then to the king.

As a teen-ager reared in Flanders, King Charles was under the influence of several preceptors: his tutor, a Flemish nobleman named Jean le Sauvage, who became royal treasurer of Spain; and a Dutch priest, Adrian Dedel, dean of the University of Louvain, who became president of the Council of the Indies, cardinal, and, later, Pope Adrian VI.

The advisory council listened to Magellan's plan and approved it in principle. The king's counselors then arranged an audience for Magellan with King Charles, warning Magellan to make it clear that he had King Emanuel's permission to seek employment abroad. The audience was highly successful. In Magellan, Charles recognized the resolute, devout, and dedicated type of adventurer he had come to admire. Magellan showed the king the letter he had received from Francisco Serrao describing the wealth of the Moluccan islands—Amboina, Tidor, and Ternate. He displayed globes showing the Moluccas in the Spanish zone of world exploitation and referring to a secret strait between the Atlantic Ocean and the South Sea, or Magnus Sinus.

There was no question about the desirability of the enterprise as a means of advancing Spanish interests and filling the royal treasury, which was chronically low. The expedition was expected to yield a profit of 250 to 400 percent. The king signed a contract with Magellan and Faleiro March 22, 1518, awarding them 5 percent of the profit of the voyage in addition to handsome salaries and titles; they were to be viceroys of all lands they discovered, and the titles were to be hereditary. Five ships were to be provided by the Casa de Antillas, and the crown was to provide the trade goods.

The royal treasury, however, had been pilfered systematically, and funds were insufficient to purchase the trade goods. These were then provided by the House of de Haro, acting for Jakob Fugger, who invested 10,000 ducats in the expedition.

THE BURGOS PLOT

While he was waiting for Aranda to provide the ships, Magellan wooed and wed Diogo Barbosa's daughter, Beatriz. Now it appeared he had succeeded beyond his dreams. He had acquired one of the most valuable commissions of the age, a rich wife, and the confidence of one of Europe's most powerful princes. But behind this facade of good fortune, an ill wind was blowing, and it threatened to wreck the whole enterprise.

Fonseca and de Haro were unhappy with the price Magellan asked and received from Charles. They objected to the percentage the king had awarded Magellan and Faleiro and to the hereditary offices of viceroy over the new lands each would acquire. These rewards conceivably could make them the richest men in Europe. The two promoters then hatched a scheme to dump Magellan and Faleiro and substitute their first candidate, Gomes, who was willing to undertake the expedition's command for salary alone and a possible bonus at a successful conclusion. The first move of the bishop of Burgos and the ex-Lisbon banker was to get Gomes on the expedition's payroll as chief pilot.

Next, Fonseca persuaded the unstable, erratic scholar Faleiro to withdraw as cocaptain of the expedition, promising him that he would be supreme commander of the second expedition to the Moluccas. With Faleiro out of the way, Fonseca persuaded the king to appoint Juan de Cartagena, the bishop's illegitimate son, as Faleiro's replacement. But Magellan was able to prevent the bishop's son from being commissioned cocaptain of the expedition. Cartagena received command of one ship, the 130-ton *San Antonio*, one of the two largest vessels in the five-ship squadron. The other was Magellan's flagship, *Trinidad*, also listed at 130 tons burden.

With command of one of the largest and best armed ships in the Armada de Maluco, Cartagena considered himself coequal in authority with Magellan and the representative of Spanish interests on the voyage. The stage was thus set for the mutinies, murder, and executions that bloodied the expedition.

Fonseca did not confine his effort to gain control of the expedition to his son's appointment. He secured the commission of one of his henchmen, Gaspar de Quesada, as captain of the 90-ton vessel *Concepcion* and of still another, Luis de Mendoza, as captain of the 90-ton *Victoria*. Mendoza was also appointed the treasurer of the expedition. Leaving as little as possible to chance, Fonseca also arranged the appointment of Antonio de Coca, who was either his nephew or another natural son, as comptroller, and of a natural son of de Haro's named Geronimo Guerra as the expedition's accountant.

In attempting to counter these moves, Magellan was only able to obtain command of the 60-ton *Santiago* for Juan Serrano, a friend or possibly a relative. Serrano is identified as Magellan's cousin and the brother of Francisco Serrao (or Serrano) by Parr, but other authorities disagree (see note 13). Magellan hired as many Portuguese seamen as he could, mainly because he regarded them as the best trained in the world but partly because they were unlikely to be influenced against him by Fonseca's captains.

Fonseca had picked Gonzalo Gomes de Espinosa to be the expedition's sergeant at arms, who would command a detachment of marines. Realizing that control of this armed force was essential, Magellan won over Espinosa, and the loyalty of the sergeant at arms became Magellan's trump card in the plots and mutinies that Fonseca set in motion.

While the expedition was being outfitted, agents of Portugal attempted to sabotage it but were foiled by Magellan's alertness to this possibility. Spies had informed the court at Lisbon that Spain was preparing to muscle into the East Indies by a westward route. Magellan received word that Emanuel was determined to head off such an incursion, even to the extent of hijacking the Armada de Maluco on the high seas. Although such an act risked war with Spain, the Portuguese could claim that the armada had entered their waters off Africa in violation of the treaty and of papal bulls. If all the ships were sunk and the crew imprisoned or massacred, there would be no rebuttal. There was little question that if Magellan could be seized, he would be tried and probably executed as a traitor to Emanuel.

Magellan proved to be a tough customer for Fonseca to push around. He defeated the bishop's efforts to replace Portuguese crewmen, loyal to Magellan, with Spanish seamen, who might support Cartagena, by enlisting Basques and by maneuvering, at the last minute, to keep his picked, Portuguese sailors.

When the little armada finally sailed from the port of San Lucar de Barrameda at the mouth of the Guadalquivir River September 20, 1519, it carried a force of 241 men and the most modern armament then available, including the new-fangled harquebuses and heavy cannon.

On the eve of the departure, Magellan sent a prophetic farewell message to King Charles: "Hail, Caesar! We who are about to die, salute you!" The ancient, gladiatorial salute was highly appropriate inasmuch as Charles had been elected Holy Roman Emperor on June 28, 1519, at Frankfurt, where he was crowned Charles V.[15] The arena into which Magellan now fared was the world ocean, the greatest part of which no European had ever crossed.

The armada's first stop was Tenerife in the Canary Islands, to top off supplies. There, Magellan received a dispatch by fast cutter from his father-in-law, Diogo Barbosa, warning him of a captains' plot to put Cartagena in command. Someone had boasted about it in Seville after the armada had sailed. Parr tells that it was the intention of the Fonseca gang to call a captains' meeting and prod Magellan, by some act of insubordination or insult, to violence, whereupon his supporter, Serrano, would be stabbed to death and Magellan would be blamed for it.[16] Magellan would then be whisked back to Spain for trial, and the armada would sail on with Cartagena in command.

Forewarned, Magellan played a cool hand when the captains' meeting opened and Cartagena arrogantly assumed the chairmanship of it. Magellan played along with Cartagena, seeming to accept his assumption of command, and the incident that was supposed to lead to a general scuffle and Serrano's murder never materialized. The Fonseca gang returned to its ships, Cartagena believing that he now held the whip hand. The armada departed Tenerife, and Magellan laid a course southward along the coast of Africa.

As a veteran of Portuguese naval-warfare tactics, Magellan was reasonably certain that Portuguese men-of-war lay in wait for him along the route the armada was supposed to take to its first transatlantic landfall, the coast of Brazil. Spies could have obtained information about the route from the Casa de Antillas, where detailed copies of the route were on file.

Ships poaching on Portuguese waters were summarily sunk, even after they were captured or surrendered. Crews were locked in the holds, and the vessels were sent to the bottom by cannon fire. Magellan was aware that his whole armada could be wiped out to a man without any outsiders knowing their fate. Dead men tell no tales.

Consequently, after a fishing boat advised him that a fleet of Portuguese *naos* was patrolling off the African coast to the south, Magellan changed course to evade the enemy ships, without advising the Fonseca captains. It was his plan to cross the Atlantic on a southwesterly course in order to reach the Brazilian coast at 30 degrees south latitude. At that point, the armada would be south of Portuguese ambushers, lying off the Brazilian coast. It would be also below Cape San Roque at the bulge of Brazil. This cape was extremely difficult to sail around late in the year because of contrary winds.

These reasons undoubtedly were good and sufficient ones to alter the planned course, but Magellan's decision to leave his captains in ignorance of his plans angered them. Although Magellan was captain general and in full command by order of the emperor, he owed the captains at least the courtesy of consultation in such a major decision. At least, so they felt. He did not trust them. His self-protective arbitrariness now provided fuel for the fires of disaffection and mutiny.

Furious at not being consulted, Cartagena sailed the *San Antonio* close to the flagship and noisily protested the course change. To his astonishment, Magellan curtly told him to keep his mouth shut and follow orders. Cartagena took the rebuff hard. He refused to make the prescribed daily salutes to the flagship, a protocol that served as a means of communication, and exhibited open disregard for Magellan's authority. Aware that he would have to deal with this man, Magellan bided his time.

It came during a sodomy trial involving one of the junior officers and a sailor. The penalty for sodomy on Spanish ships was death, but it was often waived if manpower was short and the culprits were given several dozen lashes. Magellan's change of course had taken the armada into the doldrums, where it lay, becalmed in terrific heat, for twenty-one days before the ocean currents carried the little ships into the region of the southeast trade winds. Morale was low among the crews, and Magellan knew that the Fonseca gang had been rowing back and forth to each others' ships to confer. He decided discipline was in order and imposed the death penalty on the sodomy-trial defendants, the executions to be carried out in Brazil.

Before the assembled captains, who had gathered on the flagship for the trial, Cartagena could not resist the opportunity to upbraid Magellan, and he

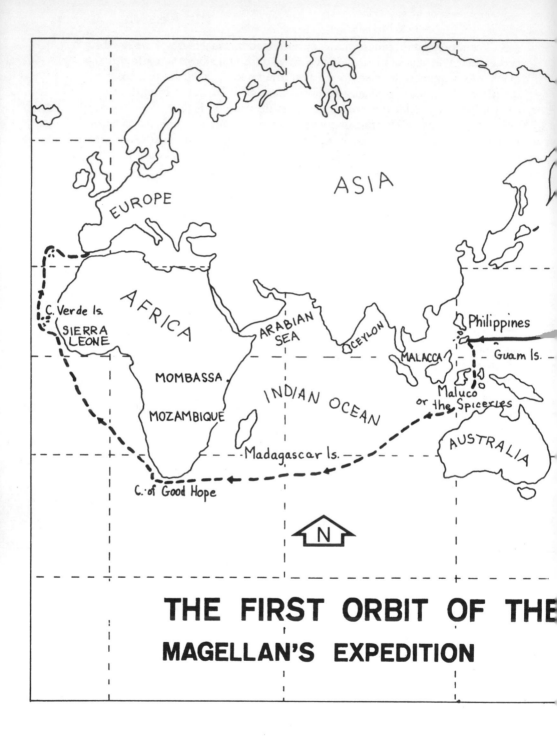

THE FIRST ORBIT OF THE

MAGELLAN'S EXPEDITION

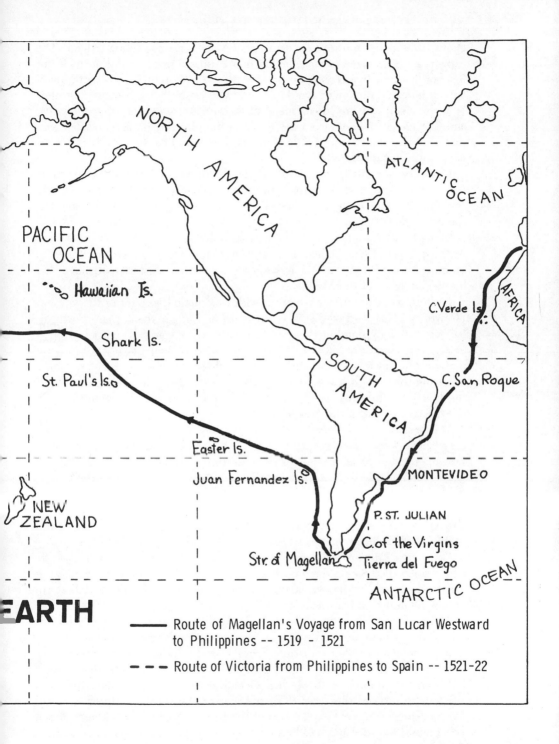

NORTH AMERICA

ATLANTIC OCEAN

PACIFIC OCEAN

Hawaiian Is.

AFRICA

C.Verde Is.

Shark Is.

St. Paul's Is.

C. San Roque

SOUTH AMERICA

Easter Is.

Juan Fernandez Is.

MONTEVIDEO

NEW ZEALAND

P. ST. JULIAN

C. of the Virgins

Str. of Magellan

Tierra del Fuego

ANTARCTIC OCEAN

EARTH

——— Route of Magellan's Voyage from San Lucar Westward to Philippines -- 1519 - 1521

- - - Route of Victoria from Philippines to Spain -- 1521-22 openly threatened mutiny. That was what Magellan was waiting to hear. The captain general seized Cartagena and had Espinosa put him in the stocks for insubordination. It was an open break with the bishop of Burgos, but Magellan felt he could no longer avoid it. Coca (who was either Cartagena's brother or first cousin) was put in command of the *San Antonio* as a sop to Fonseca, and Cartagena, released from the stocks at the pleading of his associates, was placed in the custody of Mendoza on the *Victoria*. For the time being, Cartagena was out of the way.

In December 1519, the armada entered the channel of the Bay of Santa Lucia and sailed past Sugarloaf Mountain, near the site of modern Rio de Janeiro. The armada had reached the land of Verzin, as Brazil was called in those times.

Aboard the *Trinidad* was a gentleman adventurer and observer named Anthony Pigafetta, an Italian of means and education who had petitioned to go on the expedition more or less for the ride. Some historians believe that he was an agent of the Medici.

Pigafetta kept a journal, which provides a detailed account of the voyage. He wrote: "This land of Verzin is very vast and larger than Spain, Portugal, France and Italy combined, very vast indeed." Pigafetta's journal is filled with awed comments about Saint Elmo's fire, which played around the masts of the ships during a violent storm off the African coast; about sharks following the ship to scavenge the garbage; and about the storm petrels and the flying fish he saw. As the armada crossed the equator, Pigafetta noted the disappearance of the North Star.

The armada lingered two weeks in the Bay of Santa Lucia to allow the crew shore leave among a tribe of friendly Indians and their women. The first open attempt at mutiny came after this respite, when Coca released Cartagena and the two, with their followers, tried to seize control of the armada. The uprising was quickly suppressed by Espinosa and his marines. Dismissing Coca from command of the *San Antonio*, Magellan turned the ship over to Alvard de Mesquita, his cousin. As time passed, Magellan found that his friends and relatives were the only ones he felt he could trust.

Coasting southward, the armada reached thirty-five degrees south latitude and a cape called Santa Maria on January 20, 1520. Just around it opened the great estuary of the Río de la Plata, where Magellan planned to follow up Solis's ill-fated reconnaissance of 1516.

Although orthodox geographers believed that the coast of South America (or eastern Asia) continued south to 75 degrees south latitude to the coast of Terra Incognita, or Terra Australis, enclosing the Indian Ocean, there were some who held with the German geographer, Martin Behaim, that a strait led from the Atlantic to the Indian Ocean via the Magnus Sinus. Behaim's 1492 globe showed the strait to exist between the southern tip of Asia and Ceylon, but Portuguese exploration of the Indian Ocean over the next fifteen years found that Behaim had located Ceylon too far to the east.

Magellan supposed that the strait actually lay between Brazil and Terra Australis. He was attracted to Cape Santa Maria because he believed it might be the southern tip of Brazil. It resembled in general landform the Cape of Good Hope at the tip of Africa. Beyond this cape, extruding from the hump of Uruguay, lay the great estuary, which surely must be the entrance to the strait.

With the dreadful fate of Solis in mind, Magellan ordered Serrano to sail the *Santiago*, smallest and most maneuverable vessel of the squadron, up the river to see if it became a strait. Serrano was instructed to avoid a landing. Aboard ship, he had enough firepower to fight off the cannibals if they attacked. Magellan, himself, took command of the *San Antonio* and explored the south coast of the estuary (Argentina), which he thought might be the northern extremity of Terra Australis.

Magellan sailed the *San Antonio* along the south shore as far as the site of modern Buenos Aires. He turned back only when the river narrowed and swung to the north. When he rejoined the armada, he found that Serrano had returned. Serrano reported that the "strait" had become so shallow he dared not go farther. When he tested the water, Serrano said, he found it sweet river water, not the saltwater of an interocean passage. The Río de la Plata (Rio de Solis, as Magellan called it) was indeed a river.

Nevertheless, Magellan kept the armada in the estuary for three more weeks to make sure it was not a strait. Then he issued orders to sail south once more. The captains of the Fonseca faction objected, and this time they had crew support. The air was growing colder and the seas rougher. Although it was still high summer in the southern hemisphere, the austral autumn and winter would soon overtake them. As they moved southward into subantarctic latitudes, they could expect only fogs and cold.

The dissident captains exercised their right to call for a vote on a proposition to return north to the Bay of Santa Lucia and spend the winter there among the friendly Indians and their friendly women, many of whom had formed attachments to the European visitors. Magellan, however, was able to sway the crew to his belief that the strait was surely near at hand. Once the *paso* was found, riches and the warmth of the tropical Indies could not be far away. The armada plunged southward.

For two months, the small fleet sailed on. The winds became harsh and chill; ice formed on the rigging and spars. At the end of March, 1520, the armada reached Port San Julian at 50 degrees south latitude in Patagonia, a thousand miles below the Río de la Plata.

Because the strait had not appeared, the dissident faction proposed that the armada turn east and sail to the Moluccas via the South Atlantic and Indian oceans. The armada could take a course well south of Portuguese patrols, the dissidents argued. Magellan stood firm. He vowed that he would continue sailing south to 75 degrees south latitude. Only when the armada reached that point would he consent to give up the search for the *paso*

and turn east, he announced. Long before he could have reached that latitude, however, Magellan would have encountered the antarctic ice pack.
Quite possibly, he would have discovered the antarctic peninsula, if his vessels could have survived the rough seas of the Antarctic Ocean. But no European would reach such a latitude for another two and one-half centuries.

Port San Julian was at the entrance of a gulf that Magellan explored. There
was no sign of a passage. For several weeks, as Magellan put the crews to
work careening the ships on the beach to scrape the barnacles off their bottoms and building shelters, no sign of human occupation of this hard, cold
land was observed. Then appeared the first gigantic inhabitants—true giants,
eight to eight and one-half feet tall, according to the journal of Anthony
Pigafetta. He related that the Europeans barely came up to the natives'
waists.

The giants were dressed in skins of guanaco, a relative of the llama. They
wrapped their feet in these skins, which they stuffed with straw for warmth.
The coverings made their feet look huge. Magellan named the land after
their big feet—Patagonia. Two of the giants were lured into leg-irons and
chains and taken aboard ships so that they could be exhibited in Spain when
the armada returned; but they died, along with many members of the crew,
later in the expedition. Although Pigafetta's account of the Patagonian giants
was supported by the survivors of the expedition, later European voyagers
did not see them. Were they figments of overworked imaginations, such as
the mythical Unipeds, or were they a remnant of a primitive race of giants
that later vanished?

Magellan proved to be a practical explorer. He put the crews on half rations to stimulate them to hunt for food and live off the land as much as possible so as to conserve shipboard supplies. But morale was low. It became
apparent that in spite of the secret information Magellan was thought to pos-
sess, he knew no more about this region nor where the *paso* might be than
the most illiterate sailor.

A mutinous mood spread through the armada. On Easter Sunday, 1520,
Magellan and the crew of the *Trinidad* went, armed, to celebrate mass on
shore. The mutiny broke out the next morning. Cartagena was again released by Coca. With Quesada and thirty armed men, they seized the *San
Antonio* and tied up its captain, Alvaro Mesquita. In doing so, Quesada fatally wounded the first mate, Juan de Lloriaga, who tried to stop them. By
the time Magellan became aware of the mutiny, the Fonseca gang controlled
three of the five ships: the *San Antonio,* the *Victoria* under Mendoza, and
the *Concepcion* under Quesada. Magellan retained control of the *Trinidad*
and the little *Santiago,* captained by Serrano.

During the morning, sailors rowed from the *Concepcion* to the flagship
with a letter from Quesada. It explained that the uprising was a protest
against the captain general's refusal to treat the captains in a manner becoming to their rank and to take them into his confidence. If Magellan would

mend his ways and listen to them, the letter promised, the mutineers would return to duty under his command.

Magellan responded by suggesting a conference of captains on the flagship. He sent the answer to Mendoza on the *Victoria* by Espinosa and six men. All carried concealed weapons, and they rowed deliberately over to the rebel ship. Mendoza allowed this small and apparently harmless group to gain the deck. He received Espinosa and a marine in his cabin, where he stood supremely confident, clad in armor. As he began to read Magellan's letter, Mendoza was seized by Espinosa, who plunged a dagger into his throat while the marine struck at Mendoza's legs.

At this point, a boatload of Magellan's men, led by his brother-in-law, Duarte Barbosa, pulled alongside the *Victoria* and swarmed over the rail onto the waist deck. They had little difficulty in gaining control of the ship from the crewmen, who were only half-hearted about the mutiny. Leaving Mendoza dying in the cabin, Espinosa and the marine came forth on deck and assisted Barbosa in securing the ship. Then, according to a prearranged plan, they moved it alongside the *Trinidad* and the *Santiago* to block the harbor. Now Magellan had three ships to the rebels' two. Quesada and Coca tried to sail the *San Antonio* past the blockade, but their men took cover below deck when the *Trinidad* opened fire with its batteries. Magellan then led a boarding party and seized the deck; Quesada, deserted by his men, surrendered. Only Cartagena, who had assumed command of the *Concepcion*, remained. Seeing the odds against him, he yielded.

This time, Magellan held a full court-martial, over which his cousin, Mesquita, presided as judge. Forty men, including the Fonseca gang ringleaders, were sentenced to death. Because this was 20 percent of the entire crew, Magellan commuted the death sentences to hard labor for all except Quesada, who had murdered the *San Antonio*'s first mate, and Quesada's aide, Luis de Molina, an accomplice in the crime.

In exchange for his own life, Molina agreed to serve as his master's executioner and swung the sword that decapitated Quesada. The bodies of Quesada and the slain Mendoza were chopped into quarters, according to the custom of the time, and the bloody pieces were hung on stakes ashore as grim reminders of the penalty for murder and mutiny.

Late in March, Magellan sent Serrano on a scouting expedition to the south to look for inlets that might indicate the *paso*. The little *Santiago* made slow progress against unfavorable winds and currents. About sixty miles below Port Saint Julian, Serrano reached the mouth of a river. He named it Rio de Santa Cruz in honor of the day, May 3, the Feast of the Holy Cross.

A violent storm roared out of the south. Mountainous waves ripped off the *Santiago*'s rudder and drove the vessel onto the beach. All but one of the crewmen were able to jump off the ship to dry sand before huge waves rushed up again and dragged the ship back into the sea, where it was smashed against rocks.

Without food, clothing, or supplies, the shipwrecked men faced freezing and death. Fortunately, Serrano had flint and steel in his pocket so that a fire could be started. He sent two men back to Port Saint Julian overland for help. They crossed the mouth of the river on a makeshift raft and hiked to the armada's base in eleven days, arriving so gaunt that their crewmates could barely recognize them. Magellan immediately sent a rescue party with food and supplies.

Influenced by Serrano's report that Santa Cruz offered a more sheltered port for wintering over in this frigid land than did Port Saint Julian, Magellan decided to move his winter quarters there. At least he would be nearer the *paso*—how much nearer he was to learn later.

THE STRAIT OF PATAGONIA

The armada, now four ships strong, sailed out of Port Saint Julian August 24, 1520, leaving marooned on a small island the arch-rebel Juan de Cartagena and a priest, Pedro Sanches de Reina, who had supported the mutiny. The two were given a small supply of ship's biscuits and wine. They were never seen again, at least by Europeans. In his chronicle of the voyage, Pigafetta said of Cartagena: "The captain-general did not wish to have him killed because the emperor, Don Carlo, had appointed him a captain."

The only conspirator whose lot ultimately was improved by the mutiny was Juan Sebastian del Cano. He was among those sentenced to death and later pardoned. As a result of the expedition's high casualty rate, he became captain of the *Victoria* and brought her back to Spain, eventually receiving command of a second Moluccan expedition. [17]

When the austral spring came, the armada resumed the search for the passage. The ships sailed out of the estuary of Santa Cruz October 18, 1520, once more on their interminable journey toward the "antarctic pole," as Pigafetta related it. Three days later, after weathering a polar storm, the armada was forced to turn southeastward by the trend of the land that flared out into a prominent cape. Magellan named it the Cape of the Eleven Thousand Virgins, because it was sighted on Saint Ursula's Day, October 21. [18]

The cape concealed the entrance to a wide bay. To the west, there appeared a strange landscape, a range of towering snowcapped mountains. As Magellan sailed into the embayment for a routine exploration, Gomes and the men who supported him again broached the prospect of sailing eastward to the Moluccas. Even Magellan's closest associates—Barbosa, Mesquita, and Serrano—were convinced that it was a waste of time to explore this unpromising body of water, for the backdrop of mountains made it seem unlikely that any strait would be found there.

But Magellan obstinately insisted on carrying out the search procedure that he had repeated time after time since the armada had failed to find the passage in the Río de la Plata. He ordered Mesquita and Serrano to sail their ships, the *San Antonio* and *Concepcion*, westward to see where the embayment led. While they were on that mission, Magellan and Barbosa would investigate the northern and southern shores of the bay in the *Trinidad* and *Victoria*. After five days, the vessels would make rendezvous at the Cape of the Eleven Thousand Virgins.

Pigafetta tells that the ships had hardly set out on their reconnaissances when a great storm broke. The *Trinidad* and *Victoria* were able to ride it out by "letting ourselves drift hither and thither about the bay," but the *San Antonio* and the *Concepcion* were driven hard before the wind to the west and vanished from Magellan's view. He was sure they were lost. Three days later, after the storm let up, Magellan and Barbosa saw smoke. They feared it was the signal of shipwrecked men, but a short while later, they saw the missing ships racing toward them, "with sails full and banners flying in the wind," Pigafetta related. "When they neared us in this manner," the chronicler added, "they suddenly discharged a number of mortars and burst into cheers."

They had found the passage! Where it led, to Balboa's South Sea or Ptolemy's Magnus Sinus, remained to be seen. According to Pigafetta, the discovery of the strait had been an accident. As the *San Antonio* and *Concepcion* were blown landward in the bay, they spied "a small opening which did not appear to be an opening, but a sharp turn. Like desperate men, they hauled into it." It was a channel that led into another bay. They sailed through the second bay, and at its end they found another channel leading to a third bay, larger than the first two. Buckets were lowered for water samples and the water was salt. "Very joyful, they immediately turned back to inform the captain-general. . . . Then all together thanking God and the Virgin Mary, we went to see [the strait] farther on."

Pigafetta was convinced that Magellan knew of the strait all along, because its entrance was not obvious to anyone else, and other mariners would have passed it by. It was Pigafetta's understanding that Magellan learned about the strait from the globe of "Martin of Bohemia" (Behaim) or from a copy of it in Lisbon.

Alvaro de Mesquita had sailed the *San Antonio* about ninety miles through the strait before turning back. He reported that it was narrow and deep—so deep in places that he could not find bottom. Granite cliffs flanked the narrow passages between the bays. On shore, the sailors found huts containing the mummified bodies of Patagonians, all more than six feet tall.

During the rest of October, the ships bobbed cautiously through the mountain-girt channels that Norsemen would have recognized as fjords. Then the armada reached a fork in the road. One passage led to the southeast and another to the southwest. Magellan dispatched the *San Antonio* and the *Concepcion* to explore the southeast passage. He and Barbosa took the *Trinidad* and the *Victoria* into the southwest strait, which seemed more likely to lead to the western sea. They were to meet back at the fork in five days.

Magellan and Barbosa threaded their ships cautiously between the sharp rocks of this great, flooded fault that separates the main corpus of South America from its spiny tail. The water was salty all the way. Much of the time, mist enshrouded the narrow channels and cloaked the mountains. When it lifted, there stood revealed a mountain scene of immense grandeur and beauty. Pigafetta related that the lower slopes were forested with evergreens. Clear, sparkling streams poured down through the wooded hills into the strait.

Turning to the northwest, the strait widened. On their port side, the men of the armada saw a lonely land, which Magellan was convinced was Terra Australis. It could not be Ceylon, which was tropical, he reasoned. At this season of the year, the night is only three hours long. In the darkness appeared the distant glow of campfires. Magellan called the south coast Tierra del Fuego ("Land of Fire"). He called the passage the Strait of Patagonia, according to Pigafetta; other accounts say he named it the Strait of All Saints. Only later was it named after him. At a gushing river—called the River of Sardines because so many of the small, silvery fish were caught in it— Magellan anchored the armada. He sent Espinosa, his trusty sergeant at arms, ahead with several men in a longboat to reconnoiter the strait further and to determine if it was passable to the ships.

Three days later, the longboat returned. Espinosa could be seen from afar, waving a red banner tied to a lance. When he reached hailing distance, he cried out that he found the open sea and a cape at its entrance. Magellan listened in silence as his sergeant at arms bawled out the news. "When he heard this," said Pigafetta, "the captain-general wept for joy and called that cape, Dezeado [Desire], for we had been desiring it for a long time."

Magellan then turned back to look for the ships that he had sent to reconnoiter the southeastern channel. Only the *Concepcion* awaited him at the rendezvous. There was no sign of the *San Antonio*.

For days, Magellan searched for the missing vessel, fearing that it had been sunk. Cannon was fired at intervals. Messages were left in cairns onshore in case the missing ship might pass the searchers during a fog in one of the wide embayments. The *Victoria* sailed all the way back to the Atlantic entrance of the strait. But of the *San Antonio* there was no trace.

Magellan never learned what had happened, but he had a theory. Andres de San Martin, the expedition's astrologer, divined that Gomes, still the pilot aboard the *San Antonio*, had led a mutiny against Mesquita, taken over the ship, and sailed back into the Atlantic toward Spain. It was a logical divination and turned out to be the case.

With his Armada de Maluco reduced to three ships, Magellan turned back to the west and completed the 375-mile passage between the oceans, entering the open sea November 28, 1520. Once in the South Sea, the armada enjoyed fine spring weather and good sailing to the north. The sea was as smooth as glass. Magellan, impressed by its calmness in contrast to the Atlantic, called it El Mar Pacifico.

GUAM

The northward course in the Pacific Ocean, along the coast of South America, was dictated more by winds and currents than by any navigational judgment on the part of Magellan and his pilots. The little armada was swept up above the equator to the latitudes of the southeast trades. These winds pushed the ships across the ocean on a long diagonal that took them considerably north of the Moluccas and to the Marianas and the Philippines instead.

It was a long haul for ships of the sixteenth century, which were poorly equipped and victualed. Quite possibly it was the longest voyage without a landfall Europeans had ever made. Island-hopping Polynesians had crossed thousands of miles of the western and central Pacific in their frail canoes, but they were a sea people and knew how to extract the sea's bounty; they understood its moods and currents. The Europeans were in the Pacific for the first time. Until Balboa, its existence had been ambiguous, until Magellan, its dimensions unsuspected. In terms of geographical comprehension, Magellan discovered the Pacific Ocean, and it was a hard experience.

On the armada sailed, day after day, as the weather grew warmer. It missed Easter Island, where the crews might have replenished supplies of food and water that had been exhausted before they reached the equator. Their north-by-northwest route took them over an empty expanse of ocean between the Galapagos Islands on the east and the Marquesas on the west.

For three months and twenty days there was no fresh food, Pigafetta related. When the biscuits—the main food staple—were gone, the men ate the crumbs from the bottom of the barrels. The crumbs were swarming with worms and stank of rat urine, but the men ate them. When the crumbs were gone, the starving sailors dismantled the oxhides that covered the tops of the main yard to prevent it from chafing the shrouds. The hides were eaten, too. They had become as brittle as wood from sun, wind, and rain, but the men doused them in saltwater to soften them and then cooked them over slow fires.

They ate sawdust from boards. Rats were snared and sold for a half ducat apiece. Some men died when their gums swelled so much from scurvy that they could not eat anything. Altogether, nineteen men died from the effects of scurvy and malnutrition. Among the dead was one of the Patagonian giants they had chained to exhibit back in Spain and a Brazilian Indian, also an exhibit. The second giant had been incarcerated on the *San Antonio,* and he also died before Gomes reached Spain. There is, consequently, no independent verification of these strange aborigines, at least of the ones reported by the men of the first Armada de Maluco.

On the flagship, thirty of the men were so sick and weak they could not work the ship. Pigafetta relates that, miraculously, he remained well. Presumably, he had access with the officers to a better diet than the ordinary seamen had. Pigafetta told: "We sailed about four thousand leagues [about 12,000 English miles] during those three months and twenty days through an open stretch in that Pacific sea."

Pigafetta expressed doubt that such a voyage would ever be made again. The starving men saw two desert islands, which they called the Unfortunate Isles. These were Clipperton and Clarion Islands near the South American coast. Had they continued sailing west at fifty-two degrees south latitude after leaving the Strait of Patagonia, Pigafetta reckoned, they might have sailed all the way around the world without sighting land until they returned to the Cape of the Eleven Thousand Virgins. Except for the subantarctic islands, he was right.

The Italian chronicler noted several points of interest about the southern hemisphere, unreported by Europeans before. He thought that the "antarctic pole is not so starry as the arctic." But he noted a region where many small stars were clustered together to give the appearance of two luminous clouds. Pigafetta was seeing farther than he could have imagined. The luminous clouds were galactic neighbors of our galaxy, the Milky Way, and the captain-general's name became enshrined in these distant galaxies, which became known as the Magellanic Clouds. At night, there was a cross in the heavens of "very clear stars dead west and they were evenly spaced," Pigafetta noted. Onward sailed the armada, under the Southern Cross, seemingly on an endless ocean.

When the armada reached the equator, Magellan continued sailing to the northwest, with the prevailing wind. The course would carry him north of the Moluccas, which he knew were only 4 degrees above the equator. He now explained that he was aiming for Cattigara, which the Ptolemaic maps said was on the China coast. Once he had reached that rich port and taken on provisions, he would turn back south to the Moluccas.

The explanation has made many an historian wonder what Magellan was up to. One theory is that he was looking for the Philippines, which he may have visited, or heard of, in 1512, while serving with the Portuguese fleet at Malacca. Another suggests that he was searching for lands not claimed by the Portuguese in the Magnus Sinus—rich islands called the Lequios (Ryukyus, probably, and the Island of Formosa). There, people wealthier than the Chinese were reputed to dwell, so Magellan had heard.

Before the expedition got underway, Magellan had considered a number of possible goals. The Moluccas were only one of them. The islands off the China coast might be lands referred to in the Old Testament as Ophir and Tarshish, which King Solomon and his naval partner, Hiram of Tyre, had exploited for gold, precious stones, and spices.[19]

In the fifteenth century, these lands were thought to be on the east coast of Africa. Hiram's galleys could have reached them there by sailing from the port of Eilat via the Gulf of Aqaba and the Red Sea. But when the Portuguese failed to find them, the lands kept moving farther and farther east, always eluding the searchers. Magellan considered the possibility now that they were in the vicinity of Cattigara.

There is no record of what he intended to do. However, at 12 degrees north latitude, he turned the armada west and reached Guam in the Marianas on March 6, 1521. His crews were in a terribly weakened state, many near death. The islanders were a dark, active, wiry people, the Chamorros, who rubbed their bodies with coconut oil and rejected utterly the concept of private property. When they swarmed to the ships in their outrigger canoes and clambered over the rails, they stole everything in sight, including the *Trinidad*'s small boat. The flagship's crewmen were so weak they could not interfere with the gleeful looting by the natives who knocked Magellan's men around at will.

Alarmed and then enraged by the aggressiveness of the islanders, Magellan ordered his crossbowmen to shoot them. When several of them went down with arrows in their chests, the natives fled, taking the *Trinidad*'s longboat with them. The armada shelled the native village, and then Magellan took forth armed men ashore, burned what was left of the village to the ground, and recovered the longboat. He named Guam and adjacent islands the Ladrones ("Islands of Thieves"). "Those Ladroni thought, according to the signs which they made, that there were no other people in the world but themselves," Pigafetta observed.

Unable to get supplies on Guam, the armada sailed on to the Island of Rota. Its inhabitants had been apprised of the slaughter on Guam. They paddled out toward the ships but remained at some distance. This time, Magellan was able to trade peacefully with the people of Rota and stock the ship with fruit, chickens, and pork.

The armada sailed on to the west. Magellan sought a pleasant island where he could rest the crews and allow the sick time to recover. At dawn, March 16, 1521, the lookouts sighted a high land dead ahead. Pigafetta identified it as the Island of Zamal (Samar). It lies on the eastern edge of the Philippine archipelago, which Magellan named the Archipelago of Saint Lazarus, since March 21 was the saint's day.[20]

Bypassing the island, which looked inhabited, Magellan dropped anchor at a nearby island called Homonhon, which appeared to be uninhabited. He wanted to avoid another encounter with natives. The crews of the three ships needed water and rest. Tents were set up for the sick, and one of the pigs acquired from Rota was roasted.

Two days later, a boatload of people approached the island. Pigafetta tells that these were "reasonable men," and Magellan welcomed them.

During his military service in Malacca, Magellan had picked up a loyal servant, Enriques, a Malay. He was able to act as interpreter in the widespread Indonesian language, as was one of the Portuguese pilots, Juan Lopes Carvalho, who also had served in the Indies. With communications open, Magellan quickly established friendly relations with the delegation. He gave the short, brown men red caps, mirrors, combs, bells, and ivory. They reciprocated with fish, palm wine called arrack, and coconuts. The spokesman said the delegation came from a nearby island called Suluan. It was evident that they represented a higher culture than did the naked warriors of Guam. The delegates wore gold ornaments and conducted themselves with restraint and dignity.

Magellan and his men now knew that they had reached a vast array of islands with a large population. These people had contact with the Indies and probably with China. According to Pigafetta, the archipelago lay in 10 degrees latitude "toward the arctic pole and longitude of 161 degrees from the line of demarcation." That would put it in the Spanish zone.[21] Modern reckoning would show that the armada had penetrated eight degrees thirty minutes into the Portuguese zone. But because that could not have been determined accurately for another two and one-half centuries, the question was academic.

The Suluanese eventually produced their chief, or rajah—a tattooed old man who wore two gold rings in his ears. He was escorted by an honor guard of men who wore gold bands around their biceps and brightly colored kerchiefs around their heads. "There are people living near that island who have holes in their ears so large that they pass their arms through them," Pigafetta reported.

The people were called by Moslem merchants Caphri (kaffirs, or "heathen"). Pigafetta described them as "dark, fat and painted, with waist-long, black hair." Their weapons were the dagger and spear, ornamented with gold, and "their boats were like ours." Most of the time, they went about naked, except for a breechclout, he said.

Magellan moved on. On March 28, the armada anchored near the Island of Limasawa, south of Leyte. The local ruler, or datu, was one Rajah Columbu, who became so friendly with Magellan that he piloted the armada to the rich island of Cebu. That island was more advanced than any of the others the Europeans had seen. It was inhabited by a wealthy, civilized people who evidently had trading contact with Arabs and Chinese. When the armada arrived in the harbor of Cebu, April 7, a Chinese junk lay at anchor, having disgorged a cargo of slaves and porcelain artifacts. There was now no question that Magellan had indeed found a westward path to the East Indies, but it was longer and harder than he had bargained for.

MACTAN

The rajah of Cebu was a short, fat fellow named Humabon. At first, he tried to exact tribute from the armada, but an Arab merchant who had arrived with the Chinese junk warned him that these fair-skinned people were highly destructive when aroused and could, if they wished, destroy his whole city. The Arab assumed that the Europeans were Portuguese.

Magellan's servant, Enriques, who had followed this conversation, interposed with a correction. These were not the same people who had conquered Calicut, Goa, and Malacca, but their masters. Impressed, Humabon dropped his demand for tribute, or a "port tax," as he called it.

Pigafetta relates that the rajah treated Magellan and his officers with great respect and "had three quite naked girls dance for us." The girls also played musical instruments, including a drum, gongs, and little brass bells. Pigafetta noted that the gongs were made of brass, like the bells, and came from "the regions about the Signio Magno which is called China."

Humabon, eager to please the Europeans, and 500 of his subjects were converted to Christianity en masse. They had gained the impression that the conversion would help them overcome their enemies. Magellan gave the rajah a Christian name, Don Carlo, after the emperor.

Magellan realized that he had made a major discovery of new territory. He was anxious to seal it for Spain, for the archipelago appeared to be potentially as rich as the Malay peninsula farther west. He now set out to establish a political hegemony in these islands under Humabon, the first Christian king who had sworn allegiance to Spain.

Meanwhile, his captains, Barbosa and Serrano, urged him to sail on to the Moluccas; but Magellan wanted to consolidate his discovery of the archipelago before leaving it. It was for this reason that Magellan volunteered to intervene with his armored force in a local war between two chiefs on the neighboring island of Mactan. Zula, a vassal of Humabon, complained that a rival, Cilapulapu, refused to recognize the authority of Humabon. This implied that the rebel chief rejected the suzerainty of Spain. Humabon's vassal asked for help in subduing Cilapulapu, and Magellan considered it politic to provide it.

Magellan decided to put on a demonstration of the might of European arms and armor and at the same time teach Cilapulapu a lesson. At dawn on April 27, 1521, the captain general and 49 men, including Pigafetta, waded ashore on Mactan, leaving 11 men to guard the boats. Pigafetta said that as the sky lightened, they found themselves facing a rebel force of 1,500 armed warriors. Lying offshore, Humabon commanded a fleet of 1,000 men and offered to join the attack, but Magellan bade him only to observe. It was a fatal mistake.

In armor that was invulnerable to Filipino weapons and with harquebuses and crossbows, the Europeans felt themselves invincible. The natives had dug a series of trenches in the beach, which the Europeans had to cross to reach them. Then the rebels let fly a rain of spears, arrows, fire-hardened stakes, and mud balls. Magellan sent a squad to burn their village, expecting that would take the heart out of them. But it served only to infuriate them to demoniacal energy.

The European firearms and crossbow bolts did not have the expected effect, probably because Magellan's poorly trained force opened fire at too great a distance. The missiles failed to penetrate the wooden shields of the natives or were so spent when they did that they inflicted only superficial wounds. Magellan was wounded in the leg (he already limped from an old wound received in Morocco) by an arrow. The rebels realized that the legs of the invaders were vulnerable, like their faces, and aimed their bamboo spears and fire-hardened arrows at those parts.

Slowly, Magellan and his men were forced back into the trenches they had struggled across to reach the rebels. The natives surrounded them on three sides and pushed them toward the surf. The retreat quickened. "The natives continued to pursue us and picking up the same spear five or six times hurled it at us again and again," Pigafetta wrote. "Recognizing the captain, so many turned upon him that they knocked his helmet off his head twice, but he always stood firm like a good knight, together with some others."

Magellan and eight men, including Pigafetta, retreated into the surf, holding off the mass of natives so that the rest of the force could reach the boats. Then an "Indian," as Pigafetta called all the native peoples he encountered, hurled a bamboo spear into Magellan's face. Painfully hurt, Magellan killed the assailant with a lance. Leaving it in the warrior's body, Magellan then tried to draw his sword, but his arm was too badly wounded to draw it more than halfway. Pigafetta relates:

> When the natives saw that, they all hurled themselves upon him. One of them wounded him on the left leg with a large cutlass which resembles a scimitar. That caused the captain to fall face downward, when immediately they rushed upon him with iron and bamboo spears and with their cutlasses, until they killed our mirror, our light, our comfort and our true guide. When they wounded him, he turned

back many times to see whether we were all in the boats. Thereupon, beholding him dead, we, wounded, retreated as best we could to the boats, which were already pulling off.

So ended Magellan's role in the greatest voyage in European history. He was forty-one years old when he was slain on Mactan. With his death, the expedition disintegrated.

Duarte Barbosa was elected captain general and Juan Serrano second in command of the armada. The influence of the Europeans in Cebu had evaporated with the Battle of Mactan. The rebel chief, Cilapulapu, threatened to attack Humabon unless he got rid of them. On May 1, Humabon lured the new commanders and two dozen of their men ashore, gave them a banquet with dancing girls, and then seized and murdered nearly all but Serrano. He was exhibited as a hostage to prevent cannon fire from the ships. Juan Carvalho, next in command, took over the armada and, rejecting Serrano's frantic pleas that the armada ransom him, sailed away, leaving Serrano to his fate.

Of the 241 men who had left Spain nearly two years before, only 115 remained. They were too few to man the three ships. Carvalho had the *Concepcion* beached on an island, stripped, and burned, its stores transferred to the *Trinidad* and *Victoria*. Now down to two vessels, the armada sailed on toward the Moluccas.

Carvalho, however, turned out to be an indifferent navigator in those waters but an efficient pirate. As the ships floundered about the Sulu Sea, he seized as many local vessels as he could find, looting their cargoes and enslaving any women aboard. Eventually, the armada reached Borneo, where the ships spent a month in the port city of Brunei. With a harem of captured women, Carvalho had become addicted to piracy. His stewardship of the armada became intolerable, even to his comrades. Espinosa and Del Cano overpowered him and told him he was through as captain general. Command passed to Espinosa and the one-time mutineer Del Cano.

Once more under new management, the Armada de Maluco reached the Island of Tidore in the Moluccas early in November of 1521. There they learned that Francisco Serrao had been murdered just a short time before on Ternate. They were told that he was poisoned by a native woman at the behest of the Portuguese, who had failed in several attempts to seize him.[22] The Portuguese feared that if Magellan reached Ternate, Serrao's influence would swing the allegiance of the rajah, Boleyse, to Spain.

At Tidore, Espinosa and Del Cano were welcomed by the ruler, a personable man named Almanzor, who was looking for allies to keep the Portuguese out of his realm. Both ships were then loaded with cloves—the *Trinidad* with fifty tons and the *Victoria* with twenty-six. But as they departed for the homeward voyage December 18, 1521, the *Trinidad* sprang a leak.

Repairs would take months. The ship would have to be unloaded, beached, and careened. It was agreed that Del Cano would sail the *Victoria* back to Spain at once via the Cape of Good Hope to take advantage of favorable winds at that season in the Indian Ocean, taking care to avoid Portuguese ships. The *Trinidad* finally was repaired and sailed April 6, 1522, with fifty-four crewmen, leaving a small force of marines on Tidore to establish Spain's claim. By that time, the winds had reversed, preventing Espinosa from following Del Cano's track. Espinosa had no choice but to sail back to Patagonia and work his way through the strait to the Atlantic.

En route, he discovered the Caroline Islands. After reaching the Marianas, he encountered a twelve-day storm. It battered the *Trinidad* so badly that Espinosa decided the ship was in no condition to attempt the strait. He then turned north, hoping to reach the Pacific side of Spanish Panama, where he could obtain repairs and supplies. But unfavorable winds and a shortage of food made that course inadvisable. After twenty-seven members of his crew died of hunger and disease, he turned back to the Moluccas.

Unluckily, he landed at Ternate, which the Portuguese had seized after the rajah there had been murdered by poison. The flagship of the armada and its rich cargo of cloves—enough to have paid all the costs of the entire expedition and still leave a profit (see note 17)—was captured by the Portuguese. All of Magellan's logs, charts, and diaries fell into Portuguese hands. Espinosa and his crewmen were sentenced to four years of hard labor in India as punishment for daring to encroach on a Portuguese claim. He and four others survived the imprisonment. They returned to Spain in 1526.

Meanwhile, Del Cano steered the *Victoria* in a furtive flight across the Indian Ocean at 42 degrees south latitude, where he hoped to evade Portuguese ships. His voyage was beset by famine, thirst, mutiny, scurvy, and disease picked up on the Island of Timor. For nine weeks, Del Cano and his weakened crew tried to sail around the Cape of Good Hope into the Atlantic, only to be driven back time after time by contrary winds.

The little ship finally succeeded in doubling the cape at a distance of only fifteen miles May 6, 1522, but lost its foremast in the struggle. For the next two months, Del Cano sailed northwest, not daring to put into any port for food or water as they cruised along the west coast of Africa. During that time, twenty-one men died, including a contingent of Mollucans who had signed on to help work the ship. Pigafetta, the indestructible chronicler, noted that "when we cast them [the dead men] into the sea, the Christians went to the bottom face upward while the Indians always went down face downward."

No longer willing to sail by another port without making some attempt to get food and water, Del Cano took a chance of tricking the Portuguese and put into Sancto Jacobo in the Cape Verde Islands on July 9. There they learned they had lost a day circumnavigating the world, for at Sancto Jacobo, the date was July 10.

Del Cano gave the shore party explicit instructions to say that the vessel had lost its foremast on a terrible trip across the Atlantic from the Americas, not near the Cape of Good Hope. The stratagem worked. The starving sailors received two boatloads of rice. However, a second shore party erred in trying to exchange some cloves for food and was quickly seized. Fearing the *Victoria* would be impounded, Del Cano raised sail, leaving the party of thirteen men in a tropical prison.

On Saturday, September 6, 1522, the *Victoria* entered the Bay of San Lucar; it was just two weeks short of three years after the grand Armada de Maluco had so proudly sailed away. Of the 241 men who had departed in 1519, only 18 ragged, gaunt men returned that day.

The *Victoria* sailed up the Guadalquivir River to Seville. Pigafetta reckoned that the little ship had traveled 14,640 leagues (43,920 miles) in completing the first circumnavigation of the world. He concluded: "On the eighth of September, they dropped anchor in the Port of Seville. And they shot off all artillery, gave thanks to God in their shirts, barefooted, and with torches in their hands." [23]

DRAKE

Fifty-five years later, Francis Drake, an English sea captain and privateer in the service of Queen Elizabeth I, added the epilogue to the search for the southwest passage.

As Magellan did, Drake set sail with a fleet of five ships on a voyage of circumnavigation. It was, however, a multipurpose expedition. In addition to aiming to raid Spanish commercial enterprises on the Pacific coast of the Americas, Drake carried secret instructions to look for the legendary Terra Australis. Magellan had supposed that Tierra del Fuego was a piece of the land that Elizabethan adventurers such as Richard Greynville believed extended northward in the Pacific Ocean from the antarctic pole to a latitude of 30 degrees south. There might be a southern continent as rich as the Americas, for all anyone knew.

Drake's voyage, like Magellan's, was a monument to navigational skill, courage, and luck. It took him through the Straits of Magellan and then, after a storm that left only his flagship, the *Golden Hind*, under his command, northward along the west coast of South America. He raided Valparaiso and Callao and captured a Spanish treasure ship off Mexico.

To avoid reprisal while seeking a northwest passage back to the Atlantic, Drake sailed far to the north of the Spanish bases of Acapulco and Panama.

He ranged the coast of California and put into a bay north of San Francisco Bay (Drake's Bay) for repairs and provisions. He named the region New Albion and claimed it for Elizabeth.

Drake probably sailed the *Golden Hind* as far north as Seattle before he gave up the search for the Northwest Passage and turned southwest to sail across the Pacific Ocean. He called at the Moluccas, Celebes, and Java; negotiated the Indian Ocean; rounded the Cape of Good Hope; and reached Plymouth September 26, 1580. Elizabeth knighted him aboard the *Golden Hind*.

Sir Francis had not found Terra Australis, but he had launched England on the road to world naval power. And he had completed the demolition of Ptolemy's geography to allow the emergence of the modern world.

Along with the latest maps and charts, Drake carried Pigafetta's journal when his fleet put to sea on the great voyage November 15, 1577. Coasting south along Africa and then crossing the Atlantic, the fleet reached the Río de la Plata early in April 1578 and Port Saint Julian in Patagonia in mid-winter, June 20, 1578. There he suppressed a mutiny, as Magellan had done. Drake broke up his two expendable supply ships and transferred their food and munitions to the *Golden Hind*, the *Marigold*, and the *Elizabeth*.

Drake's three ships arrived at the Cape of the Eleven Thousand Virgins August 17. They made the transit of the Straits of Magellan in seventeen days. On September 6, the fleet entered the Pacific Ocean. At once it was caught by a terrible storm. For days, the roaring gales drove the ships southward. When the storm abated, the *Golden Hind* was alone on the tossing sea, near a cluster of rocky islands. It was evident that Tierra del Fuego was not Terra Australis but part of an island cluster at the tip of South America.

Drake sailed the flagship among the cluster, vainly seeking the *Marigold* and the *Elizabeth*. But they were gone—the *Marigold* to the bottom with all hands, the *Elizabeth* back to England.

There was no Terra Australis in that latitude. Drake reported: "We fell in with the uttermost part of land towards the south pole and had certainly discovered how far the same doth reach southward from the coast of America. . . . the uttermost cape of headlands of all these islands stands near 56 degrees without which there is no main or island to be seen to the southwards but that the Atlantic Ocean and the South Sea meet in a most large and free scope." [24]

The age of Ptolemaic geography had ended.

CHAPTER III

TERRA AUSTRALIS

The next move in the European reconnaissance of the world after the discovery of the Americas and the islands of the Pacific Ocean was the search for Terra Australis, the southern continent. Two hundred years after Drake's *Golden Hind* was blown south of Tierra del Fuego into the wild seas now called the Drake Passage, European mariners were still looking for that hypothetical land.

In that period, maritime superiority had shifted from the Iberian kingdoms to England, France, and the rising Netherlands. The circumnavigation of the Earth had become an acceptable risk—so much so that a well-to-do, young Englishman, when asked if he was ready to take the conventional grand tour of Europe to complete his education, remarked: "Every blockhead does that. My grand tour should be around the world." He was Joseph Banks, and he did sail around the world, as scientist with the greatest of eighteenth-century navigators, James Cook.

Cook's three voyages (1768–1779) opened Australia, New Zealand, and the islands of Oceania and Hawaii to Western colonization and exploitation. With them, modern geography comes into focus, for they disposed of the last of the Ptolemaic myths: that Terra Australis extended into the South Temperate Zone.

James Cook was born in a mud cottage at Marton-in-Cleveland, October 27, 1728, the son of a farm laborer in North Riding, Yorkshire. He was the second of nine children and received only an elementary education. At seventy, his father learned how to read in order to find out what his famous son was doing, for Cook's journals were widely distributed.

At the age of seventeen, Cook became an apprentice to the Walker shipping firm at Whitby, where he acquired his first training in navigation. During the Seven Years War for the control of North America, Cook, in his late twenties, served in the British navy as an able seaman and then as a chart-maker. His charts of the Saint Lawrence River and the coast of New-foundland attracted the attention of admiralty officers. He rose quickly to mate and master. Unlike his great predecessors Columbus, Magellan, and Drake, he did not seek assignments; they sought him.

In the awakening of science and technology in the eighteenth century, a new motivation for discovery was born. It was an effort to investigate the nature of the environment. In that period, it was coupled with the search for new lands.

Earlier in the eighteenth century, the Astronomer Royal, Edmund Halley (1656–1742), suggested that the transit of Venus across the face of the sun would be useful in solving a perplexing scientific problem—the distance from the Earth to the sun. Simultaneous observations of this event from different points on the Earth would enable astronomers to determine the parallax of the sun. (*Parallax* refers to the distance an object appears to shift against its background when seen from different points of view. Solar parallax is the angle subtended by the equatorial radius of the earth at the distance of the sun.) From this determination, the distance of the sun could be calculated.[1]

The British admiralty undertook to send an astronomical expedition to the Island of Tahiti to observe from there the transit of Venus, which was scheduled to occur June 3, 1769. For this scientific purpose, the navy acquired a Whitby-built collier, the *Endeavour,* and summoned James Cook, then a lieutenant, to take command of it.

Tahiti had been discovered by Samuel Wallis in June 1767 and visited by Louis Antoine de Bougainville, who claimed the island for France, in April 1768. While Cook's mission marks the beginning of government-sponsored scientific expeditions, the observation of the transit of Venus was not its sole objective. Cook sailed with secret orders that were not published until 1928. They stated:

> Whereas there is reason to imagine that a continent or land of great extent may be found to the southward of the tract made by Captain Wallis in His Majesty's ship, the "Dolphin," or of the tract of any former navigators in pursuits of the like kind; you are therefore in pursuance of His Majesty's pleasure hereby required and directed to put to sea with the bark you command as soon as the observation of the transit of Venus shall be finished and observe the following instructions: You are to proceed to the southward in order to make discovery of the continent above mentioned until you arrive in the latitude of 40 degrees, unless you sooner fall in with it; but not having discovered it or any evident signs of it in that run you are to proceed in search of it westward between the latitude aforementioned and the latitude of 35 degrees until you discover it or fall in with the eastern side of the land discovered by Tasman now called New Zealand.

In the two centuries since Drake had reported that the Atlantic and the South Sea met in wide and free scope below South America, the extent of Terra Australis had been shrinking. However, the southern part of Tasmania and the west coast of New Zealand, discovered by the Dutch captain Abel

Tasman in 1642, were considered to be the northern coasts of Terra Australis.

Because of that possibility, a strong belief existed in Europe that another continent rivaling the Americas in gold and natural resources lay waiting to be found in the southern ocean. The belief was promoted in England by Alexander Dalrymple, a Fellow of the Royal Society, first hydrographer of the navy and an expert on the South Sea. A similar idea was fostered in France by Charles DeBrosse, president of the Parliament of Dijon and disciple of the naturalist Georges Louis Leclerc, Comte de Buffon.

DeBrosse had published a history of navigation to southern lands in 1756. It influenced French maritime policy toward seeking Terra Australis, especially after the loss of Canada as a French colony to the British with the Treaty of Paris in 1763. Even before that, however, the French navy sent Pierre Bouvet de Lozier to explore the southern ocean. On New Year's Day, 1739, he found a snow-covered island 1,400 miles south of the Cape of Good Hope in 54 degrees south latitude. It is still known as Bouvet Island. De-Bougainville also sought the elusive southern continent.

In England, the search, begun with Drake, was carried on in the eighteenth century by John Byron in 1764–1766 and by Wallis in 1766–1768. Both used the same ship, the *Dolphin*, and both carried secret orders to look for Terra Australis, as did Cook.

Cook set sail on his first voyage August 8, 1768. Destined to become a famous vessel, his *Endeavour* displaced 366 tons, had a deck length of ninety-seven feet eight inches, and had a width of twenty-nine feet two inches. The hold was eleven feet four inches deep. It was square-rigged on all three masts. The vessel carried a navy crew of eighty-four men and eleven civilians.

Cook reached Tierra del Fuego in mid-January 1769 and elected to sail around Cape Horn rather than through the Straits of Magellan at that season of the year. Anchoring in the Bay of Success before venturing into the Drake Passage, Cook described the natives there not as giants but as a copper-colored people of average size with long, black hair. They painted their bodies in streaks of red and black and wore guanaco or sealskin "in the same form as it came from the animal's back." Their dwellings were beehive-shaped huts and their weapons bows and arrows "neatly made." They were extremely fond of "any red thing."

When he reached Tahiti, Cook reported the persistent problem of native thievery. At one time, the natives stole the ship's quadrant—a heavy, brass instrument essential in navigation. It was recovered after a good deal of trouble.

The transit of Venus was observed June 3, 1769, on schedule by Cook along with the expedition's astronomer, Charles Green, and the botanist D. C. Solander.

Cook left Tahiti at the end of August 1769 and spent a month charting the Society Islands. He then sailed south to 40 degrees south latitude in search of Terra Australis, which, according to his journal, he never really expected to find. Seeing no sign of it, he turned west and raised the eastern coast of New Zealand's North Island October 2, 1769.

Cook determined that New Zealand consisted of two large islands separated by a sea passage, which was named for him. The inhabitants were the tough, warlike Maoris, who spoke a Polynesian language like that of the Tahitians. They called the North Island Aeheino Mouwe, and the South Island Tovy Poenammu.

The language affinity of the Maoris and Tahitians struck Cook as evidence that these people had a common origin. Was it Terra Australis? Asia? If there was a common place of origin, "it certainly is neither to the southward nor eastward," he wrote in his journal, "for I cannot persuade myself that ever they came from America; and as to a Southern Continent, I do not believe that such a thing exists except in a high latitude."

On April 19, 1770, Cook sighted the last of the supposed northern promontories of Terra Australis—Australia. The surf was too heavy to enable the crew to land, but they saw several crude canoes drawn up on the beach. Cook sailed the *Endeavour* into a wide bay, which he first called Stingray Harbor, because two giant stingrays, weighing 600 pounds each, were caught there. Later, he changed the name to Botany Bay. He anchored the *Endeavour* at an inlet north of the bay later called Port Jackson, not far from the present site of Sydney.

Coasting northward, Cook discovered the Great Barrier Reef, which lay on his starboard side. The *Endeavour* was trapped in waters between the beach and the reef. Before he was able to get clear of the trap, the *Endeavour* was nearly wrecked. The bottom was badly damaged by the sharp coral when winds drove the vessel onto the reef. The expedition was forced to spend months in Batavia in the Dutch East Indies while the ship was repaired. There Cook and his officers heard the first news of the coming revolution in America. The colonists were refusing to pay taxes.

Cook returned to England July 10, 1771, with the report that, although he had failed to discover "the so much talked of Southern Continent (which perhaps does not exist), yet I am confident that no part of the failure of such discovery can be laid to my charge."

COOK'S SEARCH CONTINUES

The experience of nearly being wrecked on the Great Barrier Reef had convinced Cook that on future expeditions he should have a second ship in reserve. On his second voyage, which began in July 1772, he took two ships. They were the 462-ton *Resolution* and the 336-ton *Adventure*. Tobias Furneaux was the captain of the smaller vessel, under Cook's overall command.

Admiralty sailing orders directed Cook to sail southward from the Cape of Good Hope to find Cape Circumcision on the land that Bouvet had found in 1739. He was to determine whether this cape was part of the southern continent. If it was, Cook was then to prosecute discoveries as near to the south pole as he could get.

If he could not find the cape, or if it was only part of an island, he was to continue south as long as he thought there was a likelihood of "falling in with a continent." He was then to proceed eastward in further search of land as well as discover "such islands as may be situated there." He was to keep in the high southern latitudes and search as near the pole as possible until he had circumnavigated the globe, returning by the Cape of Good Hope.

At Capetown, on the outward-bound leg of the voyage, Cook learned that two French ships under Yves Joseph de Kerguelen Tremarec, who had been sent by France to seek Terra Australis the previous year, had found an island in the Indian Ocean at 50 degrees south. He called it New France. (It is now called Kerguelen Island.)

Summer gales in the South Atlantic pushed Cook's two ships far to the east of the supposed position of Cape Circumcision. By December 10, 1772, the lookouts spied the huge, tabular icebergs that break off the antarctic ice sheet in midsummer and drift northward. The ice island, as Cook called it, was fifty feet high and one-half mile around, its top perfectly flat.

A century later John Murray, a Canadian oceanographer, was to inform the Royal Society in London: "Those flat-topped icebergs form the most striking peculiarity of the Antarctic Ocean. Their form and structure seem clearly to indicate that they were formed over an extended land surface and have been pushed over low lying coasts into the sea." [2]

But Cook and his observers did not realize that the flat-topped icebergs had broken off a continental ice sheet and were harbingers of Terra Australis. Sailing east and south, the vessels passed more of the ice islands. From one, the crews obtained fifteen tons of fresh water.

Nowhere in the wild southern ocean did Cape Circumcision appear. At 58 degrees south, sleet fell and froze on the rigging. "Every rope was covered with the finest transparent ice I ever saw," Cook wrote in his journal. On January 17, 1773, Cook noted:

> I continued to stand to the south and on the 17th between 11 and 12 o'clock we crossed the antarctic circle in 66 degrees 36 minutes and 30 seconds south.* The weather now was become tolerably clear so that we could see several leagues around. . . . about 4 p.m. as we were steering to the south we observed the whole sea in a manner covered with ice . . . and as we continued to advance to the south

* The antarctic circle is 66 degrees 30 minutes south.

it increased in such manner . . . that we could proceed no farther, the ice being entirely closed to the south in the whole extent from east to west-southwest, without the least appearance of any opening.[3]

In February, Cook instructed Furneaux to sail the *Adventure* to New Zealand while the *Resolution* continued the search for Terra Australis along the edge of the ice pack. By the middle of March, Cook was sailing in latitude 59 south and longitude 146 degrees 53 minutes east. He had seen no land in nearly three months. He then "bore away northeast and north, having come to a resolution to quit the high, southern latitudes and to proceed to New Zealand to look for the *Adventure* and 'refresh my people.' " All that the men of the *Resolution* had seen in the southern ocean were the ice pack, the ice islands, and brilliant displays of the aurora australis.

Cook reached New Zealand on March 25, after a sail of 3,660 leagues in 116 days "without having once sight of land." He then explored the Pacific between New Zealand and Pitcairn Island, which had been discovered in 1767; but "everything conspired to make me believe there is no southern continent between the meridian of America and New Zealand."

Cook then sailed north to the relative paradise of Tahiti and the Society Islands as the austral winter closed in on New Zealand during July and August of 1773. In the southern-hemisphere spring, he returned to New Zealand. At the end of January 1774, as summer came to the southern latitudes, he made another stab at Terra Australis. Twice he crossed the antarctic circle, but he found only ice islands.

On the morning of January 30, "we perceived the clouds over the horizon to the south to be of an unusual snow-white brightness, which we knew announced our approach to a field of ice," he wrote. When they reached the field, the mariners found that it extended east and west "far beyond the reach of our sight." Cook counted ninety-seven ice hills, some resembling a ridge of mountains, "rising one above the other until they were lost in the clouds." The outer edge of the ice field consisted of loose, broken ice, close-packed "so that it was not possible for anything to enter it." Cook noted that such mountains of ice were never seen off Greenland. He was certain that the ice was continuous all the way to the south pole or, possibly, was joined to land.

Even though he suspected that there was land beyond the ice, Cook admitted that he was not sorry to meet this seemingly impenetrable ice pack, "as it in some measure relieved us; at least shortened the danger and hardships inseparable from the navigation of the southern polar regions." He concluded:

Since, therefore, we could not proceed one inch farther to the south, no other reason need be assigned to my tacking and standing back to the north, being at this time the latitude of 71 degrees 10 minutes south and longitude 106 degrees 54 minutes west. I was now well satisfied that no continent was to be found in this ocean but what must be so far to the south as to be wholly inaccessible on account of ice.*

It was not until early in 1775 that Cook sighted an antarctic land. It was a large, mountainous island, with an area of 1,450 square miles, that lay 1,220 miles south and east of Tierra del Fuego. The island had been reported in 1756 by a Spanish ship but remained unnamed and unclaimed. Cook named it South Georgia, for George III. It was a barren, desolate place, he reported, "not a tree was to be seen nor a shrub big enough to make a tooth pick."

If there was a southern continent, Cook mused in his journal, the greater part of it must lie within the polar circle, "where the sea is so pestered with ice that the land is thereby inaccessible." It must be "a country doomed by nature never once to feel the warmth of the sun's rays but to be buried in everlasting snow and ice."

On this third and final voyage, 1776–1780, Cook was instructed to find the Northwest Passage. This effort failed, although he sailed the farthest north of anyone in the eighteenth century—to 70 degrees 44 minutes—as he had sailed the farthest south. After exploring the west coast of North America, he sailed for Hawaii, where, like Magellan at Mactan, he became embroiled in a battle with the natives and was killed February 14, 1779, at the age of fifty-one. He had seen more of the world ocean than any other man before him.

LO, ANTARCTICA!

The search for Terra Australis became more intense in the nineteenth century, and the motive for it changed. The reconnaissances of the eighteenth century had shown that Ptolemy's southern continent must lie within the antarctic circle. It must be a polar land, of dubious value for exploitation and colonization. Such a land might hold sources of wealth or be useful for naval bases in the southern ocean, where the ships of several nations hunted whales and seals. But the rhetoric of the nineteenth century suggests another motive. The location and the conquest of Terra Australis became a challenge to western man's rising capability of mastering the planet. The theme of man

* At the farthest south position he described, Cook appears to have been on the northern edge of the Bellingshausen Sea, about 125 miles north of Thurston Island and the Eights Coast of Antarctica.

against nature was dawning in the western world. Exploration became a powerful compulsion. National prestige and prowess were rewards enough to attract financing for expensive sorties into the arctic and antarctic. The Heroic Age of polar exploration was dawning.

The first sighting of antarctic continental land was the result of chance. It is not fully settled whether the first men to have seen it were Englishmen or Americans. Essentially, Antarctica was discovered in 1820, the last continent to be found by western man.

In 1819, an English skipper named William Smith was hauling freight around Patagonia in the brig *Williams,* when he was forced to head southward by a storm. He sighted a snow-covered land, later identified as one of the South Shetland Islands. Following up this sighting, the British navy sent Lieutenant Edward Bransfield in the brig *Andromache* from Valparaiso later that year to investigate. Smith went along. On January 16, 1820, they saw land in the southeast, quite possibly the coast of the antarctic peninsula. On January 29, they made another sighting, probably Trinity Island, off the peninsula coast.

The following November, Nathaniel B. Palmer of Stonington, Connecticut, the youthful skipper of the forty-four-ton *Hero,* left a fleet of New England seal-hunting vessels to look for new seal herds farther south in the waters of the Drake Passage. He sighted the coast of the peninsula southeast of Deception Island November 20, 1820, in latitude 63 degrees 45 minutes south.

The peninsula, or panhandle, of Antarctica extends northward from the great ice sheet toward Patagonia. Geologically, it is more akin to Patagonia than to the main antarctic landmass. By sea, it is more accessible than any other coast in the region and, consequently, the most likely coast to be sighted first.

That same year, 1820, two Russian ships, the *Vostok* and the *Mirnyi,* commanded by Baron Fabian Gottlieb von Bellingshausen, were scouting antarctic waters for Czar Alexander I. Bellingshausen found a large island off the peninsula coast and named it Alexander I Island.

Thus, three nations that were to develop major programs of antarctic exploration in the twentieth century first encountered Terra Australis in the same year, 1820. A new polar frontier was opened. A decade later, a British seal hunter, John Biscoe, circumnavigated the continental ice cap, an area larger than Australia.

In 1836, although the United States was engaged in exploring its own territory, Congress appropriated funds for an antarctic expedition to establish a United States presence in the region, which whalers and sealers were exploiting with increasing intensiveness. The expedition was commanded by navy Lieutenant Charles Wilkes. It consisted of six vessels in various states of seaworthiness and sailed from Hampton Roads, Virginia, in August 1838.

Wilkes probed southward along the east coast of the antarctic peninsula as far as the great Atlantic embayment of Antarctica, the Weddell Sea (named for a British sealing captain, James Weddell, who first penetrated the embayment in the brig *Jane* in 1822). Wilkes attempted to enter the embayment, but his ships were driven back by a powerful clockwise current. In May 1839, Wilkes' squadron was forced to put into Sydney, Australia, for supplies; there the poor quality of the American ships and lack of polar gear were openly ridiculed. Australian mariners warned Wilkes that the expedition was doomed if it sailed south again. Undaunted, Wilkes did just that. On January 19, 1840, he sighted land, the coast of East Antarctica.

After losing one of his ships in the ice pack, Wilkes led his squadron through the ice floes on January 30 to a bay beyond which stretched rocky land that was nearly inundated in ice, as far as the crew could see. Wilkes located it in longitude 140 degrees 30 minutes and latitude 66 degrees 45 minutes south.

He wrote in his log: "and now that all were convinced of its existence, I gave the land the name of the Antarctic Continent." [4] The land Wilkes saw lay in the Australian quadrant of East Antarctica. The whole region became known as Wilkes Land.

Wilkes was not the only one to see it. The French explorer-ethnologist Jules Sebastien Cesar Dumont d'Urville was sailing the same seas in January 1840. His expedition consisted of two ships, the *Astrolabe* and *Zelee*. They encountered the *Porpoise* of Wilkes' squadron, but, contrary to custom, no courtesies were exchanged, each side believing the other to be on a secret mission. D'Urville sighted the coast the same day as Wilkes had—January 19, 1840—and named it Terre Adelie. But d'Urville was not as confident as Wilkes was that it was the southern continent. D'Urville was concerned with art as well as science and navigation. He had acquired the Venus de Milo for the Louvre in Paris during a navy tour in the Mediterranean. King Louis Philippe had sent him on a mission to find the south magnetic pole, the precise location of which had navigational importance, and allowed him to pursue his ethnological studies in Polynesia.

The north magnetic pole had been found several years earlier by an English naval officer, James Clark Ross, in the Boothia Peninsula of arctic Canada. The antipodal pole should therefore be found in 66 degrees south latitude and 146 degrees east longitude, according to the German mathematician Johann Karl Friedrich Gauss. Once the location of both poles of the geomagnetic field was known, a precise definition of the global field was possible. Navigation by magnetic compass could be vastly improved with such data. In high latitudes, the dip of the compass could be equated more accurately with latitude.

What was not known in that period was that the magnetic poles move around, reflecting instability in the hypothetical dynamo mechanism within the Earth that is believed to create the field. The search for the south magnetic pole was the first principal geophysical investigation in the antarctic. It represented the rising influence of scientific inquiry in exploration, although, as I have indicated, the scientific goal had economic applications.[5]

MOUNT EREBUS

The most spectacular expedition in this mid-nineteenth century period was the one led by Ross. Not long after Wilkes sailed out of Sydney harbor, Ross entered it, with two magnificent sailing ships, the *Erebus* and the *Terror*. These vessels had been used in the arctic and were equipped for polar waters. They were double-hulled, with oak planking and copper sheathing, and double-decked; and they had watertight compartments.

Ross followed the meridian of 170 degrees east longitude southward. It led him into the great Pacific embayment of Antarctica after the *Erebus* and *Terror* had crunched their way through the ice pack. This embayment, now called the Ross Sea, presents one of the most beautiful marinescapes in the world. It separates West from East Antarctica, and on its western coast there rises a magnificent range of shining mountains. Beyond them lies a vast, high plateau, all ice.

In water as smooth and dark as black glass, Ross's ships sailed southward along that mountainous coast. The weather was sunny and clear, the sky several shades of blue, the deeper blue fading to a pastel blue after midnight as the sun swung slowly around the mountains but did not set. Ross and his men watched the coast slip by, alpine, lifeless, icebound. Glaciers cascaded in frozen immobility down through the mountain passes and extended giant tongues of ice into the sea. But the rocky shore was inaccessible. On January 22, 1841, Ross's ships reached 74 degrees 20 minutes south latitude, for a new "farthest south" record. It broke the farthest-south record set by Captain James Weddell of 74 degrees 15 minutes that had broken Cook's record of 71 degrees 10 minutes.

To the south arose twin volcanoes, which Ross named Mount Erebus and Mount Terror, after his ships. Erebus is an active volcano, still smoking under its mantle of ice. In Ross's time, it was erupting, sending up gouts of black smoke and flame. Beyond the volcanoes there loomed a line of white across the southern horizon, and when the expedition sailed up to it, Ross and his men saw a massive wall of ice, more than 150 feet high, stretching across the sea as far as the eye could see. Vainly, Ross sought a passage through it, but it was as impenetrable, he reported later, as the Cliffs of Dover. It was an ice shelf, now called the Ross Shelf, formed by the extrusion of the continental ice sheet over the embayment. The way south was barred, but Ross had approached within 750 nautical miles of the geographic south pole. The Ross Shelf starts at about 77 degrees 30 minutes south latitude. He had no way now of reaching it or the magnetic pole.

Although Ross had penetrated deeply into Antarctica; Wilkes and d'Urville had scouted the coastline facing Australia; and Weddell and Bellingshausen had examined the peninsula and the regions in the Atlantic, or American, quadrant of this icebound region, a full definition of what all these various sightings represented remained elusive. These explorers were like a committee of blindmen attempting to determine the nature of an elephant by touch. Only disparate parts of Antarctica had been perceived. Wilkes's conclusion that the land he saw was part of a continent was guesswork; he could not have known that it was. Ross considered the lands he saw to be an array of large, mountainous islands, like those of the arctic. Terra Australis had been found. But what was it?

In the second half of the nineteenth century, polar exploration shifted to the arctic. While the whaling and sealing industry rapidly developed their outposts on antarctic islands, the United States, Great Britain, and the Scandinavian countries probed the arctic to find the northwest passage, the old Norse Ginnungagap.

In 1872–1874, the British scientific-survey ship H.M.S. *Challenger* crossed the antarctic circle and examined the marine life and sediments in the Antarctic Ocean. From the bottom of the ocean, the *Challenger*'s powerful dredge pulled up rocks that were not oceanic at all but obviously had come from some continental landmass. They were granites, schists, and gneisses, all igneous-metamorphic rocks that comprise the structure of continents. What were they doing at the bottom of the sea? The only explanation was that they had been rafted hundreds of miles from land by icebergs that had broken off the main ice sheet at the coast and that they had sunk when the ice melted. They became an important clue to the continentality of the south polar land.

A German survey in the steamship *Grönland*, under Captain Eduard Dallmann, investigated the antarctic peninsula in 1873–1875. Americans called it Palmer Land, and the British, Graham Land. Dallmann determined that it was an archipelago dominated by a long peninsula.

No major explorations were recorded for the next twenty years. In 1893, Captain C. A. Larsen, a Norwegian, explored the Weddell seacoast in the *Jason*. In 1894–1895, another Norwegian skipper, Leonard Kristensen, sailed his vessel, the *Antarctic*, into the Ross Sea. Aboard were a Norwegian explorer, H. J. Bull, and an Australian schoolteacher, Carsten E. Borchgrevink. They discovered a beach at Cape Adare at the entrance to the embayment and landed in January 1895.

Interest in the antarctic was being rekindled. In 1895, Antarctica was the principal subject of concern at the Sixth International Geographical Congress in London. There it was defined as the most important geographical problem of the age. The mystery intrigued the London press and the public. And the government, too, began studying the prospect of renewing antarctic exploration.

Other countries picked up the antarctic challenge. In 1898, a well-equipped Belgian national expedition, led by Adrien de Gerlache, sailed boldly into antarctic waters; its research ship, *Belgica*, was beset in the ice off Alexander I Island. It was the first expedition to spend the winter in antarctic waters. The first mate of the *Belgica* was Roald Amundsen, a doughty Norwegian explorer and mariner of considerable experience in polar waters; the ship's surgeon was an American, Dr. Frederick A. Cook. Both would be heard from later.

The pace of exploration quickened. In 1899, a privately financed British-Scandinavian expedition headed by Borchgrevink reached Cape Adare in the *Southern Cross* with the purpose of wintering over there on land. A hut was set up on the beach, and the first antarctic scientific base was established. Over the winter, the scientists in the party made a continuous record of magnetic, auroral, and weather phenomena; studied the habits of penguins and seals; and investigated the only flora to be found in the region, lichens. When spring came, the expedition explored as far south as McMurdo Sound and the twin volcanoes Ross had seen. Undeterred by the ice shelf, the explorers climbed it and made a sled trip to 78 degrees 50 minutes south, 670 miles from the geographic pole.

Although the continentality of the region could not be perceived, it could be deduced from several major pieces of evidence. In 1898, John Murray, the Canadian oceanographer who had sailed in the *Challenger*, proposed that the coasts seen by Wilkes, d'Urville, and others did, indeed, represent a true continent. The rocks dredged up by the research ship clearly indicated this. And, as I have related earlier, so did the flat-topped icebergs that had carried the rocks so far out to sea, for such ice islands could only have been formed on land of vast extent—continental land. They were clues representing a new scientific sophistication that had appeared in the ancient art of exploration. With the discovery of Antarctica, a new era of scientific exploration opened, coincident with the onset of the twentieth century. It awaited only the development of new technologies in transportation, communication, and observation to convert the ancient art to a science that would unlock the secrets of nature.

HEROISM AND THE SCIENTIFIC METHOD

At the turn of the century, the scientific motif and the struggle of man against the elements were combined. It was a time when the values of der-ring-do, of struggling against seemingly insurmountable obstacles, and of self-denial and sacrifice were highly cherished in Western European society, especially in Great Britain. The whole society was reaching out toward a new destiny that encompassed the ultimate mastery of nature; and those in the vanguard, the intrepid polar explorers, were its heroes. Not only individual but national prestige were involved in daring exploits, and this intangible had real value in the politics of empire.

In 1900, a new antarctic expedition was being prepared in England. Its object was to extend the explorations of the 1899 British-Scandinavian ex-pedition to Cape Adare and McMurdo Sound, seek a new "farthest south" overland, and examine the prospects for reaching the geographic south pole. The expedition was essentially a naval enterprise, commanded by a naval of-ficer, Commander Robert Falcon Scott, who had no previous polar experi-ence. Its vessel was the steam bark *Discovery,* whose name became that of the expedition. Following the tracks of Cook and Ross, Scott sailed in July 1901 for New Zealand, where he loaded on board the crowded ship precut lumber for the construction of winter quarters in Antarctica.

In January 1902, the *Discovery* anchored in McMurdo Sound off Ross Island, a volcanic pile formed by the smoking, snow-clad volcano Mount Erebus. Quarters were erected for men and animals—dogs and ponies—on a volcanic ledge called Hut Point. When spring came in November 1902, Scott led a sled party southward across the ice shelf to 82 degrees 16 minutes south latitude, turning back only when scurvy broke out among his men. His farthest south was 464 miles from the pole. Year by year, expeditions were creeping up on it.

During its second year, the expedition's men climbed the Ferrar Glacier to the high plateau of Victoria Land. Beyond the chain of mountains (the Transantarctic Mountains) the plateau stretched endlessly westward from the coast of the Ross Sea. In two months, the traverse covered 725 miles, return-ing, exhausted, but jubilant at its progress, to Hut Point on Christmas Eve 1903.

The following spring, a relief expedition consisting of two ships, the *Terra Nova* and the *Morning,* arrived from New Zealand with orders to Scott to re-turn home. This Scott was reluctant to do because the *Discovery* had become wedged in the ice of the sound. Dynamiting and sawing the ice, Scott's crew finally freed the trapped vessel, and Scott sailed her home around Cape Horn.

On November 7, 1904, Scott presented his findings to an elite audience in Albert Hall in London.[6] Among the notables present were the United States ambassador, Joseph H. Choate, and Whitelaw Reid, editor of the *New*

York Tribune, who succeeded Choate in 1905 as ambassador. It was an historic occasion, marked with lantern slides of antarctic scenes.

The excitement and admiration the results of the expedition engendered were certainly not the least of its rewards. The total effect was to stimulate public interest in planetary exploration. Scott and his men had the world at their feet. Of longer-lasting consequence was the wealth of scientific observations.

The *Discovery* expedition presented to the world its first broad picture of Antarctica. It was a land immersed in ice, as Cook had predicted, but it was also one of lofty mountains and strange "dry" valleys that remained free of ice and snow, indicating that the ice sheet had retreated from an earlier time. Although no animals existed on land, sea- and bird-life was abundant. Life in Antarctica came from the sea, and, although penguins and the hawk-like south polar skuas nested on beaches and among rocks, they made their living from the sea. On land there existed only the most primitive of all plants, the lichen, while weird, wingless insects drifted on the winds like aerial plankton. It was not a land flowing with milk and honey, but it had a strange fascination, ever luring men back.

During the early years of the new century, several expeditions were probing the ice cap. In 1901–1903, a German national expedition led by Professor Erich von Drygalski in the sailing ship *Gauss* sought the magnetic pole on the Knox Coast of Wilkes Land but could not land there. To the east, the expedition managed to come ashore and explore a portion of the east antarctic region it named Kaiser Wilhelm II Land. During this period, a Swedish expedition led by Dr. Otto Nordenskjöld and Captain C. A. Larsen in the steam-driven whaling ship *Antarctic* explored the peninsula coast to the Weddell Sea. In the Weddell Sea embayment, they steamed southward until they were stopped by an ice barrier—the Filchner Ice Shelf.

Nordenskjöld, one of the distinguished geologists of the time, observed that the geological structure of the peninsula was similar to that of the Andes Mountains of South America. On a broad scale, the antarctic peninsula was a continuation of the great Andean fold, of which the Rocky Mountains of North America are a part.

It thus appeared as though this Andean extrusion was not part of Antarctica, but part of South America, that it butted up against the region called West Antarctica—the region in the western hemisphere opposite the Americas. Nordenskjöld's analysis of the peninsula raised a major question. Was Antarctica one continent or two?

The good ship *Antarctic* did not survive the expedition. It was crushed by pack ice and finally sank—but not before the crew had time to evacuate the doomed vessel with much of their supplies. They were marooned over the winter and then were rescued by an Argentine ship. The question of whether there was one continent or two under the ice persisted for the next fifty years.

In 1903–1905, a Scottish national expedition led by Dr. W. S. Bruce in the *Scotia* made observations in the Weddell Sea, wintered over on Laurie Island, and discovered an adjacent coast, which Bruce named Coats Land. In 1904–1905 a French expedition under Jean B. Charcot charted the coast of the peninsula; they refined this work in 1908–1910.

Gradually, the periphery of Antarctica was becoming known. It was a land locked in an ice age, analogous to the ice ages that had inundated northern Europe and parts of North America in the Pleistocene epoch of geological time, between 1 million and 25,000 years ago. Here might lie clues to the origin of ice ages. A major question was: Is the ice coming or going in Antarctica? Or, is it standing still? How long had the region been glaciated?

As these questions were considered in Europe, it became clear that although of little value in terms of wealth and exploitation potential, the antarctic region was of great significance to science. It became both the intellectual and physical challenge of the age. In Edwardian England, the physical challenge was the one that attracted private capital to finance expeditions. The great goal of derring-do was the conquest of the south pole. Although senior scientists, such as John Murray, argued that such an effort was irrelevant to the scientific questions posed by Antarctica,[7] the pole was the lodestone that attracted public interest. By the middle of the first decade of the twentieth century, the Heroic Age of antarctic exploration was in full flower.

In 1907, one of the most colorful figures in Scott's *Discovery* expedition, Ernest Henry Shackleton, went into the discovery business for himself. He raised private funds for a Shackleton antarctic expedition. His target was the pole. Shackleton had become desperately ill of scurvy on the southward traverse of the *Discovery* expedition. Scott invalided him home on the relief ship *Morning* in 1903, over Shackleton's fierce protests. Scott ran a tight ship, and a chronically ill man on a polar expedition was a liability. After Shackleton recovered, he became Scott's rival. He obtained a whaling ship, the *Nimrod*, and early in 1908, he set up a base at Cape Royds, about eighteen miles from Scott's 1902 base at Hut Point on Ross Island. Shackleton had hoped to use Hut Point, but Scott advised him that the base was not available. Scott was planning a second antarctic expedition himself.

Nearly every antarctic expedition in the heroic period experimented with novelties. Scott and Nordenskjöld used balloons to loft them 1,200 to 1,500 feet to observe the icescape. Shackleton brought an automobile, the first vehicle with an internal-combustion engine to be used on the ice cap. He also experimented with Manchurian ponies as transport animals, but he found that their hooves were poorly adapted to movement on ice.

In 1908, Shackleton marched south, with four ponies, across the Ross Ice Shelf to the Transantarctic Mountains. There, a broad highway led to the south polar plateau, 9,000 feet above sea level. It was the largest glacier Shackleton and his party had ever seen, thirty miles wide at its confluence with the ice shelf. For 100 miles it wound through the mountains, a gigantic frozen river flowing imperceptibly but with great force down through the mountain passes that it filled onto the shelf, which was cracked and crevassed by its impact. Shackleton named it the Beardmore Glacier, after one of his backers, a Glasgow industrialist, William Beardmore.

As Shackleton and three companions ascended the glacier, they realized that it must be the greatest river of ice on Earth. The climb was brutal. One by one, the ponies perished, until the men were reduced to pulling the sleds themselves. Once on the plateau, where the air was thin and every exertion forced the explorers to gasp for breath, the party had reached a vast tableland of ice. Here, to the south, lay the geographic south pole.

Determined to win glory, Shackleton and his men pushed on until their supplies ran so low they realized that soon they would not have enough to keep them alive on the homeward trek. At latitude 88 degrees 23 minutes south and longitude 162 degrees east, they turned back. They were within ninety-seven nautical miles of the pole—almost there, but not quite. The decision to retreat must have been an agonizing one, but it saved their lives.

Meanwhile, a second traverse to the north was more successful in reaching its objective—the south magnetic pole. The party was led by an Australian scientist, T. W. Edgeworth David, and it used a motor vehicle to haul supplies to a depot on the Victoria Land side of frozen McMurdo Sound. David's northern party struck out along the coast of Victoria Land and turned inland; ascended a glacier to the high plateau; and located the magnetic pole in 72 degrees 25 minutes south latitude and 155 degrees 16 minutes east longitude, about 700 miles from Ross Island.

The magnetic poles of this planet shift about, with unexplained motions of the axis of the geomagnetic field, as I have mentioned. By 1960, the pole was 1,000 miles from the spot where David's magnetized needle pointed down to it. Covering more than 1,400 miles, the party made the first geological assessment of Victoria Land, which eventually was to be recognized as the main continental landmass of Antarctica.

At the end of the decade, Western man had nearly encompassed the Earth. Americans had reached the north pole, but which of two expeditions got there first became a long-lasting dispute. The claim of Rear Admiral Robert E. Peary that he, his aide Matthew Henson, and four Eskimos achieved the geographic north pole April 6, 1909, was upheld by Congress. A rival claim by Dr. Cook that he had attained the pole a year earlier was officially rejected, but the physician-explorer pressed it nevertheless for years.

Meanwhile, as Scott prepared for his second antarctic foray, the Norwegian explorer Roald Amundsen had been preparing to be first at the north pole. After his antarctic voyage as mate of the *Belgica*, Amundsen negotiated the Ginnungagap of Norse legend—the Northwest Passage. He sailed a small vessel, the *Gjoa*, through the icy network of straits, bays, and passages across the top of Canada from Greenland to Alaska. It was a slow trip, interrupted by pauses for exploration and to extricate the ship from the ice. It took three years, from 1903–1906, but it blazed a trail that would not even begin to become economically useful until the third quarter of the century.

With the north pole in view, Amundsen purchased a fine polar exploring ship, the *Fram* ("Forward"), from Fridtjof Nansen, the famous Norwegian arctic explorer, in 1909. He expected to drift in it for several years, if necessary, from the Bering Strait as far north as the currents would take the ship, and then strike out with dog teams for the pole. His experiences in the transit of the Ginnungagap had indicated to Amundsen that this could be done.

But then Peary's announcement that he had reached the north pole burst upon the world. Amundsen reversed his field. When the *Fram* anchored in the harbor at Buenos Aires, supposedly on its way around Patagonia to the north Pacific Ocean and the Bering Sea, Amundsen sent a terse telegram to Captain Robert Falcon Scott of the Royal Navy: "Beg leave to inform you proceeding Antarctica."

Scott received the message when he reached Melbourne, Australia, en route to McMurdo Sound in the *Terra Nova,* a Dundee whaling ship with beams of oak. The *Terra Nova* was no stranger to antarctic waters. It had been one of the relief ships sent by the navy to aid Scott's first expedition in 1904. Realizing that Amundsen must have been well on his way to Antarctica, Scott pulled out of Melbourne as quickly as his supplies could be put on board. He arrived at Cape Evans, another promontory of Ross Island, in Mc-Murdo Sound, in January 1911.

After erecting winter quarters—wooden huts—for the men and animals, Scott authorized a party to sail the *Terra Nova* across the Ross Sea to its eastern coast, along the region now called Marie Byrd Land. In the Bay of Whales, an indentation in the coastal ice sheet, the *Terra Nova*'s crew spied the *Fram.* The race for the south pole was on.

VICTORY AND DEATH

Amundsen's camp at Framheim ("Home of the Fram") was about two days' journey nearer the pole than Scott's base at Cape Evans, but Scott had the advantage of following a known route, the one pioneered by Shackleton up the Beardmore Glacier, to the south polar plateau. Both expeditions were occupied during the austral summer of 1910–1911 laying in supply caches along their routes. Then both settled down for the stormy polar winter to begin the race for the pole in the spring.

Amundsen and his crew started first, on October 19, 1911, with four sleds, each one pulled by thirteen Greenland dogs. The sleds carried a total load of

3,200 pounds of food and fuel, enough for 120 days. The Norwegians crossed the ice shelf rapidly, skiing where they could and running behind the dogs over rough ice. In the mountains, they encountered exasperating difficulties, forcing them to turn back from one blind pass after another. Compared to Scott, Amundsen was an amateur in this land, but he was a master of the technique of polar travel and a farsighted organizer. Additionally, he had that magic ingredient that his ancient landsman, Leif Ericsson had—luck. Without it, nothing succeeds, or so it appears in the long history of exploration.

Eventually, the expedition struggled up to the plateau, after negotiating a region where the ice was so hard and slippery that the crew dubbed it the Devil's Dance Hall. Once on the plateau, Amundsen winnowed his final party down to four men beside himself and sent the rest back to Framheim. This was a common polar exploration tactic to save food.

The five Norwegians reached the south pole at 1,500 hours (3:00 P.M.) Greenwich Mean Time December 14, 1911. The heroes were, besides the thirty-nine-year-old Amundsen, Olav Bjaaland, Helmer Hansen, Sverre Hassel, and Oskar Wisting. Without wasting much time in ceremony on this bleak, windswept plain of ice, they turned around and drove the exhausted dogs northward back to the Fram. They reached the Bay of Whales January 25, 1912, with two of the four sleds and eleven of the fifty-two dogs they had started with.

Scott's pole party left Cape Evans two weeks after Amundsen's, on November 2, 1911, and followed Shackleton's 1907 route up the Beardmore Glacier. Delayed by storms on the plateau, the expedition fought its way slowly south. The Siberian ponies and dogs Scott had brought were unable to cope with the ice. The rough, hairy paws of Amundsen's Greenland dogs were well adapted to getting traction on ice, but Scott had been unable to get such animals, although he knew from Shackleton's experience that they were better than ponies or Siberian dogs for Antarctica.

By mid-January 1912, Scott estimated that he was 150 miles from the pole. The ponies and dogs had perished. The men now hauled or pushed the sleds with their food and fuel. For his final dash for the pole, Scott, like Amundsen, picked four men to go with him. They were Dr. Edward A. Wilson, Petty Officer Edgar Evans, Captain Lawrence E. G. Oates, and Lieutenant Henry R. Bowers. Scott sent the rest back to Cape Evans.

Agonized entries in Scott's diary summarize the rest of the tragic story. On January 16, 1912, at an elevation of 9,076 feet, the pole party found a black flag tied to a sled and the rubbish of a campsite. Sled and dog tracks were all about. Scott wrote: "The Norwegians have forestalled us and are first at the pole. It is a terrible disappointment." Scott and his exhausted companions reached the pole January 17, 1912. "Great God," he wrote, "this is an awful place and terrible enough for us to have labored to it without the reward of priority."

On the long way back to Cape Evans, Evans fell, apparently fracturing his skull, on the descent of the Beardmore Glacier. He died shortly thereafter. When the remaining four reached the ice shelf, they were pinned down in their hastily erected tent by a nine-day blizzard. They were only eleven miles from a cache of supplies, but it was hopeless to attempt to find it in the raging storm.

Oates, whose feet had become gangrenous from frostbite, limped away during the height of the blizzard and perished. Scott, Wilson, and Bowers died quietly of freezing and exhaustion in the tent. Scott's last entry in his diary was dated March 29, 1912: "For God's sake, look after our people."

Their bodies were found eight months later by a searching party from Cape Evans.

THIN ICE

Now, at last, 900 years since the Norse discovery of Vinland, the Earth had been encompassed by men of the west. They had sailed all the seas and reached the poles. What aspects of Western culture produced this planetary reconnaissance? Was there an exploration imperative in Western culture, an anomalous drive to discover? Was this activity a concomitant of the industrial revolution that began in the West? Of the Renaissance? These were phases in the intellectual and technical development of Western society. It seems more likely that the stimulus to discovery was a product of Western cultural development. In it, we can perceive a kaleidoscopic panorama of motives, changing over the centuries, from the expansion of a medieval have-not Viking society and the sixteenth-century commercial quest for the spices and wealth of the Indies to the prestige of being first at the pole. But a common denominator was perceptible: competition.

In Antarctica, a critical shift in the rationale of exploration came into focus when the race for the pole ended. Man had now achieved just about everything, except, perhaps, the top of Mount Everest and the depths of the sea, that the planet could offer. He had begun to reconnoiter the ocean basins. With the physical challenge disposed of, the intellectual challenge came to fore. For the first time in the history of exploration, the new land became a subject of intensive scientific investigation, for quite early in the game it had yielded clues that it might be a key that would unlock the secrets of the evolution of the Earth.

In spite of the hardships of the return journey, Dr. Wilson had faithfully hauled back samples of coal and of fossils he had collected in the mountains during the climb to the polar plateau. These were found in the sled, and his notes, along with Scott's diary, were found in the tent by the rescue party.

The fossils were of a southern-hemisphere tree fern called glossopteris that must have attained a height of sixty feet or more. The fern fossil is found in other lands of the southern hemisphere—in Africa, India, and South America. Encased in the rocks with the plant fossils were winged pollen grains of ancient flowering plants. Dr. Wilson's heroic collection included lumps of anthracite coal.

Shackleton's party had also seen coal in the mountains as it climbed the Beardmore Glacier. Coal posed a very great mystery. It is supposed to be derived from a woody vegetation, the buried fossil of mighty forests. When had a forest thrived in this frozen desert, where only lichens grew today on naked rocks?

Coal was the evidence that Antarctica had once basked in a temperate or subtropical zone in the Pennsylvanian or Upper Carboniferous period of geologic time, 250 million years ago. A warm, humid climate was required for a carboniferous forest. But this raised a botanical question: Could a carboniferous forest have grown in a high latitude where the nights were six months long?

In the Royal Society range of the Transantarctic Mountains, Frank Debenham, assistant geologist on the *Terra Nova* expedition, found fossils of land and freshwater plants. They indicated a humid climate and marshy landscape in the far past, a region of rapidly flowing rivers.

The evidence of drastic change in the antarctic climate gave the region special significance, for here was a key to the geologic and climatic history of the Earth. What caused the change here? Was it related to climatic oscillations in other continents?

A further question presented itself. Had Antarctica always been a polar continent? If not, had the poles moved? Had the south pole once been located in the Pacific Ocean? If not, then had the continent moved? If so, what mechanism could account for its change in position?

A shift in the Earth's axis of rotation could be accounted for by astronomical catastrophe, such as a collision between the planet and a large meteor or planetoid. Such a collision can be inferred by the Earth's axial tilt of 23½ degrees to the plane of its orbit around the sun. It can be supposed that the planet's axis of rotation once was perpendicular to the orbital plane and that it was tilted by the impact of a large body, an impact that may have created the Arctic Ocean basin.

Climatic oscillations of the degree represented by the Pleistocene Ice Ages and Antarctica might be caused by another astronomical situation: changes in the amount of solar radiation the Earth has received over time. Perhaps the sun's output has changed, although careful observations so far in this century have failed to find direct evidence that this might be the case. It is more likely that any deficit in radiation was the result of interference with the planet's reception of sunlight. One form of interference would be the passage of the solar system through an interstellar dust cloud. Another would be the heavy pollution of the atmosphere by volcanic eruptions hurling millions of tons of dust-size particles into the stratosphere, thus screening out sunlight. Industrial pollution in the modern age threatens to produce this effect.

Not only coal but the discovery of fossils of the southern hemisphere tree fern Glossopteris pointed strongly to the conclusion that Antarctica had not always been a polar, continent. Once this fact is thoroughly digested, inductive reasoning leads to the inescapable conclusion that the continent must have moved. It could not have been polar in the Pennsylvanian period.

The poles of the Earth are cold because sunshine strikes them at such an oblique angle that most of the radiation is reflected off into space before it can be transformed into heat. The poles, therefore, are heat sinks. Heat from the sun accumulates principally between the equator and the tropics (Cancer and Capricorn). It is transported by the atmosphere and oceans poleward, where it is dissipated into space. This process is part of the vast mechanism that drives the weather systems of the northern and southern hemispheres from the energy of the sun.

In the light of what is known today, the simplest explanation of a continent that produces a coal forest in one geological epoch and an ice cap in another is offered by the theories of continental drift and plate tectonics. Antarctica, once subtropical, became glaciated when it drifted into its present position over the south pole. It seems to be a simple, satisfying explanation of a great mystery.

But in 1912, the idea of drifting continents was as bizarre and heretical from the viewpoint of scientific orthodoxy as the idea of a sun-centered universe had been to religious orthodoxy in the time of Copernicus, Bruno, and Galileo. The history of science tells us that new conceptions are hardly ever welcome, that one orthodoxy changes only to another orthodoxy, that heresy never changes—only the definition of what is heretical.

When it was published in 1922, the scientific report of the Terra Nova expedition presented several conclusions, all erroneous. The first was that the antarctic ice sheet was thin compared with the mile-thick ice sheets that overlay northern Europe and North America in the Pleistocene epoch. The second was Scott's own estimate of the area of the ice cap—2 million square miles. That was large enough to astound the scientific community of Edwardian England, but not half as large as the reality. The ice cap has an area of 5½ million square miles.

The expedition's geologist, Griffith Taylor, estimated that the ice cap was only 1,000 to 2,000 feet thick. He had no way of making direct measurement. He concluded this by observing the relatively slight depth of the outlet glaciers flowing down the mountainsides from the Victoria Land plateau. Taylor's estimate was supported by the observations of two young physical scientists, Charles Seymour Wright and Raymond Priestley. It was confirmed further in later years by observations of the West Antarctic ice sheet, which undulated in such a way that it seemed to follow the contour of the land beneath it.

The depth of the ice sheet was an important quantity. It was needed to assess the Earth's water budget, for one thing. For even a thin ice cap of such an extent tied up as much water as a respectable ocean. If the ice cap melted, the release of water in the world ocean would be catastrophic, drowning, or at least flooding, the world's seaports and many of its coastal cities.

It was important to know how long the region had been covered with ice; whether the ice sheet was waxing, waning, or standing still; and the manner in which it moved over the land. There were indications in Scott's time that the Ross Ice Shelf had receded since James Clark Ross first saw it in 1840–1841. Whether the recession had been local or general could not be determined in 1912. It still eludes definition.

Whether the ice cap was coming or going was important not only locally but as a clue to worldwide climatic dynamics. If the cap was receding, it might indicate an alteration in patterns of precipitation in the southern hemisphere. Meteorologically, most of Antarctica is a desert, with average precipitation of 2.5 inches a year. A recession of the ice sheet would not necessarily imply a warming trend, but a drying one. Conversely, a worldwide warming trend would at first increase the ice cap by increasing snowfall. Only later would melting begin to decrease the ice load.

Once its fluctuations were understood, the antarctic ice cap would become a sensitive indicator of world climatic change. On a planet where two-thirds of the population is balanced on the knife-edge of famine, climatic fluctuation is of critical concern. It may have widespread effects on crop production and hence, on the destiny of whole nations and cultures.

Climatic fluctuation has happened before. The Sahara Desert was not always a desert. It is conceivable that the modern bread-baskets of the world, such as the American mid-continent and the Ukraine, could become arid, Saharan wastes. Imagine the impact of a new ice age comparable in scope to the last one, only 25,000 years ago. In the last glaciation, called the Wisconsin in the United States and the Wurm in Europe, the ice extended down over most of Canada to cover most of the midwestern and eastern United States as far south as the Ohio River. In Europe, all of Scandinavia, Germany, the Baltic countries, Poland, western and central Russia, Czechoslovakia, Austria, and Hungary were inundated, as Antarctica is today. The deepest ice of the Wisconsin glaciation was where the centers of Western industrial civilization are today. Understanding ice ages begins in Antarctica. It may be of inestimable value to future generations.

With the *Terra Nova* expedition, European nations and, later, Americans became deeply involved in the questions raised by the early years of antarctic investigation. The great question of the antarctic past seemed to lie beyond the pale of direct investigation, but there were more immediate problems that could be resolved: How much ice was there? What were the dimensions of the ice cap? Did it cover one continent or two?

THE INTERNATIONAL GEOPHYSICAL YEAR

After the south pole was won, the next popular exercise in Antarctica was the crossing of the ice cap from the Weddell Sea to the pole and from there to the Ross Sea. Dr. Wilhelm Filchner, whose name is memorialized in the ice shelf at the southern end of the Weddell Sea embayment, led a German expedition to attempt the crossing of Antarctica in 1912. His ship, the *Deutschland*, became beset in the ice, and the plan had to be abandoned.

Shackleton made a similar attempt in 1914. But his ship, the *Endurance*, also became stuck in the ice. Unlike the *Deutschland*, which eventually was freed, the *Endurance* was crushed and sank. Shackleton and his men had to make their way by longboats to Elephant Island in the South Shetlands. From there, Shackleton and a small force took one of the boats and sailed 800 miles across the Scotia Sea to South Georgia, where there was a coal depot for whaling ships. Unhappily, Shackleton and his men beached their boat on the wrong side of the island and had to climb a 9,000-foot mountain range to reach the station, where they could radio for help. The entire crew was ultimately rescued by a Chilean ship.

Meanwhile, airplane reconnaissance began in Antarctica. Between 1928 and 1930, Sir Hubert Wilkins, the British explorer, attempted an airplane reconnaissance of West Antarctica, but he was forced back time after time by bad weather. Also in 1928, Rear Admiral Richard E. Byrd established a base near Amundsen's old camp on the Bay of Whales. He called it Little America, and from it he flew sorties over the region of West Antarctica he named Marie Byrd Land. In November 1929, Byrd, Bernt Balchen, A. C. McKinley, and Harold June flew from Little America to the south pole and back, a round trip of 1,500 air miles.

With air transportation, Antarctica exploration became simplified and accelerated. It was now possible to resupply expeditions out on the ice or perform rescue missions by air and to make long-range aerial surveys. Byrd led the United States back to the antarctic, which the country had seemingly forgotten about since Wilkes' day. Byrd's expeditions in 1933–1935 and 1939–1940 paved the way for effective long-term exploration of the continent and of the seas around on a rational basis.

In earlier years, explorers used most of their energy pushing, hauling, or driving dogsleds in polar regions. There was no other way to travel. Scientific investigation, such as detailed geologic examination of exposed rocks and of mountain structure, was always limited by the primitive logistics of transportation. So was the amount of scientific equipment a traverse party could carry.

Although the introduction of the automobile to Antarctica by Shackleton was only a demonstration, it showed that specialized motor vehicles were useful for safe and efficient transportation across the ice. Scott had experimented briefly with a tracked vehicle, but he did not use it; yet this was the shape of antarctic transportation to come. The development of the tractor, on the farm, and in warfare as the tank, produced polar vehicles that could haul men and supplies thousands of miles.

Finally, with the icebreaker ship, transportation technology enabled large expeditions to move into the antarctic, set up semipermanent bases there, and carry out continuous observations over several years.

The modern period of antarctic exploration was ushered in by the International Geophysical year, 1957–1958, with a grand invasion of the ice cap by twelve nations. Sixty bases were set up all around the continent by Argentina, Australia, Belgium, Chile, France, Japan, New Zealand, Norway, South Africa, the Soviet Union, the United Kingdom, and the United States.

In preparation for the United States effort, coded as Operation Deep Freeze, the navy icebreaker U.S.S. *Glacier* crashed its way into McMurdo Sound through the receding ice of the austral spring of 1955. The vessel unloaded men and supplies on Ross Island for the construction of the principal United States base in the antarctic, the U.S. Naval Air Facility at McMurdo Sound. It was not only a base but also a scientific station with an airport capable of landing the largest transports in the world. It was a port of entry to a continent for science.

Six other bases were constructed in the next two years. They were Amundsen-Scott Station, at the geographic pole; Hallett Station, at Cape Adare; Wilkes Station, on the Budd Coast of Wilkes Land in the Australian quadrant; Ellsworth Station, on the Filchner Ice Shelf on the Atlantic side; Little America V, at Kainan Bay on the Ross Sea Coast of Marie Byrd Land; and Byrd Station, in the interior of Marie Byrd Land. (Little America V was near the site of Amundsen's Framheim, but the Bay of Whales, the landmark of the site, had disappeared.) More than 3,000 men, 200 aircraft, and 300 vehicles—airplanes, tractors, trucks, and jeeps—were used in this continental construction program. The seven bases were tied together and to navy communications in Washington by radio.

With thousands of men working and exploring in Antarctica, the development of the region proceeded rapidly. Sir Vivian Fuchs, the British scientist-explorer, executed the crossing of Antarctica from the Weddell Sea to the Ross Sea via Amundsen-Scott Station in 1957–1958, with the aid of Sir Edmund Hillary, conqueror of Mt. Everest, who laid in caches of food and fuel for Fuchs's party between the pole and McMurdo Sound.

During the eighteen-month period of the IGY, from July 1957 to December 31, 1958, most of the general physiography of Antarctica was revealed. The first United States traverse in 1957 demolished the thin-ice theory that had characterized the ice cap for more than forty years. A young geophysicist, Charles R. Bentley, who had recently received his doctorate from Columbia University, and two graduate students in geophysics, Vernon H. Anderson of the University of Wyoming and Ned Ostenso of the University of Wisconsin, set out January 28, 1957 on a 650 mile traverse from Little America V to Byrd Station. They drove three Tucker Sno-Cats—tracked vehicles with cabins that had been developed for oversnow traveling in the High Sierras of the United States and adapted for Greenland by the U.S. Army.

The youthful investigators used the explosion-seismology method of determining ice depth. The technique sounded ice depth by recording the travel time between the surface and rock bottom of seismic or sound waves generated at the surface by an explosion. Moving inland from Kainan Bay, the party found that the ice increased in thickness from a few hundred feet to 3,500 feet. While the elevation of the ice surface rose as the party rolled eastward, the depth increased even faster, indicating the existence of an oceanic basin underneath the ice. Near Byrd Station, the ice was found to be 8,200 feet thick, although the surface elevation was hardly 5,000 feet. There was a basin, or trough, 3,200 feet below sea level. The discovery of deep ice in West Antarctica upset calculations that had stood unchallenged for years. It pointed to a dramatic increase in the assessment of the Earth's water budget.

Albert P. Crary, deputy chief scientist of the U.S. Antarctic Research Program, circumnavigated the Ross Ice Shelf, which he found to be 210,000 square miles, and ascended the Skelton Glacier to the high plateau of Victoria Land.

Pushing westward toward the Soviet Union's Vostok Station about 1,000 miles away, Crary and his party made soundings that showed the land underneath the ice lay at sea level. But as they moved westward, their elevation increased from 6,000 to 9,348 feet. Victoria Land appeared to be a vast cake of ice of about 1 million square miles. Crary's soundings of the south polar plateau confirmed other measurements showing that it consisted of ice 9,000 feet deep. The land lay at sea level or slightly below, depressed, as in Victoria Land, by the enormous weight of ice.

At the Russian Vostok Station in East Antarctica, Russian seismologists reported depths of 11,217 feet and an average depth of 8,700 feet. A French expedition traveling inland from Charcot Station in Wilkes Land found ice depths of 9,000 feet.

By the end of 1960, the program of seismic soundings, started early in the IGY and continued beyond its nominal extent, indicated that the ice sheet had an average depth of 8,000 feet—eight times the estimate in 1912. It had a volume of about 8 million cubic miles. It was an ocean of frozen fresh water on land, an ocean the size of the North Atlantic. This assessment now showed that there was 20 percent more water on Earth than previously had been supposed.

On the Atlantic side, a traverse party led by Edward C. Thiel, of the University of Wisconsin, explored the Filchner Ice Shelf at the head of the Weddell Sea and the mountains to the south of it. The shelf turned out to be nearly the size of the Ross Ice Shelf on the Pacific side, about the size of France. Thiel's traverse charted the subice structure of the region and found that the ice had been higher in the past in the area of the Pensacola Mountains and the Dufek Massif. One of the most promising young geologists in antarctic research, Thiel was killed in an airplane crash at Wilkes Station in 1962.

A post-IGY assessment of Antarctica by Thiel, Bentley, Ostenso, and Crary presented a new picture of the region.[8] Geologic evidence showed that Antarctica actually consisted of two different provinces welded together by a 5,500,000-square-mile ice sheet.

Mainly facing the Atlantic Ocean and in the western hemisphere was the province called West Antarctica. Except for ranges of volcanic mountains on the north, most of the interior region (Marie Byrd Land) was sea bottom. If the ice was stripped away, West Antarctica would consist of a chain of mountainous islands and a sea stretching to the Transantarctic Mountains. The peninsula would appear to be a sea-girt archipelago dominated by a long, mountainous island extending possibly to the south polar plateau.

Mainly facing the Pacific and Indian Oceans was a province called East Antarctica because it lay principally in the eastern hemisphere. In land area, it was slightly larger than Australia. Its basement rocks were older than any of those found in West Antarctica, although they appeared younger than similar rocks in other continents. On this continental foundation of metamorphic and igneous rocks (gneisses, schists, and granites) lay a succession of sedimentary and volcanic rocks. The sequence in which these were found was an important clue to the mystery of how this land, once obviously warm and open to the sun, came to be imprisoned in an ice age.

The sedimentary rocks, formed by the deposit of sediments in streams of shallow seas, were called the Beacon Group. They were principally sandstones as old as 350 million years (Devonian). The igneous or volcanic rocks were called the Ferrar Group. They were younger, about 150 million years old (Jurassic). Between the Beacon sandstones and the younger volcanics were beds of tillite—aggregations of rocks swept up by glaciers—indicating the existence of an ice sheet 270 to 350 million years ago. It was not the same ice sheet that exists now, for overlying the tillite were younger rock strata that held coal and the fossil glossopteris trees of Pennsylvanian and Permian time that bespoke of a warm climate. The climate had oscillated back and forth from polar to temperate-subtropical several times.

These sequences of rocks were not peculiar to East Antarctica. They have been found all over the southern hemisphere, showing a relationship in the far past of all the southern landmasses. One of the senior geologists in the antarctic program, Campbell Craddock, of the University of Wisconsin, concluded: "This succession of distinctive rock types can be matched, at least in part, in Australia, India, Madagascar, Africa and South America. The character and distribution of these ancient glacial beds imply the presence of Paleozoic ice sheets of continental dimension." * [9]

ANCIENT GONDWANALAND

The geologic evidence supported an old idea—that continents drift about on the surface of the Earth and thus alter their relationship to the sun. This would account for the antarctic ice sheet in the present and subtropical forests and other evidence of a warm climate in the past.

Continental drift was first proposed by Francis Bacon (1561–1626), who noticed from the earliest mappemondes (world maps) showing the New World that the bulge of Brazil (Cape San Roque) looked as though it might have once fitted in the armpit of Africa.

In 1885, Eduard Suess, an Austrian geologist, proposed that parts of Africa, Madagascar, and peninsular India had been joined. They formed a supercontinent. "We call this mass Gondwanaland † after the ancient Gondwana flora which is common to all its parts. This country is incomparably older than North America. Indo-Africa is the great table land of the Earth. [10]

Building on this Indo-African connection, a more elaborate hypothesis of continental drift was proposed in 1912 by Alfred Lothar Wegener, professor of meteorology and geophysics at the University of Graz, Austria. His thesis was:

> He who examines the opposite coasts of the South Atlantic Ocean must be struck by the similarity of the shapes of the coastlines of Brazil and Africa. Not only does the great, right-angled bend formed by the Brazilian Coast at Cape San Roque find its exact counterpart in the re-entrant angle of the African coastline near the Cameroons but also south of the corresponding points, every projection on the Brazilian side corresponds to a similarly shaped bay on the African side and vice versa. [11]

* The Paleozoic era is the earliest division of geologic time when complex life forms existed. It began 500 million years ago and lasted 300 million years.
† The term *Gondwana* is derived from a rock formation in India, and the formation in turn is named for an ethnic group called the Gonds.

Wegener went further than to suggest merely a southern hemisphere supercontinent. He proposed that all the continents were once joined in a single landmass. He called it Pangaea. In the northern hemisphere, Europe was joined to North America through Ireland, Iceland, and Greenland; in the southern hemisphere, Africa, Antarctica, Australia, India, and South America were joined.

Over time, Pangaea broke up, forming the South Atlantic Ocean with the separation of Africa and South America and the North Atlantic Ocean as North America rotated away from Europe and Africa. In the southern part of Pangaea, Antarctica formed the center piece. As this Gondwana fragment of Pangaea broke up, Africa, India, and Australia moved away from each other; South America moved westward. Antarctica then rotated over the south pole, where eventually it acquired an ice cap.

Evidence collected by the National Science Foundation research ship *Eltanin* and other vessels suggests that Antarctica and Australia were joined as late as only 40 million years ago, according to Craddock. The ice cap, he estimated, was formed at least 7 million years ago, judging from the fact that volcanic rocks overlie a glaciated surface in the coastal mountains of West Antarctica.[12]

In the first half of the twentieth century, Wegener's theory of continental drift and sliding was widely regarded as a crackpot idea by practical geologists. It was difficult to imagine how the continents, composed of a mass of crustal rocks twenty to sixty miles thick, could move about on the underlying rock mass called the mantle. The crust was analogous to the skin of a golf ball, the mantle to its hard, rubberoid interior, and the core to the ball's hard center—except earthquake-produced seismic waves indicated that a large part of the planet's core was liquid, possibly molten iron. With this conception of the Earth's structure and lacking a source of energy to move landmasses, orthodox geology considered Wegener's theory nonsense. But the evidence on the surface of the Earth was difficult to ignore.

In 1937 a South African geologist, Alexander L. Du Toit, published a Gondwanaland hypothesis in which he remarked: "The role of the Antarctic is a vital one. . . . The shield of East Antarctica constitutes a 'key piece'— shaped surprisingly like Australia, only larger—around which, with wonderful correspondences in outline, the remaining 'puzzle pieces' of Gondwanaland can, with remarkable precision, be fitted." [13]

Du Toit's reconstruction of Gondwanaland, comprising all the lands of the southern hemisphere, shows Antarctica as the center piece. It was also the center piece in the evolution of drift theory. For clues pointing to Gondwanaland as a reality appeared almost as soon as men landed in antarctic lands. The first clues were fossil ferns, mollusks, and conifer trees found on antarctic islands in 1893 by Captain C. A. Larsen, the master of the sailing ship *Jason*. Snail-like fossil fauna were discovered by members of the *Belgica* expedition. They were identified at the University of Chicago in 1903 as three species of gastropods whose fossil remains are also found in southern India.[14]

On Scott's 1901–1904 expedition, Hartley T. Ferrar, geologist, found fossils of glossopteris tree trunks and coal seams in the Prince Albert Mountains of Victoria Land. Raymond Priestley, of that expedition, described tree trunks twelve to eighteen inches in diameter fossilized in the sandstones of Victoria Land.

Shackleton found thick seams of anthracite coal in the sandstone cliffs rimming the Beardmore Glacier. And there were coal and fossil plants in the thirty-five pounds of samples that Dr. Wilson laboriously hauled back from the pole in 1912 to the Ross Ice Shelf.

In addition to the geologic clues showing that the structure of the southern continents was consistent with a single large landmass having flora and fauna in common, there was an additional line of evidence pointing to an ancestral supercontinent. It was the Earth's magnetic field, first described in 1600 by William Gilbert, physician to Elizabeth I, in the treatise "De Magnete."

The magnetic clues were chiefly in the igneous rocks, those formed from the cooling and crystallization of a melt. Mixed in with the silicates was usually a small amount of magnetite (Fe_2O_4), which became magnetized by the Earth's magnetic field as the rocks cooled. Iron and titanium oxides in molten rock are nonmagnetic when very hot. But they become magnetic in the Earth's field when they cool down to a critical temperature, called the Curie point. It ranges from 200 to 680 degrees centigrade. Since these rocks crystallize at 1,000 degrees Centigrade, they are magnetized after they harden in place. These igneous (and also some sedimentary) rocks retained a memory of the geomagnetic field's orientation at the time they cooled from a lava flow, whether it was 10 years or 10 million years ago. The information was stored in them as it is in a computer.

The magnetic orientation in igneous rocks of the same age has been found to vary remarkably in the continents that once formed Gondwanaland. Fossil magnetism in a piece of Tasmanian granite 400 million years old pointed to a magnetic pole thousands of miles away from that indicated by a rock formation of similar age in South Africa.[15] This evidence suggests that these landmasses have moved in relation to each other in the 400 million years since the rocks were magnetized, inasmuch as the age of the rocks tells us that they were magnetized about the same time.

The magnetic orientation of rocks formed within the last 25 million years indicates that the magnetic poles have been located generally in geographic polar regions in that time. This suggests that the continents have maintained present positions relative to each other, generally, since then.

Over a longer period, 300 to 400 million years, the magnetic poles have wandered all over the Earth between the equator and the axis of rotation, according to the magnetic orientation of rocks in major land formations. This suggests that the continents have moved in relation to the magnetic poles, in addition to the motion of the magnetic poles around the geographic poles.

In the southern hemisphere, investigators have found that the ancient magnetic axis can be realigned with the geographic poles (or axis of rotation) by a partial reassembly of Gondwanaland. When the entire continental jigsaw puzzle is reconstructed, the magnetic poles are generally aligned with the spin axis, although the polarity is often reversed, as I will relate in a moment. That is, in some periods of ancient time, the north magnetic pole was where the south magnetic pole is now, and vice versa. The estimated rate of magnetic pole wandering indicates that North America and Europe were joined 300 million years ago and have been separating at the rate of several centimeters a year.[16]

Despite geologic, biologic, and magnetic evidence of continental drift, leaders in the geophysics community remained skeptical about it during the first half of the twentieth century. A leading British geophysicist, Sir Harold Jeffreys, of Cambridge University, contended that the crust was far too rigid to permit drifting. Below it were 1,800 miles of crystalline rock. How could continents drift through it? What was the source of energy for such massive movement?

THE PLASTIC PLANET

In the 1930s, laboratory studies of heat flow and the behavior of solids under heat and pressure hinted at the answer. Under certain conditions of heat and pressure that were believed to exist within the planet, solid rock could become plastic and flow, even in the solid state, as ice does. A Scottish geologist, Arthur Holmes, and a Dutch geophysicist, F. A. Venning Meinesz, proposed that the heat of the Earth's interior (from the decay of radioactive isotopes) produced giant convection cells in the mantle. Convection caused the rocks to flow at a very slow rate.

This idea slowly gained support. But it was not until the ocean floors were probed after World War II that the theory of mantle convection became the keystone in a new theory of geodynamics. From it has evolved the conception of the Earth's crust as an assemblage of plates that move apart and butt up against or grind against each other as they are rafted about on the convecting mantle.

The new geodynamic theory of plate tectonics was developed in four decades of research. One of the spectacular findings in its evolution was the discovery of the mid-Atlantic ridge, a gigantic undersea mountain system, in the 1950s by the late W. Maurice Ewing and the oceanographic research team he headed at the Lamont-Doherty Geological Observatory of Columbia University. Further investigation of the world ocean by Lamont, the Scripps

Institution of Oceanography, and the National Science Foundation revealed that the mountain system was global in extent, running 40,000 miles through the basaltic floor of the oceans and seas. Surveys of the ridge system show it to be an enormous mass of jumbled peaks and scarps rising two miles above the abyssal plain in the Atlantic Ocean and somewhat less in the Pacific, where it was first called the East Pacific Rise.

In the center of the ridge lies a deep rift, twelve to thirty miles wide, from which mantle material is slowly extruded onto the ocean floor by convection. This global system, hidden beneath the seas, has numerous branches. In the Indian Ocean, they run through the Red Sea and divide again to form the Dead Sea, the Jordan Valley, and the rift valley of east Africa. A Pacific Ocean branch runs through the Gulf of California and appears on land as the San Andreas Fault and, probably, the Imperial Valley.

In the 1960s, Harry H. Hess, of Princeton University, and Robert S. Dietz, of the United States Coast and Geodetic Survey, proposed in independent papers that the oceanic ridge and rift systems were created by rising flows of magma (molten rock, such as lava), which spread outward on both sides of the ridge to form new ocean floor. This process, called sea floor spreading, pushed the older, basaltic sea floor away from each side of the ridge system. As the floor moved, the continents, rising above it like huge plateaus, moved with it.[17]

The Americas moved one way; Europe and Africa moved another. This process can be assumed to account for the breakup of the world continent, Pangaea, and later, of its southern hemisphere component, Gondwanaland.

Maurice Ewing and his brother, John, proposed in 1959 that all continental material was collected in one hemisphere by an early system of mantle current. A second current then developed and broke the continental mass into fragments. These settled into the present continental configuration and are still moving.[18]

One obvious problem in sea floor spreading was where the old sea floor went. Some investigators considered the possibility that the Earth actually was expanding in circumference by this mechanism. The problem was resolved by assuming that as rapidly as new ocean crust is formed from the ridge-rift system, old crust is being pushed into the deep ocean trenches, a convenient repository for both the crust and the theory. Presumably, it is returned in this way to the mantle.

The sources of energy for this slow convulsion of the planet are heat and gravity. Heat is provided by the decay of radioactive elements, principally uranium, thorium, and potassium, and has been accumulating since the Earth was formed some 4.5 billion years ago. As the mantle is heated, the hotter material, being lighter, moves upward, being pushed there by the cooler material, which, being denser, sinks toward the center. This is convection. The mantle is visualized as convecting in titanic waves thousands of miles long.

In the aeons this has been going on, there may have been more than one Pangaea. Landmasses may have been assembled and disassembled by this process a number of times. The most recent breakup of Pangaea occurred near the end of the Triassic period, about 195 million years ago, according to one hypothesis.[19] The world continent split into two segments. One consisted of both Americas, Eurasia (except India), and Africa. It was called Laurasia and West Gondwana. The other, called East Gondwana, included Antarctica, India, Australia, New Guinea, and New Zealand. India separated from East Gondwana and drifted northward to butt into Asia. North America was forced away from South America and Africa by the formation of the North Atlantic rift, but it did not separate from Europe until the Tertiary period at the beginning of the Cenozoic era, some 65 million years ago. About 100 million years earlier, during the Upper Jurassic or Lower Cretaceous periods, South America moved away from Africa, and Antarctica separated from Australia and New Guinea.[20]

REVERSED POLES

Confirmation of sea floor spreading, as of drift, has been found in the Earth's magnetic record. One of the astonishing revelations in this record is evidence showing periodic reversal of magnetic poles. About 700,000 years ago, the *north* magnetic pole was in Antarctica and the *south* magnetic pole somewhere in northern Canada. In the last 3.6 million years, there have been nine reversals of the magnetic poles. And each of these reversals is recorded in the oceanic rocks on either side of the ridge-rift system.

Investigators of the Scripps Institution of Oceanography found that magnetic polarity alternates in the rocks on each side of the ridge. It forms a striped pattern extending for great distances. The pattern is symmetrical on each side of the ridge-rift system.[21]

The striped pattern is the result of outflow of magma from the Earth's interior at different times. As the magma cooled on the ocean floor, its iron and titanium oxides were magnetized in the direction of the magnetic field at the time. When the field reversed, the reversal was coded in the "magnetic memory" of the rocks.

Magnetic reversal has been known for a long time. Bernard Brunhes, a French physicist, found volanic rocks with reversed polarity in 1906. Reversed-polarity rocks were found in Japan in 1929 by Motonori Matuyama. For many years it was believed that some mechanism within the rocks caused the polarity to reverse.

In fact, this possibility was investigated by researchers at the University of Tokyo and the Philips Research Laboratories in the Netherlands. But further tests of the magnetizing process in several laboratories have confirmed that magnetic reversal generally is the result of the mysterious switching of the total magnetic fields of the Earth.[22]

Why the Earth's field reverses every so often has become one of the big questions in geophysics. It challenges the most generally accepted theory of the dynamo process, by which the field is believed to be created. This theory says that the molten iron-nickel core of the Earth functions like a dynamo in an electric power generating plant. Convection currents in the rotating core supply the necessary motion, and the electrical currents that result create the magnetic field.

Magnetometer surveys of the rocks on either side of the ridge-rift system show a sequence of major normal and reversed polarity "epochs." These are named after scientists who have investigated the phenomena. We are now living in the Brunhes Normal epoch, about 700,000 years old. That is the age of the oldest rocks with normal polarity in the striped sea floor pattern on either side of the ridge. The age of the rocks was determined by radioactive decay of potassium[40] to argon[40]. Prior to this epoch, rocks in the striped pattern show reversed polarity, in the Matuyama Reversed epoch, which extends into the past for an additional 2.5 million years. Before that, the striped pattern reveals the Gauss Normal epoch, extending back to 3.3 million years. And before that, there is the Gilbert Reversed epoch, extending beyond 3.6 million years ago.

Between these major epochs, there were brief fluctuations of polarity, which are called polarity events and lasted only a few thousand years.

The striped normal-reversed polarity pattern not only confirms the theory of sea floor spreading as a result of mantle convection but provides a rough time scale for the process. The size of the Atlantic Ocean changed in each of the epochs as spreading forced the continental masses, or plates, apart.

The magnetic observations show that magnetic reversal occurs relatively quickly, in a period of fewer than 5,000 years. There is some evidence that the strength of the magnetic field gradually diminishes, as it seems to have been doing in the last century, until it finally shuts off. Then it comes on again, gradually gaining in strength, with reversed polarity.

Investigators from the Scripps Institution of Oceanography and the Lamont-Doherty Geological Observatory have taken deep cores out of the floor of the Bellingshausen Sea with a normal-reversed polarity record going back to 3.6 million years. It parallels the sequences of epochs and events in the rocks on each side of the ridge system.

During the millennia when the field was attenuating or shut down entirely, the Earth would be without the great magnetic umbrella that shields the biosphere from ionizing radiation in the solar wind and cosmic rays. The magnetic shield extends outward 40,000 miles on the sunward side of the planet. It forms a long, tenuous tail to beyond the orbit of the Moon on the side opposite the sun.

What happens to life on Earth when the shield is down? When the radiation environment increases sharply? Several scientists have speculated that with the rise in radiation dosage in the biosphere, wholesale mutations would take place in terrestrial life. New species would arise; others would perish. In fact, the Bellingshausen deep cores showed major changes in the assemblages of the fossils of microscopic sea creatures near a magnetic polarity change.[23]

Perhaps genus *Homo sapiens* came into flower as a magnetic field reversal mutation 700,000 years ago or earlier. It is only a speculation, but it indicates how intimately the evolution of man may have been affected by the geophysical contortions of the Earth.

THE FOSSILS AT COALSACK BLUFF

The earliest antarctic evidence for continental drift, in the form of coal and the carboniferous tree fern, Glossopteris, was found in the Transantarctic Mountains. It was particularly appropriate, then, that the faunal evidence that finally nailed down the reality of continental drift was found there, too.

During the six decades that sailors, explorers, and scientists had trod the frozen continent, not a single shred of evidence that land animals had ever dwelled there was found. Then, suddenly, a fossil bone turned up in December 1967 in the Transantarctic Mountains. It was found by Peter J. Barrett, a New Zealand graduate student employed by the Institute of Polar Studies of Ohio State University, high on Graphite Peak, about thirty miles east of the Beardmore Glacier. Barrett and another member of the Institute, David Johnston, were making a geological reconnaissance of the peak when Barrett spied a piece of "foreign" material embedded in a sandstone layer of Triassic age (about 200 million years ago) called the Fremouw Formation. It looked like a fossil bone. Although not trained in paleontology, Barrett was aware that the discovery of any animal fossil would be an historic event. He carefully chipped the three-inch grayish piece out of its niche. When he and Johnston returned to camp, Barrett showed the fossil "thing" to Ralph Baillie, a geologist who had some background in vertebrate paleontology. Baillie pronounced it to be a fossil bone, all right. It was a critical find, this first piece of evidence that land animals had once inhabited Antarctica. It was destined to make a major contribution toward confirming continental drift. But what was it?

Baillie packed the fossil bone in cotton and put it in a tin box. When the party returned to Christchurch, New Zealand, the port of embarkation for McMurdo Sound, Antarctica, he declared the contents of the box as a bone rather than rock fossil to customs officials. Agricultural inspectors promptly sequestered the fossil and put it in a deep freeze for the duration of the party's stay in New Zealand to avoid possible contamination. The government of New Zealand is wary about the introduction of pests into the two islands, and the fact that the fossil was probably 250 million years old did nothing to allay official concern.

When Barrett returned to the Institute of Polar Studies at Columbus, Ohio, he and an English geologist, David H. Elliot, sought the opinion of one of America's leading paleontologists on the identification of the bone. He was Edwin Harris Colbert, then curator of vertebrate paleontology at the American Museum of Natural History in New York City. "Barrett and Elliot thought they had something and they called me up long distance," Dr. Colbert said. "I don't know why they just happened to pick on me." [24]

Colbert identified the bone as a piece of the lower jaw of an ancient amphibian called a labyrinthodont because of the structure of its teeth. This creature evolved from air-breathing fish ancestors at the end of the Devonian period of geologic time, 340 million years ago. It existed for about 140 million years and died out at the end of the Triassic period. [25]

Where there was one Triassic fossil bone, there must be many more, Colbert reasoned. During his long career, he had dug them out of sedimentary rocks in South Africa and India. Now that a single fragment had been found in Antarctica, the implication was literally earthshaking. These were freshwater creatures. They had no way of crossing oceans; yet, they were found in widely dispersed continents. The probability of faunal proof of Antarctica's connection with Gondwanaland was now very high.

Although he was retiring from the American Museum, Colbert asked the National Science Foundation to consider a small paleontological expedition to look for more fossils in the vicinity of Graphite Peak. The proposal was approved by the NSF as part of its continuing Antarctic Research Program for the austral summer of 1969–1970.

Colbert picked three younger men to go with him: William J. Breed, curator of geology at the Museum of Northern Arizona, Flagstaff; James A. Jensen, curator of the Earth Sciences Museum, Brigham Young University, Provo, Utah; and John S. Powell, a student at the University of Arizona. The four-man paleontological expedition was made a part of a twenty-man geological research group under the scientific leadership of David Elliot. It was scheduled to examine the geology and paleontology of the Princess Alexandra range of the Transantarctic Mountains near the Beardmore Glacier.

In September 1969, the NSF announced that "scientists from three institutions will join in a search through remote, ice girdled mountains in Antarctica for fossil evidence that the world's continents once were one." A similar release was issued to the press by the U.S. Navy, which had the mission of providing food, shelter, and transport for scientists in the NSF's Antarctic Research Program.

"The inclusion of Dr. Colbert and his group was in part an act of faith on the part of NSF," Elliot commented.[26] "The likelihood of coming across something was, I think, somewhat marginal in their opinion. Their [the Colbert team] inclusion was done on the possibility that if something was found, you were making the best use of all the logistics." *Logistics* is the operative word in antarctic exploration—indeed, in all modern exploration. Without adequate life support and transport, nothing operates in the environmentally hostile regions modern man is now investigating, from the seabed to the Moon. The first antarctic paleontological expedition suffered logistical setbacks, but it did have another essential element . . . luck.

A temporary camp was set up by Navy Seabees * in the mountain region about sixty miles from the Beardmore Glacier on a relatively crevasse-free stretch of ice called the Walcott Névé, a tributary of the extensive Lennox-King Glacier. The névé was selected because it provided an accessible landing strip for the ski-equipped C-130 (Hercules) turbojet aircraft on flights from the U.S. Naval Air Facility on Ross Island at McMurdo Sound.

The camp consisted of four well-insulated Jamesway huts. These are long, semitubular buildings, first cousins to the Nissen huts of World War II; they became the principal early shelter of the U.S. antarctic program. They were delivered in sections to the névé and set up in a matter of hours by the Seabees.

The Beardmore Station, as the camp was called, was seventy-five miles from Graphite Peak, the paleontological target, but transportation there was to be provided by three navy turbo-helicopters. The only geological feature of interest nearby was a series of nunataks (mountaintops protruding through the ice) about five miles away.

Elliot, Colbert, and most of the party arrived at the Beardmore camp in a Hercules transport November 22, 1969. They were late, having been delayed in New Zealand and at McMurdo Sound by bad weather and a radio blackout induced by sunspots. When heightened solar activity results in the damping out of radio transmissions in Antarctica, the navy grounds its aircraft there. Emissions of energetic particles by the sun disrupt the ionosphere in polar regions. The ionosphere is the electrified region of the upper atmosphere that reflects radio signals around the curvature of the Earth.

The helicopters had not yet arrived. After spending Saturday, the first day, settling in, Elliot and some of his colleagues decided to take a look at the nunataks Sunday morning. These peaks formed a broken series of cliffs, bluffs, and rock-strewn slopes running about four-fifths of a mile roughly east and west with a maximum height of about 600 feet above the snow surface.

---

* Derived from *CB*, or Construction Battalion, a force created in World War II to build navy installations on land. The Seabees built all U.S. antarctic stations during and after the IGY.

The north-facing slopes were mostly free of ice and snow. They were in the lee of the winds and storms blowing off the polar plateau to the south. The slopes exhibited a familiar geologic record, characteristic of southern lands, consisting of sandstones and siltstones deposited by ancient streams and carboniferous coal beds six to eight feet thick.

It was a bright, sunny morning, and the antarctic summer temperature was about the same as that on a cold, sunny day of a midwestern winter. It was a perfect day for a reconnaissance, and the geologists, after frustrating delays, were raring to go. "So we set out in the morning, at least a half dozen of us, in the motor toboggans," Elliot related. "Some question arose as to just exactly what part of the sequence was represented in these cliffs. As a result of this dispute, we wanted to check out exactly what the rocks were."

Parking the toboggans at the foot of a conspicuous nunatak that an earlier party of New Zealanders had dubbed Coalsack Bluff, Elliot and his colleagues climbed about halfway up the debris-strewn slope. As Elliot began examining the sandstones, he saw bone fragments encased in them—not just one, but many. Coalsack Bluff was a graveyard of extinct fauna. "It was pure serendipity," Colbert said. "They all came back about lunch time and Dave said he thought he had bones. He showed them to me and sure enough, that is what they were. We all went over to the bluff and that was it. We spent the rest of our time there, getting those bones."

The paleontologists did not reach Graphite Peak that season. When the three helicopters arrived, one of them crashed. Fortunately, no one was hurt, but the 'copter was a total loss. The crash was attributed to a broken drive shaft in the tail rotor. The drive shafts in the other two machines were removed and flown back to New Zealand for inspection. Eventually, they were returned to the Beardmore camp and reinstalled, but helicopter transportation was greatly restricted. In Antarctica, the navy rule was that one helicopter had to remain at base as a rescue backup while the other was out on the ice. With three helicopters, two could have been flown on mission at any one time, but with two, only one could be used at a time.

However, the good luck at finding the bones at Coalsack Bluff kept the paleontologists busy for the entire summer season. At the outset, bones of the same species of labyrinthodont amphibians represented by Barrett's 1967 discovery at Graphite Peak were found at Coalsack Bluff. On December 4, the jawbone of a mammallike reptile called Lystrosaurus appeared. It was another historic discovery. For fossil remains of Lystrosaurus, a four-footed, chunky animal, about four to five feet long, are typical of Lower Triassic sedimentary rocks of South Africa, peninsular India, and Eastern China, Colbert said. The reptile has a heavy skeleton; a barrel-shaped body; short, stocky legs; broad feet; and a short tail, as Colbert has reconstructed it. The head is remarkable, with eyes and nostrils placed high in the skull and a beaklike upper jaw like that of a turtle. The mouth is toothless except for two large tusks, one on each side.

The first identifiable specimen of *Lystrosaurus* found in Antarctica. Right maxilla with tusk. Amer. Mus. Natl. Hist. No. 9302. From the Lower Triassic Fremouw Formation, Coalsack Bluff.

Lystrosaurus skull in rock. Amer. Mus. Natl. Hist. No. 9515. Fremouw Formation, Halfmoon Bluff, Shackleton Glacier.

Partial right ilium of *Lystrosaurus*. Amer. Mus. Natl. Hist. No. 9318. Fremouw Formation, Coalsack Bluff.

Left femur of *Lystrosaurus*. Amer. Mus. Natl. Hist. No. 9321. Fremouw Formation, Coalsack Bluff.

Restoration of *Lystrosaurus* by Margaret
Colbert. From *The Age of Reptiles* by
Edwin H. Colbert, copyright © 1965 by
Edwin H. Colbert. Reprinted by permission
of W. W. Norton, New York, and
Weidenfeld and Nicolson, London.

Skeleton of *Thrinaxodon in situ*. (Natural
mold in the rock.) Amer. Mus. Natl.
Hist. No. 9500. Fremouw Formation,
Mt. Kenyon, Shackleton Glacier.

Front of skull of *Thrinaxodon*. Amer.
Mus. Natl. Hist. No. 9529. Mt. Kenyon,
Shackleton Glacier.

Lystrosaurus is classed in an infraorder of reptiles called dicynodonts, which means having two doglike teeth. Although its geologic time span was relatively short (ranging from about 250 to 200 million years ago), the dicynodont reptiles were numerous and widespread. Of special significance to continental drift theory, Lystrosaurus was a plant eater and appears to have thrived mainly in the stream beds of tropical and subtropical lands.

Its discovery in South Africa, India, and China was of interest to specialists in paleontology; but its discovery in isolated Antarctica was sensational, for it virtually proved continental drift, the most controversial theory about the Earth since Copernicus.

It happened that on the day the Lystrosaurus skull fragment was found in Coalsack Bluff, Laurence M. Gould, dean of American antarctic scientists, who had begun his career there as a geologist with Admiral Byrd, flew into the Beardmore camp for a visit. He was celebrating the fortieth anniversary of his first antarctic expedition. When he heard about the Lystrosaurus skull, he got on the radio and called the National Science Foundation in Washington with the news.

In his assessment of the Lystrosaurus find, Colbert wrote: "Here, with these small bones of land-living reptiles we had indisputable proof that in early Triassic time, Antarctica was connected to Africa." [27] For, he added, these animal fossils were found also in the Great Karroo—a huge, shallow basin in South Africa north and east of the Cape of Good Hope—and in Triassic beds of the Panchet Formation of the Ranigani coalfields near Asansol, India.

Gould commented: "Dr. Colbert's Lystrosaurus not only dated a continent but it is also the keystone of the evidence for the reality of Gondwanaland." No further proof was needed for the former existence of Gondwanaland. [28] Further, the existence of Lystrosaurus fossils in the Tunghungshan beds of Sinkiang, China, seemed to add that part of Asia to the Gondwanaland complex.

In addition to Lystrosaurus and the labyrinthodont amphibians, the sediments of Coalsack Bluff yielded the bone fragments of another group of reptiles called thecodonts. They were related to modern crocodiles and were the ancestors of the dinosaurs of the upper Triassic and Jurassic periods. "It was evident," Colbert said, "that the fossils were just like they were in Africa. Finding them was just plain luck and, of course, luck comes into all this. How many pieces did we get? I estimate about 450 to 500." Although technically the property of the National Science Foundation, the fossil bones were stored for analysis at the Harold S. Colton Research Center, Museum of Northern Arizona at Flagstaff, where Dr. Colbert retired—and then went back to work as curator of vertebrate paleontology. They will be housed permanently at the American Museum of Natural History, New York.

During the austral summer of 1969–1970, Colbert, at age sixty-four, was as active and energetic as his younger colleagues in their twenties and thirties, Elliot said. It was exhausting work, scrambling around on the slopes, Colbert recalled. For every step upward, you would slide back two.

The following year, another paleontology group investigated sediments about 120 miles southeast of Coalsack Bluff at nunataks on the McGregor Glacier, a tributary of the Shackleton Glacier. On the very first day, one of the geologists found the impression of a skeleton in the sediments. The principal paleontologist on the expedition, a South African scientist named James W. Kitching, identified it as the skeleton of Thrinaxodon, a small, carnivorous, mammallike reptile about the size of a weasel. Like Lystrosaurus, Thrinaxodon was characteristic of the Karroo beds in Africa. In addition to the bones of these creatures and more Lystrosaurus bones, the paleontologists at McGregor found the bones of a third reptile, called Procolophon.[29]

Colbert, who did not go on the 1970–1971 outing, received the fossils in Arizona, where he undertook the long process of classifying and identifying each bone, a monumental task. In this work he has reconstructed, in imagination, what the antarctic landscape was like 200 to 300 million years ago. At that period, the regions now covered with ice lay warm and open to the sun in a tropical or subtropical zone of this planet.

Colbert has visualized the landscape as low lying, abounding with lakes, streams, and ponds. Many of the reptiles that left their bones in the Fremouw Formation sediments that later became uplifted to form part of the Transantarctic Mountains lived in streams hardly more than twenty to thirty feet wide, for the most part. There, a forest grew of coniferous trees, a good deal like the ones in the Petrified Forest, Colbert surmised. The Glossopteris, fernlike trees, were gone then. They existed much earlier, in Permian time.

After seventy years of first intermittent and then continuous exploration, Antarctica evolved into a vast outdoor laboratory. But although its investigation illuminated much of the geophysical history of the Earth, the region still held its secrets. Now that early reptiles had been found there, what of later ones? What of early mammals? Were they hidden in the strata above the Triassic beds? Would it be possible to learn from fossils when the southern continent had drifted over the pole and when it had become devoid of land animals until the advent of man?

The United States, Great Britain, France, the Soviet Union, Japan, Argentina, Chile, and other nations have pursued these questions on a diminishing scale since the great effort of the IGY. But then the exploits of scientists in the last land frontier of the planet were drowned out in the breaking wave of the space age. In 1957, western technology began to penetrate a new environment, the interplanetary medium, at first with robots and then with men.

In Antarctica, men sought to unravel the mysteries of the Earth. But in space, they sought to perceive the processes of creation.

 PART II

ANOTHER SEA

CHAPTER IV

THE ENTERPRISE OF THE MOON

The reconnaissance of the Earth was achieved with the exploration and the scientific colonization of Antarctica in the 1960s. By 1966, the Second International Oceanographic Congress, in Moscow, reported that most of the planet's ocean bottom had been mapped.

A popular myth now held that the human condition called the *exploration imperative* sought new worlds to conquer. It was a mystical way of explaining the forces of competition and of struggle for survival that motivated an intelligent species to investigate its natural environment in an ever-widening radius. Beyond the Earth, the exploration imperative became the "extraterrestrial imperative." [1]

It was convenient to assume that some inborn genetic trait other than the cultural, economic, and political forces that could be perceived "programmed" man to explore and expand his habitat. But what a thousand years of human exploration and exploitation had demonstrated, from Vinland to Antarctica, was the irresistible drive of intraspecific competition. The way men responded to it—in camel caravans, in outrigger ocean-going canoes, in *knarrs*, in Iberian *naos*, or in great iron ships—was determined by their culture and level of technology.

The new worlds of the twentieth century were highly visible. There they were, shining islands in another sea: pearly Venus near the horizon; Mars glowing red in the night; the blazing beacon of Jupiter; distant Saturn with its rings; the Moon, its mountains, dark "seas," and bright "continents" plainly visible through even small telescopes and field glasses.

In the second half of the twentieth century, the Space Age dawned. The mystique of an extraterrestrial imperative is not required to account for it. The Space Age is a perceptible consequence of the same old, oft-discredited motives that impelled Norse voyagers to find Newfoundland, dispatched Columbus and Magellan on the Enterprise of the Indies, impelled Drake and Cook on their global quests, and sent Scott and Amundsen racing to the south pole. In the modern world, intraspecific competition bred two world wars in the first half of the twentieth century. In the second half, in a sublimation called the Cold War, it boosted men to the Moon.

Although the concept of interplanetary voyaging, especially of a trip to the Moon, has existed since Lucien of Samosata, a Greek philosopher, described an imaginary lunar voyage 1,800 years ago, the Space Age is the direct outgrowth of the two world wars and the weapons technology they stimulated. In World War II, the combatants produced new weapons that made space flight inevitable as a product of military competition. Germany invented the V-2, the first operational liquid-fuel rocket. The United States invented the nuclear bomb, which, when coupled with the rocket for delivery, became the most powerful weapon in history. Radar, another essential for space flight, was developed by Allied and German science about the same time.

With the defeat of the Axis powers and the exhaustion of Western Europe in World War II, the United States, undamaged by the war except in its Pacific Ocean possessions, and Russia, which had suffered vast war damage, emerged as the dominant world powers. The postwar scene became polarized into free and Communist-controlled worlds. With the rapid dissolution of the old European empires in Africa, India, and Southeast Asia, a Third World of developing nations came into being. Communist and anti-Communist forces competed for its allegiance, backed by the Soviet Union and mainland China on the one hand and the United States on the other. The ensuing wars in Korea and Indochina expressed the intensity of this contest at its human frontiers.

When the second half of the twentieth century opened, the United States and the Soviet Union confronted each other at several points around the world, from the thirty-eighth parallel in Korea to Berlin. As the foreign affairs specialist Joseph G. Whelan, of the Library of Congress, has observed: "The principal objective of the United States was to preserve a world order acceptable to the common interests of free people; the USSR sought to destroy the order and to transform it into the Soviet Image, with its distinctive governmental and economic form and totalitarian value systems. The resulting clash of interests and forces produced the cold war.[2]

The exclusive possession of the atomic bomb by the United States from 1945 to 1949 and the means of delivering it to centers in the Soviet Union by B-29 bomber fleets from bases in Western Europe were important stabilizing factors in the uneasy postwar era. With a tight grip on Eastern Europe, Stalin pushed hard for nuclear-weapons equality with the United States and Great Britain. Russia had no convenient bases near the contiguous United States, and an air assault from bases in eastern Siberia, to which Alaska was exposed, would be detected long before it reached the border by the U.S.-Canadian radar fences—the Distant Early Warning (DEW) line covering the polar cap, the mid-Canada Line and the Pine Tree net across the northern tier of states.

It was inevitable that the Russians would turn to long-range rockets as a means of striking its number-one competitor or, in Russian terms, of countering a strike from America. When the Russians developed nuclear bombs in 1949 and thereafter, their rocket technology, which was much more developed than the West suspected, was directed toward producing a powerful intercontinental ballistic missile.

THE ROCKET'S RED GLARE

In the arsenals of history, the rocket is the oldest form of artillery after the catapult or ballista. Centuries before Sir Isaac Newton formulated the principle of rocket propulsion in 1687 (Newton's Third Law of Motion states that for every action there is an equal and opposite reaction), the Chinese, Tartars, and Moors were shooting rockets at foes. In the thirteenth century, Chinese defenders of the city of Kai-fung-fu used rockets against besieging Mongols. The Hindus of Mysore fired rockets against British forces at Seringapatam in 1792 and again in 1799.

Early in the nineteenth century, Major William Congreve, an inventor as well as an artillery man in the British army, developed a war rocket with a range of 2,000 yards. It was used to fire bomb Boulogne, Copenhagen, and Danzig and in the Battle of Leipzig in 1813. The British fired Congreve rockets against Americans at the Battle of Bladensburg and at Fort McHenry, outside of Baltimore, in 1814. The "rocket's red glare" of Francis Scott Key's "The Star Spangled Banner" memorializes that episode.

The Congreve rocket used a long stick to stabilize its flight. About 1845, another English inventor, William Hale, conceived the idea of installing curved fins in the blast stream of a rocket to spin-stabilize it. During the Mexican War (1846–1848), American troops used the Hale rocket, but it went out of style with improvements in breech firing field artillery. In his novel *From the Earth to the Moon* (1864), Jules Verne employed a supercannon to launch his explorers to the Moon. H. G. Wells used the same device to send explorers into space in *The Shape of Things to Come* (1933). In literature, space flight became the hallmark of an advanced society.

The idea of using a rocket for interplanetary travel was proposed seriously in 1903 by a Russian schoolteacher, Konstantin Eduardovich Ziolkovsky (1857–1935). He is not only a space flight pioneer, but the patriarch of three generations of dreamers and schemers of space travel.

Ziolkovsky lost his hearing at the age of nine as the result of scarlet fever. Unable to attend school because of this handicap, he educated himself in mathematics and the natural sciences. The habit he acquired early of independent study and thinking freed him from the technical dogma of the period. It allowed his brilliant, imaginative mind greater scope than if he had been locked into a conventional curriculum.

His great work is *Exploration of the Universe with Reactive Devices*, first published in 1903 and extensively revised by the author in 1926, in which he analyzed the problems of space flight. He considered life-support systems; several types of propulsion, including liquid hydrogen; and the energy of radium. He proposed multistage rockets as a means of lifting heavy payloads of the Earth. In 1890, he built the first wind tunnel; but no one paid much attention to it, and he settled in the city of Kaluga to teach school and develop his ideas of space travel.

His practical book on rocket travel was preceded by fiction and fantasy writing. One of these was a booklet called *On the Moon*. Another was *Dreams About the Earth and Sky*. Probably the most quoted line in all of his writing is this short statement: "The Earth is the cradle of mankind; but one cannot remain forever in the cradle." [3] It appeared to Ziolkovsky, as well as to others who came to share his views in Europe, that space travel was man's destiny. Now that the means—reaction engines—were at hand, the time had come to begin to realize it.

But for decades, Ziolkovsky and his ideas shared the fate of other pioneers who were ahead of their time. His theoretical work was ignored during most of his life; only in his later years was it recognized. After his death, the government built a museum memorializing his work at Kaluga. A group of cosmonauts made a pilgrimage there to open it in 1965.

In the United States, a less theoretical and more practical approach to rocketry was pursued by Robert H. Goddard, professor of physics at Clark University, Worcester, Massachusetts. He began testing solid-fuel rockets in 1915. He, too, considered the transport potential of rocket propulsion, but he refrained from speculating about its interplanetary possibilities. In 1919, the Smithsonian Institution in Washington, D.C., published his classic work, *A Method of Reaching Extreme Altitudes*, in which he described the modern theory of rocket propulsion. With publication of the paper went a grant of $5,000 to finance his research.

Goddard's visualizations were as powerful as those of Ziolkovsky (of whom he had never heard), but they were couched in less romantic terms. He perceived the rocket as a long-range strategic weapon, and he tried to sell the U.S. Army on the project of developing it. Ordnance experts rejected the idea, largely on the grounds that rockets were unreliable and uncontrollable. In vain, Goddard tried to persuade military artillery experts that it was possible to devise precise steering and stabilization systems for rockets so that they could strike targets over very long distances. But in 1916, when Goddard approached the U.S. Army, neither it nor any other army was ready for rockets. The German army had developed two long-range weapons in World War I: the zeppelin and the Paris gun, or "Big Bertha," a super-long-range cannon with poor accuracy.

On March 16, 1926, Goddard successfully fired the first liquid-fuel rocket at Auburn, Massachusetts. It flew only 184 feet, but, as the NASA historian Eugene M. Emme noted, this shot was to rocketry what the first flight of the Wright brothers at Kitty Hawk was to aviation.[4] The liquid-fuel rocket engine—burning gasoline, kerosene, or alcohol with liquid oxygen—was the forerunner of modern steerable ICBMs and deep-space rockets.

Goddard worked mostly alone. With a substantial grant from the New York banking family of Daniel Guggenheim, who became interested in Goddard's work at the suggestion of Charles A. Lindbergh, the inventor was able to develop the basic mathematics and physics of rocketry and test them.

A rocket can hardly be designed, constructed, or launched today without infringing on one or more of the 214 patents Goddard obtained, according to the rocket pioneer G. Edward Pendray.[5] In addition to being first to develop a liquid-fuel rocket engine, Goddard was the first to employ gyroscopic stabilization for rockets (1932) and use deflector vanes in the rocket engine exhaust tube for steering. He received the first United States patent on the idea of the multistage rocket in 1914; he proved in 1915 that a rocket engine will provide thrust in a vacuum (as Newton's Third Law predicted); he developed the principle of the World War II bazooka in 1918, but the army filed the plans away. He developed the first self-cooling rocket engines, variable thrust engines, and fuel pumps. He forecast jet engines for aircraft and proposed a rocket mail service.

On July 7, 1929, Goddard fired a rocket containing an aneroid barometer, thermometer, and camera. The camera was focused on the other instruments and photographed the readings. The engine burned for 18.5 seconds, lifting the rocket casing and instruments 90 feet and a horizontal distance of 171 feet. Unfortunately, complaints from spectators about the noise brought the law down on Goddard. The state fire marshal enjoined him from making further tests in Massachusetts.

He moved to the wide open spaces of New Mexico and set up an experiment site near the town of Roswell, with the financial aid of the Daniel and Florence Guggenheim Foundation. From 1930 to 1941, Goddard and a crew of technicians he gathered around him worked on liquid rockets. They developed nearly all the devices and the systems later found in the German V-2.

By 1938, Goddard had constructed a liquid-fuel rocket that reached an altitude of 4,215 feet. By 1941, it reached 9,000 feet. Goddard's rocket, *Nell*, was quite similar in operation to the V-2 the Germans fired at London in 1944–1945. The differences were mainly in fuel and size. The V-2 burned alcohol; Goddard's rocket burned gasoline. Both used liquid oxygen as the burning agent, or oxidizer. The V-2 was 46 feet long; Goddard's rocket, 22 feet long. Both used centrifugal pumps to inject fuel into the combustion chamber and a small rocket motor to drive the pumps; and both had the same arrangement of tanks, pumps, and turbines. Both used gyroscopes for stabilization, and both had internal vanes, which deflected the exhaust stream for steering, as well as external stabilizing vanes. Both had the regenerative cooling system.[6] It is a method of cooling the combustion chamber to prevent its walls from melting or eroding under high temperatures and pressures.

The origin of regenerative cooling is diffused in Europe and America. The principle was demonstrated in Vienna and Berlin early in the 1930s. In America, a working regenerative rocket engine was demonstrated in 1938 by James Wyld, an engineer, who was president of the American Rocket Society. The blast chamber was encased in a metal jacket. The fuel, kerosene, was pumped into the space between the chamber and the jacket and then forced upward through holes to spray into the blast chamber, where it was mixed with oxygen and ignited. Heat of the burning fuel in the chamber was carried away by the fresh fuel flowing around it. Goddard developed a regenerative liquid rocket engine in his own research and obtained a patent on it.

The manner in which rocket research in one country pollinated development in others in the 1930s, until military security was clamped down, is not clear; but it is well known that experimenters read each other's published papers and discussed technical problems freely before rocket development was brought under tight military control.

Walter R. Dornberger, who served as chief of rocket development in Germany from 1931 to the end of World War II, contends that Goddard's work was of little help in the development of the V-2, because his patents were not available.[7] Yet the similarity between Goddard's Roswell rocket and the V-2 raises the question: Who got what from whom? It does not seem likely that Goddard acquired any technology from the Germans, and his patents were closely guarded. Could this have been a case of parallel development, where similar solutions were found to similar engineering problems?

Wernher Von Braun, who directed the development of the A-4 (V-2) at Peenemünde, recalled: "Around 1930 when I was 18 years old and a member of the German Society for Spaceflight (Gesellschaft fur Weltraumforschung), Dr. Robert Goddard was one of the great international names in the concept of flight through space and I counted him among my boyhood heroes." [8]

Although he had read Goddard's booklet A *Method of Reaching Extreme Altitudes* and, later, articles quoting Goddard in aviation journals, Von Braun said, "at no time in Germany did I or any of my associates ever see a Goddard patent." He added: "I was not even aware of the fact that Goddard worked in the field so dear to my own heart, namely, liquid propellants, let alone that even as early as 1926 he had successfully launched the world's first liquid propellant rocket."

On April 25, 1959, Von Braun, then director of the Development Operations Division, U.S. Army Ballistic Missile Agency, spoke at the dedication of the Goddard Rocket Collection of the Roswell, New Mexico, Museum and Art Center. He left no doubt about Goddard's lead in rocket development. He noted that the American inventor demonstrated an automatic gyroscope control mechanism in 1932 and flew the first rocket under gyroscope control in 1935. He credited Goddard as the first not only to use vanes mounted in the rocket exhaust stream for steering but also to develop and patent the multistage rocket.

As NASA deputy associate administrator for planning, Von Braun appeared before a Senate space committee hearing March 16, 1970, and testified: "In 1950 when I had the first opportunity to examine Dr. Goddard's many patents, I was virtually overwhelmed by the thoroughness of his early work and found many design solutions in the V-2 rocket already covered."

THE AGE OF INNOCENCE

The early period of rocket development—from the turn of the century to 1932, when the German army turned to the rocket as a weapon whose development was not forbidden by the Versailles Treaty—could be called the Age of Innocence. It was characterized by a romantic notion of the rocket's promise as an interplanetary mode of transportation. Perhaps the dream represented an escape from the disillusion and drabness of postwar Europe.

In 1924, Ziolkovsky and several associates organized in Moscow the Society for Studying Interplanetary Communication. One of the associates was Friedrich Arturovich Tsander, an engineer from Riga, and another was Mikhail K. Tikhonravov, an artillery technician. As the membership grew, the pioneers formed a development organization called the Group for the Study of Reactive Propulsion (Gruppa Isutcheniya Reaktivnovo Dvisheniya, or GIRD) in 1928.

Tsander became a leading figure in GIRD. He and other technical men conducted rocket experiments in their spare time in the basement of a Moscow apartment building. They developed a liquid-fuel engine with sufficient thrust to propel an experimental airplane. In August 1933, they launched the first Russian liquid-fuel rocket, burning jellied gasoline and oxygen to an altitude of 400 meters (1,300 feet).

Tsander died suddenly of typhoid fever in 1933 and was succeeded as the leader of the Moscow experimenters by Sergei Pavlovich Korolev, a young engineer. It was not until thirty-three years later, on the occasion of Korolev's death on January 14, 1966, that the Soviet government formally identified him as the chief designer of Rocket Cosmic Systems. His role in the Russian rocket development program had been secret until then.[9]

In 1931, a Leningrad section of GIRD was organized under the direction of Y. I. Perelman and Professor Nikolai A. Rynin. Four years later, it was amalgamated with the Leningrad Laboratory of Gas Dynamics (GDL). From this merger arose the Soviet Institute for Research into Jet Propulsion, with Korolev as chief. The government was now in the field of reaction engines.

By that time, the German army was well into rocket experimentation on its own. In Germany, early rocket development was characterized by the same kind of romanticism as in Russia. In 1928, the Society for Space Travel (Verein fur Ramschiffahrt, or VfR) was founded by Johann Winkler and two associates in the back room of a restaurant, according to Willy Ley, one of the charter members. Another founder was the Rumanian counterpart of Ziolkovsky and Goddard, Hermann Oberth. He was born in 1894 in the Saxon town of Hermannstadt, in a German-speaking area of Transylvania that was then part of Rumania. Oberth became a professor of mathematics at the Mediash High School in the province.

In 1923, four years after Goddard's *A Method of Reaching Extreme Altitudes* was published, Oberth wrote a small book entitled *The Rocket into Interplanetary Space*. Whether he was influenced by Goddard's book is questionable. Ley suggested that Oberth probably was unaware of Goddard's work, which had a limited circulation.[10] An unknown in scientific and technical circles, Oberth had to pay part of the cost of printing his book. But it quickly gained a wide circulation.

Oberth boldly asserted that the present state of science and technology (in 1923) made it possible to build machines that could rise above the atmosphere, go into orbit around the Earth, and even fly to the moon and to other planets. Moreover, such machines could be designed to carry men and could become profitable as an engineering enterprise, he said.

In contrast to that uninhibited approach, Goddard's treatise was a factual, nonspeculative, restrained document. Even when he revised it a quarter of a century later, just before his death, Goddard remarked: "Finally, the subject of projection from the Earth and especially a mention of the Moon must still be avoided in dignified scientific and engineering circles, even though projection over long distances on the Earth's surface no longer calls for quite so high an elevation of the eyebrows." [11]

Oberth described the general nature of a spaceship, which he called *Model E*. He discussed the problem of weightlessness in space flight and proposed a space station. Goddard had thought about these problems, too. He had considered the prospects of reaching Mars and the dangers of meteors hitting the ship. But he excluded these speculations from A *Method of Reaching Extreme Altitudes.*

In addition to rocket enthusiasts, Oberth's work attracted a number of critics, including astronomers who argued that there was no such thing as recoil propulsion in the interplanetary medium—there was nothing to "push against." Presumably, these savants discounted Newton. Also, it was argued, space flight inevitably would prove fatal for human beings, for as soon as a man left Earth's atmosphere, he would be "squashed" by the gravity of the sun.[12]

Like Ziolkovsky and Goddard, Oberth proposed the development of liquid-fuel rockets for long-distance shots. Despite its critics, Oberth's book rallied a number of space enthusiasts around him. One was Walter Hohmann, the city architect of Essen-on-the-Ruhr, who wrote a book of his own, *Attainability of Celestial Bodies.*

Within a year after its founding, the VfR had more than 500 members. Among them were the German rocket developer and promoter Max Valier; the Russian, Professor Rynin, who was writing a whole encyclopedia of interplanetary travel; and a French engineer, Robert Esnault-Pelterie, who founded an "astronautics" branch of the Societe Astronomique and coined the word *astronautics* in the process. Other early members were the Austrian aviation theorist Eugen Sänger, author of a pamphlet on *Rocket Flight Technique* in 1933, and an engineering student at the University of Berlin, Wernher Von Braun.

In 1929, Oberth appeared in Berlin as a technical consultant to the motion picture producer Fritz Lang, the German counterpart of Cecil B. DeMille. Lang was producing a science fiction movie called *Frau im Mond* ("Woman in the Moon"). Willy Ley described the premiere of the movie in Berlin as a glittering social event attended by all the big names in arts, letters, and government with everyone in formal dress. In France, meanwhile, a banker, André Hirsch, posted 5,000 francs a year as an award to the person who most effectively advanced space travel.

In contrast to the "lost generation" psychology of the post-World War I decade that depressed many young people in Europe, the rocket craze and space travel energized thousands of others. It was another kind of reaction to the disillusionment and grim conditions of the postwar years. The space enthusiasts of the period between the world wars were characterized by their youth, intellectual interest in science and mathematics, and romantic daydreams of rocketing about the solar system. Many were undergraduate or graduate students in the universities or technical institutes or young instructors or teachers. Most of them were outside the scientific establishment, whose guardians looked down their noses at the idea of space travel—a puerile daydream. In these early years of space enthusiasm, rocket development was privately financed and encouraged by André Hirsch, for instance, in Paris, and the Guggenheim family in New York. Developers operated on the Columbus-Magellan model, petitioning governments and financiers to underwrite the discovery of new worlds.

In 1932, as the VfR experimenters in Berlin and those of GIRD in Moscow began to get their rockets off the ground, the military establishments of Germany and of Russia became interested. The idea of a long-range rocket as a strategic weapon appears to have entered military thinking in Europe in that year.

In Russia, Lenin had authorized construction of an aeronautics research center (AGI), which became the Russian counterpart of the United States National Advisory Committee for Aeronautics (NACA) in the 1920s. According to Colonel Gregory A. Tokaty, a Russian rocket specialist who emigrated to England, fifteen institutions for basic research grew out of the AGI.[13]

Among them were the Central Institute of Aerospace Propulsion Systems; the All-Union Institute of Aerospace Materials; the Flight Research Institute; and the State Scientific Research Institute Number 1, which concentrated on rockets. A Central Bureau for the Study of Rockets (BIRP) was created in 1924. An All-Union Society for the Study of Interplanetary Flights (OIMS) was also established in that period.

Among the younger members of these groups were Boris Sergeivich Stechkin, an AGI engineer who later became a member of the Soviet Academy of Sciences and head of the Department of Aerospace Propulsion of the Marshal Nikolai E. Zhukovsky Academy of Aerodynamics of the Soviet air force; Y. V. Kondratyuk, who in 1928 proposed the idea of aerodynamic braking to permit the reentry into the atmosphere of a spacecraft from orbit; and Tsander, who worked on jet and rocket engines.

During the fifteen years between the Russian Revolution of 1917 and the beginning of rocket development by the German army in 1932, sophisticated rocket research was carried on in Russia, along with aeronautics research. Americans were not generally aware of this because of the lack of communication between the two societies that persisted until World War II. Ignorance of Soviet rocket development contributed to the shock and amazement in America when the Russians launched the first satellite in 1957.

Political power struggles in Russia as well as its isolation from the West tended to obscure also its academic accomplishments and tribulations. The purges following Stalin's final seizure of power in 1929 took their toll of scientists and engineers. Members of the BIRP and OIMS were suddenly and inexplicably branded enemies of the regime. Tokaty said, "Naturally, these happenings confused the work of the Soviet rocketeers, but it was for a short period only and the government was far from abandoning its rocket interest."[14] A more critical view of Stalin's interference is given by a Russian expatriate journalist, Leonid Vladimirov, who sought asylum in England during a visit to London in 1966.

Most of the leaders of the Institute for Research into Jet Propulsion were liquidated by Stalin's secret police, except Korolev, according to Vladi-mirov.[15] One of those executed was Georgi Langemak, inventor of the famous Katusha war rocket, along with his entire design group. One man, A. G. Kostikov, was left alive for a time to continue the weapon's develop-ment. Later, Vladimirov said, Kostikov was given an award and then ex-ecuted like the others.

Korolev was linked with Mikhail Tukhachevsky, the deputy commissar for military and naval affairs, who was shot during the purges as a German spy. But Korolev was spared, Vladimirov believed, because the engineer had been a student of the great aircraft designer Andrei Tupolev.

In 1938, according to Vladimirov, Tupolev, his wife, and his leading engi-neers were imprisoned—Korolev along with them. Stalin ordered that all of Tupolev's people be put to work for the state instead of being wasted before a firing squad. Korolev worked in a prison office attached to an aircraft fac-tory in Moscow, and when the Nazis invaded Russia, he was transferred to Omsk, in Siberia, along with Tupolev and his staff. There, the entire group continued its work, as prisoners. Then, after Tupolev's dive bomber, the TU-2, proved effective, he and his staff were pardoned. They returned to Moscow and continued their work as civilian employees of the government. Korolev was released in 1945 and awarded the Badge of Honor for his work in developing jet engines, according to Vladimirov's account.

THE TRANSATLANTIC ROCKET

In Germany, the VfR rented a proving ground for rocket experiments from the city of Berlin in 1929. It was located in a suburb, Reinickendorf, but proved to be too small for testing larger rockets. In 1932, the Army Board of Ordnance opened its own rocket testing ground at Kummersdorf, twenty miles south of Berlin. Chief of the rocket section was an artillery captain, Walter R. Dornberger. He hired as his assistant one of the VfR enthusiasts, Wernher Von Braun, twenty, a graduate student in physics at that time at the University of Berlin.

Although the early experimentation of the VfR had been noticed by Ger-man army ordnance officers, Major General Karl Becker, ordnance chief, was more impressed with the work of Goddard and liquid-fuel rocket tech-nology than with the dreams of theoreticians aiming for interplanetary travel.

Becker and Dornberger regarded the rocket as a possible extension of long-range artillery. The rocket for space travel at this juncture became a strategic weapon. But before it could be useful in war, the rocket had to undergo an evolutionary development in which such problems as overheating, steering, and reliability were solved.

One of the early technical problems in liquid-fuel rockets was the rapid melting of the metal walls of the exhaust tube from the intense heat of the exhaust gases that propelled the rocket. Goddard found that instead of directly melting the tube walls, the exhaust eroded the metal, flaking metallic particles away until the wall collapsed under the pressure of the expanding gases.

The German VfR experimenters tried cooling the tube by immersing it in liquid oxygen (297 degrees below zero, Fahrenheit), but that did not work. The liquid oxygen boiled so fast the tank blew up. The VfR then tried water-jacket cooling. Goddard had tried that, too; it did not work either. The problem was solved by the invention of the regenerative cooling system. The fuel served as a coolant, circulating around the exhaust tube, before it was pumped into the combustion chamber to be ignited. In the process of cooling the exhaust tube, the fuel was warmed, and that promoted combustion when the fuel was mixed with liquid oxygen. Again, the invention of regenerative cooling raises the question: Who got what from whom? [16]

According to Tokaty, who was chief rocket scientist of the Soviet government in Germany in 1946–47, Russian investigators found the "secret" plans of a liquid-fuel rocket designed and built by Tikhonravov in 1934 in the files of the German Air Ministry.[17] However, Tokaty said that Tikhonravov published a good deal, and his book *Rocket Technique* (1935) was especially enlightening about his work.

The development of the V-2 (which was called the A-4 in technical parlance) began in 1932 at the Kummersdorf test center. V-2 was the German Ministry of Propaganda's name for the rocket Vergeltungswaffen Zwei, ("Vengeance Weapon Two"). The conception of the weapon was that of an extension of the Paris Gun of World War I. That huge railway gun could throw twenty-two pounds of high explosives seventy-eight miles. It was designed to bombard Paris and thus crush French morale, but it never was brought near enough to reach the city.

The Board of Ordnance settled on a rocket that would throw 100 times the payload of the Paris gun—2200 pounds, or a metric ton. Its range would be double that of the Paris gun, or 156 miles. By a process of calculation involving an accommodation with narrow roads and railway tunnels through which the weapon would have to be transported, the dimensions were set at a diameter of 9 feet and a length of 46 feet. A thrust of 25 metric tons (55,000 pounds) was required to loft a warhead of one metric ton a distance of 156 miles. In 1932, the maximum thrust obtained from liquid-fuel rockets was just short of 1,000 pounds.[18]

The first model of the war rocket, the A-1, displayed an unanticipated technical problem when it blew up at the first launch attempt. The designers had used compressed gas to force fuel and oxidizer into the combustion chamber, but that system was inadequate. They found it necessary to develop a pumping system that would deliver 1,100 gallons of alcohol and 1,000 gallons of liquid oxygen a minute to the chamber.

A steam-driven pump was built, the steam generated by the decomposition of hydrogen peroxide by liquid potassium permanganate. Toward the end of 1932, a redesigned rocket, the A-2, was launched to an altitude of 6,500 feet. Now, the reorganizing German army had a genuine ballistic missile in sight.

By the end of 1936, the rocket program boasted a staff of 100 engineers and technical people. It became known as the Department of Special Ordnance Devices. Far from the "madding crowd" of spies, saboteurs, and Gestapo agents, the new department acquired a development center on the island of Usedom in the Baltic Sea, off the mouth of the River Peene. The army leased the site from the town of Peenemunde.

The stabilization and steering of the rocket in flight were the next development problems. The English inventor Hale had shown a century earlier that vanes in the exhaust stream could stabilize the rocket. Goddard had installed movable vanes in the exhaust to guide his vehicle, and the Peenemunde group used that system.

The internal-vane guiding system was built into the next model, the A-3. It developed 3,300 pounds of thrust, had a burning time of forty-five seconds, and reached an altitude of seven and one-half miles and a range of eleven miles. A combination of internal vanes and external fins was then adopted in the next model, the A-4, which, after hundreds of tests, became the operational rocket called the V-2. At the time it was first launched against Paris and then London in early September 1944, it was 85 percent reliable.

Launched from sites on the Dutch coast, V-2s fell on England and on liberated areas of France and Belgium during the fall and winter. It followed the terrifying V-1 "flying bomb" that began hitting random targets in London on June 12, 1944. The V-1 was a relatively slow-moving, pilotless jet airplane, launched by a catapult and steered by a primitive autopilot. The Luftwaffe had developed it at much lower cost than the V-2. Although the V-1 was vulnerable to being shot down by antiaircraft fire or fighter airplanes as it putt-putted along at low altitudes at 190 miles per hour or less, it was as effective as the V-2 as a terror weapon.[19]

The V-2, or A-4, was not the end of the line of Peenemunde rocket plans. The Dornberger-Von Braun group had plans for the construction of a transatlantic rocket, the A-10. It was a two-stage vehicle that would be capable of dumping a ton of high explosives on New York City. The first stage would have 440,000 pounds of thrust for fifty seconds. The second stage was a winged version of the A-4 designated the A-9. The composite vehicle would be seventy-two feet tall with a diameter of twelve feet. Its lift-off weight would be 87 metric tons. The war ended before the A-10 could be built, but the conception was fifteen years ahead of the analogous United States ICBM, the *Titan II*. Twelve years later, Von Braun told the U.S. Senate Preparedness Investigating Subcommittee that at the rate of progress in 1944–1945, the Peenemunde engineers could have developed an operational ICBM by 1950.[20]

When World War II ended, the Peenemunde group was ten years ahead of the United States and the Soviet Union in rocket development. Early in 1945, as Russian armies approached Peenemunde, Dornberger, Von Braun, and their associates elected to surrender themselves and their engineering documents to the United States rather than fall into the hands of the Russians. They considered themselves the torchbearers of a new engineering science. As Dieter Huzel, an electrical engineer on the team, wrote later: "They [the V-2 engineering documents] represented years of intensive effort in a brand new technology, one that would play a profound role in the future course of human events." [21]

It was the consensus of this group that the United States offered a more enlightened and politically secure technical environment in which to continue their work than did the USSR. This decision led the group to cooperate with the U.S. Army in the roundup of German technicians, tools, blueprints, manuals, and more than 100 V-2 rockets in various stages of completion in "Operation Paperclip." The first contingent of seven emigres from Peenemunde arrived at Fort Strong, Massachusetts, in September 1945. They were later transferred to Fort Bliss, Texas, where they were joined in December 1945 by 55 more members of their team. Eventually, 118 V-2 engineers and technicians signed contracts to work for the U.S. Army.

Soon after he was brought to the United States, Von Braun was asked by an Army Ordnance intelligence interrogator how the A-4 rocket worked. "I replied you could have asked your own Professor Goddard 10 years ago," he recalled (in a personal communication). "He replied that he had never heard of Goddard."

Using the Germans as a nucleus, the U.S. Army created its own rocket-development group. Test stands and a blockhouse were built at the White Sands Proving Ground in New Mexico, about 110 miles west of Goddard's experiment station at Roswell. The U.S. Army began flying the V-2.

When the Russians reached Peenemunde, they found the cupboard bare. According to Tokaty, the Soviet Union did not get a principal V-2 rocket engineer or administrator, nor did they get a complete rocket production line.[22]

Stalin was angered at the Russian failure to grab the cream of V-2 technicians and technology as the Americans had done, according to Tokaty. He quoted the premier as complaining: "We defeated Nazi armies. We occupied Berlin and Peenemunde. But the Americans got the rocket engineers. What could be more revolting and inexcusable? How and why was this allowed to happen?" [23] Tokaty concluded from inspection of V-2 technology that in theory, the Russians were not far behind Germany and, in some respects, ahead of the work at Peenemunde. But so far as practical development was concerned, he said, "we were behind the Germans."

The Russians rounded up more than 2,000 German technicians and shipped them, under nominal contracts, to rocket and aircraft research centers in Russia. The consensus of Germans who returned to their homes in 1950 and thereafter was that they were allowed to contribute relatively little to rocket development. Von Braun confirmed this in 1957–1958 when he testified before the Senate Preparedness Subcommittee. [24] Russian experts said they didn't need the Germans. Nevertheless, the V-2 remained the prototype missile in Russia, as in the United States, for five years.

Under Korolev, as chief designer, the V-2 was modified and the improved version, called the *Pobeda* ("Victory"), was uprated to thirty-five tons of thrust, with a range of 558 miles. The rocket was used for upper-atmosphere scientific probes in Russia. The U.S. Army used V-2s for the same purpose at White Sands.

In terms of Russian military strategy, the *Pobeda* was not the answer to the quest for a long-range strategic weapon. Considering Russia's geographical position and satellite countries, the rocket's short range made it virtually useless as a weapon. Tokaty quoted Soviet Air Marshal Zhigarev as telling him in Berlin in 1946: "We must admit that our V-2 type rockets do not satisfy our long-term needs; they are good to frighten England, but should there be an American-Soviet war, they would be useless. What we really need are long-range, reliable rockets capable of hitting target areas on the American continent. This is the aim that should dominate the minds and efforts of your own group." Tokaty also quoted Georgi M. Malenkov as saying, at a meeting of aircraft and rocket designers in the Kremlin, March 14, 1947: "I am not happy with our V-2s. We cannot rely on such a primitive weapon. Our strategic needs are predetermined thousands of miles away." [25] At a meeting considering the development of intercontinental jet bombing aircraft and rockets, Stalin said: "Do you realize the tremendous strategic importance of machines of this sort? They could be an effective straightjacket for that noisy shopkeeper, Harry Truman. We must go ahead with it, comrades. The problem of the creation of trans-Atlantic rockets is of extreme importance to us." [26]

Stalin ordered the reorganization of rocket research under a State Commission for the Study of the Problems of Long Range Rockets (PKRDD). Members were Ivan A. Serov; Tokaty; Mstislav V. Keldysh, later president of the Soviet Academy of Sciences; M. S. Kishkin; and V. I. Stalin, the Premier's son. An Academy of Rocket Artillery Sciences was created under Lieutenant General Anatoly A. Blagonravov.

By the end of 1947, two long-range rocket development programs had been drafted, one under Tokaty, the other under Korolev. Tokaty's group worked on a three-stage liquid-fuel rocket for high altitude and orbital flights. He said that had his group been permitted to continue the project without "interference," the Soviet Union could have put a satellite into orbit by 1952. But for reasons having nothing to do with the project, Tokaty related, "we found ourselves in a difficult position." [27] Toward the end of 1947, work on the project was paralyzed by political arrests. Tokaty and others left the country.

Korolev's program went forward to create the ICBM. Two considerations dictated the development objectives. The rocket had to be powerful enough to reach North America and to carry a heavy atomic bomb. To achieve this performance, Korolev set his goal on a rocket that developed 500 metric tons (1,100,000 pounds) of thrust. It would be twenty times as powerful as the V-2 and three times more powerful than any rocket developed in the United States up to 1961.

Under Korolev worked a talented team of engineers: Valentin Petrovich Glushko, Aleksei M. Isayev, and Tikhonravov. The first engine they developed was a cluster of four combustion chambers called the RD 107. This design—the cluster—characterized the big Russian rockets for two decades. The clustering of engines also was used in the Saturn rockets by the Von Braun team.

The RD 107, with its four exhaust nozzles, was designed to produce 102 tons of thrust. A second engine, the RD 108, was developed, also with four combustion chambers in a cluster, with 96 tons of thrust. To get the 500 tons of thrust he wanted, Korolev had to cluster the clusters. The RD 108 was inserted into the central core of the rocket, and four cones, each containing an RD 107 engine cluster, were strapped around the core cylinder, giving the structure a skirted appearance. Thus, Korolev's ICBM, which western observers called the A-1 (A for Aggregate), had five engine clusters, each with four combustion chambers and nozzles—a total of twenty nozzles. All twenty engines, burning kerosene and liquid oxygen, were brought up to full thrust at lift-off. As this multiengine rocket gained altitude, the RD 107 strap-ons dropped off, leaving the RD 108 in the central core thrusting. With the addition of a second stage, the Russian A-1 ICBM became the A-2. It had a thrust of 600 tons (1,230,000 pounds).

This powerful launcher was apparently ready for flight-testing as early as 1954, before the United States, with its long-range bombing fleet, its bases in Western Europe and Turkey, and its DEW (Distant Early Warning) line across Canada, thought urgently about ICBMs. The United States did not fly a rocket of comparable thrust until the test flight of the Saturn 1 on October 27, 1961. The Russians had a lead of seven years in big rockets.

THE MISSILE GAP

Obviously, then, the "missile gap," for which the Democrats blamed the Republicans in the presidential election campaign of 1960, was real, although, by 1960, the U.S. Air Force had begun to close it with the development of the Atlas and Titan ICBMs, and the Von Braun team was catching up to the Russian A-1 with Saturn. The Saturn was not a military missile. Using it for one was like swatting a fly with a sledgehammer. It was a deep space launcher.

Hindsight shows us that the missile gap was a result of divergent concepts of strategic warfare, reflecting differences in the geographical vulnerability of the adversaries. In the immediate postwar years, the American concept of strategic warfare centered on air power. Vannevar Bush, America's chief military scientist during World War II, opposed rocket development. The rocket was too inaccurate to carry a nuclear bomb to a target, he contended. Bush, who was president of the Carnegie Institution of Washington during this period, was probably the most influential scientist in the United States then, except for Albert Einstein. He told the U.S. Senate Special Committee on Atomic Energy during hearings in December 1945 that it was unlikely that a rocket could be aimed accurately enough to hit a city across the ocean. He said: "I don't think anybody in the world knows how to do such a thing. And I feel confident it will not be done for a very long period of time to come." [28]

But within fifteen years, which is not such a long period, inertial guidance systems for missiles, aircraft, and spacecraft, of pinpoint accuracy, would be developed at the Massachusetts Institute of Technology, where Bush had been dean of engineering before assuming the presidency of the Carnegie Institution.

There were other scientists' opinions. The talented Hungarian aerodynamicist, Theodore von Karman, of the California Institute of Technology, an air force adviser, proposed that the range of the V-2 be increased thirty times to launch a satellite.

If American military experts were concerned with what the Russians were doing in rocketry in the early 1950s, there was no outward sign of it. Robert L. Perry, historian of the Air Force Systems Division, observed that it was a precept of American strategy that the only possible opponent of the United States, the Soviet Union, was incapable of devising an advanced technology and was in a near comatose condition as a result of war damage. [29]

Secrecy in the Soviet Union served admirably to foster this illusion. During the first decade after the war, the Russians were launching the uprated V-2s from a center at Kapustin Yar, on the left bank of the Volga River. They built an ICBM launch area east of the Aral Sea in the Republic of Kazakhstan. They referred to it as the Baikonur Cosmodrome, although it was at least 230 miles southwest of the town of Baikonur and near the village of

Tyuratam. (To establish world-record claims for its manned flights, the USSR eventually had to reveal the date, time, and place of takeoff and landing under the *Code Sportif* of the Federation Aeronautique Internationale.) Like the identity of the chief rocket designer, Korolev, the location of the ICBM launch center was not disclosed for many years. This security was motivated by the fear that the chief designer might be kidnapped or assassinated by jealous rival powers and that if the location of the Baikonur Cosmodrome were known, it would be a prime target in the event of war. A third Soviet launch site was developed near the town of Plesetsk, south of Archangel.

These sites were identified in the west by a process of reconstructing the ground tracks of Soviet satellites. It was done by satellite-tracking agencies in Great Britain, the United States, and Japan, and partly by a group of London school boys as a mathematics exercise.

Rocket work at White Sands also was classified. However, in his annual report of 1948, U.S. Secretary of Defense James E. Forrestal revealed that a Committee on Guided Missiles had recommended that efforts by each of the armed services to develop satellites be limited to studies and component designs. This was the first official indication that the United States was seriously considering satellites.

One source of semiofficial Soviet reaction to this inadvertent disclosure expressed cynical indignation at the very thought of satellites. The Russian journal *New Times* referred to "madman Forrestal's idea of an Earth satellite" as an "instrument of blackmail." The article attacked America's "Hitlerite ideas" of developing rockets, and especially the "fantastic idea of reconnaissance satellites."

Aside from the V-2, the Army Ordnance Corps sought other missile designs. It financed work in that direction by the Jet Propulsion Laboratory, formerly the Guggenheim Aeronautical Laboratory, at the California Institute of Technology. JPL was headed by von Karman. Working with him were William H. Pickering, a New Zealand born physicist, and Homer J. Stewart, professor of Aerospace engineering at the institute.

JPL developed the WAC Corporal, which was fired to an altitude of 235,000 feet from White Sands on October 11, 1945. From this vehicle, the Aerobee sounding rocket was developed for the Office of Naval Research by Johns Hopkins University. The Aerobee was destined to become a second stage of the ill-fated Vanguard.

In February 1949, the WAC Corporal was clamped to the V-2 as an upper stage and launched to an altitude of 244 miles from White Sands. Then, on July 24, 1950, a WAC Corporal-V-2 combination called Bumper-WAC was successfully launched from a sandy spit on the east coast of central Florida called Cape Canaveral. (The name means cape of reeds. Ponce DeLeon charted it as he sailed along the Florida east coast in 1547 to establish a base at Saint Augustine.) The air force had acquired it in 1949 as a missile-launching site. It overlooked a stretch of the Atlantic Ocean extending 6,500 miles to the south-southeast between South America and Africa. The stretch became the Atlantic Missile Range.

At Huntsville, meanwhile, the army's Von Braun group developed a 200-mile missile called the Redstone after the Redstone arsenal, on whose acres of red mud the Marshall Space Flight Center later arose. The engine for this rocket came from one developed from the V-2 by North American Aviation, Inc., for an unmanned bomber called the Navaho. The Navaho was a $700 million project of the air force that never got off the ground.

The army gave North American Aviation's Rocketdyne Division a contract to modify the Navaho engine for Redstone, and the end product was the H-1 engine, a roundabout descendant of the V-2. This engine eventually became the clustered power plant for the Saturn 1. Redstone, meantime, was developed as an intermediate-range ballistic missile.

During 1953–1954, radar observations from Turkey, plus other intelligence reports, warned the Pentagon that Russia was making rapid progress with the rocket called the A-1. Within a short time, these reports predicted, the Soviet Union would have launch vehicles capable of carrying nuclear bombs to the United States.

What was America doing about long-range rockets? Not much in the mid-1950s. The air force had been working on an ICBM called the Atlas since 1951, but it had been bogged down by the necessity of creating the technology for building rockets before it could put one together. In February 1954, the Strategic Missiles Evaluation Committee of the Air Force recommended prompt development of an ICBM. The committee was headed by John von Neumann, an engineer-mathematician at the California Institute of Technology. Von Neumann was certain that a U.S. ICBM could be developed in time to counter the USSR's ICBM threat if money and talent would be mobilized for such a project.

The committee underlined the urgency of the competition. It probably had some effect on the air force, but it did not result in a crash program. Despite intelligence reports to the contrary, it was difficult to overcome the notion that the Russians, after all, were a society of peasants with a horse-and-cart technology and very little indoor plumbing.

The air force ICBM was predicated on the payload of a lightweight thermonuclear bomb to be delivered over a range of 5,000 miles. At the time it contracted for the Atlas, the air force also let contracts for a second, somewhat more powerful, ICBM called the Titan. On June 11, 1957, thirty months after its final configuration had been approved, the Atlas was ready for its first test. But on the first launch the Atlas 4-A failed, because of "thrust decay." On December 18, 1958, the air force launched an entire Atlas ICBM, weighing 8,750 pounds (minus propellants), into orbit. This shot was called Project Score. The vehicle carried a radio that played a tape-recorded Christmas message to the people of Earth from President Eisenhower for thirteen days. The words of peace and good will toward men, and so on, implied another message addressed to Russia. It said: "We've got an ICBM, too." The missile gap was closing.

The first Titan ICBM passed its flight test down the Atlantic Missile Range February 6, 1959. With its intermediate-range Thor missile, also developed in this period, the air force had a "stable" of rockets capable of plastering the USSR with nuclear bombs once the launchers were fully operational. By the middle of 1960, when they were ready, the military missile gap was virtually closed, but the Russian A-1 launcher still was much more powerful than the Atlas and the Titan. This did not give the Russians advantage in strategic bombing, but it did give them superiority in launching spacecraft.

Consequently, despite the relatively rapid development of the Atlas, Titan, and Thor missiles, the Russians remained ahead in large boosters at the end of the 1950s. The A-1 and A-2 rockets were capable of putting up five-ton manned vehicles in orbit and of sending heavy scientific reconnaissance packages to the Moon, Venus, and Mars. Because of this lead in rocket development, the Russians maintained a lead in manned flight until Project Apollo began to fly in the fall of 1968.

The effect on Americans of the early Russian superiority in space, once it was demonstrated, was traumatic. It shook up the nation as nothing else had since Pearl Harbor. Again, Americans were caught napping, and, in a dynamic era of escalating military technology, that was profoundly disturbing.

The response to the trauma was the onset of the greatest technological competition in history: the space race.

FELLOW TRAVELER

Although the Department of Defense had reacted to its awareness of the Russian ICBM by speeding up work on Atlas and Titan, the long-standing proposal to put a satellite into orbit stirred minimal response. Satellite proposals from the army, navy, and air force had been presented periodically since 1948, but the Pentagon had been unable to find an urgent reason to justify the cost.[30]

The idea of space flight generally was not quite acceptable to the defense bureaucracy during the first postwar decade. In the early 1950s proposals by scientists that the United States undertake a program of space exploration were ridiculed and hooted down at meetings where they were brought up, Lloyd V. Berkner recalled ten years later when he was chairman of the Space Science Board of the National Academy of Sciences.[31]

During the eight years of the administration of President Dwight D. Eisenhower, the national mood was not conducive to the fanciful ideas of space flight. The ex-boss of General Motors, Charles Wilson, was secretary of defense, and he liked to have all four wheels on the ground. He characterized the feat of putting a satellite in orbit as a useless stunt. What would it be good for? He would not be concerned, he said, even if the Soviet Union did it first.[32]

Nevertheless, the idea of a satellite fascinated scientists planning the International Geophysical Year, a worldwide effort of sixty nations to take stock of the global environment during an eighteen-month period of intensive research from July 1, 1957, to December 31, 1958.

At its third general assembly in Rome in October 1954, the Special Committee for the IGY recommended that satellites be considered "in view of the great importance of observations of extraterrestrial radiations and geophysical phenomena and in view of the advanced state of rocket techniques." [33]

The recommendation was transmitted to President Eisenhower by Alan T. Waterman, director of the National Science Foundation. The president took no action on it. Meanwhile, evidence that the USSR was planning a satellite accumulated. Early in 1954, Alexander N. Nesmeyanov, president of the Soviet Academy of Sciences, issued a statement that Soviet space technology now was capable of putting up a satellite and also of sending a spaceship to the Moon.

In April 1955, the Russians announced the formation of the Permanent Interdepartmental Commission for Interplanetary Travel as an arm of the Astronomical Council of the Academy. Moscow radio said that in addition to the satellite, Russian scientists had conceived of a radio-controlled vehicle like a military tank that would explore the surface of the Moon. That conception seemed ridiculously far out to American observers, but it was realized in fifteen years. But then, who in 1955 would have imagined that only sixteen years later two Americans would be riding about the Moon in an electric jeep, having the time of their lives?

Nevertheless, the political merit of planning a satellite for the International Geophysical Year (IGY) penetrated the reserve at the White House toward space projects. On July 29, 1955, United States plans to perform this feat were announced by the National Science Foundation, the National Academy of Sciences, and the Department of Defense. On July 30, the USSR announced that it, too, was planning to loft one or more satellites during the IGY. The space race was on, but during that long, unusually hot summer, few construed these announcements as indicating the onset of such a contest.

As I have mentioned earlier, satellite proposals from the armed services had been simmering on the back burner of national policy since 1946. As preparations for the IGY went forward during 1954, two proposals reached the Defense Department. The Army's Von Braun missile men and a Navy group presented Project Orbiter, calling for the launching of a ten-pound navy satellite into orbit by the army's newly developed Jupiter C missile.

Another branch of the navy, the Naval Research Laboratory, offered a rival scheme—the Vanguard project. It called for a three-stage rocket that would thrust a twenty-pound satellite into orbit. The first stage would be a Viking rocket that the Glenn L. Martin Company developed for the navy. Viking reached an altitude of 158.4 miles at White Sands, May 24, 1954. The second stage was to be the Aerobee, which the Office of Naval Research was using to make soundings of the upper atmosphere. The third stage would be a small, solid-fuel rocket.

Early in 1955, the Defense Department appointed an ad hoc committee of civilian consultants to weigh the proposals. The air force had offered the Atlas as a satellite launcher, but the offer was dismissed on the grounds that preparing the vehicle as a satellite launcher would interfere with its development as a missile. Besides, the Atlas was not far enough along to warrant confidence in its performance.

When the Eisenhower administration decided to attempt a satellite launching for the IGY, the ad hoc committee's decision assumed more urgency. Against strong minority dissent, a majority of the members selected the Vanguard. Their decision was influenced by the consideration that Vanguard could be presented to the world as a nonmilitary vehicle designed specifically for a peaceful, scientific mission, in contrast to the Jupiter C, an intermediate-range ballistic missile. It was a feature of Eisenhower's policy that the United States should demonstrate to the developing nations and to the world at large that rocket development could be used to advance the welfare of mankind as well as to threaten it.

Untroubled by such qualms, the Russians went ahead with plans to launch their satellite with the powerful ICBM they had developed. By April 1956, the Russian A-1 launch vehicle was ready for flight testing at the secret launch site in Kazakhstan. But the Russians made no secret of their intention of exploring space. Principal figures in the Soviet Academy's space commission were identified by *Vechernaya Moskva*, a Moscow evening newspaper,[34] as Leonid I. Sedov, Peter L. Kapitsa, and V. N. Ambartsumyan—scientists well known to the American scientific community.

During the summer of 1955, Sedov predicted that the Soviets would have a satellite in orbit in two years. Only a few people took this seriously—those who knew the Russian scientist and knew that he knew what he was talking about. On Capitol Hill and at the White House, Russian intimation of satellite plans was taken as boasting, despite a warning to the contrary from the Central Intelligence Agency.[35] Eisenhower's principal assistant, Sherman Adams, publicly discounted the importance of being the first to put up a satellite.[36]

On August 3, 1957, Russia launched its ICBM on a successful test flight, which was announced by TASS, the official news agency, August 26. Observers in the Defense Department knew then it was just a matter of time until a satellite went up.

The space shot that shook the world was fired from Tyuratam early in the morning of October 5, 1957. It launched *Sputnik I* ("Fellow Traveler I"), a 22.8-inch sphere of aluminum alloy weighing 184 pounds. The size of the satellite was insignificant compared with that of the ICBM core that went into orbit with it. The core vehicle was the size of a railroad Pullman car.[37]

Radios on the first man-made satellite transmitted a steady signal on 20 and 40 megacycles at 7.5- and 15-meter wavelengths. The "voice" of *Sputnik* was picked up all over the world, from ham radio stations in Chicago to a research ship in the Antarctic Ocean.

News of the satellite broke in Washington on the night of October 4, local time, in a dramatic way. Scientists from thirteen nations had been attending a satellite conference at the National Academy of Sciences during the day. Many were conveniently assembled at a cocktail party at the Soviet Embassy when the news reached them. It did not come from the Russians, but from Lloyd V. Berkner, a member of the President's Special Committee for the IGY. He got it from the Washington Bureau of the Associated Press, which telephoned him for comment.

The scientific community was stunned. Members of Congress expressed astonishment and dismay. Although aware of Soviet satellite-launching capability, the United States diplomatic and military establishments seemed to be taken by surprise; they did not expect it so soon. The press screamed, commentators roared, critics howled. Reaction rolled across the country like a tidal wave. Editorial writers wondered how a supposedly backward, static, Communist society, without even an automobile industry of any consequence, had suddenly launched the space age!

Educators, pundits, and politicians began to look critically at the assumption that the United States had the most advanced technology. As *Sputnik I* orbited the Earth at an altitude of 560 miles, its radios beeping cheerfully, the prestige of the Soviet Union soared with it.

A senior specialist in national defense for the Library of Congress, Charles H. Donnelly, noted: "The American public badly underestimated the capabilities of Soviet scientists and engineers, especially in the military field, because it was difficult to understand how a nation with such rudimentary plumbing, for example, could possibly produce complex, precision machines equivalent to our own. . . . it took the dramatic appearance of Soviet satellites in our skies to prove how wrong our estimates of the Soviet capabilities had been." [38]

A month later, as America was still reacting to the shock of *Sputnik I*, the Russians launched *Sputnik II*, a 1,121-pound vessel that went into orbit with its carrier rocket. *Sputnik II* had a life-support system and a passenger, a mongrel female dog, Laika ("Barker"). Monitoring of the placid animal's cardiovascular and respiratory responses by radio showed that the life-support system worked. Significantly, she showed no ill effects from the multiple-gravity stress of the launch nor from weightlessness. In orbit, she moved about, took food from an automatic dispenser, and barked now and then. Instruments aboard the satellite reported on radiation and micrometeors in the region of the orbit, an ellipse ranging from 140 to 1,038 miles. *Sputnik II* transmitted data for seven days and then fell silent. Laika survived for that period, but when she perished was not known. After 163 days, *Sputnik's* orbit decayed, and the vehicle plunged back into the atmosphere, where it flashed briefly like a big meteorite and was consumed.

The shot clearly pointed out the direction in which Russian space technology was heading—manned flight. Chief designer Korolev wrote: "The study of biological phenomena made during the space flight of a living organism, something done for the first time in *Sputnik II*, is of tremendous interest." [39]

The United States did not match the 1957 Sputniks in total weight of payload and carrier rocket in orbit until January 29, 1964, when the Saturn 1 vehicle, SA-5, with a live second stage, inserted the stage weighing 37,900 pounds into a 160-by-476-mile orbit.

Sputnik II repeated the "message" of the first Fellow Traveler—that the Russians now had the capability of delivering a nuclear bomb anywhere in the world.

EXPLORER I

On November 8, 1957, President Eisenhower, in a nationwide radio and television address, admitted that the Sputniks represented "an achievement of the first importance." But even though the Russians were "quite likely ahead in some missile and special areas," he said, reassuringly, "the overall military strength of the free world is still greater than that of the Communist countries." The president then showed the television audience the scaled-down nose cone of an ICBM that had been launched in August on a reentry test by a Jupiter C down the Atlantic Missile Range and recovered at sea.

The Jupiter C (for composite) had been built by the Army Ballistic Missile Agency (ABMA), which replaced the Guided Missile Development Division of the Army Ordnance Corps in 1956. Major General John B. Medaris, a blunt-spoken artillery man, was named commander, and Von Braun became technical director. The German team simply continued its rocket work for the army under a new agency.

On the same day as Eisenhower's address of reassurance to the nation, the new defense secretary, Neil H. McElroy, who succeeded Wilson, instructed

Medaris to prepare backup rockets to launch two satellites during March 1958—in case Vanguard failed. The Von Braun people and Medaris were delighted. They had been proposing this for months. They had a Jupiter C in the hangar. It could be made ready for launching as early as January 30, 1958. Medaris later contended that the army had the capability of launching a satellite in September 1956 but was thwarted by the Defense Department on the theory that satellite launching was Vanguard's exclusive role.[40]

On Friday, December 6, 1957, Vanguard was launched on its first all up flight test, with a satellite aboard. If the test had been successful, the satellite would have gone into orbit. But seconds after the first stage ignited and started to lift, the vehicle fell back and blew up. The Russian press hooted. The British press laughed, referring to Vanguard as *Kaputnik* and *Flopnik*. A Tokyo newspaper called the debacle a Pearl Harbor for American technology. That was rubbing it in hard.

Now the Von Braun team and Medaris at Huntsville were ready to rush to the rescue, a contingency they had foreseen. McElroy had asked for two backup launches; Medaris offered four in a program called 416—four Jupiter C launches for $16 million.

The first of the backup rockets was *Missile No. 29*, a Jupiter C consisting of an uprated Redstone first stage, a cluster of eleven small Sergeant solid-fuel rockets for the second stage, a cluster of three Sergeants for the third stage, and a single Sergeant for the fourth. The satellite was combined with the fourth stage, and both together formed a tube six feet eight inches long and six inches in diameter. When the fuel in the rocket end of the tube burned out, the tube weighed 30.8 pounds, including an 18.13 pound payload of scientific instruments, two radios, two antennas, and batteries. The scientific instruments above weighed only 11 pounds. They were designed to measure micrometeors, temperature at various altitudes and in orbit, and cosmic rays. The radiation experiment consisted of a single Geiger counter that would measure the intensity of energetic, cosmic-ray particles in space near the Earth. It was provided by James A. Van Allen, chairman of the Physics Department at the State University of Iowa.

Throughout January, the army prepared to launch *Missile No. 29* from Cape Canaveral. The first launch attempt was scrubbed January 29, 1958, because of high winds. The next day the winds died down and the missile was launched at 10:47 P.M., Eastern Standard Time, January 30, 1958. All the upper stages fired precisely on time. According to all the calculations, the satellite, *Explorer I*, would go into orbit. But this could not be confirmed until the satellite's radio signal was picked up at listening posts in California, showing that *Explorer I* had circled the Earth from Florida. Shortly before 1 A.M., Eastern Standard Time, the radio voice of *Explorer I* was picked up in California, and the Jet Propulsion Laboratory reported that the first American satellite was truly in orbit. The army's spirits soared. Von Braun's only comment was that the signal had been received eight minutes later than his people had calculated it would be. He could not understand why. Everyone else was hysterically happy.

The Geiger counter data from this first shot provided the earliest clue to the greatest discovery of the IGY—the existence of a zone of high-energy radiation trapped in the Earth's magnetic field beyond the atmosphere—the Van Allen radiation belt.

The success of *Explorer I* was reassuring, but then Vanguard failed a second time a few days later. On March 17, 1958, however, Vanguard finally worked. It lofted a 3.25-pound satellite, the size of a grapefruit, into an elongated orbit of 405-by-2,462 miles. Although the Communist bloc ridiculed this tiny machine, it turned out to be one of the most useful satellites of the early Space Age.

Vanguard's tiny radio, powered by photovoltaic (solar) cells, continued transmitting for six years. Tracking the satellite by means of the radio signal enabled geophysicists to refine the figure of the shape of the Earth. They found that it was faintly pear-shaped, with the stem of the pear toward the north pole. Vanguard made it possible for the first time to observe the pressure of the stream of sub-nuclear particles emanating from the Sun—the solar wind—on the path of the satellite. Small though it was, *Vanguard I* was an elegant experiment. It demonstrated a capability that became of paramount importance in the space race: reliable electronics.

The ABMA, meanwhile, went on launching Explorers. *Explorer II* did not reach orbit, because the fourth stage failed to ignite. However, *Explorers III* and *IV*, launched March 26 and July 26, 1958, did go into orbit. The radiation data they obtained confirmed the existence of the radiation belts.

After its hard-won success in March, Vanguard experienced a run of bad luck. The rocket failed to put another satellite into orbit on each of the next five launches. Then it orbited *Vanguard II* for eighteen days in February 1959 and *Vanguard III*, a 100-pound satellite, the following September. After that, Vanguard vanished from the Space Age. In picking it over the Jupiter C, for whatever reason, the ad hoc committee majority had backed the wrong horse.

ACTION AND REACTION

The year following Sputnik was one of agonizing reappraisal in the United States—reappraisal of its science, its technology, its educational system, its ability to meet new challenges, and its defense strategy. The revelation of a high military technology in the Soviet Union was shocking. For the first time since the War of 1812, the eastern cities of the United States could be threatened with bombardment by a foreign power.

The development of Russian nuclear bombs, and of Russian rockets to deliver them, threatened America's insular security. The Sputniks challenged, symbolically, virtually every aspect of American life, especially technology and education, and the vitality of the free world. In Washington, changes began to happen.

The development of the nuclear bomb had created a new technoscientific dimension in military affairs. To help him understand what was going on in it, President Truman established the President's Science Advisory Committee (PSAC) in 1951. The committee's function was to advise him on scientific and technical matters impinging on national and particularly on military policy.

Under its first chairman, Oliver Buckley, a former president of Bell Telephone Laboratories, the committee reported to the president through the director of defense mobilization. As Jerome B. Wiesner, who was President Kennedy's science adviser, has noted, it was not until Sputnik shocked the nation into reappraising its support of science that PSAC moved into the White House, where it became more effective in its advisory role.[41] The position of special assistant for science and technology was created in the White House so that a scientist became a part of the president's staff as science adviser. James R. Killian, of the Massachusetts Institute of Technology, became science adviser to President Eisenhower and also served as PSAC chairman. Essentially, it was a revival of the ancient kingly prerogative of having an astrologer, magician, shaman, or medicine man handy to interpret the portents of obscure phenomena. This oracular service in the White House was finally discontinued by President Nixon in 1973, by which time the uneasy partnership between science and politics was dissolved. That, however, came nearly twenty years later. The period from 1950–1960 saw the onset of the scientific revolution in America, a process growing out of the Atomic Age and generating the concepts of the Space Age. The events that characterized it, as listed by Wiesner, were the atomic bomb, which multiplied explosive power by a factor of a thousand; the thermonuclear bomb, which raised this by a factor of another thousand; the ballistic missile, which reduced reaction time to intercontinental attack from hours to minutes; and the electronic computer, which made it feasible to replace human control with automated controls that were many times faster.[42] These were the developments that revolutionized warfare on one hand and made space flight technically possible on the other.

It is reasonable, then, to perceive the development of space exploration as a result of this technology of warfare or, put another way, the technology of competition.

Five days after *Sputnik I* went into orbit, a special committee of the Air Force Scientific Advisory Board recommended the development of second generation ICBMs that could be used as space boosters, although the first generation had not yet got off the ground. The committee went blue sky with proposals. It proposed that the air force develop reconnaissance, communications, and weather satellites, and even missions to the Moon. These ideas fermented rapidly in the air force, which began to think of itself as also a space force, and adopted *aerospace* in its unit nomenclature.

A committee of academic and corporate scientists and air force officers, headed by the nuclear physicist Edward Teller, who had a leading role in developing the thermonuclear bomb, was appointed by the secretary of the air force, James H. Douglas, to propose an action plan for space. The committee came up with a five-year plan for unifying all space activity in the Department of Defense under the wings of the air force.

The year 1958 produced a hailstorm of space projects. The principal focus was on manned space flight, and the common ultimate objective of that activity was a trip to the Moon. One of the astonishing happenings of this Sputnik-Explorer period is the transformation of political, military, and public attitudes toward a manned flight to the Moon. In two years, the notion of putting a man on the Moon was metamorphosed from an unacceptably romantic one to a feasible though distant goal. Sputnik and the American reaction to it accomplished that. If the Russians were going to send men into space, perhaps to the Moon, as *Sputnik II* suggested, the United States must follow. The question was: How?

The air force had been tinkering with a space airplane concept called Dyna-Soar, a vehicle that could be boosted into orbit by a rocket and then glide back to Earth like an airplane. Dyna-Soar was pushed as one way to get the jump on the Russians by putting a man into orbit first. Although Dyna-Soar later became as extinct as its Jurassic homonym, the dinosaur, it proved to be the ancestral concept of the Space Shuttle, the ground-to-orbit aerospace vehicle that NASA began to develop in the 1970s to supersede Apollo.

Another approach to a manned space vehicle was investigated by engineers of the Pilotless Aircraft Research and Development Division of the National Advisory Committee for Aeronautics. NACA was a government agency that had been conducting research in aviation technology since 1915. It had research centers at Langley, Virginia; Cleveland, Ohio; Edwards Air Force Base, in Southern California; and Moffett Field, California, near San Francisco. At Langley, the Pilotless Aircraft researchers developed the concept of a wingless, nonlifting, cone-shaped capsule as a manned satellite. It could be boosted into orbit by an ICBM, reenter the atmosphere with the protection of a heat shield, and descend by parachute to a soft landing.

At the beginning of 1958, there were, in addition to the two ways to fly a man in space, the rudiments of three satellite booster programs. They were based on the Army Ballistic Missile Agency's Jupiter C, the Naval Research Laboratory's Vanguard, and the air force ballistic missiles, Atlas, Titan, and Thor.

The air force appeared to be the favored service to develop manned space flight. It ordered its Air Research and Development Command (ARDC) to prepare a comprehensive five-year space program, as recommended by the Teller committee. The ARDC came up in January 1958 with plans for reconnaissance, communications, and weather satellites; recoverable scientific capsules that could be scooped up as they descended by parachute by aircraft; a manned spacecraft testing program; a manned space station in Earth orbit; and, finally, a manned base on the Moon.

The ARDC then invited eleven aircraft and missile firms to a closed conference at Wright-Patterson Air Force Base near Dayton, Ohio, to discuss plans for a manned satellite. In addition to Dyna-Soar and the capsule, a third approach was considered—an advanced version of the X-15, the high-flying experimental rocket airplane.[43] It was clear to investigators that an ICBM-boosted capsule could be developed faster than an orbital version of the X-15 or an ICBM-boosted Dyna-Soar. But the Air Force was not to make the decision on which way to go.

Meanwhile, with the success of its Jupiter C as a satellite launcher, the Army Ballistic Missile Agency sought a major role in space. It reminded the Defense Department that the Von Braun team had a plan to build a deep space rocket with a million pounds of thrust by clustering engines already developed. Huntsville called it the Saturn project, perhaps because it was farther out, from a technical point of view, than the Jupiter, in the scheme of major planet nomenclature. In its initial configuration, the Saturn would have a first stage powered by eight H-1 Redstone-derived engines, developing a total of 1.3 million pounds of thrust in the earliest model.

Beyond the Saturn rocket, the Von Braun team had another scheme. It proposed launching a man in a capsule into a suborbital flight that would reach 150 miles altitude and then come down by parachute, to be recovered by a ship. It was called Project Adam, because it would put the first man into space, if only for a few minutes, on a ballistic flight down the Atlantic Missile Range. Although Project Adam became the blueprint for Project Mercury's first two suborbital flights, it was several years ahead of its time. The Defense Department turned it down. Critics at NACA ridiculed it as a version of the circus stunt of shooting a lady out of a cannon.

President Eisenhower and his advisers saw the need to organize these divergent and competitive programs under a single managing agency. In February 1958, he instructed Secretary McElroy to set up the superagency that would coordinate all Department of Defense space projects. It was called the Advanced Research Projects Agency (ARPA). It did not seem to exert much influence at first. In March 1958, the Ballistic Missile Division of the Air Force, under the command of Major General Bernard A. Schriever, proposed an eleven-step program to put a man on the Moon. It was the first detailed lunar landing scheme, and it ended the reluctance in the Defense Department to speculate on the Moon as a goal of manned flight.

The Air Force BMD program began conservatively enough with animal experiments in orbit, a la Laika. It then called for a manned orbit of the Earth, assuming that the animal experiments confirmed the belief that weightlessness would not be hazardous to health. Next, an instrumented capsule would be rocketed around the Moon, followed by manned circumnavigation of the Moon and, finally, by a manned landing on the Moon.

NASA IS BORN

If the military services, segments of the press, and others seemed to overreact to Sputnik, the White House seemed to underreact. President Eisenhower had expressed concern about the U.S. lag in missile development, but Sputnik did not seem to unnerve him at all. "Our satellite program has never been conducted as a race with other nations," he said.[44] But many members of Congress and leaders of business and industry did not share the president's equanimity about the Russian lead in space. It was plain to that mythical person, the man-in-the-street, that the Sputniks had caused the United States to lose face and had seriously undermined its image as the world's leading technological society.

Feelings of frustration and anxiety were being expressed everywhere: by politicians, by editorial writers and newspaper columnists, and by radio and television commentators, all tending to project an image of a do-nothing, inert, nonreacting national administration. The term *missile gap* began appearing in critical columns, and the Democrats quickly seized it as a campaign issue. It signified a lapse in national defense capability as well as a loss of national prestige, which had a dollar value in foreign markets.

These feelings and criticisms shortly became transformed into an urgent need to catch up with and surpass the Russians. America had to compete with Russia, not only in missiles, but in satellites, to preserve its image. This urge to competition was nothing new in the world. It had many of the characteristics and concerns of the maritime contest between Spain and Portugal in the fifteenth and sixteenth centuries and between England and France in the eighteenth century.

Meanwhile, Congress had begun to investigate the nature, causes, and consequences of the space and missile gap. In January 1958, the Preparedness Investigating Subcommittee of the Senate Armed Services Committee, after extended public hearings on the missile program, came up with recommendations that included the establishment of an independent space agency. This idea was supported by the National Academy of Sciences, representing the nation's scientific establishment, and the American Rocket Society, which had become a prominent spokesman for the technical community. By April 1958, Congress had received twenty-nine bills concerning space programs and their management. "Almost everyone assumed that some sort of thorough-going reform legislation, probably creating an entirely new agency, was needed if the United States was to overcome the Soviet lead in space technology," the official history of NASA remarked.[45]

No one was more aware of the delays and excess costs of rivalry among the armed services than President Eisenhower. He did not dispute the recommendation for an independent space agency. His only concern was that it should be civilian. The wartime Allied supreme commander had formulated a consistent policy that outer space should be used only for peaceful purposes. He had expressed this sentiment a number of times, and he repeated it in a letter to Soviet Premier Nikolai Bulganin dated January 12, 1958. That policy, indeed, had influenced the selection of Vanguard as America's entry into the satellite sweepstakes.

In the spring of 1958, the White House did respond to the growing national demand for a competitive space program by sending up to Capitol Hill on April 14 a bill creating a new civilian space agency, the National Aeronautics and Space Administration (NASA). It had the blessing of the White House Advisory Committee on Government Organization, headed by Nelson Rockefeller, and the President's Scientific Advisory Committee, headed by James R. Killian. In March 1958, the PSAC had promulgated a rationale for the space program that NASA had been created to carry out. The PSAC cited the "compelling urge for man to explore and discover," the need for defense capability, national prestige, and "new opportunities for scientific observation and experiment." PSAC membership included Berkner, Wiesner, George B. Kistiakowski, James A. Doolittle, Edwin F. Land, and Herbert F. York.

Congress passed the National Aeronautics and Space Act in July 1958, and the President signed the bill July 29. T. Keith Glennan, president of the Case Institute of Technology, Cleveland, Ohio, was named the first administrator, and Hugh Dryden, head of NACA, deputy administrator. NASA absorbed NACA's laboratories and test centers in Virginia, Ohio, and California, and the veteran agency's 8,000 employees. It took over the Vanguard, Explorer, and other ARPA projects and the Jet Propulsion Laboratory. The army was reluctant to let go of the Von Braun group at Huntsville, but, finally, it, too, was transferred to the NASA in 1959, and a portion of acreage and structures of the Redstone Arsenal was set aside as the George C. Marshall Space Flight Center. With the transfer of Von Braun's group to NASA went a prize package—the Saturn rocket, the most successful and reliable launch vehicle in the American inventory.

America was now in the space race, but the Russians stayed ahead. *Sputnik III* had been fired into orbit May 15, 1958, weighing 2,926 pounds. It was a complete geophysical laboratory for the observation of electromagnetic fields and particles in space near the Earth. The United States did not match it until it put up the first Orbiting Geophysical Observatory (OGO I) in 1964.

Adding an upper stage to its Sputnik launch vehicle, the Soviet Union began throwing a series of "cosmic rockets" at the Moon in 1959. The first, *Luna I*, was launched January 2, 1959, and was supposed to crash-land a 3,245-pound-package consisting of the upper-stage rocket shell and 800 pounds of instruments on the lunar surface. The payload was designated *Mechta* ("Dream"). It missed the moon by 3,700 miles and went into orbit around the sun, the first artificial "planetoid" in the solar system. *Luna I* returned data on the solar wind until it ceased broadcasting.

The Russians tried to hit the Moon again by launching *Luna II* September 12, 1959. It carried an 858-pound automatic interplanetary station bearing the hammer-and-sickle emblem. This time, the aim was good, and the vehicle crashed into the Mare Serenitatis ("Sea of Serenity").

Meanwhile, the United States was shooting at the Moon, too, but with poorer luck. We rang up a sequence of five failures with payloads ranging from thirteen to eighty-seven pounds between August 1958 and March 1959. Designed by the Defense Department's Advanced Research Projects Agency and inherited by NASA, this early Moon-shot program was designated as Pioneer. From its discouraging beginning, the Pioneer program evolved into one of the greatest scientific and technical achievements in history, as I will relate later, but in its early years, it was a source of embarrassment.

On the first launch attempt, the Thor-Able rocket blew up over Cape Canaveral. Two more Pioneers reached altitudes of 70,717 and 63,580 miles, respectively, before falling back into the ocean. Another fell on Africa when the third stage of the Thor-Able launch vehicle failed to ignite. On the fifth try, March 3, 1959, *Pioneer IV*, weighing a mere thirteen pounds, was lofted into a solar orbit by a Juno II (an uprated Jupiter) rocket after sailing by the Moon at a miss distance of 37,300 miles. We were not fated to hit the Moon until April 1962, when *Ranger IV* went out of control and came down on lunar far side, the side we cannot see from Earth. But in October 1959, Russia received radio facsimile photos of far side from its 614-pound camera satellite, *Luna III*, which was launched October 4, 1959, on the second anniversary of *Sputnik I*.

NASA, meanwhile, assigned top priority to getting a man into space. Robert R. Gilruth, the former director of NACA's Langley Laboratory, was appointed head of a special space task group. The mission of the STG was to put a man into orbit as soon as possible. The STG drafted plans for a manned-satellite program that called for the early development of a one-man space capsule along the lines proposed by three engineers of the Pilotless Aircraft Research Division of NACA in March 1958. The engineers were Maxime A. Faget, who became chief spacecraft designer for NASA; Ben-

jamin A. Garland; and James J. Buglia. The spacecraft design adopted for
Project Mercury essentially was their idea.

The capsule would be launched by an ICBM from Cape Canaveral and return by parachute. In shape, it was a truncated cone, nine feet seven inches
long from the top of the cylinder, where the parachutes were stored, to the
base of the heat shield, where its diameter reached six feet two inches. Six
solid-fuel rockets were mounted at the base of the heat shield. Three would
be fired to separate the capsule from the rocket when orbital velocity was
reached; the other three would be fired by the pilot or by radio control from
the ground, to "de-orbit" the vessel for a water landing. By firing the latter
three rockets in the direction of flight, the flight path would be changed from
one going around the Earth to one that intersected the Earth at what NASA
called a preplanned landing point.

Having thus reduced part of the energy imparted to the spacecraft by its
launch vehicle, the retrorocket system would be jettisoned, and the remainder of the energy would be taken out of the flight by friction with the
atmosphere and transformed into heat, to be dissipated by the heat shield.
The falling spacecraft would then be stabilized by a drogue and slowed by a
sixty-three-foot ringsail parachute that would lower the vehicle to the surface
of the sea. A pneumatic landing bag between the heat shield and the cabin
was added later to cushion the shock of impact.

The capsule was equipped with a fiber glass contour couch, also invented
at Langley, by Faget, William M. Bland, Jr., Jack C. Heberlig, and others.
It was designed to ease gravitation stress at launch and deceleration on reentry. Controls were complex. The vehicle had a dual-control system consisting
of eighteen gas thrusters. These enabled the pilot to maneuver it in pitch (up
and down), yaw (right and left), or roll (turning on the long axis). The "attitude," or position, of the craft relative to the Earth or to its direction of flight
was critical for retro-rocket fire, the braking maneuver to reenter the atmosphere. Faulty alignment of the vessel at the time of retrofire could cause it
to overshoot or undershoot the splashdown zone, where the recovery ship
was waiting, by tens to hundreds of miles. Alternatively, misalignment could
cause the craft to strike the top of the atmosphere at an angle at which it
would carom off into a higher orbit. In that case, the pilot could be stranded
in orbit for a period of time exceeding his oxygen supply. Or, reentry would
be made at a point where he would land a thousand miles or more from the
preplanned impact area.

In the tiny cabin, the pilot was supplied with pure oxygen at five pounds
per square inch pressure as breathing atmosphere. Oxygen alone was easier
to monitor than as part of a two-gas mixture of oxygen and nitrogen, which
the Russians were using in their heavier one-man spacecraft, called Vostok
("East"). Pure oxygen also saved weight, an important consideration in the
American program, which relied on the Atlas to loft the Mercury spacecraft
into orbit. The Russian capsule was lifted by the Sputnik A-1 launcher,

which had two to three times the thrust of the Atlas.

Untroubled by weight restrictions to the extent that NASA had to consider them, the Soviet vehicle carried a two-gas atmosphere at 14.7 pounds pressure per square inch—the normal sea level pressure, and came down via parachute on land. However, in the Vostok, the pilot bailed out before touchdown, using an aircraft ejection seat system.

Once the main features of the man-in-space effort had been settled, the problem of naming it was considered. Gilruth liked Project Astronaut. That designation was overruled on the theory that it focused too much attention on the pilot at the expense of the human pyramid of engineers and technicians required to launch him into orbit and the program's significance to mankind. The Greek Pantheon had been exploited in naming the military missiles: Jupiter, Juno, Atlas, Titan (except for the brief digression into Scandinavian mythology for Thor) and for the new, deep-space rocket, Saturn. What could be more appropriate than *Mercury* for the first one-man vehicle? Mercury was the grandson of Atlas, wore winged sandals and cap, and generally was known as a speedy fellow. He was also reputed to be the patron of clever thieves. Most people in NASA accepted the image of the messenger of the gods as appropriate for the thrusting of man into the heavens. Also, the White House did.

The initial Project Mercury timetable, as devised by Gilruth and his flight director, Christopher Columbus Kraft, Jr., called for the first manned ballistic flight to be launched atop a Redstone rocket April 26, 1960 (as per Project Adam). The first manned orbital flight, launched by an Atlas, was slated for September 1, 1960. After that, it was planned to launch several, possibly four more, Mercury flights, extending time to seventeen or eighteen orbits, a full twenty-four hours, depending on how the pilots were affected by free fall on the shorter trips. This schedule proved to be optimistic. It did not reckon with delays caused by the inevitable failures that come from creating a new technology.

In addition to developing the capsule and testing it, NASA established a round-the-world flight control and communications system to monitor and, if necessary, control the orbital flight. The system was a network of seventeen land- and ship-based radio stations stretching across the Atlantic Ocean from Cape Canaveral to Grand Canary Island, across Africa, the Indian Ocean, the Pacific (Canton Island and Hawaii), Mexico, California, Texas and back to Eglin, Florida. The tracking network was evolved from a simpler system set up for Vanguard to receive scientific data in both the northern and southern hemispheres. It was later to be augmented for the Gemini and Apollo missions. The Mercury network was a unique development in communications. The Russians had nothing like it. The network provided controllers at Cape Canaveral with global, though intermittent, communication with the capsule pilot and, when necessary, the ability to control the flight of the capsule through any station in radio view of it. The control center was tied in by telephone land lines with a central NASA computing and communication station near Washington, D.C. This was a Goddard Space Flight Center at Greenbelt, Maryland, where two IBM 7090 computers determined the present and future positions of the spacecraft continuously.

During 1959 and 1960, test failures plagued the development of the Mercury capsule, triggered press criticism—especially in the technical journals—and made officials extremely cautious about publicity.

There were some bright spots in this picture, however. A flight test of the Mercury capsule's ablation heat shield was successful September 9, 1959, despite the partial failure of the Atlas 10-D booster. The heat shield was adapted from missile nose cone technology. It was a mix of resin and glass that ablated or flaked away when heated, carrying the heat with the flakes. The shield was designed to protect the spacecraft during reentry from atmospheric friction heating as high as 5,000 degrees Fahrenheit. It worked perfectly.

Then, on December 4, 1959, the escape tower system and the mechanism separating the capsule from the launch vehicle passed tests on a launch from the Langley flight-testing station on Wallops Island, Virginia. The escape tower was a small rocket affixed to the top of the capsule. It was designed to pull the capsule away from the launch vehicle when triggered by a launch-vehicle failure during lift-off. The capsule would be lifted to sufficient altitude so that it could land safely in the Atlantic Ocean on its parachute. In a nominal lift-off, the tower was jettisoned at altitude. The launch vehicle was a sawed-off rocket called *Little Joe,* which was devised especially for the Mercury test program. On this test, a Rhesus monkey named Miss Sam was the passenger and survived undamaged.

Monkey tests had shown that low acceleration loads were harmless, if uncomfortable, to animals. Two monkeys, Abel and Baker, were launched 1,700 miles down the Atlantic Missile Range by a Jupiter C in the spring of 1050. They survived, but with a display of indignation.

The first suborbital flight test of the capsule July 29, 1960, went up in smoke when the Atlas booster unaccountably blew up one minute after lift-off from the Cape. That was the day NASA headquarters picked to announce plans for a three-man space ship called *Apollo.* It was programmed to carry three men on a long orbital flight and, perhaps, around the Moon. The test failure in Florida did not brighten the prospect, however.

A second suborbital test attempt, this time aboard a Redstone, failed November 21, 1960. The Redstone engine mysteriously cut off seconds after it was ignited, and the rocket and spacecraft fell back, triggering the escape tower and parachute system.

At last, on December 19, 1960, the capsule was launched on a true suborbital test to an altitude of 130.68 miles. It splashed 243.8 miles down-range in the Atlantic Ocean, where the Navy recovered it in fifteen minutes. It reached a velocity of 4,909.1 miles an hour, less than one-third of the zip needed to go into orbit, but the main objective of the test—the integrity of the structure, heat shield, and landing system—was happily realized. The Mercury capsule was a "go" spacecraft.

A second Mercury-Redstone test, launched January 31, 1961, was also successful. This one carried a thirty-seven-pound chimpanzee named Ham, who survived, somewhat dazed but angry. Then on February 21, 1961, another capsule went up to an altitude of 114 miles aboard an Atlas ICBM and landed 1,431.6 miles down the Atlantic missile range in the first successful demonstration of an orbital-type launch.

Next up would be a man, on a short suborbital flight. NASA began recruiting a corps of astronauts from the flying services—Air Force, Navy, and Marines—in 1958. Candidates had to be less than forty years old, less than five feet eleven inches tall, in top physical and psychological condition, have a bachelor's degree or its equivalent, be a graduate of a test pilot school, and have 1,500 hours of jet aircraft flight time. From fifty-six candidates, seven men were selected for training as astronauts in Project Mercury. They were Malcom Scott Carpenter, thirty-six, a Navy lieutenant commander; Leroy Gordon Cooper, Jr., thirty-two, an Air Force captain; John Herschel Glenn, Jr., thirty-eight, a Marine Corps lieutenant colonel; Virgil I. (Gus) Grissom, thirty-three, an Air Force captain; Walter M. Schirra, Jr., thirty-six, a Navy lieutenant commander; Alan B. Shepard, Jr., thirty-six, a Navy lieutenant commander; and Donald K. Slayton, thirty-five, an Air Force captain. The physical and psychological tests these men passed were probably the most detailed, protracted, and, perhaps, uncomfortable in the history of aviation medicine. The main personality and neurological characteristics the selection process emphasized were coolness in an emergency, high intelligence, quick reaction time, emotional stability, individuality, ability to cooperate with others, and willingness to accept long hours of special training and testing. These generally followed the behavior pattern of the American test pilot subculture, from which the Mercury Seven were drawn. That subculture dominated the flight-selection process throughout the development of manned space flight, to exclusion, except in one instance, of scientists who were trained as astronauts.

THE SELLING OF THE MOON

Halfway around the world, the Russians, too, were testing their manned spacecraft and training their cosmonauts. Against NASA's 3,000-pound Mercury capsule, the Soviet State Commission for Space Flight developed a spherical capsule which, with reentry and landing systems, weighed 10,000 pounds. The cabin alone weighed 5,500 pounds. The Vostok vehicle was being tested in orbit with animals, insects, and plants aboard while the Mercury was undergoing aerodynamic testing on suborbital flights. Cosmonaut recruiting and training were in progress in the Soviet Union at about the time that astronaut recruiting and training were going on in the United States.

Although Vostok was ahead of Mercury in development, the sharp edge the Russians had was their significantly more powerful booster, the rocket designated by Western observers as A-1. The twenty-engine monster could send a big, heavy Russian payload to the Moon; orbiting the Vostok was no problem at all.

The spacecraft was tested in five successive Sputnik launches, starting with *Sputnik IV*, launched May 15, 1960. It put the five-ton Vostok in a 193-by-228-mile orbit with a simulated passenger load. The cabin was not recovered, however, as a result of a misfire of the retro-rocket engine that pushed it into a higher orbit. This gave rise to the rumor that a cosmonaut had perished on that flight.

Sputnik V, the second Vostok test, was launched in a 189-by-210-mile orbit on August 19, 1960. It carried two mongrel dogs, Strelka ("Little Arrow") and Belka ("Squirrel"), a colony of mice, some rats, houseflies, and plants. After eighteen revolutions of the Earth, the capsule was brought down by radio commands to a landing only six miles from the designated landing site.

Lieutenant General Nikolai P. Kamanin and chief designer Korolev, who directed the cosmonaut program, were in no hurry to send up a man, according to the Russian space historian Evgeny Riabchikov.[46] That was a fortunate attitude, for *Sputnik VI*, launched December 1, 1960, with two more dogs, mice, insects, and plants, burned up on reentry, giving rise to another rumor that cosmonauts had perished. Rumors were rife concerning the Russian program because of the secrecy that surrounded it. The Russians never reported a failure. Consequently, even successes in their program were subject to doubt, until proof was provided.

While the causes of the *Sputnik VI* reentry failure were being investigated, the Soviets tried two shots to the planet Venus, which Americans had touched with radar. The first shot, launched February 4, 1961, was logged officially as *Sputnik VII*. It was supposed to send a heavy probe to Venus from a second-stage rocket in a parking orbit around the Earth, but the orbital stage failed. On February 2, 1961, *Sputnik VIII* tried the maneuver a second time. It succeeded in boosting a 1,415-pound reconnaissance vehicle to the vicinity of Venus from Earth orbit, a magnificent feat at the time. But radio communication failure fouled the flight of *Venus I*. Communication with it was lost en route to the pearly planet, and it flew on past Venus into solar orbit. This type of failure was to plague Russian interplanetary missions for the next fifteen years.

On March 9, 1961, *Sputnik IX* went up, with the fourth Vostok. It carried a dog, Chernushka ("Blackie"), guinea pigs, and mice, plus a wooden dummy representing a man. It reentered and landed safely after one orbit. Three weeks later, *Sputnik X* roared off the Baikonur (Tyuratam) Cosmodrome, carrying a dog, Zevesdochka ("Litte Star") and another dummy pilot. Two live cosmonauts observed the launch. One was a twenty-seven-year-old senior lieutenant in the Soviet Air Force named Yuri Alekseyevich Gagarin, a fighter pilot. The other was a twenty-five-year-old Air Force pilot, Gherman Stephanovich Titov.

Next up was a man. The state commission set April 12, 1961, as the date for the first manned orbit flight. Suborbital flight was never considered. It was orbit or nothing. Gagarin was selected as pilot of *Vostok I* and Titov as his backup. The day of the launch was clear, and a small group of air force officers, engineers, and officials assembled to watch it—a far cry from the teeming thousands that observed the United States manned launches from Florida.

Vostok I was boosted smoothly into a 112-by-203-mile orbit at an inclination of sixty-five degrees to the equator. Gagarin did some piloting of the craft, but the retrofire over Africa that brought *Vostok I* down from its one-orbit flight was automatic. Just 108 minutes after the launch, the first man in space landed in his parachute in a field near the village of Smelovka. To the woman and little girl who watched him descend in his orange space suit, helmet, and huge parachute, he must have looked like a visitor from another planet. The Vostok, still hot, landed some distance away. Farm workers rushed to the scene, but a helicopter appeared and snatched the hero away for a debriefing. Man was now in space.

The Gagarin flight was no surprise to NASA nor to the Pentagon. After all, Premier Khrushchev had predicted it the previous September, when he came to New York to do some politicking at the United Nations. But it produced a new wave of dismay and criticism in the United States. Now, however, there was no one to blame in the White House. Eisenhower was gone, and a new Democratic administration ruled the roost, with a majority in Congress and a new president, John F. Kennedy, who had made a campaign issue out of the missile and space gap. What was he going to do about it now?

President Kennedy had taken office with a new slogan: The New Frontier. It referred to new social and economic goals, but it could be taken literally to mean the physical frontier man was preparing to cross—into interplanetary space.

In the process of setting up his administration, Kennedy replaced the NASA administrator, Glennan, with a North Carolina lawyer, James E. Webb. For a time, Webb had served as director of the Bureau of the Budget under President Truman; he was in the oil and aircraft industries, and he knew his way around Congress as well as anyone. But he had neither technical nor academic background. Divesting himself of his business interests that would be construed to be in conflict with his new post, Webb threw himself with astounding energy into the job of getting NASA moving. The mood of public anxiety and criticism gave Webb the public support he needed. And he had friends in Congress, especially among the Oklahoma and Texas Democrats. If Kennedy believed that what NASA needed was not another distinguished scientist as leader, but a salesman, he was right. Webb turned out to be a super salesman.

In my judgment, Webb was the man who sold the Moon. Hindsight has not altered this opinion. He knew not only how to deal with members of Congress, but with lofty academicians. They, at first, looked down their noses at him; later they acquired respect for him as the federal administrator who gave graduate study in the sciences the greatest boost in history. Webb could handle press criticism without becoming angry, sarcastic, or imperious. He talked and talked and talked. The press corps dubbed him "the fastest mouth in the South." But he made sense, especially to the business and industrial communities. Fortunately, in persuading Congress to finance manned space flight, he had a powerful ally: the Soviet Union. Russian space successes were worth billions of dollars to NASA. Without them, U.S. manned space flight might well have been confined to Earth orbit.

At last, Project Mercury was ready to send up its first man. Alan Shepard was selected for the suborbital ride. The morning of May 5, 1961, dawned hot and clear, and the Redstone rocket, with Mercury perched atop it, stood on its launch pad, pointing skyward a fateful finger. More than a few of the 700 spectators assembled in a clearing in the palmetto scrub of Cape Canaveral had the impression that here was a human sacrifice on the altar of technology, a man shortly to be encompassed in a pillar of fire.

Conscious of the national image and of a watching world, NASA had christened the capsule *Freedom VII*, saluting the seven astronauts. The countdown went to zero, and the Redstone ignited in a gout of smoke and flame. It lifted slowly, almost magically, off the pad. In the flimsy grandstand, where the press was assembled, and from the crowd around it, came first applause, then screams and shouts of "Go, baby! Go!" Up she went into the high blue sky, arcing over the ocean and out of sight behind wisps of cirrus cloud.

Freedom VII reached a top speed of 5,180 miles an hour and a peak altitude of 116.5 miles. From that point of vantage, Shepard saw that the Earth was, indeed, a sphere, mottled a gorgeous blue and white. As Shepard fired the thrusters to turn the capsule around so that it would descend heat shield first, he could look back at a tan coastline on the far horizon.

Freedom VII landed in a calm sea fifteen minutes after launch 303.8 miles down range and was picked up by a helicopter that deposited it on the flight deck of the aircraft carrier *Lake Champlain*. Shepard emerged to become the hero of the hour. The success of the flight, with its enormous publicity, took the sting out of Gagarin's orbital flight, but it could not erase the fact that Russia was still ahead in space.

The Shepard flight took some of the pressure off NASA and the new Kennedy-Johnson administration to close the space gap. Immersed in earthly problems, such as the direction in which the Castro revolution in Cuba was moving, the problem of nuclear arms control and testing, and the state of the national economy, Kennedy was not primarily concerned with accelerating the space program in the first months of his administration. Johnson picked up the reins of the National Aeronautics and Space Council, which had been drifting toward the end of the Eisenhower administration, and assumed command of this influential, policy-shaping body as chairman.

With the council, the establishment of NASA, and the establishment of special space committees in the House of Representatives (Committee on Science and Astronautics) and the Senate (Committee on Aeronautical and Space Sciences), the political and administrative apparatus for space programs as a major government undertaking had been created during the Eisenhower administration. All President Kennedy had to do was use it. But this he did not do in the early months of 1961. What this elaborate apparatus lacked was a single, top-priority, organizing objective. Only the president could provide it—and make it stick.

The Eisenhower administration had not been oblivious to the prestige factor in space technology. In 1960, *Echo* had been launched into a 1,000-mile orbit as a passive communications satellite. It was a 100-foot-diameter balloon of mylar plastic that inflated itself beyond the atmosphere. Its size and reflectivity made it easy to see at night from any part of the planet over which it passed. A radio aboard broadcast a taped message from President Eisenhower promising that the United States would continue to make the scientific results of space experiments freely available to all people.

But Eisenhower's policy did not countenance a space race, which he believed was irrelevant. Members of his staff kept in step with this attitude. One of his special assistants for foreign trade characterized Sputnik as "a silly bauble in the sky" and pointed to an American supermarket exhibit in Zagreb, Yugoslavia, as a more significant demonstration of national productivity. [47]

While NASA's Office of Manned Space Flight, eventually headed by George M. Low (this segment of NASA underwent several metamorphoses between 1958 and 1962), was making a study of lunar landing problems, the President's Science Advisory Committee was estimating the cost. The PSCA came up with a bill of $20 to $40 billion. President Eisenhower's Commission on National Goals issued a warning against being "driven by nationalistic competition into extravagant programs which would divert funds and talents from programs of equal or greater importance."

This attitude was fairly prevalent in the Eisenhower administration and carried over into the Kennedy administration before the Gagarin flight. In fact, toward the end of 1960, a negative attitude toward manned space flight beyond Project Mercury was gaining force. In submitting the NASA budget to Congress for the 1962 fiscal year, the Eisenhower administration stated: "Further tests and experimentation will be necessary to establish if there are *any valid scientific reasons* for extending manned space flight beyond the Mercury program."

This view was not confined to Republicans. It was shared by influential persons in the incoming Kennedy administration. One in particular was Jerome B. Wiesner, of the Massachusetts Institute of Technology, who had served as Kennedy's science adviser during the election campaign and was slated to continue this role in the White House.

Wiesner had headed an ad hoc committee in 1960 that had reviewed the nation's defense and space posture for the candidate. The committee's report was not enthusiastic about the prospects of Project Mercury. It recommended that Mercury should be downgraded because it emphasized one phase of space activity at the expense of others. The report advised Kennedy to "stop advertising Mercury as our major objective in space activities. Indeed, we should make an effort to diminish the significance of this program to its proper proportion before the public, both at home and abroad." [48]

When President Kennedy took office, not only had the prospects for manned space flight dimmed considerably, but the project itself seemed to face an uncertain future. If manned space flight was to get off the ground in America, it needed another shock treatment. Gagarin's flight provided it. Shepard's flight doubled the dose. These events and their impact turned the White House around. Although he respected Wiesner's views, Kennedy tended to follow his own political instincts when they ran counter to advice he received from specialists.

During the spring of 1961, the new administration began to perceive that space was involved as a factor in the major problems the nation had to deal with. In the national economy, space work was a growing part of the employment picture, especially in aircraft, automotive, and chemical industries. There was no question that an expansion of the space program would take up the slack there.

In education, the revelations of Russian space technology led to comparisons between the educational systems of the United States and the USSR. Critics of American education suddenly found it to be deficient in the teaching of science and mathematics compared with the Russian system. A new emphasis on science teaching in the secondary schools appeared. The National Science Foundation began to plan for a major national effort to upgrade curricula in mathematics, biology, chemistry, physics, and earth science in the high schools.

In February 1961, reacting to the concept that space was the cutting edge of scientific and technological development, the Space Science Board of the National Academy of Sciences adopted a platform on "Man's Role in the National Space Program." The ultimate aim of the program, the board stated, should be the scientific exploration of the Moon and planets, and man must be included. "Every effort should be made to establish the feasibility of manned flight at the earliest opportunity," the board said.[49] Berkner was chairman of this group, which included Harold C. Urey, 1934 Nobel laureate in chemistry; Van Allen; Harrison Brown; Bruno Rossi; and Joshua Lederberg, a 1958 Nobel Prize winner in physiology and medicine.

April 1961 was the political nadir of the new administration. A week after Gagarin's triumph came the Bay of Pigs debacle, in which a U.S.-supported attempt to overthrow the Castro dictatorship in Cuba was ignominiously routed. On April 25, 1961, a test of the Mercury spacecraft on an Atlas ICBM failed because of a malfunction in the rocket's guidance system, throwing doubt on the timing of the first orbital flight, but not affecting Shepard's Mercury-Redstone flight, which was scheduled ten days later.

On the international scene, space prowess was a factor in negotiations for nuclear arms control and a ban on testing that was poisoning the atmosphere. Kennedy was preparing to meet Khrushchev in Vienna for discussions about the test ban and Berlin. As Helen Fuller, of the *New Republic* magazine, noted, "A bold new undertaking that would demonstrate national self confidence had definite appeal at that moment." [50]

President Kennedy turned to Vice-President Johnson and asked him, as Space Council chairman, where the United States stood in the space race and what it could do to improve its position. Kennedy's inquiry was in three parts: Could we beat the Russians (1) by putting up a manned space station? (2) by sending a crew on a flight around the Moon? or (3) by landing a man on the Moon and bringing him safely back? [51]

Johnson turned to NASA for answers. Von Braun, who had become director of the Marshall Space Flight Center, where the Saturn was being built, was ready with an answer. Indeed, he had been ready for a long time. "We have a sporting chance of sending a 3-man crew around the Moon ahead of the Soviets," he said in a memorandum dated April 29, "and an excellent chance of beating the Soviets to the first landing of a crew on the Moon." [52]

This estimate reflected lunar mission planning that had already been done. The planning considered a lunar flyby circa 1967 and a landing in 1968, based on the progress of an advanced Saturn rocket—not the Saturn 1, which was being developed at the time, but a much larger vehicle still in the planning stage.

By the end of 1959, NASA had drafted a ten-year program of manned space flight. It called for a manned orbital space station, circumlunar flights in 1966–1968, and a landing in 1971. In response to the vice-president's inquiry, NASA headquarters officials advised that there was little chance of being first to make a circumlunar flight because the Russians appeared to have a launch vehicle capable of boosting a capsule around the Moon, or soon would have one.

But a manned landing on the Moon required a launch vehicle much more powerful than any the Russians had demonstrated. NASA officials believed that with its superior technology and industry, the United States could develop a Moon-landing rocket as soon as or even before the Russians could do so. On the basis of this reasoning, NASA headquarters recommended that there was a good chance of beating the Russians to a manned lunar landing—if Congress would spend the money it would take. NASA had projected the cost of a ten-year manned lunar landing program at $21.3 billion. If this was speeded up, the cost would rise, perhaps to $33.7 billion, for a landing as early as 1967.

Vice-President Johnson made a careful canvass of opinion. The military and space people he consulted were unanimous in favor of a spectacular manned shot, preferably one to the Moon. Secretary of Defense Robert S. McNamara seconded Webb that manned space flight was the most effective way to restore American prestige vis-à-vis the Soviet Union. Prestige was justification enough for sending men to the Moon, from that viewpoint, even if such a venture could not be justified on scientific or military grounds.[53] General Schriever, an influential voice in the military establishment, urged the lunar landing. Strong support for manned space flight came both from the House and the Senate. Representative Overton Brooks (D-Louisiana), chairman of the House Committee on Science and Astronautics, asserted in a memorandum to Johnson May 4, 1961: "We cannot concede the Moon to the Soviets, for it is conceivable that the nation which controls the Moon may well control the Earth." [54] The chairman of the Senate space committee, Senator Robert S. Kerr (D-Oklahoma), a friend and former business associate of Webb, enthusiastically supported the expansion of the manned space program.

Johnson meticulously sounded out Republican minority leaders on the House and Senate committees and found support there. Business and industry leaders were enthusiastic. The country had to get moving, they told Johnson. Johnson believed he had detected a national consensus in favor of action, and he reported his findings to the president. This impression was greatly enhanced by the wave of enthusiasm and approval created by Shepard's flight. Kennedy perceived that the time was ripe for a bold decision. He made it and communicated it to Congress in a State of the Union message May 25, 1961.

He called upon the nation to commit itself "to achieving the goal before this decade is out of landing a man on the Moon and returning him safely to Earth." It was the ultimate demonstration of the "New Frontier" outlook that Kennedy hoped would characterize his administration. "If we are to win the battle that is going on around the world between freedom and tyranny," he said, "if we are to win the battle for men's minds, the dramatic achievements in space which occurred in recent weeks should have made clear to us all, as did the Sputnik in 1957, the impact of this adventure on the minds of men everywhere who are attempting to make a determination of which road they should take. Now it is time to take longer strides, time for a great new American enterprise."

The enterprise of the Moon was launched.

CHAPTER V

GENESIS

In the atmosphere of the Cold War, President Kennedy's call for a manned lunar landing as a national goal was a summons to arms. Sputnik and Vostok had military as well as scientific impact on the Western alliance. Sputnik, in 1957, had amounted to a military and a political victory in the framework of the Cold War; Gagarin's orbital flight enhanced it dramatically.

These events and the American reaction to them generated a political climate in Washington in which the summons seemed reasonable. Certainly, such a declaration would have sounded bizarre four years earlier; before Sputnik, it would have sounded irrational. Hindsight makes it clear that President Kennedy's decision to send men to the Moon was a response to Russian moves that were believed by many members of Congress to have profound military implications. In this respect, the decision was a move on the international chess board. Sputnik was a knight in this game, as two staff members of the House Select Committee on Astronautics and Space Exploration (later called Science and Astronautics) saw it.[1] The staffers, Frank B. Gibney and George J. Feldman, cited Admiral Mahan's naval doctrine of the "fleet in being" as a deterrent. The idea refers to an aggregation of warships that remains in the harbor and never has to sail out—if it's powerful enough to be feared by a potential enemy. Sputnik and Vostok symbolized a space power in being. If the United States was to fulfill its role as the champion of the West, it was required to match such a fleet. To do so, of course, necessitated a command decision from the top. The Kennedy summons provided it and launched a national effort that would create a national space power in being in developing the means of flying men to the Moon and bringing them safely back to Earth.

Without the Moon decision, the creation of a national space agency was insufficient to develop such a power in being, or to counter the effects of Sputnik. In absorbing the "good, gray National Advisory Committee on Aeronautics," Gibney and Feldman said, NASA did not strike out on a Manhattan-District-style effort, as many members of Congress expected. Glennan, the first administrator, appeared simply to be transposing NACA's deliberate "ruminative research" in aeronautics to aerospace; NASA was adding an aerospace component to aeronautics. In the view of Gibney and Feldman, Glennan did not perceive NASA's role as an operations one, but rather as one confined to research and development. But political and military planners were convinced that a more aggressive program of development had to be adopted if the United States was to overtake the Soviet Union in space capability. It was not until after the administration changed in 1961 and the Gagarin flight lengthened the Soviet lead that this view prevailed. President Kennedy's call to arms focused it on a distant but realizable objective.

Under Webb's energetic direction, NASA was prepared to implement the presidential dictum immediately. In partnership with the state of Oklahoma, whose senior senator, Robert S. Kerr, was an influential member of the administration as well as Senate Space Committee chairman, NASA staged a national briefing on a projected space program at the Oklahoma State Fairgrounds in Tulsa. The First National Conference on the Peaceful Uses of Space opened the day after the Kennedy call to arms. At a banquet where 600 guests each received a scroll attesting that he was an "A-OK Astronaut of Oklahoma" (the term A-OK was attributed to Alan B. Shepard by John A. "Shorty" Powers, NASA's Voice of Project Mercury, during Shepard's flight), Webb disclosed some of the background of the president's lunar policy:

> It was the decision of the President that the key to retrieving our position lay in determining that we could no longer proceed with the Mercury one-man spaceship as if it were the end of our program, but that we must, even in a tight budget situation, present to Congress the urgent necessity for committing ourselves to the giant boosters required to power the larger craft needed to accommodate crews of several men on long voyages of deep space, lunar and planetary exploration.

Webb described a huge rocket called Nova that would boost men to the Moon. It would be "60 feet taller than a football field is long," he said. Nova was the king of a tribe of Saturn rockets, the first of which, the Saturn C-1, was being built "in-house" (by NASA) at the Marshall Space Flight Center at Huntsville, Alabama. The developer was the Von Braun team. The Saturn C-1 cluster of eight H-1 engines in its first stage would, as previously mentioned, deliver 1.3 to 1.5 million pounds of thrust. Advanced versions of the boosters were visualized as the Saturn C (for configuration) 3, delivering 3 million pounds of thrust, and a C-5 which would deliver 7.5 million pounds. The Nova would be even more powerful. Upper stages using hydrogen-fueled engines were in development, but first, NASA had to create a reliable hydrogen engine. A small version called the RL-10 was being developed for a rocket called Centaur, designed as a second stage atop the Atlas.

The Oklahoma conference served essentially as a rally to focus national attention on the Moon declaration and explain its rationale to the electorate. Major General O. J. Ritland, commander of the Air Force Space Systems Division, compared the American position in space in 1961 to "the attitude we held toward the airplane in 1910." He quoted an editorial from the magazine *Scientific American* of that period, which branded predictions of air travel as "the wildest exaggeration." The trouble with assessments like that, said Ritland, is that they fail to consider the development of technology.

From the National Academy of Sciences, a voice was heard saying: "One gets a little tired these days of reading about Russian space supremacy." That was the sentiment of Lloyd V. Berkner, chairman of the academy's Space Science Board.

The Oklahoma conference inaugurated a series of annual national conferences on space development. These continued until 1966. By that time, the increasing technical complexity of space programs alienated public interest, and the function of discussing them was taken over by technical and scientific societies at their annual meetings.

NASA GROWS UP

Equipped with a far-out but highly visible goal—the Moon—NASA began to expand. From NACA, it had inherited four high-quality research centers: The Lewis Center at the Cleveland Airport, specializing in propulsion; the Langley Laboratories at Langley, Virginia; the Ames Research Center at Mountain View, California; and a test center at Edwards Air Force Base, California.

Additionally, the agency developed the Marshall Space Flight Center on the grounds of the Redstone Arsenal in the mountains of north Alabama as its main rocket development center. In Florida, adjacent to the Air Force Missile Test Center on Cape Canaveral, an 80,000-acre site on Merritt Island was purchased by NASA for development as a manned rocket launching base—a space port. In the suburban New Orleans area of Michoud, NASA leased a huge factory building for the production of Saturn rockets. The structure had been erected during World War II by the government for the construction of an oversized wooden airplane, the *Spruce Goose*, which was abandoned after a prototype was built. Eastward, at Bay Saint Louis, Mississippi, NASA bought up 1,000 acres of pine scrubland as a test site for the Saturn rocket engines.

In September 1961, Webb announced that the agency had selected a site twenty-five miles southeast of Houston, Texas, on the Gulf plain, for the construction of the Manned Spacecraft Center for the training of astronauts and the control of all manned space flights. Although there were no technical nor logistical reasons for establishing the center in Texas instead of on the ample space port acreage that NASA was acquiring in Florida, there were political ones of some consequence.

Lyndon B. Johnson, the vice-president and the chairman of the National Aeronautics and Space Council, and Representative Albert Thomas, a Houston Democrat who presided over the House Appropriations Subcommittee on Independent Offices and was a member of the House Committee on Science and Astronautics, along with another Texas Democrat, Representative Olin E. Teague, were powerful influences in the agency's decision to locate the center in Texas. There was no irrefutable logic in this selection. It simply followed the pork-barrel tradition.

A tract of 1,020 acres was deeded to NASA by Rice Institute of Technology, which had received the land from the Humble Oil Company, exclusive of mineral rights. NASA also purchased an additional 600 acres from Rice at a cost of $1.4 million to bring the total acreage to 1,600. Rice had acquired the 600 acres from Humble in exchange for thirty-three acres of industrial property the institute owned near Houston. The gyrations set off a miniature land boom on the salty Gulf plain midway between Houston and Galveston. Real estate values doubled, tripled, and quadrupled for a time with the prospect of development. In two years, a handsome campus of sixteen buildings arose on the plain, surrounded, eventually, by well-designed middle-income residential communities. Some day, if NASA's astronaut-training and launch operations are consolidated in Florida, as logic suggests they should be, this Houston center may become a university.

While NASA was building an administrative empire on the ground, its Space Task Group pushed preparations for the second manned suborbital flight, *Mercury-Redstone IV*. On the morning of July 21, 1961, Air Force Captain Gus Grissom squeezed into the tiny cabin of the Mercury capsule *Liberty Bell VII* and was boosted to an altitude of 118 miles by the thundering Redstone rocket.

When *Liberty Bell* splashed down in the Atlantic Ocean, some 303 miles southeast of the cape, the spacecraft hatch blew off prematurely and water began pouring into the cabin. Grissom scrambled out of the capsule and floated near it. For a few moments, he paddled around easily, buoyed up by his flight suit. Suddenly, he noticed he was sinking as he watched a helicopter hovering above him. His flight suit began to ship water through an open vent, and its steadily increasing weight began to drag him down as he struggled in the water to grab a horse-collar sling that was lowered to him from the helicopter. The air blast of the helicopter blades kept pushing him away from the sling; finally the pilot maneuvered it to within his grasp. *Liberty Bell* was too weighted down with water in the cabin to be hoisted out of the sea. Only a line hitched to it from the aircraft kept it from sinking. When it became plain that the helicopter could not lift the half-swamped vessel out of the water, the line was cut, and the spacecraft sank to rest on the bottom with the hulks of Spanish galleons and pirate ships.

Spiced by Grissom's brush with drowning, the flight of *MR-IV* was hailed by the nation's press as another milestone on America's march to the Moon. The premature opening of the hatch after splashdown was never fully explained. Grissom said he armed the explosive charges that blow the hatch outward, but that he had not fired them. An early transcript of his radio conversation with the Mercury Control Center indicated that he was actually "blowing the hatch," but a later, corrected version quoted him as saying merely that he was getting ready to blow the hatch. The incident was not treated as a malfunction of the hatch detonation system, and NASA simply revised procedures to avert a recurrence of the accident. With the spacecraft at the bottom of the sea, there was no opportunity to examine the mechanism.

Project Mercury was now ready for orbital flight. The Space Task Group and Webb advised the White House and Congressional leaders that they were scheduling the first American manned orbital flight for late December 1961. The pilot would be John Herschel Glenn, Jr., lieutenant colonel in the Marine Corps.

In August, the Soviet Union scored another triumph in the space race. On the morning of August 6, 1961, Major Gherman S. Titov, twenty-five, was launched from Tyuratam in a five-ton spacecraft, *Vostok II*, into an elliptical orbit of 110-by-159 miles. He landed the following day after completing seventeen and one-half revolutions of the Earth. It was a new blow to American optimism. It made the suborbital flights look puny by comparison.

In the launching of *Vostok II*, Titov apparently experienced none of the delays that had wearied Shepard and Grissom during holds and restarts in the Mercury countdowns. He felt the pull of five gravities and then the release of free fall. A moment after the Vostok engines shut down and the boost phase of the flight ended, Titov experienced several seconds of spatial disorientation during the transition to weightlessness. Afterward, he related: "Suddenly, there was a dead silence. I was in space! Suddenly, the instrument panel swam off somewhere. I could not figure out where the Earth was, what position I was in, but in a few minutes, everything was in its place." [2] "This is Eagle," Titov then reported to the ground. "I feel magnificent."

Titov related that when he "took the wheel" to guide the spaceship manually, its response to changes in attitude was so smooth that he thought he could go off then and there to other planets. "Night came like the darkness of a tunnel which one enters in an automobile or a train and daylight appears as if turned on by a rheostat, like the house lights being turned up in a theater." [3]

On the fifth revolution, Titov experienced nausea, a condition that worried the Russian space medics. That reaction had not been predicted. It raised the possibility of vestibular (inner ear) problems that might impose a limitation on manned space flight. "In order to quiet my naughty vestibular system, I cautiously found the most comfortable position in the chair and fainted," his autobiography says. The word *fainted* was later listed by the publisher as an error and was changed to *remained still*.

When he recovered from the bout of nausea, Titov tested the flying performance of his five-ton cosmic machine. He found that it responded to the "wheel" like a well-built fighter aircraft. During communication periods with the ground, he received a congratulatory message from Yuri Gagarin, who was visiting the Canadian industrialist, banker, and philanthropist Cyrus S. Eaton, in Canada. Eaton's sumptuous lodge at Pugwash, Nova Scotia, was the scene in 1957 of the initial Pugwash conference between Western and Soviet Bloc scientists in an Eaton-financed effort to establish a dialogue among intellectuals across the iron curtain.

Titov was full of praise for the Vostok machine. The cabin, he said, had the temperature, pressure, and humidity of a health resort. I would not have expected him to complain, but this description was composed after the flight in an autobiography written in collaboration with a ghost writer. Titov's comments must be viewed, functionally, as propaganda. But the images of gallantry and infallibility this prose projected were no more chauvinistic than those of NASA's public information machine, with its breakfast-food champion image of the astronaut, who was constantly being "honed to a fine edge" by delays and frustrations that would have driven ordinary mortals up the wall.

Titov tried to sleep. He found that as soon as he dozed off, his arms would rise up and hang in the air. It was only after he tucked his hands in the seat belt that he was able to fall asleep. But when he awoke, he found his hands in the air again. "What can you do?" he asked.

By the thirteenth revolution, Titov had become accustomed to the sensation of weightlessness. He decided to take photographs of the ground during his "free" period with a movie camera. "It is very handsome, our Earth," he reported. "At every turn, new colors, new spectra, irreproducible panoramas. The outlines of the continents, mountains and forests were clearly to be seen. The ribbons of the big rivers, the seas and the large lakes gleamed."

On the seventeenth revolution, *Vostok II* was positioned automatically for retrofire and landing, with its retro-rockets pointing in the direction of flight. Unlike the Mercury, with its heat shield aft, the entire globular surface of Vostok was shielded by ablative material that flaked off as it was heated by atmospheric friction during reentry and thus carried the heat away.

Retrofire restored the feeling of weight. Objects that had been floating in the cabin—the movie camera, the logbook, a pencil, the camera exposure meter—settled down to the floor. The vessel's frame heated as it plunged downward through the upper atmosphere. Titov found the cabin immersed in flame. The braking system (parachutes) worked precisely, and at an altitude of several kilometers, he turned on the landing system.[4]

After Titov was ejected in his seat from the descending spaceship, he saw it coming down below him. It was falling almost twice as fast as he was on its big parachute. Titov's seat chute lowered him gently to the ground beside a railroad embankment. "Bump. And I was on my feet," his autobiography related. Three motorcyclists came up running at full speed, calling: "Are you Titov?" "I am Titov," the cosmonaut replied. "Good stuff, Titov!" they shouted.

COUNTDOWN FOR GLENN

The seventeen and one-half-orbit flight of Gherman Titov was the third shock to the United States' self-image of technological ascendancy. If there was any doubt now about the effectiveness of Russian space technology, the flight of *Vostok II* erased it. Military observers noted that the high inclination of the Vostok flight path (64 degrees 56 minutes from the equator) put the ship over nearly all of the United States during the seventeen revolutions. Although Titov had little time for effective reconnaissance with his movie camera, the mission demonstrated Soviet capability of carrying out detailed observations of the United States with manned vehicles as well as with Kosmos satellites, some of which were reconnaissance machines.

Looking back on this period a decade later, the British astronomer Sir Bernard Lovell characterized the Russian space achievements as "developments which could have vital military, commercial and political consequences." It was fortunate, he added, that the Kennedy administration and members of Congress realized this. From a technological view, Sir Bernard said, the two Russian manned space flights had tilted the balance of power between the superstates toward the Soviet Union. Thus, "the landing of men on the Moon and their safe return to Earth became a prestigious goal." [5]

From an American viewpoint, the Moon declaration put the Gagarin and Titov flights into the perspective of the preliminary rounds of a nine-year contest in which victory would not be determined until the end. It thus postponed the finality of the Russian achievements and attempted to subordinate them to a distant main goal. History might record that the Soviet Union put the first man into orbit, but the Moon declaration implied that a more sophisticated indicator of technological prowess was the capability of landing men on the Moon and bringing them safely home.

Although the Russians appeared to avoid any direct response to Kennedy's lunar strategy, they did not reject the notion of a Moon race. At public appearances and at press conferences, cosmonauts alluded to a lunar landing and predicted that Russians would be first to accomplish it. But no official statement was made on this subject, either pro or con. This was consistent with Soviet policy of refraining from any announcement prior to a launch—and useful policy it was. Failures and aborts were never mentioned.

So far as Russian space successes were concerned, these became the grist for the Soviet propaganda mill. But repeated claims of space superiority and the use of space spectaculars for political propaganda depended on competition; they required a competitor, and the United States filled that role. By the same measure, the American program was sustained on competition, too. It was nourished by those successes that fed the Soviet propaganda machines. Without Sputnik or the Vostoks, there would have been no declaration of the Moon, for there would have been no demonstration to which the nation could react. So long as the Soviet Union presented a challenge, Congress would appropriate funds to meet it in the belief that Russian gains in the Cold War threatened United States security and world position.

"The prestige factor as a political ingredient of Soviet space activities in the Cold War setting can remain a valid principle only so long as this competitive situation exists," a Senate space committee staff report noted.[6] Consequently, a denial of competition would reduce the political effect of space spectaculars—and there was no denial from the Soviet Union. Neither was there any confirmation. The moon race was defined by the existing situation—both sides competing in manned and automatic vehicles.

Addressing workers at a tractor factory in Yugoslavia in 1963, Nikita Khrushchev said: "When people talk about the mightiest country in the world, they say that there are two giants in the world: the Soviet Union and the United States. This is not a bad acknowledgment of our successes in the last 46 years: If one considers that manned flights in space are the summit of the development of science and technology at their present stage, then here we have already overtaken the United States." [7] During his visit to the United States in the fall of 1963, Yuri Gagarin and the Soviet ambassador, A. F. Dobrynin, asserted that the Soviets would land a man on the moon by the end of the decade, whatever the United States did.[8]

Although Titov's seventeen and one-half orbits had effectively upstaged the planned three-orbit flight of John Glenn in December, tension mounted in the space agency as problems with the spacecraft and with the Atlas rocket cropped up. NASA was under unique pressure to perform—as much, perhaps, as a military force preparing to meet an adversary. Essentially, a failure of *Mercury-Atlas VI*, the first American attempt to fly a man in orbit, would be a defeat in the Cold War. In their program, the Russians had the cover of secrecy. NASA did not. Its own public information apparatus began rolling out handouts that inevitably generated a public expectation of success.

Before the summer of 1961 ended, the Glenn mission was postponed—slipped, in NASA parlance—until January 1962. The engineers responsible for determining the conditions under which *MA-VI* would be launched were veteran NACA executives. They were imbued with a sense of perfection, evolved from long experience with the truism that manned flight, in the atmosphere or out of it, is singularly unforgiving of error. To the extent that they could perceive problems in the booster and spacecraft, they resolved them. They left nothing knowingly to chance, for it was their experience that a considerable element of chance existed that could not be perceived or foreseen. It lurked in the unexpected, the unplanned, the unforeseen, the accidental. That was enough to cope with. No foreseeable gamble would be taken if it could be prevented.

That was the creed of the triumvirate that ruled Project Mercury: Robert R. Gilruth, the director; Walter C. Williams, associate director in charge of operations; and Christopher Columbus Kraft, Jr., deputy director of operations. They were dealing with a rocket that would be committed to boosting a man for the first time when it launched John Glenn. The Atlas D was "man-rated" in technical terms, but this still was its first manned test. They were dealing with a spacecraft that had been tested with a man in it only in suborbital flight, that had not subjected a man to the full stress of reentry at orbital velocity.

In order to prevent nature from interposing problems, the directors set weather minimums high. They required that cloud cover be restricted to two-tenths—no more. The directors wanted to observe the early stages of powered flight up through the atmosphere. Sea conditions in the splashdown area of the western Atlantic Ocean, to the southeast of the Bahama Islands, had to be calm enough to allow the navy to retrieve the spacecraft from the water without risk. The rocket, the spacecraft, and the astronaut had to be in perfect condition. All systems—meteorological, mechanical, and physiological—had to be "go" before the Mercury directorate would authorize a launch. Another "go" condition was that the round-the-world network of eighteen tracking stations had to be operational, so that the Mercury Control Center on Cape Canaveral could be in radio communication with the spacecraft at key points on each orbit.

All these conditions made a firm launch date problematical. In December, NASA announced that *Mercury-Atlas VI* would not be launched before January 23, 1962. The launch date then began to slip, as difficulties in the checkout of rocket and spacecraft persisted. It slipped to January 25, 26, and 27, where it held.

Early on the morning of January 27, after a predawn breakfast of steak and eggs that was to become traditional on launch day, Glenn struggled into his twenty-pound, $4000 pressure suit. He rode in a van from Hangar S, the astronaut headquarters on the cape, to Launch Complex 14, where the Atlas stood wreathed in oxygen vapor with the Mercury spacecraft and its escape tower steeple on top. Both rocket and spacecraft were enclosed in the steel embrace of a service tower. Glenn rode up the tower elevator to the capsule level and promptly squeezed feet first into the cabin of *Friendship VII*.

At the press site, 8,000 feet from the launch pad, more than 1,500 news correspondents representing the news media of the United States, Canada, Mexico and Latin America, Western Europe, and Japan had assembled to record the event for newspapers, radio, and television. As the countdown proceeded toward the launch, torrents of news copy rolled out of portable typewriters to be dispatched over teletype machines or dictated by telephone, and hurricanes of words went out over radio, television, and telephone circuits. This was the largest concentration of news media reporters, commentators, and photographers in history. All eyes were turned toward the distant Atlas missile with the manned spaceship replacing its warhead. Beyond the cape, more than 250,000 men, women, and children had assembled on the Atlantic beaches to watch the launch.

A brief power failure was reported from Mission Control, and the countdown was held until power was restored. But during the hold the weather closed down. Clouds rolled over the cape, and the bright sky went dark. Weather minimums were exceeded. Thirteen minutes before countdown would have reached launch time, the launch was scrubbed. Mercury Control announced a delay of at least two days. Then a leak in the Atlas fuel tank was discovered, and the launch was repostponed until February 13, then to February 14, and, after a spell of rainy, cloudy, weather, until February 20.

Once more Glenn went through the prelaunch ritual of the formal breakfast, the final physical examination, the suiting up, and the predawn trip from the ready room to Pad 14. Holds were called to replace a defective transponder in the rocket (a device to amplify the return of radar signals used to track the rocket) and to replace a broken bolt in the spacecraft hatch that somehow had escaped detection earlier. The early morning was cloudy; but as the sun rose, the skies cleared. The service tower was rolled away from the rocket and spaceship. They stood silhouetted against the morning sky like a finger pointing out the road that man was now beginning to travel.

At 9:47 A.M., Eastern Standard Time, February 20, 1962, the first American was launched into orbital flight around the Earth. At 75,000 feet, *Mercury-Atlas VI* passed through the region of maximum dynamic pressure (Max Q) to which the vehicle was subjected on its exit from the atmosphere. "Have some vibration," Glenn reported, "through Max Q and smoothing out real fine. Flight very smooth now. Sky looking dark outside. Cabin pressure is holding at 6.1 [pounds per square inch]. The gees [gravities] are building up to six."

The Atlas began to pitch over from an oblique flight path to one almost parallel with the ground as it approached orbital velocity of five miles a second. When the main booster engine cut off at two minutes twelve seconds, Glenn reported that the gee force had dropped to 1.25. The rocket continued to accelerate, however, on its two sustainer and vernier engines. Suddenly, Glenn felt a thump, heard a bang, and saw smoke. It was the escape tower being jettisoned.

The astronanut reported fuel, oxygen, cabin pressure, and the falling gee load to Alan Shepard, his ground contact, or "capsule communicator" (Cap Com). The Atlas sustainer engines cut off. With a mild thump, three solid propellant rockets at the rear of *Friendship VII* ignited and shoved the spacecraft clear of the Atlas. Now free, the capsule was turned around automatically so that it would fly with its heat shield forward. Glenn was now facing rearward. He could see the whole panorama of the Florida coast and the gray sea below, the view partly hidden by pearly masses of cloud gleaming in the sun. "Oh, that view is tremendous," he said. "Roger," said Shepard. "You have a go, at least 7 orbits." *Friendship VII* was in elliptical orbit of 100 by 158.7 (nautical) miles.

Glenn suffered none of the disorientation or nausea that Titov had reported. Instead, he felt comfortable, and he felt elated. "This is a very comfortable zero gee," he said. "I have nothing but a very fine feeling. It just feels very normal and very good."

Although the orbit *Friendship VII* was flying was calculated to be secure for seven orbits before it began to decay (as a result of friction with gases beyond the sensible atmosphere), the spacecraft timer was set to fire retro-rockets at four hours thirty-two minutes and twenty-eight seconds after lift-off. At that time, Glenn would be in his third revolution of the Earth and in radio view (contact) with the Mercury ground station at Kauai, Hawaii.

As *Friendship VII* arced high above the Atlantic, Glenn looked through a periscope that enabled him to see forward. He reported that the horizon was a brilliant blue. He could see the Canary Islands and, beyond, the shoulder of Africa. Dust storms were visible swirling over the Sahara Desert. Over Nigeria, Glenn took control of the ship and yawed it sixty degrees to the left and right. He reported that he felt fine when queried by the ground station at Kano. Moments later, he was talking to the ground crew on Zanzibar, and, from there, the spacecraft flew "in the blind" over the Indian Ocean and into nightfall. Zanzibar told him that the results of his automatic electrocardiogram, radioed to the ground along with telemetered data on the performance of spacecraft systems, were excellent. Nothing to worry about. Glenn wasn't worried. He practiced a sequence of head movements to test whether they would induce vertigo, dizziness, or nausea, but he experienced none of these effects. Mercury directors were relieved to find that on his first revolution, Glenn was entirely free of adverse physiological symptoms. It could now be assumed that Titov's symptoms of disorientation and nausea were individual responses to the new environment. Mercury directors were not aware at the time that the Vostok spaceship was spin-stabilized; the Mercury was not. The spin might have produced the symptoms Titov reported. On later flights, U.S. spacecraft were rolled around their long axes to avoid overheating of the side exposed to the sun. No adverse effects were noted.

A shipborne communications station in the Indian Ocean asked Glenn again if he had any feelings from weightlessness as *Friendship VII* passed within radio view. "Negative," he said. "I feel fine so far." Astronaut Gordon Cooper, stationed at Muchea, Australia, called the spacecraft next. Glenn reported he could see ground lights and the illuminated outline of a city below. It was Perth, whose residents turned on all their lights to salute the voyager. Glenn passed down his thanks for the beacon, a welcome visual contact with the people on the ground.

Still, no ill effects from weightlessness, he reported, and vision was normal. Woomera airport turned up its floodlights, but Glenn could not see them because of clouds. Woomera ground station advised Glenn that his telemetered blood pressure read 126 over 90, a healthy pressure.

Friendship VII flew a northeasterly track across the Pacific Ocean, and the pilot talked to the Mercury station on Canton Island. As Glenn opened a tube of applesauce and squeezed some into his mouth, he glanced into the periscope and saw the rising sun. "Oh, the sun is coming up behind me in the periscope, a brilliant, brilliant red," he said, speaking into the blind. Canton heard him.

It was during this first Pacific pass that Glenn reported sighting the mysterious luminous particles that suddenly appeared around his ship like fireflies. The particles glowed white, green, and yellow and seemed to have a motion of their own, independent of the ship. The mystery persisted after the flight, generating imaginative theories of a species of space life afloat above the atmosphere or a cloud of silicates from a volcanic eruption in orbit around the Earth. The actuality was more prosaic. The "fireflies" were particles of frozen exhaust globules from the vessel's attitude-control thrusters. They danced away from the ship at sunrise as the sun's heat began to vaporize the frozen exhaust residues that either clung to the ship or traveled in orbit with it.

On his second revolution of the Earth, Glenn reported intermittent problems in the small gas thrusters that controlled the vehicle's attitude. The thruster that caused the vessel to yaw to the right failed to function in the automatic-control mode. But Glenn found he could control this motion manually.

Meanwhile, Mercury Control monitors became alarmed by an indication that the spacecraft's landing bag had been accidentally deployed. If so, the astronaut was in serious jeopardy. The rubberized canvas bag was designed to become a pneumatic cushion and absorb the shock of landing on the water by filling with air during descent through the atmosphere once it was released from the capsule wall.

During flight, the bag was pressed flat against the rear wall of the spacecraft by the heat shield, which was held in place by mechanical clamps. After reentry and during parachute descent, the pilot released the clamps by pressing a switch. The release allowed the heat shield to drop four feet away from the capsule's rear wall and the bag to extend so that it could inflate.

If the bag actually was deployed, the heat shield was no longer close enough to the vessel to protect it against the 5,000-degree-Fahrenheit heat of reentry friction. In that case, *Friendship VII* would become a blazing meteorite in seconds once it hit the sensible atmosphere.

Whether or not the bag had become accidentally deployed was not clear to Mercury controllers. The deployment signal had been reported intermittently by some ground stations, but not by all of them. The control center at Cape Canaveral considered that the signal might be false, but controllers could not afford such an assumption. They thus regarded it as an emergency. However, Glenn remained unaware of the problem. Nothing on his console indicated landing-bag deployment. When he passed over Canton Island on the second revolution, the station operators there advised him that they had no indication that the bag might be deployed.

This was Glenn's first inkling of what the ground was worrying about. "Did someone report the landing bag could be down?" Glenn asked. "Negative," replied Canton. "We had a request to monitor and to ask you if you heard any flapping." Glenn said he heard none. Had the ground concern about the landing bag been triggered by his reports of the "fireflies?"

At Cape Canaveral, a conference was called to consider emergency procedures in case the landing bag had come loose. It was decided to instruct Glenn to retain the retro-rocket package after the rockets had been fired to slow the vessel for reentry instead of casting them off. The retro-rockets were set flush against the heat shield and held in place by metal straps. The straps normally would be cast off to jettison the rockets after they discharged. By keeping the retropack in place after firing, Glenn could also keep the heat shield tight against the spacecraft even if the landing bag clamps were open. This strategy injected a new element into the reentry phase of the flight. It had never been considered before, but both NASA and contractor engineers believed that it would work.

As Glenn passed within range of the Hawaiian ground station on Kauai on his third revolution, he was advised of the landing bag problem. He had some time to think about it before he heard the voice of astronaut Walter M. Schirra, Jr., from Point Arguello, California, telling him: "Keep your retropack on until you pass Texas."

Friendship VII began its final pass over the United States, and the spaceship clock ticked down to retrofire. The braking rockets ignited with a thump. The Mercury station at Corpus Christi, Texas, instructed him to keep the retropack on all the way through reentry. This required Glenn to make a manually controlled reentry with the added burden of the retropack.

Alan Shepard "came on the line" and explained that cape flight directors were not sure whether or not the bag had deployed but advised it was the consensus that it was both possible and advisable to reenter with the retropack on. Shepard reminded Glenn to keep the capsule at zero angle for reentry. At the time of retrofire, it had been inclined with the nose down for maximum braking effect.

Arcing downward, *Friendship VII* reentered with a growing red glare that became brilliant and intense as the retropack vaporized. "A real fireball outside!" Glenn called as his radio transmission was blacked out by a wall of ionized air that formed around the vessel from the heat of atmospheric friction. When communication was restored, Glenn heard Shepard calling him from the cape: "How you doing?" "Oh, pretty good," said Glenn. "That was a real fireball. I had chunks of that retropack breaking off all the way through."

Friendship VII splashed down at 2:45 P.M., Eastern Standard Time—four hours, fifty-five minutes, and ten seconds after lift-off. It bobbed in the Atlantic swells a mile from the U.S.S. *Noa*, a destroyer, which was waiting to hoist the spacecraft aboard. The United States had qualified in the manned space flight sweepstakes.

CARPENTER, SCHIRRA, AND COOPER

The second United States manned orbital flight, *MA-VII*, was launched on the morning of May 24, 1962, with Malcolm Scott Carpenter, thirty-seven, a navy lieutenant commander, in the pilot's couch. It was essentially a repetition of Glenn's flight—three revolutions of the Earth and a splashdown in the Atlantic. However, there was a cliff-hanging variation.

Like Glenn, Carpenter experienced no disorientation or nausea. He rolled the vessel repeatedly. He allowed it to drift to see what it would do. It simply rolled and tumbled slowly. But the motion had no effect on Scott Carpenter.

In experimenting with the task of aligning the ship with the horizon by using a reticle, a scale etched on the cabin's forward window, Carpenter reported a discrepancy between the horizontal alignment he obtained visually and that on the automatic control system's horizon scanner. Alignment was critical for retrofire, when the retro-rockets had to be pitched up at the correct angle to assure that the vessel would arc down to the planned impact zone.

Assuming that the automatic scanning system was defective, Carpenter put the ship in retrofire attitude by manual control, but difficulty in overriding the automatic system caused him to fire the braking rockets manually several seconds late. As a result, *Aurora VII* was fated to overshoot the splashdown point. Carpenter reported that he did not get the "boot" when the rockets fired that Glenn had reported, but merely experienced a "gentle nudge." To flight controllers at the cape, the report suggested improper alignment for retrofire for the Atlantic landing.

Aurora VII did, indeed, overshoot its landing zone by 250 miles. It splashed down at 12:41 P.M., in an empty ocean, out of radio contact with the recovery vessel and the cape. Fearing the spacecraft was leaking and feeling hot and extremely uncomfortable, Carpenter opened the hatch and climbed out. He inflated a rubber life raft, moored it to the spacecraft, and made himself comfortable in it. He then started up a small but powerful radio beacon, designed to attract help. Within six minutes, the beacon signal was picked up by a navy search airplane, and thirty-four minutes later, he heard the aircraft overhead and signaled to it with a mirror. Never had a shipwrecked mariner received such prompt attention. The whole world was looking for him. A considerable amount of tension had been built up at the cape during a forty-one-minute period when Carpenter's whereabouts were undetermined. Fragments of a telemetry signal picked up at the cape indicated that *Aurora VII* had come down in one piece, but Mercury Control issued no public statement until the navy Neptune P2V aircraft reported that it had sighted *Aurora VII* and a gentleman sitting in a life raft beside it. After two hours, a helicopter arrived from the aircraft carrier U.S.S. *Intrepid* to pick up the gentleman and fly him to the carrier for a triumphal return.

In contrast to *MA-VII*, the flight of *MA-VIII*, *Sigma VII*, October 3, 1962, became as uneventful as a textbook mission, after a flight suit overheating problem was solved. The pilot, Walter Marty Schirra, Jr., thirty-nine, brought the spacecraft down after six revolutions just 9,000 yards from the aircraft carrier U.S.S. *Kearsarge* in the Pacific Ocean. Doubling the time in orbit had no ill effect on Schirra, but the excess heat and humidity in the flight suit during the first revolution had made him uncomfortable until he managed to correct the situation by experimenting with suit controls.

With these three missions and twelve orbits of experience, the Space Task Group engineers concluded that their technique of orbital flight and recovery was safe and that the mercury spacecraft was a viable machine. This was the first hurdle of the lunar mission. Once the technology was developed, the challenge became one of increasing sophistication and scale.

Mercury directors were now ready to test the spacecraft on a longer mission of twenty-two revolutions. Air Force Major Leroy Gordon Cooper, Jr., thirty-six, was selected to fly the extended mission in *MA-IX*, which he named *Faith VII*. Cooper was launched May 15, 1963, on the thirty-four-hour flight. Like Titov, Cooper found that he had to anchor his arms at his sides to keep them from extending upward or outward when he slept. In the tiny Mercury cabin, allowing his hands to dangle anywhere near the control console risked the inadvertent flipping of a switch.

Cooper's flight suit overheated, as Schirra's had, but he managed to re-

duce the temperature to a comfortable level. However, the suit's dehumid-
ifier was not working properly, and moisture collected in the suit, making
the pilot feel wet and clammy.

As he began his nineteenth revolution, with a good view of the Miami
area, Cooper reported a sequence of autopilot malfunctions that required
him to make a manual reentry. He aligned the ship on the twenty-second
revolution, fired the braking rockets, and splashed down three miles from
the *Kearsarge* in the Pacific.

So ended Project Mercury, nearly five years and more than $384 million
after it started. The money and the effort had put the United States on the
road to the Moon, but the Russians, meanwhile, had made dramatic gains.
They had developed a technique of group flight, with two ships in nearby orbits.

THE REPRODUCTION EXPERIMENT

Vostok III, with Andrian Gregoryevich Nikolayev in the pilot's couch, was
launched from Tyuratam August 11, 1962, on a flight of 94.4 hours—nearly
four times longer than the *Vostok II* mission. The next day, on August 12,
Vostok IV was launched, piloted by Pavel Romanovich Popovich, as Nikolayev began his seventeenth revolution. The timing and the inclination of the
launch were calculated to bring the two vessels close together at a point in
their respective orbits, a juxtaposition called rendezvous.

Nikolayev, whose call sign was *Falcon*, and Popovich, whose sign was
Golden Eagle, reported feeling well. Neither reported any sign of nausea,
vertigo, or disorientation. The pilots dined on "normal" food for the first time
in free fall instead of the toothpaste-tube-style rations and dehydrated food
packs well-meaning food technicians were inflicting on the American astronauts. The Russians had chicken, veal, and pies, which they praised as
delicious. They landed six miles apart on the same day near Karaganda,
Nikolayev after sixty-four orbits, a new space record, and Popovich after
forty-eight.

Although *Falcon* and *Golden Eagle* came within four miles of each other,
their craft were not equipped to link up. This required onboard propulsion
systems powerful enough to enable the vehicles to raise orbital altitude as
well as lower it by retrofire. The object of the exercise was to determine
whether launch accuracy made it feasible to attempt rendezvous and docking
without extensive maneuvers in orbit. In 1962, rendezvous in Earth orbit
was considered both in Russia and in America as an essential maneuver for a

lunar flight. If the Soviet space establishment had elected to use Earth-orbit rendezvous to go to the Moon, it had demonstrated the capability of doing it, according to Norman V. Petersen, the technical director of the Air Force Flight Test Center at Edwards Air Force Base, California. (Earth-orbit rendezvous is a method of assembling lunar flight components—such as fuel tanks, a landing vehicle, an interorbital spacecraft—in a low Earth orbit for the journey to the Moon. This procedure would require accurate, sequential launches, like those of *Vostoks III* and *IV*, as well as the capability of docking.) Petersen told the House Committee on Science and Astronautics: "I would certainly concur . . . that everything they have done to date supports a capacity for orbital assembly in space, and I am just hazarding a guess that this is the route they may take." [9]

Although Nikolayev and Popovich could not make physical contact, they could see each other at closest approach and communicate by both two-way radio and television. Each of the spherical five-ton vessels looked like a small moon to the pilot of the other. Their closest approach was logged officially at 6.5 kilometers and the maximum separation, 3,000 kilometers (1,800 miles).

The first group flight underscored the Russian lead in manned space flight, but it was not entirely clear what the double flight was designed to accomplish beyond demonstrating a potential for rendezvous and extending time in orbit. Although the launch accuracy the USSR space systems displayed was impressive, rendezvous was only a preliminary step toward docking in orbit. Docking was never achieved in the Vostok series.

Western observers at the time were undecided as to whether to interpret the group flight as a preliminary to a manned lunar flight program or as a test of the capability for intercepting a satellite in orbit by means of a shot from the ground. Observers in Washington leaned toward the view that the flight was "a successful exercise in Earth orbital rendezvous technique for a Moon landing." [10] Soviet academician Keldysh, frequently a spokesman for space policy, commented: "The flights in Vostok 3 and 4 mark a notable stage on this road which brings us closer to the realization of interplanetary flights." [11]

The climax of the Vostok program was the second group flight in 1963. The pilots were Lieutenant Colonel Valery Fyodorovich Bykovsky and the first female cosmonaut, Valentina Tereshkova, a twenty-five-year-old textile worker whose hobby was parachute jumping. She was accepted for cosmonaut training, although she was not a trained pilot, from a group of adventurous women who responded to a call for women volunteers to participate in space flight programs. Tereshkova had been thrilled by Gagarin's flight and had become fascinated by space flight. Her parachute experience, which included, of course, familiarity with the sensation of free fall, helped qualify her.

Bykovsky was launched in *Vostok V* June 14, 1963, and Tereshkova in *Vostok VI* two days later. Their closest approach was five kilometers (three miles). Both spacecraft landed in the region of Karaganda June 19, Bykovsky after eighty-one revolutions and Tereshkova after forty-eight. Despite the new flight record set by Bykovsky, world attention and admiration was focused on the attractive space woman, who, as the *London Daily Express* noted, became "the soaring symbol of feminine emancipation." A few months after the group flight, the world wondered if more was involved in the mission than a test of spacecraft and launch systems.

On November 3, 1963, cosmonaut Tereshkova and cosmonaut Andrian Nikolayev, the bachelor pilot of *Vostok III*, were married. The next year, cosmonaut Tereshkova-Nikolayev gave birth to a daughter weighing six pounds thirteen ounces. No abnormalities were reported in gestation or birth. The child was normal. It appeared that space travel had no effect on germ plasm, ova, or postflight conception and fetal development.

As of the end of 1975, Valentina Tereshkova remains the only woman to have flown in orbit. None has been recruited by NASA. Of the women inducted into the Soviet program, none but Tereshkova has been scheduled for flight in the twelve years up to this writing. It has been supposed by some Western observers that her experience satisfied an experiment on the effect of orbital flight on human reproduction. And with that assumed experiment, the Vostok program ended.

In America and Russia, a new phase of manned space flight began in 1964–1965. The United States produced an advanced version of the Mercury capsule, a two-man vehicle called Gemini, and the Soviets built a larger and more advanced version of Vostok called Voskhod. Both were intermediate steps in the further development of larger, more complex vehicles. These were the three-man Apollo in the American program and the Soyuz, capable of flying two or three men, in the Russian.

As the second round of the space race opened in 1964, the Soviet Union still held a commanding lead. Each competitor had flown six pilots, but there was a disparity in flight experience. At the end of Project Mercury, NASA had flown a total of 34 orbits and logged a cumulative flight time of 53 hours and 26 minutes. The six Russian pilots had flown 259 orbits and had logged 382 hours and 21 minutes in space. By that time, the missile gap was closed, but the space flight gap was still open.

SATURN

Developing spacecraft and learning to fly them in orbit was only half the battle for the Moon. The other half was the construction of a rocket capable of lifting at least 50 tons on a translunar flight path. As employees of the

Army Ballistic Missile Agency in 1958, the group of expatriate Germans headed by Wernher Von Braun had started the development of a super-rocket, the Saturn, to match Soviet big boosters. Like the Russian rockets, Saturn would use a cluster of engines.

The prototype of the C-1 was 80 feet long and 21½ feet in diameter. It was built in the shops of the Redstone Arsenal—later the Marshall Space Flight Center—at Huntsville, Alabama. Test models were then constructed and carried by barge from Marshall to Cape Canaveral via the Tennessee and Mississippi rivers, the Gulf of Mexico, around the Straits of Florida, and up through the Intracoastal Waterway to the Banana-Indian rivers estuary to Launch Pad 34. Only the first stage was "live" for the initial test on October 27, 1961. When dummy second and third stages were added, the Saturn C-1 stood 162 feet tall, dwarfing the 90-foot Atlas and Titan missiles, which were the largest in the air force inventory. Saturn was not designed as a weapon. It was the first rocket built specifically for space travel. Although some military potential was ascribed to it, none was ever realized. The Saturn family of rockets was developed specifically to win the space race.

On the morning of October 27, 1961, the first Saturn C-1 stood ready for launching on an eight-minute test flight down the Atlantic Missile Range. Of crucial importance was the performance of its eight H-1 engines in the "live" first stage. Three years of development had gone into this vehicle, initially authorized by the Advanced Research Projects Agency of the Department of Defense and later inherited, with the Von Braun group, by NASA.

In early tests, the H-1 engines were rated at 165,000 pounds of thrust instead of the design thrust of 188,000 each, giving the vehicle a first stage thrust potential of 1.3 million instead of 1.5 million pounds. Air Force public relations officers passed out plastic earplugs to an assembly of 300 news correspondents. The roar of the eight engines firing in unison would be the loudest ever heard at the cape.

Ignition produced an enormous gout of orange and yellow flame, as blinding as the sun. The first Saturn rose smoothly as the ground shook, arced high over the ocean on the long comet's-tail of its exhaust, and vanished behind distant clouds. Performance of all eight engines was flawless.

"So far as we know," said Robert C. Seamans, Jr., then NASA deputy administrator, "The Soviets have boosted vehicles weighing 750,000 to 800,000 pounds. Our vehicle weighed 925,000 pounds. Their booster [the Vostok launcher] would not have lifted the C-1 you saw today."

The "booster gap" was closed. But the C-1 was only the beginning of a deep space rocket program. It could lift 25 tons to orbit, with a second stage, but it could not lift 75 tons (NASA's 1961 estimate of Apollo's weight) to the Moon. A more powerful version of the Saturn was required for that chore. It would be the C-5, with a first stage of five clustered F-1 engines developing 1.5 million pounds of thrust each for a total of 7.5 million pounds; a second hydrogen-burning stage with a cluster of five J-2 engines putting out 1 million pounds of thrust; and a third stage with a single J-2 engine developing 200,000 pounds of thrust. This was the Moon rocket, as tall as the Wrigley Building in Chicago, the largest and most powerful vehicle ever built. Except as the American response to Cold War challenge and competition, it had no military purpose at all. Its only function was to boost men to the Moon.

THE DEBATE

During a twenty-two month hiatus between the end of Project Mercury and the first of Project Gemini's ten manned missions, doubts about Kennedy's lunar commitment and its cost flared into a national debate. Critics of the commitment, in Congress and in the scientific community, regarded the lunar adventure as a digression, an anomaly in national policy, with no foreseeable return on an enormous investment of at least $21 billion.

The critics did not accept the theory that international and ideological competition demanded such a response to Soviet space successes. Instead, many thoughtful and articulate observers regarded the Moon "madness" as an exhibition of nationalistic machismo, and space competition itself as an empty imperialistic gesture.

Liberals were suspicious of the program because of its semimilitary aspects. The members of the growing corps of astronauts, for example, were military pilots. Those intellectuals who regarded technological development in virtually every field as a threat to humanistic values denounced Project Apollo as a diversion of national resources from welfare and antipoverty programs, which had been chronically underfinanced. The Kennedy administration, they complained, had its eye on the moon rather than on the problems of poverty and illiteracy. Much of this criticism implied that if only the space program was abandoned, funds would become instantly available to cure the nation's social ills.

Historically, the complaint was chronic. The same kind of criticism delayed the first voyage of Columbus. Opponents of his mad scheme might have argued that the proceeds of the jewels Isabella was said to have pawned should have been invested in the educational system of fifteenth-century Spain, a system that taught that the Earth was the center of the universe.

Few of Apollo's critics regarded its scientific potential as worth a fraction of its cost. Fewer still accepted manned space flight as an evolutionary step in mankind's technoscientific development, a rationale that had motivated Space Age pioneers in the period between the world wars when dreams of interplanetary travel were the motive for rocket research.

Among the political liberals, many criticized space work as a costly project of the military-industrial complex, as, indeed, it was; but few of these critics considered that competition in space was a surrogate for armed conflict. In the context of that competition, the moon program was a keystone of the foreign policy of the Kennedy and Johnson administrations. In such a raison d'être lay the seeds of the manned flight program's dissolution, for once the Moon race was won, support for the costly program would dissolve.

The polarization of attitudes toward manned space flight produced curious alliances. Extremists on the right and left denounced it as militarism and as conspicuous waste, while conservatives, jingoists, and middle-of-the-roaders supported it. Big Business and Big Labor united in support of the lunar adventure, although so-called opinion leaders were ambivalent. The division showed that many political liberals were, technologically, conservative and that many conservatives were, technologically, progressive.

Liberals pointed out that space flight was essentially an "establishment" enterprise. The little people—the poor, the illiterate, the forgotten people of America—had no stake in it. Of what advantage was it to an Alabama sharecropper for America to be first on the Moon? The space program was robbing the poor, their leaders said. If the billions being spent on space were distributed among the poor, poverty would disappear, at least for a time.

Critics found numerous applications for space funds. The money could be used to cure cancer, build schools, provide better housing, feed welfare clients, supply hot lunches to every needy school child, and so on. Before Congress, NASA spokesmen cloaked the moon project in the raiment of defense when they pleaded for funds for Apollo. Defense was relatively untouchable, although the money it consumed could also build schools and housing and feed children.

In this period, the only argument that appealed to intellectuals was muted before Congressional committees. Apollo provided man with an opportunity to commence the scientific exploration of his extraterrestrial environment in situ. Such an investigation was essential to his understanding of the forces that shaped his habitat. And understanding his environment was the first step toward conserving it, as his increasing numbers seemed to demand.

But so far as overt debate went, this rationale was subordinated to the political and military exigencies of the moment. We were going to the Moon to win a battle in the Cold War. It appeared that blind response to competition, not rational foresight, was pushing man toward a mastery of the environment that was essential for his long-term survival. It was tempting to construe this as the working of the mystic forces of evolution and to say that man's fate lay literally in the stars. In terms of the origin of the elements, he had descended from them, a product of eons of biochemical evolution; and now he was taking the first feeble steps to spread out among them. The idea was romantic and exciting. Many space planners shared it privately, but not publicly. The time for dreaming was past. This was the time for doing, and that required practical men.

Although the Space Science Board of the National Academy of Sciences-National Research Council had given its blessing to Apollo, many critical voices in the scientific community were raised against the program. They complained that research funds needed in the laboratory were being squandered on hardware; that man's presence was not essential, nor especially important, in space vehicles; and that the Moon program was merely a military adventure that depleted federal resources for science. NASA officials thus found themselves obliged to defend not only space investigation in general but the manned program in particular.

All of these criticisms, both general and particular, discounted the political basis of Apollo and overlooked the historical reality that the mainstream of exploration by Western people had been motivated by competition. Intraspecific competition was an irresistible force for expansion. Apollo was an expression of it.

In the Soviet Union, where the leadership had been committed to space research since the end of World War II, despite the massive problems of postwar reconstruction, approximately 3 percent of the gross national product was allocated to space programs, according to data given the Senate space committee.[12] In 1964, the Soviet outlay for space research and development amounted to about $4.5 billion—about $1 billion less than the United States was spending that year on its total program, including Apollo.

Like some of their counterparts in America, Russian scientists had complaints about the funding emphasis on space, according to the American physicist Robert E. Marshak. "Russian colleagues in other fields of science constantly refer to the extent to which the Soviet space program drains off funds and personnel which might otherwise have been alloted to their programs," he wrote in 1963.[13]

During hearings by the House and Senate space committees on the NASA budget for the 1964 fiscal year, Webb found it necessary to make a vigorous defense of the space program in terms of its bearing on national power and prestige. Before the House committee on March 4, 1963, he argued that there was no economy in allowing the Russians to get ahead. Costs could be kept at $5.5 to $6 billion for the fiscal year 1964 "unless the Russians start doing something which makes you want to speed up." [14]

Webb then lapsed into a rhetorical justification of the program, which reflected the administration's attitude: "I happen to believe that this nation is engaged in a great contest with the Russians as to which form of government can effectively do the things that will build power." [15]

During 1963, President Kennedy found it advisable, in the light of growing criticism of space costs, to reiterate his commitment to the Moon. At his press conference of March 21, 1963, he stated: "We are expending an enormous sum of money to make sure that the Soviet Union does not dominate space. We will continue to do it." [16]

At another press conference, April 24, he was asked if he saw cause to reconsider the commitment in the light of the debate about the wisdom of the lunar program. He stated firmly that nothing had changed his attitude and that it would be a mistake to interfere with the development of Apollo by cutting expenditures. [17]

There was no ambiguity in the view of the lunar program by the president and the vice-president. It was a military necessity that they equated with national security. Webb had expressed this view in his March appearance before the House committee, saying: "My own view is that if we do not have a position of pre-eminence in space at the bargaining table of the nations or in the minds of the world's leaders, the decisions that bring peace or war are not apt to be of our making."

The vice-president, Lyndon B. Johnson, went a step further in a speech in Dallas. He warned that the lunar venture was a necessary risk because "failure to go into space was even riskier." If we do not succeed, we may not be first on the Moon, first in space, or first on the Earth, he said. [18] In this view, he implied that not being first among the hosts of the nations of the Earth would be catastrophic. This Roman self-image was an important ingredient in the determination of the Kennedy-Johnson administrations to push Project Apollo to a successful conclusion.

To critics who characterized the space race as "adolescent," Webb replied: "If it is adult of us to accept the role of second best to the Soviet Union, let us hope that this nation can maintain a position of perpetual adolescence." [19]

In the fall of 1963, doubt was raised by the critics that the Russians actually intended to land a man on the Moon. It was fanned by an ambiguous statement from Nikita Khrushchev at a press conference October 25, 1963, with journalists from developing nations. Asked about Russian lunar plans, the premier replied.

> It would be very interesting to take a trip to the Moon but I cannot at present say when this will be done. We are not at present planning flights by Cosmonauts to the Moon. . . . I have a report that the Americans want to land a man on the Moon by 1970 or 1980. Well, let's wish them success. . . . We shall take their experience into account. We do not want to compete with the sending of people to the Moon without careful preparation. It is clear that no benefits would be derived from such competition. [20]

This oracular comment seemed to indicate on one hand that the Russians were not involved in a race with anyone to put a man on the Moon, but it did not definitely say that Russians were not going to make the attempt. Perhaps Khrushchev realized that an ambiguous declaration was the best way to confound the Americans. Because Russia held a significant lead in space technology, there was no reason to boast of future intentions. It was the consistent policy of the USSR space directorate never to reveal plans in advance—a policy that, in contrast to NASA's practice of publicizing its intentions, served to conceal failures both of launches and entire programs.

A fortnight after his press conference, Khrushchev was asked, November 6, 1963, by a delegation of visiting American businessmen, why the Soviet Union was giving up a lunar landing. He replied: "We have never said that we are giving up our lunar project. You're the ones who said that." [21]

The question of whether the Russians were going to the Moon or not was further complicated by the report of the British astronomer Sir Bernard Lovell and its aftermath. In a letter to Hugh Dryden, deputy NASA administrator, dated July 23, 1963, Professor Lovell said that on a visit to Russia he had been told by Mstislav V. Keldysh, president of the USSR Academy of Sciences, that plans for a manned lunar landing had been cancelled. He quoted Keldysh as saying that fear of solar radiation and the lack of a sure method of bringing cosmonauts back alive from the Moon had led to this decision. Keldysh, he added, believed that instrumented probes could provide adequate scientific data. [22] However, on October 10, 1963, Keldysh denied, in an interview on Radio Prague, that he had told Lovell anything of the sort. "Professor Lovell obviously came to this conclusion by himself as we had never said this," Keldysh stated. [23]

In the light of these conflicting pronouncements, Webb admitted to the House Independent Offices Committee at an appropriations hearing in October 1963 that "we have no way of knowing what the Russians will do or what the competition will be." [24]

Consequently, the NASA administrator took a cautious defense stance before Congress, interpreting the Kennedy commitment to the Moon as signifying that the national goal was becoming the world's leading space-faring power, not merely being first on the Moon.

In the fall of 1963, the Grumman Aircraft Engineering Company, which was the prime contractor for the lunar excursion module, the vehicle that would ferry men between the orbiting Apollo mother ship and the surface of the Moon, had a poll taken on attitudes toward Apollo. Most opinion leaders surveyed by the polling organization Fuller, Smith & Ross, Inc., were not sold on the political advantages of a United States lunar landing by 1970. They predicted that any gains from winning the lunar sweepstakes would be short-lived and hardly worth the cost. But among the general public, nearly 50 percent was satisfied with the space program and the lunar goal and 25 percent wanted to accelerate it. Less than one-third believed that it should be slowed down or given a lower priority on the scale of national needs. [25]

In general, the mass media of communication in America supported the Moon program and found in it a wealth of feature material. *Life* magazine made a contract with the Mercury Astronauts to purchase their personal-experience stories, and the Corporate Educational Division of Field Enterprises, Inc., publisher of *World Book Encyclopedia*, later joined in the agreement. NASA approved these arrangements on the theory that the astronauts had the right to sell their private memoirs so long as this arrangement did not come into conflict with their obligation to make public their experiences at postflight press conferences. The *Life* magazine stories were highly entertaining, ostensibly narrated by the astronauts but actually put together by professional writers. Postflight press conferences could not compete in detail and in color with these exclusive accounts. A number of metropolitan daily newspaper editors who sent their own correspondents to Cape Canaveral to cover major launches complained about the private deal. It appeared to critics that astronauts would not talk unless they were paid. Interviews with them were difficult to arrange, and even when one was granted, their stereotyped, stilted responses made indifferent copy. I believe the *Life*-Field Enterprises arrangements with the astronauts were consistent with competitive journalism, although as a reporter for a Field Enterprises newspaper, the *Chicago Sun-Times*, I received no benefit whatever from them and found myself in the same position as every other correspondent from a nonfavored publication. Although it was part of the news division of the Field Enterprises organization, the *Sun-Times* itself did not benefit from the *World Book* deal. However, I was in a position to observe the results of the Field Enterprises arrangements with the astronauts, and I concluded that the financial problems outweighed the advantages. The space program was open enough so that anyone who did his homework in space science and technology could cover it adequately. The main story line was the one that was visible. The rest, including much of the "inside" material fed to syndicated columnists and television news personalities, was so much fluff, with no particular significance.

In brief, the space story was so big, so magnificent, so obvious that no one who kept his eyes open and paid attention could miss it. But, although the *Life-World Book* deal did not deprive any aggressive journalist of opportunity to learn what was going on, it contributed to a process of alienation between NASA and newspaper editors and correspondents that was to continue through Apollo.

Among the influential proponents of the lunar effort were leaders of the scientific community who believed that space exploration was essential to scientific development. One was Harold C. Urey, professor of chemistry at the University of California, La Jolla. He told a Senate space committee hearing on national space goals that he approved a program that would make the United States preeminent in space. Failure to achieve that, said Urey, "would either indicate a certain corrosion of character which I would not like to admit or it would indicate that corrosion of character is coming in the future and that if that is the sort of spirit that this country has, that sooner or later it will be second rate." [26]

Another witness at the Senate committee hearing on space goals was Berkner, then president of the Graduate Research Center of the Southwest. The conquest of space, he said, has acquired "an enormous international political value. The nation that can achieve and retain space superiority will have won the equivalent of a war in demonstrating the superior viability of its system in the eyes of the world." Viewing the space race as an ideological contest, Vice-President Johnson remarked that "a failure in space would be the costliest failure in our national history." [27] Shortly before he was assassinated, President Kennedy told a rally in Fort Worth: "We believe that the new environment, space, the new sea, is also an area where the United States should be second to none." [28]

GEMINI

In an article entitled "Manned Space Stations," which was published in *Izvestia* in 1964, Major General Nikolai L. Kamanin, commander of the cosmonaut training school, and an engineer, I. N. Bubnov, laid out the following program of Soviet lunar exploration: [29] A soft landing on the Moon by an automatic station, 1964–1965; manned circumlunar flight, 1966–1967; a three-man space station, 1967–1970; manned lunar landing, 1968–1970; manned flights to Mars and Venus, 1975–1980; manned landing on Mars, 1980–1990.

The program was ambitious inasmuch as neither rockets nor spacecraft existed in 1964, in Russia or in the United States, that were capable of flying men around the Moon and back. Both countries, however, were rushing to develop automatic vehicles that could be soft landed on the moon—a contest Russia was to win in 1966 with *Luna IX*.

Although the Kamanin timetable was considered highly speculative, it had some propulsive force on the American program. It was now possible for NASA officials to point at a Russian plan. Although unofficial, it had as much authority behind it as Sedov's pre-Sputnik predictions that the Soviets were planning to put a satellite into orbit.

During 1964, a second-generation American spacecraft was in construction, the two-man vessel called Gemini. It had to be maneuverable in orbit to accomplish rendezvous and docking with another vehicle, a requirement of a lunar journey. It had to be more than a capsule. It had to be a vessel that men could navigate in space—a spaceship.

Like Mercury, Gemini was roughly bell-shaped, with the crew compartment in the tapered end, or reentry section. In the wide section, called the adapter, a complex system of maneuvering rocket engines was housed, along with fuel and oxygen tanks. Gemini obtained electrical power from fuel cells that produced electrical current chemically by mixing hydrogen and oxygen, with water as a by-product. These devices greatly extended its service time in space, compared with the storage battery power supply in Mercury. Weighing 8,300 pounds, two and one-half times the weight of Mercury, Gemini was 20 percent larger, and its cabin had 50 percent more volume. The astronaut couches were placed side by side in the familiar pilot-copilot arrangement of an aircraft cockpit. With the adapter section, Gemini was nineteen feet long and ten feet in diameter. It was smaller than the early Vostoks, which were twenty-two feet long and twelve to fourteen feet wide. It was also somewhat lighter. The Vostoks weighed about 10,000 pounds and were spherical rather than conical.

Instead of the steeple-shaped rocket escape tower that Mercury carried to pull the capsule away from the launch vehicle in the event of a malfunction on the pad, Gemini had ejection seats for emergency escape on the pad or during launch. Otherwise, the crew remained in the cabin for landing. Early Gemini design included a stowable paraglider or Rogallo wing (designed by Francis M. Rogallo, of the Langley Research Center) that could be deployed for a glider-style landing on a runway after the craft had reentered the atmosphere. However, the time and cost required to develop the new landing device persuaded NASA to abandon it and use the reliable Mercury parachute-water recovery system.

Gemini was developed with remarkable speed and confidence at the McDonnell Aircraft Company plant in Saint Louis. If Mercury was designed for a chimpanzee, with its automatic controls, Gemini was built for man. In Gemini, the pilot had much more to do in controlling the craft than in Mercury. He actually flew the vessel. For maneuvering in space, which meant changing orbit, Gemini carried an orbital attitude maneuvering system (OAMS). It consisted of sixteen thrusters. Two with 100 pounds of thrust provided forward acceleration to increase altitude, two with 85 pounds of thrust provided deceleration to lower altitude; four 100-pound thrusters enabled the craft to move sideways, up, or down; and eight 25-pound engines provided pitch, roll, and yaw control. Aft, in the retrograde segment of the adapter section, were four solid propellant rocket engines. These were ripple fired in overlapping sequence for the deorbiting maneuver that would bring the spacecraft back to Earth.

After retrofire, the reentry section, consisting of the crew compartment and parachute descent system, was separated from the adapter, which was literally thrown away and destroyed by the heat of reentry. The reentry section, equipped with a Mercury-style heat shield, was controlled during the turbulence of reentry by eight twenty-five-pounds-of-thrust jets with which the crew could control the capsule's attitude. The pilot could operate the thrusters with a hand controller or allow the autopilot to fire them.

The conical nose of Gemini, which contained the drogue and 84.2 foot main parachute, also was equipped with an electrical connector and latches for docking with another vehicle in orbit. In the Gemini project, the docking target was an Agena rocket, the second-stage vehicle that the air force had developed for its Atlas and Thor boosters. By docking with a previously orbited Agena in a low Earth orbit, Gemini would acquire a second booster that could lift it to very high altitudes. Theoretically, it was possible to attain a circumlunar orbit by this method of Earth-orbit rendezvous with a sufficiently powerful booster. Agena could not do the job, but more powerful upper-rocket stages, powered by the new, hydrogen-oxygen engines, could put the two-seater spacecraft around the moon on a free return trajectory—a flight path that would bring it back to Earth for a landing.

As the Gemini project opened, Earth-orbit rendezvous was the method NASA planners contemplated for the lunar landing, and Gemini was the first step in developing the technique; similarly, the Vostok group flights appeared to be the USSR's first step in that direction.

As Gemini was being prepared for its first manned launching aboard the air force's Titan 2 missile, a more powerful booster than the Atlas, the Soviet State Commission for Space Exploration unveiled its new spaceship, Voskhod ("Sunrise"). This improved vehicle was launched October 12, 1964, from Tyuratam on a seventeen-orbit flight with three cosmonauts: Vladimir Komarov; Konstantin P. Feokstistov, a scientist; and a physician, Boris B. Yegorov. It was the first multiman space flight. During the mission, the crewmen took off their flight suits and luxuriated in a shirt-sleeve environment. *Voskhod I* reentered on its seventeenth revolution and landed on parachutes, with the crew remaining inside instead of being individually ejected as in the Vostok.

Six months later, on March 18, 1965, the Russians launched *Voskhod II*, with two men aboard: Aleksei A. Leonov and Pavel A. Belyayev. During the second orbit of the seventeen-orbit flight, Leonov, wearing a newly designed space suit, crowded into an airlock where pressure was reduced from the sea-level pressure, oxygen-nitrogen atmosphere of the Voskhod cabin, to the vacuum of space. He then climbed out of chamber when Belyayev opened the hatch and floated at the end of a tether for ten delightful, exhilarating minutes to become the first space-walker or, in this instance, floater.[30]

Leonov shoved himself about fifteen feet from the vessel. He photographed the Earth and ship while an automatic television camera observed him. He assumed horizontal and vertical positions with ease, experiencing no vertigo or nausea.

At a postflight press conference, Leonov said that as he drifted beside the ship, he felt exhilaration. When he tugged ever so lightly on the tether that kept him from drifting off, he returned to the metal wall of the ship so swiftly that he felt it necessary to protect his helmet visor with his gloved hands from striking the vessel. One day, he predicted, cosmonauts would maneuver outside of their spacecraft like deep-sea divers, using portable propulsion systems.[31]

The flight of *Voskhod II* came just five days before astronauts Virgil I. (Gus) Grissom and John W. Young flew the first Gemini mission. Leonov's space walk had the effect of upstaging the introduction of the second-generation American spacecraft and reminding Congress and the public that the Russians were still ahead. The National Aeronautics & Space Council secretary, Edward C. Welsh, commented: "This is a logical extension of the manned space program that they have. It helps them to maintain the lead they have over us in manned space flight. It shows that they have a space suit sufficiently well developed and designed to permit men to move outside their spacecraft." [32] Representative George P. Miller (D-California), chairman of the House Space Committee, said : "I don't think they have done anything that we have not planned. But they have gotten ahead of us. This shows we will have to tighten our belt and get along." [33]

The Russians lost no opportunity to make political use of Leonov's feat. The cosmonaut-training detachment commander, General Kamanin, cited Voskhod as an example of the superiority of the Soviet space program. He pointed out that the improved Russian vessel weighed 6,000 kilograms compared with Gemini's 3,175 kilograms and that it flew at a peak altitude of 500 kilometers compared with Mercury's top altitude of 285 kilometers (reached by Schirra in *MA-VIII*. Soviet vessels could make soft landings on land, he added, whereas the American ones had to splash down in the sea. The Voskhod (A-2) booster, he continued, developed 650 metric tons (1.4 million pounds) of thrust compared to the 240 metric tons (528,000 pounds) developed by the two-stage Titan 2 launcher. Belyayev told the postflight press conference of March 27, 1965: "Our Soviet man was the first in the world to step out directly into outer space. Is this not proof of the superiority of the Socialist system over the capitalist one? Of Soviet science and technology over bourgeois science and technology?" [34]

CRUISE OF *THE MOLLY BROWN*

On the morning of March 23, 1965, astronauts Grissom and Young climbed into the first of the manned Gemini spacecraft, *Gemini III*. Nearly two years had passed since Gordon Cooper's thirty-four-hour flight in *Mercury-Atlas IX*. In the roomier two-seater, which they had christened *The Molly Brown*, they waited for the ignition of the ninety-foot, two stage Titan 2 rocket that would boost them into orbit on the first manned test of the new vehicle. The spacecraft was named for the musical comedy, then popular, *The Unsinkable Molly Brown*. The title, not the plot of the musical, suggested Grissom's narrow escape from drowning after the splashdown of *Mercury-Redstone IV*, July 21, 1961. NASA headquarters executives and Manned Spacecraft Center chiefs dropped the practice of naming vehicles in Gemini and referred officially to the flights by number, starting with III and ending with XII. The name *Molly Brown* stuck to *Gemini III*, however, although it did not convey an image that agency executives considered appropriate.

The Titan lifted on a swirl of pale violet fire from Pad 19 at 9:24 A.M., Eastern Standard Time. Both stages of the missile fired smoothly and injected *The Molly Brown* into an oval orbit of 100-by-139 miles altitude. On their first revolution, the pilots saw the friendly lights of Perth, Australia twinkling far below in the abyssal dark.

As they approached the end of their first revolution, the crewmen performed the first orbit change. Grissom fired the 100-pound OAMS thrusters in the direction of flight for seventy-four seconds. The braking effect reduced velocity by 50 feet a second and lowered the vessel's apogee (peak altitude) from 139 to 105 miles to make the orbit more circular. The maneuver was the first step toward making rendezvous with another vehicle in orbit.

On the second revolution, Grissom changed the orbital plane one-fiftieth of a degree by firing the 100-pound thrusters to nudge the vessel out of plane. On their third and final revolution, he and Young tested their ability to fly the spacecraft to a designated splashdown area in the Atlantic Ocean after reentry.

Gemini was designed to have lift as it passed through the high atmosphere at supersonic speed. Its offset center of gravity enabled the pilots to increase or decrease the lift vector by rolling the vessel around its long axis. In this way, they could control the length of their descent arc. They could extend it by 200 miles by rolling to a heads-down position, or shorten it a similar distance by flying heads up. The lift vector could be neutralized by continuously rolling the vehicle so that its descent would follow a ballistic arc.

A small computer aboard Gemini figured the amount of roll or "bank angle" required to carry the capsule to a predetermined splash point. In *Gemini III*, Grissom and Young found themselves at the beginning of the learning curve in the art of descent navigation. Their reentry on their third revolution was smooth enough, but their descent control was somewhat imperfect. They splashed down fifty-eight miles short of the impact area where the aircraft carrier *Intrepid* waited for them.

Nevertheless, the flight of *The Molly Brown* was a notable success. Leonov's space walk on *Voskhod II* five days earlier had been a hard act to follow, but as a parallel to *Voskhod I* the flight of *Gemini III* showed that NASA was catching up. The space agency moved fast to duplicate Leonov's feat on the next mission, *Gemini IV*. The Gemini flight suit was modified to protect a man outside the vehicle and fitted to air force Major Edward H. White, II, thirty-four. He and air force Major James A. McDivitt, thirty-five, were the crew of the second Gemini space mission.

On the morning of June 3, 1965, the two Air Force officers climbed into the Gemini cabin and were boosted uneventfully into orbit on a flight programmed for four days. Their first task was to attempt to make rendezvous with the second stage of the Titan 2 rocket after separating from it. The Titan second stage was a sizable target, twenty-seven feet long and ten feet in diameter. It was equipped with a flasher beacon to make it more visible.

Again, at the beginning of the learning curve in orbital navigation and control, the crewmen found that maneuvering the Gemini close to the dead rocket stage was harder than it looked. McDivitt, the command pilot, found that it took more fuel than expected to remain near the rocket, which kept tumbling away from the spacecraft as though propelled by some agency of its own. After half of the OAMS fuel was spent, the ground advised the crew to abandon the attempt to keep "station" with the rocket.

After an orbit of preparation, the astronauts depressurized the Gemini cabin as they passed over Australia about four hours after launch, protected by their space suit life-support systems. Because Gemini's cabin atmosphere was pure oxygen at five pounds per square inch, there was no need for an airlock, Voskhod-style. Once the Gemini cabin atmosphere was exhausted into space, all White had to do was to open the hatch above his seat and step outside into the interplanetary medium.

White first stood up in his seat, his head and shoulders extending above the craft. Then, as Gemini IV passed north of Hawaii, he stepped outside. He propelled himself to the end of his tether with a portable gas thruster that somebody had named a "Zot" gun, in comic strip parlance. For a few minutes, White practiced with the gun. He reported enthusiastically that by controlling one's pitch and yaw one could actually move from point A to point B. With his trusty Zot gun, the space-suited pilot was mobile in all directions like a fish in the sea. He was a miniature spaceship. It was a science fantasy dream come true, and White relished every second of it, moving about with glee until his Zot gun ran out of gas.

White experienced no symptoms of disorientation, vertigo, or nausea. In fact, his rambling happy monologue directed to McDivitt and the ground suggested euphoria. The first American space walker—or, more accurately, swimmer—remained outside as Gemini IV crossed the California coast; passed over Texas, where McDivitt reported sighting Galveston Bay; and sped beyond the east coast toward Bermuda. It took the combined coaxing of McDivitt and the ground controllers to persuade White to come back into the capsule so that the hatches could be battened down before dark. White yielded to these entreaties, complaining that returning to his seat after floating wild and free in space was "the saddest moment of my life." Shortly after noon of June 7, 1965, on their sixty-third revolution, McDivitt and White splashed down, about fifty miles short of the planned impact area.

Next up was *Gemini V*, scheduled to fly an eight-day mission that would set a new record for man in orbit. The mission took off from Pad 19 on the morning of August 21, 1965, with Cooper and Charles (Pete) Conrad, Jr., thirty-five, a lieutenant commander in the navy, aboard.

A sequence of minor difficulties starting with a malfunction in the fuel cell battery power supply threatened to curtail the flight, but the flight director, Kraft, kept it going while the crew managed to deal with the problems. On August 26, Cooper and Conrad surpassed the five-day flight record of Bykovsky in *Vostok V*. After that, thruster trouble appeared in the OAMS system, and again the pilots were kept busy proving their ingenuity by devising means to compensate for it.

Gemini carried a detachable pod, which contained a radar transponder, a device that amplifies and reflects a radar signal back toward the source. The transponder made the small pod "visible" to the Gemini radar at a considerable distance. Deployed in orbit, the pod was to be used as a rendezvous target. However, after setting the pod free so that it would drift away from the spacecraft, the crew preoccupation with fuel cell trouble delayed the rendezvous exercise so long that the batteries powering the pod transponder were exhausted before rendezvous maneuvers could be started.

The pod experiment was the first of a series of abortive efforts to use various devices as rendezvous targets. Equipment malfunctions and failures harrassed the Gemini pilots through most of the ten-flight program. Nevertheless, the program succeeded in its basic purpose. In it, astronauts learned how to fly in space.

On the morning of August 29, after 120 revolutions and eight days in orbit, Cooper and Conrad brought *Gemini V* down in the Atlantic Ocean southwest of Bermuda. The United States now held the manned space flight endurance record.

The main experiment on this flight involved the condition of the crew after prolonged exposure to zero gravity. Both astronauts were able to walk when they returned, a result the medical team had reason to hope for but could not ascertain without an actual flight experience. Eight days in orbit was long enough for a flight around the Moon, and *Gemini V* proved that such a mission was physiologically feasible.

The unresolved rendezvous problem still confronted the Gemini curriculum in astronautics. The next exercise was to link up with an Agena rocket that would be placed in orbit before the Gemini lift-off.

The Agena was launched from Pad 12 on Cape Canaveral by an Atlas ICBM on the morning of October 25, 1965. Astronauts Schirra and Thomas P. Stafford, thirty-five, a major in the air force, sat in *Gemini VI* on Pad 19 waiting for radar confirmation that the Agena had entered the planned 185-mile circular orbit.

The exercise called for making rendezvous with the Agena and docking with it on Gemini's fourth revolution. Once the linkup was made, the Gemini crew could control the Agena's 16,000 pounds of thrust engine by means of electrical interconnections in the docking assembly. By firing the Agena engine, the crew could then boost the joined vehicles to higher altitudes.

In the earlier stages of the Apollo program, as I have related, this method of rendezvous in Earth orbit was contemplated as a means of using an orbital booster for the push to the Moon. By 1965, however, Earth-orbit rendezvous had been abandoned as a strategy for landing on the Moon in favor of a plan calling for rendezvous in lunar orbit, which I will describe in the next chapter. Even so, the technique of rendezvous and docking in orbit was essential whether it took place around the Earth or around the Moon. It was required for lunar flight and for the development of a space station.

The series of malfunctions that plagued Gemini from the beginning frustrated the rendezvous-docking test on the *Gemini VI* mission. After separating from the Atlas, the Agena vanished from the radar screens. Chaff that appeared on the screens indicated that the rocket had blown up when its engines ignited. Gemini Control waited, however, for a report from Australia, where radar scanned the heavens for the missing rocket. The report was, "No joy"—the rocket was not detected.

Mission Control then postponed the mission, and after hours of waiting to be launched, Schirra and Stafford climbed down from *Gemini VI*. The exercise was rescheduled for December.

Meanwhile, NASA went ahead with plans to launch *Gemini VII* on a fourteen-day flight to determine how men would tolerate a lunar landing mission approaching that duration. Air force Major Frank Borman and navy Commander James A. Lovell, Jr., both thirty-seven years old, were the crew. *Gemini VII* was launched on the afternoon of December 4, 1965. Then, on the morning of December 12, after *Gemini VII* had been in orbit eight days, Schirra and Stafford climbed back into *Gemini VI* to chase *Gemini VII* as a rendezvous target. It was indeed a target of opportunity, but the bad luck that had pursued Gemini all year persisted. The Titan 2 engines shut down suddenly after ignition, and Schirra and Stafford came close to ejecting from the capsule until they realized that the big rocket had failed safe.

The third attempt to launch *Gemini VI* succeeded in putting the vehicle into orbit on the morning of December 15. On the third revolution, Schirra announced that he "locked on" to *Gemini VII* with his radar. During midafternoon that day, he eased *Gemini VI* to within one foot of *Gemini VII*. The first American group flight rendezvous had been achieved, seemingly with ease once the vehicles functioned properly.

In *Gemini VII*, Borman and Lovell reported that they could see a sign in the window of their companion spacecraft. The sign did not quite reflect the magnitude of this historical moment, but it bore a message: "Beat Army." Schirra, a master pilot, flew *Gemini VI* around *Gemini VII*, and he and Stafford continued formation flight for a total of twenty hours and twenty-two minutes. On December 16, the crew of *Gemini VI* broke formation and reentered, coming down thirteen miles west of the carrier *Wasp*.

Upstairs, Borman and Lovell continued on their appointed rounds. For comfort, they removed flight suits and stripped down to their underwear. On the morning of December 18, 1965, they reentered and splashed down in the Atlantic about 700 miles southeast of Cape Canaveral. Theirs was another new record in space—330 hours and 35 minutes, just 5 hours and 25 minutes short of a full 14 days. On the deck of the carrier *Wasp*, their legs felt heavy and rubbery, and they walked as though trudging through a swamp. But they walked! The postflight physical examinations and an exhaustive series of tests showed physiological changes, but these reverted to normal after the crewmen returned to Houston for rest and debriefing. There was no doubt now that, so far as his ability to tolerate zero gravity was concerned, a trained man was physiologically able to endure a flight to the Moon lasting up to two weeks.

Rendezvous and docking with an Agena rocket were finally accomplished on March 16, 1966, by Neil A. Armstrong, thirty-five, a civilian test pilot, and Major David R. Scott, thirty-three, of the air force. They linked up with the rocket on the fifth revolution of *Gemini VIII*. But soon, the trouble that persisted intermittently in this program reappeared.

After docking, the crew tried out the secondary propulsion system of the Agena to turn the joined vehicles ninety degrees. Then, twenty-seven minutes after docking, the joined vehicles began an uncontrolled rolling motion of their own. The roll was accompanied by pitching and yawing. In vain, the pilots attempted to stabilize the joined vehicles by sending commands to the Agena secondary propulsion system. For a while, the crew succeeded in damping down the gyrations, but not for long; they resumed, becoming more violent as the crew sought to regain control.

Fearing that Gemini would be ruptured by the violent swinging and turning, the crew hastily undocked from the Agena, which they assumed was causing the trouble. But that assumption was wrong, as they realized as soon as Gemini was free of Agena and began to gyrate more violently than ever. It was the Gemini OAMS thrusters that were firing wildly, presumably because of some electrical malfunction, not the Agena's. As long as it was docked to the Agena, the Gemini oscillations were damped somewhat by the mass of the rocket; free of the rocket, the spacecraft seemed to go wild.

Armstrong and Scott managed to get partial control of their ship by using the reentry control system. Mission Control instructed them to make an emergency land in the Pacific Ocean. Gradually, the astronauts regained control over the OAMS systems and asked consent to continue the flight, but flight rules required a landing once reentry thrusters were used. If the crew had to resort to emergency use of the reentry control system again during orbital flight, fuel consumption in the emergency might compromise the system's capacity to control the capsule during reentry.

Gemini VIII landed in the swells of the western Pacific Ocean between Okinawa and Japan at 10:23 P.M. Eastern Standard Time that event-filled day. The crew was recovered by a navy destroyer, the *Mason,* and taken to Okinawa. Because the adapter section where the OAMS problem was located was jettisoned before reentry, there was no way of determining precisely what had caused the thrusters to fire out of control. An electrical short circuit was later cited as the probable cause.

The third attempt in the Gemini program to dock with an Agena was frustrated May 17, 1966, when a malfunction in the Atlas booster's guidance system prevented the Agena from achieving orbit. The breakdown left Stafford and navy Lieutenant Commander Eugene A. Cernan, thirty-two, sitting disconsolately in *Gemini IX* without a target. The mission was scrubbed.

Anxious to keep the Gemini program moving along, NASA did not wait until the air force could provide another specially rigged Agena; it substituted a makeshift target. It consisted of Gemini parts, including a docking mechanism. It was launched June 1, 1966, but *Gemini IX* did not leave the pad until June 3, delayed by computer trouble.

On their third revolution, Stafford and Cernan made rendezvous with the twelve-foot target and saw that a shroud, designed to protect the vehicle during flight through the atmosphere, had not been jettisoned. Two jawlike segments of the shroud had opened partly and then had become stuck in that position. Stafford reported that the contraption looked like an "angry alligator." Docking was not possible with the shroud in the way, but he and Cernan practiced rendezvous with the "weird machine" and at one point came within a foot of it so that Cernan could photograph the opened jaws.

On the program was a space walk, to be executed by Cernan. It was designed as a test of a spaceman's ability to do useful work outside the ship in free fall. Cernan climbed out of the ship on June 5. He attempted to don a backpack maneuvering unit as soon as he was free of the hatch, but in struggling to get his bulky spacesuit arms through the harness, he breathed so hard that his face plate became fogged, and he could not see. Abandoning the backpack, Cernan found that once his air conditioning system was overloaded with moisture, the fogging of the face plate persisted. This and other minor problems made it impractical to continue attempting to perform specific tasks. After an hour and twenty-six minutes of exhausting effort, Cernan returned to his seat.

Stafford landed *Gemini IX* in the Atlantic Ocean within two miles of the *Wasp.* Descent piloting had improved, but Manned Spaceflight executives and astronauts realized there was a considerable amount of work to be done in learning how to work in free fall outside a spacecraft.

With *Gemini IX,* the program's rendezvous difficulties ended. On *Gemini X,* John Young and air force Major Michael Collins, thirty-five, made rendezvous with their target Agena five hours and twenty-one minutes after launch

July 18, 1966. This time, no problems appeared after they docked.

Young fired the Agena's main engine, which boosted the joined vehicles to 458 miles above the Earth. It was a new world record. Opening the hatches, Collins stood up in his seat and took photographs of stars in ultraviolet light for Professor Karl Henize, astronomer. Henize later joined the corps of astronauts as one of a group of scientist-astronauts.

Collins' open-hatch photography chore was curtailed, however, by the infiltration of an eye irritant in the breathing oxygen. It had the effect of tear gas, forcing the crewmen to close the hatches, repressurize the cabin with fresh oxygen, and take off helmets. The irritant was later identified as a residue of a chemical compound used on the face plates to inhibit fogging.

On the third day of the flight, Young undocked from the Agena and adjusted his orbit to make rendezvous with the *Gemini VIII* Agena, the rocket that had been hastily abandoned by Armstrong and Scott in March. He pulled up alongside the derelict second stage but made no attempt to dock with it. The crew then depressurized the cabin, and Collins climbed out. Using the Zot gun, he pushed himself across a three-foot gulf separating the vehicles and climbed on the rocket. He retrieved a cannister of microorganisms that had been carried aloft in March in a test of their ability to survive space conditions. Among the organisms were T-1 bacteriophage, some of which had survived four months in space. Dwindling fuel persuaded the crew to cut the EVA (extravehicular activity) time from the planned fifty-five to thirty-five minutes. Young and Collins brought *Gemini X* down to an Atlantic landing July 21, 1966.

The following September 12, 1966, the climax of Project Gemini was achieved. Conrad and Lieutenant Commander Richard F. Gordon, Jr., thirty-six, of the navy, made rendezvous and docked with their Agena target on the first revolution of *Gemini XI*. After testing the performance of the joined vehicles, Gordon climbed out of the capsule on the fifteenth revolution and tied the rocket to the spacecraft with a 100-foot nylon rope. When the vehicles were later undocked, the tether would prevent them from drifting more than 100 feet apart.

The purpose of the maneuver was to determine whether Earth's gravity would stabilize the attitude of the tethered vehicles if they were aligned vertically with the ground. In theory, a vertical alignment would result in a gravitational gradient wherein gravitational force would be greater on the lower part of the system than on the upper part. If the theory worked out in practice, a large space station could be anchored in orbit this way.

Gordon was scheduled to perform two hours of extravehicular activity, but, like Cernan, he was blinded by perspiration that fogged his face plate as he struggled to do routine tasks. Unable to see, he finally had to climb back into the cabin after forty-four minutes.

When the cabin was repressurized and the crewmen removed their helmets, Conrad fired the Agena engine. It boosted the joined vehicles to 850.5

miles, a new altitude record. He then reduced altitude to 180 miles with a retrograde burn of the Agena.

On the thirty-second revolution, Conrad aligned the vehicles vertically in reference to the ground for the gravitational-gradient experiment. He then undocked and backed away from Agena. The two vehicles remained tethered but the tether itself would not become taut. Instead, a big bow formed in the line and persisted despite the crew's effort to straighten it out by moving the Gemini back and forth. Conrad advised the ground that the tether looked like a skip rope.

He then fired the Gemini OAMS thrusters to start the vehicles rotating around each other like the ends of a dumbbell turning on its long axis. Immediately, the tether jerked taut. And gradually the motions of the vehicles were damped out as they revolved around each other every nine minutes. The rotation produced 1.5 thousandths of a gravity, it was estimated, causing a pencil afloat in the cabin to settle against a rear wall.

After two hours of playing this game, Conrad released the tether from Gemini by firing a small explosive charge, and he and Gordon watched the rope wind itself around the Agena. They landed September 15 in the Atlantic Ocean about 700 miles southeast of Cape Canaveral.

In Gemini, the physical exertion of EVA had proved more difficult than anyone had anticipated. With no place to stand, the astronaut trying to work outside the ship had to brace one set of muscles against another to turn a screw or a bolt. If he used a hammer or mallet, he had to clutch a handhold as he swung the tool so that the blow would not push him away from the vessel. In free fall, Newton's law that every action has an equal and opposite reaction worked with a vengeance. The simple act of tightening a nut with a wrench could cause the workman to rotate with the turn of the tool.

There was one more opportunity in the program to tackle the problem of working in EVA—*Gemini XII*. The astronaut scheduled to perform EVA on the final mission was air force Major Edwin E. (Buzz) Aldrin, Jr., thirty-six. He rehearsed his EVA maneuvers for months in a swimming pool, coached by Cernan and Gordon.

Gemini XII was boosted into orbit on the afternoon of November 11, 1966. Lovell, the command pilot, caught the target Agena on the third revolution. However, a telemetry indication from the rocket of a defective fuel pump forced the crew to abandon an attempt to use the Agena engine.

On the morning of November 13, Aldrin stepped out of the capsule to examine the problem of working while falling free around the Earth. He was careful at the outset to avoid overloading his air-conditioner with body heat. As his mentors had advised, he took it easy. Moving on to Agena, he picked up a tether stowed there and fastened it to Gemini. He climbed back aboard Gemini and cleaned the windshield of dirt he supposed was picked up during the powered flight up through the atmosphere. But most of the dirt, Lovell told him, was on the inside of the window.

Using foot restraints and a body tether on the adapter section, Aldrin found he could turn bolts without turning himself around. For two hours and nineteen minutes, he worked carefully and completed simple tasks such as attaching and detaching electrical connectors and mechanical devices that had been affixed to the adapter for this exercise. The training paid off. Aldrin proved that it was possible for a trained man to work in free fall. It meant that men could construct large space stations in orbit, provided that conventional techniques of metalworking, such as welding and brazing, could be applied in the airless environment of zero gravity. Experiments to determine whether these processes could be carried on in orbit were five years downstream from Gemini. By the end of 1966, however, Americans had learned techniques that later would enable them to repair a space station seemingly hopelessly disabled and make it habitable for months.

After Aldrin returned to the cabin, Lovell undocked and repeated the gravitational-gradient experiment that had been attempted on *Gemini XI* with such curious results. This time, after an initial period of rolling, the linked vehicles, which formed a system 145 feet long pointing Earthward, finally stabilized. It took about three hours for the oscillations to damp out.

Lovell then brought *Gemini XII* down November 15 to an Atlantic landing within sight of the carrier *Wasp*. Gemini was completed. It was difficult for experts to recall any program in the history of flight that had started so trouble-ridden and succeeded so well. Gilruth, the manned space flight chief, summed it up: "In the 10 manned flights in 18 months, we did all the things we had to do as the prelude to Apollo."

THE BLUE PLANET

Two years passed. On the morning of December 24, 1968, three men fell toward the moon at 2,700 miles an hour after entering for the first time the region where lunar gravity predominates over that of Earth. They were the crew of *Apollo VIII*—Borman, Lovell, and William A. Anders, thirty-five, a major in the air force.

Launched by the mighty Saturn 5 on the morning of December 21, 1968, *Apollo VIII* coasted in low Earth orbit with the Saturn third stage attached. The crew then fired the attached third stage (S4B) on their second revolution over Australia. It accelerated the twenty-five-ton Apollo spaceship from 25,400 to 35,400 feet a second, nearly Earth-escape velocity. They separated from the rocket stage and entered an elongated orbit with an apogee of 240,000 miles. It would take them around the leading edge of the moon and, unless they changed it by firing the powerful Apollo rocket engine, would bring them back to Earth.

The outbound flight appeared to be uneventful until the second day, when NASA revealed that Borman had become mysteriously ill, with the symptoms of nausea and vomiting. Questioning of the crew by Dr. Charles A. Berry, the manned space flight medical director, elicited admissions from Lovell and Anders that they had experienced some queasiness when they took off their space suits and began moving about the cabin.

The medical team at the Manned Spacecraft Center, Houston, attributed the mild symptoms experienced by Lovell and Anders to motion sickness. Their queasiness soon passed. But Borman's condition was alarming. By the second day, *Apollo VIII* had passed beyond the Earth's magnetic field—the planet's great shield against much of the radiation that streams toward Earth from the sun and other stars. Man was now traversing the breeze of particles from the sun called the *solar wind* for the first time. It was a new exposure. Borman's symptoms were similar to those of the onset of radiation sickness. However, instruments aboard *Apollo* did not indicate any radiation levels that could be considered dangerous, even when *Apollo VIII* flashed through the Van Allen radiation zone.

Borman quickly recovered, however. Houston concluded that whatever had smitten him could not be attributed to the environment of cislunar space. At 3:59 A.M., Central Standard Time, December 24, Apollo reached the point of closest approach to the Moon, *pericynthion*. The crew burned its service propulsion system engine for four minutes, six and one-half seconds to drop the vessel into a lunar orbit of 69.5 by 194.3 miles as it rounded the far side of the Moon.

From those distances, men looked at the surface of the Moon for the first time as a massive landscape that filled nearly all of their field of view. To Lovell, its color was gray, like plaster or beach sand. Borman and Anders saw the dead panorama of mountains and craters as a grim, forbidding, dry place—a desert of planetary proportions.

Apollo VIII passed over the basin called the Sea of Fertility, and the crewmen looked down into the crater Langrenus. Instead of the sharp peaks and scarps depicted in pre-Space Age artists' conceptions of the lunar landscape, they saw an undulating surface. The rims of craters and the crests of mountains were rounded off. There were hills like sandpiles and, at their bases, rocks strewn about as though rolled down the hills by a careless giant.

The series of lunar reconnaissance vehicles dispatched to the moon between 1964 and 1968—*Ranger, Surveyor,* and *Orbiter*—had prepared man for such scenes with the closeup photographs the automata radioed to Earth. But seeing it in situ was still surprising. Erosion was at work on the airless, waterless Moon—in what form could merely be surmised. Perhaps the ancient hills and crater rims had been sanded down by the infall of micrometeoroids or by the solar wind that blew directly on the naked lunar surface.

On their third revolution of the Moon, the crewmen burned the Apollo engine again to circularize their orbit at sixty-nine miles—the altitude from which later expeditions would descend to the surface in a landing vehicle called the lunar module.

Beyond the lunar horizon, the astronauts saw a moon-sized Earth, a blue-white marble afloat in a black cosmos. How small and fragile it seemed. On the Blue Planet, it was Christmas Eve. Borman, Lovell, and Anders took turns reading passages from the Book of Genesis in the Old Testament. From this lunar Sinai, the words, "in the beginning," crossed the heavens to the blue planet on the magical weave of the Apollo communications network. The passages from Genesis were recited in the flat tones, terse syllables, and hesitations of tired men—men unaccustomed to reading aloud, except to their children; men looking down for the first time on the cratered wilderness of the lunar world.

The inconceivable had happened. The Cold War, the space race, the politics of hegemony, and the struggle for security—all had conspired to produce the spectacle of three men circling the Moon and reading from the Bible on the radio on Christmas Eve. Who could have predicted that in 1961?

From the Moon, the television images of the distant Earth enabled mankind to perceive his habitat from a cosmic perspective for the first time. The perception imparted a new, historic credibility to the conception of One World, a planet of limits and bounds.

Apollo VIII won the race to lunar orbit, but its real victory lay in giving mankind a clear, visual image of the abode of life, the Blue Planet, a lone haven in the immensity of solar space.

On the circumlunar voyage of *Apollo VIII*, Western man completed the reconnaissance of the Earth that had begun a thousand years before. Ahead lay the first land fall in the cosmic sea.

CHAPTER VI

VICTORY
AND RETREAT

In the euphoria generated by the dramatic flight of *Apollo VIII* in lunar orbit, the haste with which that mission was hustled off to the Moon was generally overlooked. The risks were high. And the decision of NASA to accept them indicated the pressure under which the agency labored, not only to meet the Kennedy deadline but to forestall a Russian "first" around the Moon.

Indeed, compared with the caution that characterized the Soviet program, *Apollo VIII* seemed reckless. It carried men to lunar orbit on the first manned launch of the Saturn 5 and on the second manned test of the Apollo spacecraft. Moreover, *Apollo VIII* went to the Moon without the lunar module, which could serve as a "lifeboat" in case of a breakdown in the Apollo life-support system. Such a breakdown did occur sixteen months later, on the flight of *Apollo XIII*, when an oxygen tank exploded. Then, the LM's life-support system saved the crew from suffocation. A similar accident on *Apollo VIII* would have doomed its crew.

In addition to life support, the LM also provided an auxiliary engine to lift the crew out of lunar orbit and send Apollo back to Earth in the event the Apollo Service Propulsion System (SPS) failed. There was no such backup on *Apollo VIII*. It was certainly NASA's biggest gamble. *Apollo VIII* appears to have been an impulsive digression from an otherwise conservative plan. It was designed originally as an Earth-orbit mission, to follow a similar one on *Apollo VII*, the first manned test of the spacecraft.

The decision to try for lunar orbit on *Apollo VIII* was hatched in the summer of 1968, three months before the first manned test could be carried out. Although it suggests considerable engineering confidence in the earlier performance of the Saturn-Apollo system, there is little in the performance history of either rocket or spacecraft to suggest readiness for a lunar journey in

1968. In fact, the performance record indicated that neither vehicle was ready. This is what had happened.

When Project Gemini ended in December 1966, the development of the Apollo was moving ahead well, or so it seemed. Apollo had profited from Gemini, which was not only a learning experience for the astronauts but for engineers and contractors, too. Each Gemini flight had exhibited malfunctions in mechanical, electronic, and propulsion systems. With proper analysis, these problems could be avoided or, at least, reduced in frequency in Apollo. If Mercury was a "Model T" and Gemini a "Model A"—then Apollo was a new Cadillac.

Meanwhile, the development of the Saturn 5 moon rocket, with 8.75 million pounds of thrust in three stages, was progressing well. A first flight test of this 6-million-pound vehicle, 363 feet tall, was in sight in the third quarter of 1967.

Early in 1967, the crew of *Apollo I* was already deep in training and had moved from the Manned Spacecraft Center in Houston to the Kennedy Space Center in Florida to commence vehicle tests on Launch Pad 34. Gus Grissom was flight commander. His fellow crewmen were White and Roger B. Chaffee, a thirty-one-year-old lieutenant commander in the navy. They had been picked to take *Apollo I* on her maiden voyage of up to fourteen days in Earth orbit.

On the morning of January 27, 1967, *Apollo I*, with the factory number 012, was being tested as it sat atop its Saturn 1B launch vehicle. After lunchtime, Grissom, White, and Chaffee donned flight suits and helmets and climbed into the command module to rehearse a portion of the countdown.

Communications kept dropping out intermittently during the rehearsal. The afternoon passed quickly. Suddenly, the crew in the launch control room was alerted by a surge of alternating electric current. It was 6:30 P.M. One minute later, a voice was heard from the command module yelling, "Fire!" But the communications were so poor, what followed was barely intelligible. A voice was heard saying, "I've" or "We've" and then "got a fire in the cockpit." Then, "We've got a bad fire . . . let's get out . . . open 'er up . . . we're burning up."

Before the pad crew could respond, the Apollo cabin split open with a gout of flame. Smoke poured out. Technicians struggled to undo the outer hatch. This seemed to take forever. When they got it open, the inner hatch, designed to open inward, was blocked by an obstruction inside. It was the body of one of the crewmen. Peering within, the pad technicians saw a vision of hell: smoke, heat, prostrate forms in flight suits. More than five minutes had passed, and there was no hope anyone could be alive.

Grissom, White, and Chaffee had been asphyxiated by the infiltration of toxic gases, principally carbon monoxide, into their breathing loops. Apollo 012 was a smoking hulk. Only a miracle prevented the flames from igniting the solid rocket in the overhead escape tower. The launch vehicle, Saturn 204, was unscathed.

A review board concluded that a short circuit, caused by exposed wiring, emitted a hot, electric arc. It ignited the plastics in the cabin—materials that were fire-resistant in a normal oxygen-nitrogen atmosphere but inflammable in the pure oxygen atmosphere of the cockpit. Under the conditions of the January 27 test, the board found, the Apollo cabin was a deathtrap. Not only did it present an unrecognized fire hazard, but it also failed to provide a means of quick egress for the crew. There was simply no way for the crew to escape once the cabin began to burn.

The Apollo Review Board found numerous deficiencies in design and quality control of the spacecraft. It blamed both the prime contractor, North American Aviation, and NASA for the accident. A combination of carelessness and overconfidence had deluded contractor and NASA engineers into believing that all was well with Apollo and blinded them to its deficiencies, despite a critical report warning that all definitely was not well during an earlier development phase of the spacecraft. At the end of 1965, Major General Samuel C. Phillips, Apollo program director, submitted a report to NASA headquarters complaining about contractor delays in meeting performance milestones and about hardware "degradation" as a result. The report was not made public until after the fire.

The immediate impact of the disaster was a purge in North American's top management and a minor shuffling of executive posts in NASA. A hostile Congress and an indifferent chief executive might have put the space agency out of business at that point, but such attitudes never materialized. Confessing culpability, the agency and the contractor threw themselves on the mercy of the public. There was no serious effort to cover up the cause of the tragedy, and the *Review Board Report* seemed to me to be an admirable piece of frank disclosure.

Changes were made in the Apollo command module to enable the crew to get out more quickly and easily. The more flammable plastics were replaced by less flammable ones. Many experts urged the space agency to redesign the life-support system for a sea level atmosphere of oxygen and nitrogen, such as Russian spacecraft used, pointing out that in a normal mixture, the plastics would not have blazed. But the delay of such a changeover militated against it. Apollo would continue to have a pure oxygen atmosphere at five pounds per square inch pressure while in space. On the launch pad, a mixture would be used during testing and countdown. Then, when the vessel was launched, the mixture would be gradually "bled off" and replaced with pure oxygen.

In altering the spacecraft to reduce fire hazard, NASA found money it previously did not seem able to lay hands on to make a number of additional changes and corrections in the vehicle that were not related to the fire but that greatly improved reliability. Reworking of the spacecraft was started promptly after the investigation; nevertheless, twenty-one months were to elapse from the time of the fire before a crew would finally make the first flight test.

Russian commentaries laid the cause of the fire to reckless American haste to win the race to the Moon. Then, tragedy struck on the Russian side April 23, 1967, when Colonel Vladimir M. Komarov of the Red air force was killed in the crash of *Soyuz* ("Union") *I*, a new manned spacecraft he was testing. The lines of the parachute fouled during the vehicle's descent after a seventeen-and-one-half-orbit flight, and the vessel plunged to the ground. Both sides had paid with blood sacrifice.

During that fateful period, a new and more powerful launch vehicle appeared in Russia. Western observers called it a D-1-e, a term signifying their belief it had three stages. It was thought to be at least as powerful as the Saturn 1.

It was used to launch *Kosmos 146* on March 10 and *Kosmos 154* on April 8, 1967. The spacing between these flights—about a lunar month—suggested that they were precursors to a circumlunar flight program called Zond, which began sending Soyuz-type spacecraft around the moon the following year. Zond also referred to unmanned interplanetary vehicles launched to Mars and Venus, unsuccessfully, in 1964.

Then, in the fall of 1967, the Soviets launched two unmanned Soyuz-type vessels, which docked. The first, *Kosmos 186*, was boosted into Earth orbit October 27, and the second, *Kosmos 188*, was lifted October 30 on a path that brought it to within fifteen miles of the first. The first Kosmos then docked with the second by autopilot. After three and one-half hours, the vessels undocked and were brought down separately to soft landings. It was a notable exhibition of precision launching and docking in Earth orbit. Was the object a lunar or space station preparation? No one in the United States could be sure.

Then it was America's turn to put on a demonstration.

THE BIG SHOT

With its recovery from the fire, the Apollo program began to accelerate, and the space agency announced it would conduct an "all up" test of the Saturn 5 on November 9, 1967. Scheduled to fly on the mission called *Apollo IV* were all three stages of the big Saturn, number 501, and Apollo spacecraft. As it stood poised on Launch Pad 39A that morning, Saturn 501 was the most powerful rocket ever built. Five F-1 engines in the first stage would develop 7.5 million pounds of thrust. Five J-2 hydrogen engines of the second (S-2) stage would produce 1 million pounds of thrust. The single J-2 engine of the third (S4B) stage would put out 200,000 pounds of thrust.

The launch of the Saturn 5 at precisely 7 A.M., November 9 (on time!), was an earsplitting experience for the 600 news media and other observers at the Kennedy Space Center. The thirty-six-story rocket with *United States* painted on it in bold red letters looked like the Washington Monument taking off from the Mall. The earth shook. At the press site, three and one-half miles away, the steel grandstand shivered, telephones jumped up and down in their cradles, and the roof and window of the Columbia Broadcasting System's television trailer caved in on commentator Walter Cronkite, who nevertheless persevered in describing the stupendous scene of that huge rocket rising like Judgment Day on its pillar of fire.

Later, analysis of the Saturn 5 revealed a problem. Oscillations had appeared in the first stage, causing some shaking or "pogo-ing" of the launch vehicle until the first stage engines cut off. Otherwise, all ninety-five engines on the launch vehicle and spacecraft performed in a nominal way.

Apollo directors were elated with the results of the all-up test, which the contractors had publicized as "the Big Shot." But the seeds of trouble were there. On the next test of the Saturn 5, April 4, 1968, the pogo effect was more severe. Although Saturn 502 succeeded in establishing *Apollo VI* in a low Earth orbit, two serious malfunctions were recorded that would have aborted a lunar mission. Two of the five engines on the second (S-2) stage cut off prematurely, and the third (S4B) stage failed to restart in orbit as it would be required to do on a lunar flight. The pogo effect in the first stage engines was suspected as the cause of both malfunctions, in which ruptured fuel lines were indicated by postflight review of telemetry.

By the end of April, Marshall engineers believed they had found a fix for pogo in the first stage, where it produced a longitudinal acceleration (shaking) of 0.72 gravities. The pogo effect also induced a dangerous, sideways sway in the lunar module, which was carried just behind Apollo in the S4B (third) stage. Pogo was the effect of oscillations in the first stage liquid oxygen line induced by vibrations in the rocket structure. It was not noticed during static firings on the ground because the vehicle was prevented from vibrating extensively by being clamped to the test stand. The oscillations in the oxygen line were damped out by installing an accumulator in the liquid oxygen line prevalve. The accumulator injected a neutral gas (helium) into the line to cushion oscillations of flow. Subsequently, pogo also appeared in the S-II (second) stage of the Saturn 5. It was abated also by installing an oxygen line accumulator.

Once this fix was determined, NASA officials saw no reason to delay a manned flight test of Apollo aboard the Saturn 5. On August 19, 1968, Sam Phillips, Apollo program director, announced that the second manned flight of

Apollo—*Apollo VIII*—would be launched by Saturn 503 in December. It would follow the first manned Apollo test in October—*Apollo VII*—which would be lifted into Earth orbit by the smaller of the two Saturn rockets, the Saturn 1B. The smaller Saturn had never exhibited the pogo effect. In fact, it proved to be the most reliable launch vehicle in the American inventory.

Saturn 5, however, was another kind of beast, and the decision to entrust a crew to it on its third launch, without a flight test of the pogo fix, seemed risky enough; the decision to send them to the Moon tempted fate. Yet by August 19, that decision had been reached.

The decision was strongly motivated by the belief that the Russians could spring a manned circumlunar flight in 1968. The probability was seemingly enhanced by the launch of *Zond IV* March 2, 1968, followed by a second automatic docking April 15 of *Kosmos 212* and *213*, all thought to be Soyuz prototypes. Western observers were impressed. They considered *Zond IV* a diagnostic test of a vehicle capable of carrying a crew of three around the moon.

The fate of *Zond IV* was not disclosed. On September 14, 1968, *Zond V* was launched from the Baikonur Cosmodrome on a circumlunar flight involving two mid-course corrections. It swung around the Moon at a distance of 1,210 miles from the surface and raced back to Earth, reentering the atmosphere over the south pole. It splashed down at night in the Indian Ocean, where it was recovered by a waiting Soviet vessel using radio locating devices and brilliant searchlights. The vehicle was then carried to Bombay, where it was transferred by truck in a sealed container to the airport. Russian cargo aircraft flew it back to Baikonur.

The consensus of Western observers was that *Zond V* was clearly a Soyuz prototype, designed for a lunar mission. It consisted of a recovery module, in which the crew lands, and a service module containing propulsion and life-support systems. It lacked only the workshop module that the advanced Soyuz carries. In 1971, the Russians released drawings confirming the Soyuz-like configuration of *Zond V*, with solar panels extended. The vehicle carried turtles, flies, plants, and bacteria to determine radiation effects. No deleterious effects were reported from the circumlunar test.

Zond VI was launched November 10, 1968, by a D-1-e launcher into a parking orbit and then propelled moonward by the firing of the third stage rocket, to which it remained attached until it left Earth orbit. It rounded the Moon at a distance of 1,400 miles and returned to Earth, where it made an initial reentry over the south pole, skipped out of the atmosphere in a maneuver that reduced its velocity from 24,300 miles to 16,796 miles per hour, and reentered the atmosphere again to land in the Soviet Union.

The aerodynamic braking technique that *Zond VI* demonstrated seemed to be more sophisticated than the American recovery system of a high-speed ballistic reentry and parachute descent to an ocean splashdown.

With the flight of *Zond VI*, the impression that the Russians were preparing for a manned circumlunar flight gained strength. By November, however, the lunar-orbit flight of *Apollo VIII* was set; the astronauts were in rigorous training for it; the prospect had been well publicized, and the risk was being amortized on an "if we can do it" basis of small steps. The first step led to Earth orbit. If all was well, the next step was the circumlunar boost from Earth orbit with a second burn of the Saturn S4B. The trajectory would carry the spacecraft around the Moon and back to Earth if nothing further was done. If all seemed to be going well on the outward-bound journey, especially if the Apollo engine performed nominally on in-flight test firings, then Mission Control at Houston would give a "go" for the braking maneuver that would drop the vehicle into orbit around the Moon. The initial elliptical orbit would later be circularized at about sixty-nine miles altitude, and the crewmen would observe and photograph the surface, preparing the way for a later landing mission. They would then fire the Apollo engine to lift the vehicle out of lunar orbit and send it racing back to Earth for a Pacific Ocean splashdown. That was the plan. It could be aborted if anything went wrong with the Apollo at any point along the way until the vehicle fell into lunar orbit. Then if the Apollo engine failed to restart and lift the vehicle out of lunar orbit or if the life-support system malfunctioned, the crew was doomed, because there was no lunar module with its backup propulsion and life-support systems available for a December flight.

APOLLO VII

The sixteen-ton lunar module had undergone its first test in Earth orbit January 22, 1968, on the mission called *Apollo V*. The launch vehicle was Saturn 204, to which *Apollo I* had been mated when the fire erupted. The performance of the descent engine, designed to lower two crewmen to the surface of the Moon, was compromised by a computer error. However, the ascent engine, which would boost the lunar explorers back upstairs to rejoin the orbiting Apollo command and service module, performed satisfactorily. NASA pronounced the LM a "mature spacecraft."

Next up, as I have related, was *Apollo VI*, which brought the pogo problem in the Saturn 5 first stage into sharp focus. While that difficulty was being resolved, the space agency rolled out the trusty Saturn 1B with *Apollo VII* on top and prepared for the first manned flight test of the Apollo spacecraft.

Apollo VII was launched October 11, 1968, with Schirra; air force Major Donn F. Eisele, thirty-eight; and Walter Cunningham, thirty-six, a civilian test pilot, aboard. It flew eleven days without exhibiting any notable problems, one of the few "textbook" flights in the United States space program. It was not simply beginner's luck, but a consequence of the Apollo fire investigation, which led NASA to make nearly 100 fixes in the spacecraft that otherwise might not have been made.

The mission displayed the first television scenes of an American crew tumbling and swimming about the cabin in orbital free fall. Schirra and Cunningham came down with colds, and testy dialogue was heard between Schirra, the commander, and Mission Control, disputing who was running the show up there. Schirra insisted that as commander, he was—an issue that Mission Control artfully dodged. It was Schirra's last space flight. Schirra retired from NASA in July 1969. He held the rank of captain in the navy.

Schirra tested Apollo's maneuverability by executing a transposition and docking maneuver with the S4B rocket stage, which is the second stage on the smaller Saturn 1B. On a lunar landing mission, the LM was carried into orbit by the S4B just behind the command and service modules. After the S4B boosted these vehicles out of Earth orbit toward the Moon, the Apollo separated from the rocket stage. The crew then turned it around (transposition) and nosed the conical end of the command module back to the S4B to latch on to the lunar module (docking). The crew then backed off, pulling the LM clear of the rocket stage. Thus attached, the LM and Apollo command and service modules headed for the Moon, with the spent rocket stage tumbling along Moonward also, on a diverging path.

Because there was no LM on *Apollo VII*, Schirra's transposition-and-docking maneuver was merely a rehearsal to show what Apollo could do. The crew was delighted with the spacecraft's performance.

Although the clean performance of *Apollo VII* seemed to reduce the element of risk in the lunar orbit goal of *Apollo VIII*, it did not compensate for the lack of a lunar module. That lack seemed to emphasize the acceleration of the lunar landing program.

Before *Apollo VIII*'s lunar mission was conceived, the flight was scheduled to be an Earth orbit test of all components of a lunar landing mission: the Saturn 5, Apollo spacecraft, and the lunar module. However, when the LM designated to fly with *Apollo VIII* arrived at the Kennedy Space Center in June 1968, it was found to have electronic problems. These could not be corrected in time for a December flight. It was doubtful that the LM could be made ready for space before February 1969.

Thus, when the Apollo directorate decided to send *Apollo VIII* to the Moon in December, it faced the question of going without the LM and its backup life-support and propulsion systems. The alternative was to postpone *Apollo VIII* until February 1969.

Why did the Apollo directorate decline to postpone the mission two months and wait for the LM? Why was December the magic month? Why did the NASA administration consent to risk a lunar orbit disaster that could have delayed a manned lunar landing for years, or even shut down the whole program?

No doubt, there was concern about the possibility of manned Zond flight early in 1969. There was concern, too, about making a reconnaissance of the lunar gravitational field, which was distorted by mass concentrations below the surface of the great, dark basins.

The "lumps and bumps" in the field, causing unexpected accelerations of vehicles in lunar orbit, had been observed in tracking Lunar Orbiter camera spacecraft two years earlier. They complicated the guidance and navigation program for landing a lunar module. Unquestionably, that was a factor in rushing the flight for December. There is yet another factor in this curious *Apollo VIII* equation, a domestic political factor.

The Kennedy-Johnson era that produced Project Apollo was coming to an end in 1968. President Johnson had announced, dramatically, before the Democratic National Convention in August, that he would not seek another term. December 1968 was the last chance to achieve even a partial fulfillment of the grand lunar goal in Johnson's term of office. The first manned flight around the Moon would live in history longer, perhaps, than anything else in Johnson's administration—longer than the Chicago convention riots and their aftermath. At least it would brighten, if successful, the last dismal months of the LBJ era.

For the troubled Lyndon B. Johnson, beset with rising antiwar and racial protest, with rebellious youth and with crumbling political support, the flight of *Apollo VIII* was a last hurrah.

In any case, the genesis of the *Apollo VIII* mission came one morning in August 1968 in the office of Robert R. Gilruth, director of the Manned Spacecraft Center (now the Johnson Space Center) in Houston. It was a hot day, as it always is in Houston in August, but the office was air-conditioned, as one would expect in an agency whose mission it is to hone the cutting edge of modern technology.

Among those present was Christopher Columbus Kraft, Jr., flight director at the Center, who later recalled that as soon as there was a consensus that a lunar orbit flight was feasible, Gilruth picked up the telephone and called Wernher Von Braun, the director of the Marshall Space Center at Huntsville, Alabama. Kraft related: [1]

> Bob [Gilruth] said that if we're going to do this, we've got to get Von Braun's co-operation because he's got this Saturn 5 problem. [This referred to the pogo effect in the first stage. By August 1968, the fix was determined but had not been fully tested.]
>
> So, he got Wernher on the phone, and said, "what are you doing this afternoon?" He [Wernher] said, "well, we're busy here with Sam Phillips talking over the problems on the Saturn 5." And Bob said, "we'd like to fly over right now and we have a proposal we'd like to make to you and see what you think about it."

We got in the airplane around noon and arrived there [at Huntsville] in two and one-half hours. We got Sam Phillips and broached the plan to him. Well, they [Phillips and Von Braun] thought the plan was super. It was a great idea. We didn't have to do any convincing at all.

They thought they could probably get the Saturn problems worked out—they thought they knew what the pogo problem was. They felt fairly confident they could get it fixed and they thought it was a heck of a great idea.

The next step was to sell the idea to George E. Mueller, then NASA associate administrator for manned space flight, and administrator Webb. This was not so easy to do, Kraft recalled. Gilruth, who retired as Center director in 1972, recalled that at first, Mueller, Webb, and President Johnson, the final arbiter of the lunar orbit flight, were opposed to it.[2]

"They did not want to do it," Gilruth said. "It was only [as a result of] the triumph of logical argument that they agreed, that the risk was not any greater than for any other lunar mission, and the payoff was very real. They were reluctant to do it because they had the feeling that there was a change in plans—people are always reluctant about any change in basic plan." Gilruth asserted that the main reason for moving ahead so quickly "was to put our landing schedule ahead, not to be first to the Moon, although I had in the back of my mind that being scooped by a half-baked Zond flight to the Moon would have a tremendous psychological effect. It would have really downgraded the landing."

He added: "I'm sure they were planning a Zond [manned] flight before our landing and when we flew in December it was too soon for them to make it. I feel that it [Apollo VIII] was justified on the basis of let's learn all we can about the Moon, let's photograph the landing site and make sure that all the gravitational problems are solved." This referred to gravitation anomalies in the Moon apparently resulting from concentrations of mass (mascons) below major basins.

Gilruth said there was "no doubt in my mind they were going to fly a man around the Moon." He added: "That was the beautiful thing about Apollo VIII. It was not originally scheduled so it had an element of surprise." [3]

According to Charles S. Sheldon, chief of science policy research for the Library of Congress, the Russians subsequently announced that Zonds IV, V, and VI were all aimed at perfecting a manned spaceship to go around the moon.[4] But, in contrast to the boldness of the Apollo VIII gamble, the Russians appeared to have doubts about the safety of a lunar mission and continued to send unmanned vehicles on circumlunar flights. On December 10, 1968, Academician Blagonravov, an influential voice in the Soviet space program, was quoted on Moscow radio as saying that further unmanned tests would be required before man could be sent around the Moon.

Eleven days later, Apollo VIII was launched, on the hot Florida morning of December 21, before 800 news correspondents and observers at the Kennedy Space Center. In preflight briefings, Mueller and Phillips had emphasized the variable goals of the mission. If all went well in Earth orbit, Mission Control at Houston would signal a "go" for Translunar Injection (TLI). This meant a second burn of the S4B's hydrogen engine to accelerate the Apollo spacecraft out of low orbit and into a loop 238,000 miles long that would take it around the Moon and back to Earth. And then, if all went well, Mission Control would signal the crew to fire the Apollo engine to brake velocity and allow the craft to fall into an ellipitical lunar orbit that would later be circularized.

After the smoke of the thunderous launch had vanished and the bright spark of the departing Saturn 5 rocket engines had disappeared behind the high clouds over the Atlantic Ocean, the silence of expectation fell over the press site. Would Apollo try for the Moon? During its first revolution around the Earth, all systems were reported as working normally. Frank Borman advised Mission Control that the ride to orbit on Saturn 503 had been smooth and easy.

As *Apollo VIII* commander, Borman was the key crew figure in the decision to try for lunar orbit. He could have blocked it if he had believed it too much of a gamble. Another astronaut whose support was essential was Donald K. (Deke) Slayton, the Project Mercury astronaut who had been kept from space flight by a heart rhythm irregularity. Slayton was astronaut crew chief. Kraft recalled:

> Deke said that he could get the crew ready. We had already talked to Borman about his ability to plan and to get ready to go to the Moon. It was my opinion that if we were going to go, we ought to put the vehicle in orbit around the Moon because there was so much more for us to learn in an operating sense. We had to convince Frank that we ought to go into orbit around the Moon rather than just fly a circumlunar mission, because there was a hell of a difference in the risk they would have to take. At first, he wasn't very happy about that. We got together and talked about it and I explained to him what we were up to and why we needed to do it. So he bought it.

Now Borman, Lovell, and Anders were flying in orbit around the Earth, awaiting a "Go!" from Mission Control for TLI. Each was too preoccupied with his spacecraft to be acutely aware of the peril of a journey no man had ever begun before. It was as audacious as the first voyage of Columbus across the uncharted poison sea. Yet they were test pilots, and this was a test. But what a test! No one could be sure about the effects of radiation beyond the protecting umbrella of the Earth's magnetic field, and they would clear this protection 40,000 miles out.

The Russians had sent mice and insects in their Zonds to test radiation effects, with ambiguous, apparently negative results. America was sending men. There were new navigation problems to be resolved, such as the lumps of gravitational anomalies in lunar orbit. The Soviets had been flying their unmanned vehicles around the Moon for months to investigate navigation problems. Now the Americans were sending a crew on the first attempt to fly a spacecraft in lunar orbit and bring it back. If Apollo's engine failed in lunar orbit, the crew would perish before the eyes of a world powerless to help, and each moonrise would memorialize the mission's fate.

At the crowded press site, the NASA commentary on the progress of the flight during the first revolution of the Earth boomed out intermittently from the loudspeakers. The crew was coming back over Florida to begin their second revolution. News correspondents, press agents, industry observers, politicians, stage and screen personalities, and socialites milled around the press and VIP compounds, chatting in small groups or queuing up for hot coffee or cold soft drinks. Some dozed, outstretched, on the Saint Augustine grass. Busses were already leaving the press site to return spectators to their motels at Cocoa Beach. As *Apollo VIII* approached Australia on the second revolution, Borman and Lovell could be heard talking to Houston. All systems were working perfectly.

Then, the voice of astronaut Michael Collins, the capsule communicator at Houston, came over the press site loudspeakers saying, conversationally: "Apollo, Houston. You are go for TLI." They were "go" for the Moon. But the words seemed to be lost on the milling, chattering throngs. There was no stentorian rhetoric, roll of drums, blast of trumpets. There was just a rattle of typewriters and telephones as correspondents put new tops to their stories.

Southwest of Hawaii, the S4B's J-2 engine flared into life and lifted *Apollo VIII* out of its 118-mile orbit on the 238,000 mile journey to the Moon. "You are go," Collins said, noting the telemetered performance of the S4B and the acceleration of *Apollo VIII*. "You look good." "Thank you, Michael," said Frank Borman.

It was Borman who began the reading from the Book of Genesis that Christmas Eve in lunar orbit. Seven years later, Chris Kraft remembered the tension he felt early Christmas day waiting for the signal that would tell Mission Control the Apollo engine had fired behind the Moon to boost *Apollo VIII* out of lunar orbit and send it home. "The longest 20 minutes I ever spent in my life was waiting for the SPS [service propulsion system] to burn around the back side of the Moon. I remember very vividly when they came around and Jim Lovell said, 'There really is a Santa Claus.' I'll remember those words as long as I live." *Apollo VIII* was the pivot of the whole Apollo lunar landing program, Kraft added. "From there on, we really knew what we were doing."

SOVIETS IN EARTH ORBIT

The Zond circumlunar program lost its urgency when *Apollo VIII* returned from lunar orbit, Charles Sheldon noted.[5] Nevertheless, the Russians continued shooting Zonds around the Moon, with *Zond VII* in August 1969 and *Zond VIII* in October 1970. They were unmanned.

With *Apollo VIII* safely and gloriously ensconced in history, the Apollo directors moved confidently toward the lunar landing in the summer of 1969. There seemed to be no likelihood that the Russians could get to the Moon first, and the public statements by Soviet officials reflected a change in direction in manned flight, away from the Moon and toward an Earth-orbit space station.

An eighteen-month hiatus in Russian manned flight after Komarov was killed ended October 25, 1968, only three days after the splashdown of *Apollo VII*, with the launch of *Soyuz II*. This vehicle was flown as an unmanned rendezvous target for *Soyuz III*, which was launched the next day with cosmonaut Georgiy T. Beregovoy as pilot. He maneuvered *Soyuz III* to within 650 feet of *Soyuz II* and then landed October 30 after sixty-four orbits.

In January 1969, the Russians accomplished their first docking of two manned spaceships. *Soyuz IV*, piloted by Lieutenant Colonel Vladimir A. Shatalov, was launched January 14, and *Soyuz V* went up the next day crewed by three cosmonauts: Lieutenant Colonels Boris Volynov and Yevgeny Khrunov and an engineer, Aleksey Yeliseyev. The accuracy of the launches brought both vessels fairly close. On the thirty-fourth revolution of *Soyuz IV*, Shatalov docked with *Soyuz V* by manual control after both vessels were steered to within 325 feet of each other by their autopilots.

As both Soviet ships orbited the Earth in the docked configuration, Khrunov and Yeliseyev climbed out of *Soyuz V* and, one at a time, made their way by holding handrails to an open hatch aboard *Soyuz IV*. It was the first crew transfer in space history. Although the vessels remained docked only four hours and thirty-five minutes, the Russians hailed the docking and the crude, outdoor transfer of crewmen from one vessel to the other as a demonstration of the world's first space station.

But *Apollo VIII* was still a hard act to follow, one seemingly beyond Soviet technical capability at the time. There were no further indications, verbal or engineering, that the Russians were going to send men to the Moon. Gradually, the West became aware that a superrocket, the so-called G launch vehicle, which the Russians were believed to be developing to surpass the mighty Saturn 5, was stalled on the ground. The rumored development of the G launcher had worried American observers since 1967, but nowhere did it appear.

Lunar Module 3, for which *Apollo VIII* had not waited, was tested in earth orbit on the ten-day flight of *Apollo IX*, March 3 to 13, 1969. The crewmen were Scott, McDivitt and Russell L. Schweickart, thirty-three, a civilian aeronautical engineer. To distinguish them in orbit, Mission Control awarded the Apollo command and service module the call sign *Gumdrop*, and the lunar module, *Spider*.

Once in orbit, McDivitt and Schweickart entered *Spider* through a connecting tunnel from *Gumdrop*, separated the LM from the mother ship, and tested the descent and ascent engines. As noted earlier, the LM is a two-stage vehicle. Its lower, or descent, stage has a rocket engine designed to enable it to land softly on the moon from lunar orbit. Its upper, or ascent, stage has another rocket engine designed to lift it off the moon for the return to the orbiting Apollo CSM. The astronauts ride in the ascent stage. When they lift off the moon, they use the descent stage as their launch pad.

In Earth orbit, McDivitt and Schweickart jettisoned the descent stage by firing the ascent stage engine in simulation of a lunar lift-off. Continuing to fire the ascent engine, they made rendezvous with *Gumdrop* and docked. Now both Americans and Russians had accomplished the docking of two manned vessels, but the apparent purposes differed. The Russian exercise in January pointed toward an eventual space station. The American maneuver in March rehearsed the landing on the Moon.

Apollo IX was lifted by the fourth Saturn 5, and there was no complaint about the performance of the launch vehicle. On the fifth launch of that great rocket, Stafford, Young, and Cernan rode *Apollo X* to lunar orbit May 18–26, 1969, for the final prelanding test of the lunar module. For call sign distinction, the Apollo CSM was dubbed *Charlie Brown* and the LM, *Snoopy*, giving that particular comic strip a niche in space history.

Stafford and Cernan detached *Snoopy* from the CSM and took the LM down to a mountain-grazing altitude of 47,000 feet above the surface, while Young remained at the helm of *Charlie Brown* in a 69-mile orbit. Again, the descent and ascent engines were tested. Stafford and Cernan jettisoned the descent stage and flew the ascent stage back to Apollo, just as the *Apollo IX* crew had.

To several astronauts, it seemed incredible that the *Apollo X* lunar module would descend to 47,000 feet without landing. However, the successful flight of *Apollo VIII* may have been a factor in making *Apollo X* a dry run for the LM, inasmuch as *Apollo VIII* had eased the pressure of a Soviet attempt to send men around the Moon. It was obvious that the Russians were in no position to attempt to land a crew on the Moon. Caution now was an affordable luxury.

During late 1968, it was not clear to the astronauts themselves which crew would be first to attempt the landing. It could have been Stafford's (*Apollo X*), Armstrong's (*Apollo XI*) or Conrad's crew (*Apollo XII*). It appeared to Michael Collins, the *Apollo XI* command module pilot, that the jump from *Apollo VII*, the first manned test of Apollo in Earth orbit, to *Apollo VIII*, the first manned lunar orbit flight, was greater than the jump from *Apollo IX*, the first test of the LM in Earth orbit, to the landing.[6] From the command module pilot's point of view, the most worrisome part of the mission was the lift-off of the LM from the moon on the proper rendezvous trajectory. A malfunction of the gyroscopes in the LM could put the vehicle on a flight path that was out of plane from that of the command module, thus presenting both the lunar module and command module pilots with a truly hairy rendezvous problem.

In listening to the air-to-ground dialogue on these flights, I was struck by the apparent difference in the reactions of the *Apollo VIII* and *Apollo X* crews to their closeup views of the lunar surface. On *Apollo VIII*, Borman, Anders, and Lovell seemed to view the surface with awe and some foreboding. It appeared to them to be a vast, cratered desolation, gray and utterly barren, a lifeless, horrendous wilderness. But the crew of *Apollo X* saw something else on the moon. They perceived beauty and majesty in the mountain chains, the sinuous rilles, the cratered basins. On the second visitation by man, the lunar aspect had changed, and, as the Apollo program continued, it became progressively more exciting, more beautiful, and, to explain this phenomenon, more familiar.

TRANQUILITY

At thirty-two seconds past 4:17 P.M., Eastern Daylight Time, July 20, 1969, the first men landed on the moon in the lunar module *Eagle*. They were Armstrong and Aldrin, both veterans of Gemini. Armstrong, the flight commander, was the first to climb down the LM ladder to the powdery topsoil of the Mare Tranquillitatis. At the foot of the ladder, there was a three-foot drop to the ground. Armstrong paused a moment, noted the position of the LM footpads, and stepped off. "That's one small step for man," he said, "one giant leap for mankind." Later, NASA corrected the transcript to read, "one small step for *a* man," presumably under the impression that the article had been omitted in transmission. But the corrected version is not what Armstrong really said, as those of us who heard him will testify. It is not a big point. But if those words are to go echoing down the centuries, or to be carved in granite, he should be quoted accurately.

One of the most delicate problems of the *Apollo XI* mission had nothing to do with technology. It dealt with which of the two astronauts, Armstrong or Aldrin, would be the first man to set foot on the Moon. The third member of the expedition, Michael Collins, who has discussed this matter in his own book,[7] was out of the running, because, as command module pilot, he was fated to remain in orbit in the CSM *Columbia* without setting foot on the Moon at all.

The issue of the precedence had been determined at the Manned Space-craft Center well in advance of the flight on the following basis: As mission commander, Armstrong should be first ashore. A thousand years of history said so.

Politically, some importance was attached to having Armstrong step out first, because he was a civilian. That seemed to underscore the civilian, nonmilitary nature of the enterprise. On the other hand, Aldrin was a colo-nel in the air force. He came of a military family. His father, Edwin E., was a retired air force colonel. Had Aldrin been first out, domestic and third world critics could have exploited a "militaristic" aspect to the event, for whatever it was worth as anti-American propaganda.

On the other hand, the U.S. Air Force could have claimed that distinction forever—a great asset to recruiting. Some pressure was put on the people at Houston to have Aldrin climb down the ladder first, but the veteran civilian engineers in charge of the Center stuck to their guns. Gilruth recalled:

> That decision was made right here when I was director of the Center. It was made by George Low, Deke Slayton and Bob Gilruth, and it was announced to the press. Crew selection had to be ratified by Mr. [James E.] Webb [NASA adminis-trator], but what the crew did was a decision that was made right here. It was a good decision. I have no reason to regret it. I can see how someone might be disappointed. The commander clearly should be the first out. You would have to have a lot of reasons for not having the commander go out first. There may have been some lobbying on the part of some people to have the decision changed, but there was no way it was going to be changed.

Behind these careful words, the gist of the story is that air force proponents tried to persuade Gilruth, through Webb and others, to alter the prece-dence, and he refused, telling them, in effect, to mind their own business.

With the words, "Tranquility Base, the Eagle has landed," the United States won the space race and established itself as the world's leading space power. The entire mission went without a significant hitch.[8] There was, how-ever, a Soviet move toward the Moon that many of us who observed the *Apollo XI* mission believed was a ploy to upstage the American landing. If so, it was a clever one, because it struck at the weak link in the Apollo program—it's huge cost—by trying to demonstrate a cheaper way of explor-ing the Moon with automatic vehicles.

On July 13, 1969, three days before *Apollo XI* went up, the Russians launched *Luna XV* to the Moon. Now the launch date and flight plan of *Apollo XI* were known months in advance, but no notice was given of *Luna XV*. When its flight was detected by tracking monitors, there was some uneasiness at NASA headquarters. It did not appear that the Russians were flying a manned vessel to the Moon, but the possiblity they were attempting to land a probe suggested a maneuver to counter the impact of an Apollo landing. The only clue to the purpose of *Luna XV* was a report on Moscow radio that the vehicle was designed to study the lunar environment—including the gravitational field and the chemical composition of the rocks—and to take surface photos.

On July 17, the day after *Apollo XI* was launched, *Luna XV* was dropped into lunar orbit. Mission Control at Houston then became concerned about the possibility of interference by the Russian craft with the oncoming Apollo—electronic interference, more realistically, because in the vast reaches of cislunar space, any likelihood of collison was quite remote.

The man to resolve this problem was Frank Borman, who had been assigned to Washington as liaison with the White House. He had just returned from a goodwill tour of the Soviet Union, where he had been the guest of the Institute for Soviet-American Relations. Borman telephoned academician Keldysh personally in Moscow and was advised that the orbit of *Luna XV* would not intersect the published trajectory of *Apollo XI*. Later, he received a cable from Keldysh advising that *Luna XV* had been inserted into lunar orbit shortly after noon, Moscow time, July 17, with an orbital period of two hours and thirty seconds. The orbit was altered twice after that, and on July 21, as Armstrong and Aldrin left Tranquility Base in the ascent stage of the *Eagle* to rejoin *Columbia*, the Russians signaled *Luna XV* to land in Mare Crisium ("Sea of Crises"). It crashed there at a velocity of 300 miles an hour.

The purpose of *Luna XV* has not been divulged up to this writing, but, judging from later Soviet automata, it may have carried a radio-controlled reconnaissance vehicle designed to roll about on the surface, take pictures, and make soil tests. In any case, if it had worked and if Apollo had failed, it would have embarrassed the United States. But *Luna XV* failed, and Apollo won the greatest contest in the history of technology.

Ironically, the victory on the Moon disposed of Apollo's strongest suit—the space race. Once the race was won, there was no urgent reason to continue Apollo at a high funding level, and, although the scientific exploration of the Moon was now under way, the political purpose of the project had been served.

Around the world, the American victory enhanced the American image in the industrial societies, but the impact of Apollo on the third world was dulled by the anti-Americanism generated by United States intervention in Viet Nam. English became the main language of space science and technology in Europe and in non-Communist Asian countries. In the USSR, space officials became more conciliatory toward long-standing American proposals for cooperative ventures in space and exchanges of scientific data. A new atmosphere of détente was generated.

TRANSITION

The days of Project Apollo now were numbered. In the second half of 1969, a time of troubles was overtaking the United States. It was paced by the seemingly hypnotic compulsion of one national administration after another to plunge the nation ever more deeply in the revolutionary struggles of Southeast Asia and, ultimately, into the most questionable and unpopular war in American history.

Beset at home by dissent approaching a revolutionary ferment among the young intellectuals in the universities and by rising concern about racial tension, poverty, and crime, the Congress quickly lost interest in the great space adventure. The administration of President Nixon continued the cutback in space funding requests that had begun even before the landing.

With the landing on the Moon, another change appeared. The whole pattern of exploration changed. The image of the explorer as a solitary hero pitting brain and brawn against the elements to challenge nature faded away. It was replaced by a federal bureaucracy that managed a team. The men who landed on the Moon and later began to explore it were the players. The team, in turn, formed the apex of a social pyramid comprising the scientific, technical, and industrial power of a whole society. Exploration of the Moon was no longer an example of individual derring-do, but of national prowess. The explorer himself was largely controlled, puppetlike, by an electronic string that tied him to Mission Control.

It took 5,000 men and women to launch a lunar landing mission from the Kennedy Space Center, Florida. Thousands more were involved in tracking the spaceship to the Moon and back. Around the world, at Canberra, Australia; Goldstone, California; and Madrid, Spain, the 85-foot and 210-foot diameter antennas of the Deep Space Network kept radio and television communications open between the Earth and Moon.

The creation of an apparatus to fly men to the Moon and back required the organized effort of a major fraction of society. At the peak of the Apollo program, in 1966–1967, a contractor and civil service work force numbering 420,000 persons was employed in it. This included 90,000 scientists and engineers, 20,000 industrial firms, and 100 universities.[9]

The transition from individual to organized exploration had appeared in the eighteenth century, with the voyages of Captain Cook. However, the individual effort, in which the hero could still be identified as an entity apart from the society supporting him, still survived in the early twentieth century, in polar exploration, as I have related earlier.

But that image faded after World War II, when the application of new technologies not only mechanized the exploratory process but substituted scientific for personal goals. With the advent of the International Geophysical Year, exploration became a full-fledged scientific enterprise, in which the individual and his goals were subordinate to the objectives of scientific committees and government bureaus. Space exploration enlarged and accelerated this process. Yet, although the heroic age of exploration had ended with the IGY, the public-affairs component of NASA made a conspicuous effort to revive it in the personna of the astronauts. Their flight successes were treated as individual achievements and triumphs. They were idolized, heroized, and exhibited around the world in a manner that would have had done justice to Columbus, Magellan, Drake, or Cook. But as each of them invariably confessed, they were merely the apex of a social and technical pyramid, the extension of an industrial organism.

In space, from the beginning, the individual was encompassed by the group. Space flight was an exercise in military style discipline, social coordination, and industrial organization. The submergence of individual roles and judgments to those of the leadership and the bureaucracy it served was the main reason that several scientist-astronauts quit the program even before it became apparent they would never have a chance to fly.

On the Moon, the astronauts followed a flight plan so detailed that any deviation from it required a justification to Mission Control at Houston. Each lunar mission was rehearsed in more detail than a stage play, with even less leeway for extemporaneous performance. For the most part, the activities of the lunar explorers were carried out in full view (by television) of Mission Control and with constant radio communication during the periods that the explorers were outside the lunar module.

Under these circumstances, the men on the Moon became consenting marionettes, subordinating their own will and often their judgments to the wisdom and judgment of the flight plan, or, in an emergency, to the decisions of the group back at Mission Control. There were no Amundsens nor Scotts in space. The explorer was, in reality, the bureaucracy, and the astronaut was its representative.

Once the lunar landing that had seemed so remote in 1961 was accomplished, critics of manned space flight asked if it had been worth the cost. According to NASA, the accrued costs of the Apollo Program through July 31, 1969, came to $21,349,000,000. The most costly part of it was the Saturn family of launch vehicles—the Saturns 1, 1B, and V—costing $7,940,000 in total. The Apollo spacecraft cost $6,939,000,000 to develop to lunar flightworthiness. [10]

As to the worth, no bookkeeping method existed to determine it. The United States now had a space transportation system that enabled men to explore the Moon in a limited way. It had been the dictum of the scientific establishment that such an enterprise was essential if science was to attack the most significant scientific question of the age: the origin and evolution of the solar system. What this might yield could hardly be calculated in currency.

THE POST-APOLLO PROGRAM

Before public indifference had displaced the euphoria generated by the landing at Tranquility, a program for the post-Apollo period was made public in September 1969 by a space task group appointed by President Nixon. Essentially, it was an effort to design a plan for the next thirty years, and, like all advance planning, both social and technological, it could not take into account unpredictable changes in public attitudes and moods. Consequently, the 1969 Report of the Presidential Space Task Group reflected a triumphant mood that was going out of style when the report was made public.

Inasmuch as the Earth has only one moon, being the first to land men there was a hard act to follow, as Wernher Von Braun pointed out. But the space task group had in mind an act that would top it: a manned landing on Mars in the early or late 1980s, depending on how much money the nation was willing to spend to develop a Mars landing program.[11] This recommendation followed the principle of striking while the iron was hot. But it failed to stimulate public interest. The public had not responded to the exploration of the Moon—only the race to get there first. Once the race was won, the moon reverted to songwriters and scientists. Scientific interest in Mars was hardly sufficient motivation for Congress to consider seriously a manned mission there in the foreseeable future. Unfortunately, the Soviets had not revealed any plans to fly men to Mars.

Of more immediate significance, however, the report offered a blueprint of a more economical manned space transportation system than Apollo. In addition to the high cost of developing rockets and spacecraft, the cost of deploying them in a transportation system was high because they could be used only once. The space task group offered the concept of a reusable vehicle that could shuttle between the ground and orbit on repeated missions. This concept assumed the inevitable shape of a rocket-boosted airplane and acquired the inevitable title of *The Shuttle*.

Members of the group were three men long identified with the space effort: Robert C. Seamans, Jr., former deputy NASA administrator under Webb and then secretary of the air force; Thomas O. Paine, NASA administrator who had succeeded Webb in 1968; and Lee A. DuBridge, former president of the California Institute of Technology, who had become Nixon's science adviser. The chairman was Vice-President Spiro T. Agnew, by virtue of his position as chairman of the National Aeronautics and Space Council.

The program that the group presented to the White House attempted to make a Mars mission economically palatable by establishing it as an end-option of a multipurpose space transportation system that could be developed in increments during the 1970s. Instead of building a huge superrocket such as the *Nova* to lift a manned vessel to Mars, the group proposed development of an incremental system that could be used for Earth orbit and lunar missions as well as for interplanetary ones. (The *Nova* was conceived as a super-Saturn 5 but never developed.)

The first increment was to be the two-stage shuttle. It would be lifted into orbit by a recoverable and reusable rocket stage and be able to reenter and land horizontally on a runway, like an airplane.

A second increment was a space tug, which would operate outside the atmosphere and never land. It would move payloads brought up to low Earth orbit by the shuttle to higher orbits, such as the synchronous orbit at 22,300 miles altitude, where the Communications Satellite Corp. stationed its satellites. A third increment was a basic space station module housing six to twelve persons. Several modules could be joined to create a multimodule space station. The basic module could be used also as the crew quarters of a lunar or interplanetary vessel. A fourth increment was a nuclear-powered transfer stage designed to move payloads, such as the space station module, from Earth to lunar or to Mars orbit. A modification of the tug could be developed to land men and supplies on the Moon and a modification of the shuttle called Mars Excursion Module (MEM) to land them on Mars. Manned lunar or interplanetary transportation via these increments presupposed the existence of an orbital base or large permanent space station in Earth orbit.

In a report by NASA to the space task group, a decision to develop the MEM would have to be made in the 1974 fiscal year if the United States accepted a commitment to launch men to Mars in 1981 or 1983.

The first increment, the reusable shuttle, would replace virtually the entire inventory of nonreusable rockets such as the Thor, Atlas, Titan, and Saturn as space boosters for NASA and the air force. It would reduce the cost of putting payloads in orbit from $600–700 to $100 a pound, according to NASA estimates.[12] Cost of delivering *Explorer I* to orbit January 31, 1958, has been estimated by NASA at $1 million a pound. This was reduced to $1,000 a pound by the Saturn 5 ten years later. It would enable the air force to deploy special-purpose satellites quickly instead of waiting up to thirty-eight months for the delivery of a launch vehicle such as the Titan 3-C.[13]

The space shuttle could be used again and again. It could make fifty or more flights a year instead of being thrown away after each mission like the $200 million Saturn 5/Apollo.

At the beginning of 1970, the NASA directorate perceived the space shuttle as the answer to a rational space transportation system. Operating like a commercial airliner, it would deliver passengers, cargo, scientific and applications satellites, and deep-space probes on a schedule to their space destinations. Charles W. Mathews, NASA deputy Associate Administrator for Manned Space flight, predicted: "Ultimately, the space shuttle would become a part of a larger transportation system which would extend in future years the benefits of reusability to the Moon and later to the exploration of the solar system. Under such expansion, the space shuttle would carry passengers and freight to the space base where they would transfer to other vehicles for flights to the Moon or beyond." [14]

The earliest a Mars mission could be developed for launching on a minimum-energy trajectory to the red planet was 1981 or 1983, the space task group calculated. In order to exercise this option, NASA would have to reach a decision to develop the shuttle in 1972, so that the vehicle would be operational by 1977. Also, the group estimated, a space station would have to be operating in orbit by 1975. A start on the Mars excursion module would have to be made by 1978, although NASA called for the start earlier.

Funding for the earliest Mars option would run from $4 billion a year in 1971 to $5.7 billion in 1976 and $9.4 billion in 1980. These levels might be reduced by delaying the Mars landing until the late 1980s or 1990s, the task group reported.

The space task group also outlined a broad program of unmanned planetary reconnaissance. It included a Mariner mission to Mars orbit in 1971–1972; a Mariner mission flying by both Venus and Mercury; and a "Grand Tour" mission in the late 1970s that would fly by Jupiter and use its gravitational field to boost the spacecraft on to Saturn, Uranus, and Neptune. Such a flight was possible in the 1977–1979 period due to the alignment of the major planets.

It was generally considered in NASA, as well as by members of the space task group, that although a manned flight to Mars was as feasible in terms of 1970 space technology as a flight to the Moon was in 1961, there was a considerable difference in the political acceptability of the ventures. The task group stated:

> The United States and the USSR have been widely portrayed as "in a race to the Moon" or as vying over leadership in space. In a sense this has been an accurate reflection of one of the several strong motivations for United States space program decisions over the previous decade. . . . For the short term, the race with the Soviets has been won. . . . The attitude of the American people has gradually been changing and public frustration over Soviet accomplishments in space, an important force in the nation's acceptance of the lunar landing in 1961, is not now present.

Although new Soviet achievements would not have the same impact as those in the past, the task group conceded, the Soviets have continued to develop capability for them. The group warned that despite failures in the Soviet program and the "preemptive effect" of *Apollo XI*, "there is no sign of withdrawal or retrenchment from the public arena of space activity" by the Soviet Union.

The task group urged acceptance of "the long term goal of manned planetary exploration as an important part of the future agenda of this nation in space." It would serve as a focus for the "precursor" programs: the shuttle, the tug, the nuclear stage, the space station module, and the planetary landing craft, the group said. And it would continue United States leadership in space.

A staff writer for *Science,* the weekly publication of the American Association for the Advancement of Science, noted: "Today, in the wake of the successful Apollo [XI] mission, President Nixon and Congress face a critical question of space policy not unlike that which confronted President Kennedy and the Congress in 1961. . . . Now it is up to Nixon to say Yes, No or Maybe to the question of whether to send men to Mars in the early 1980s." [15]

How would Nixon respond? On September 15, 1969, the President's press secretary, Ronald L. Ziegler, briefed the press on Nixon's answer. It sounded like "yes," but actually it was "maybe." [16] He agreed that the United States should send men to Mars—eventually. But it should not launch a costly crash program to do it. The briefing conveyed the impression that although a timetable for a Mars landing had not been adopted, a flight early in the 1980s was out of the question.

The post-Apollo space program occupied Nixon's attention only intermittently in the latter half of 1969 and early 1970. As time passed and domestic problems intensified, Nixon's enthusiasm for space exploration, which had peaked during *Apollo XI,* began to wane, along with that of the public.

APOLLO XII

Meanwhile, *Apollo XII* executed the second lunar landing mission with spectacular success November 14 to 24, 1969, even surviving a lightning stroke during the launch through storm clouds from the Kennedy Space Center.

The crew consisted of Conrad and Gordon, Gemini veterans, and navy Commander Alan L. Bean, thirty-seven, a space rookie. Gordon remained in lunar orbit aboard the Apollo command module, *Yankee Clipper,* while Conrad and Bean landed in the lunar module, *Intrepid,* in Oceanus Procellarum on November 19, 1969. Their touchdown was 600 feet from an historic landmark and mission target—the reconnaissance spacecraft *Surveyor III.* It had made a soft landing on the slope of a crater April 20, 1967, and had returned photos and soil data. The flight plan called for Conrad and Bean to hike over to the Surveyor and examine it for the effects of the lunar environment, along with other tasks. The landfall at 2.94 degrees south latitude and 23.45 degrees west longitude was 954.4 statute miles west of Tranquility Base in a similar "mare," or lowland, basin region.

Compared with the two hours and thirty-two minutes that the Armstrong-

Aldrin team had spent on the first lunar EVA, Conrad and Bean were scheduled to extend extravehicular activity to two three-and-one-half hour periods separated by a nine-hour sleep period. They actually were outside a total of seven hours and forty-six minutes. During the first EVA period, they collected fifty pounds of soil and rock, set up a television camera which failed—presumably because the lens inadvertently was turned toward the blazing sun—and deployed six scientific instruments. One was a solar wind collector—a strip of aluminum foil on a pole—similar to a device that Armstrong and Aldrin had set up (to trap particles) at Tranquility Base. The other instruments were an array of seismometers to detect moonquakes or meteor impacts; a magnetometer to measure a magnetic field, if any existed; a solar wind spectrometer, which recorded the flux and chemical identity of charged particles in the solar wind and ionosphere; and atmosphere detectors to sniff out gases at the surface. The instruments were powered by a radioisotope thermoelectric generator, which produced seventy-three watts of electricity. On their second EVA, Conrad and Bean reached *Surveyor III*, which they found coated with a film of fine tan dust. They cut off pieces of the television cable and tubing and extracted instrument glass, which they took with them for analysis at the Lunar Receiving Laboratory at Houston.

Conrad and Bean lifted smoothly off the Moon in the *Intrepid* ascent stage November 20 and rejoined Gordon in *Yankee Clipper*, leaving the stage adrift in lunar orbit. Mission Control then fired *Intrepid*'s ascent engine and sent it crashing on the surface to provide a seismic signal for the seismometers the explorers had set up at their landing site. The impact caused the moon to ring like a gong with reverberations lasting more than one hour.

President Nixon outlined his space policy March 7, 1970, in a statement issued at the Key Biscayne, Florida, "White House." He listed six objectives. These were to continue the exploration of the Moon; to carry out unmanned reconnaissance of the planets, and eventually to send men to Mars; to devise cheaper space transportation, namely the shuttle; to extend man's capability to live and work in space in an experimental space station (Skylab); to expand the practical uses of space in the form of Earth resources technology satellites that could monitor the Earth's surface and encourage greater international cooperation. No date was hinted for the "eventual" manned mission to Mars, and it was not cited as an objective thereafter.

NASA administrator Paine told a press conference at Key Biscayne that he had recommended a manned Mars mission in 1986. But Nixon never confirmed such a date. Paine projected seven more lunar landings in Apollo, with a recess in the Apollo lunar program during 1972, when Skylab, the experimental space station, would be flown in low Earth orbit to test a crew's ability to endure orbital free fall for a period of fifty-six days. Skylab was not a prototype of the modular space station proposed by the space task group but a cut-rate job converted from an empty hydrogen tank of the S4B, the third stage of the Saturn 5 or second stage of the Saturn 1B. It would be placed in orbit by a Saturn 5, containing an oxygen-nitrogen atmosphere at sea level pressure, and then boarded by a crew docking with it in an Apollo, to be launched separately. As I will relate later, Skylab had a number of scientific and industrial purposes, but its principal one was to provide a testing chamber for the effect on man's physiology of long-duration zero gravity (free fall). It was essential to determine what the effect might be before a manned flight to Mars could even be considered in a free-falling spaceship. It was technically possible to induce artificial gravity in a manned capsule by rotating it, but such a development was regarded as extremely costly.

In the 1976–1977 period, Paine said, the first of the six- to twelve-man space station modules would be placed in Earth orbit. In 1977, an instrumented unmanned vehicle would be launched on the grand tour of the outer planets, and in 1978, the first nuclear rocket was to be launched.

Asked about the future of the Soviet space program, Paine characterized it in Churchill's terms as: "a mystery wrapped in an enigma." He said, "We know that they are continuing to move toward the Moon" and had made "substantial statements" about cosmonauts visiting the planets.

RETREAT FROM THE MOON

On the afternoon of April 11, 1970, *Apollo XIII* was launched from the Kennedy Space Center toward a region of the Moon called the Fra Mauro Formation, where geologists and chemists attached to the program as principal investigators hoped that rocks older than those found in Mare Tranquillitatis and Oceanus Procellarum could be collected. Lovell, then a captain in the navy, was in command. His partner on the moon was to be Fred Haise, Jr., thirty-six, a civilian, the pilot of the lunar module, *Aquarius*. John L. Swigert, thirty-four, another civilian test pilot, was to remain in lunar orbit in the command module, *Odyssey*.

Shortly after 9:00 P.M., Central Standard Time, April 13, when Odyssey-Aquarius was more than halfway to the Moon, the Number 1 oxygen tank in the Apollo service module exploded, damaging the Number 2 tank, which began to leak badly. The tanks supplied oxygen not only for life support but also for the three fuel-cell batteries that produced electricity for the space ship by an oxygen-hydrogen reaction. With half of the oxygen supply gone and the other half leaking out to space, the crew lost its main source of power and breathing gas and became dependent on battery power and emergency oxygen—which were limited.

When the magnitude of the disaster was realized at Mission Control, the landing was aborted, and the flight path of *Apollo XIII* was altered so that the crippled vessel could swing around the Moon and head back to Earth in the boomerang mode. The crew retreated into the ascent-stage cabin of the lunar module, *Aquarius,* for breathing-oxygen and power, rigging up an emergency carbon-dioxide absorber at the suggestion of Mission Control. As Odyssey-Aquarius approached the Moon, Lovell fired the descent propulsion engine of *Aquarius* to accelerate the return. Splashdown was targeted for the mid-Indian Ocean, but a recalculation of the trajectory at Houston showed that with a second burn of the descent engine, a central Pacific Ocean landing could be made earlier. This correction was made. As the damaged vessel neared Earth, the crew returned to the Apollo command module for reentry, using emergency oxygen supplies. They cast off *Aquarius,* which could not, of course, reenter, because it had no heat shield, and landed smoothly, on the afternoon of April 17, 1970. The aircraft carrier *Iwo Jima* was standing by to pick up the frustrated and weary astronauts.

It was the only close call in the lunar flight series, and, like the *Apollo I* fire, it had resulted from a sequence of events that never were anticipated. Had this accident happened aboard Apollo VIII, as I have indicated earlier, the crew could not have survived.[17]

Apollo XIV was delayed while alterations were made in the Apollo service module to avert another blowup. In September 1970, two missions were cut from the Apollo program as a result of budget retrenchment reducing NASA's $3.6 billion request for the 1971 fiscal year to $3.27 billion. The number of planned landings was thus curtailed from nine to seven. With the *Apollo XIII* landing abort, only four landing opportunities remained in the program. In vain, the science community protested. The Space Science Board of the National Academy of Sciences and the Lunar and Planetary Missions Board of NASA declared to Congress that the reduction in missions impaired the ability of the Apollo program to answer "first order scientific questions."

With the cutback in Apollo, the more exotic features of the space task group's program began to fade away. The nuclear rocket propulsion program, which was nearly completed, was halted. That meant an indefinite postponement of the projected nuclear transfer stage for interorbital flights. It also meant the indefinite postponement of a Mars mission that would use nuclear-hydrogen or nuclear-electric propulsion for the journey from Earth to Mars orbit.[18]

An electronics research center that NASA sought to establish at Cambridge, Massachusetts, to improve spacecraft and rocket electronics was phased out of the budget and out of existence. NASA also placed its White Sands, New Mexico, test facility on standby status at the western end of the army's White Sands Missile Range. The lunar module and the Apollo service module's reaction control system engines had been tested there.

With the decline in the budget, the space work force, both contractor and civil service, which had numbered 420,000 in the 1969 fiscal year, dropped to 190,000 in the 1970 fiscal year and to 140,000 at the end of fiscal 1971.

On July 29, 1970, Paine resigned as administrator to return to the General Electric Company, from which he had come to NASA. He told a news conference at the San Clemente White House that the cuts had not influenced his decision. However, there was little doubt about his concern for the program. He advised the House Committee on Science and Astronautics that "The NASA Fiscal Year 1971 authorization and appropriation request is lower than the budget that my colleagues and I would prefer to defend." [19]

Paine's resignation was not unexpected. He was a holdover Democrat in a Republican administration that was intensely and excessively patronage-minded. Moreover, Nixon's White House troops tended to regard the erudite, sometimes visionary engineer with suspicion. There was too much of the space romantic about Paine for their taste: He wanted to send men to godforsaken places like Mars. For his part, Paine received an impression that he was becoming a political liability to NASA and that his continued presence in the role of administrator would dampen its funding chances. Five years later, he told me: "I was in the position of a general managing a retreat. How would we retreat from Apollo in the most orderly way?" [20]

In the space task group report, he had managed to hoist a trial balloon after *Apollo XI* to see whether Congress and the public would continue to support a bold, imaginative program involving a Mars mission, space stations, and a lunar colony. The answer, he recalled, came back loud and clear, from the news media, the government, from Congress. Boldness was the right attitude in the early days of the Kennedy administration, when the United States had suffered such Cold War reverses as the Soviet manned space flight lead and the debacle of the Bay of Pigs. But with *Apollo XI* and *Apollo XII*, the United States had regained its preeminence as the world's technological leader. The urgency that required a bold response had vanished; it was no longer necessary to be bold.

Before the landing on the Moon, there had existed a real danger that the Soviets might miscalculate America's technoscientific and industrial capability, as Japan and Germany had in 1941, Paine believed; but after *Apollo XI*, the danger passed. Apollo was a factor in stabilizing the geopolitical situation and winding down Cold War tensions in the 1960s and early 1970s, in Paine's view, and a factor in détente. Stabilization was further advanced by improvements in the surveillance satellites, which, Paine noted, are still the technological basis on which arms control agreements can operate.

The retreat from the Moon meant the indefinite postponement of a manned mission to Mars. It meant the cancellation of nuclear rocket development, which would have been required for Mars. Modular space stations and lunar colony plans went into cold storage. What was salvaged among the space task group recommendations was the shuttle plus some early planning for a space tug.

Looking back to the fifteenth century, Paine recalled that the maritime ascendancy of Portugal grew out of the research in navigation and geography and the development of better ships by Prince Henry. His work created the transportation capability to make long voyages on a reasonable basis, Paine noted. "I liken Apollo to a Viking ship," Paine said. "It's close, but not quite able to support colonization. To pursue space exploration in manned vehicles on a reasonable basis, we must have something beyond Apollo. We must have the shuttle."

VULKAN AND LUNOKHOD

To the dwindling space audience in America, the "rest of the Apollo program" that followed the cliff-hanger of *Apollo XIII* was anticlimax. But technically and scientifically, the last four lunar landing missions were brilliant exploits. They provided a wealth of information about the Moon that enabled scientists to approach a consensus on its origin and evolution, as I intend to show in a later chapter on Apollo's scientific results. But before completing the Apollo flight log, I think we ought to take note of what the Russians were doing in Earth orbit while we were on the Moon.

In the autumn of 1969, the Russians lowered their sights, so far as manned flight was concerned, from the Moon to the development of a manned space station, using the Soyuz spacecraft as the means of transportation to Earth orbit. Lunar and planetary exploration would be carried out by automated vehicles. For the time being, cosmonauts would not venture beyond the environs of Earth.

On October 11, 12, and 13, 1969, three Soyuz spacecraft were launched into orbit from Baikonur, carrying a total of seven men. *Soyuz VI* was piloted by Lieutenant Colonel Georgiy Shonin, and Valeriy Kubasov was flight engineer. Kubasov experimented with a welding unit and had some success with the electron-beam process of welding metal, but arc welding efforts were later reported to be uncertain. The experiment called Vulkan underscored an oft-mentioned Russian intention of erecting a large station in Earth orbit by welding prefabricated sections. The mission lasted five days.

Soyuz VII, launched October 12, carried docking equipment. Its three-man crew consisted of Lieutenant Colonel Anatoly Filipchenko and two engineers, Vladislav Volkov and Lieutenant Colonel Viktor Gorbatko. This vehicle was designated as the passive docking target of *Soyuz VIII,* which went up October 13 with pilot Shatalov and Yeliseyev, flight engineer. Shatalov, it will be recalled, piloted *Soyuz IV* the previous January to a docking with

Soyuz V. He made a rendezvous with *Soyuz VII*, and the two vehicles remained close, in group flight, as the Russians called it, or *station keeping*, the NASA term, for two days. Docking was not achieved, however. Whether it was attempted was not divulged. So ended the Soviet manned flights for 1969.

At midnight June 1, 1970, *Soyuz IX* was launched from Baikonur with Andriyan Nikolayev as pilot and Vitaliy Sevastyanov as engineer. This was the first night launch in the Soyuz program. Visiting in Moscow at the time, Neil Armstrong saw it on television. The Russians maintained their policy of barring foreigners from their Baikonur Cosmodrome, with the exception of General Charles de Gaulle in 1966 and his successor as president of France, Georges Pompidou, in 1970, the only foreign officials to visit the Kazakhstan launch center in that period. These visits highlighted the Franco-Soviet rapprochement that weakened NATO and strained France's ties with the United States.

Soyuz IX set a new orbit endurance record of eighteen days. When it landed in Kazakhstan June 19, 1970, Nikolayev and Sevastyanov reportedly had more difficulty in readapting to Earth's gravity than had Borman and Lovell after the fourteen-day flight of *Gemini VII*, which had set the old record five years earlier.

In the late summer of 1970, the Russians tried their luck in picking up a sample of Moon soil by automated lander and returning it to Soviet territory. The ill-fated *Luna XV* had been followed by two more landing attempts that failed in 1969—*Kosmos 300*, launched September 23, and *Kosmos 305*, launched October 22, 1969.

Persistence eventually paid off on *Luna XVI*, launched September 12, 1970. The two-stage lander, weighing 4,145 pounds and standing thirteen feet high, came down successfully in Mare Fecunditatis ("Sea of Fertility") at 0 degrees 41 minutes south latitude and 56 degrees 18 minutes east longitude. It carried a radio-controlled drilling arm that collected a soil sample at a depth of fourteen inches and deposited it into a sterile container on the vehicle's ascent stage.

After twenty-six hours and twenty-one minutes on the ground, the ascent stage bearing the soil sample lifted on September 21 and flew back to Earth. About 30,000 miles out, the recoverable capsule separated from the carrier rocket that had propelled it home from the Moon and made a ballistic reentry, landing in the USSR September 24. The capsule contained 101 grams of lunar soil, or about 3½ ounces.

Elated, the Soviet space directorate announced that this technique was the one they had designed to reconnoiter the planets, as well as the Moon, without wasting men on such chores. This policy echoed faintly in the flight of *Zond VIII*, which was launched October 20, 1970, to the vicinity of the Moon. It took pictures in color and in black and white of both the Moon and the Earth, returning over the north pole to an Indian Ocean splashdown. A similar photographic mission had been performed by *Zond VII* in August 1969. So ended the Zond program, the suspected precursor to a manned lunar mission that did not materialize.

Luna XVI was followed November 10, 1970, with the launching of *Luna XVII*, which landed in Mare Imbrium November 17 at 38 degrees 17 minutes north and 35 degrees west. The lander was a flat platform weighing 1,667 pounds with ramps on each side. Down one ramp rolled a vehicle called *Lunokhod I*, which looked as though it had been designed by an illustrator for Jules Verne. It resembled nothing so much as a nineteenth-century bathtub on eight wheels covered by a convex lid. From it protruded antennas, four television cameras, and a mechanical arm designed to test soil density.

The remarkable fact about this weird-looking contraption was that it worked. Each of the eight wheels was powered independently by an electric motor. The vehicle had a suspension system designed to give it stability on rough ground festooned with potholes or small craters. It was controlled 238,000 miles away by a four-man crew in Russia. The controllers could drive it at two speeds both forward and backward. Sensors automatically halted the vehicle if it was about to encounter an obstacle that the controllers could not see in the television screen, which displayed the view of the four television camera "eyes" of this little monster. The cameras permitted closeup or distant views in all directions, stereo and panoramic.

The lid on the tublike chassis contained an array of solar cells on its underside. During the lunar day, the lid folded outward to face the sun. At night, it closed down to protect the solar panels from damage by meteors, dust, or the vast drop in temperature that comes with sundown on the Moon. During the long lunar night, the vehicle was warmed by a radioisotope heating system.

Between November 12 and 23, *Lunokhod I* traveled 640 feet and transmitted fourteen closeup photos and twelve panoramic views to Earth. Parked during the night, it extended a French-built laser reflector, designed to reflect a tight laser beam back to Earth. Beams were aimed at it by both French and Russian observatories.

On its second lunar day of operation, starting December 8, *Lunokhod I* traveled 5,587 feet in 2 weeks. (Because the Moon rotates around its axis once in 27.3 days, a lunar "day" is nearly 2 weeks long. During the lunar night, the vehicle was shut down for nearly 2 weeks.) It radioed to Earth thirty-three surface panoramas and seven astronomical photos to pinpoint its location. During January, the vehicle was piloted back to its landing platform, having made a round trip of 3,655 meters (11,878 feet).

In addition to performing lunar observations, which showed that the region had been covered by a succession of lava flows, *Lunokhod I* was equipped with an instrument that made X-ray spectrographs of stars and with instruments that reported the energies of incoming solar protons, electrons, and alpha particles (helium nuclei). Although the machine was designed to operate through three lunar days (a total day-night period of three months), it actually functioned for eleven lunar days. The experiments ended with its shutdown at the end of the eleventh day, September 15, 1971. During the ensuing night, the radioisotope heaters failed, and the robot explorer was not reactivated.

According to the analysis made for Congress, Lunokhod traversed a total distance of 10,540 meters (33,280 feet), or 6.3 miles.[21] It transmitted more than 20,000 television pictures and more than 200 panoramas. It made more than 500 tests of the mechanical properties and more than 25 chemical analyses of the soil.

By way of comparison, the Senate space committee's staff report on the two Luna missions noted that although they cost about one-fourth as much as Apollo lunar missions, their scientific return was considerably less: "it was hard to escape the conclusion that an Apollo flight at roughly $400 million each out-of-pocket, bringing back 200 pounds of documented samples selected with care over some miles of terrain, should have far greater scientific merit for analysis than a *Luna XVI* flight at roughly $100 million bringing back a sample of 3.5 ounces selected at random." [22]

However, despite the Luna program's relative bargain-basement approach to lunar exploration, Lunokhod appeared to be the most sophisticated vehicle of that period for automated, lunar reconnaissance. NASA had considered the development of a similar robot vehicle in a project called Prospector. But that concept was revised to the manned electric car called Rover, which was carried to the Moon on the last three lunar missions of Apollo.

The United States did not produce an automatic vehicle of comparable complexity to the Lunas until the Viking Project, designed to send an orbiter to Mars and land a sophisticated scientific laboratory on the surface in 1976 to conduct an automated geophysical reconnaissance and seek chemical evidence of life.

The Soviets continued the Luna program until 1973, with mixed results. *Luna XVIII*, a sample-return vehicle, was launched September 2, 1971, entered lunar orbit September 7, and landed September 11 in the rugged, mountainous region of the Apollonius Highlands north of Mare Fecunditatis. Radio communication broke off with the landing, and the assumption is that the vehicle was wrecked in the rough country. The site was selected for a sample of the light-colored highland soil, believed to be older than the dark basaltic maria sampled by *Apollos XI* and *XII* and *Luna XVI*.

On September 28, 1971, the Russians launched *Luna XIX*, apparently an orbital reconnaissance vehicle not designed to land. According to *Izvestia*, the semiofficial Russian newspaper, *Luna XIX*'s mission was to study the gravitational field of the Moon; locate mass concentrations (mascons), which had the effect of distorting the field; measure the radiation environment in low lunar orbit; and take readings of gamma radiation (from radioactive elements) emanating from the surface.[23]

A second attempt to grab a highland sample was made on *Luna XX*, launched February 14, 1972. It landed seven days later in the Apollonius region, where *Luna XVIII* had failed; extended a hollow drill; and bored into the rocky soil and rubble to obtain a deep core. Then the hollow drill, with the core, was withdrawn into the ascent stage of the lander, and the stage lifted off, using the descent stage as the launch pad, as the lunar module did, for the return to Earth. Recovery of the landing capsule in the USSR was handicapped by a snowstorm, but the core was retrieved and flown to the Soviet Lunar Receiving Laboratory for analysis. The amount of soil returned was not disclosed, but American experts supposed it was on the order of the *Luna XVI* sample of three and one-half ounces.

The last of the Lunas in the Apollo lunar period was *Luna XXI*. It was launched January 8, 1973, following the *Apollo XVII* mission, and it reached lunar orbit January 12. It was then landed in the crater Lemonnier at the eastern edge of Mare Serenitatis, where it discharged *Lunokhod II* down its ramp to the surface. The machine rolled about through four day-night cycles, reporting on soil analyses and taking closeup and panoramic photos. To a limited extent, it supplemented the exploration of the *Apollo XVII* astronauts at Taurus-Littrow in an adjacent mountainous region.

APOLLO XIV

After the debacle of *Apollo XIII*, the detailed investigation of its origin and evolution, and the "let it never happen again" fixes to the Apollo service module, the scientific exploration of the Moon was put back on the rails with the launch of *Apollo XIV* January 31, 1971. Its destination was again the Fra Mauro Formation.

Apollo XIV's lunar module, *Antares*, landed February 5 in a shallow valley at latitude 3 degrees 40 minutes 24 seconds south and longitude 17 degrees 27 minutes 55 seconds west, about 110 miles east of the *Apollo XII* landfall. Nearly 1,000 miles to the northwest, in the Imbrium Basin, *Lunokhod I* was rolling slowly over uneven ground, its controllers 238,000 miles away stopping it now and then to take soil mechanical measurements. Traffic on the moon definitely was picking up.

Out of *Antares* climbed Alan Shepard, now forty-seven years old and a captain in the navy, who, ten years earlier, had put America's toe into space on the first suborbital flight of Project Mercury. Still jaunty and able, Shepard was followed down the ladder by navy Commander Edgar Dean Mitchell, forty-one. Upstairs, in lunar orbit, rode air force Major Stuart A.

Roosa, thirty-seven, making his appointed rounds in the command module, *Kitty Hawk,* and taking pictures of the surface.

Two extravehicular activity sessions were scheduled on this mission. On the first one, Shepard and Mitchell set up the television camera, taking care to keep the lens pointed away from the sun. A televised record of their activities was transmitted to Earth. They erected the Apollo lunar scientific experiment package (ALSEP) instruments, which included the solar wind collector, ionosphere and atmosphere detectors, active and passive seismometers, and a laser reflector similar to one brought to Tranquility by Armstrong and Aldrin.

The "active" seismometer experiment called for the deployment of sound detectors, or geophones, on the ground, wired to a recording device that transmitted the signals to Earth. The seismic signals were made by the explorers themselves, using a device called a thumper, which fired a sequence of explosive charges. The detonations sent waves through the subsurface strata, and recordings of the type and velocities of the waves provided clues to the subsurface lunar structure. In addition, the explorers set up rocket grenades that would be fired by radio signal from Houston after they had left the Moon.

This was the first attempt to make seismic soundings by the technique of explosion seismology on another planet. It had been done routinely in Antarctica, where, as related earlier, the method had revealed the true depth of the ice cap.

Meanwhile, the S4B rocket, which had propelled the Apollo Moonward, was guided so that it would crash on the Moon and generate seismic signals for the *Apollo XII* seismometers in Oceanus Procellarum. The fifteen-ton spent rocket struck 103½ miles from the *Apollo XII* instruments and produced a strong ringing signal in the subsurface rocks.

On February 6, 1971, after a sleep period, the lunar explorers climbed down from *Antares* for a second EVA. This time, they made their way to a feature called Cone Crater, towing geology tools and other equipment on a two-wheeled rickshawlike cart elegantly styled in NASA nomenclature and cost accounting as a modularized equipment transporter, or MET for short. On their return to *Antares,* Shepard exhibited a number-six golf iron affixed to the staff of a soil sample collector and, bringing forth a white golf ball, attempted to drive it down the lunar fairway—one-handed. The bulky moon suit inhibited a normal two-handed swing. On the second stroke, Shepard hit the ball and sent it sailing 100 yards or so. It was a delightful if capricious bit of nonsense that lent a casual air to that complex and exhausting mission.

Shepard and Mitchell set a new EVA record of nine hours and nine minutes of outdoor activity, compared with seven hours and forty-six minutes on *Apollo XII* and two hours and thirty-two minutes on *Apollo XI.* They splashed down in the Pacific Ocean February 9, 1971. After their twenty-one-day period of quarantine without any sign of lunar organisms, living or fossil, the quarantine procedure inaugurated on the return of *Apollo XI* was dropped. Every test biologists and biochemists could think of had been applied to lunar rocks, soils, and returned astronauts on the first three lunar missions for the detection of lunar microbes or viruses. None were found. The Moon was as sterile as the beginning of creation, although chemical compounds that were identified as precursors to amino acids were found in the lunar soil.

THE ROVER BOYS

The *Apollo XIV* "rickshaw" was succeeded by the amazing lunar Rover as surface transportation on *Apollo XV,* which was launched July 26, 1971. The lunar module, *Falcon,* landed July 30 on a lava flow between the Apennine Mountain front and a shallow, winding canyon called the Hadley Rille on the eastern edge of the Imbrium Basin at 3 degrees 39 minutes 10 seconds east longitude and 26 degrees 6 minutes 4 seconds north latitude. Down from the *Falcon's* porch climbed Scott, now a full colonel in the air force. Lieutenant Colonel James B. Irwin, forty-one, followed him. Then the two of them struggled mightily to unpack that multimillion-dollar Rover, the second surface vehicle to be landed on the moon (after *Lunokhod I*) but the first manned car on another planet. In lunar orbit rode air force Major Alfred M. Worden, thirty-nine, in the Apollo spacecraft *Endeavour* (named for Captain Cook's ship, *Endeavour,* which he sailed around the Earth in 1768–1771), making scientific observations and taking photographs of the regions below his orbital track.

The Rover was a two-seater, four-wheeled car, with the lines of a beach buggy. It was ten feet long and three and one-half feet high. Its wheels were made of a piano wire mesh, and each was powered individually by a one-fourth horsepower electric motor, supplied with current by batteries. Lunokhod, it will be recalled, was powered by solar panels. With a Moon weight of seventy-six pounds, Rover had a top speed of eight miles per hour. In addition to radio equipment, it mounted a television camera and parasol antenna. It could go forward or in reverse and could be steered by the front or the rear wheels. Three of these vehicles plus training equipment and spares were built by the Boeing Company at a cost of $21 million. Rover essentially was a manned spacecraft, designed to provide mobility on the surface of the moon.

Scott and Irwin explored the Apennine Mountain front and the lip of the great rille in three traverses in the Rover over a period of three days. They made extensive soil surveys and managed to insert heat probes partway into drill-resistant soil to record the flow of heat from the interior.

Again, this mission set new records. In their three EVAs, Scott and Irwin logged eighteen and one-half hours outside and increased stay time on the lunar surface from *Apollo XIV*'s thirty-four hours to sixty-six hours fifty-four minutes.

The Apollo command and service module *Endeavour* carried a thirty-one-inch box, which was released from the ship into lunar orbit and was destined to remain there after the crew departed in the *Endeavour*. The small "subsatellite" carried an S-band transponder, which facilitated its tracking from Earth by amplifying radar signals it reflected. Changes in the subsatellite's orbital acceleration over points on the Moon's surface would serve to refine Houston's model of the lunar gravitational field. In addition, the subsatellite carried a magnetometer, to detect any magnetic field associated with the Moon, and solar wind detectors. It was a smaller version of *Luna XIX*, performing similar experiments. The *Apollo XV* crew splashed down in the Pacific Ocean August 7, 1971, bringing back 77 kilograms (169.4 pounds) of lunar soil and rock.

In comparing the American and Russian lunar exploration programs at this stage of their development, the staff report of the Senate space committee estimated that the cost of *Lunokhod I* (*Luna XVII*) was probably $100 million, compared with $450 million for *Apollo XV*, including the Rover. *Lunokhod I* weighed 1,667 pounds and Rover, 1,540. (Earth weight including 460 pounds for the vehicle and 1,080 pounds payload, consisting of two astronauts and their gear.) Although Lunokhod traversed a total distance of only 6.5 miles, the *Apollo XV* Rover covered more than seventeen miles. In terms of automation and remote control, Lunokhod was a more sophisticated vehicle. *Apollo XV*, however, combined the features of *Lunas XVI, XVII*, and *XIX*. It returned more geophysical data than all of the Lunas combined, plus the ingredient that cannot be duplicated robotically: human observation on the scene.

SALYUT

While American astronauts walked and drove on the Moon during 1971, Russian cosmonauts practiced with a new space station in Earth orbit called Salyut ("Salute"). Launched by a D-1 Proton booster April 19, 1971, *Salyut I* was established in Earth orbit as a rendezvous and docking target for *Soyuz X*.

The Soviet space station weighed about twenty tons. It was sixty-five and one-half feet long (with Soyuz docked) and divided into three sections. First was a transit section through which cosmonauts entered and left the station from and to Soyuz. Beyond it was a cylindrical compartment thirteen feet in diameter with places for four men. Beyond that was a compartment containing life support, communications equipment, and the station's power system. The station was self-propelled by means of rocket engines that could change its orbit, and propellant (fuel and oxidizer) was stored in spherical tanks behind the main working compartment. The source of electric power was a pair of solar panels, similar to those on the Soyuz.

On April 23, 1971, *Soyuz X* was launched from Baikonur with a crew consisting of Colonel Shatalov, engineer Yeliseyev, and another engineer, Nikolai Rukavishnikov, thirty-nine, whose function was to conduct tests. Early April 24 (Moscow time), the crew docked with Salyut but did not board the space station. They separated Soyuz from the station after five and one-half hours and returned to Karanganda, USSR, April 25. Shatalov reported that he had difficulty in docking with the station and had to fire the Soyuz engines repeatedly to achieve it. Presumably, the flight was a test of the docking system.

Next up was *Soyuz XI*, which was launched June 6, 1971. At first, the mission went very well, with no hint of the tragedy that was to befall it at the end.

The crew, consisting of Lieutenant Colonel Georgiy Dobrovolski, forty-three, commander; Viktor Patseyev, thirty-seven, test engineer; and Vladislav Volkov, thirty-five, flight engineer, docked with *Salyut I* June 7 and entered the station for a three-week stay. They logged a total of twenty-three days, seventeen hours, and forty minutes orbiting the Earth, to set a new space endurance record. Patseyev even observed his thirty-eighth birthday on board.

On June 29, the crew returned to *Soyuz XI*, separated it from the station, and, early June 30, fired the spacecraft's braking engine to return home. That is the last time their voices were heard. When the seven-minute braking burn ended, communication ceased. The silent Soyuz reentered the atmosphere, deployed its parachute, and, as it neared the ground, fired its retro rockets under automatic control. When the hatches were opened, the crew was dead in the couches.

All that has been definitely ascertained about the disaster is that the crewmen suffocated as the result of a sudden loss of pressure. Why the atmosphere in the recovery module suddenly whooshed away into space has never been pinned down. Was it a defective hatch seal? Was human error responsible? Western observers suspected a defective seal.

Soyuz was grounded thereafter for twenty-seven months while modifications were made. These, in effect, converted the vessel from a three-man to a two-man spacecraft, because one of the couches was removed to make room for extra life-support equipment.

During the hiatus in Russian manned flight, Project Apollo came to end with the flights of *Apollos XVI* and *XVII* in 1972.

THE HIGHLAND MISSIONS

The last two lunar missions were sent to highland regions to seek both the oldest and the youngest rocks on the Moon and to test a supposition that volcanic activity on the moon may have continued later than the 3-billion-year-old lava flows that had filled the mare basins. With increasing precision of navigation and flight experience, landfalls in mountainous areas now seemed less hazardous than they had appeared earlier in the program.

Southeast of the center of the Moon lay the light-colored highland region called Descartes. There the *Apollo XVI* lunar module, *Orion*, landed April 20, 1972, at 8 degrees 59 minutes 34 seconds south latitude and 15 degrees 30 minutes 47 seconds east longitude.

Commander of the expedition was John Young, now a navy captain and a veteran of both Gemini and prelanding Apollo missions. With him on the Moon was air force Lieutenant Colonel Charles M. Duke, thirty-six, while navy Lieutenant Commander Thomas K. Mattingly, II, thirty-six, remained aloft in lunar orbit in the Apollo command and service module, *Casper*.

The flight to the Moon had been plagued by relatively minor malfunctions, but then when the crew reached lunar orbit and prepared for landfall, a serious problem developed. Attempting to circularize *Casper*'s orbit on the thirteenth revolution of the moon, Mattingly noticed a malfunctioning circuit in the backup steering system of the vessel's main rocket engine. This was the engine that would be called upon to boost the Apollo spacecraft out of lunar orbit for the return home.

Although the primary steering system was in good order, mission rules required that the backup system be functional too before the lunar module was released for the lunar landing. If the backup system was out of order, the LM would not be allowed to land, because its powerful descent engine would then be needed as the backup. Mission Control would not take any chances of leaving a crew marooned in lunar orbit, especially at this stage of the game, when all seemed to be going so well.

After hours of consultation, NASA and contractor engineers decided that the malfunction in the backup steering system would not prevent that system from being used in an emergency. Young was then given a "go" for landing in *Orion* with instructions to get a night's sleep and begin exploration the next day, April 21. One other difficulty remained: The main (S-band) steerable antenna on *Casper* was jammed, requiring the crew to use the less effective omnidirectional antenna to communicate with Houston. However, they would be able to transmit television and voice communications through the Rover's S-band dish antenna when the auto was unpacked on the Moon.

On the first EVA, Young and Duke set up a new instrument—an ultraviolet camera spectrograph—on a tripod in *Orion*'s shadow, so that it could photograph stars in ultraviolet light. The explorers then buried a second set of heat-flow experiment probes, but Young tripped over a cable and wrenched it out of the probe connector. It could not be fixed, and the astronauts apologetically wrote off the experiment.

However, they were successful in taking deep-core samples of the highland soil. The next day, they made a Rover traverse across rough country, carrying a magnetometer, which detected localized magnetic fields of surprising strength. The implications of that finding and others related to it will be discussed later.

On their third EVA, they sought ancient, volatile gasses believed trapped in the perpetual shadows below rock overhangs and in depressions where sunshine never reached. In those dark places, intense and unwavering cold might have preserved primeval gasses that otherwise would have been dissipated by the sun's heat.

In total, they traversed 27 kilometers (16.5 miles) of the region. At one point, they drove the Rover at a top speed of 10 miles an hour. On the surface seventy-one hours, their EVA time totaled twenty hours and fifteen minutes. When they lifted off from Descartes April 23, 1972, they took 96 kilograms (211.2 pounds) of rocks and dirt with them. They splashed down in the Pacific Ocean April 27, 1972.

No evidence of volcanism younger than that in the maria basins was found at Descartes. However, photographic studies of another highland region in the Taurus Mountains bordering Mare Serenitatis suggested to the geologist-astronaut, Harrison H. (Jack) Schmitt, thirty-six, that evidence of later volcanism might be found there.

Schmitt was the only member of the group of scientist-astronauts recruited in 1965 who went to the Moon. He was a geologist specializing in lunar structure and at long last he was selected as lunar module pilot in the crew of *Apollo XVII*, bound for a region in the Taurus highlands near crater Littrow. Eugene Cernan, a veteran of *Gemini IX* and *Apollo X*, commanded the mission. The command module pilot was navy Commander Ronald E. Evans, thirty-eight, like Schmitt a space rookie.

Apollo XVII began the project's final lunar journey with a spectacular Saturn 5 launch in the early morning darkness of December 7, 1972, after a two-hour-forty-minute delay caused by an automatic sequencer problem in the terminal countdown. This did not affect the flight to the Moon.

The lunar module, *Challenger* (named for the famous British research ship H.M.S. *Challenger,* which laid the foundation of modern oceanography a century ago) landed in a narrow valley at 20 degrees 9 minutes 20.5 seconds north and 30 degrees 44 minutes 58.3 seconds east. Cernan and Schmitt lost no time in setting up the mission's experiments and in extracting the Rover from the *Challenger*'s descent stage, while Evans sailed by in lunar orbit in the command and service module, *America.*

Cernan and Schmitt brought the most sophisticated array of instruments to Taurus-Littrow yet assembled for a lunar mission. It included a radio transmitter-receiver system to probe the soil to the depth of a kilometer with high-frequency radio waves, mainly in search of reflections that would indicate subsurface ice. Two gravity meters were deployed, one to measure changes in the gravitational field along traverses in the Rover and the other, to record gravity waves propagated through the galaxy. The explorers deployed an array of geophones and set eight explosive charges to be detonated after they departed. They sank a neutron probe into a drill hole to measure the production of neutrons at depth by the penetration of energetic cosmic ray particles.

These experiments, along with the *Apollo XVI* ultraviolet camera spectrograph, presaged the eventual use of the Moon as a platform from which to observe the universe. In his search for evidence of late volcanism, Schmitt found deposits of glassy orange soil that seemed, at first, to be of late volcanic origin, until subsequent analysis showed it was quite ancient.

Cernan and Schmitt spent seventy-five hours on the moon, twenty-two hours and four minutes of it exploring the valley of Taurus-Littrow in the Rover and on foot. When they splashed down in the Pacific Ocean December 19, 1972, they brought 110 kilograms (242 pounds) of rock and soil samples with them, including the mysterious orange glass, which had a strange story to tell.

Apollo XVII was the end of manned lunar exploration in this century but not of the Apollo program. Four more flights of that spacecraft lay ahead before it was mothballed in 1975, and they would open another era of the Space Age.

CHAPTER VII

DÉTENTE

The splashdown of *Apollo XVII* on December 19, 1972, not only ended the lunar missions of Project Apollo after eleven years but also marked the end of an era. With its page-one report the next day, the *Los Angeles Times* carried an overline stating: "Spaceflight Epoch Over." The end of Apollo was the end of Part One of the Space Age. By the end of 1972, Part Two was well into the planning-and-development stage, and it would occupy the balance of the twentieth century. So far as manned flight was concerned, the American retreat from the Moon shortened the focus to Earth orbit. Supplanting the space race motive was the practical one of applying the technology of manned flight to environmental reconnaissance and research and to the uses of contemporary civilization.

Three major programs constituted manned flight activity in the immediate post-lunar period. First was the development of the Space Shuttle, a ground-to-orbit, rocket-boosted airplane about the size of a medium-range jet airliner such as the DC-9, which was authorized by President Nixon early in 1972. As reported earlier, the Shuttle was the first unit of a modular space transportation system. By 1980, when it was scheduled to be in operation, it would not only supplant Apollo but also most of the space launch vehicles in the United States inventory. Next was Skylab, a glossy title for the Saturn Workshop program that was started in the mid-1960s to convert the third (S4B) stage of the Saturn 5 into a roomy manned space station. It was scheduled to go into orbit in 1973–1974. Third was the long-sought joint manned orbital flight with the Russians—the Apollo-Soyuz Test Project, or simply ASTP.

After ten years of stalls, rebuffs, and diplomatic maneuvering by the USSR, the United States secured an agreement for the joint Apollo-Soyuz flight, to take place in mid-1975. It materialized out of the Nixon-Kosygin summit meeting in Moscow in May 1972. Although the USSR was concerned principally with promoting a general European conference, the summit opened the door to cooperative manned spaceflight and terminated the era of competition that had characterized—and motivated—Part One of the Space Age.

The Russians had been saying all along, especially during their early rebuffs of proposals from Kennedy and Johnson, that détente in orbit must come from détente on the ground. But a number of people in NASA had a different view. Looking back at negotiations in which he was involved as director of the old Manned Spacecraft (Johnson) Center at Houston, Gilruth remarked that "the Russians never would have agreed if we hadn't beat them to the Moon." [1]

The Agreement on Cooperation in Space between the United States and the USSR was signed May 24, 1972, in a period when the Russian Soyuz was grounded and undergoing redesign following the *Soyuz XI* accident. A month before the summit, *Apollo XVI* had executed the daring and successful mission to the lunar highlands of Descartes with impressive results. In the manned flight context, the Russians were down and the Americans were up. If the time had come for détente in orbit from a political point of view, it had also arrived from a technical one, and the Soviets now could lose nothing in a joint venture.

NASA's plan for promoting international cooperation in space exploration not only for the sake of détente but also to share costs was approved by President Nixon during an informal meeting July 24, 1969, aboard Air Force 1, as Nixon flew across the Pacific Ocean to welcome the crew of *Apollo XI* on its return from the moon. Aboard the presidential airplane were Secretary of State William P. Rogers; the president's foreign affairs counselor, Henry Kissinger; and NASA administrator Tom Paine.[2] To get the ball rolling, Paine transmitted America's post-Apollo plans to academician Keldysh and suggested that the two countries look into potential joint programs and missions.[3] Keldysh responded "favorably."

It was the season for such a plant to grow. The balance of space achievement had reversed since 1961, when Nikita Khrushchev had let pass President Kennedy's euphoric suggestion in Vienna, "Let's go to the Moon together." [4] Kennedy later formalized the proposal in a speech to the United Nations General Assembly September 20, 1963. But the Russians did not move beyond a polite, ambiguous response. Congress reacted, though. The House of Representatives nailed a rider to the NASA Appropriation Bill for the 1964 fiscal year restricting the use of funds for a joint lunar landing without specific congressional approval.[5] It was, after all, the era of the Cold War and one of its principal effects, the space race.

Cooperation between the two space faring powers developed slowly and in most instances as the result of American initiatives. Rhetorically, the way was paved in part by United Nations General Assembly Resolution 1721 of December 20, 1961, which called for international cooperation in space in principal and encouraged bilateral agreements. This led to negotiations between Hugh L. Dryden, deputy NASA administrator, and academician Blagonravov. They provided for exchanges of satellite data on weather, magnetic fields and the sun, and medical results of manned space flights. In addition, the USSR was encouraged to use the passive communications satellite *Echo II* for communications experiments (by bouncing radio signals off the big orbiting balloon). However, Cold War politics militated against any effective implementation of the Dryden-Blagonravov accords, and exchanges were minimal.

After the Air Force 1 conference, however, the concept of an international flight began to take shape. In April 1970, Paine proposed to Blagonravov a cooperative effort to develop space rescue capability. It would require apparatus that would allow American and Russian vessels to dock with each other and with each other's space stations.

In May 1970, Paine followed up the proposal by asking Philip Handler, president of the National Academy of Sciences in Washington, to pass the proposal on to Keldysh, president of the Soviet Academy of Sciences. Paine then talked to Keldysh directly at the end of July, and Keldysh agreed to arrange a meeting in Moscow to consider it in the fall.

From this record, it appears that NASA was pushing for cooperation after any strategic need to take the intiative had passed. However, it was an essential aspect of NASA's total mission to achieve international cooperation in space. The reaches beyond the Earth's atmosphere offered mutual advantages to the adversaries, and there was no reason to extend the Cold War there. Consequently, after the landing on the Moon, NASA had a role as an agency of détente, and Paine was implementing it with the consent of the White House. Beyond this, it was clear to everyone in the space program that the costs of ambitious space projects required international participation. Interplanetary manned flights needed international financing.

The long-sought meeting on space rescue materialized October 26–28 in Moscow and resulted in an agreement that both sides would commence the design of a docking system that would be compatible for their capsules and space stations. Three joint working groups were formed.

In January 1971, a second meeting was held in Moscow on general aspects of cooperation in space science and applications. Agreements were reached to exchange lunar samples and data on Mars. Subsequently, lunar soil and rock samples were exchanged between the *Apollo XI* and *XII* collections and the *Luna XVI* sample and between the *Apollo XV* and *XVI* collections and the *Luna XX* sample. Data from the U.S. *Mariner IX* and USSR *Mars II* and *III* reconnaissances of Mars were also exchanged.

In June 1971, the suggestion that a compatible docking system be constructed specifically for the Apollo and Soyuz spacecrafts was approved at a meeting between George M. Low, NASA deputy administrator, and Keldysh. Working groups met in Houston to look into the technical requirements.

Late in November 1971, three joint working groups met in Moscow to plan a "possible" joint Apollo-Soyuz test mission. They met again the following spring to talk about the compatible docking system. Then, in April 1972, Low went to Moscow to confirm the American interest in the desirability of an Apollo-Soyuz test mission and set up with the Soviets an understanding on how it would be managed and operated.

By mid-May, Working Group 2 had defined the compatibility of radio guidance, optical, and communications systems. It was necessary that the Apollo and Soyuz crews be able to communicate with each other as well as with their own ground stations. Radio and optical guidance systems had to match for rendezvous and docking.

When the joint flight agreement was signed at the summit meeting May 24, 1972, the main details of the Apollo-Soyuz Test Project were settled. It had been agreed that the linkup required a docking module, which would be manufactured by the United States (by Rockwell International, the Apollo prime contractor). The cost was $250 million. The module would be carried into orbit by the more powerful Apollo spacecraft and Saturn 1B launch vehicle, and Apollo would do most of the maneuvering for rendezvous and docking because it could carry more fuel than Soyuz could. For its part, the USSR space agency would equip the Soyuz spacecraft to be used in the mission with apparatus that would enable it to mate with the docking module; would fly a pre-mission test, using a Soyuz; and would have a backup Soyuz ready for launching in case the prime vehicle failed or Apollo's launch was unduly delayed.

It was agreed at a meeting in October 1972 that both vessels would be launched July 15, 1975, with Soyuz going up seven and one-half hours before Apollo, and that all phases of the flight, from launch to touchdown, would be covered by television. The Russians wanted to launch first for purely navigational reasons. The launch timing would enable the Soyuz spacecraft to be within communication range of Soviet ground stations during the critical docking phase of the flight, which would occur over Western Europe. For compatibility, American television equipment was installed in Soyuz. The July 1975 flight period happened to coincide with the windup of the Conference on Security and Cooperation in Europe, which began in Geneva in 1973 and ended in Helsinki July 19, 1975.

NASA'S CABIN IN THE SKY

As technical preparations got underway for the linkup and the American and Russian crews began their training, NASA moved ahead on its two other manned projects, Skylab and the Shuttle. Skylab was a test of the feasibility of a permanent space station for the long-term study of the Earth, the sun, and other stars and of man's ability to withstand long-duration flights in zero gravity. Although manned flight to Mars had been dropped from NASA's agenda, there remained a need to know for future planning whether human beings could survive a trip of seven to nine months in weightlessness.

America's "cabin in the sky" evolved not from a manned spacecraft, as the Soviet Salyut station did, but from a rocket, the Saturn S4B stage. Wernher Von Braun, director of the Marshall Space Flight Center, talked about using the empty tank of an orbiting Saturn stage as a manned vehicle during the early days of Saturn rocket development. The idea was first published in a report by the Douglas Aircraft Company that proposed that the S4B be used as an "orbital house." [6] The stage was twenty-one feet eight inches in diameter and fifty-eight feet seven inches long. Its main structure was the liquid hydrogen tank, a cylinder forty-eight feet long that contained 63,000 gallons of liquid hydrogen for the rocket's J-2 engine. When emptied of hydrogen in orbit, the tank could serve as a roomy cabin with more than 10,000 cubic feet of space, about the equivalent of a five-room house. On the lower end of the hydrogen tank was the oxygen tank, holding 20,000 gallons of liquid oxygen. When emptied, this tank could be used for waste disposal or storage.

The S4B concept was pushed by NASA's manned space flight chief, George E. Mueller. It could be deployed quickly and utilized excess Apollo-Saturn hardware from the lunar program. By 1965, the Orbital Workshop plan was merged with a proposal to convert the Apollo CSM into a manned solar observatory, with telescopes mounted on the service module. The basic design joining both the Workshop and the Apollo Telescope Mount (ATM) was first sketched by Mueller August 19, 1966, as a cluster consisting of the Workshop; airlock; docking adapter, to which an Apollo CSM was docked; and a solar telescope and camera array (see sketch on page 239). Earlier, the Workshop had been a feature of the Apollo Extension System (AES) program, which had contemplated space stations and bases on the Moon, and its successor, the Apollo Applications Program (AAP), which was inaugurated in 1965 to figure out ways of using the Saturn-Apollo transport system so as to keep it in business (and in production) indefinitely.

The day before the *Apollo I* fire, a general outline of the AAP was presented at a press conference in Washington, on January 26, 1967. It did not survive very long after the fire January 27, but it was ambitious. AAP called for the launching of four Saturn 1Bs and four Saturn 5s a year. It also called for establishing two S4B Workshops, one in a low orbit of 250 to 300 miles and the other in a geostationary orbit at 22,300 miles altitude, where the sta-

Hand sketch of early Skylab concept by Dr. George E. Mueller, August 19, 1966. Signed by Davy Jones for G. E. Mueller.

tion would move around the Earth at the same rate as the planet's rotation, thus appearing to hang over one point on the equator. Communications satellites of the Comsat Corporation are placed in geostationary orbits.

The key element of AAP was a NASA decision "to use, modify and expand present Apollo systems capabilities rather than move toward whole new developments." [7] The decision would have frozen the Apollo-Saturn system indefinitely if it had not been reversed in 1969 by the space task group's recommendation to phase out Apollo after the lunar missions and develop a reusable system, starting with the Shuttle. Paine had predicted that the Shuttle would reduce payload-launch cost from $1,000 a pound on the Saturn 5 to $10 a pound by the 1980s. [8]

AAP was scrapped when the Shuttle was born, but the Saturn Workshop survived, mainly because it was a relatively economical project and provided use for surplus Apollo spacecraft and Saturn rockets.

SCHEME 1: THE "WET" WORKSHOP

The initial Workshop plan called for the launching of five Saturn 1B rockets. First up would be the S4B Workshop, which would propel itself into orbit as the second stage of the Saturn 1B. Then, when its propellant residues were dumped into space, the vehicle would be transformed into a habitable space station by the first crew to reach it.

Of course, the big hydrogen tank would be modified before the launch. An airlock would be mounted on the front end, at the point where the lunar module was attached on a flight to the Moon. A docking adapter would be mounted on the forward end of the airlock. Hinged on the rocket's side would be huge wings containing photovoltaic (solar) cells to provide electrical power. Folded during launch, the wings would be extended when the vehicle reached orbit. Inside, an aluminum grid floor would divide work and housekeeping areas. Hinged panels would be installed before the flight that could be opened to form compartments after the big tank was evacuated of fuel. The grating floor would not impede the flow of liquid hydrogen during powered flight, the engineers on the project said.

A mock-up of this remarkable combination of rocket and space station was put on display at the Marshall Space Flight Center, Huntsville, Alabama. Thousands of school children and adult visitors saw it and were permitted to peek inside. It was an astonishing structure, a huge cylinder propped up vertically in a hangar shop, bisected horizontally by the grating, which would serve as a floor on both sides. In orbit, visitors were told, it was possible for the crewmen to stand on both sides of the floor, anchored by shoe cleats, their heads pointing in opposite directions and their feet separated only by the grating. Children who were able to visualize that situation learned a lesson in physics they were not likely to forget.

Fully fueled as a rocket and partially outfitted as a space station, the S4B would be launched from Pad 37B at the Kennedy Space Center and would propel itself into a circular orbit of about 250 or 300 miles. Most of its propellant would be expended in this process; the remainder would be vented by radio command from Houston. The next day, a three-man crew would be launched in an Apollo from Pad 34 by a second Saturn 1B. The crew would dock the Apollo at the docking adapter of the now empty S4B, flush out residual hydrogen with nitrogen gas, pressurize the great hydrogen tank with oxygen at five pounds per square inch, and then enter it through the airlock.

Once inside the "spent stage" Workshop, the crewmen would find themselves in a two-story structure that they could readily convert into a home in orbit by deploying partitions and folding doors to compartmentalize the tank. The shell was even equipped with a fire retardant liner on the inside and a meteoroid shield on the outside. The meteoroid shield was designed to prevent high-velocity dust particles from penetrating the tank walls and also served as a shade to keep the direct glare of the sun from heating up the Workshop's interior.

Running the length of the tank was a "fireman's pole." It enabled the crewmen to move hand over hand from one end of the Workshop to the other. The pole passed through a square "manhole" in the aluminum grid divider, which was either floor or ceiling, depending on the position of a crewman's head.

The forward part of the tank was a work area, with 181 square feet of floor space. Crew quarters aft included 137 square feet for the sleep compartments and 56 square feet for food preparation and waste management. There was a small kitchen and pantry; toilet facilities were better than on Apollo but not deluxe; and crewmen slept in a hammock that could be zippered shut to prevent the sleeper from drifting around the compartment. The sleepers appeared to be standing up, but, since there was no sensation of gravity in free fall, sleeping was as comfortable in one direction as in another. There was also a "space shower." It was contained in a cylinder of waterproof cloth. Suction at the bottom drew off the water.

At the end of a twenty-eight-day tour, the first crew would put the Workshop on "stand by" and return in the Apollo to Earth. Four months later, a second crew would return, this time to spend fifty-six days in the Workshop. Six months after they departed, a third crew would dock for another fifty-six-day tour. The stay times were multiples of the fourteen-day flight of *Gemini VII* in 1965.

The fifth launch of the Saturn 1B would bring up an unmanned Apollo spacecraft equipped with solar and astronomical telescopes. The third crew aboard the Workshop would remotely guide the Apollo telescope mount to a docking at a side port on the Workshop's multiple docking adapter. The telescope mount was expected to provide the most effective instrumentation to study the sun in the history of astronomy.

SCHEME 2: THE "DRY" WORKSHOP

The spent stage, or "wet" Workshop (because it went into orbit filled with liquid hydrogen), was planned to fly as a "live" stage on Saturn 1B during the prelunar landing period when all of the Saturn 5 production rockets were tagged for lunar missions. With the reduction in the number of Saturn 5 test flights that had been programmed in 1968 and the subsequent cutback in lunar missions, the big Saturn became available as a booster for the Workshop.

The first and second stages of the Saturn 5 could put the entire Skylab "stack" into orbit "dry"—without propellant. It would be lifted as payload. The "stack" included the Workshop, airlock, docking adapter, and the eleven-ton solar observatory (Apollo telescope mount). The observatory would have been boosted separately under the wet scheme. This meant that the station could go up completely equipped with breathing gases (4,930 pounds of oxygen and 1,320 pounds of nitrogen) plus 6,000 pounds of water and 1,470 pounds of food. In orbital operations, the Workshop atmosphere, at 5 pounds per square inch pressure was a mixture of 74 percent oxygen and 26 percent nitrogen. This provided the crew with the same amount of oxygen they would breathe at sea-level pressure. All furnishings, lockers, scientific equipment (including the telescopes), and industrial apparatus could be installed before the launch. In the wet stage, some of the supplies and equipment would have to be hauled in Apollo. Following the Saturn 5 launch of the dry Workshop, three Saturn 1B rockets would be needed to boost the three crews up to the Workshop in Apollos.

NASA's decision to shift from the wet to the dry Workshop was announced July 22, 1969, as the crew of *Apollo XI* was heading back to Earth from the Moon. Naturally, it made little impression at the time.

The prime contractor for the dry Workshop was the McDonnell Douglas Corporation, Astronautics Company, at Huntington Beach, California. The corporation's eastern division, at Saint Louis, was prime contractor for the airlock. The cylindrical airlock module carried the oxygen and nitrogen tanks and housed the Workshop controls and displays. It also contained equipment for electrical power distribution, data processing, communications, and several experiments. A Program Office was established in NASA's Office of Manned Space Flight under William C. Schneider. Overall responsibility for developing the project was assigned to the Marshall Space Flight Center. Leland F. Belew was project manager.

The airlock, ten feet in diameter and seventeen and one-half feet long with its five-and-one-half-foot connecting tunnel, was designed not only as a means of entry and egress between Apollo and the Workshop but also to enable astronauts to go outside the Workshop to perform maintenance and collect film from the solar observatory cameras.

Like all of the structures comprising Skylab—the solar observatory, the multiple docking adapter, and the workshop itself—the airlock module was big. It weighed twenty-five tons and contained 613 cubic feet of work volume. The multiple docking adapter, built by the Denver Division of the Martin Marietta Corporation, was 17½ feet long, 10 feet in diameter, weighed six tons, and provided 1,140 cubic feet of work space. The ATM solar observatory, designed and built by the Marshall Center, was 14.7 feet long and 11¼ feet in diameter. It contained no work space other than outside footholds and film access hatches and was controlled from the docking adapter. The observatory carried four solar array wings, which were deployed, windmill style, in orbit. The photovoltaic cells on the wings covered an area of 1,200 square feet and converted sunlight into ten and one-half kilowatts of electricity, which kept eighteen nickel-cadmium batteries fully charged to feed the observatory's instruments. The windmill panels could also feed electricity to the Workshop—a contingency that saved the mission, as it turned out. Finally, there was the Apollo spacecraft itself, weighing fifteen and one-half tons, with a work volume of only 366 cubic feet.

In order to grasp the size of this first American space station, one must visualize it in orbit, with the Apollo spacecraft docked at the forward end. The whole cluster that comprised Skylab totaled 118.5 feet (36 meters) in length. It weighed 100 tons and provided 12,763 cubic feet of conditioned work space. More than four times the weight and volume of the 25-ton Salyut space station, Skylab was the largest construction placed in orbit as of this writing. It went up only fifteen years after the 31-pound *Explorer I*.

Like Apollo, Skylab was an ad hoc project. It was designed for a single objective. As a model for a permanent facility, it was infertile and would not be the progenitor of future space stations. That is regrettable, I believe, because it was an astonishing achievement, both technically and scientifically.

However, not many of us who witnessed its launching by the thunderous Saturn 5 on the afternoon of May 14, 1973, would have bet on that outcome when, a few minutes after the giant rocket cleared the tower, reports came in that Skylab was in trouble.

Watching Skylab depart from Pad 39-A was the first crew whose Apollo spacecraft was ready to fly atop a Saturn 1B. The smaller Saturn stood propped up on a 128-foot tall launch pedestal at Pad 39-B, three miles away from the empty Saturn 5 pad.

Crew commander was Conrad, veteran of *Apollo XII*, *Gemini V*, and *Gemini XI*. He was now forty-two years old, a navy captain. His fellow crewmen were navy Commander Paul J. Weitz, forty, pilot, and Dr. Joseph P. Kerwin, forty-one, a navy physician of commander rank, the science pilot. Neither Weitz nor Kerwin had flown in space before. With Kerwin, Skylab had a doctor in the house, a wise precaution for the first twenty-eight-day mission.

REPAIRMEN IN ORBIT

Hardly had the Saturn 5 vanished into the cirrus clouds over the Atlantic Ocean and the ground stopped shaking when trouble showed up. At sixty-three seconds into the flight, Mission Control at Houston received telemetry indications suggesting that the aluminum meteoroid shield attached to the Workshop had come loose and that one of the Workshop's two solar array wings was no longer folded against the hull in the launch position.

Controllers worried and waited for further developments. At 591 seconds after launch, the Skylab cluster separated from the second stage of the Saturn 5. It coasted into orbit 8 seconds later at an altitude of 435 kilometers (270 miles) and an inclination of 50 degrees to the equator, as planned. Its orbital path would pass over most of the habitable world save Canada and Scandinavia in the northern hemisphere and Patagonia in the southern hemisphere. It circled the Earth every 93 minutes.

When orbit was reached, controllers maneuvered the huge structure into a gravity gradient attitude by means of small control thrusters on the Workshop. These had been retained from the S4B structure, but the main J-2 engine had been removed. As mentioned earlier in the Gemini program, the gravity gradient attitude is a method of orienting a vehicle in orbit so that one end points toward the center of the Earth. The slight increase of gravitational force on the end nearer the center of Earth kept that end of the 118½-foot cluster pointing groundward.

Controllers then turned on the Workshop refrigerator to preserve the frozen foods. The shroud covering the observatory and the docking adapter was cast off. The windmill array of the observatory's four solar cell wings was opened outward by radio command. Each wing was 43.4 feet long and 8.7 feet wide. As the 164,160 silicon solar cells on all four caught the full sunlight, electricity began to flow in the electric power system.

The controllers then turned their attention to the meteoroid shield, an aluminum sheet 25-thousandths of an inch thick that was designed to prevent high-velocity dust particles from penetrating the Workshop hull and also to shade it from the sun. During launch, the shield was supposed to be held against the hull, but in orbit it was to be moved out about five inches by the release of torsion bars.

The indication during launch that the shield had deployed prematurely had alerted controllers to the likelihood of a problem—and they found it. There was no telemetry confirmation on the first revolution of Skylab that the shield was in a raised position. Moreover, there was no indication that the two solar cell wings on the Workshop had unfolded from the launch position. Each wing was thirty-one feet long and twenty-seven feet wide, and the two carried 147,840 solar cells producing about 12.4 kilowatts of electricity for the Workshop. The 147,840 cells on the Workshop solar array system were two-by-four centimeters each, while two-thirds of the observatory's windmill SAS cells were two-by-two centimeters each and one-third, two-by-six centimeters each. The solar cells on the Workshop array thus covered more area and, hence, produced more electricity than the larger number on the windmill SAS. With the solar observatory windmill providing 10.5 kilowatts, the total solar power available for Skylab was supposed to be 22.9 kilowatts—more than enough for all planned operations. But without the Workshop wing arrays, the space station's source of solar electricity was reduced to the 10.5 kilowatts of the observatory windmill array. This was not enough to run a complete mission.

The launch of the first crew was postponed for ten days while Schneider, Skylab program director; Rocco Petrone, Marshall Center director; Kraft, now director of the Johnson Space Center; and NASA and contractor engineers sought to analyze the problem and see what could be done.

Their analysis concluded that the shield had been ripped off during powered flight through the atmosphere and had taken one solar wing along with it. [9] With the shield gone, the Workshop was exposed to the full glare of the sun. Inside, the temperature climbed rapidly toward 200 degrees, F. It threatened to overwhelm the refrigerators, spoil food and medicines, and, if it rose above 300 degrees F., to cause the emission of a toxic gas from the polyurethane insulation that was bonded to the Workshop's interior walls.

The priority task, Schneider reasoned, was to lower the temperature. Controllers maneuvered the Workshop by radio to point its broadside away from the sun. Unhappily, the maneuver reduced the amount of solar energy the windmill solar panels atop the observatory would receive and, hence, cut electrical power; but it also reduced the temperature inside the Workshop to 130 degrees F.

The next objective was to invent a sun shade that would replace the shield and could be erected by the first crew on the Workshop hull. Three different types of big awnings were hastily devised by technicians at the Johnson

Center in Texas, the Marshall Center in Alabama, and the Langley Center in Virginia. Each was designed to be carried in Apollo to Skylab and installed over the Workshop by the crewmen before they moved into the Workshop to set up housekeeping.

However, even if an effective sunshade could be rigged—and nothing like that had ever been attempted—the dismal fact remained that the only power source, outside batteries, was the observatory windmill array. It could not provide enough electricity to operate fully the observatory and the Workshop, too. However, one of the Workshop's solar wings appeared to be intact, but still folded against the hull. The crew would have to take a look at it and see whether it could be deployed by human muscle power. If it could be, the billion-dollar Skylab mission might still be viable.

Conrad, Kerwin, and Weitz, meanwhile, stood by, taking part in consultations and discussions of first one scheme and then another to rig a sun shade on the overheated Workshop. The idea that at first seemed most likely to succeed was hatched by Conrad's next-door neighbor, Jack Kinzler, director of technical services at the Johnson Center.

Kinzler started with four telescoping fiber glass fishing rods acquired at a sporting goods store in downtown Houston. Constructing a model of a device he had in mind, he arranged them on springs so that when they were folded up into a vertical bundle like the ribs of a closed umbrella they could be released to spring out ninety degrees around a central pole and spread a flat canopy.

Telescoped into short lengths and folded around the telescoped central pole, the rods and canopy could be packed in a small container. The model looked feasible; then the task was to construct a larger version that could be carried up in Apollo and deployed on the Workshop by the crew.

The project involved 135 employees in Technical Services. Kinzler borrowed engineering and drafting services from other divisions of the Center. Parts that his people could not make in the shops were hastily fabricated by several Skylab contractors. In a few days, Kinzler had a model ready for testing.

The name of the game was speed, he related. "Our problem was to do a four to six months' job in a week." [10] The Kinzler "fix" was an outsized parasol. When opened, it would spread a canopy twenty-two by twenty-four feet over the sun-facing side of the Workshop.

The main advantage of this device over others being developed feverishly at Marshall and Langley was that it could be erected from inside the Workshop through a scientific instrument airlock. It simply had to be tailored to fit inside a canister that had been designed to pass through the airlock. The parasol thus obviated the risk and loss of time of trying to rig a shade outside the Workshop in bulky space suits.

The operational model of the Skylab parasol used one-and-three-eighth-inch diameter aluminum tubing for the ribs, which collapsed in four-foot sections. It was packed like a parachute in the science canister, a rectangular box eight and one-half inches on a side and fifty-three inches long. Because the science port was ten feet off the center of the outer hull area that the parasol was to cover, the center pole of the shade had to be off-center, too.

While the parasol was in construction, tools were assembled at the Marshall Center to enable the crew to free the apparently stuck solar wing. The toolbox included a long-handled cable cutters, a shears, and a long-handled boathook. It was the consensus of experts that the folded wing was held down by debris and metal from the shorn-off meteoroid shield, which had become wrapped around the wing's main beam. Once freed, the beam might be pushed out away from the hull by the expansion of a spring-loaded, liquid-damped "actuator," a device resembling a shock absorber with an internal piston and a stiff external spring. But, if the fluid was frozen in the actuator, the beam would not move. In that case, crewmen would have to break the actuator and pull the wing out by hand. That seemed to call for some fancy footwork on the outside of the Workshop hull in the bulky space suits. Could they do it? No one knew. As an experiment in man's adaptation to space, Skylab was proving more rigorous than NASA expected.

Once the main beam was extended away from the hull, wing sections would be thrust out from the beamlike window shades by additional actuators—assuming their fluid was not frozen. If it was frozen, Skylab could be rotated so that the extended wing beam would be in the full glare of the sun. Heated sufficiently, the fluid would extrude the solar panels. All fixes and operations were tested by engineers and astronauts in a large water tank at the Marshall Center. Under water, in a stage of neutral buoyancy, a man in a space suit can experience a simulation of many of the working conditions in orbit. Practiced repeatedly in the Huntsville tank were unfolding the parasol frame, cutting the aluminum strap, pulling open the solar array beam with a rope, and, for a later fix, deploying solar canopy poles.

The parasol in its canister and the tools were loaded aboard Apollo along with extra supplies of food and medicines to replace those that might have been spoiled by high temperature.

Skylab Day 12 dawned hot and cloudy May 25, 1973, and Conrad, Kerwin, and Weitz climbed into Apollo CSM 116. The Saturn 1B lifted at 9:00 A.M., eastern daylight time. They made rendezvous with Skylab promptly and transmitted television pictures of the big station on a pass across the United States. As Houston had feared, the damage was nearly catastrophic. The meteoroid shield was gone. One solar wing had been sheared off, and the other was held fast by a bar of aluminum that was bent over the main wing beam.

After a fly-around inspection of Skylab, Conrad moored Apollo to the docking adapter temporarily while the crew took a lunch break and conferred with Houston on the strategy of freeing the stuck wing. Conrad executed a "soft dock" by latching the spacecraft's extended probe in the adapter drogue to achieve "capture." However, the spacecraft and adapter docking rings were not latched, as they would be in a "hard dock."

Conrad undocked after lunch and backed Apollo away. Then he maneuvered the spacecraft so that Weitz could reach the wing with the boathook by standing up in the hatch. The command module was then depressurized, and the hatch opened. Weitz leaned out and caught the wing beam with the boathook while Kerwin held his legs lest he pull himself out of the hatch when he tugged on the wing.

As Conrad kept Apollo hovering close to the Workshop hull, Weitz could see that the wing beam was held by a three-quarter-inch strip of aluminum that was bent around it. But, strive as he might, he could not pull or pry the strip loose with the boathook. One difficulty was the lack of a stable platform to stand on. Archimedes said that with a lever long enough and a place to stand, he could move the Earth. Weitz had the lever, but he did not have a firm place to stand; for as he struggled with the aluminum bar, he simply pulled the CSM closer to the Workshop, forcing Conrad to keep firing the thrusters to back away. A large quantity of fuel was being used in this way, apparently to no avail.

The crew closed the hatch, repressurized their cabin, and sat down to think and to talk things over with Houston. It was decided that they should postpone the solar wing job for the time being and enter the Workshop to deploy the parasol. Conrad moved the CSM in to dock with the space station, but this time the docking probe's capture latches would not engage the adapter drogue. After several attempts, Conrad backed the CSM off. He and his crew struggled into space suits and depressurized the cabin. They then removed the forward hatch through which the docking probe was deployed and took the probe apart, but they were unable to make it work. They finally accomplished a hard docking without the probe by easing the CSM flush against the adapter so that their docking rings made firm contact, activating the twelve latches that clamped the two rings together. It had been a long, hard, and frustrating day, and Houston advised the crew to get a night's sleep.

The next morning, after breakfast, the astronauts donned gas masks and crawled into the airlock tunnel, testing for noxious gases that Workshop engineers feared might have been given off by overheated polyurethane insulation. The tunnel was clear. Weitz then entered the Workshop and inspected the interior for an hour and fifteen minutes. Except for the heat, the interior was in good order, he reported. There was no trace of toxic gases, possibly because Houston had taken the precaution of flushing out and replacing the Workshop atmosphere before the crew boarded.

When Weitz reported all was well, Conrad and Kerwin joined him inside the Workshop. The temperature hovered between 125 and 130 degrees Fahrenheit, but the humidity was so low that all three found they could work there for hours without serious discomfort.

Prospects for the mission looked better, and the crew immediately prepared to erect the parasol through the scientific airlock, which faced the sun. The canister was fitted into the port, and the parasol was slowly extruded outside in the folded position. When the four aluminum tube ribs were clear, they sprang out from the off-center pole, and the huge umbrella spread a mylar canopy over about 500 square feet of the Workshop. It was nearly perfect, except for one loose corner, and it worked. The temperature in the Workshop began to fall. Six days later, it had dropped to a shirt-sleeve eighty degrees.

The crew attacked the formidable job of freeing the solar wing on Skylab Day 25, June 7. Conrad and Kerwin struggled into their space suits and squeezed outside through the airlock with the tools. Careful to avoid snagging his space suit on the jagged remnants of the meteoroid shield, Conrad took up a position near the wing and tied a rope to a slot in the wing beam. The other end of the rope was secured to an airlock fixture. He then manipulated the long-handled cutters so that their jaws were clamped on the piece of aluminum bent around the wing beam. By pulling on a lanyard, Conrad forced the jaws to close, and they severed the aluminum bar. At once, the wing beam moved out twenty degrees. But, as engineers at Houston had feared, the actuator that was supposed to drive the beam outward ninety degrees had become stuck. Conrad and Kerwin then pulled the beam out with the rope, breaking it loose from the stuck actuator.

Skylab was then maneuvered so that the extended beam would be in the full wash of sunlight. After three and one-half hours outside, Conrad and Kerwin returned to the Workshop. They had completed the most difficult repair in the history of space flight. And their effort paid off. The sun warmed the frozen fluid in the hydraulic dampers on the actuators on the wing beam so that gradually the fluid melted and allowed the segments containing hundreds of silicon solar cells to extend outward into the sunlight. Six hours after the astronauts had deployed the wing beam, all thirty solar cell panels were extended, and the wing was generating peak power of 7,000 watts.

At Houston, the capsule communicator, Russell L. Schweickart, called up the Skylab mechanics and said: "Everybody down here wishes they could reach up and shake hands with you." Director Schneider told a news conference: "We feel we're back on a fairly nominal mission."

ANOTHER FIX

Despite the power shortage during the first thirteen days of their tour before the Workshop wing was put into service, the Conrad team was able to complete eleven Earth-resources experiments out of fifteen scheduled, gathering principally photographic data on the lands and oceans over which they flew. They were able to make astronomical observations, collect film during their sortie outside from the observatory, and follow a schedule of exercises and physiological tests. Test results were passed down to Houston.

But the Mr. Fixit role of the astronauts did not end with the deployment of the parasol and the solar wing. One of the eighteen battery chargers that recharged the observatory batteries from the solar windmill array failed. It would not draw power from the windmill because of a stuck relay, according to the engineers' diagnosis. Conrad was asked to see what he could do.

On Skylab Day 37, which was June 19, 1973, he climbed outside through the airlock armed with a hammer and whacked the charger, which was on the exterior of the observatory. That freed the stuck relay, and immediately the charger began passing 240 watts of electricity into the observatory's power system.

On Skylab Day 40—June 22—Conrad, Kerwin, and Weitz closed out the Workshop, figuratively turned out the lights, entered the Apollo CSM, and undocked. They flew Apollo around Skylab for a last look, now regarding the crippled space station with its single Workshop wing and the slightly askew parasol sunshade with feelings of pride. The mylar plastic canopy seemed to be deteriorating in the sun, and the next crew would have to erect another, more permanent shield—which had already been constructed and packaged at the Marshall Space Flight Center. But the station was habitable now.

Having bested adversity, the first U.S. space station crew returned to Earth. Aside from their historic accomplishment of repairing a badly damaged space station, the men of Skylab 2 had racked up a new world record of twenty-eight days in orbit. And they all felt fine.

THE SECOND MANNED MISSION: SKYLAB 3

The first manned occupation of Skylab was designated officially as Skylab 2 because the unmanned launching of the space station had been recorded as Skylab 1. Some of the news media, however, referred to the first manned visit as Skylab 1, and that accounts for confusion in Skylab mission designations. I will follow the official record. The Skylab 3 crew was composed of navy Captain Bean, the commander, now forty-three and a veteran, with Conrad, of *Apollo XII;* Owen K. Garriott, Ph.D., forty-two, an electrical engineer and astrophysicist; and Major Jack R. Lousma, thirty-seven, of the Marine Corps. Garriott and Lousma were taking their first trip to orbit. The program called for a fifty-six-day tour.

The second crew was launched at 7:10 A.M., Eastern Daylight Time, July 28, 1973, which was Skylab Day 76. Bean flew CSM 117 around the station to inspect the condition of the entire stack. All appeared to be well, but he flew so close to the Workshop that the exhaust from Apollo's attitude control thrusters caused the parasol to flap, and Mission Control advised him to shear off lest the canopy be blown loose. The thruster exhaust could also deposit an unwelcome film on the solar cell surfaces and reduce their efficiency. Bean backed away and then docked with the adapter.

As the crew prepared to enter the Workshop, a leak was detected in the reaction control thruster system of Apollo. It was traced to Quad B, one of four clusters each consisting of four thruster nozzles by which the spacecraft was steered. By firing selected thrusters, the vehicle could be made to roll, yaw left or right, or pitch up or down. In addition to attitude control, the quads could be fired simultaneously or in pairs for minor velocity changes in separating from the booster or in rendezvous and docking. They were especially critical in orienting the spacecraft properly for reentry and for separating the command module from the service module before the command module plunged into the atmosphere for splashdown. Consequently, a defective quad threatened the safety of the astronauts on the return flight. Quad B was turned off to conserve propellant.

Once inside the space station, the crewmen were smitten by motion sickness, from which they recovered gradually. Then new mechanical problems showed up. A pressure leak developed in a pump. On August 4, Skylab Day 83, Quad D on Apollo's reaction control system was found to be leaking fuel. Propellant supply valves were closed. Now, two of the RCS clusters were out, and the safety of the mission was seriously compromised. For a time, Schneider and Kraft considered terminating the mission while Apollo was still navigable, but they decided to continue it. Concern was eased by a space rescue capability in Skylab that had not existed before. Because its life-support system could sustain three men for 150 days, Skylab made rescue possible by allowing sufficient time for a rescue spacecraft to be counted down and launched. It took forty-eight days to prepare a rescue Apollo for launch, and if preparations began immediately after the lift-off of the prime vessel, the backup spacecraft would be ready to go before a fifty-six-day mission was completed.

NASA promptly prepared to mate Apollo CSM number 118 with its Saturn 1B launch vehicle and alter it for a rescue contingency; otherwise, it would be used for the third manned mission.

The day after Quad D went out, a leak in the Workshop's primary coolant loop was detected in telemetry received at Houston. Bean was notified, and the crew searched for it, but they could not find it inside the vessel. The next day, August 6, they went outside to look, but they still could not find it. Lousma and Garriott retrieved film canisters from the solar observatory cameras and installed fresh film. Then, warmed up by this effort, they prepared for their major extravehicular activity task—erecting a "permanent" twenty-two-by-twenty-four-foot sun shield over the parasol.

The Marshall Space Flight Center sunshade consisted of a mylar canopy coated with silicone rubber stretched over an A-frame. The frame was formed by two fifty-five-foot aluminum poles. Garriott assembled these by fitting together five-foot sections as he stood, anchored in foot restraints, near the airlock hatch. As he fitted the sections together, he passed the pole out to Lousma, who had anchored himself near the observatory by means of a portable foot restraint.

After assembling the poles, Garriott inserted their ends into the sockets of a V-shaped base plate, which he had attached by means of C-clamps to a strut on the observatory ladder. The poles then extended over the workshop in the form of a huge V. Hauling on ropes passed through pulleys at the far end of each pole, Lousma hoisted the mylar canopy along the poles like a sail. One of the ropes kept twisting around a pole. But eventually, the rectangular canopy was stretched out and secured.

Lousma and Garriott then repaired an ultraviolet spectrometer and set up a space dust collector. When they went back inside, they had logged six and one-half hours on the outer hull performing demanding tasks. Neither reported feeling exhausted. Crews were now mastering the knack of working outside a vessel in free fall.

Additionally, this crew made repairs, replacements, or adjustments to the hot water system, the video tape recorder, an ergometer pedal (for measuring energy expended doing work or exercise), and a mirror used in an experiment. They installed a supplementary rate gyroscope packaged in the adapter, but intermittent gyroscope problems cropped up from time to time in the Workshop, threatening the stability of the big vehicle and requiring the crew to fire thrusters to maintain attitude control during experiment periods, especially when they were trying to make multispectral photographs of the lands and seas below.

On August 23, the 102nd day of Skylab, pressure in the primary cooling system dropped so low that the pump had to be shut down. The laboratory continued to be cooled by the secondary system, but it was found to be leaking. On the ground, technicians assembled a servicing kit, complete with instructions. It was to be carried up by the third crew, which would make the repair.

The next day, a four-and-one-half-hour EVA was performed to install a supplementary rate gyroscope in the adapter and interconnect gyroscopes in the observatory with a cable. A third EVA, lasting two hours and forty-five minutes, was performed September 22. On September 25, the 135th day of Skylab and the 59th of the mission, Bean, Lousma, and Garriott closed the Workshop, donned pressure suits, returned to the CSM, and successfully reentered the atmosphere using only two of the four quads of reaction control system thrusters. The second Skylab crew splashed down in the Pacific Ocean 230 miles southwest of San Diego, having set a new space record of fifty-nine days, eleven hours, and nine minutes.

The crew brought back more than 74,000 photographs of the sun and more than 16,800 of the Earth. In an experiment suggested by a high school student, a spider named Arabella (*species Araneus diadematus*) demonstrated that it could spin a web in a weightless environment about as well as on the ground. The experiment received more attention from the mass media than any other.

The astronauts tested a maneuvering unit inside the Workshop, a gas-propelled "Buck Rogers" device invented half a century ago in science fiction. They did not attempt to use it outside. Eventually, spacemen building large structures in orbit, such as a big space station or solar energy collector, would require such a means of locomotion.

Of all their chores, the Earth-resources experiments seemed to intrigue the crewmen the most. They photographed a quiescent volcano in New Zealand and Mount Aetna in Sicily, which was smoking. They could identify Crater Lake in Canada as an impact feature, gouged out by some ancient meteor. Occasionally, they had clear views of New York City and Long Island, of Land's End at the southern tip of England, of the mountains of Wales, and of London immersed in fog. Then one day, when Britain was not obscured by clouds, they could see the whole of the British Isles.

They looked down upon the central valley of California and sighted Bakersfield and San Francisco. Eastward, they saw Lake Meade, the Hoover Dam, and the blight of Las Vegas on an otherwise tawny desert; they saw the Grand Canyon, which exhibited a dendritic pattern of furrows not unlike the river valleys of Mars, as revealed in the photographs by *Mariner IX*.

As they crossed the Alps, after photographing Rome and Naples, they noted changing color patterns. There were the green and brown reaches of Eastern Europe on orbits that took them over Tashkent, the Himalayas, the high plateau of Tibet, the Gobi Desert, Korea, Japan, and the Pacific. At the orbital inclination of fifty degrees to the equator, they passed as far north as Winnipeg and as far south as Magellan's old landfall of San Julian in Argentina. From the snows of Fujiyama to the glow of Mauna Loa, the island chains of the Pacific flowed beneath their track.

"We never lost our desire to work hard," Jack Lousma recalled in the postflight news conference. "We were always motivated to get the maximum out of ourselves and out of the equipment. We never experienced any loss of morale."

If there was a low point in the mission, Bean said, it was that period after they had recovered from five days of motion sickness and were just beginning to feel good and do some work when the quad problem of the CSM threatened to cause an abrupt end to the mission. But that contingency was not considered long at Mission Control. Their spirits soared when director Kraft told them they could stay aloft.

SKYLAB 4: COMET KOHOUTEK

The final visit to Skylab was launched on the morning of November 16, 1973, on Skylab Day 187. Aboard CSM 118 were Lieutenant Colonel Gerald P. Carr, forty-one, of the marine corps, commander; Edward G. Gibson, Ph.D., thirty-seven, an engineer; and air force Lieutenant Colonel William R. Pogue, forty-three. Gibson was designated as the science pilot and Pogue as pilot, but their duties aboard the Workshop were more or less interchangeable.

The third mission originally was scheduled to last fifty-six days. It was extended to sixty days and then in weekly increments to eighty-four days so that the crew could take unprecedented photographs from space of a new comet—Comet Kohoutek. It was the first Apollo space mission on which all crew members were space rookies.

The comet was discovered March 7, 1973, by Lubos Kohoutek, a Czech astronomer using a 31-inch Schmidt telescope at the Hamburg observatory. It was then about 5 astronomical units from the sun, or about as far from Earth as the orbit of Jupiter. At perihelion, its closest approach to the sun, December 29, 1973, the comet was expected to swing around the sun at 0.14 AU (13 million miles). At that time, it was expected by some astronomers to be almost as bright as the full moon, giving them an unusual opportunity to study its structure and chemical composition. It was named Kohoutek, after the man who first sighted it.

As it turned out, Comet Kohoutek was a highly overrated heavenly exhibit, but predictions of its size and brilliance during its approach to the inner solar system excited the scientific community. It was a bit of serendipity for Skylab, and the tour of Skylab 4 was delayed as well as extended to enable the crew to observe it. Although ground-based telescopes would also be used to observe the comet, instruments in space could see it more clearly, because they were free of the light-scattering and untraviolet-absorption properties of the atmosphere.

The United States had three space vehicles aloft from which comet observations could be made: the Orbiting Solar Observatory (OSO), the Orbiting

Astronomical Observatory (OAO), and Skylab. Of the three, Skylab was undoubtedly the most effective, for it carried a coronagraph that made it possible to photograph the comet closer to the sun than any other instrument could see it. The Skylab White Light Coronagraph was a ten-foot optical system, eighteen inches in diameter, that obtained thousands of pictures of the solar corona—and revealed structure never before seen. It imprinted these on thirty-five-millimeter film and also displayed them on television monitors in the Workshop. It was designed to obtain photos in visible light up to six solar radii (3 million miles). A movable disk in the instrument blocked the solar sphere so that the coronal light could be seen, as in an eclipse, flaring around the occulted solar disk.

Carr, Gibson, and Pogue docked with Skylab on the third attempt. During the rendezvous, Pogue had become nauseated, and, despite his resort to medication (lomotil), the nausea became worse. Because this upset had also afflicted the three crewmen on the second manned mission, it was believed to be a consequence of overactivity in weightlessness before the astronauts could adjust to it or get their "space legs." Consequently, the third crew had been advised to remain in the command module a full day after docking before entering the Workshop.

The crewmen entered the Workshop on the second day of their mission and noted a message addressed to them on the teleprinter, which was used to update the activities schedule. "Jerry, Ed and Bill," it read, "welcome aboard the space station Skylab. Hope you enjoy your stay. We're looking forward to several months of interesting and productive work."

In the crew quarters, the new arrivals found three space dummies awaiting them. One sat on the bicycle exerciser, another in the lower body negative pressure cabinet, and a third on the toilet. They were space suits stuffed with extra clothing—a memento from the Bean crew. By the third day, Pogue's indisposition cleared up, and by the sixth, the Workshop was fully activated.

On the seventh mission day, November 22, Gibson and Pogue donned pressure suits and went outside to perform a remarkable six and one-half hour EVA tour. They operated a camera designed to photograph dust and debris around the station, erected a device to detect cosmic ray particles coming into the solar system from beyond Uranus, deployed sheets of foil to collect nuclear particles that precipitated out of the magnetosphere, repaired an antenna, and retrieved film from solar observatory cameras that had been exposed during the inter-mission period.

On the eighth day (Skylab Day 195), they took photos of the brightening comet out of the CSM window with a thirty-five-millimeter Nikon camera fitted with a fifty-five-millimeter lens. For the next ten days, they continued to photograph the comet every twelve hours. On the ninth day, they adjusted Skylab's orbit to take photographs of the Earth, using the thrusters on Apollo, and they replaced a television monitor.

During the first ten days, Gibson and Pogue had lost between four and five pounds, while Carr had gained one-half pound. Body height increased from one and one-half to two inches with the relief of gravitational pull on the vertebrae. Orbital flight would appear to be the prescription for sufferers of "bad backs" resulting from narrowed spaces between intravertebral discs.

The crew performed three more EVAs. The second sortie, on Christmas day, lasted seven hours. On their third, December 29 (Skylab Day 231), two crewmen spent three hours and twenty-eight minutes photographing the comet and the sun while standing on the Workshop hull in foot restraints. They had photographed a partial solar eclipse on December 23. On the fourth EVA, February 4, 1974, Carr and Gibson went outside to retrieve film from the observatory cameras and collect the foil used in the cosmic ray and magnetospheric particle collections, along with thermal control coatings. Passive thermal control of space vehicles could be accomplished by paints and other types of coating that reflected or absorbed heat from the sun. Gold was a favored thermal coating material. Skylab tested cheaper substitutes. Another item they brought inside with them was a sample of material that might be used in a solar sail to propel a future interplanetary vessel. The sailcloth sample had been exposed on the observatory. Theoretically, a spacecraft could be accelerated by light pressure or the solar wind from the sun by hoisting a sail in orbit. Finally, they emplaced particle collection casettes on the observatory's sun shield. These might be collected on a future visit, although none were scheduled. The outing lasted five hours and nineteen minutes, making the crew's EVA total twenty-two hours twenty-one minutes.

The crew spent two days closing out Skylab, stowing equipment and loading recorders, tapes, film canisters, and apparatus aboard the Apollo command module. The space station was then being stabilized by two cranky control moment gyroscopes, the third one having failed earlier in the mission. Other problems were appearing. The shower unit stopped working a week before the end of the tour, and the visual tracking system on the infrared spectrometer, used in Earth-resources observations, failed about that time.

The third manned mission produced no alarms nor excursions as had the earlier two. However, on the mission's seventy-third day, or January 29, 1974, Skylab, in a 267.9-by-274.8-mile orbit, passed within 4 miles of *Orbital Vehicle 32*, a Department of Defense satellite that had been in orbit since October 28, 1966. It might be called a "near-miss." (I was advised later that the orbits of both Skylab and *OV-32* had been plotted carefully to make sure they would not collide.)

On February 7, 1974, the eighty-third day of their tour, the crew burned the Apollo CSM reaction control thrusters for three minutes to boost Skylab's orbit to 282.9 by 270.25 miles, adding a year to its orbital lifetime, which was calculated in the new orbit at nine years. The next day, February

8, they turned off all the primary systems except electricity, closed the adapter hatch after them as they entered the Apollo command module, and separated from their home away from home after eighty-four days, one hour, and fifteen minutes—a new world record.

They had conducted forty-five Earth-observation programs, twenty materials-processing experiments, seventeen science demonstrations, and two press conferences. They had amassed data on forty-five miles of magnetic tape and 200,000 images of the sun. And they had taken the first photographs of a comet from space. They splashed down in the Pacific Ocean at 10:17 A.M., central daylight time, February 8, 1974, and when they emerged from the command module on the deck of the carrier U.S.S. *New Orleans*, they could still walk—but not well.

Houston then maneuvered Skylab in a gravity gradient posture with the adapter pointing up. Controllers switched off electrical power, and on February 9, the final command was radioed to Skylab, turning off telemetry.

Nine men had spent 171 days, 13 hours, and 14 minutes aboard Skylab, and from it NASA learned the rudiments of space station technology. A great deal of new information was acquired about the sun, especially the corona; an enormous number of scientific observations were made, and important industrial processes were tested in zero gravity. The most significant learnings, however, concerned human beings.

The medical results of the three manned missions seem encouraging. Although there were individual differences among the crew members, the third crew, which performed the most exercise, emerged in the best physical condition and readapted to normal gravity soonest. Cardiovascular, skeletal, and muscle tests showed no significant deterioration in any of the crews.

Generally, crew health was good. A daily private medical conference was conducted between flight surgeons at Houston and the crew. There were no clinically serious illnesses nor injuries, a summary medical evaluation showed. The first crew exhibited a decrease in appetite initially, followed by weight loss; the second crew experienced "general malaise" for three days, and one member vomited for one day. One stye, two boils, and recurrent nasal congestion were reported. Two of the third crew had a "general malaise" for three days, and one reported vomiting for one day; also, they complained of recurrent head and nasal congestion and sleep problems.

Earlier in the space program, there had been concern about bone mineral losses and muscle atrophy, which had shown up as early as Project Mercury. But the long Skylab stays resulted in only "moderate" losses of calcium, nitrogen, and other nutrients, the evaluation stated. Bone mineral losses did not occur in the radius and ulna (forearm bones) in any of the crewmen, but losses of calcium from the heel bone (os calcis) resembled losses noted in bedrest studies of similar duration, it added. Although all three crews lost weight, the Skylab 4 crew lost the least—1.4 kilograms (3.08 pounds) or less per man. Caloric requirements appeared to be about the same in orbit as on the ground, contrary to the belief that they would be less in orbit.

Loss of red blood cell mass, noted on Apollo flights, was progressively less on each of the Skylab missions. The mean loss was 14 percent for the first crew, 12.3 percent for the second, and 6.8 percent for the third. However, plasma volume losses did not show a similar tendency. Among the first crew, two showed no plasma loss, and one showed a loss of 10 percent. All three members of the second crew showed a 10 percent plasma loss, and the third crew exhibited losses of 13, 16, and 19 percent. Postflight return of red cell mass was more rapid in the second and third crews than in the first.

Studies of the cardiovascular systems of the crewmen by techniques of inflight vectorcardiography and echocardiography did not indicate any "clinically significant patterns" nor functional deterioration. Muscle function was maintained progressively better with each mission, in accordance with the increase in the amount of exercise from thirty minutes a day on the first, to one hour on the second, and to one hour thirty minutes on the third.

The studies noted an increase in height and reduction in stomach and chest circumference. A large shift of blood and tissue fluids occurs in zero gravity from the legs to the upper portions of the body, the evaluation noted.

The evaluation concluded: "The medical experiments data analyzed to date [1974] and the observations made during and after the flight do not indicate any major medical constraints for continued extension of man's duration in space." However, it cautioned, programmed exercise was found necessary to maintain the optimum capability for satisfactory readaptation to normal gravity. "The Skylab crewmen demonstrated that man can fully adapt to a weightless environment, perform in an efficient and effective manner, and then readapt to the one-G environment. A major milestone in the manned space flight program has been accomplished."

Next up in the manned flight program was the great international mission in which the American Apollo and the Russian Soyuz would link up in orbit. It, too, was a major milestone.

SOYUZ AND SALYUT

Although the Russians were first up with a space station (*Salyut I*, launched April 19, 1971), it hardly approached Skylab in size, habitable volume, and scientific grandeur. Yet Salyut was a continuing program, whereas Skylab was technologically a mule—a sterile hybrid.

The Soviets launched *Salyut II* from the Baikonur Cosmodrome April 3,

1973. The station, without Soyuz docked, was 33 feet long and 13 feet in diameter, with 3,500 cubic feet of work space and launch weight of 20 tons. With Soyuz attached, the "stack" was 64 feet long and weighed 25 metric tons, or 55,125 pounds. The station alone was not a quarter the size of Skylab.

Soon after *Salyut II* reached orbit, ground controllers experienced problems in controlling it. On April 14, 1973, it broke up into twenty-one pieces, one large and twenty small ones. These reentered as fireballs May 28. The cause of the breakup was not disclosed.

On September 27, 1973, twenty-seven months after the *Soyuz XI* tragedy, a redesigned *Soyuz XII* was launched on an orbital test flight with Vasily G. Lazarev, an air force test pilot and surgeon, and Oleg G. Makarov, a design engineer, as the crew. This vehicle was the first of the "new" models. It carried two twelve-foot solar wings aft for electrical power and weighed 14,960 pounds, less than one half the weight of Apollo.

Soyuz consisted of three modules, compared with Apollo's two (the command service modules). Crew couches in Soyuz were located in the descent module, a cone-shaped pressurized compartment that contained the control panels and the landing system (parachute and retro rockets). It was connected by a hatch to the spherical orbital module, on the forward end of the stack—a work and recreation area for the crew that could be used also as an airlock for extravehicular activity with the descent module closed off. The third element was an instrument module, unpressurized, at the rear. The three modules measured twenty-four feet in length and seven and one-half feet in maximum diameter; in outline they appeared faintly Byzantine.

Unlike Apollo, with its pure oxygen atmosphere at five pounds per square inch, Soyuz carried a normal oxygen-nitrogen atmosphere at sea level pressure (14.7 pounds per square inch). Generally, it stocked consumables for a five-day flight; Apollo stocked them for eleven to eighteen days.

Lazarev and Makarov put *Soyuz XII* through its paces for two days. They tested a new pressure suit, which cosmonauts would be required to wear during launch and reentry to prevent another asphyxiation accident as on *Soyuz XI*. When the test was completed, Soyuz once more was back on the rails as the Soviet Union's third generation manned space vehicle. *Soyuz XIII* was launched December 18, 1973, on an eight-day mission with Lieutenant Colonel Pyotr Klimuk, thirty-three, and Valentin Lebedev as crew. The mission confirmed the reliability of the new Soyuz, and the crewmen observed the comet Kohoutek, which the third Skylab crew was photographing at the same time.

The third Russian space station, *Salyut III*, was launched June 25, 1974. On July 3, *Soyuz XIV* went up to dock with it the next day. The crewmen, Colonel Pavel Popovich and Lieutenant Colonel Yuri Artukhin, both forty-three, spent two weeks in *Salyut III*. During that mission, the Soviets deployed an Atlantic Ocean tracking network consisting of three elaborately instrumented ships: the *Vladimir Komarov*, the *Kegostrov*, and the *Morzho-vets*.

Next up was *Soyuz XV*, August 26, 1974. The mission was crewed by Lieutenant Colonel Gennady Sarafanov, thirty-two, and Lev Demin, forty-eight, an engineer and also a grandfather—the first grandfather to go into orbit. American observers suspected that Sarafanov and Demin intended to set a new Russian record of forty-five or sixty days aboard Salyut, but after forty-eight hours, Sarafanov brought *Soyuz XV* down for a night landing August 28. General Shatalov, the cosmonaut crew chief, explained that the flight was a night landing test, but admitted that Soyuz was unable to dock with *Salyut III* because its rate of approach was too high.[12]

A new "international" docking mechanism was installed on *Soyuz XVI*, which was launched December 2, 1974, as a test of all Soyuz systems for the mid-1975 Apollo-Soyuz Test Project. The vessel was identical to *Soyuz XIX*, the vehicle that the Soviets were preparing for the linkup, and both countries tracked it.

The crew, Colonel Anatoly V. Filipchenko, forty-six, and Nikolai N. Rukavishnikov, forty-two, an engineer, checked the docking gear with a simulated docking ring. No attempt was made to dock with *Salyut III*, because the new docking modification was designed for the Apollo docking module. After six days in orbit, *Soyuz XVI* returned to Kazakhstan. Russian and American experts who reviewed the flight declared that all tests were satisfactory.

Salyut IV was then launched December 26, 1974, destined to become the most successful space station in the Russian series. On January 11, 1975, Colonel Aleksiy Gubarev and Georgiy Grechko, an engineer, went up in Soyuz XVII, docked with the station, and spent thirty days there. When they landed February 9, they proclaimed *Salyut IV* a habitable and comfortable station.

A second effort to achieve a forty-five- to sixty-day stay was made in the spring of 1975 with the launch of Lazarev and Makarov in a Soyuz, April 5, but the flight was aborted before the spacecraft reached orbit because of a failure in the third stage of the launch vehicle. The cosmonauts came down safely in Siberia after a ballistic flight across the eastern Soviet Union.

The launch failure triggered concern by American space observers about the Soyuz launch for the ASTP, and NASA officials inquired about the cause—an unprecedented inquiry. Chester M. Lee, a retired U.S. Navy Rear Admiral, who was NASA director of ASTP, reported that the failed rocket had been described by the Russians as an older model. He said that he had been assured a modernized launch vehicle would be used to put *Soyuz XIX* into orbit.[13] The Soyuz involved in the abort was not designated by number.

Next up was *Soyuz XVIII*, with Lieutenant Colonel Klimuk and Sevastyanov, the engineer, aboard. It was launched May 24 and docked with *Salyut IV*. The two cosmonauts entered the station and settled down for a two-month stay that would last through the Apollo-Soyuz mission. Sevastyanov was the flight engineer on *Soyuz IX*, which had flown eighteen days in June to set a new world record then. He was well known in the USSR as a television commentator on science. To Sevastyanov must go the distinction (if any) of being the first journalist in space.

SPACELAB AND SHUTTLE

During this period when Skylab and Salyut were being demonstrated, Western Europe entered the space station sweepstakes with a new space station concept called Sortie Lab and later, Spacelab. It took the form of a pressurized cylinder somewhat smaller than Salyut plus adjoining open platforms or pallets on which instruments could be mounted. Spacelab was conceived by NASA as prime payload for the Shuttle. NASA proposed that Europe build it to be flown in the Shuttle's big sixty-foot cargo bay.

The Spacelab-Shuttle partnership between Western Europe and the United States grew out of Tom Paine's visit to London, Paris, Bonn, and Rome in October 1969 to promote greater European participation in the United States post-Apollo program. Paine and his staff visited Australia and Japan to invite their participation also in 1970.

The time was ripe for such a deal. In the United States, now that the space race was over, money was becoming ever harder to get for space projects. Plans for developing a space station after Skylab were shelved in the Nixon administration. The Shuttle hung by a thread. The original concept of two reusable Shuttle stages, a booster and orbiter, had been modified to that of a less costly rocket-boosted airplane with recoverable solid-fuel booster rockets. There were no funds at all for a reusable space tug, the next in the series of reusable vehicles in the 1969 space task group blueprint for the future. The tug was essential to hoist payloads that the Shuttle could deliver only to low orbit into geostationary orbits—especially communications satellites.

Initially, Paine had proposed that Europe build the tug. The idea appealed to the European Launcher Development Organization (ELDO), a partnership of seven nations created in 1962 to develop satellite launchers for Western Europe.

The transition of European participation in NASA's post-Apollo plans from the tug to Spacelab reflects the rise and fall of ELDO. The idea of a multinational European effort to build satellite launchers—and thus free Europe of dependence on NASA to launch European research satellites—was proposed by the United Kingdom in 1960. At that time, the British decided to halt development of their Blue Streak missile as a weapon of war; the British Isles were protected by American-built Thor IRBMs. The government offered the Blue Streak as the first stage of a multistage rocket, to be financed and developed jointly by Western European nations.

France supported the idea and offered a launcher it was working on, the Coralie, as the second stage. West Germany agreed. It proposed its Astris rocket as the third stage. Italy joined and offered to build the first series of satellite test vehicles. Belgium enrolled to provide ground guidance stations, and the Netherlands came into the partnership with the mission of setting up long-range telemetry links. The seventh partner was Austria.

Test facilities were provided at first at the Woomera rocket range in Australia and later at a near-equatorial launch site at Kourou, French Guiana. A joint budget of 70 million pounds sterling was provided. However, the financing base was changed to a monetary unit (MU) equaling the United States dollar.

The convention under which these arrangements were worked out entered into force May 1, 1964. From then on, inflation and management and technical problems dogged the program and ultimately defeated it.

By 1965, the development program, which contemplated a series of *Europa* rockets, broke through the 70-million-pound ceiling. Costs were recomputed to 400 million monetary units (MMU), but that did not suffice long. In 1966, the ELDO Ministerial Conference raised the ceiling to 626 MMU. By 1973, the development cost of *Europa II* had escalated to 771 MMU.

ELDO was authorized to develop three models. *Europa I* was the first, designed to put a one-ton payload in low orbit. *Europa II* was an uprated version with the mission of lifting 450 pounds to geostationary orbit (at 22,300 miles altitude) from Kourou launch center. A third model, *Europa III*, with enough thrust to put 1,500 pounds in geostationary orbit, was started.

The testing program opened with promise. Five launches of the first stage were successful. Then, on two tests in 1967, the second stage failed. In 1968, the third stage failed; in 1969, it failed again. In 1970, the last test launch from Woomera, the launch vehicle failed to orbit a satellite, but otherwise its performance was more encouraging than the earlier tests. It was at this point that NASA administrator Paine appeared in Europe with the proposal that ELDO build the tug.

On November 5, 1971, *Europa II* was launched from Kourou and exploded 150 seconds after lift-off. It was the shot that sank ELDO. In mid-1972, NASA withdrew its offer of ELDO participation in the tug and proposed instead that Europe build Spacelab as a payload for the Shuttle, a program in which ELDO would not be involved. European engineering teams that had spent two years on preliminary tug designs were left high and dry. But that was only the beginning.

Later in 1972, the Germans pulled out of the Europa rocket program, concluding that: "the financial effort required for launchers was too high in relation to the small number of satellites which the Americans might refuse to launch." By the end of the decade, the West German government predicted, the United States Shuttle "would have made our launches actively pointless." [14]

The reasons the ELDO rocket development program bogged down are illustrated by the report of a review commission that was set up in November 1971 to investigate the cause of delays and difficulties in the development of *Europa II*. "The Europa II project bears the mark of the historical and political circumstances that have attended its implementation and resulted in a highly unintegrated design consisting of stages built nationally and practically independent of one another." [15]

The lack of coordination could have been corrected by efficient management, the report said, but it wasn't. The report noted also a tendency to resort to national agencies in placing contracts, a circumstance that effaced the secretariat's technical authority. In short: Technical authority was inadequate for the secretariat to carry out an effective managerial function; the internal organization of the secretariat was "inefficient," and "pressures exerted on ELDO by member states did nothing to improve this state of affairs."

These difficulties conferred upon ELDO a Tower-of-Babel image, and member states became disenchanted with the experiment of building a rocket by diplomacy. ELDO, its former secretary-general observed candidly, "was inspired more by the need to find some use for a rocket already wholly developed by one country—namely, the United Kingdom's "Blue Streak," which had just lost its military raison d'etre—than by any real resolve to make Europe self-sufficient in the satellite launcher area." [16]

Europa II was reorganized. ELDO then began work on *Europa III*, but members had become "disinclined to believe in the need for Europe to build its own launchers." [17] The Europa III program was cancelled by the European Space Conference in Brussels in December 1972. The conference assigned to France the responsibility for developing a heavy launch vehicle, called Ariane, with financing from ELDO members. Then in April 1973 the ELDO Council halted the *Europa II* program, and ELDO was without a mission.

Meanwhile, a second European space group called ESRO (European Space Research Organization) was formed in 1964 to build the satellites that ELDO's rockets were designed to launch. But because ELDO was not getting off the ground, most of the satellites were launched by U.S. Scout and Thor-Delta rockets and the French Diamant launcher. ESRO consisted of Belgium, Denmark, France, West Germany, Italy, Netherlands, Spain, Sweden, Switzerland, and the United Kingdom. Austria, Norway, and Ireland had observer status.

ESRO's main technical facilities were housed in the huge European Space

Research and Technology Center (ESTEC) at Noordwijk, Netherlands, on the duney coast of the North Sea between Amsterdam and The Hague. Satellites were designed, built, and tested there. ESRO manages an operations center at Darmstadt in West Germany and a rocket range in northern Sweden. It operates telemetry receiving stations in Belgium, Alaska, the Falkland Islands, and Spitzbergen.

The rise and fall of ELDO, which finally was merged with ESRO in the new European Space Agency, had shown clearly that the main problem in multinational development of complex vehicles such as big rockets was managerial, not technological. NASA executives became aware of this, and it was one reason they withdrew their proposal that Europe develop the Space Tug.

However, ESRO showed promise of learning from the mistakes of ELDO, and ESRO-ELDO officials made it clear to NASA that a tight technical management would be appointed and headquartered at ESTEC if Europe decided to build Spacelab. Technically, that vehicle was well within the state of the art of the European aircraft industry. Politically and economically, it offered Europe a piece of the action in manned space flight.

An agreement among ESRO members setting up the financial basis for Spacelab was drafted in March 1973. Nine ESRO members committed themselves to the project: Belgium, Denmark, France, West Germany, Italy, the Netherlands, Spain, Switzerland, and the United Kingdom. Austria, which was not an ESRO member, joined later. Funding was set at 380 million accounting units, an international monetary standard. In 1973, it was based on an equivalence of 1 AU to $1.302.

There followed an intergovernmental agreement between the European group and NASA "concerning the development, procurement and use of a space laboratory in conjunction with the Space Shuttle System" in August 1973. It identified NASA and ESRO (later ESA) as cooperating agencies. A Memorandum of Understanding dated August 14, 1973, was signed by chiefs of ESRO and NASA, paving the way for the partnership to start in June 1974.

Spacelab was characterized by ESRO as one of two "special projects." The other was the Ariane rocket, which France was building. It was insurance that Europe would have an independent capability of launching scientific, meteorological, and communications satellites, even though the Shuttle was available as a common carrier for the same tasks.

Contracting Spacelab construction followed the ESRO custom of awarding work to each member state in proportion to its contribution to the project. It was not the most effective way of getting the best work, but it appeared to be an inescapable political necessity. In a somewhat different way, NASA also followed this practice, awarding contracts and establishing centers on a geopolitical basis. This was the reason, for example, the Lyndon B. Johnson Space Center was located in Texas, rather than in Florida, where there was plenty of room for it on the acreage that NASA bought in Merritt Island for the Kennedy Space Center.

In Spacelab, West Germany contributed the largest share of the funding, 53 percent, and also got the lion's share of the work, including the prime contract. Next was Italy, with 18 percent; France, 10 percent; the United Kingdom, 6.3 percent; Belgium, 4.2 percent; Spain, 2.8 percent; Netherlands, 2.1 percent; Denmark, 1.6 percent; Switzerland, 1 percent, and Austria, 1 percent.

The Spacelab prime contractor was a West German firm, ERNO/VFW Fokker of Bremen, which won a competition for the job with another German firm, MBB (Messerschmitt, Bölkow-Blohm). ERNO is a subsidiary of VFW Fokker whose shareholders in 1974 included the Northrop Corporation in California, the United Aircraft Corporation in Connecticut, the Krupp and Heinkel interests in Germany, and the Algemene Bank in Amsterdam. Each of the competitors had its own array of major subcontractors and consultants. Two American firms, McDonnell-Douglas and TRW, served as consultants to the ERNO team. Some of the MBB team members were called in to perform specialized work after the contract was given to ERNO. Messerschmitt was engaged to help develop an instrument-pointing system so that Spacelab telescopes and other instruments could be aimed precisely at objects (the sun or other stars) the scientists want to observe. The pointing system had to be integrated with the Shuttle orbiter stabilization and guidance system—as indeed the entire Spacelab article had to be integrated with the Shuttle.

In this program, therefore, Europe not only undertook to build a space vehicle but also to create an international manufacturing complex requiring unprecedented coordination. Beyond this, every system had to be compatible with the Shuttle Orbiter, extending the coordination requirement across the Atlantic to American Shuttle contractors. Spacelab and Shuttle thus became the largest international manufacturing program in the history of civilization. It was also the most advanced undertaken by Western people. Direct telephone dialing was opened between ESTEC in Holland and the Marshall Center in Huntsville, and teams of engineers shuttled back and forth between Houston or Atlanta and Schipol Airport, Amsterdam—from which it is hardly a forty-minute drive to ESTEC.

With the Spacelab partnership, the Shuttle became more secure as a continuing program. It had acquired no small international political importance. The final design was an orbital aircraft called the Orbiter; it was about the size of a DC-9 jet liner, with a pressurized compartment for a three-man crew and four scientists forward and an unpressurized cargo bay 18.5 meters (60 feet) long and 4.6 meters (15 feet) in diameter. This was ample to carry Spacelab with a maximum length of 15 meters (47.75 feet) and diameter of 4 meters (13 feet) in all its three configurations.[18]

The Orbiter, with a wingspread of 78 feet, was designed to be boosted vertically off a modified Saturn 5 launch pad by two solid-fuel rockets and its own three hydrogen-oxygen engines. At lift-off, this combination was to develop 6.7 million pounds of thrust. (Saturn 5 developed 7.5 million pounds of thrust at lift-off.) After firing for 125 seconds, the two solid-fuel rockets would be detached and descend on parachutes from an altitude of 25 miles to be recovered in the Atlantic Ocean for refurbishment and reuse. At 50 miles altitude, the 155-foot hydrogen fuel tank serving the Orbiter engines would be jettisoned. It would not be recovered. To return, the Orbiter would deorbit by the retrofire of its maneuvering engines, and, after reentry, glide to landing on a 3-mile concrete runway at the Kennedy Space Center. The runway was completed in 1975.

The Shuttle Orbiter prime contractor was the Rockwell International Corporation, which as North American Aviation, then North American Rockwell, had been Apollo prime contractor. The initial contract negotiated in April 1973 amounted to $477.4 million. The Orbiter's three main hydrogen-oxygen engines designed to develop 470,000 pounds of thrust each were awarded to Rockwell's Rocketdyne Division. The external fuel tank contractor was Martin Marietta, and the solid rocket boosters contractor, the Thiokol Chemical Corporation. Aerojet General Liquid Rocket Company was engaged to build the orbital maneuvering system (OMS) engines; the Marquardt Company, the reaction control system (RCS) thrusters; and the Grumman Corporation, the big delta wing. The total contract team numbered 130 major firms.

Attached to its fuel tank and erected vertically on the launch pad, the Shuttle would stand 184 feet high. The Orbiter alone was 122 feet long. Launch weight was 4.4 million pounds. Landing weight was to be 187,000 pounds. Although the Shuttle was being designed to deliver 65,000 pounds to a 100-nautical-mile- (115 statute miles) orbit, it could return only 32,000 pounds. With a safety margin, maximum return weight would be held at 25,000 pounds. Spacelab was designed to meet that constraint.

HOUSTON, THIS IS SOYUZ

As Europe went to work on its first manned spacecraft in 1974 and America went ahead with the first orbital airplane, a new era of détente and cooperation in space bloomed between the United States and the USSR with the advent of the Apollo-Soyuz test project. Layer by layer, the wraps of secrecy were peeled off the Russian manned space program. Pilots, engineers, and technicians on each side trained for the joint flight at each other's manned space flight centers at Houston and Moscow and in Florida and Kazakhstan.

The universal docking module that would enable the Apollo and Soyuz to mate was built by Rockwell. It provided an airlock that was required to equalize pressure during crew transfers from one vessel to the other.[19] Normally, the Soyuz atmosphere was at sea level pressure, 14.7 pounds per square inch. It was reduced to 10 pounds per square inch to facilitate crew transfers to and from Apollo, with a 5 pounds per square inch pressure.

Compatible radar, optical ranging, and television systems were installed on the two spacecraft. The crews, too, were compatible. Over their training period, they developed an easy-going, cameraderie. As space men, they were members of an elite fraternity. Professionally, their interests were identical. Their military backgrounds were similar.

The Apollo commander was Tom Stafford, now forty-four, a brigadier general in the air force. He was a veteran of Gemini VI, Gemini IX and Apollo X. The command module pilot was Vance DeVoe Brand, forty-four, a navy-trained, civilian test pilot. Donald K. (Deke) Slayton, now fifty-one, was docking module pilot. One of the original Project Mercury astronauts, Slayton had been scheduled to fly the second Mercury orbital mission until he was grounded by the medical staff because of a heart rhythm irregularity. He remained in the astronaut office at Houston, in the role of boss astronaut, hoping that some day he would be cleared for orbital flight. In 1972, the medical opinion that had kept him from space flight was reversed and he was assigned to the Apollo-Soyuz mission.

The Russian commander was the ebullient, artistic Colonel Alexey Arkhipovich Leonov, the space walker of Voskhod II. Now forty-one, he had become a well-known figure in Europe. At the first International Conference on the Peaceful Uses of Space in Vienna in 1968, Leonov was highly visible as a member of the Soviet delegation, giving corridor interviews in the Hofburg Palace. The engineer in the two-man crew was Valeriy Nikolaevich Kubasov, forty, a veteran of the Soyuz VI mission. Their vessel was *Soyuz XIX.*

Curiously, the Apollo spacecraft had neither a name nor mission number. It could have been called *Omega* since it was the last Apollo to fly.

To avoid confusion, Americans spoke Russian when they addressed their Soviet colleagues, who spoke English when they talked to the Apollo crew. Learning Russian was part of the training for Stafford, Slayton, and Brand. During 1974, both crews trained with the other's space equipment. The Americans were required to become familiar enough with the 7-ton Soyuz so that they could fly it if necessary. Conversely, the Russians learned to fly the 16-ton Apollo. On ASTP, the Apollo CSM weighed 32,490 pounds (14,737 kilograms), and Soyuz weighed 14,960 pounds (6,800 kilograms). With the docking module, which weighed 4,436 pounds, attached, the total Apollo CSM-DM payload was 36,926 pounds (16,784.5 kilograms). Following the flight of *Soyuz XVI* in December 1974, the Russians reported that tests of the reduced cabin pressure and of the docking system were satisfactory, and Soyuz was ready.

At the end of February 1975, NASA inspectors found hairline cracks in the fins of the eight-year-old Saturn 1B that was to launch Apollo on its final flight. All eight fins had suffered from stress corrosion in storage and had to be replaced.

In May 1975, the Russians lifted the curtain on their flight control center at Kaliningrad, fifteen miles northeast of Moscow, and allowed foreign news correspondents to tour it. It was described as a six-story, U-shaped brick and sandstone building in a walled compound with an electrically controlled gate.[20] Completed in 1970, it was used to control the flight of *Soyuz XII*. A world map covered one wall in the main control room, with the locations of Soviet tracking stations and ships pinpointed on it. There were five rows of consoles arranged in ascending banks, like those at the Johnson and the Kennedy Space Centers. A three-room suite had been set aside for nine American controllers, who would be on duty there during the joint flight, supplementing those at Mission Control, Houston. They could monitor both Apollo and Soyuz and also converse with Houston.

During May also another layer of Soviet space secrecy was peeled away when a group of NASA technicians and officials headed by George M. Low, deputy administrator, and Glynn Lunney, the ASTP technical director for NASA, toured ASTP-related facilities (only) at the Baikonur Cosmodrome. The consensus of the Americans was that Soviet testing equipment was ten to fifteen years behind that at the Kennedy Space Center, but that the Baikonur (or Tyuratam) center was much larger than the Merritt Island Launch Area (MILA) and the Kennedy Space Center in Florida.

The NASA contingent was housed in a cosmonaut hotel in the city of Leninsk, south of the Cosmodrome. The Americans were transported in a bus each morning to the engineering building near the primary Soyuz launch pad. At the end of the working day, they were bused back to the fenced hotel compound.[21] Photographs were not permitted in Leninsk nor in the area of the Soyuz launch site. The NASA technicians complained they could not even enter the parking lot of the Soyuz engineering building without a Russian security agent.

Overall, the group received the impression that the Baikonur launch complex was developed to accommodate space activity on a grand scale. It was laid out in the form of a Y. Railroad tracks branched off from the main access road and rail line, and the visitors saw passenger trains taking workers to and from the Cosmodrome. The *Soyuz XIX* launch pad was located at the end of the main stem of the Y. The NASA group was informed that a backup Soyuz was ready on another pad about twenty miles away. It would be launched if *Soyuz XIX* was forced to land or abort before the docking could be carried out or if the Apollo launch was delayed more than five days after *Soyuz XIX* was launched. There was no backup for Apollo at the Kennedy Space Center.

During the visit, five days of flight simulation exercises were held. The

NASA flight director, M. P. "Pete" Frank, later told a press conference that whenever a problem arose, the Russian group exhibited a great deal of caution in adopting any solution to it. "We severely underestimated the time it takes to assimilate agreement between the two countries on any problem," he said.[22]

The science program for the joint flights seems to have been devised with the objective of getting the maximum return from the mission—and from both crews. There were twenty-seven experiments, five of them requiring joint efforts by the two crews. Essentially, the experiments were designed to yield more information about the effects of weightlessness and the near-Earth radiation environment on living organisms and to use the two space vehicles as observatories for studies of the sun, the galaxy, and the Earth. Most of the experiments were extensions of those previously done on Apollo, Soyuz, Skylab, and Salyut, except for the joint experiments, which required two maneuverable space vehicles.[23]

LET'S GO!

Soyuz XIX was launched at 3:20 P.M. Moscow time (8:20 A.M. Eastern Daylight Time) July 15, 1975, from the launch pad where Yuri Gagarin had been boosted on the first manned orbital flight fourteen years before. During the final moments of the countdown, Leonov and Kubasov had been joking with the ground crew as they reclined in the couches of the Soyuz descent module. To calls of "good luck" from the ground technicians, Leonov responded, "to the devil!" The kerosene-liquid-oxygen propellant ignited in a gout of brilliant flame, but the A-2 rocket was held down until full thrust was built up by all twenty engines. "Let's go!" cried Leonov. Then up they went, smoothly, into an orbit 117-by-142 miles high, with an inclination of 51.8 degrees to the equator. The 51.8 degrees of inclination put Soyuz in an orbital plane through which the Kennedy Space Center passed every twenty-three hours and thirty-five minutes with the rotation of the Earth. To avoid fuel-costly plane change, Apollo had to be launched at the same inclination. An on-time launch of Apollo seven and one-half hours after Soyuz lift-off would lead to rendezvous on Apollo's twenty-ninth revolution and to docking fifty-one hours and fifty-five minutes after Soyuz lift-off. Tracking data were passed by Russian ground and, later, ship stations to Apollo Mission Control at Houston and Launch Control at the Kennedy Space Center, where the Apollo countdown was proceeding.

On its third orbit,* *Soyuz XIX* passed over the United States, and Leonov was advised that all was going well in the Apollo countdown. Apollo was scheduled to lift off Pad 39-B at 3:50 P.M., Eastern Daylight Time, seven and one-half hours after Soyuz's launch. This timing represented a compromise that enabled the Soviets to observe the docking from their ground stations. NASA could observe it from a ground station in Madrid and by the ATS-6 satellite.

During the *Soyuz XIX* passes over the United States, Houston relayed communications between the Russian spaceship and Mission Control, Moscow. But there was some initial difficulty in the communications.

> MCC,M: Soyuz, Soyuz, this is Moscow. Congratulations on achievement of orbit.
> Kubasov: Moscow, this is Soyuz 2.†
> MCC,M: Soyuz 2, we've been calling you for several minutes. How do you read?
> Kubasov: We didn't have our transmitter turned on. We didn't have time to turn it on. We wanted—we should have turned it on. Yes?
> MCC,M: You have to do it yourself—turn on the transmitter.
> Leonov: We were just busy flying so we didn't have time.

This exchange must be interpreted as partly in jest. Kubasov, a trained engineer, certainly was intimately familiar with the Soyuz communications equipment; however, cosmonauts were not accustomed to communicating with Moscow while flying over the United States. During the early phase of the mission, the Soyuz crew made routine tests of the orientation and guidance systems. Moscow wanted to know the results.

> MCC,M: How did the tests go?
> Kubasov: Tests? We're now monitoring the system after testing.

The dialogue between a Soviet spacecraft and its control center, made public, at least in the United States, for the first time, gave the impression of an easy, nonchalant attitude on the part of the crew and a mother-hen concern by the controllers at Moscow.

Meanwhile, at the Kennedy Space Center in Florida, the largest assemblage of international news media since the launch of *Apollo XI* six years ear-

---

* The circumnavigation of the Earth in a spaceship was figured differently by Russians and Americans. NASA referred to it as a "revolution," or "rev," which was counted by each crossing of the meridian at 80 degrees west longitude, where Cape Canaveral is located. Since the Earth is rotating eastward during the ninety minutes or so a spacecraft is circling it in low orbit, a rev is actually more than 360 degrees. It may cover 384 degrees. The Russians measure their orbit from ascending node to ascending node, a tour of 360 degrees without reference to the ground. On every fifteen revolutions, Apollo would complete the equivalent of sixteen Soyuz orbits. This discrepancy was not important, however, because both sides used as standard reference Ground Elapsed Time (GET), based on the Soyuz launch.
† There were two Soyuz vehicles in orbit. *Soyuz XVIII* was docked with *Salyut IV* during the flight of *Soyuz XIX*.

lier milled around the press site and crowded into the roofed race-track-style grandstand to get out of the broiling sun. In the launch control room sat the Soviet ambassador, Anatoly Dobrynin, with NASA administrator Fletcher.

The countdown of Saturn 210, the thirty-second Saturn launch vehicle to go into space since October 27, 1961, moved down to ignition on time. The eight first-stage kerosene-oxygen engines erupted in a sunburst of flame, and the last Saturn scheduled to fly lifted Apollo spacecraft number 111, the last of its kind to go into orbit, smoothly off the pad. Flight control shifted to Houston as Stafford announced "tower cleared."

> Houston: Roger, Tom. You've got good thrust in all engines. You're right on the money.
> Stafford: Thirty seconds and we're on our way.

Two minutes and twenty seconds after lift-off, the first stage of the Saturn 1B burned out at an altitude of thirty-six miles. The S4B second stage ignited two seconds later. From the ground, it could be seen as a distant bright spark in the blue bowl of the sky. The Apollo crew felt a surge of acceleration.

At Houston, the capsule communicator, Richard H. Truly, a navy commander, advised: "Thrust is up on the S4B. Looking real fine." Truly was one of several pilots who had been in training for the Manned Orbital Laboratory, an air force project, which was cancelled in 1968. He joined the NASA corps of astronauts in 1969.

> Stafford: Roger. Five minutes. Looks good on board, Dick. And we've got some beautiful sights.
> Slayton: Roger! Man, I tell you, this is worth waiting 16 years for. Got a beautiful view here, Dick!

At the Launch Control Center, administrator Fletcher and Ambassador Dobrynin vied in congratulating the crew. "It was a very nice job," the ambassador commented. "All good things come to an end," Fletcher added, "and it seems like this is an appropriate time for the Saturn launch program to end."

Apollo, attached to the S4B, was inserted into an orbit close to the nominal one planned, 93 by 104 miles. Seventy-three minutes after launch, the command module pilot, Brand, separated the Apollo CSM from the S4B, turned it 180 degrees, and nosed it into the S4B adapter to dock with the docking module. He then backed off, pulling the docking module away from the rocket. Apollo was now ready for rendezvous, and that process commenced with a sequence of maneuvers that first circularized the orbit at 105 miles and then reshaped it into an oval 145 miles high at the highest point (apogee) and 104½ miles at the lowest (perigee).

On the morning of July 16, Leonov burned the Soyuz engine for 28.4 seconds to circularize the Russian vessel's orbit at 140 miles (actually 139.15). During the remainder of that day, both crews were occupied with performing experiments. The next day was Docking Day, or, as a Polish news correspondent suggested during a press conference in Moscow, the day of the "Peace Orbit."

On the morning of July 17, the Apollo crew made two orbit adjustments that brought Apollo within visual range of Soyuz through the sextant telescope. Brand reported to Houston: "He's just a speck right now, hard to distinguish from the stars." Stafford put in a call for Soyuz in Russian. Then, suddenly, a voice in Russian-accented English burst through the static:

Hello, hello, everybody!
Stafford: Valeriy!
Brand: Valeriy, Hi!
Valeriy Kubasov: Hi to you, Tom and Deke! Hello there, Vance!

At 9:15 A.M. Central Daylight Time, with a short blast from its engine, Apollo entered a roughly circular orbit of 127.6 by 126.5 miles. It was inside of and nearly coelliptic with the 193.5-mile-high orbit of Soyuz. Having the inside track, Apollo was moving faster than Soyuz and rapidly overtaking the Russian ship. Both crews were trying to communicate with each other, but ground transmission on radio frequencies close to theirs broke in. These were later identified as calls from the airport control towers at Los Angeles International and Heathrow, London, and from a Moscow radio station broadcasting weather bulletins. The interference abated only when both spaceships passed out of its reach.

Leonov: Apollo, Soyuz. What is the range now [between the ships]?
Stafford: 48 miles.
Leonov: Okay. I'm docking on time!
Stafford: Okay, I understand you. Go for docking.
Leonov: Our beacon is on.
Stafford: All right. I see it.

At 10:14 A.M., Central Daylight Time, Brand fired the Apollo engine for $^8/_{10}$ second, boosting the ship's apogee to 139.5 miles—the altitude of Soyuz. Ascending toward its new apogee, Apollo rapidly closed to within 2,000 feet of Soyuz. Apollo then matched Soyuz's velocity with an 18.9-second burn of its reaction control system thrusters, which circularized Apollo's orbit to conform to that of Soyuz. The two vessels were now flying in the same path facing each other (station keeping), Apollo on its twenty-ninth revolution, Soyuz on its thirty-fifth orbit. The braking maneuver added velocity to Apollo, but the effect was to slow it relative to Soyuz. In space flight, the higher the orbit, the slower a satellite appears to be moving around the Earth.

Suddenly, a picture from Apollo's television camera appeared on the monitors at Houston. It was fuzzy at first, then magnificently clear. Standing out starkly against the black sky appeared Soyuz, light green in color, with its bright solar cell wings flashing. It appeared to hover just above the docking module like a segmented dragon fly. Off to the side appeared the distant white puffballs of cloud over the Atlantic Ocean.

Houston: Looks real pretty.
Stafford: Soyuz, this is Apollo. How do you read?
Leonov: Real fine.
Stafford: Da ["Yes"]. Please tell us when you begin your maneuvering [in Russian].
Leonov: Soyuz initiating orientation maneuver. Ready?
Stafford: Da. Very slowly [in Russian].
Leonov: Visual orientation initiated.
Stafford: Roger.
Leonov: Soyuz docking system is ready.
Stafford: We are also ready. Apollo is ready [in Russian].
Leonov: Do you see spacecraft?
Stafford: Yes. We see it. It is very beautiful. We see your periscope [in Russian].
Leonov: The maneuver is completed. Visual orientation established.
Houston: Good show [referring to the TV picture]. Looking fine.
Stafford: I'm approaching Soyuz.
Leonov: Oh, please! Don't forget your engine! [He meant, don't forget to brake to avoid a collision.] [Laughter.]
Stafford: Less than 5 meters [in Russian].
Houston: Deke, can you close down the f stop some? [The vessels had turned toward the sun, and its glare was washing out the television picture.]
Stafford: Three meters. One meter. Contact! [Russian]
Leonov: Capture!
Stafford: We also have capture. We have succeeded. Everything is excellent [Russian].
Leonov: Soyuz and Apollo are shaking hands now.
Stafford: We agree.
Houston: Apollo, Houston. Deke, when you have a chance, we'd like to close down the f stops. We do have a good picture but it's too bright. Yeah. Right there, Deke. We copied Aleksey saying you are holding hands and we see it, too.
Stafford: Soyuz, this is Apollo. Initiating the traction. [Apollo's docking guide ring was retracted to bring the surfaces of the structural rings together so they could be firmly latched.]

The docking was completed as eight hooks in the Apollo ring were engaged with those of the Soyuz ring. The vessels were then hard docked, forming a rigid assembly sixty-six feet long, joined by the docking module.

Stafford: Docking complete, Dick. Docking is completed, Houston [in English].
Leonov: Well done, Tom. It was a good show. We're looking forward now to shaking hands with you in board Soyuz.
Stafford: Thank you, Aleksey. Thank you very much. And to you, Valeriy.

The first international docking took place six minutes ahead of schedule at 11:09 A.M., Central Daylight Time, as both vessels flew over the Atlantic

Ocean 640 miles west of Portugal, heading toward the Bay of Biscay. They continued on, joined, over the Loire Valley of France and the cities of Nantes, Paris, Luxembourg, Frankfurt, and Lodz; they crossed the USSR between Minsk and Kiev.

As the vessels passed over the Baikonur Cosmodrome, Slayton entered the docking module to prepare it for the Russians. This required boosting the pressure from Apollo's five-psi (pounds per square inch) atmosphere to Soyuz's ten-psi atmosphere. Slayton was struck by a very strong odor of something burned and called Stafford.

"Deke smells something that's pretty bad in the Docking Module," Stafford advised Houston. "It smelled like cordite or burnt glue or acetate." Stafford then advised Leonov of the problem. After considering it for a few minutes, Houston suggested that a small electric furnace might be the cause. It was mounted on the module wall, and the crew had used it to run experiments on zero gravity convection in metal melts and on the recrystallization of partly melted germanium. Houston suggested that one of the hot samples may have scorched some velcro material. As he continued to investigate, Slayton reported that with the module opened up, the odor was rapidly diminishing. However, Houston advised Stafford and Slayton to wear oxygen masks while inside the module.

Then another anomaly occurred. The master alarm was triggered in Apollo, indicating a sudden drop in pressure in one of the big oxygen tanks in the service module. It was the same alarm that signaled the bursting of the oxygen tank on *Apollo XIII*, forcing the abort of the first mission to Fra Mauro. But telemetry reaching Houston showed normal pressure in the oxygen tanks. Controllers advised that the alarm probably was set off by faulty instrumentation, and the matter was dismissed as an emergency.

As the joined vehicles arced over the Atlantic on Apollo's thirtieth revolution, the television camera picked up Slayton and Stafford working in the docking module. They had closed off the Apollo command module and had added nitrogen from a storage tank to equalize the pressure in the docking module atmosphere with that of Soyuz.

During docking module chores, communications faded between Soyuz and Apollo. Houston could not hear Soyuz at all. The problem had to be relayed to the Soyuz crew by way of Moscow, which was in voice contact with the ship. The cosmonauts were advised to adjust their VHF transmitter. When they did, Leonov's voice suddenly boomed out, saying: "Hey, Tom. Hatch 4 is open." It was the hatch on the Soyuz side of the docking module tunnel. Now all that remained was for the Apollo crewmen to open Hatch 3, on their side of the tunnel. The docked spaceships entered Apollo's thirty-first revolution.

Stafford reported that he and Slayton had completed "step 23" in preparing to open Hatch 3 and were starting on "step 24." That should have indicated to observers some of the complexities of the docking system.

Slayton asked: "Soyuz, how do you read? I am ready to open Hatch 3. Okay! I'm opening Hatch 3." At once, the helmeted head of Leonov appeared in the tunnel. "Ha, ha!" he cried, a big smile on his round face. Stafford called, "Come in here and shake hands. Come in, please." He and Slayton peered into the Soyuz cabin and noticed piles of cables and hoses. It was a familiar sight—spaceships always had piles of cable lying around. Stafford noted: "Looks like they've got a few snakes in there, too. They're almost as bad off as we are." Then in Russian, Stafford said: "Aleksey, our viewers are here. Come here, please. Glad to see you!"

The television camera showed Leonov squeezing into the tunnel from Soyuz and pulling himself into the airlock. This scene reminded me of the one ten years before showing Leonov emerging from the airlock of *Voskhod II* to become the first man to float in space—the first "space walker." Both scenes suggested birth; they symbolized man's emergence from the womb of Mother Earth or, as Ziolkovsky said eighty years earlier, from the cradle.

Kubasov floated through next. The Russians wore leather helmets with white flat tops, and the Americans wore helmets with a narrow white band. That was one way to tell them apart. In space flight headgear, all men seem to look alike.

"Deke, Tom," said Leonov breezily. "Very glad to see you." "This is Soyuz—and the United States," responded Slayton. They all laughed delightedly. The big job was done. They had made it. No one had fouled up. They had made history. "Valeriy," Stafford called. "Come here. Valeriy. How are things?" "Hello," said Kubasov. "I see you."

Houston cut into this exchange with the advice that, "We've got a good picture of the hatch and you people inside there in the tunnel." Houston then relayed a message of congratulation from Leonid Brezhnev, the Soviet leader. It said in part: "It could be said that the Soyuz and the Apollo is a prototype of future orbital space stations . . . Détente, positive movement ahead in Soviet-American relations have created the proper conditions for the first international space flight."

After the televised handshakes, Stafford and Slayton made their way with Leonov and Kubasov into the Soyuz orbital module, where the four hunched around a tiny table, to the accompaniment of stage directions from Houston. President Ford was going to congratulate everybody. Houston instructed Slayton to give his headset to Leonov so that the Russian commander could hear the president. The TV picture was great, Houston added, except it was upside down. "Oh, Jesus, I'm sorry," said Stafford. He flipped it right side up. Crews frequently flew heads down. It made no difference in orbit, but it looked queer on television.

Houston: The astronauts are on the line, sir.
President Ford: Gentlemen, let me call to express my very great admiration for your hard work, your total dedication in preparing for this joint flight. All of us here

in Washington, in the United States, send to you our very warmest congratulations for your successful rendezvous and for docking and we wish you the very best for a successful completion of the remainder of your mission. . . . It's taken us many years to open this door to useful cooperation in space between our two countries. And I'm confident that the day is not far off when space missions made possible by this first joint effort will be more or less commonplace.

Ford then conducted impromptu interviews with the members of the two crews. He asked "General Stafford . . . uh, Tom, now that you've had an opportunity to test the new docking system, do you think it will be suitable for further international manned space flight?"

> Stafford: Yes, sir, Mr. President, I sure do. Out of the three docking systems I've used, this was the smoothest one so far. It worked beautifully.*
> Ford: About 3½ hours ago, I sat here in the Oval Office and watched the docking procedure. It looked awfully simple from here. I'm sure it wasn't that simple for the five of you.
> Stafford: . . . it's a lot . . .
> Ford: Yes, Tom. Let me say a word or two if I might to Colonel Leonov. The docking was a critical phase of the joint mission. Colonel, could you describe it and would you describe the reaction of the crews on meeting in space after such a long preparation?
> Leonov: Mr. President, I'm sure that our joint flight is the beginning for future considerations in space between our countries. Thank you very much for very nice words to us. We'll do our best.

Ford then turned to Slayton, from whom he elicited this advice to the young: "Decide what you want to do and then stick to it." Slayton certainly practiced what he preached, Ford noted, having waited to fly in orbit since 1959. From Brand, the White House interviewer obtained a comment on the value of ASTP training, and from Kubasov, a comment on the tolerable quality of space food.

Following the presidential interview, Stafford used the remaining ten minutes of television time to present the cosmonauts with five metal flags, to which Leonov responded: "Thank you very much for these expensive presents." †

Crewmen then took pictures of each other and sat down around the little table to eat a hearty Russian meal featuring borscht. They signed certificates attesting to the first international flight for the Federation Aeronautique Internationale in Paris, the official international record-keeping body for air and space flights. Amid the flurry of amateur photography after dinner,

---

* Stafford referred to the Gemini and Apollo docking systems.
† NASA had moved its Applications Technology Satellite 6 from a geostationary position over the equator at 94 degrees west longitude from which it could relay television programs to Rocky Mountain regions, Northwest Canada, and Alaska to 35 degrees east longitude, where it hung over the eastern shore of Lake Victoria, Kenya. From there, ATS-6 could relay radio and television from both spacecraft along 55 percent of the flight path. In addition, fourteen U.S. ground stations, including the USNS Vanguard, supported the mission. The Russian network included nine ground stations, with two ships, the *Yuri Gagarin* and the *Sergei Korolev*.

medallions that had been divided into halves carried by each crew were joined and exchanged.

Like good soldiers, the American and Russian crewmen faithfully acted out all the planned ceremonials that their respective space bureaucracies had planned for them. Listening to them at Mission Control, Houston, that legendary afternoon of July 17, 1975, I had the clear impression that they were enjoying themselves immensely, fully conscious of the historic impact of their words and acts, and also taking care not to overdo it.

Three more transfers were scheduled, and the second began early Friday morning, July 18. Brand went to Soyuz, where he lunched with Kubasov on sauerkraut soup, meat, black currant juice, plums, strawberries, and coffee. Leonov pulled himself into the Apollo command module, where he joined Stafford and Slayton for a meal of potato soup, beefsteak with barbecue sauce, strawberries, almonds, and tubes of macaroni and cheese. This was topped off with a strawberry drink.

THE BIGGEST RIVER IN THE UNIVERSE

In the Soyuz orbital module, Brand and Kubasov adjusted the television camera as the linked vessels arced northeastward across the South Atlantic Ocean and passed over the Ivory Coast of Africa, the Sahara Desert, and Libya. Brand announced that Kubasov was preparing to narrate in English a television tour of that part of the world.

As they cleared Africa and crossed the Mediterranean, Kubasov called: "Houston, Houston, this is Soyuz. How do you read me?"

Houston: [to Brand] We read him well.
Brand: Okay, Bo, I think we're about ready to go here.* Looks like we're coming up over the Black Sea and right now, Valeriy is getting in position. He's ready to tell you a little about his homeland, the Soviet Union, a very big country. . . .
Leonov: I see my airfield where I go 10 years ago. . . .
Kubasov: Dear American tee vee people, you show feelings about the Soviet Union. Some of you visited my country and you enjoyed the beauties of its cities and towns, rivers, forests, mountains and fields. Aleksey Leonov and me visited the United States several times and really did enjoy its beautiful landscape.
Brand: Are you reading him, Bo?
Houston: Roger. We hear Valeriy.
Kubasov: Roger. It would be wrong to ask which country is more beautiful. It

* Air force Lieutenant Colonel Karol J. Bobko, capsule communicator on duty at the time. Like Truly, he was a transfer to NASA from the discontinued Manned Laboratory program of the air force.

would be right to say there is nothing more beautiful than our blue planet. . . .
Our spacecraft, Soyuz, is approaching the USSR territory. Our country occupies
one-sixth of the Earth's surface. Its population, over 250 million people. It consists
of the 15 United Republics. The biggest of them is the Russian Federal Republic
with the population of 135 million people.
    Leonov: Valeriy, please tell our people about me!
    [Laughter.]
    Kubasov: Aleksey, where are we flying now?
    Leonov: Past the Volga. Just past the Little Volga.
    Kubasov: We are approaching the Volga River now. This river is the biggest in
the universe. At the moment we are flying over the place where the Volgograd city
is. It was called Stalingrad before. In winter 1942–43, German fascist troops were
defeated by the Soviet Army here. Three hundred and thirty thousand German
soldiers and officers were killed and taken prisoner here.

Switching to Russian, Kubasov said he couldn't finish his travelogue in the
three minutes remaining for transmission on the ATS satellite. Leonov established contact with Mission Control, Moscow, and continued the commentary, speaking in Russian. His words were translated into English as he
spoke.

    Leonov: I am now in the Command Module of the Apollo spacecraft. I am here
together with Deke Slayton and Tom Stafford. We are flying over the Soviet
Union's territory and we are observing everything which is speeding by below us.
We began our observations over the Crimean Peninsula and now we're approaching the Ural Mountain range. It's a beautiful Earth below us, blue, covered with
light cloud.
    Moscow: Would you do that in English, please?

Leonov continued to declaim about the beauties of the Earth in Russian.
Moscow insisted he speak English, but he kept on in Russian. Brand interrupted: "It's a very long tour over the Soviet Union," he said. "We're still
passing over it. The eastern part here is steppe or desert and there's just a
lot of country here, a lot of farm land down here on the steppes, apparently.
I think very shortly we'll be at the Pacific. And here's some more words from
Valeriy who was noting that the flight path passed over the Baikonur launch
site."

    Leonov: [in English] By the way, three years . . . three days before, Valeriy and
me was launched from this Baikonur launch pad.
    Kubasov: We are going to land here after the mission. This part of Kazakhstan
was not cultivated until 15 years ago. Today, it is one of our breadbaskets. A new
city, Kaliningrad, appeared here. It was only 10 years ago. Not far from here
begins the Siberia, the biggest part of our country, rich in natural resources.
    Houston: Command pilot, Houston.
    Leonov: We are over mountains now.
    Brand: Okay, go ahead.
    Houston: We've been getting a good picture here. We can see the clouds and
the mountains pass below. You might tell Valeriy we've been enjoying it.

During the luncheon that followed the travelogue, Houston received an instructive television demonstration of Leonov squirting potato soup into his mouth from a bulb. That was the only way to eat soup in orbit.

> Stafford: How's the soup, Aleksey?
> Leonov: Houston, this is Soyuz commander. How do you read me? Hey, Bo! How do you read me?
> Houston: I read you well.
> Leonov: Okay, Houston. Just now, right now, Tom, Deke and me are in the Apollo spacecraft. We fill with lunch. It is a good lunch. I like it very much, but it is mostly the same. The best part of a good lunch is not what you eat, but with whom you eat. Just now I eat my space food with my very good and very nice old friends, Tom and Deke. I have potato soup, strawberries and steak, bread and cold tea. I like it very much.

With that speech, the linked spacecrafts passed out of communications range as they crossed over Indonesia.

ON THE RIGHT, VIRGINIA

Early Friday afternoon, July 18, the third crew transfer was made. Leonov returned to Soyuz with Stafford, and Brand went back to Apollo with Kubasov. Moscow then called up Stafford and asked him to make a statement to open a press conference with reporters in Moscow and Houston. When the two crews faced each other in the docking tunnel after Hatch 3 was opened, Stafford said he had this thought: "When we opened this hatch in space, we were opening a new era in the history of man."

Leonov added: "This work became possible in the climate of détente and developing . . . between our two countries. This is why it is an important step on the endless road of space exploration by the joint effort of all mankind."

Leonov then exhibited sketches he had made of Stafford, Slayton, and Brand. They were the work of a first-rate artist. One of the press conference questions asked Kubasov was what was the most important thing he and Leonov were learning on the first international space flight.

"First of all," the engineer replied, "we found out that we [U.S. and USSR crews] can work together in space and cooperate."

These words expressed the intent of the joint flight so succinctly they might well be engraved in stone as a benchmark of the twentieth century.

Later that afternoon, Brand performed a six-minute travelogue for viewers in the Soviet Union as the joined spacecraft flew along the United States east coast on Apollo's forty-sixth revolution. Brand gave his dissertation in Russian. It was translated at Houston as follows:

Brand: Dear television viewers, at the present time we are going to make a little tour over the eastern part of the United States. This place developed about 200 years ago. Here, most of the industrial concentration of the United States is located. . . . At the present time, we're flying over sunny Florida. It's a very warm climate in Florida, over 200 sunny days a year. Here is located the Kennedy Space Center. [Clouds obscured part of the view.] At the middle of your screen we see North Carolina. Only 72 years ago the first airplane flew in this state. On the horizon, we see the Blue Ridge Mountains.

On the right there is the State of Virginia. . . . We now can almost see Washington, to the left of us. Of course, this is the capital of the United States, the political and cultural center. To the left now, you can see New York. Around us also we see several other states—Massachusetts. In 1920, Dr. Goddard flew one of his first rockets there. . . . New England is to the north and in the center of our screen we saw a lot of cloudiness, so we couldn't really tell enough.

Moscow: Thank you, Vance.

There followed another exchange of medallion halves, which the crewmen joined together. The medallions were destined for museums in Moscow and Washington. Stafford presented fir tree seeds to Leonov. More flight documents were signed by Brand and Kubasov. After a considerable effort to adjust the television camera, Leonov made another speech, to the accompaniment of stage directions from Houston.

Leonov: Good evening, dear television friends. It is 2200 hours [10:00 p.m.] Moscow time. The terminating activities are going on aboard our two spacecrafts and we will have our fourth and final transfer soon. . . .

Houston: Still lower. A little lower [referring to the camera].

Leonov: The joint operations include Tom Stafford's transmittal to me of a box of seeds of very fast growing pine trees . . . also an exchange of medals. One half of the medal was placed on the Apollo spacecraft and the second half of the medal was placed on the Soyuz spacecraft. And now here together in an orbit of the Earth we will be connecting these two halves of the medal. . . .

When these ceremonies were concluded, the crewmen shook hands and returned to their own ships. Hatch 4 on the Soyuz side of the docking tunnel was closed at 4:06 p.m., central daylight time, July 18, and Stafford closed Hatch 3, sealing the tunnel, twenty seconds later. After thirty minutes of closeout chores in the docking module, Stafford and Slayton returned to the Apollo cabin for the sleep period.

Early Saturday, July 19, after breakfast, the two vessels undocked, and Apollo took up a position 164 feet away from Soyuz to block out the sun so that Leonov and Kubasov could take photographs of the solar corona. Later, the two vessels maneuvered for a second docking, with Soyuz the active partner this time. In the active mode, Soyuz extended its docking guide ring and, after capture, retracted the ring to lock the two vehicles firmly together.

The ships remained docked until 10:28 A.M., when they undocked for the last time. Apollo then maneuvered around Soyuz, testing the ability of the crews to track each other's ships visually with the aid of beacons and a spotlight. Each crew then photographed the other's vessel Saturday afternoon, and Apollo increased its separation from Soyuz with a short burn of RCS thrusters.

The first international linkup in manned space flight had ended happily. Henry Shapiro, the United Press International correspondent in Moscow, summarized it this way: "It may be no exaggeration to describe the Apollo-Soyuz flight as the most successful cooperative peacetime venture in the history of the two nations."

Soyuz continued in orbit until Monday morning, July 21, when it was televised landing in Kazakhstan with a puff of dust kicked up by retro-rockets. Out popped Leonov and Kubasov, waving jubilantly to a crowd of recovery technicians and to the camera.

Apollo continued in orbit until Thursday afternoon, July 24, 1975, when it reentered and splashed down in the Pacific Ocean six years to the day after the splashdown of *Apollo XI* on its return from the first manned lunar landing.

THE CLOSE CALL

When the crewmen stepped out on the deck of the recovery ship, the U.S.S. *New Orleans,* and made their "glad to be back" speeches, neither President Ford, who welcomed them, nor television viewers were aware that they had experienced a brush with death during the parachute descent. This was not disclosed until the next day.

A condition in which the crew could have been asphyxiated in the cabin was precipitated during the descent by an unaccountable failure to turn on the automatic Earth landing system at the right time. As a result, nitrogen textroxide gas, which is toxic, permeated the cabin atmosphere on the way down. When Apollo hit the water, it overturned into what NASA calls "stable position 2." The conical top end was under water, and in that position the blowers could not clear the noxious fumes out of the cabin.

During the five minutes it took the spacecraft flotation bags to inflate and turn the spacecraft right side up, the crew was exposed to gas contamination in the cabin atmosphere. Stafford unstrapped from his couch, lowered himself to the top of the control console, and crawled around behind the couches to extract oxygen masks from a drawer in the aft bulkhead. Brand, meanwhile, fainted, apparently from sudden blood pooling in the legs rather than from the gas; but Stafford and Slayton slapped an oxygen mask over his face and turned the oxygen flow up high as they donned their own masks. Brand came to in a moment. Prompt use of the masks may have saved the crew's lives, or at least prevented serious lung damage.

After the command module righted itself in the water, Stafford turned on the blower and cleared the gas out of the cabin. Coughing by the crew could be heard over the communications system, and later they noticed burns on their hands. But the gas did not incapacitate any of them, and it was not until welcoming ceremonies were over that Stafford reported the problem.

Flight surgeons then hustled the crewmen into sick bay, and the carrier sped to Honolulu, where Stafford, Slayton, and Brand were put to bed at Tripler Army Hospital for a detailed examination.

What had caused gas to enter the cabin? It was another of those unforeseen, unpredictable happenings that have appeared from time to time in the Apollo program. During the descent, Brand was supposed to push two switches that activated the Earth landing system at 30,000 feet altitude. But he failed to do it. Stafford or Slayton were supposed to make sure that Brand pushed the switches by reading off the checklist of landing items to him. According to NASA ASTP Director Lunney, Slayton called for the landing switches, but Brand apparently did not hear him because of noise and a loud squeal in the cabin.[24]

Activation of the switches at 30,000 feet would have set up this sequence of events. At 24,000 feet, the reaction control system thrusters, which had been firing to stabilize the craft through reentry, would shut off. Then the parachute system cover would be jettisoned. Two seconds after that, two drogue parachutes, each 16 feet in diameter, would blossom forth to slow the command module's descent. At 10,000 feet, three 83½-foot-diameter main parachutes would be yanked out by pilot parachutes. They would reduce impact on the water to a gentle splash.

Slayton was watching for the drogues to appear at 24,000 feet so that he could photograph them. When they didn't appear, he told Brand to hit the drogue deployment button. Brand hit it, the parachute cover blew off, and out came the drogues.

But—because the Earth landing system had still not been turned on—the reaction control system thrusters were still active when they should have been off. As the drogue parachutes came out and caught the air, the capsule began to swing, and the computer kept the thrusters firing to control these oscillations.

Stafford realized something was amiss and shut off the propellant, but residual nitrogen textroxide oxidizer in the thrusters was blown into the cabin.

That occurred because a pressure-relief valve had opened at 24,000 feet. It allowed outside air to flow into the cabin to equalize the five pounds per square inch pressure inside with rising air pressure outside. As the outside air poured in, it brought the gas residue in the thrusters in with it. As soon as the crew noticed the gas, Slayton acted quickly to put up the oxygen flow, which helped reduce the effects of the fumes; but the three crewmen could not avoid inhaling some of it.

None of them realized the Earth landing switch oversight until the capsule had fallen to 11,000 feet, just before main parachute deployment. At last, the Earth landing system was turned on, but Stafford feared it might not get the main parachutes out on time. He manually deployed them, and they came out six seconds later than they would have had the automatic system been activated on time. As a result, the spacecraft hit the water slightly harder than it might have normally and rolled over to "stable position 2," which further aggravated the gas problem.

After ten days under observation in Honolulu, the crew returned to Houston, where Brand contended that he, alone, was to blame for the oversight, and Stafford and Slayton insisted they were to blame, too.

The accident resulted in an unexpected bit of serendipity. Detailed lung X-rays taken at Tripler revealed the presence of a small tumor in Slayton's left lung. Surgeons recommended immediate exploratory surgery to look for cancer. Slayton counted himself "damn lucky" that the tumor had escaped detection before the flight; otherwise he never would have realized the long-awaited space flight. On August 26, the fifty-one-year-old astronaut underwent surgery in Houston. The tumor was found to be benign.

So ended the saga of Apollo. It began in an era of intense competition. It ended in a global demonstration of cooperation between the former space rivals. The epilogue came July 31–August 1, when the chiefs of thirty-five nations, including Ford and Brezhnev, signed the final document of the Conference on Security and Cooperation in Europe, the so called Declaration of Helsinki. A political statement of intent, the document sought to stabilize the existing geopolitical configuration of Europe. In this respect, it was the most ambitious attempt at a general European settlement since the Congress of Vienna in 1815. Multilateral preparatory talks had begun in November, 1972. In 1973, they opened formally at the foreign-minister level in Geneva. They were completed July 19, 1975. Détente in orbit was a concomitant of détente on the ground.

But, before winter, the old rivalry would be resumed, in political struggles in Africa and in Portugal. Only in space had it abated. Or had it? In August and September 1975, NASA launched two pairs of orbiter-lander spacecraft to Mars. In October, Soviet vehicles landed on Venus, and this time they returned photos of a dim, rocky landscape, the first of a hellish surface where lead could exist only in liquid form.

Press reaction in the United States and Europe was mixed. The political aspect of the flight was generally approved; the scientific side was generally regarded as irrelevant. The Chinese Communist newspaper, *Peoples Daily*, termed the ASTP "a duel in space" in which each side sought to learn the other's secrets. In an editorial in the journal *Aeronautics and Astronautics*, United Nations Secretary-General Kurt Waldheim cited the application of space technology to reduce tensions and observed that space developments "can go far in unifying mankind." [25]

The results of the ASTP are not difficult to assess. It proved that irrespective of future political developments, the technology of space cooperation was certainly viable.

 PART III

THE NEW
WORLDS

CHAPTER VIII

THE SEARCH FOR CREATION

After the crew of *Apollo XVII* returned from Taurus-Littrow, the lunar-module pilot, Harrison H. (Jack) Schmitt, the only professional geologist to go to the Moon, put the lunar adventure into this perspective: "The probability is very great," he said, "that the synthesis of the geology of Apollo and Luna will become one of the fundamental turning points in the history of all science." [1]

At the end of eight years of reconnaissance, beginning with *Ranger VII*, which radioed the first closeup pictures of the Moon's surface before it crash-landed in July, 1964, and ending with *Apollo XVII* in December 1972, our knowledge of the Moon had become enriched with two basic discoveries.

First, it was ascertained that there was no evidence of life on the Moon, present or fossil. No sign of microorganisms, algae, nor lichens was found. The moon was sterile. Life had never evolved in its waterless wastes.

The surface appeared to have been depleted of organic compounds. However, six amino acids, which are building blocks of living material, were found in laboratory hot-water extracts of the lunar dust. The amino acids reported by Sidney W. Fox, director, Institute for Molecular and Cellular Evolution, University of Miami, were glycine, alanine, glutamic acid, aspartic acid, serine, and threonine. The precursors of amino acids were present on the Moon as in meteorites; when water was added, amino acids formed. The early stages of biochemical evolution were thus represented but it never reached the amino acid stage because there was no water. [2]

Second, the Moon could not be characterized simply as a piece of the Earth's mantle, as George Darwin, second son of Charles Darwin, suggested in 1895, or simply as an unevolved planetesimal, as others believed in the early twentieth century. It was a planet in its own right, with a crust, a mantle and a core. In the far past, it had its own magnetic field.

Because of similarities with the Earth in its internal structure, the Moon seemed to represent early phases of planetary evolution. Up to a point, it was analogous to the evolution of the Earth, but only up to a point. Major processes of its evolution had stopped 3.2 billion years ago.

Like the Earth, the Moon is chemically layered, and extensive surface features, mainly on the Earth-facing side, have been molded by volcanism. In other respects, it is unlike the Earth. There are conspicuous differences in the bulk chemistry of the Moon, the crust of which is considerably thicker than Earth's and contains a higher proportion of the radioactive elements uranium, thorium, and potassium.

Basalt that paves the lunar basins looks like basalt on Earth but varies chemically. Lunar basalt is richer in iron and titanium and poorer in alkali elements than terrestrial basalts.

Both mountains and basins appear to have been formed by different processes on the two bodies. Lunar mountains and mare (sea) basins were created by the impacts of giant planetesimals or meteors. The mountains of the Moon are arranged in concentric rings around the great basins.

Terrestrial mountains and basins are now believed to have been formed by the movements of crustal plates over the mantle, although it is easy to believe, as some geophysicists do, that the Pacific Ocean basin was created initially by the impact of a giant planetoid—as Hudson's Bay and the Arctic Ocean Basin might have been.

When Galileo Galilei looked at the Moon through his homemade telescope in 1610, he saw mountains, basins, and the light-colored regions called the "terrae," or highlands. Because of their dark color, which suggested water, he called the basins "maria," or seas. The largest one on near side is called an ocean—Oceanus Procellarum, the "Ocean of Storms."

What flowed into them, as we learned in the eight years of lunar exploration, was not water, but molten lava. It congealed and formed basaltic rock, first identified chemically by *Surveyor V* in 1967.

That discovery provided the initial clue that the Moon had undergone chemical differentiation, like the Earth. This is a process whereby the lunar material was heated and thoroughly cooked to a molten soup. Lighter elements float to the top and form a scum. On a planetary scale, the scum cools to become a crust. The heavier elements sink to the center of mass, to become a core. In between, there is the bulk of the planet—the mantle.

Because both the Earth and the Moon exhibit this structure, it appears reasonable to expect that other terrestrial planets do—that this is the basic form planetary evolution takes, not only in our solar system but in all those with terrestrial planets. Thus, the results of the exploration of the Moon imply a cosmic uniformitarianism in the evolution of planets, with local variations. It is a satisfying thought, because it suggests that there is order in the universe and that we, having merely ventured as far as our own Moon, can already perceive it.

The eight years of investigation of the Moon by automated and manned space vehicles has resulted in a scenario that may change later on but currently goes like this. The Moon formed, as all the planets did, from a ring of dust and gas around the sun, the solar nebula. The nebular hypothesis goes back to Immanuel Kant and Pierre Simon de Laplace in the eighteenth century. Not much has been discovered either to verify or refute the basic idea since then. In the process of its accretion, probably from smaller globs of material or planetesimals, the Moon grew extremely hot. Most of it, perhaps all of it, became molten. On the surface, the scum formed the crust; the heavy materials sank toward the center. The time? About 4.5 or 4.6 billion years ago.

Imagine the scene then, as astronaut-geologist Schmitt has: "About 4.6 billion years ago, when the Moon was approximately its present size, the sun probably set on a glowing, splashing sea of molten rock. Storms of debris still swept this sea, mixing, quenching, outgassing and remelting a primitive melted shell. This outer shell and possibly the entire Moon appear to have been melted by the great thermal energy released by the last violent stages of the formation of the terrestrial planets." [3]

The Moon cooled. Its surface was pummeled then by giant meteors and planetoids. Some may have been pieces of rocky material hurled into the inner solar system during the formation of the giant planet Jupiter, or they may have been pieces of the Moon itself, broken away when the protomoon was seized by the Earth, hurled into distant orbits around the Earth, and finally recaptured as the Moon spiraled outward away from the Earth as a result of tidal friction—a process many experts believe is still going on at a rate laser beams can measure.

The great bombardment, unaccountably focused on the Earth-facing (near) side of the Moon, reached a peak about 3.9 billion years ago. The Imbrium Basin was probably formed then, Apollo data indicate. The planetoid that created it and raised the Apennine Mountain chain must have been the size of the island of Cyprus.

At the end of this cataclysmic period, which lasted about 100 million years, another episode of cooking followed. Much of the upper portion of the Moon became molten, heated this time by the radioactive decay of potassium, uranium, and thorium in the crust.

Into the great basins oozed the molten rock. It filled them as water filled the ocean basins on Earth. In the light of this analogy, Galileo's conception of the lunar basins as seas is not so far off the mark. They were, for a time, seas of glowing lava. When it cooled, the seas became permanently frozen.

The light-colored lunar highlands consist of another kind of rock, a feldspar called anorthosite. This discovery was a surprise. Anorthosite, which is rare on Earth, was not expected on the Moon. It represents a phase of early crustal evolution through which the Earth presumably passed but which is now nearly buried and obliterated on Earth. But there it is on the Moon, forming a major portion of whitish highlands.

A third type of rock was found on the Moon. Geologists called it KREEP, an acronym for certain constituents—potassium (K), rare-earth elements, and phosphorus. KREEP also is rich in uranium and thorium. These rocks appeared to be concentrated in the Procellarum and Imbrium basins. There was a fourth species, called breccia, an aggregate of fragments welded by heat and pressure.

By what process were the potassium, the rare-earth elements, the phosphorous, uranium, and thorium concentrated in the KREEP rocks? Was it analogous to the concentration of metal ores on Earth, where the process was just faintly understood? Was it uniform in the terrestrial planets? These questions were of intense interest to the geologist; their solution would be of inestimable economic value in prospecting for metals. This point was elaborated in a report by the Lunar Science Institute, Houston, on Apollo scientific results (1972):

> Chemically, this lunar crust is unlike the great bulk of the continental crust of the Earth, but it has some fundamental similarities to the relatively rare bodies of gabbroic igneous rock from which are drawn the Earth's rare but vital deposits of nickel, platinum and titanium. Such terrestrial ore deposits are the products of concentration by geochemical processes from unknown sources, probably layers within the deeper Earth which formed early in its chemical evolution.
>
> Studies of the lunar crust promise basic information on how the raw materials of a newly formed planet undergo processing that leads to a concentration of elements. The concentration process which probably functioned also on Earth appeared to have begun in the earliest phases of planetary evolution.

By the end of Apollo, only a fraction of the 840 pounds of lunar soil and rocks returned by the six landing missions had been analyzed. The most striking general observation was the lack of water. As a consequence, the lunar rocks have different electrical, sound-transmitting (seismic), and optical characteristics than Earth rocks.

Not only was water missing from the lunar rocks, but they were found to be deficient in all relatively volatile (light) elements (hydrogen, oxygen, lead, etc.). There are several hypotheses: (1) they were vaporized and lost to space by heating after the Moon was formed; (2) they were driven off from lunar material during the accretion process; or (3) the Moon was formed in a volatile-poor but refractory-rich region of the solar nebula.

The third hypothesis is favored by some investigators because it accounts for the finding that lunar rocks have more than the cosmic share of refractory elements—those which vaporize at high temperatures. The scarcity of volatile elements and the relative overabundance of refractories, including potassium, uranium, and thorium point to its accretion in a different region of the solar nebula than the region where the Earth formed. If that was the case, the Moon must have been captured by the Earth. But the capture theory is loaded with unanswered questions. The big one is, "How?" The dynamics of capture are highly controversial. One difficulty is that if a body of lunar size approached close enough to the Earth to be captured, it would be broken up into many pieces by tidal stresses imposed by the Earth's gravitational force. The distance at which this would occur is called the Roche limit (named for Edouard Roche, a nineteenth-century French mathematician). The limit has been calculated at 2.88 Earth radii, or 11,401 miles from the center of the Earth. If it is taken into account, capture theory must cover the likelihood of the Moon's breakup and its subsequent reassembly in Earth orbit. One attractive feature of such a two-phase operation is that the final period of the reassembly phase might account for the massive bombardment that created the maria basins and big craters.

However, like other theories of where the Moon came from, the capture hypothesis has another hurdle if it must rely on the conclusion that the Moon accreted in a different part of the nebula, possibly closer to the Sun, than the Earth. Oxygen isotope studies show the likelihood that both the Earth and Moon grew in the same nebular neighborhood.

Obviously, the scientific mission of the Apollo program to discover the origin and evolution of the Moon was only partly realized by the end of the program. A great deal about the evolution of the small planet was learned, but the program failed to answer the question of origin definitively enough to establish a consensus of scientists.

Lunar scientists can speak confidently now about the internal structure of the Moon, the chemical composition of its crust, the processes that formed the crust, and its general history. But they can only speculate about its origin. Apollo and its Luna supplement were only the beginning of man's effort to understand the chemistry of creation.

THE EMBARRASSMENT

In 1961, when President Kennedy called for a manned lunar landing, the Space Science Board of the National Academy of Sciences nominated the origin of the Earth, the Moon, and the solar system as the most challenging scientific questions of the age. Many scientists believed that the answer to the origin and evolution of the Earth, where evidence of the first billion years has been erased by volcanic and tectonic reprocessing, might be found on the Moon, where they expected that parts of the primeval crust escaped alteration after the small planet was formed. For this reason, the scientific community, or most of it, supported the Apollo Program, even though its major goal was political. Many devout members of the lunar science team were bitterly disappointed when the Apollo lunar exploration program was cut back in 1969 after its political mission had been fulfilled.

But the Moon was not the Rosetta Stone of the solar system. It was an anomaly in terms of several theories. In a uniformitarian scheme of condensation in a solar nebula where temperature falls with distance from the Sun, the denser planets should be nearer the Sun and the liquid or gaseous planets farther out. It works out that way, in general, except for the Moon.

A scenario accounting for this arrangement has been sketched by John S. Lewis, Massachusetts Institute of Technology. It starts with the solar nebula heating up as it contracted. The sun was formed. Close to it all material existed as gas. As cooling set in, compounds condensed into solids in a sequence determined by their vapor temperatures and pressures.[4]

Precipitating out of the gas first were the refractory materials that vaporize only at the highest temperatures, namely the oxides of calcium, titanium, uranium, thorium, and so on. As temperatures in the nebula dropped off with increasing distance from the sun, next to condense was metallic iron; next was magnesium silicate (enstatite). Next, sulfide gases reacted with iron to produce iron sulfide, or troilite (FeS). Next to condense was a mineral called tremolite, a hydrous silicate containing calcium and water. Next, a ferric oxide dissolved in silicates to form the mineral pyroxene and a ferromagnesian silicate mineral called olivine. Farther out, water vapor condensed as ice.

Thus, Mercury should be rich in iron because it was formed at temperature too high for silicates to condense. Its density suggests it may contain 60 to 65 percent iron. At the orbit of Venus, magnesium silicate condensed, forming a planet less dense than Mercury. Earth accreted of materials that condensed at slightly lower temperatures, including the water-bearing mineral tremolite and sulfur. For that reason, Earth has water and Venus probably has not.

Less dense than Mercury, Venus, and Earth, Mars formed in a region where there was no metallic iron (in this scenario), but plenty of tremolite. The abundance of tremolite would give Mars five or six times more water than the Earth has per unit of mass, but most of the water may be bound up in minerals; otherwise, Mars could be entirely covered by an ocean several kilometers deep (if it had an atmosphere dense enough to hold liquid water on the surface).[5]

As a result of this condensation sequence, the terrestrial planets exhibit a density profile that generally is inversely proportional to their distance from the sun. The density of Mercury is 5.441 grams per cubic centimeter; of Venus, 5.227; of Mars, 3.97. Earth, however, has a density of 5.516, making it the densest planet. But these figures may reflect compression resulting from the greater mass of the Earth, largest of the terrestrial planets. An uncompressed density calculation alters the figures to conform better to the condensation-density sequence. The uncompressed densities have been figured for Mercury as 5.4; Venus, 4.7; Earth, 4.4 and Mars, 3.7.[6]

What about the Moon? With a density of 3.34 grams per cubic centimeter, it becomes an embarrassment to this elegant condensation model. Clearly, the model says that the Moon formed in another part of the solar system than the Earth and was then captured—unless: it coagulated from planetesimals that were hurled into the inner solar system by Jupiter and somehow congregated in Earth orbit; it fissioned from the Earth's mantle, which has a density similar to that of the Moon's bulk density; or it coagulated in Earth orbit from a cloud of silicates left over from the accretion of the Earth.

At the end of the Apollo program, these were the most widely discussed theories of the origin of Moon—just as they were before the program started. Although the capture theory appeared to be the predominant one circa 1975, the evidence acquired in eight years of reconnaissance and exploration does not provide enough constraints to rule out any of them. Consequently, the origin of the Moon may be considered the "other shoe" that is yet to be dropped.

LUNA, RANGER, AND SURVEYOR

So far as it has gone, the investigation of the Moon has been an inductive process, like the investigation of a crime, in which certain generalizations (such as its origin and evolution) are sought from data. As the investigation, which began with simple photographic reconnaissance, proceeded to higher and higher levels of sophistication and complexity, the definition and scope of the scientific problem became apparent. The problem could be defined as the understanding of the creation; the scope was the solar system. The solution lay beyond the Earth and its unaccountable Moon.

Lunar reconnaissance from space began with the Soviet's *Luna III*, which photographed the far side for the first time in 1959 and revealed a cratered moonscape, but one significantly different than astronomers were accustomed to seeing through their telescopes on the near side. A principal difference was the lack of the large dark areas that characterized the near-side basins.

Ranger VII plummeted into the outfall from the crater Tycho and radioed 4,308 photos before it crashed July 31, 1964.[7] Closeup photos taken from an altitude of 1,600 feet showed craters nested within craters. They disclosed that some agency, the solar wind or space dust bombardment, had caused erosion on the Moon.

Two more crash-landing camera vehicles followed in 1965. *Ranger VIII* came down in Mare Tranquillitatis and *Ranger IX* in the crater Alphonsus. They transmitted a total of 17,259 photos to Earth.

Winning the race to soft land the first unmanned vehicle on the Moon, the Soviet *Luna IX*, a 220-pound craft with a camera, touched down automatically in Oceanus Procellarum near the crater Reiner February 3, 1966. The photos it sent back revealed a crumpled bed of dark rock that looked like lava. It was a scene that shocked the proponents and adherents of the theory that the Moon had accreted cold and was stone cold dead.

Four months later, *Surveyor I* landed June 2, 1966, in southwestern Procellarum. NASA had hoped to beat the Russians to an automated soft landing, but problems in the development of Surveyor delayed its launch. It was, however, a larger and more productive reconnaissance vehicle than Luna. The first of the 11,240 photos it returned to Earth showed a gentle, rolling landscape, with low hills in the middle distance and far mountains. Few visionaries expected the Moon to look like that. Generations of science fiction illustrations, based on an assumption that erosion was absent on an airless, probably waterless Moon, had depicted jagged peaks and scarps with knife-blade edges. Instead, there appeared a desert scene, pocked by craters with nicely rounded rims. Close up, the lunar soil around the Surveyor footpads resembled that of a freshly ploughed field, with rocks and clumps strewn about. The lunar topsoil, or "regolith," was a surprise.

After *Surveyor II* failed, *Surveyor III* landed April 20, 1967, in eastern Procellarum. There, also, it viewed a gentle, rolling landscape.

Surveyor IV failed, but *Surveyor V* was a triumph. It landed September 10, 1967, in southwestern Mare Tranquillitatis. In a small gold box it carried a chemical analyzer that identified major chemical elements in the soil by bombarding them with alpha particles (helium nuclei). The manner in which the particles were scattered or reflected by the target atoms indicated their chemical identity.

After 900 minutes of data from the little gold box, Anthony Turkevich, of the University of Chicago, and his coexperimenters, James H. Patterson, of the Argonne National Laboratory, and Ernest Franzgrote, of the Jet Propulsion Laboratory, concluded that *Surveyor V* was resting on basalt. The rock was chemically similar, but not identical, to basalt on Earth. It was volcanic rock.

This discovery was the first proof that the lunar surface had been cooked. It set the stage for discoveries that were coming later. The findings of *Surveyor V* were the dawn before sunrise. *Surveyor VI*, which landed in the Sinus Medii November 10, 1967, confirmed basalt. *Surveyor VII*, which came down in the highlands north of Tycho January 10, 1968, reported a feldspathic rock of a chemistry different from lowland basalt, but a rock that was also a product of the cooking process.

It was apparent to some scientists, although not to all, that the Moon had undergone an evolution similar to that of the Earth. Its primeval material had been reprocessed by internal heating that had melted, remixed, re-melted, and mixed again the early mineral combinations.

It now seemed reasonable to think that the evolution of the Earth and the Moon had proceeded as a cosmochemical process that was determined by several parameters: the size and composition of the primordial body; its distance from the sun; and the availability of raw materials from the nebula. Compared to Earth, the Moon might be considered a case of arrested development. After 1.3 billion years from the Moon's formation (4.5 billion years ago), chemical processing of rocks had stopped, and surface sculpting by impacts had died down. Lunar activity was thus short-lived compared with Earth, which remains active after 4.5 billion years.

Beginning with data from Surveyor, the investigation of the Moon posed a scientific challenge that became more complex and demanding every year. Nothing short of an antarctic-style research program—with semipermanent scientific bases on both the near and far sides, a global transportation system, and continuous resupply from Earth—would resolve the fundamental questions of origin and development. A thorough geological survey might take a century.

The events between 1964 and 1972 were just a beginning. Between August 10, 1966, and the end of January 1968, NASA sent five camera spacecraft to lunar orbit. The lunar orbiters photographed about 99 percent of the moon. From their reconnaissance, NASA selected eight landing sites for Apollo astronauts. The Orbiter photos and other data enabled the U.S. Geological Survey to construct a complete photomap of lunar near side and identify on it the principal geological features.

The Orbiter program provided a serendipitous discovery about the lunar interior. By tracking the 850-pound *Lunar Orbiter V*, scientists at the Jet Propulsion Laboratory noticed peculiarities in its orbit. The trackers were William L. Sjogren, Paul M. Miller, and Peter Gottlieb. At certain times, it seemed to accelerate. This could be attributed only to a gravitation effect. At six places on the Moon, gravitational attraction was higher than average. These places happened to be circular maria: Imbrium, Serenitatis, Crisium, Nectaris, Humorum, and Aestatum. Each appeared to contain concentrations of excess mass—the "mascons." Following an initial report on this phenomenon, more mascons were detected by anomalies in the *Orbiter V* flight path in crater Grimaldi, Mare Humboldtianum, Mare Orientale, Mare Smythii, and two small, unnamed maria.

The mascons were interpreted differently by the "cold moon" and "hot moon" schools of theory. Proponents of the cold moon thought the mascons represented the buried masses of planetoids or meteors that had gouged out the basins. Hot-moon theorists argued that the buried masses were concentrations of congealed lava that had filled the bottoms of the basins and cracked substrata.

By the end of 1968, the controversy over whether the Moon was hot or cold reached its height. The cold-moon "school," headed by Harold Urey, of the University of California, La Jolla, who was highly regarded as the dean of cosmochemists in America, believed that the Moon had accreted cold and had undergone major alteration from impacts. The "hot mooners" pointed to evidence of volcanism reported by the alpha-scattering experiments on the Surveyors. But it was possible, some chemists argued, that the basalt was a preaccretion product and that the differentiation had occurred in the nebula before the Moon coagulated.

This controversy was related to an older one concerning the origin of the craters. One school insisted they were volcanic; another maintained that they were the products of impacts. The volcanists argued that if impacts had scarred the Moon, they would have battered the Earth even more severely, because the Earth would have exerted six times the gravitational attraction of the Moon on cosmic debris falling into the Earth-Moon system. But where were the scars on Earth? The "impacters" answered that the scars were nearly all obliterated by continuing tectonic processes that accounted for the rise and erosion of whole mountain systems and the creation of oceans.

The Ranger photos, which revealed craters in all sizes, plainly supported the impact theory so far as basin and crater formation were concerned. But the volcanists were right, too. Both processes had been at work on the moon, and both, presumably, were involved in the formation of planets.

THE MARBLE IN THE SKY

The first human beings to observe the lunar surface close up with the naked eye were the astronauts of *Apollo VIII*, Borman, Lovell, and Anders. Their photographs resolved objects four times smaller than those of the Lunar Orbiters. Vertical photography from *Apollo VIII* with a 250-millimeter lens as recorded on color film SO-368 showed craters as small as 17 meters in diameter. It is possible to resolve craters approximately 60 meters in diameter in high-resolution Lunar Orbiter photos. They revealed in more detail than ever before the differences between lunar near side and far side. The far-side basins and craters were largely devoid of the massive basalt fill that patterned the near side.

In the analysis of the *Apollo VIII* photos, a NASA report stated that they depicted "probable" impact craters, especially those named Humboldt and Ziolkovsky.[8] But they also showed crater chains similar to those produced by volcanism on Earth. However, the report qualified, some of the chains might be considered the product of a secondary bombardment by rocks splashed out of primary-impact craters by massive projectiles falling on the moon from space.

Perhaps the most significant photographic contribution of *Apollo VIII*, as I suggested earlier, was its magnificent visualization of the Earth as a lone blue-white agate in a black sky. The pictures of Earth rising over the lunar horizon, of the half-Earth, or of the full disk of the Earth looking no larger than the Moon does from Earth provided all mankind with the visual realization that his habitat is indeed one world spinning in a vast sea—a world that he despoils at his peril. Now it was perfectly clear to anyone who looked that the wages of ecological sins are extinction.

Apollo XI reinforced this new percept. Aside from its political objective to beat the Soviets to a manned lunar landing, *Apollo XI* was equipped to enable its crew to perform limited scientific chores. These were to collect rocks and dirt, deploy a seismometer, set up an optical corner reflector that would reflect a laser beam from Earth back to its source, and rig a sheet of aluminum foil to trap nuclear particles of the solar wind. Additionally, the crewmen were to take photographs, on the surface and from orbit, using a stereoscopic camera for closeup views on the surface, and they were to drive two hollow tubes into the regolith (topsoil) to obtain cores that would show how the regolith was layered.

Anxiety at Houston to get Armstrong and Aldrin off the surface at Tranquility Base and back home alive limited the amount of documented soil collecting the two explorers could accomplish. Documented samples had to be photographed in situ and their orientation established before they were picked up. It was important for scientists who were to examine them to be sure which side was exposed to the sun and solar wind.

The total extravehicular activity time on the surface of two and one-half hours was partly taken up by ceremonials, such as planting the flag and engaging in a radio telephone conversation with President Nixon. Armstrong and Aldrin performed all their major tasks setting up the seismometer and the laser reflector and bagging 24.1 kilograms (53.68 pounds) of rocks and dirt, which were hauled by spacecraft, ship, aircraft, and truck to the Lunar Receiving Laboratory at the Johnson Space Center, Houston.

The seismometer, consisting of four units that would respond to vibrations in the Moon, and the laser reflector were crucial instruments in probing the lunar interior. Essentially, the seismometer was a set of ears that "heard" seismic or sound waves traveling through the lunar interior from moonquakes or impacts, transposed them into electrical signals, and transmitted the signals by radio to Earth. In general, the velocity at which the waves traveled through the Moon indicated the density of the material through which they passed.

Because the seismic sounding of another planet was a new art, the functioning of instruments delicately enough attuned to record astronauts' footfalls was an unknown quantity. On Earth, seismic sensors are set firmly on piers in underground vaults, as far from man-made noise as possible. On the Moon, the package had to be set out on the surface, but there was a great advantage: Compared with the Earth's background noise of human activity, storms, tidal waves, and volcanic rumblings, the Moon was a silent planet. For example, the launching of the Saturn 5 was comparable in sound production to the explosion of the Indonesian volcano Krakatoa in the nineteenth century.

The 100-pound seismometer package erected by Armstrong and Aldrin functioned for twenty-one days with a high degree of sensitivity before it failed. The main purpose it served was to prove the feasibility of planting a network of such instruments across the face of the Moon as a means of probing the interior structure.

The laser reflector made it possible for astronauts and physicists to refine certain physical parameters about the Moon, such as its mean distance from the Earth to within a few meters; variations in its orbit; its libration, or wobble; and, from this, its moment of inertia, a mathematical quantity that would indicate the existence of a core.

This information could be ascertained with precision by aiming a laser beam at the Tranquility Base reflector from the Earth and observing its return. Ruby lasers were installed in the 120-inch telescope of the Lick Observatory, Mount Hamilton, California, and the 107-inch telescope of the McDonald Observatory, Mount Locke, Texas.

In contrast to an ordinary light source, the laser emits a "coherent," or organized, beam of light with great energy. Aimed at Tranquility Base, the beam illuminated a spot about two miles in diameter encompassing the mirror, which reflected some of the light back to the telescope from which it emanated. Because the speed of light is precisely known, the round-trip time could be converted to a precise measure of distance.

The lunar laser reflector experiments also would yield physical information about the Earth. Over time, they would provide a measure of the rate of continental drift and of variations in the Earth rate of rotation, which affects the length of the day; eventually, they would furnish evidence pro or con for the hypothesis that the Moon is receding from the Earth.

On July 22, 1969, two days after Armstrong and Aldrin emplaced the seismometer, a transmission on the order of a moonquake signal was received by Houston. Members of the seismic experiment team saw evidence in the seismogram of layering on the Moon, indicating the existence of a crust and mantle. The members were Maurice Ewing and Gary Latham, then of the Lamont-Doherty Geological Observatory; Frank Press, of the Massachusetts Institute of Technology; and George Sutton, University of Hawaii. The event stimulated excitement and speculation among the lunar scientists as the first men on the Moon sped Earthward for their Pacific splashdown.

Vainly, the scientists waited for a repetition of the moonquake, but nothing came. Later analysis of the July 22 signal raised doubts about its authenticity as a moonquake or impact. There were indications that it might have been a malfunction or "glitch" in the instrument rather than a recording of an external event.

Whether or not it was such an event, later developments in the Apollo Program showed that the team was right the first time: The crust-mantle structure they thought they had perceived in the apparently spurious seismogram from Tranquility Base did indeed exist.

Photographs taken by Collins in the Apollo CSM, *Columbia,* further enhanced the view of lunar far side. Moreover, they contributed to the realization that the dark maria were certainly younger than the light-colored highlands. This could be deduced from the fact that maria were much less pocked with craters. From such a comparison, it could be concluded that the bombardment rate had dropped dramatically after the maria were flooded by outpourings of lava.

Scientists on the lunar sample analysis team could hardly wait for the twenty-one-day quarantine period to end to get their hands on the rock and soil samples. (Astronauts returning from the first three lunar landing missions were quarantined twenty-one days from the time of lift-off from the Moon as a precaution against contamination by possible lunar microorganisms. The practice was abandoned after no sign of life on the Moon was found.) By measuring the radioactive decay of potassium^{40} to argon^{40} in the rocks from Tranquility, the team established that they ranged in age from 3.5 to 3.7 billion years. From this range, it could be inferred that crustal melting in that region occurred 800 million years after the Moon accreted and persisted at least 200 million years.

Inasmuch as there were fewer craters in the basalt than in the highlands, it appeared that the cratering of the Moon tapered off at or earlier than 3.7 billion years. The frozen lava covered the earlier scars.

Chemically, laboratory analysis of the maria rocks confirmed the results of Surveyor's alpha-particle analyzer. They were rich in iron and titanium and poor in sodium and carbon, and they lacked water, compared with Earth rocks. These samples showed also that the Moon was richer in uranium and thorium than the standard cosmic abundance, as determined by analyses of meteorites and the spectra of solar gases.

The abundance of radioactive elements in the crust at Tranquility suggested that if it was Moon-wide, the heat accumulated from the decay of these elements would have been ample to produce the lava flows in the basins.

Although incomplete, the *Apollo XI* findings led to a widespread view among experimenters that the outer part of the Moon, at least, had been melted to produce the maria. Whether there was more than one heating episode and whether it involved the whole Moon were questions that 115 domestic and 75 foreign principal investigators representing 88 institutions in the lunar-sample program (budgeted for the 1970 fiscal year at a cost of $9 million) hoped to learn.

THE MAGNETIC MYSTERY

The expedition of *Apollo XII* in mid-November 1969 to Oceanus Procellarum returned basaltic rocks that were younger than those of Tranquility. They were dated as having crystallized from a melt 3.2 billion years ago—a half billion years later than the oldest of the Tranquility rocks. It now appeared the lunar volcanism had lasted 500 million years.

Conrad and Bean landed amid some rubble that had been splashed out of the big crater, Copernicus. Analysis of the samples indicated that the crater was relatively young—only 900 million years old.

When the expedition departed, the lunar module that ferried them from the surface up to the orbiting Apollo-CSM was sent crashing to the surface by radio command from Houston to generate seismic waves for the *Apollo XII* seismometers. All three instruments that Conrad and Bean had set up with painstaking care recorded the impact and its astonishing results. The Moon rang like a bell. For nearly an hour, the reverberations continued from that blow. The experimenters were fascinated. Earth had never yielded a response like that!

The crew of *Apollo XII* had brought a magnetometer to the Moon. It confirmed findings in the *Apollo XI* rocks of a weak magnetization. The *Apollo XII* instrument detected a local magnetic field at the landing site in Procellarum of thirty-six gammas, about a thousandth of the Earth's magnetic field. A similar finding had been reported in April 1966 by the Soviet lunar orbiter *Luna X*. In 1967, NASA put *Explorer XXXV* into lunar orbit with a magnetometer, but it did not confirm the Soviet data.

Now, the new magnetic evidence indicated the existence of a global magnetic field in the Moon at some time in the past. The importance of this indication was that it implied the existence of a metallic core in the Moon, further evidence of its structural resemblance to Earth. In theory, the Earth's magnetic field is generated by dynamo action involving its rotation and iron core. Whether or not the Moon had an iron core or, as some speculators thought possible, an iron sulfide core, its present slow rotation rate does not suggest an active dynamo comparable to Earth's. However, it was reasonable to believe that tidal interaction with the Earth had slowed the Moon's axial rotation dramatically to the present period of twenty-eight days. Consequently, the dynamo theory could be satisfied to some extent by supposing a global magnetic field was generated by the Moon in the far past, when it was presumably rotating more rapidly.

The Russians, meanwhile, achieved automated sample return with *Luna XVI* during the hiatus between the *Apollo XII* and *XIV* missions. Basalts that the Soviet sample grabber brought back from Mare Fecunditatis yielded a crystallization age of 3.4 billion years, between those of Procellarum and Tranquillitatis.

On the *Apollo XIV* mission to the Fra Mauro Formation January 31 to February 9, 1971, Shepard and Mitchell set up a passive seismometer and supplemented it with an active one consisting of a string of sound sensors called geophones. The string was laid out on the ground and recorded sound waves generated by an astronaut-operated explosive device called the "thumper." These seismic sources were to be supplemented after the crew left the Moon by grenades fired by radio command from a mortar box left at the site.

The active seismic experiment was analogous to the seismic-sounding technique of probing the depth of the antarctic ice sheet during and after the International Geophysical Year. On the Moon, it provided information about the depth and composition of the crust.

The Fra Mauro Formation, on the eastern edge of the Procellarum Basin, appeared to consist mainly of throw-out from the planetesimal impact that had excavated the Imbrium Basin to the north.

This material, it was hoped, would consist predominantly of rocks with a different mineral composition from the predominant basalts returned by *Apollos XI* and *XII*. The dating of the rocks that were considered to be Imbrium debris yielded a probable date of 3.9 billion years for the Imbrium impact. Chemically, they varied, as expected, from the maria basalts. They had a lower concentration of iron, titanium, manganese, and chromium and more silicon, aluminum, and sodium than the mare basalts. They were at least 200 million years older than the oldest mare rocks yet found.[9] But they were not ancestral; chemical divergence showed that basalts could not have been derived from them by a later process of remelting and cooling.

From this finding, the *Apollo XIV* science report concluded, neither the mare nor the nonmare regions of the Moon so far reconnoitered were representative of the planet's bulk composition; instead, what the scientists had seen so far were rocks that had been reprocessed by melting and cooling episodes from material within the Moon that represented its early bulk composition.[10]

Further evidence that the lunar rocks had been magnetized by an early magnetic field was found at Fra Mauro. Shepard and Mitchell left a laser reflector there as well as a set of seismometers. With these instruments, the lunar scientific community had made a start toward "wiring" the Moon for sight and sound at three places. On the flight back to Earth, Shepard,

Mitchell, and Roosa busied themselves with experiments in electrophoretic separation, convection, and composite-casting in zero gravity. These tests were the forerunners of more elaborate ones in the later Apollo, Skylab, and the ASTP missions, all aimed at investigating a new technology of separating particles such as proteins, colloids, and cells; manufacturing alloys, and growing crystals of the highest purity in a weightless environment. These experiments, which received little public attention, had the potential of providing a much-needed industrial purpose for space activity. When they splashed down, the *Apollo XIV* crewmen were the last to undergo quarantine.

THE FIRST 500 MILLION YEARS

On *Apollo XV*, July 26 to August 7, 1971, Scott and Irwin investigated three geological features on the eastern edge of Imbrium: a small mare called Palus Putredinus ("Marsh of Decay"), on which they landed; the Apennine Mountain front; and a sinuous canyon called the Hadley Rille. They made the first manned motorized sortie on the Moon, driving the two-seater, battery-powered jeep called the Lunar Roving Vehicle (LRV).

The Rover extended the radius of a manned lunar traverse from a mile to 6 miles. It logged 28 kilometers (17.3 miles) of travel as the astronauts cruised around the plains region between the Apennine front and the great rille.

While Scott and Irwin set up another seismometer array and pounded heat-flow detectors in the regolith, Worden orbited the Moon in the CSM, *Endeavour*. He made surface observations with X-ray and gamma ray sensors. They marked the distribution of chemical elements, especially radioactive species. Additionally, a "subsatellite" released in lunar orbit from the CSM measured solar particles.

On the slopes of Mount Hadley, a massive mound of horizontally layered debris from the Imbrium impact rising to 14,625 feet, the space-suited explorers collected samples of breccia, consisting of ancient mineral fragments or "clasts" embedded in a fine-grained matrix. Strewn about the Moon, it represented a fourth rock type, with basalts, KREEP, and anorthositic feldspar. Of particular interest were the clasts, which had crystallized, for the most part, eons before the Imbrium impact.

"Through the clasts in the breccias, we began to see vaguely into the first half-billion years of lunar evolution," Schmitt reported.[11] He surmised that these ancient fragments, some more than 4 billion years old, represented a period when the outer shell of the Moon was melted to a depth of 100 kilometers.

During the first Lunar Science Conference at Houston in January 1970, observers were somewhat mystified by data showing that the 3.7-billion-year-old basalt rocks returned by *Apollo XI* were younger than soil particles or "fines" that had been picked up with them. Some of the fine material checked out as more than 4 billion years old.

That was a puzzling situation to those of us nongeologists who were accustomed to thinking of soil as the product of erosion of adjacent rock. On the Moon, the fines were not necessarily derived from the rocks embedded in them; often they were the debris of some titanic collision that had hurled material out of the depths of the Moon for hundreds of miles. Thus, a 3.7-billion-year-old rock could be deposited in material 4.5 billion years old.

The Plain of Hadley was underlain by a series of lava flows that the *Apollo XV* Preliminary Science Report noted were about the age of those in Oceanus Procellarum. Scott and Irwin set up the third laser reflector on the plain, establishing a north-south base line for measurements from Earth with reflectors in the Sea of Tranquility and Fra Mauro.

The heat-flow experiment, although not properly implanted because of soil resistance, yielded interesting results. It registered heat flowing out of the depths of the Moon at a rate about one-half the average for Earth. The summary report, prepared by the Johnson Space Center, Houston, noted that the *Apollo XV* heat-flow results indicated a content of radioactive elements substantially higher than that of Earth. The heat-flow experiment investigators, headed by Marcus G. Langseth, Jr., were more conservative. They concluded that if the observed lunar heat flow originates from radioactivity, then the moon must be more radioactive than the classes of meteorites that have formed the basis of Earth and Moon models in the past.[12]

CORE OF THE MATTER

Each of the lunar landing missions had provided more insight into the evolution of the Moon. It was possible with seismic data to define the extent of the crust, mantle, and core. Seismic results showed that the crust—on the near side—was 60 to 65 kilometers thick, two to three times the thickness of Earth's continental crust. Beyond the crust, an intermediate region, the mantle, extended inward about 1,000 kilometers, and the remainder appeared to be a soft core, partly molten, of silicates or iron sulfide. On the far side of the Moon, the crust was believed to be much thicker, possibly up to 150 kilometers.

In the maria, the crust was divided into a layer of basalt about twenty kilometers thick beneath the regolith, or layer of broken topsoil. Below twenty kilometers, the crust appeared to consist of coherent or "competent" rock of the type that geologists call anorthositic gabbro, a species of feldspar composed chiefly of calcium-aluminum silicate.

An upper mantle of iron-rich silicates extended from the base of the crust to a depth of 200 kilometers. Below that, the seismic data indicated a silicate rock type similar to that found in chrondritic meteorites. The lower part of it might be melted. If so, it would explain a sequence of weak moonquakes that were recorded by the Apollo seismometers on the Moon at times when the Moon was near perigee, its closest approach to the Earth, in its orbit. The quakes were interpreted as the result of a shifting of this deep liquid from the increased tidal pull of the Earth near or at perigee.

Evidence for the molten core was found in the failure of some lunar seismic stations to record "S," or "shear," waves from impacts on lunar far side. Pressure, or "P," waves were detected from these events, but not the S waves, which cannot pass through liquids.

In February 1972, the Soviet Union's second lunar sampler, *Luna XX*, descended near the Apollonius C crater south of Mare Crisium and 120 kilometers north of the *Luna XVI* landfall in Mare Fecunditatis. It returned to the USSR soil and rock samples similar to those brought back two months later by the crew of *Apollo XVI* from the Descartes region of the lunar highlands.

Soviet scientists reported that the Apollonius rocks hardened from a melt about 3.9 billion years ago. This was also about the age of older rocks found at Fra Mauro and, during the spring of 1972, in the Descartes highlands. It was the supposed time also of the Imbrium impact.

The heat of impact, the shock of impact, and the pressure either melted and recrystallized older rocks or reset their radioactive "clocks" to show the time of the impact. Thus, rocks picked up at various landfalls on lunar near side with apparent ages of 3.9 billion years seemed to bear witness to some frightful event that took place at that time. The favored explanation among principal investigators was that this was a period when "hell broke loose" on the Moon—when the bombardment of planetesimals reached its height. The cratering record of the near side seems to confirm that idea.

Apollo XVI headed directly for the true highlands, in the region north of the crater Descartes. The mission of April 16–27, 1972, carried another subsatellite to the moon, equipped with a camera for orbital photographs. Astronauts Young and Duke landed in the lunar module, *Orion,* on a relatively smooth surface called the Cayley Formation, adjacent to mountains and ridges of the Descartes highlands.

Overhead, the command module pilot, Mattingly, continued the work of geochemical mapping from orbit in the CSM, *Casper,* with an X-ray fluorescence spectrometer and the gamma ray spectrometer. The X-ray instrument sensed fluorescent, or secondary, X rays, which were generated by the interaction of solar X rays with chemical elements in the topsoil. Because the energy of the secondary X rays varied with each element (and the variation was known), the energy spectra recorded by the spectrometer identified the elements in the area over which the CSM was orbiting. Both *Apollo XV* and *XVI* X-ray results told the same story: The highland crust was mostly anorthositic gabbro. Presumably, this material covered the whole Moon before the maria basins were excavated by bombardment of planetoids and later paved with volcanic basalt.

Significantly, breccias picked up from Descartes and the Cayley plains yielded ages of 3.9 billion years. It appeared also to some investigators that the earliest extrusion of mare basalts could be pushed back to 3.8 or 3.9 billion years.[13] Consequently, the period of volcanism that produced the intermittent lava flows could have extended 700 million years. There was no evidence of volcanism younger than 3.2 billion years, the youngest age of the Procellarum rocks collected by *Apollo XII*.

The search for younger volcanics was a dominant theme in the last mission, *Apollo XVII* (December 7–19, 1972). Schmitt, the first professional scientist to visit the Moon, landed with Cernan in the valley of Taurus-Littrow—"near the coast of the great frozen sea of Serenitatis." [14]

The site was adjacent to the Taurus Mountains and the Littrow craters. When he climbed down the ladder from the lunar module, *Challenger*, Schmitt found himself in a geologist's heaven. He and Cernan drove their Rover, packed with scientific equipment, in an expectant search of evidence of volcanism more recent than 3.2 billion years ago.

For a while, the astronauts believed they had found it with the discovery of orange glass deposits at the edge of a crater. But later analysis proved the glass was quite old. It was allied chemically and compositionally to green glass picked up by Scott and Irwin at the Apennine Mountain front.

However, both glasses turned out to be intensely interesting. Condensed on them were unexpected volatile materials—bromine, silver, zinc, cadmium, and thallium. They were extremely rare in the Moon, thought to be depleted in all volatile elements and entirely lacking in water.

The discovery of the glasses, with volatiles condensed on them, suggested that deep within the Moon, or in some unexplored region, there might be zones of volatiles. The six Apollo landings and the Soviet grab samples had barely grazed the surface of the planet. Characterizing the whole Moon from these pinpoint reconnaissances on only one hemisphere was like trying to determine the physiography of Africa from a half-dozen widely separated visits.

The rocks Cernan and Schmitt collected were predominantly basalts and breccias. The oldest breccias contained clasts consisting of the remnant of crystallization from the primeval melted shell, Schmitt noted.[15] One clast composed of a crushed rock of magnesium olivine exhibited an apparent crystallization age of 4.7 billion years, the geologist said. In the valley, the explorers found some of the oldest mare basalts on the Moon—50 to 100 million years older than the oldest obtained from the Mare Tranquillitatis.

By the end of the Apollo lunar missions, the predominant view among lunar scientists held that the Moon was clearly a "differentiated" body; it had been cooked, at least the outer parts had. The question then was: When did the major cooking occur? The basaltic events, starting at 3.8 or 3.9 billion years ago, were a "recent" manifestation of internal heating by radioactive decay; but there were earlier heating events, on a larger scale, which had differentiated the parent rocks from which the basalts were descended. The source of heating was speculative.

Some investigators believed that the major episode of melting and of differentiation occurred early in the Moon's history, perhaps during its accretion. They suggested that it accreted rapidly from hot planetesimals, probably in a hot part of the solar nebula or in an extended and hot terrestrial atmosphere.[16]

Schmitt visualized the Moon of 4.6 billion years ago as "a sea of molten rock." [17] Most of the chemical differentiation probably occurred during the formation and cooling of the outer shell, it was speculated. During that time, volatile elements might have been lost.

One popular scenario proposed that the Moon was formed in a hot part of the solar nebula, where volatile elements existed in a vapor state. Heavy bombardment during the first 600 million years of the moon's history created the basins, and the climax of the barrage was reached at 3.9 billion years. Then, a pulse of heating in the upper crust, doubtless caused by radioactive decay, remelted the crust and upper mantle rocks. Molten lava poured out of cracks and fissures punched in the crust by bombardment and filled the maria basins. These volcanic episodes continued for 700 million years, dying out 3.2 billion years ago. Since then, the surface of the Moon has been battered and gardened by infalling debris, but it has not been altered further, apparently, by volcanism.

WHAT HAVE WE LEARNED?

One of the most curious consequences of lunar exploration so far is that in spite of the mass of physical evidence accumulated about the Moon since 1964, there is not enough to exclude any of the major theories of its origin. I have touched on this question earlier, but I believe the comment of Don L. Anderson, of the California Institute of Technology, summarizes this circumstance nicely: "All the classical theories of lunar origin are still with us—capture, fission and dual planet accretion," he said.[18]

Chemical differences in the compositions of the Earth and the Moon can be explained if the Earth formed in a dense part of the nebula and the Moon in a less dense part. In that case, the Moon was captured, a process no one (at this writing) seems fully to understand.

However, the differences can be accounted for also if the Moon is a by-product of the formation of the Earth. That idea eliminates the fuzzy dynamics of capture, which a number of thoughtful scientists find hard to accept. [19]

W. M. Kaula, of the University of California, Los Angeles, has proposed that the Moon accreted from a cloud of dust, gas, and planetesimals around the Earth. Planetesimals near the Earth collided initially to form the proto-Moon, which then swept up all other loose materials. [20] The process took about 1,000 years. Heat, generated by the energy of colliding planetesimals, led to melting and differentiation of the outer layers, forming the crust. Kaula speculated that some of the material involved in these Moon-forming collisions was hurled at high velocities into the inner solar system by Jupiter during its formation.

In an extrapolation of the capture theory, S. Fred Singer, a geophysicist serving as deputy assistant secretary of the department of the interior in 1970, proposed then that the capture of the Moon 4.5 billion years ago led to profound changes on the Earth resulting in the development of life. Tidal friction heated the Earth's interior, resulting in volcanic outgassing that produced the atmosphere and the oceans. The Moon, in turn, was also heated by this process. [21]

At the outset of the Apollo program, many scientists believed, as did Brian Mason and William G. Melson of the Smithsonian Institution, that: "We expect to reconstruct the story of the origin and evolution of the Moon which will also provide significant information about the early history of the Earth and entire Solar System." [22] But that goal is still a long way off. It is possibly as far away as Neptune and Pluto.

What did we learn about the Moon that we did not know before the $33-billion Apollo program started? Fundamentally, we found out that it was a partially evolved planet; but more specifically, scientists at the Lunar Science Institute, Houston, have cited the following points: [23]

There was no knowledge of a lunar crust, analogous to the crust of the Earth, before Apollo. The Moon was considered predominantly as an unlayered body, undifferentiated, like a meteorite.

The presence of processed anorthositic rock comprising most of the lunar crust was "totally unexpected," the institute report noted. It characterized anorthosite, a product of early cooking, as "rare and enigmatic" on Earth. Its occurrence on the Moon suggested that it had been common on the Earth at one time and represented an evolutionary stage through which the Earth has passed.

Prior to the Apollo landings, scientists assumed that the terrestrial planets condensed from the same kind of material as that in chondritic (stony) meteorites, which reflect the abundances of the elements in the Sun. The primeval stuff was processed by cooking after the planets accreted.

Examination of the lunar samples led some investigators to believe that the materials making up the Moon were precooked when condensation took place; they were already fractionated so that certain elements, notably the refractory (heat-resistant) ones, were concentrated.

It is assumed that the fractionation took place in the inner solar system, where the rocky or terrestrial planets condensed, in a region rich in silicates but low in volatiles. Farther away from the sun, in a cooler region of the nebula, the major planets formed of the lighter elements—giant Jupiter, ringed Saturn, huge Uranus, and icy Neptune. Pluto remains a mystery.

Planetologists have rationalized this scheme as a temperature-condensation profile, obeying well-known chemical laws and influenced by processes not so well known. The cosmochemical rules exhibited by the profile have been more clearly delineated by the exploration of the Moon.

In this solar system scheme, our planet, Earth, no longer appears unique, but it appears typical of a class of planetary bodies that undoubtedly exist by the millions through space and time in the universe.

The exploration of the Moon thus has given us more reason than ever before to suppose that there must be many "Earths" beyond our own solar system. It has broadened the base of the expectation that somewhere "out there" exist other forms of sapient life, other cultures, and, perhaps, other space-faring species.

Could we have learned as much about the Moon from Soviet-style automated landers as we did from Apollo? No, said Stuart Ross Taylor, Australian National University, a pioneer in lunar rock chemical analysis. In his book, *Lunar Science: A Post-Apollo View*,[24] Taylor has pointed out that ground truth had to be established by explorers as a matrix for interpreting the data provided by automata.

Ground truth is verification by human observation in situ. The collection of documented and oriented rock samples was an essential feature of the process of unraveling lunar-surface history from a myriad of clues—many contradictory, many obscure.

As Taylor observed, lunar-surface materials were extremely complex and mixed. He concluded that if lunar samples had been limited to such small collections as the 130 grams returned by *Lunas XVI* and *XX*, the sequence of lunar history revealed by Apollo—especially basin excavation and volcanism that filled the maria with lava—might not have become apparent for many years. "Now, with hindsight," he said, "we know exactly how to deal with a small, unmanned, lunar sample return, as was demonstrated on Luna 16 and 20 material. We can now contemplate an unmanned sample return from Mars, Mercury or other similar bodies with some confidence in our ability to ask the correct, scientific questions. This is the immediate legacy of the manned Apollo missions."

Most scientists in the lunar program share this view.

THE NEW SUN

After the moon, Skylab focused on the sun. The 171 days that three successive crews of astronauts spent aboard the Workshop resulted in more detailed solar data than had been collected during the entire history of observing the sun. At least one solar flare was observed from beginning to end. More details of the solar corona's structure were revealed than ever before.

The three missions dramatized also the advantages of manned observation of the Earth from an orbital platform. They demonstrated the feasibility of manufacturing purer alloys and crystals in zero gravity than is possible on the surface under 1 gravity.

Although accounts in mass media emphasized the time crewmen spent repairing the space station and its equipment, only 10 percent of the total stay time was actually required for maintenance and repair. At least 25 percent of the time the nine astronauts were aboard Skylab was devoted to experiments in solar physics, stellar astronomy, space physics, Earth observations, the life sciences, and materials processing experiments. The balance was required for eating, sleeping, exercise, and personal hygiene. As Ernst Stuhlinger, former deputy director, science, of the Marshall Space Flight Center, has pointed out, the amount of time crews spent on scientific work and maintenance-repair amounted to at least one-third of their stay time in orbit. It thus equalled an eight-hour work day every day they were aboard without any days off.[25]

The solar observatory cameras, telescopes, and spectrographs provided views of the sun that Earthbound observers cannot see from the ground because of the interference of the atmosphere.

The white light coronagraph, two cameras that photographed in the light of glowing hydrogen atoms, three ultraviolet spectrographs, and two X-ray telescopes viewed a region of the electromagnetic spectrum from 2 to 7000 Angstroms, from the shortest X rays through the visible light window. (The Angstrom, named for a Swedish scientist, A. J. Angstrom, is a unit of electromagnetic wave length equaling one ten-billionth of a meter, or 10^8 centimeters. Visible light wave lengths range from 3,850 to 7,600 "A." Radiation with wave lengths less than 100 A are classed as X rays.)

These instruments greatly enlarged the view of processes in the sun by enabling scientists to photograph what was going on through the X ray, ultraviolet, and extreme ultraviolet "windows" in addition to the narrow window of visible light. Similar instruments had been deployed on high-altitude balloons, sounding rockets, and sun-viewing satellites. Those on Skylab were generally more sophisticated. They provided a continuous record of solar activity and, unlike satellite data, the photographs and tapes could be returned to Earth for processing.[26] The instruments were used also to study the atmosphere of Mercury and the Comet Kohoutek.

Skylab was operated as a manned space station during a supposedly "quiet" period of the eleven-year solar cycle, but the view of the sun from space showed plenty of action. The corona, the crown of light that flares around the edges of an eclipse, showed changes in photos taken only forty seconds apart.

From the corona comes the solar wind, which blows among the worlds. Before Skylab, it was generally supposed that the outer corona was fairly homogenous. Changes in it appeared to be slow. The X-ray cameras revealed sequences of rapid change. Transient loops of material appeared in the corona—loops the size of the sun itself. About sixty of these features were seen. Some lasted for weeks after rising rapidly out of the photosphere, the blinding, bright disk below the corona. Material in the loops expanded at an estimated speed of 400 to 500 kilometers a second.

Frequently, the loops were accompanied by eruptive prominences in the chromosphere, a region of the sun between the corona and the photosphere. These events represented invisible nuclear and electromagnetic processes within the solar sphere.

Skylab's coronagraph made it possible for the first time to observe these features as they began, evolved, and subsided. The instrument was fitted with a metal disk to cover the blinding photosphere and thus create an artificial eclipse. Before such an instrument was invented, astronomers and physicists had to wait for the Moon to eclipse the photosphere so that the corona and the chromosphere could be seen in some detail. During the joint Apollo-Soyuz mission, as noted earlier, Apollo served the purpose of blotting out the photosphere by maneuvering between Soyuz and the Sun so that the cosmonauts could photograph the corona.

In the corona, where temperatures range from 6,000 to 2 million degrees Kelvin, the atmosphere of the sun expands, attenuates, becomes an electrified material called a plasma, and, hence, interacting with the great magnetic fields generated by the Sun, spirals outward, pulling lines of magnetic force with it. This is the solar wind. It has been detected as far out as the orbit of Jupiter; undoubtedly it blows far beyond.

For the first time, Skylab made it possible to study the phenomena of "holes" in the corona in detail. The holes were discovered in X-ray photos taken from sounding rockets and later by Orbiting Solar Observatory satellites. The X-ray and ultraviolet telescopes aboard Skylab showed the holes as dark areas against the bright disk. It was speculated that coronal holes may be the region from which the solar wind is ejected.[27]

Solar physicists had observed that the corona changed from one eclipse to the next, but they were surprised by the rapid rate of change when it was monitored from Skylab. The coronagraph showed a more dynamic corona than scientists suspected. It underwent changes in form from minutes to months.[28]

Two kinds of transient alterations occurred. One was a rapid rearrangement of material. The other produced a brightening of a part of the corona. It indicated that new material was being emitted from the interior into the field of view. These "mass ejection" transients took the form of bright loops that ascended outward and were frequent.[29]

The nuclear-magnetic processes these observations reflect remain to be delineated by theoreticians. For the great engine of the sun can be studied only by its effects in the photosphere, the chromosphere, and the corona. Below the photosphere, in the star's radiative interior, the hypothetical nuclear fusion reaction and its chain of transformations remain forever hidden.

DAYS OF THE COMET

The crewmen of Skylab 4 had a good, long look at the Comet Kohoutek. They brought a special electronographic camera with them when they docked their Apollo CSM with the station. The camera could be operated from inside or outside the Workshop.

The instrument revealed that as the comet neared the sun, the visitor was encapsulated in a huge cloud of hydrogen larger than the sun. Evidently, the hydrogen was emitted by the photodissociation of water and other molecules containing hydrogen as the comet heated up. At perihelion passage (nearest the sun), the comet produced about a ton of hydrogen a second, and the total outgassing may have released more than a million tons of hydrogen.[30]

Identified also in the comet were atoms and molecules of carbon, oxygen, sodium, silicon, calcium, iron, copper, nitrogen, carbon dioxide, and water. Particles of silicon about ten micrometers in diameter were observed. These findings supported the long-held theory that comets are mostly dirty snowballs of ice and dirt.

Kohoutek's Comet had two tails. The main one was the gas cloud blown away from the sun by light pressure and the solar wind. It was the familiar tail that follows the main body of the comet inbound and precedes it out-bound, always pointing the way the solar wind blows. The second tail was a stream of dust. It had been part of the original tail and persisted in pointing rearward as the comet rounded the sun and commenced its outbound jour-ney. Outbound, while the gaseous tail pointed away from the sun, the dust stream, or "antitail," pointed toward the sun, its particles less affected by the solar wind.

From the length and form of the antitail as reported by the Skylab crew, the size of particles ejected from the nucleus was estimated at 0.1 to 1 millimeter. This was the first indication that comets lose particles large enough to account for meteor showers.[31]

Kohoutek's Comet added greatly to the storehouse of data about comets, which seem to represent the oldest class of objects in the solar system and also the class least changed through time. Observations of Kohoutek from Skylab and from the ground confirm a model that assumes comets have the cosmic abundance of the elements except for some depletion of hydrogen. The bulk of the comet consists of hydrogen, carbon dioxide, and water. Ma-terial in the nucleus was probably never heated above 100 degrees K. for any period of time, other than perihelion passage, and therefore represented primordial condensate from a nebula.

Which nebula? It was speculated by Marshall Space Flight Center inves-tigators that Kohoutek's Comet could have been formed in the solar nebula or in a part of some distant interstellar cloud.[32]

EREP

For observation of the Earth, Skylab was turned away from the sun so that the Earth instruments pointed groundward. The Earth Resources Experi-ment Package (EREP) consisted of six cameras and radiation sensors that ob-served in the visible, infrared, and microwave regions of the spectrum.

The instruments were a multispectral camera capable of photographing ground areas in visible and infrared light simultaneously; an Earth terrain camera using high resolution color film; an infrared spectrometer; a mul-tispectral scanner; a combination microwave radiometer and radar altimeter; and an L-band radiometer.

The two camera systems, the spectrometer, and the scanner were used to examine croplands, forests, geological formations, lakes and rivers, and the oceans and assess their condition. The cameras took pictures in black and white, color, and infrared of land and water scenes that revealed evidence of vegetation blight; ocean currents; areas of pollution, especially noticeable in the Great Lakes region; sedimentation at the mouths of rivers; and the sprawl of urban areas. The spectrometer and scanner looked at the surface in the visible, near, and far infrared regions of the spectrum and taped the radiations that were reflected or emitted from the ground.

The instruments mapped areas of vegetation, such as forests and croplands; indicated soil moisture and water pollution; and recorded surface temperatures. Essentially, their feasibility for monitoring large areas of the planet from orbit was being tested. The results seemed promising.

The radiometer recorded sea conditions, ice cover on the Great Lakes, seasonal changes in vegetation, and floods and rainfall. It also provided engineering data for designing space radar altimeters. The L-band radiometer measured the brightness temperature of the ground, which varies with cloud cover, landscapes, and ocean surface features (an index of thermal conditions on the ground or in the atmosphere).

In its total performance, the EREP represented a precision method of maintaining a watch over the habitability of Earth. Any change likely to affect large areas would be recorded and analyzed by the system. With it, the spread of blight, of insect swarms, of industrial contaminants, of oil slicks at sea, of grass and forest fires, of flooding and drought, could be monitored daily by an orbiting space station.

The materials-science investigation consisted of fourteen experiments designed to observe the effect of weightlessness in manufacturing such items as semiconductors and in metal processing. The experiments were done in a workshop chamber that could be vented to space.

To apply intense, localized heat, an electron beam gun was used. For uniform sample heating, a furnace was installed. It was loaded with the experimental materials and set for a specified heating program. When samples were cooled, the crew stowed them for the return to Earth, where they would be analyzed.

The results of these highly technical experiments were spectacular. In one test, indium antimonide was melted inside the chamber and then allowed to cool. This is a semiconductor alloy that solidifies in crystalline form rather poorly under Earth gravity. The crystals are not fully homogenous. Convection currents, caused by gravity, disrupt uniform crystal growth. They also create defects in the structure of the crystal lattice. Undisturbed by gravity in Skylab, however, the indium antimonide sample cooled as a single homogenous crystal.[33]

In another experiment, a germanium selenide crystal grown on Skylab reached ten times the size of Earth-grown crystals. Its surface was virtually free of defects. Similarly, mixtures of gold and germanium, which are coarse and show large-scale segregation when alloyed on Earth, cooled to a fine uniform solid in Skylab.

"All experiments dealing with materials in space convincingly proved that the weightless environment of orbital flight indeed offers to the materials scientist an exquisite tool unavailable on Earth but full of promise for further experimentation and discovery," Stuhlinger reported.[34]

SUN, MOON, AND ICE

Although studies of the Earth, the Moon, and the sun tend to be specialized, the data we have gathered from each contribute to the understanding of the others—and of the totality of the environment of man, which is the solar system.

In the exploration of Antarctica, investigators found evidence that the ice cap was somewhat larger in the past than it is now. It is possible that it swelled during the time of the last ice age, which receded only 12,000 to 14,000 years ago in the northern hemisphere. In Antarctica, scientists hoped to find the mechanics of intermittent ice ages through which the Earth has passed; but they have failed so far—just as lunar scientists have not been able to realize their early expectation of deciphering the origin and evolution of the solar system from the exploration of the Moon.

As scientists have moved from one frontier to another, from Antarctica to the Moon, the great answers continue to elude them and to beckon them ever farther into the unknown.

Like the riddle of the Moon, the basic unsolved riddle of the antarctic ice cap is its origin. How did it start? What factors caused the glaciation of a land that once, in the far past, sported a subtropical forest that ultimately became transmuted into thick beds of anthracite coal? There were several hypotheses: continental drift over the south pole from a warmer latitude; passage of the Earth through a sun-obscuring cloud of dust that was sufficient to start a self-sustaining glacial period; or periodic changes in the sun's output of heat and light.

The hypothesis that changes in the luminosity of the sun account for ice ages was not taken seriously by many climatologists because of a prevailing view that the time scale for any waning or waxing of the solar constant $(1.36 \times 10^6$ ergs a second) would be billions of years. However, like so many scientific propositions that somehow become enshrined as dogma, the solar constant may not be so constant as many scientists have believed.

At Tranquility Base, Armstrong and Aldrin found a scattering of glassy patches atop clumps of soil at the bottom of shallow craters, and Armstrong photographed them. They looked like frozen drops from a hot liquid, ranging in size from one-half millimeter to one centimeter.

Astronomer Thomas Gold, of Cornell University, observed that these glazes were oriented in the same direction. He suggested that they could have been caused by an intense burst of solar heating—a sudden increase in the sun's luminosity by a hundredfold. Gold proposed that the drops were evidence that the sun emitted a nova-like burst of energy no more than 30,000 to 100,000 years ago, which he reckoned was the probable age range of the glassy patches.[35] Such an outburst would have swept away the helium from the top of Earth's atmosphere and perhaps the entire atmosphere of Mars, Gold speculated.

Gold's theory attracted interest and argument, but not much support. Opponents contended that the droplets might just as well have been sprayed in the splashout of a meteor impact, congealing when they hit the ground. If the droplets came from the same splash, it would explain their orientation. Additionally, information about solar-flare activity on the sun over geologic periods of time was obtained in lunar-surface material. It was interpreted as evidence that flare activity has not changed appreciably in several million years.[36]

To some orthodox scientists, the idea that our sun is a variable star was heresy. The predominant theory of stellar evolution predicts that the luminosity of a star changes only at intervals of billions of years—as long as the age of the Earth. Consequently, the theory rules out short-term variations in luminosity.

But the theory is challenged not only by Gold's controversial hypothesis of lunar glass but by a remarkable experiment undertaken by Raymond Davis, Jr., of the Brookhaven National Laboratory, a government facility operated by the Energy Research and Development Administration (ERDA). The experiment was designed to detect nuclear particles called neutrinos, which nuclear theory predicts are emitted by the sun with such energy that they pass through the Earth like sunlight through a plate glass window. Nearly all matter is transparent to neutrinos.

So far, Davis's experiment has failed to detect the neutrinos that theory says it should. Is the experiment wrong? Or is the theory? A number of astronomers have become fascinated by the problem.

The neutrinos that Davis is trying to catch (an effort that seems like trying to hold a red-hot rivet in a paper bag) are emitted by the decay of boron[8], a product of thermonuclear reactions in the heart of the sun. Neutrinos cannot be trapped, but they can be detected by their effects. The collision of a neutrino with chlorine[37] would convert the chlorine to argon[37], which is detectable by its radioactivity.

Using this principle, Davis filled a big tank with 100,000 gallons of perchlorethylene—a cleaning fluid of chlorine compounds—and put it 5,000 feet underground in the Homestake Gold Mine, South Dakota. The purpose of locating the neutrino detector so far underground was to protect it from vagrant cosmic rays, which can also cause nuclear reactions by atomic collisions.

But argon is not being produced in the tank, implying neutrinos are not being emitted at the rate expected. Are the physical principles on which the experiment is based wrong? Or, as the University of Chicago physicist Eugene N. Parker, a discoverer of the solar wind, suggested: "Perhaps the luminosity of the sun goes up and down over a period of a million years or so. We recall the ice ages." [37]

Inasmuch as the theory of stellar evolution fails to meet the neutrino test, astronomer R. K. Ulrich, of the University of California, Los Angeles, concluded: "We must concede that solar luminosity varies on a time scale of less than billions of years." [38] Investigations of this phenomenon by the Smithsonian Astrophysical Observatory and other institutions have been inconclusive, Ulrich said.

Direct observations from Skylab and scientific satellites are much too short-term to illuminate this riddle. The lunar evidence is hardly conclusive. So far on Earth, we have little evidence that ice ages in the northern and southern hemispheres are contemporaneous, as they well might be if solar luminosity dropped off from time to time.

There is another place to look for evidence: Mars. Photographs from the *Mariner IX* Mars orbiter have shown evidence of climatic changes on the Red Planet. Some experts have suggested Mars is presently locked in an ice age. On the scale of geologic time, Earth is just easing out of one. If the time scale of Martian climatic change can be determined, a correlation with changes on Earth might furnish new evidence about the luminosity constant of the sun.

Clues to its possible variability in Antarctica, on the Moon, in the Homestake Gold Mine, and on Mars inevitably beckon man to more distant shores. In the thousand years of exploration by Western people, there were always farther ports of call.

At the end of 1975, two reconnaissance vehicles called *Viking I* and *II* were heading toward them, for landfalls at Chryse and Cydonia on Mars. But meanwhile, the space science community had its first closeup look at the master planet of the sun's family, Jupiter.

"Man," said Jack Schmitt, "has made the universe an accessible part of his environment." [39]

CHAPTER IX

THE LIQUID PLANET

The idea of reconnoitering the outer planets—Jupiter, Saturn, Uranus, Neptune, and Pluto—evolved slowly during the 1960s. It was developed in a set of scientific objectives by the Space Science Board of the National Research Council of the National Academy of Sciences in a sequence of studies. They pushed the theme that understanding the nature of the outer planets was essential to understanding the nature of the solar system, and that was the goal of the whole space game. Although investigating the Earthlike planets—the Moon, Mars, Venus, and Mercury—and studying the sun was a fair beginning, the board pointed out that the major part of the sun's planetary system lay beyond the orbit of Mars. Jupiter alone contained two-thirds of the mass of the nine planets.

A good deal was known about Jupiter from Earth observation. It exhibited a large, powerful magnetic field, a "prodigious" source of internal energy, and an atmosphere in violent motion, the board stated.[1] It seemed to be gaseous, composed mainly of hydrogen—a sunlike planet that somehow had never evolved into a star but had remained in a state between a star and a planet. The evolutionary significance of Jupiter was speculative, but fascinating. What did it represent in terms of cosmic evolution?

"It is the center of a large family of circling satellites, as diverse in their properties as are the planets themselves," the board study said. The scale of the satellite systems of these big outer planets was awesome.

Jupiter has thirteen satellites (a thirteenth moon was identified by Charles Kowal, of the Hale Observatory, Mount Palomar, California, in 1974); Saturn has ten, in addition to its spectacular rings; Uranus has five; and Neptune, two. The satellite families of Jupiter, Saturn, and Uranus are analogs of the solar system itself. Two of the inner satellites of Jupiter are about the size of the planet Mercury, and two others approximate the size of our Moon. Titan, a moon of Saturn, and Triton, a moon of Neptune, also are close to our Moon in size. In the late 1960s, when plans to investigate the outer solar system were being made, Titan was the only moon known to have an atmosphere.

"The state of our knowledge of the outer solar system is fragmentary and limited," the study admitted, "this part of the solar system must be fully explored." The board considered low-, medium-, and high-cost programs of exploring the outer planets. The favored program was the high-cost one. It called for the development of a special space vehicle called the Thermoelectric Outer Planet Spacecraft (TOPS). It would weigh about 1,400 pounds, generate its own electricity from the radioactive decay of plutonium[239] in a thermoelectric generator, and cost about $440 million to develop. NASA had invested $25 million up to 1971 in a study of TOPS.

If the space agency elected to follow the high-cost road to the outer planets, it would also have to develop a launch vehicle for TOPS. The air force's Titan 3-C, with a Centaur upper stage, was one possibility. There were other upper stage propulsion systems that had yet to be developed.

One was solar electric propulsion. The system converted sunlight by means of photovoltaic cells to electricity to accelerate ions through a thrust tube. The emission of the charged nuclear particles yielded a puny thrust in space, but over a period of time, the cumulative effect produced respectable acceleration. This was one version of the "ion drive" of science fiction. Several types of ion engines were developed by NASA in the early 1960s, and one was tested as an attitude-control device on a weather satellite. The problem was a power source. Photovoltaic conversion of sunlight by solar cells was not promising at large distances from the sun. At Jupiter, the intensity of sunshine is hardly one twenty-fifth that at the Earth. The radioisotope generators that NASA and the Atomic Energy Commission had developed to provide direct current for satellites and instruments on the Moon were inadequate for large electric propulsion systems. A small-scale nuclear reactor power plant would be required to provide the electricity for a large ion engine.

Another propulsion system that was further along in development in the 1960s was the NERVA (Nuclear Engine for Rocket Vehicle Application). It was in an advanced state of development by the AEC, NASA, and private contractors by 1968 and had undergone tests that year at the Nuclear Rocket Testing Station at Jackass Flats, Nevada. The engine consisted of a small nuclear reactor five feet long and three feet in diameter that heated hydrogen to 4,000 degrees F. The hot gas was expelled through a nozzle to produce powerful thrust.

Such an engine had been visualized as ideal for outer planet flights. The technology was straightforward, and the engine worked. But it never got into space and eventually was abandoned. One reason was the problem of launching a nuclear reactor from Cape Canaveral. The hazard was unacceptable, even to the most gung-ho nuclear power enthusiasts. If the launch vehicle failed, either on the pad or during powered flight, the dispersal of radioactive debris in the atmosphere or in the Atlantic Ocean could be disastrous. There was only one safe way to operate nuclear propulsion in space. It was to launch the spacecraft with an unfueled reactor and insert the fuel in orbit. That required manned operations in orbit quite beyond the scope of the outer-planets program.

Without discussing such problems as these, the Space Science Board report estimated that an ion engine, powered by solar cells, could be developed for $90 to $200 million. It would send 1,300-pound payloads on direct flights to Saturn in 2.3 years, Uranus in 5.2 years, Neptune in 7.3 years, and Pluto in 10 years. A nuclear powered ion engine would boost heavier payloads to Uranus, Neptune, or Pluto, on direct flights, in less than 4 years. Development cost was estimated at $285 to $515 million.

There was a low-cost road to the outer planets, and it did not require exotic propulsion systems nor the TOPS program. It utilized a modification of the existing Pioneer class spacecraft, which had been designed to measure particles and fields in space near the Earth. As a near-Earth monitor, Pioneer weighed 140 pounds and carried 40 pounds of scientific instruments. Its cost was modest, and it could be easily launched by medium-sized rockets.

The vehicle could be modified for a Jupiter flyby without a great deal of expense. Four thermoelectric generators providing a total of 150 watts of power could be added. Spacecraft weight could be raised to 560 pounds at launch including 65 pounds of experimental equipment.

The question of durability had been partly answered by *Pioneer VI*, launched in 1965. By 1971, it had been operating for six years.

And by that time, two Jupiter-class Pioneers were being built by TRW Systems Group, at Redondo Beach, California. They were designated as *Pioneers F* and *G*. NASA spacecraft are given letter designations before launch; after successful launch, they are given numbers. *Pioneer F* was due to be launched from Cape Canaveral early in 1972, and *Pioneer G*, early in 1973, on 600-day, 620-million-mile arcs to Jupiter. Once successfully launched, they would be known as *Pioneer X* and *XI*, respectively. The launch vehicle for the Jupiter Pioneers was the trusty Atlas Standard Launch Vehicle, with a Centaur second stage on top and solid-propellant "kick" stage on top of that.

There was also another way—a cheaper way—of reaching the outer planets beyond Jupiter than developing costly ion propulsion systems. That was to use Jupiter's immensely powerful gravitational field to accelerate the spacecraft like a missile from a sling. The slingshot effect could send the vehicle clear out of the solar system or to any of the other outer planets, depending on its flight path and point of closest approach (periapsis) to Jupiter.

Theoretically, it was possible to use the slingshot effect again and again, from planet to planet, to reach Saturn, Uranus, Neptune, and Pluto. In the 1960s, an Illinois Institute of Technology group had calculated "Grand Tour" missions on which a vehicle would pass these planets at times when they were aligned on the same side of the sun. The earliest time when a Grand Tour would be possible was 1977. Once the spacecraft reached Jupiter, it would be boosted on to Saturn by Jove's gravitational energy. Saturn would send it on to Uranus, Uranus to Neptune, and Neptune to Pluto. After that, it would enter interstellar space. If the spacecraft was not aligned on a course to Saturn or to any of the other outer planets, it would simply fly out of the solar system after encounter with Jupiter.[2]

Gravitational assist was a simple but powerful technique of getting places in space. With precise navigation and plenty of time, it made interstellar flight possible—or so it seemed. The possibility could be tested by the Jupiter Pioneers.

Before the more expensive TOPS missions were undertaken, the hazards of navigation to the outer planets could be assessed by the lower-cost Jupiter Pioneers. The two known hazards were the Asteroid Belt, a supposed zone of rocks and abrasive particles stretching 270 million miles between Mars and Jupiter, and the radiation zone at Jupiter. Whether space vehicles could negotiate the asteroidal obstacle course and survive the high-energy trapped radiation in Jupiter's extensive magnetosphere were as uncertain in 1971 as whether Columbus could reach India by sailing west in 1492. There was a strong body of opinion that Pioneer would never make it through the Asteriod Belt, just as there was that Columbus would never make it across the Atlantic. And once at Jupiter? Zap! Pioneer's electronics might be extinguished in Jove's trapped-radiation belts.

ABANDONING THE PLANETS

NASA's decision to fly *Pioneers F* and *G* to Jupiter was a compromise between the demands of the scientists and the money requirements of the manned flight program. Each year since 1965, the Space Science Board's recommendation for planetary reconnaissance on a more ambitious scale than the budget allowed had become more insistent. NASA was pouring most of its resources into Project Apollo.

The conflict between manned and unmanned missions became particularly intense during this period. Essentially, the issue was not intellectual; it was political. NASA programs were subject to the political as well scientific goals of the administration. Historically, its counterparts in earlier ages of exploration were the Casa de Contratacion ("Board of Trade") of Spain in the fifteenth century and the British navy in the eighteenth and nineteenth. The

Casa de Contratacion acted as royal agent in outfitting the fleets of Columbus and Magellan. The British navy funded Cook, Ross, and Scott. These agencies served the interests of government. They served science only insofar as the scientific community was able to influence government.

In the 1960s, scientific and utility satellites (i.e., weather and communications satellites) had secondary and tertiary place in the national space program, for the focus was on Apollo. And the voyages of Apollo began as a political response to unexpected early Russian space successes. They were motivated by competition, just as the voyages of Columbus and Magellan had been.

Vainly, the critics of Apollo protested that science was given only the leavings of the manned space flight program. By the end of the 1960s, the influence that academic scientists had wielded in shaping national policy, especially in weapons development and arms control, was fading rapidly.

Under Presidents Eisenhower, Kennedy, and Johnson, a "hot line" existed between the scientific establishment and the White House. The National Academy of Sciences was influential in directing national science policy—except where it came into conflict with political objectives, such as the race to the Moon. The liaison was maintained through the White House Office of Science and Technology and the president's science adviser. Until the election of 1968, the scientific community had access to the president through this apparatus. After that, the apparatus began to lose its influence with the president. Mr. Nixon, although enthusiastic about the lunar landings, did not solicit the views of the intellectuals. In 1972, he abolished the apparatus, and the scientists were dismissed from the White House. The functions of the Office of Science and Technology were relegated to the director of the National Science Foundation, who, at that time, was H. Guyford Stever. But his contact with the president was not direct. It was mediated by a member of the White House staff. The connection between the scientists and the president, which arose out of necessity during World War II, was broken.

This severance appeared to be a concomitant of fading public interest in space exploration as a national adventure, which accompanied its loss of political urgency after the landing on the Moon. Once the competition was taken out of space exploration, its fund-raising appeal to Congress dropped markedly. As I have shown earlier, NASA's budget was contracted to the $3-billion-a-year level in 1970 from nearly twice that in 1965. Anyone who wanted to visit the outer planets would have to take the low-cost road, with Pioneer and Atlas-Centaur technology. TOPS and exotic ion propulsion were shelved, along with the whole NERVA project. Thus, *Pioneers F* and *G* offered the only realistic means of inspecting the outer planets in the first half of the 1970s.

Even though many scientists decried the competitive motivation of the Apollo program, they did not dispute its efficacy in fund raising. In its issue of December 15, 1967, the magazine *Science*, published by the American

Association for the Advancement of Science, raised the competition motif in an editorial by James A. Van Allen entitled: "Are we to Abandon the Planets to the Soviet Union?"

Van Allen noted that during the previous five years, the United States had launched only five planet missions; three of them (*Mariners II, IV,* and *V*) were successful in reconnoitering Venus and Mars. He noted that the Soviet Union had succeeded in dropping a probe to the surface of Venus (*Venera IV,* June 12, 1967) and was moving ahead with planetary exploration plans that are "both ambitious and increasingly competent," while the United States was allowing its own competence in planet exploration to lag, "and is thus abandoning in situ study of the planets to the Soviet Union."

As though in response, NASA administrator Webb told the House of Representatives Committee on Science and Astronautics two months later that: "We are initiating the development of two additional Pioneers to explore the Solar System beyond the orbit of Mars, out toward the orbit of Jupiter." [3]

These were *Pioneers F* and *G.* Initially, they were designed to fly out to four astronomical units, not to reconnoiter Jupiter, which is at five AUs. Webb said they would be launched in the 1973 time period. They would take up a solar orbit at four AUs, in the region between Mars and Jupiter. They would reconnoiter the Asteroid Belt and measure the gradients of the solar wind and cosmic rays out there. In this context, *Pioneers F* and *G* did not fulfill a Jupiter reconnaissance.

A Jupiter mission of the Atlas-Centaur class had been proposed by NASA's Lunar and Planetary Missions Board as part of a larger program of planetary exploration. But NASA had nothing to send to Jupiter, except the two new Pioneers. These could be fitted for planetary flyby reconnaissance and launched to Jupiter by Atlas-Centaur. That is what the space agency decided to do. It would satisfy the scientists and it wouldn't cost much more than flying to 4 AUs.

Van Allen appeared before the House committee February 20, 1968, to advocate the Jupiter project funding. He was aware that it was deeply in the shadow of the Apollo program, which was being accelerated to attempt the lunar landing in mid-1969. He said: "Now, throughout the lifetime of NASA, the dominant national goal in space was to land a man on the Moon and return him safely to Earth. We all hope and pray that the national commitment to complete the Apollo program successfully will be discharged within the next two years. Following that, we will be free for the first time in nearly a decade to develop a more rational, though doubtless less dramatic, program in space exploration."

Although President Kennedy's decision to go to the Moon was a popular one, he conceded, it excluded "a more rational" program of scientific investigation and technological development. "Aren't we saying here that it was basically a political decision in the realm of international politics—world politics?" asked Representative Charles A. Mosher (R-Ohio). "And since it was basically a political decision, it has distorted scientific judgments ever since?" "Yes, sir," replied Van Allen. "I agree with that. At the same time, I do think it did represent, and perhaps very well continues to represent, the interests of a large number of citizens of the United States."

Representative Joseph E. Karth (D-Minnesota) asked Van Allen if he did not agree that considerations other than scientific ones were involved in space policy, and that one important consideration was international politics. Of course he agreed, said Van Allen.

> Representative Lester L. Wolff (D-New York): You said that you would like to see America first in the various areas. Doesn't that perpetuate space race priorities?
>
> Van Allen: I don't mind being accused of helping perpetuate the idea of a space race. I think it is fundamental that the United States should be the best in anything it undertakes. We would be ahead of the USSR if we launched to Jupiter in 1972. We have technical superiority in telecommunications and in small, nuclear power supplies.
>
> Representative James G. Fulton (R-Pennsylvania): This would give us a clear first in exploration of the larger planets?
>
> Van Allen: I think that is likely. The mission depends on the development of a SNAP [Space Nuclear Auxiliary Power] power supply. The scheme proposed uses a SNAP-27 RTG [radioisotope thermoelectric generator], the same as proposed for the 1970 lunar landing package.

The Iowa scientist explained that his "highest professional interest" was focused on Jupiter, "the only planet in the Solar System which is electrically, dynamically active." "It approaches the size of a star," he said. "From the standpoint of physical dynamics, it is the most interesting."

Van Allen's pitch to the committee was a hard sell for understanding the evolution of our solar system and all solar systems. That was what the outer-planets investigation was all about. But, as Van Allen told the committee, the outer planets had not received the attention from NASA that their importance dictated. The emphasis in the planetary program was on Mars, largely because of the expectation of finding life there. "I would bet against that possibility," Van Allen said.

The following day, February 21, 1968, John E. Naugle, NASA associate administrator for space science and applications, appeared before the committee to explain that the agency was ready to modify the trusty Pioneer spacecraft design for Jupiter when Congress approved requested funds for that purpose in NASA's 1969 fiscal year budget.

The following August, the National Academy's Space Science Board, under the chairmanship of Harry H. Hess, of Princeton, proposed a planetary exploration program for 1968–1975 that paid particular attention to Jupiter. The outer planets were important because the big ones—Jupiter, Saturn, Uranus, and Neptune—appeared to have their original atmospheres. Earth, as we know, does not. Its primitive reducing atmosphere, which may have been similar to Jupiter's, was replaced by the products of outgassing from the interior; the breaking down of water molecules in the high atmosphere by solar ultraviolet light into oxygen and hydrogen (with the hydrogen escaping to space and the oxygen remaining); and plant photosynthesis, which releases oxygen from carbon dioxide.

The Jovian atmosphere probably was the same as the material of the solar nebula, from which the solar system formed, members of the board reasoned. Thus, they said, "the composition and structure of the atmosphere of Jupiter may serve as criteria for understanding theories of the evolution of the Solar System."

THE RADIO SIGNALS

Jupiter has been observed for more than 360 years, ever since Galileo Galilei turned his primitive telescope toward it at Padua on January 7, 1610, and discovered its four larger moons. In 1675, a Danish astronomer, Olaus Roemer, worked out the velocity of light from observing those satellites. He noticed that times of their eclipse by the planet came sixteen minutes and forty seconds later when Jupiter was on the opposite side of the sun from Earth than when the big planet was on the same side as Earth. This meant that it took their light sixteen minutes and forty seconds to cross twice the radius of the Earth's orbit, or 186 million miles. By dividing sixteen and two-thirds minutes into 186 million, anyone can find the speed of light—186,000 miles a second (186,000,000 ÷ 1,000 seconds).

The four large moons of Jupiter are known as the Galilean satellites for Galileo, although he may not have been the first person to see them. A German astronomer, Simon Marius, observed the moons December 29, 1609, but he did not publish his findings as Galileo did, according to some accounts.[4] Although Marius is not generally credited with their discovery, he did name them Io, Europa, Ganymede, and Callisto in the classical tradition and in order of their nearness to the planet. Jupiter's fifth moon, Amalthea, was discovered by E. E. Barnard in 1892. It is quite small, only 150 miles in diameter compared with the planet-sized Galilean satellites, and it orbits Jupiter at a distance of only 113,000 miles from the big planet's center.

Seven more moons were discovered after that, all smaller than even Amalthea. They were named Hestia, Hera, Demeter, Andrastea, Pan, Poseidon, and Hades. The last four orbit in the opposite direction from the other nine and may be asteriods captured by Jupiter; they are 13 and 14 million miles out. The thirteenth satellite, also in retrograde orbit, was first observed in 1974 at the Mount Palomar Observatory in California.

Observation of Jupiter for three and one-half centuries has yielded enough information, most of it in the last fifteen years, to make it a fascinating object of study. By far the largest of the sun's planets, its mass is one-thousandth the mass of the sun. It is almost a sun in its own right, but not quite. Jupiter can be called a star that never made it. But among planets of the solar system, it is a giant. It has twice the mass of the next largest planet, Saturn, and 318 times the mass of the Earth.

The diameter of Jupiter through its considerably flattened poles is 82,967 miles (133,516 kilometers), more than ten times that of Earth. Through its bulging equator, the diameter of the Big Planet is 5,767 miles (9,280 kilometers) more than at the poles. That is a considerable bulge, and it tells us something about the planet's composition.

One reason the poles are flattened and the equator bulges is the planet's rapid rotation. The Jovian "day" is nine hours and fifty-five and one-half minutes, except at the equator; there it is five minutes shorter—nine hours and fifty and one-half minutes. An object on the Jovian equator would be moving at an orbital speed of 25,000 miles an hour relative to a point in space—or twenty-five times faster than an object on Earth's equator.

Compared with Earth's average density of 5.5 grams per cubic centimeter (or 5.5 times the density of water), Jupiter's average density is just 1.33 times that of water. It appears to be a liquid planet with a gaseous atmosphere and a rocky core of possibly several Earth masses.

Consequently, although Jupiter's mass is 300 times that of Earth, its volume is 1,317 times that of Earth. The bulk of the Big Planet is thought to be metallic hydrogen in a liquid state.[5] Hydrogen is the principal constituent of Jupiter; helium was believed to exist in significant proportion, but could not be detected from Earth. Compounds such as methane, ethane, acetylene, and ammonia were observed in the clouds and the upper atmosphere. In fact, the brightness of the cloud tops was attributed to ammonia crystals.

Jupiter is a spectacular planet. In good telescopic color photos, it is striped by bands of red, yellow-brown, and pearl gray, and these represent cloud formations afloat in the high atmosphere. The most conspicuous marking on it is the Great Red Spot, a brick-red oval that seems to ride above the cloud deck in the South Tropical Zone. The oval is about 30,000 miles long and 8,000 miles wide. Sometimes it has the contour and color of a red-lipped mouth—one that could swallow two or three Earths, with room to spare.

The Red Spot has been around a long time. It was described in 1664 by Robert Hooke, an English astronomer. Since then, it has disappeared for a time and then reappeared, always in the southern hemisphere. In 1878, it was strikingly visible, but it faded in 1883, reappeared, and then faded again at the turn of the century.

There have been a number of ideas about the Red Spot. To some observers, it looks like a solid mass afloat on the clouds; to others, it has the appearance of a column of gas flowing over a mountaintop.

Jupiter is just about the largest planet possible, in the opinion of Fred L. Whipple, director of the Smithsonian Astrophysical Observatory. "If it were much more massive," he said, "it would shrink in size because of the formation of a dense core of degenerate matter, or, if more massive still, become a radiating star." [6]

A number of experts did not believe that the sun's heat was enough at five AUs to account for the conspicuous turbulence of the Jovian atmosphere, which was highly visible through the telescopes. They suspected a source of internal heat. The question of whether Jupiter was radiating heat was an intriguing one, because it had cosmologic significance. The decay of radioactive elements, which accounts for the internal heat of the Earth, Moon, and, probably, of Mars, judging from its huge volcanoes, was not considered a likely source of internal heat for Jupiter, because its low density precluded a sufficient concentration of heavy elements to heat up its great volume. If Jupiter was hot, the heat must be the leftover of some evolutionary phase of the planet, possibly primordial heat from its accretion.

Whipple and others believed that the apparent atmospheric turbulence, which they thought might account for the Great Red Spot and other smaller red spots and eddies in the atmosphere, must be energized by heat emissions from the depths of the planet. It was stretching the imagination to think of volcanoes on Jupiter, in view of its low surface density, but, as Whipple noted, "It is difficult to postulate another type of source for such strange, persistent clouds." [7]

In 1955, radio noise from Jupiter was detected by two radio astronomers, Bernard F. Burke and Kenneth L. Franklin, of the Carnegie Institution of Washington. As other radio astronomers tuned in, it became apparent that Jupiter was one of the strongest radio-wave emitters in the sky. Three types of signals characterized these emissions. One type is in the decametric (tens of meters) wave-length range. It seems to come in short, energetic bursts, which, strangely enough, can be correlated to certain positions of the near moon, Io, in its orbit around Jupiter. These emissions seemed to be produced by powerful electric discharges in the Jovian atmosphere. As Whipple described them, "The great radio noise bursts from Jupiter correspond in energy to a billion simultaneous lightning flashes on the Earth and seem to be of very short duration, a small fraction of a second."

A second type of signal was received in the decimetric band (tens of centimeters). It was thought to be produced by charged nuclear particles around Jupiter, suggesting the existence of trapped-radiation zones in a powerful magnetic field, by analogy with Earth's magnetosphere and Van Allen Belts. The shortest wave signals, of less than a few centimeters, were thermal radiation, produced by molecules vibrating in a warm part of the atmosphere.

Study of the signals led to several conclusions: that Jupiter rotated as a solid body; that it had an extensive and powerful magnetic field, perhaps five to ten times stronger than Earth's; and that it had belts of high-energy radiation that presented a hazard to any spacecraft venturing close to the planet.

The Owens Valley Observatory, of the California Institute of Technology, found that the radiation was polarized in a plane, indicating the existence of a dipole magnetic field as matrix of the radiation. The field seemed to be tilted nine degrees to the Jovian axis of rotation. This was the first evidence of a magnetic field on another planet.[8]

Jupiter was an exceptional object of study. As Whipple noted, "All the dynamic problems of the entire Solar System are reproduced with Jupiter's family of satellites." [9] There were some differences, though. In "Sol's system," the larger planets are the more distant ones, while in Jupiter's, the larger satellites are the nearer ones. Nevertheless, the distribution of densities was similar for Sol and Jove; the denser Jovian satellites are the nearer ones, just as the denser, terrestrial planets are those closer to the sun. This arrangement fits the prevailing theory that refractory elements in the solar nebula condensed at high temperatures nearer the sun, whereas the lighter, volatile elements were driven outward by heat and radiation-pressure to condense in cooler distant regions. Thus, with notable exceptions, the dense planets are in the inner solar system. The notable exceptions are two of the Galilean satellites, which are of greater density than our Moon (Io, in fact, has a higher density than Mars); the five small but high-density satellites of Uranus, one of which, Titania, has a higher apparent density than the Earth; Neptune's lunar-sized satellite, Triton, with the approximate density of Mercury; and the Earth-sized planet, Pluto, with about the same density as Earth.

Although Pluto and the heavy outer-planet moons may have condensed in the inner solar system, according to the theory, they are certainly not there now. How did they get where they are? Perhaps these moon-sized objects, which Harold Urey has suggested may have been the nuclei of the planets, had highly eccentric orbits that took them near the sun at one focus and to the outer reaches at another, where they were captured by their respective primaries.

But it is also easy to think of Io, Europa, Ganymede, and Callisto as products of Jupiter itself, their formation and densities influenced by the primordial heat of the great planet at an early time when its output of heat was much greater than now.

As early as 1961, Urey summarized the Jovian problems that a reconnaissance would attempt to resolve.[10] He said:

> Certain features of Jupiter have been puzzling us for years. Weather bands are understood as circulation on a rapidly rotating planet under the heating action of the Sun, but the great Red Spot which appears to be floating in some way on the surface is a very great puzzle. Also, the burst of radio emissions from somewhere deep below the visible surface has been most interesting in recent years. Observations of the radio emissions suggest that the planet has an ionosphere, a magnetic field of at least 2 Gauss [about three and one-half times Earth's surface field of 0.6

Gauss at the poles] and that the sources of the radio bursts rotate with the surface of an invisible body.

Although a direct approach may not be feasible, use of one of Jupiter's satellites as an observation point would avoid the extremes of gravity, if such a feat became possible.

THE JOVIAN PIONEERS

For a nation that was spending $33 billion to send men to the Moon, a reconnaissance of Jupiter with (relatively) low-cost Pioneer-class spacecraft was a poor man's effort. In view of the risks—the Asteroid Belt and the Jovian radiation belts—perhaps the economical approach was the most logical. The Pioneer program goes all the way back to the beginning of the Space Age. It was started in 1958 as a series of lunar probes by the Advanced Research Projects Agency of the Department of Defense (ARPA). ARPA made one attempt to launch a spacecraft called Pioneer aboard a Thor-Able rocket August 17, 1958, but the first stage failed. The object, as mentioned previously, was to send the payload to the Moon. En route, it would radio data about particles and fields in the interplanetary medium.

Later in 1958, when NASA was created by Congress, the program was shifted to the civilian agency. NASA's maiden launch effort was carried out with partial success October 11, 1958, with *Pioneer I*, an eighty-four-pound spacecraft that was boosted to 70,717 miles altitude by a Thor-Able rocket. It, too, was a moonshot, but its orbit decayed October 12, and it fell back to Earth after radioing forty-three hours of data.

On November 8, 1958, NASA launched the eighty-seven-pound *Pioneer II*, its second lunar probe, but the third stage of the Thor-Able rocket failed.

Cutting back spacecraft weight to thirteen pounds, NASA took another shot at the Moon December 6, 1958, with *Pioneer III*. The launch vehicle, a Juno 2, lifted the small payload to about 63,500 miles. The *Pioneer III* fell back, after returning some radiation-belt data.

Pioneer IV, NASA's fourth attempt to hit the Moon, was a thirteen-pounder, also. Launched March 3, 1959, it passed within 37,300 miles of the Moon and went into solar orbit.

Using a bigger Atlas-Able rocket, NASA then attempted to launch a bigger Pioneer, weighing 372 pounds, to the Moon, November 26, 1959. The shot failed when the payload shroud broke away forty-five seconds after lift-off.

Pioneer V was the first truly successful deep-space reconnaissance vehicle. Weighing ninety-five pounds, it was boosted into solar orbit by a Thor-Able rocket March 11, 1960. It ranged 22.5 million miles away from the Earth, and its little radio played back data on the solar wind until June 26, 1960, when it fell silent.

With *Pioneer V*, the basic mission of this type of vehicle was firmly established. It was a deep-space sounder, a reconnoiterer. As related earlier, the moonshot effort was shifted to the Ranger crash-landing camera vehicles during the early 1960s.

Pioneer does not enter the space logs again until December 16, 1965, when *Pioneer VI*, a 140-pound interplanetary-medium monitor, was launched by a Delta rocket into a solar orbit between .814 and .985 AUs— several million miles closer than Earth to the sun. By this time, not only had launch-vehicle technology improved launch reliability, but advances in instrumentation, spacecraft construction, and radiation shielding conferred longevity on spacecraft. *Pioneer V* had lasted three and one-half months. *Pioneer VI* was still transmitting in 1975.

Pioneer VII was launched by a Delta August 17, 1966, into a solar orbit just beyond Earth's. *Pioneer VIII* was boosted December 13, 1967, into a solar orbit almost the same as Earth's, from 1 to 1.1 AUs. *Pioneer IX* was hurled November 8, 1968, into a solar orbit about three-fourths of Earth's distance from the sun. Like *Pioneer VI*, all were operating in 1975, although partial failures had been experienced on some instruments. Since 1958, Pioneer had matured as a reliable, long-lived machine. It was its extraordinary survival value that made this spacecraft a candidate for outer-planet scouting.

Pioneers F and *G* were designed for lifetimes of at least two years, but NASA hoped for more. With Jupiter's slingshot effect, they could go sailing off to Saturn or clear out of the solar system. A ten-year lifetime might yield the first data on what lay beyond the solar system frontier.

Without the knowledge of Jupiter's magnetic field and intense radiation belts, deduced from radio signals, the Jovian Pioneers would have been seriously misdesigned, the Radio Astronomy Panel of the NASA's Astronomy Missions Board noted.[11]

The spacecraft were built by the TRW Systems Group, an old-line aerospace firm at Redondo Beach, California. They were designed by H. A. Lassen, of that company, as lightweight, durable, spin-stabilized space vehicles. The design is purely functional and purely Space Age. No one would have the remotest idea what these things were before the Space Age. I dare say that not many people in the world would be able to identify them if they saw the Pioneers today.

To the uninitiated, *Pioneers F* and *G* look like big metal umbrellas, with hexagonal boxes clustered behind them and with booms and struts sticking out at odd angles. Prior to 1958, they probably could have been sensations in an exhibition of modern art.

The nine-foot-diameter umbrella dominates the vehicle. It is the high-gain antenna and it has to be big to direct an eight-watt radio signal to Earth over distances of 520 million miles and more and receive a response. At Pioneer's closest approach to Jupiter, it would take a radio signal traveling at light speed forty-six minutes to reach Earth.

Behind the umbrella, two ten-foot-long trusses extend outward from an hexagonal compartment twenty-eight inches long and fourteen inches deep. They carry the RTGs (radioisotope thermoelectric generators) and hold them away from the instruments that the radioisotopes might affect. A boom twenty-one feet long extends also out of the compartment. It carries the magnetometer, holding it well away from the vehicle's electronic and radio-isotope interference.

In the center of the nine-foot antenna dish is the horn-shaped medium-gain antenna. There is a third antenna on the spacecraft, an omnidirectional one, facing aft. "Forward" on this vessel is the way the high-gain umbrella antenna and medium-gain horn antenna are pointing. That is the way the vehicle is mounted in the ten-foot-diameter shroud of the Centaur second stage of the Atlas-Centaur launch vehicle. When first released to space, Pioneer is flying with its umbrella and horn facing forward, its aft omnidirectional antenna pointing toward Earth. The omniantenna is good enough at near-Earth distances, but as the vehicle goes farther away, Pioneer must be turned 180 degrees, so that the high- and medium-gain antennas face Earth. In this attitude, the sensors and particle telescopes the vehicle carries point in the direction of travel from their housing in the hexagonal compartment. It thus flies "backward" to Jupiter.

From the edge of the horn antenna to the end of the aft-facing omniantenna in the rear, Pioneer is nine and one-half feet long, just six inches more than the width of the high-gain antenna. It looks a great deal like the Hollywood conception of H. G. Wells's time machine in the movie *The Time Machine*, except there is no place for anyone to sit in it. Most of the experiments are in a small hexagonal box attached to the twenty-eight-by-fourteen-inch compartment containing spacecraft equipment and electronics. The two compartments and the big umbrella are built of lightweight but strong aluminum honeycomb, a material used in many different kinds of spacecraft, including manned ones.

A "minimum energy" flight to Jupiter is possible from Earth every thirteen months. For *Pioneer F*, the first launch opportunity was between late February and early March, 1972. *Pioneer G* could go thirteen months later.

KILROY WAS HERE

There were three main objectives of the Pioneer thrusts: to explore the interplanetary medium beyond the orbit of Mars, which had never been sampled; to investigate the Asteroid Belt as a navigation hazard; and to explore the environment of Jupiter. If the Pioneers survived those dangers, they could proceed outward and keep on sending data. NASA considered that whatever it received beyond Jupiter would be gravy.

With the energy imparted to the spacecraft by Jupiter's gravitational boost, *Pioneer F* would sail into interstellar space, to wander through the galaxy. Its instruments would tell experimenters when it crossed the frontier of the heliosphere, the region controlled by the sun, and what there was beyond.

Pioneer carried a plaque identifying it as the product of a civilization on the third planet of the star called Sol. The message was engraved on a gold anodized aluminum plate six by nine inches attached to the antenna support strut. It was addressed to any being intelligent enough to decipher it. It pictured a naked man and a naked woman, the man's hand raised in a sign of peace, the female standing submissively beside him. Behind them was sketched the outline of the vehicle. It showed the location of Sol relative to fourteen pulsars and the center of the galaxy. It depicted the scheme of the solar system and the flight path of spacecraft. To convey to an alien mind the size of the spacecraft and of the species that built it, the plate contained two clues: a schematic of the hyperfine transition of neutral hydrogen, which provides a universal unit of time and material length, and the binary equivalent of the decimal eight. An intelligent species would be expected to know the wavelength of hydrogen (eight inches in our common measure). Multiplied by the binary representation of eight, which is engraved beside the female, it gives her height (sixty-four inches in our terms).

Any extraterrestrial being who sees the plaque would have to be at least as clever as Carl Sagan and Frank Drake, the Cornell University astronomers who designed the plaque, to get the message—a cosmic version of "Kilroy was here." There is also a possibility that our descendants might find this strange artifact thousands of years hence as they flit among the stars and try to deduce from it the ancestral culture that wrought it—as we do with the ancient shards and glyphs of bygone cultures.

From 150 proposals, NASA picked eleven instruments to be carried to Jupiter. Five measured subatomic particles in several energy ranges; two detected dust and debris from sand grains to planetoids; two detected electromagnetic radiation in the infrared and ultraviolet regions of the spectrum; one measured magnetic field strength; and one was a combination polarimeter and television camera that would photograph the planet, line by line, with the spin of the spacecraft.

The helium vector magnetometer was extended away from Pioneer electronics on a twenty-one-foot boom. It was designed to measure the interplanetary magnetic field (which originates in the sun) en route to Jupiter and the Jovian field at the planet. The instrument was sensitive enough to perceive fields ranging from 0.01 gamma to 140,000 gamma. (One gamma is

1/100,000th of a Gauss, a unit of field intensity. Earth's field ranges from 0.4 to 0.6 Gauss, or 40,000 to 60,000 gammas.) The principal investigator was Edward J. Smith, of the Jet Propulsion Laboratory.

Until the advent of the Jupiter Pioneers, the outer limit of man's observations of particles and fields in the solar system was the orbit of Mars. What lay beyond? How far does the solar wind blow? How far does the sun's magnetic field reach? As the sun's influence wanes, are incoming galactic cosmic rays more intense? The Pioneers carried five particle detectors to examine the solar wind, cosmic rays, and particles trapped in the Jovian magnetic field.

Through a window in the dish antenna, an instrument called a plasma analyzer looked back toward Sol. Solar wind particles, or plasma, moving faster than the spacecraft would enter holes in the analyzer and pass between two plates that would measure their energy, direction, and numbers. The experiment would indicate how the solar wind changed in the outer reaches. John H. Wolfe, Pioneer project scientist at Ames, was the principal investigator.

Four other instruments looked at the energy and chemical composition of cosmic rays coming from the sun and from the galaxy and at radiation (actually, solar-wind-charged particles) trapped in the magnetic field of Jupiter.

The charged-particle-composition experiment carried four detection systems. Two were particle telescopes. They looked at nuclei moving through interplanetary space and could identify the chemical composition of the nuclei in a range of eight elements from hydrogen to oxygen. The instrument could also identify the hydrogen isotope, deuterium, and two helium isotopes, helium[3] and helium[4].

This experiment also included two new types of sensors. They measured very high intensities of trapped radiation in the magnetosphere. The principal investigator was John A. Simpson, of the University of Chicago.

The Pioneers carried a second cosmic-ray-trapped-radiation detector, designed by the Goddard Space Flight Center. It could identify cosmic ray nuclei of the ten lightest chemical elements and measure protons and electrons in several energy ranges. The principal investigator was Frank B. McDonald, of Goddard.

Van Allen had a third particle detector aboard, a highly sophisticated version of the Geiger tube he and his colleagues used on *Explorer I* just fifteen years before. The instrument consisted of an array of seven small Geiger tube telescopes. It was designed to observe the energies and distribution of trapped protons and electrons and particle showers in the magnetic field.

A fourth instrument also analyzed trapped radiation. It used five detectors to measure charged particles over a broad energy range: electrons up to 100 million electron volts (MeV) and protons to 350 MeV. The principal investigator was R. Walker Fillius, of the University of California, San Diego.

Two detectors aboard the Pioneers were designed to map the rock, sand, and dust densities in the Asteroid Belt, which stretched for 270 million miles along the flight path between Mars and Jupiter. One detector consisted of four telescopes that measured sunlight reflected by meteoroids. Each telescope contained an eight-inch mirror and photomultiplier tube. The tube converted light into electrical signals that would be radioed to Earth. If one object was seen by three of the telescopes, its distance, trajectory, velocity, and relative size could be calculated. The instrument could detect objects as big as distant asteroids several miles in diameter or as small as dust particles several feet away. The principal investigator was Robert K. Soberman, of the General Electric Company, Philadelphia.

The second Asteroid Belt "analyzer" was a meteoroid-impact detector. It covered six and one-half square feet on the back of the main antenna dish. The detector consisted of thirteen panels, each with eighteen sealed cells, pressurized with argon and nitrogen. When a shell was punctured by a dust particle, it would lose gas at a rate proportional to the size of the hole. The instrument recorded penetrations by objects with masses of one-billionth of a gram up to pea-sized gravel. Principal investigator was William H. Kinard, of NASA's Langley Research Center.

The identification of the constituents of Jupiter's atmosphere and their relative amounts was the object of two experiments. At Jupiter, an Ultraviolet Photometer would scan the atmosphere and cloud tops. Changes in the intensity of ultraviolet in the sunshine spectrum that was reflected into two photocathodes on the instrument would indicate the amounts of hydrogen and helium the photometer was seeing.

Although helium was assumed to be part of the Jovian atmosphere, it could not be detected from Earth, because our atmosphere screened out the ultraviolet wavelengths that helium reflected. The photometer also could detect the existence of polar auroras on Jupiter. Beyond the Big Planet, it would continue to measure the amount of hydrogen in the heliosphere by the scattering of the ultraviolet in sunlight by hydrogen atoms. The principal investigator was Durrell L. Judge, of the University of Southern California.

Of crucial importance was the heat balance of Jupiter. It was to be determined by an infrared radiometer, an instrument that measured radiation in the infrared band of the electromagnetic spectrum. Although infrared radiation from planets can be seen by Earth telescopes, some wavelengths are absorbed by the atmosphere, just as some of the ultraviolet is. Most of Jupiter's infrared is emitted at wavelengths of twenty to forty micrometers, which are absorbed in our atmosphere.

The two-channel radiometer measured infrared in two bands: fourteen to twenty-five and twenty-five to fifty-six micrometers. It could determine the temperature of the disk of Jupiter and provide data on the planet's heat balance. Earth telescopes had indicated that Jupiter emits more heat than it gets from Sol. The radiometer would check this with a precise measurement. The principal investigator was Guido Munch, of the California Institute of Technology.

The instrument expected to produce the most spectacular results was the imaging photopolarimeter, a scanning TV camera capable of taking pictures in two colors, red and blue, and of transmitting them to Earth.

The camera's optical system consisted of a 2.54-centimer (1-inch) diameter telescope, a calcite prism, filters to separate the red and blue components of light reflected from Jupiter, relay optics, and detectors that would sense polarized light.

The IPP was actually three instruments in one. It had the function of measuring zodiacal light while the Pioneers were in interplanetary space. It could measure the intensity and polarization of light reflected from planets. And, finally, it could photograph Jupiter by means of spin-scan imaging. That is, the one-inch lens would scan a horizontal segment of Jupiter as the spacecraft was slowly spinning. Thomas Gehrels, of the University of Arizona, Tucson, was the principal investigator. [12]

Two experiments did not require special instrumentation. One was the measurement by Pioneer's S-band radio beam of the density of the Jovian atmosphere at several different altitudes. The beam was the spacecraft radio signal. Refraction or variation in the frequency of the beam caused by atmospheric and ionospheric interference as the Pioneer spacecraft passed behind the Big Planet indicated atmospheric and ionospheric density and, to some extent, chemical composition, supplementing the ultraviolet photometer. The spacecraft radio also served in a celestial mechanics experiment. This consisted of tracking the Pioneers and noting variations in their velocities to a fraction of a millimeter a second by recording minute changes (Doppler) in the signal wavelength.

Changes in spacecraft acceleration in the Jovian system were the result, of course, of the gravitational effects of Jupiter and its major moons. From the magnitude of these effects, the masses of the planet and its satellites could be calculated with considerably more accuracy than Earth-based observation made possible. John D. Anderson, of JPL, was the principal investigator.

The Pioneer spacecraft radio was an astonishing electronic voice. It transmitted at a power of only eight watts—the power used by one of a string of Christmas tree lights; yet it reached 513.3 million miles from Jupiter to Earth. Fortunately, NASA's Deep Space Network of tracking stations and antennas was completed in time for the Jupiter mission. It consisted of three 210-foot- (64-meter) diameter dish antennas around the world. There was one at Goldstone, California, in the Mojave Desert; a second at Madrid, Spain; and a third at Canberra, Australia. Pioneer was in radio view of at least one station all the time, and often its tiny signal could be received by two.

During tracking periods, velocity data were received once each minute, and as each Pioneer passed the moons, even at distances of millions of miles, their perturbation of the little spacecraft's flight path would be sensed and interpreted as evidence of their masses. When each vehicle neared Jupiter, its acceleration would not be minuscule; it would be dramatic.

Electric power for each Pioneer mission was supplied by four SNAP-19 (Space Nuclear Auxiliary Power) thermoelectric generators. These had been developed by the Atomic Energy Commission and JPL. The generators were fueled with plutonium[238]. Heat from its decay was converted into electricity. The four generators produced a total of 155 watts of electricity, more than enough. The spacecraft required only 100 watts, including 26 for the scientific instruments. But the extra power would not last, for as the Pioneers flew on month after month, and, eventually, year after year, the power would diminish steadily until there would be no reserve at all—just enough to keep the vehicle "alive."

A THEOLOGICAL ANSWER

Between Earth and Mars, the trip was expected to be uneventful for Pioneer. Beyond Mars, the spacecraft would encounter a region of supposed hazard, the Asteroid Belt. It was believed to be thickly populated with rocks of all sizes, from planetoids such as Ceres (with a diameter of 635 miles, or 1,022 kilometers) or Vesta (313 miles, or 504 kilometers), to clouds of silicate and metallic dust. The Asteroid Belt traditionally had been considered an obstacle course to passage to the outer planets. Moving in the ecliptic plane, a spacecraft had to go through it; attempting to fly above or below it was beyond the technology of the Pioneer spacecraft, for it would require far more energy than the Atlas-Centaur could provide.

If Pioneer survived the belt, it would next encounter menacing high-energy radiation once it entered the magnetosphere of Jupiter, extending millions of miles from the planet. The builders of Pioneer had provided some radiation shielding. Had they provided enough? No one knew the actual intensity of the Jovian radiation belts. Only approximations could be made. Radiation intensities in the Jovian magnetosphere was one of the main questions that the *Pioneers* F and G were designed to answer.

Van Allen, the principal investigator for the radiation belt experiment, was optimistic about Pioneer's chances for survival in the Jovian high-energy radiation zone. "It's controversial," he admitted, "but the present consensus is, yes, it probably will survive. As a reference for the design of my instrument, I used data from the high altitude explosion of a nuclear bomb in 1962 over

Johnston Island in the Pacific Ocean. This explosion, code name Starfish, produced a temporary radiation belt in the vicinity of Earth that more nearly resembled what we may expect at Jupiter than any feature of Earth's natural radiation belt." [13]

Van Allen surmised that the magnetic field at the surface of Jupiter was about ten Gauss, about eighteen times that of the Earth. Consequently, it was estimated that the intensity of trapped charged particles in the field could be 10,000 times that of particles in Earth's field, and their energies fifty times greater.

As preparations went forward to launch *Pioneer F* between February 27 and March 1972, NASA staged a series of press conferences in an effort to generate public interest in the mission through the mass media. It was a time when public interest in space projects was fading. Even the manned flights to the Moon, although more spectacular than ever, had lost their novelty and, consequently, much of their audience.

Although the Jupiter mission was a milestone in the history of exploration, it attracted little attention from the general public. It was lost in the rising turbulence of the 1972 presidential election campaign, mounting public pressure for the disengagement of troops from Viet Nam, and the domestic problems that long, dreary war exacerbated.

In this general atmosphere, a news conference was held at the University of Chicago in February 1972. Two of the principal investigators for the Pioneer mission, John Simpson and James Van Allen, as well as Charles F. Hall, the project manager, conducted the briefing.

Newspaper, radio, and television reporters zeroed in on the risks of the mission. These gave the story a better chance of being printed or aired than a straightaway recital of the scientific objectives, for the mission to Jupiter had to compete with crime, politics, sex, and scandal. These items sell newspapers and get time on the electronic newscasts in Chicago, as in other major cities; science does not. A science story without a "gee whiz" angle tended to get lost in the newsroom shuffle. Luckily for Pioneer, there were asteroid and radiation perils to lend a smidgin of suspense. Hall commented:

> We don't know whether the Asteroid Belt is a severe hazard or not. From the ground, we can look at perhaps 2000 objects, the largest one being 500 miles in diameter, the smallest, a mile or so. We can see those from the ground. Knowing there is that much debris of that size, one can infer that there must be many orders of magnitude more debris of the pea and BB size.
>
> If there is and if the spacecraft is moving at perhaps 10 miles a second and one of those little BBs hits it, it could penetrate almost any shield you might think about.
>
> I've seen a 1 gram piece of plexiglas shot into a solid steel mass at 44,000 feet per second—roughly the velocity we're talking about. It cut a hole that was about as big as my hand in this solid steel mass.
>
> Press Question: At this time, do we know if human passengers could survive in the radiation belts of Jupiter?
>
> Van Allen: We do not know even if an instrument can. Clearly, any kind of

manned flight to the outer planets is an exceedingly remote practical possibility, because the general tendency is toward a one-way trip. It's very difficult to find volunteers for a one-way trip. Missions that require close fly-bys, like the one we're planning, are very likely impossible for any foreseeable kind of manned spacecraft.

Question: What about *2001*? [The query referred to the motion picture *2001*, a science fiction account of a manned trip to Jupiter on a spaceship piloted by a mad robot.]

Van Allen: I don't think they took all this into account. [Laughter.]

Was there a practical payoff for this mission?

Simpson fielded the question. He explained that one of the intellectual objectives of the mission was to find out how nature accelerates particles. This is something that scientists are trying to do in particle accelerators, or atom smashers, costing hundreds of millions of dollars. In space, and out near Jupiter, the particles and the mechanism that boosts them to nearly the speed of light can be observed.

With this information, science would have a powerful tool to develop a nuclear fusion power generator. It would, in theory, solve the energy crisis. It would enable man to substitute deuterium, which is abundant in the oceans, for oil and gas as fuel to generate electricity.

People are working on fusion, Simpson explained. They have been for years. The main problem is containing the fusion reaction—the reaction that apparently produces the sun's energy in a magnetic field. There is no other way known to contain it. "The principal problem today is the same problem we had in the beginning, namely to hold the plasma in the magnetic field long enough to get the power out," Simpson said. "The instabilities of magnetic fields and the detailed understanding of how particles move in a magnetic field are still very fluid problems. It may turn out that this [the knowledge of how nature does it] is one of the fruitful, quick returns."

Beyond fusion, a more detailed knowledge of Jupiter's atmosphere and its energy processes would help us understand how our own atmosphere operates. A better understanding of the physics of the heliosphere—the region of the sun's influence in interplanetary space—would improve our ability to predict weather and climate, Simpson suggested. "There is also the hope," he added, that "we will learn the source composition of cosmic radiation in the galaxy and thereby learn something of the origin of the elements."

Press Question: Okay, but what do we tell the beer and pretzels audience we have watching television? How do you explain it to them?

Van Allen: I teach a large course in freshman astronomy and one of the first things I tell them is that you can take away the whole universe except the Sun, and maybe the Moon, and you wouldn't know the difference, living on Earth.

Now this is a good technique for weeding the ribbon clerks out of the course, because if they think I'm going to tell them something practical, I just want to make it clear right away that I'm not.

I think that is basically what underlies this investigation. It is an investigation in astronomy. I've learned a long time ago not to claim that I'm doing anything practical, because as soon as you do, you're accountable for delivering on what you claim and I'd much rather say personally that this mission is an investigation in astronomy and that we think it will be intellectually very interesting. I know for a fact that there's a very wide segment of the population in the United States that is interested in astronomy for no practical reason. Just for pure knowledge, understanding what the universe is all about.

I think that all of us are here to do something besides eat and sleep. I think that using our heads is one of the things we're here for. That's a kind of theological answer. But I believe it very deeply myself. If we don't believe in what I've just been saying, we don't believe in education.

600 DAYS TO JUPITER

The Jupiter launch window opened February 27, 1972. The "launch window" is the period of time of the day, month, or year when the geometry of the solar system makes it possible to hit a moving target (the Moon, Mars, Jupiter, etc.) with a missile fired from a moving platform (the Earth launch site). The missile is aimed at a point in the target's orbit where the target will be when the missile gets there. Atop its 417,000 pounds of thrust Atlas-Centaur launch vehicle at Cape Canaveral, *Pioneer F* was ready to go on a flight path that would curve 160 degrees around the sun and cover a distance of 620 million miles to within two Jupiter radii (86,000 miles) of the big planet.

Launch was scheduled at 8:52 P.M. Eastern Standard Time that day. The countdown went smoothly during the early evening hours until it reached T (for launch time) minus fifty-nine minutes, when blockhouse electrical power failed. By the time it was restored, the launch window was still open, but the winds had risen too high to permit the launching. High winds delayed the launch February 28 and March 1. Finally, at 8:49 P.M. Eastern Standard Time, March 2, 1972, the Atlas-Centaur lifted off the Florida coast on a pillar of brilliant golden-orange fire that could be seen for miles in the balmy winter night.

As *Pioneer F* sped skyward over the Atlantic Ocean, its official designation changed to *Pioneer X*—a customary NASA procedure to identify by number vehicles successfully launched for the records. Powered flight through the atmosphere took seventeen minutes. When final cutoff of the third, or "kick," stage came, the quarter-ton Jupiter probe was rushing away from Earth at nine miles a second (about 32,114 miles an hour). It was moving faster than any other object ever launched into space.

The first breath-holding event, after the launch, from the point of view of the observers, was the unfolding of the twin booms on which the nuclear power units were mounted and then the extension of the magnetometer boom. These had been folded inward, within the ten-foot-diameter Centaur shroud, during the launch phase. Slowly, the small servo motors extended the booms. A failure there would have aborted the mission. The extension of the booms slowed Pioneer's spin to 4.8 revolutions a minute.

In its launch position, as noted earlier, the nine-foot dish antenna on *Pioneer X* faced forward, away from the Earth, and radio communication with the vehicle was conducted through the small omnidirectional antenna that pointed Earthward.

The attitude and spin of the vehicle were fully controllable by radio signals activating the gas jets on the dish antenna rim. Early in the flight, controllers at the Ames Research Center, in California, to whom navigation control passed after the launch, maneuvered the vessel so that it was shielded from direct sunlight and consequent overheating by the dish antenna—like a parasol turned inside out. Later, the concave side of the dish was turned toward Earth as the spacecraft receded from the sun and the overheating threat diminished.

Spiraling outward from Earth, *Pioneer X* zipped across the orbit of the moon in eleven hours—a run that took seventy-four and one-half hours for *Apollo XVI*, launched seven weeks later. Course analysis showed that the launch was so accurate that a correction of only 31 miles per hour in velocity was needed to bring *Pioneer X* within 86,000 miles of Jupiter's cloud tops at a point fourteen degrees below the equator.

The course correction was made March 7. A second small change was made March 23 and 24 in two stages to adjust the flight path so that *Pioneer X* would pass behind the moon Io and then approach Jupiter 4,000 miles closer—to within 82,000 miles of the cloud tops. The purpose of flying behind Io was to determine, by its occultation of Pioneer's radio signal, whether the moon had an atmosphere and an ionosphere. If all went well, then, *Pioneer X* would reach Jovian periapsis or closest approach to Jupiter—at 8:30 P.M., Pacific Standard Time, December 3, 1973.

Two days after launch, the cosmic ray telescope was turned on by radio command. One by one, the other instruments were activated. The data they radioed back showed they were working properly.

When *Pioneer X* crossed the orbit of Mars, May 25, just eighty-four days after launch (*Mariner IX* had taken four times as long to get there), the imaging photopolarimeter (IPP) was pointed sunward, toward the region of zodiacal light. This is the faint glow seen in Earth's skies just after sunset and just before dawn (the false dawn). The IPP was then turned in the opposite direction, away from the sun, to look at the *gegenschein,* or counterglow, which appears in the direction away from the sun. These phenomena had been studied on the manned space flights. Early on, some theorists held that the glows were caused by dust held in Earth orbit, but later observations showed that the glows were much more widespread in the solar system. By the time

Pioneer X flew, the phenomena were generally believed to be the refraction of sunlight by dust particles throughout the interplanetary medium. The Pioneer IPP saw them as far out as Mars orbit. The observations knocked down theories that the *gegenschein* was caused by a dusty or gaseous tail trailing from Earth, corresponding to the planet's magnetic tail.

On July 15, 1972, 135 days after launch, *Pioneer X* entered the Asteroid Belt. Nothing changed. Asteroid and meteoroid detectors showed no increase in dust, sand, or larger rocks. On August 2, the spacecraft passed within 5.5 million miles of a rock called Palomar-Leyden, about a half-mile in diameter. It came within 5 million miles of a planetoid named Nike, which is 15 miles in diameter, on December 2. It never came any nearer to any other detectable object.

During the summer of 1972, while *Pioneer X* was in the belt, its instruments observed the rush of radiation from big solar storms on August 2 and 7. At the Johnson Space Center, Houston, a scientist speculated that the August storm generated enough energy to supply the United States with electricity, at its present rate of consumption, for 100 million years. It was an interesting, if unverifiable, estimate.

These solar events were observed also by four other *Pioneers—VI, VII, VIII,* and *IX,* all in solar orbit near the Earth. *Pioneer IX* saw the highest solar wind speeds ever recorded—2,235,000 miles an hour—whipping past the Earth. The velocity of the subatomic particles had dropped to about half this value when they reached Jupiter-bound *Pioneer X* about seventy-six hours later as the little vehicle was motoring along within the dreaded belt.

Between 250 and 300 million miles from the sun, *Pioneer X* traversed the supposedly densest part of the Asteroid Belt. For a week, the density of dust particles, which had been unchanged since Pioneer began its flight, rose slightly. Then it declined to earlier levels, which were about the same inside the belt as outside. The spacecraft then emerged from the supposed region of the belt in February 1973 at a distance of 340 million miles from the sun (or 247 million miles from Earth's orbit). It was now on the high road to Jupiter.

On the evening of April 5, 1973, *Pioneer G* was launched from Cape Canaveral and became *Pioneer XI* once it was established in a stable flight path. It had the same instrument array as *X* except for the addition of a flux-gate magnetometer to supplement the helium magnetometer initially installed. The flux-gate magnetometer was supposedly more sensitive to magnetic field effects at distances much closer to the planet than *Pioneer X* was destined to penetrate.

STRANGENESS BEGINS

Now two reconnaissance vehicles were moving toward Jupiter and the great beyond. On November 8, 1972, *Pioneer X* crossed the orbit of Hades, outermost of Jupiter's twelve known moons, at 14.7 million miles from the center of the Big Planet. It was now in the Jovian system. The next day, it crossed the orbit of another outer moon, Pan, 14 million miles from the Jovian center.

Accelerating now as it approached Jupiter, *Pioneer X* crossed the orbits of three "middle" moons—Demeter, Hera, and Hestia (7.3 to 7.1 million miles out)—on November 22. Principal investigators were now converging on the Ames Research Center at Mountain View for the encounter sequence.

On November 26, *Pioneer X* passed through the bow shock wave, which is formed at the junction of the solar wind and the great magnetic field of Jupiter. This was recorded by the magnetometer and by particle detectors showing a region of turbulence analagous to that of an ocean wave breaking on a beach. This boundary was at 109 Jupiter radii (Rj), or 4,733,128 miles from the planet's center.

At that point, strangeness began. Suddenly, the bow shock vanished. The magnetometer ceased reporting the magnetic field. *Pioneer X* had somehow flown out of the field. Later, the bow shock reappeared. The magnetic field reappeared. It became clear that the magnetosphere was inflating and collapsing like a cosmic balloon, millions of miles in extent, that was pushed inward by solar wind pressure and expanded outward again as the pressure dropped off. The word investigators conjured up to describe this effect was *squishy*. It was not elegant, but it was apt. The magnetosphere of Jupiter was squishy.

By the end of November, *Pioneer X* was deep into the field. Early on December 3, fourteen hours before periapsis, *Pioneer X* crossed the orbit of the planet-sized moon Callisto, 1.1 million miles out. It swept through the orbit of Ganymede, another of the planet-sized moons, twelve and one-half hours before closest approach. At noon, it entered the high radiation zone at five Rj, or 217,115 miles out, after passing the orbit of Europa, 372,000 miles out, and the orbit of the big moon, Io, at 221,000 miles out.

Periapsis came at 8 P.M., Pacific Standard Time, December 3, 1972. *Pioneer X* approached to 81,000 miles of the cloud tops (5,000 miles closer than originally planned). At that point, its speed was 22.7 miles a second (82,000 miles an hour). Then, as it swung away from Jupiter on its departure trajectory, *Pioneer X* passed behind Io for one minute and thirty-one seconds. Its eight-watt radio signal indicated that the moon had both an atmosphere and a surprisingly dense ionosphere, a region of charged particles in the moon's upper atmosphere.

An hour later, *Pioneer X* passed behind Jupiter, and the main occultation experiment began. The radio beam passed through successive layers of the

Jovian atmosphere until the rising density of the hydrogen-helium planet blocked it out. The period of occultation lasted sixty-five minutes. When the signal was reacquired at Earth, controllers and a crowd of visitors at Ames were relieved to see that *Pioneer X* was still "alive and well." Radiation had not killed it, as some feared, but had damaged the optical part of the meteoroid experiment and caused several weird effects.

Pioneer X had broken the trail to Jupiter. After passing the orbit of Pluto in the late 1980s, it would head out of the solar system toward another sun, called Aldebaran, in the constellation of Taurus.

SOME SURPRISES

There were surprises in Pioneer's scientific results. The first was the lack of any significant increase in dust and debris in the Asteroid Belt. This raised the question of whether or not the term *Asteroid Belt* is an overstatement of what is acutally out there between Mars and Jupiter. So far as *Pioneer X* was concerned, the region presented no hazard to navigation. Some people had thought it would turn out to be impenetrable.

Another surprise to the cosmic ray physicists was the finding that the intensity of galactic cosmic rays does not increase out toward Jupiter as they surmised it would. This indicates that the strength of the solar wind and magnetic field does not diminish with distance as rapidly as supposed.

The squishiness and great extent of the Jovian magnetosphere were surprising. The field is reversed, compared to Earth, so that a compass needle on Jupiter would point to the south magnetic pole. The existence of an ionosphere at Io was unexpected. Also, Pioneer detected a cloud of neutral hydrogen extending out from the moon along its orbital path some 120 degrees. These findings led to speculation about a powerful electrical current passing between Jupiter and Io to form a half-million-mile, 100,000-volt circuit as the mechanism that modulates the decametric radio emissions from Jupiter's lower atmosphere.

Jupiter's magnetic field, the *Pioneer X* data indicated, encompassed a region of space with a diameter of 420 Rj (18,237,660)—about 70 percent of the distance between Earth and Venus.[14] Like Earth's field, the Jovian field is tilted to the spin axis of the planet. The radiation belts of Jupiter were thousands of times stronger than those of Earth, as expected. The density of dust increased near Jupiter, also as expected, because of its powerful gravitational attraction.

John Wolfe, of Ames, characterized the atmosphere as "warm and extended, rich in hydrogen." The occultation, infrared, and ultraviolet experiments showed that it was feasible to send probes deep into the atmosphere, even at the current level of technology, Wolfe said.

Flowing parallel to the equator was an intense sheet of electrical current in the outer magnetosphere, Smith, of JPL, reported. He characterized the magnetic field not only as "squishy" but "lumpy"; its strength varied at different locations from two to fifteen Gauss. It expanded and contracted so much that *Pioneer X* crossed and recrossed the field boundary seventeen times.[15]

One of the major discoveries of the flight was that Jupiter is the source of the mysterious "galactic electrons" that have puzzled space scientists since they were first detected near the orbit of Earth by an interplanetary monitoring platform in 1964.

According to John Simpson, of the University of Chicago, these electrons, in an energy range of 3 to 12 million electron volts, were thought at first to originate from some undetected source outside the solar system. The particle detectors aboard *Pioneer X* identified their source as Jupiter's magnetosphere. They showed a ten-hour period of variation, corresponding to Jupiter's rotation. "There it was," Simpson said. "We've been monitoring Jovian trapped radiation for years and never knew what it was."

Van Allen's findings confirmed his surmise that the trapped-radiation belts of Jupiter were analagous in density and energy to the artificial-radiation belt produced by the 1962 Starfish high-altitude nuclear bomb test. Because *Pioneer X* had been designed to withstand hard radiation based on that model, it survived the Jovian belts. The density of electrons with energies above 60,000 electron volts was 5 billion per square centimeter per second in the inner belt.

The outer magnetic field and radiation zone had the shape of a disk that seemed to flap up and down as *Pioneer X* passed in and out of it. The wobble amounted to twenty degrees every ten hours, the period of Jupiter's rotation. The high-intensity radiation was sensed in an inner belt. It formed a doughnut-shaped ring around the planet and was contained by the powerful inner magnetic field.

In point of size, the inner belt extended about 800,000 miles from the top of Jupiter's ionosphere. The outer zone extended beyond it in a flattened ring for another 1.3 million to 6 million miles (as it is compressed and inflated). The outer zone is about 445,000 miles thick.

The celestial-mechanics experiment of John Anderson, JPL, yielded precise gravity data that enabled the experts to refine previous estimates of the masses of Jupiter and the Galilean satellites. Of some significance was the fact that *Pioneer X* periapsis came one minute sooner than calculated, showing that Jupiter's mass was somewhat greater than the preflight assessment.

The new data pegged Jupiter's polar diameter at 82,967 miles and its equatorial diameter at 88,734 miles. The ratio of the polar flattening to the equatorial diameter turned out to be ten times that of the Earth, mainly because Jupiter is mostly in a fluid state and rotates more than twice as fast as Earth does.

The observations confirmed an average density for Jupiter of 1.33 grams per cubic centimeter. It was a fluid planet. The relative masses and densities of the four Galilean satellites were determined from the experiment, and these enhanced the analogy between the Jovian moons and the planets of the solar system.

Expressed in terms of the mass of our Moon, which is $1/81$ the mass of the Earth, the mass of Io, the closest of the Galilean satellites, is 1.22 lunar masses; the mass of Europa is 0.67; Ganymede, the largest of the satellites, is 2.02; and Callisto, 1.44. (The nearest satellite is tiny Amalthea, 113,000 miles from the center of Jupiter. Amalthea was too small to be seen by Galileo's thirty power telescope and, hence, is not a "Galilean" satellite.)

Of special significance are the densities of these moons in relation to their distances from the planet. In terms of grams per cubic centimeter they are: Io, 3.5; Europa, 3.14; Ganymede, 1.94; and Callisto, 1.62.

The significance of the decrease of density of these moons with distance from the planet is the indication that they were formed when Jupiter was very hot. As mentioned earlier, the heavier elements (silicon, iron, nickel, which are refractory at high temperatures, would have condensed closer to the planet than the volatile elements (hydrogen, helium). At one time, Jupiter may have radiated like a weak star, although it never was massive enough to have started a thermonuclear reaction that would have caused it to radiate like the sun. The source of heat, presumably, was gravitational—the energy accumulated by the compression of accreting molecules in the solar nebula.

The density-with-distance arrangement of the Galilean satellites is analogous to that of the terrestrial planets, as I have pointed out previously. The exception is our Moon. With its low density (3.3), it ought to be out there between Mars and Jupiter, possibly among the Galilean satellites, but it isn't. It's right here, close to Earth. None of the theories of the origin of the Moon—including capture, fission, or the ring hypotheses explains the density anomaly. Our Moon fits into the Jovian satellite scheme (between Io and Europa) more neatly than it does in the terrestrial planet scheme. Could it have come from there—or from somewhere beyond Mars—if it was captured? Is our Moon possibly a displaced satellite of Jupiter?

BLACKOUT OF IO

As *Pioneer X* passed through the Jovian satellite system, the IPP relayed back to Earth photographs of Ganymede and Europa. But as it approached Io, deep in the radiation zone, false commands, which were generated by the radiation, caused the camera to miss Io entirely. The IPP responded to at least ten spurious commands caused by the high radiation. It was as though Jupiter had seized control of the spacecraft to inhibit picture taking!

When controllers at Ames realized what was happening, they radioed a sequence of commands to reconfigure the IPP so that closeup pictures of Jupiter would not be lost. Because of the forty-six-minute time lag in transmissions, the commands were repeated periodically to reverse the Jovian commands even before they could be detected from spacecraft telemetry back at Earth. By December 2, 1973, the photos of Jupiter exceeded in detail the best ever taken from Earth.

The imaging of Ganymede, with a resolution of 240 miles, showed features that look like lunar maria. There is one mare region in the center of the moon and another at the south pole, each about 480 miles in diameter—about twice the surface area that the 1-inch camera lens could resolve. The north polar region was brighter than other areas, possibly indicating frost or ice. Europa was too distant for surface detail to be recorded. As with Earth's Moon, Ganymede's maria indicated an episode of volcanism. So did the lava plains of Mercury and the great volcanoes on Mars. Volcanism seemed to be a characteristic of Earthtype bodies in the solar system.

Io's hydrogen cloud was seen by the ultraviolet photometer. It extended about sixty degrees on either side of Io in the moon's orbital plane, like gaseous horns. Darrell Judge, of the University of Southern California, the principal investigator, compared the hydrogen torus to a partly-eaten doughnut in shape. He thought it was probably formed by atomic hydrogen, created by the interaction of Io and the protons it swept up from the plasma in the Jovian magnetic field. The protons were neutralized by the addition of electrons collected from the moon's surface.

Such a phenomenon was new and exciting to the chairbound explorers at Ames. The Jovian system indeed was a new ball park. There, the big moons orbited inside a massive magnetic field where particles from the solar wind were trapped and accelerated to high energies. Earth's field does that, too, but not on such a grand scale; and Earth's Moon lies far outside the main body of the terrestrial magnetosphere, except for its tenuous "tail" through which the Moon passes.

The IPP photos brought the clouds of Jupiter closer than man had been able to see them through the most powerful telescopes on Earth. The first polarimeter measurements indicated that the clouds of the North Tropical Zone, part of the Equatorial Zone, and the Great Red Spot were all elevated regions. The lowest cloud elevations were in the North and South Temperate Zones. There appeared to be a range of fifteen kilometers (nine miles) in these elevations.[16]

Tom Gehrels, of the University of Arizona, characterized the turbulence in the massive atmosphere as thermally driven from below as well as from the sun. Jupiter's internal heat generated the atmosphere bands of bright belts and dark zones. The bright bands were cloud tops, probably ammonia crystals; the dark zones were gaps in the clouds.

Jupiter exhibited an entirely new meteorology, for the infrared radiometer showed that the planet was emitting twice as much heat as it received from the sun, so that the planet, itself, was driving the convection of its own atmosphere. Saturn shows similar banding and may be hot below. Venus, which is known to have very high surface temperatures, exhibits a similar banded cloud cover.

The IPP looked down deep into the Great Red Spot and saw the structure of a hurricane. It was not unique. There were smaller versions of it, Gehrels said. He and his colleagues interpreted the "spots" as areas of whirling, rising clouds, pushed up from below by convection and then subsiding.

The Great Red Spot is always seen in the southern hemisphere of Jupiter. There is a smaller Red Spot in the northern hemisphere, but it is not as extensive nor as colorful as the big one. The smaller Red Spot appeared to be only 3,000 miles long compared to the 30,000-mile extent of the Great Red Spot, towering 5 miles above the surrounding cloud tops.

There was now a consensus among investigators that the Red Spots were hurricanes, semipermanent ones, in the atmosphere. The Great Red Spot had been waxing and waning for at least 300 years. Although the forces that produced it could be assumed to be analogous to those that create hurricanes on Earth, they were much longer lasting. Changes in the Jovian atmosphere went more slowly than on Earth. Imagine a terrestrial storm lasting for centuries! How could life exist? On Jupiter, even the most ardent believers in the possibility of life had to agree that it could have evolved only in quiet regions—certainly not in those massive storms.

NO PLACE FOR MAN

The ultraviolet photometer observations indicated a cloud deck 150 miles thick and an atmosphere consisting of 82 percent hydrogen, 17 percent helium, and 1 percent other gases about 600 miles deep. At the lower boundary of the atmosphere, the gaseous hydrogen became liquid under the pressure of the vast volume of gas. About 15,000 miles deeper, under a pressure of 3 million (Earth) atmospheres, the liquid hydrogen made a transition to a metallic phase, in which electrons were stripped from the hydrogen molecule. The liquid-metallic hydrogen was electrically conducting.

This conception of the planet's structure was explained at a NASA news conference in Washington, D.C., September 10, 1974, on the general findings of *Pioneer X*. The model was accepted by the entire Pioneer experiment team.

Investigators visualized the liquid-metallic hydrogen region as seething with turbulent motion from the energy of Jupiter's rapid spin. This condition created a dynamo effect, generating electrical currents that produced the magnetic field. At the center of the planet, it was supposed that there might be a rocky core equivalent to the combined masses of Earth, Venus, and Mars. To account for Jupiter's magnetosphere, the scientists had to invoke metal—in this case, a metallic phase of hydrogen. The evidence for the metallic center was the field itself. The low overall density of Jupiter would not support a hypothesis of a massive iron core. Thus, the two requirements, in theory, for a planetary magnetic field were met by Jupiter—a conducting medium and a relatively fast rotation.

As *Pioneer X* cleared the magnetosphere of Jupiter after the second week of December 1973, the ultraviolet photometer began to see another phenomenon: the glow of interstellar hydrogen gas flowing into the solar system from the great beyond. In a thousand years, man had pushed the "great beyond" back a half billion miles, from the seas beyond Greenland to reaches beyond Jupiter. There, *Pioneer X* was headed in the early weeks of 1974.

It appeared that *Pioneer X* had barely escaped debilitating damage in the Jovian radiation zone. The intensity of the trapped radiation within 80,000 miles of the planet was close to the small vessel's tolerance level.

At the September 10, 1974, news conference, Wolfe was asked whether man could venture into the Jovian system. *Pioneer X* received a radiation dose of 500,000 rads, he estimated. That is more than a thousand times the death dose for a human being. (Rad is an acronym for radiation absorbed dose. The International Committee on Radiological Protection cites five rads as the maximum dose a human being can safely absorb over a period of thirty years. Some experts regard this as ten times too high.) A manned voyage to the system could not safely approach Jupiter any nearer than the orbit of Callisto, 1.1 million miles out, without considerable radiation shielding, Wolfe said. Even then, when Callisto passed through Jove's extended current sheet of energetic electrons, "One would probably have to duck for cover."

On September 10, *Pioneer XI* was fewer than ninety days from Jupiter. Its observations in the interplanetary medium and the Asteroid Belt confirmed those of its predecessor. It was announced that *Pioneer XI* had been targeted to pass only 26,725 miles from the Jupiter cloud tops, more than three times closer than *Pioneer X*. However, because its periapsis would take place at high latitude in the northern hemisphere, where it would look down on the north pole of Jupiter, *Pioneer XI* would be irradiated for a shorter time than *Pioneer X*, although the radiation dose would be higher. It was believed that the shorter exposure time would compensate for the higher dose.

And then, as it departed Jupiter, *Pioneer XI* would be accelerated by the Big Planet's gravity to Saturn, where it would pass between Saturn's innermost ring and the surface of the planet on September 5, 1979. This would be an extraordinary feat of interplanetary navigation, carrying out the pool-ball, carom effect visualized years before; but it would work, all right, if *Pioneer XI* could survive the radiation during its brief encounter with Jupiter.

The encounter would take place exactly one year after that of *Pioneer X*—on December 3, 1974.

PIONEER XI

Pioneer XI crossed the Jovian bow shock wave on the evening of November 25, 1974 (California time), at a distance of 4.8 million miles from the center of Jupiter. It made its first entrance into the magnetosphere the next day, at a distance of 4.3 million miles. Once again, the ballooning and contraction of the magnetic field created the illusion that the spacecraft was going in and out of it. Early on November 27, Pioneer once more seemed to be in interplanetary space for a time. Then it recrossed the bow shock and reentered the field November 29. Even though the solar wind at Jupiter blows with only 1/25 the pressure it exerts at Earth's orbit, it is strong enough to push the magnetosphere 2 million miles inward at times.

Pioneer XI approached the planet 45 degrees to the left of sun line, thus providing a new view of Jupiter. As the IPP slowly photographed the planet, Jupiter began to grow in size on the television screens at the Ames Research Center.

On November 30, 1974, Jupiter appeared to be the size of a softball, flattened at the top and bottom. The next day, *Pioneer XI* crossed the orbit of Callisto. Jupiter slowly swelled in size in the television monitors, which carried the transmission, rectified, of the spacecraft camera.

As *Pioneer XI* approached Io, there was interest in the possibility that it might detect a hypothetical "flux tube"—a line of magnetic force extending in the magnetosphere between Jupiter and the moon and carrying a powerful electric current of perhaps 100,000 volts. This hypothesis was developed as a possible explanation of the manner in which Io modulated the forty-megahertz decametric radio waves, which something on Jupiter (possibly atmosphere lightning) emits with a power of 100 million watts.

During a series of preencounter news briefings at Ames, James W. Warwick, a radio astronomer of the University of Colorado, explained how such a current could be produced. Jupiter's magnetic field rotates with the planet fifty-four meters a second faster than Io revolves around the planet. Consequently, the magnetic field sweeps across Io at fifty-four meters a second, and magnetic lines of force cut through the moon. Io itself is conducting. It has an ionosphere through which a current can pass. It thus becomes an electrical generator, with a gradient of hundreds of thousands of volts.

The current flows out of Io and down the conjectural flux tube into the ionosphere of Jupiter, passes through it, and returns along a magnetic line of force to the opposite hemisphere of Io to complete a circuit.

The whole idea is fantastic enough to intrigue the most confirmed skeptic. Since the eighteenth century, it has been known that if you spin a metallic object between the poles of a magnet, you produce an electric current. Io, cutting across magnetic-force lines, might be expected to produce an electric current, also. Because it is immersed in a magnetic field, the moon is obviously connected to Jupiter by magnetic lines of force, along which a current might flow. All this is conjured up by a hypothesis of the moon's modulation of those powerful radio signals.

Warwick and others hoped that *Pioneer XI* would fly close enough to Io's assumed "flux tube" to detect a current with its magnetometers. But a recalculation of Pioneer's flight path showed, alas, that it would miss the supposed flux tube by four minutes; it would pass the region swept by the flux tube four minutes before the flux tube swept by. Still, the magnetometers might detect a powerful electric current if it was actually flowing through the tube at hundreds of thousands of amperes.

By noon, Monday, December 2, Jupiter had grown in the TV monitor to the size of a beach ball, gloriously banded in hues of red, reddish brown, gray, and gray-white. The Great Red Spot glowed like the pupil of a giant eye surrounded with mascara.[17]

Pioneer's velocity rose by the minute. During Tuesday, December 3, it was racing obliquely through the denser regions of the radiation zone. At 9:21 P.M. that day, *Pioneer XI* reached periapsis, 26,000 miles above the clouds of Jupiter. It was moving then at a velocity of 107,000 miles an hour. However, the spacecraft had passed around the edge of Jupiter by that time (although its radio signal was still being received because of the forty-six-minute time lag) and entered forty-three minutes of blackout as it was occulted by Jupiter.

The time computed for periapsis was off by 11 seconds—on a flight that had taken 607 days and covered an arcuate flight path of 620 million miles.

During the radio blackout, there was a buildup of tension in the control room at Ames. NASA officials were on hand for the encounter, including the agency administrator, James C. Fletcher. In tow was a group of VIPs whom the space agency invited to witness the climax of the encounter.

At twenty-four minutes after 10 P.M., Pacific Standard Time, the suspense ended when a calm voice remarked over the public address system: "Okay, we got it." The eight-watt radio signal from Pioneer had been picked up again after the spacecraft cleared Jupiter.

A check of the instruments showed that Jupiter had seized temporary control of *Pioneer XI* as it had of *Pioneer X* the year before. The plasma analyzer went through fifteen mode changes as a result of spurious commands. "We turned it off to let it calm down," said Charles Hall.

The infrared radiometer also went through a series of mode changes, against the will of Earth, and 40 percent of its north pole data was lost. Ames had to send thirty commands to restore it to normal function. Even the meteoroid detector registered "hits" that were patently false.

Yet, despite *Pioneer XI*'s closer approach, it received less radiation than *Pioneer X* because of its oblique angle of passage through the magnetosphere and a faster transit of the high-radiation zone. Magnetometer readings indicated a field strength of about four Gauss at the Jovian surface. There was no evidence of the hypothetical Io flux tube. *Pioneer XI* sped on to its next target, Saturn.

The Pioneer program had come a long way in ten years. John V. Foster, the director of development at Ames, recalled that *Pioneers X* and *XI* had originated as modest deep-space probes. They were not at first designated for Jupiter. Now, one was going clear out of the solar system and the other was headed for ringed Saturn.

"That's really milking a couple of little, deep space shots a long, long way," said Foster. "No reason we can't explore the whole Solar System with Pioneers."

CHAPTER X

VIKING

Nine hundred and seventy-five years after the first Norse reconnaissance of North America, a new "Viking" voyage of exploration was being prepared on the coast of Central Florida. As the Ides of August 1975 approached, two elaborately instrumented space vehicles, *Viking A* and *Viking B*, and their Titan 3-E launchers were being counted down at the Kennedy Space Center.

Their destination, glowing dull red in the night sky, was the planet Mars.

The principal purpose of the new Viking mission was a search for evidence of life on Mars in the form of microorganisms. However, at a prelaunch symposium on the prospects of success, Joshua Lederberg, the Nobel laureate in physiology and medicine in 1958, cited the possibility that a living thing might appear in the television camera transmission in the form of a cactuslike desert plant.

Each landing module of the two Viking spacecraft was equipped with a "biological instrument"—an automated, chemical laboratory for the detection of microbes on Mars. Each instrument could perform chemical experiments with Mars soil samples at the level of a university graduate student.

If the highly complex equipment worked, if microorganisms did exist on Mars, chemical evidence would reveal them, provided they could carry on metabolism in the environment of the Viking laboratory, which was more Earthlike than Martian. If they could not or if they were sufficiently dissimilar to Earth organisms, the experiment would not register them.

However, along with Lederberg and Carl Sagan, several members of the Viking scientific team hoped that the camera would pick up a bushlike structure or two, with leaves, to conduct photosynthesis, as well as roots to collect moisture and minerals from the soil. No liquid water could exist on Mars, because the atmosphere was too thin to hold it; but some might be trapped in the Martian regolith, a topsoil that resembled that on the Moon. Some-

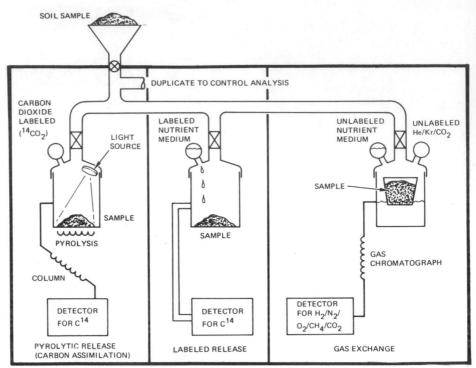

SOIL SAMPLE

DUPLICATE TO CONTROL ANALYSIS

CARBON DIOXIDE LABELED ($^{14}CO_2$)

LIGHT SOURCE

LABELED NUTRIENT MEDIUM

UNLABELED NUTRIENT MEDIUM

UNLABELED He/Kr/CO_2

SAMPLE

SAMPLE

PYROLYSIS

SAMPLE

GAS CHROMATOGRAPH

COLUMN

DETECTOR FOR C^{14}

DETECTOR FOR C^{14}

DETECTOR FOR H_2/N_2/ O_2/CH_4/CO_2

PYROLYTIC RELEASE (CARBON ASSIMILATION)

LABELED RELEASE

GAS EXCHANGE

(TEST CELLS CONTAIN MARTIAN ATMOSPHERE)

Schematic of life detection experiment system on Viking Lander. *Courtesy TRW, Inc.*

thing like a cactus was the logical kind of plant for a cold desert like equatorial Mars, where the Vikings were to be landed—one at the confluence of ancient river valleys and stream beds, the other under a hood of polar clouds.

Intellectually, every member of the Viking team realized that the chance of finding life, or evidence that it ever existed, was small. Emotionally, many team players scored the prospect as a "probable." There were endless arguments pro and con. During the countdown, they were heard at daylong discussions in the Kennedy Space Center auditorium. They were continued by members of the team in the hot August evenings as they sprawled on the beach and stood waist-deep in the surf of a warm, turgid ocean, where life on Earth began.

Viking was by far the largest and most expensive interplanetary excursion the United States had attempted. Its cost, about $1.1 billion, was twice that of an Apollo manned landing on the Moon, although, of course, the cost of the whole Apollo program was more than thirty times that of Viking.

The search for life on Mars could, from one point of view, be considered a billion-dollar gamble. The Soviet Union had made seven attempts to land reconnaissance craft on Mars. So far as the return of usable surface data was concerned, they all failed. In 1974, *Mars VI* had sent back a tantalizing clue to the presence of a large concentration of argon in the Martian atmosphere before communications blacked out.

The argon hint—and that's all it was, a hint—suggested that at some time in the past, Mars had a much thicker atmosphere than it has now, which is only one two-hundredth the density of Earth's atmosphere on the average and much too thin for liquid water. This clue to a formerly denser atmosphere supported a theory that the atmosphere and hydrosphere of Mars presently are frozen at the poles, principally in the north polar ice cap; that Mars lies sleeping in an ice age; and that climatic conditions oscillate on Mars more severely than on Earth, so that there were times when the Martian environment made it possible for life to develop. Pursuing this theory of Mars as the once and future abode of living organisms, the Viking life detection scenario offers a prospect that some organisms adapted to the climate change that produced the arid, cold desert that Mars is now. An Earthly parallel to conditions in the tropical zones of Mars is the dry valleys of Antarctica. Nothing grows there. The only living things are a few itinerant scientists, dispatched to study the region by the National Science Foundation. And even they leave at the end of the antarctic summer.

At the prelaunch symposium there were strong feelings of optimism and of skepticism. But whether or not life was found, Viking lander instruments would provide invaluable information, such as the chemistry of the soil and the internal structure of the planet.

OLDER SCENARIOS

Since the earliest times, Mars has been the subject of numerous scenarios and fantasies, each reflecting the mythology of the culture in which it evolved. It was the vengeful Nergal of the Chaldeans, the Ares of the Greeks, the Mars of the Romans. In the Greco-Roman pantheon, Mars was personified as the god of war. The "martial" aspect of the Red Planet persists in the symbolism and language of many cultures.

One of the curiosities of science is the literary reference to the two moons of Mars 156 years before they were discovered. In *Gulliver's Travels*, a satire that critics sought to counter by giving it to children to read, Jonathan Swift told how "The Laputan astronomers have likewise discovered two lesser stars or satellites which revolve around Mars."

Gulliver's Travels was published in 1721. The two tiny asteroidal moons of Mars were discovered in 1877 by the American astronomer Asaph Hall, who used the twenty-six-inch refracting telescope of the U.S. Naval Observatory in Washington, D.C. How could Dean Swift have known about them? Or did he invent them, along with the Laputan astronomers?

Mars has been singularly productive of invention and fantasy. Hall reached into mythology to confer names on the moons. He called the inner one Phobos ("Fear") and the outer one Deimos ("Flight") after the mythological horses yoked to the chariot of the ancient war god.

The year 1877 was exceptionally good for seeing Mars. The Red Planet came within 35 million miles of Earth, as it does every fifteen to seventeen years. Only Venus comes closer—26 million miles. It was the year that the Italian astronomer Giovanni V. Schiaparelli sighted linear features on Mars that he described as "canali" ("channels"). So arose the legend of the Martian canals.

Schiaparelli, director of the Brera Observatory, at Milan, mapped the *canali*, which appeared to form a network across the planet. Although he is commonly credited with the discovery of these features, they were seen by others earlier. The papal astronomer Fra Pierre Angelo Secchi observed them in 1858, and the German astronomer Johannes Schroeter noted the linear markings during observations between 1785 and 1802.

However, the main scenario of life on Mars was based on Schiaparelli's publication of his *canali* sightings. It led to fantasies of Mars as a dying planet whose civilized inhabitants are reduced to drawing water from the polar ice caps by means of a network of canals they have constructed to irrigate their fields and supply their cities.

Drawings by Schiaparelli and others depict such a geometric pattern. The Italian astronomer did not think of the *canali* as canals, however, but as large rivers that seemed to divide the surface of the planet into a number of islands. In 1879, he reported seeing double lines of *canali*.

Like the Martian moons detected by Swift's Laputan astronomers, the nineteenth-century *canali* are difficult to explain. The supposed network was as fictitious as the existence of Laputans; nevertheless, like the moons, channels do exist on Mars, but not the network Schiaparelli and others described.

The *canali* scenario was enhanced by Percival Lowell—wealthy Bostonian, amateur astronomer, and brother of the poet Amy Lowell. He founded the Lowell Observatory in the clear air of Flagstaff, Arizona, not far from the Grand Canyon. Lowell saw the *canali*, too, and mapped their geometry. He was convinced that they were work of intelligent beings.[1]

The canal illusion was amplified by another nineteenth-century American astronomer, William H. Pickering. Observing Mars through the Harvard Observatory telescope at Arequipa, Peru, he identified 200 dark areas where the canals seemed to intersect. He called them "oases," another reference to the idea of a planet perishing of dehydration.

More than 600 canals were mapped by Schiaparelli and Lowell. Both astronomers realized that the limit of resolution of their telescopes on Mars was about fifty miles. Lowell acknowledged that the *canali* were thus much too wide to be canals or even river valleys. He thought of them as croplands, irrigated by waterways that were too narrow to be seen from Earth but that ran for hundreds of miles. This notion acquired a degree of credibility with the observation of seasonal darkening of some areas on Mars, which began near the pole in the local Martian spring and spread toward the equator as spring advanced. Schiaparelli did not share Lowell's conviction that the *canali* were artificial; as he continued to study them, he was convinced they were natural features.

The trouble with the *canali* hypothesis, however, was that the lineaments were not always visible. Those seen during one period of observation were absent on another. In 1909, George Hale, an American astronomer, reported that he looked for canals on Mars with the new sixty-inch reflecting telescope on Mount Wilson, California, and failed to see any.[2] E. M. Antoniadi, a French astronomer, reported a similar experience in 1913, saying: "the astronomer of the future will sneer at these wonders and the canal fallacy, after retarding progress for a third of a century, is doomed to be relegated to the myths of the past." [3]

Nevertheless, some observers continued to see canals. Combining photography and direct seeing, V. M. Slipher, of the Lowell Observatory, asserted in 1927 that the canal network did, indeed, exist. Confirmation was reported by R. J. Trumpler, of the Lick Observatory, in the late 1920s and by Edison Pettit at Mount Wilson in the late 1940s and 1950s. Correlating photographs and eyeball observations through the telescope, Trumpler depicted the extensive canal network of Schiaparelli and Lowell. In 1955, Pettit reported canal images on a number of Mars photographs taken in 1954.[4]

Thus, for more than three-quarters of a century, the canal illusion persisted in scientific observation of Mars. Lowell's conviction that the canals represented the efforts of an intelligent species to survive adverse climatic conditions had a profound influence, both in science and in literature. Lowell's books *Mars and its Canals* (1906) and *Mars as the Abode of Life* (1908) provided an authoritative source for mass media Sunday-supplement fantasies about a Martian civilization. In science fiction, Mars became a colonial domain of Earth. The concept of an intelligent species on the Red Planet and its mythological identification with conflict together with the dying-planet hypothesis supplied the backdrop for the most famous of all the Mars fantasies: H. G. Wells' *War of the Worlds* (1898) and the radio adaptation of the novel forty years later by Orson Welles and his Mercury Theater. The realistic dramatization of a Martian invasion of Earth created a brief hysteria in the radio audience, especially among those who tuned in late and caught the "news bulletins" that Welles concocted to dramatize the Martian landings in New Jersey.

In the 1920s, when the canal dispute divided Mars observers, Edgar Rice
Burroughs produced a legendary Mars with a barbaric civilization and
strange beasts. Burroughs' "Barsoom" and its "towers of Helium" (a city, not
a gas) represent, perhaps, the ultimate, or at least most profitable, exploitation of the canal scenario, along with the numerous low-budget movies depicting Martians as scantily clad girls and desperate scientists bemoaning the
fate of the dying planet.

I do not believe these fantasies çan be dismissed as irrelevant to the scientific investigation of Mars—and also of Venus, Mercury, and Jupiter. They
are part of a lore that has played a part in motivating the study of these
realms beyond the Earth. That lore unquestionably was a part of the boyhood reading experience of some senior scientists in the space program. It is
an essential ingredient of the romanticism that led to the invention of space
flight—the romanticism that has characterized exploration for the last millennium.

Science and fiction interact. The motif of a dehydrated Martian civilization
can be traced to a supposition that Mars is "older" than Earth. That is, it developed earlier. The supposition derives from the hypothesis of William
Thomson, Lord Kelvin, that the terrestrial planets cooled from a molten
state as the Sun contracted, so that those more distant from the Sun cooled
first.

From that viewpoint, Mars is "older" than Earth and Venus "younger," in
terms of cooling. Mars, therefore, could be considered as a desiccated, withered planet, while Venus would be a hothouse, a primitive steaming jungle.
These were scenes projected in the science fiction of the early twentieth century, before planetary reconnaissance started, and they are not so far off the
mark. Mars is a cold, dry desert. Venus actually is as hot as the fundamentalist conception of hell. But Mars is not "older" than Earth in terms
of planetary evolution. So far as its development can be observed, it appears
to be younger. About Venus nearly everything has to be learned or verified.

Still, the idea of Mars as an abode of life is a persistent one. It was the underlying motive for the Viking expedition to see if life ever developed on
Mars—a goal most biologists consider a very long shot.

The concept of life on Mars was reinforced by the similarities of Earth and
Mars, despite their differences in size. Mars' 4,200-mile diameter is only 53
percent of Earth's; its mass is one-tenth Earth's, and its density is nearer the
Moon's than Earth's. Martian gravity is about two-fifths that of Earth.

Otherwise, the Red Planet rotates on its axis almost as fast as Earth does.
The Martian day is twenty-four hours, thirty minutes, and thirty-five seconds
long (in Earth terms). The equator of Mars is inclined twenty-four degrees to
the plane of its orbit, strikingly close to Earth's inclination of twenty-three
and one-half degrees to the ecliptic plane. Consequently, Mars has seasons.

The Martian seasons are longer than Earth's, because the Red Planet's
year is 687 (Earth) days. It is half again Earth's distance from the sun, at

1.524 astronomical units. Also, because Mars' orbit is much more eccentric than Earth's, the length of the seasons differs markedly in the northern and southern hemispheres. The northern hemisphere has a long spring of 199 days and the southern, a correspondingly long autumn. The northern summer and southern winter last 182 days; the northern autumn and southern spring last 146 days; and the northern winter and southern summer last 160 days.

Although the southern winter is twenty-two days longer and summer twenty-two days shorter than those seasons in the northern hemisphere, the eccentric orbit of Mars brings the planet nearest the sun (perihelion) during the southern spring and summer. At perihelion, Mars receives 44 percent more radiation from the sun than at aphelion (the point most distant from the sun).[5] The result is that the southern summer is hot enough to cause all but a small residue of the southern ice cap to melt or vaporize, but a substantial portion of the northern ice cap remains solid throughout the northern summer.

This situation, as events will show later, seems to have an important bearing on the question of whether life has developed on Mars—or whether it could have.

Although the thickness of the Martian polar caps is conjectural, they cover a larger percentage of the total area of Mars at fullest extent than Earth's present ice sheets cover on Earth. At full winter extent, the south polar cap on Mars covers the polar region to 50 degrees south latitude and the north polar cap to 60 degrees north latitude. At maximum, the antarctic ice sheet barely reaches 67 degrees south latitude. However, the antarctic and Greenland ice sheets don't dwindle in the summer as the Martian caps do. The significance of the size of the Martian caps to life prospects is the conjecture that they store much of a former atmosphere and hydrosphere of Mars.

All of these factors, along with the canal mythology, stimulated a strong interest in the reconnaissance of the planet in Russia and the United States. The Soviet Union attempted two Mars reconnaissance launches in 1960, but neither got out of Earth orbit. A third in 1962 also failed to leave Earth orbit. Finally, on November 3, 1962, the Russians announced that a 1,976-pound craft called *Mars I* was on its way to fly by the Red Planet, but communications failed long before it got there.

The United States fared better. The first effective reconnaissance mission was the Mars flyby of *Mariner IV*. This 575-pound octagonal box, sprouting solar panels for electric power, fled past Mars July 14, 1965, and radioed twenty-two photographs back to Earth.

When these were enhanced so that some surface detail could be seen, they sent a shock through the scientific community. What appeared was a dim replica of the Moon—a cratered, potholed landscape, undeniably lunar. In the southern hemisphere, where it was winter, the crater rims gleamed white with frost. So dismal did this vision appear that no form of life recognizable on Earth could be imagined to inhabit that landscape.

Launched November 28, 1964, by an Atlas Agena rocket, *Mariner IV* carried a dust detector, plasma probe, radiation detectors, and a magnetometer, in addition to a television camera. Data were transmitted to Earth by an eight-watt radio. *Mariner III*, launched earlier, had failed. A protective shroud did not come off the spacecraft after it cleared the atmosphere, thus preventing communication, and the flight was written off.

As *Mariner IV* passed behind Mars, it sent the radio signal through the atmosphere. The extent to which the frequency and amplitude of the signal were distorted by the atmosphere could be measured precisely at the receivers. The average density of the Martian atmosphere could be calculated from these effects.

The results of this "occultation" experiment were even more discouraging than the photos to life enthusiasts. They indicated a density of 10 to 20 millibars—about 1 to 2 percent that of Earth's atmosphere (1,013 mb. at sea level, or 1 "bar"). And even that calculation was optimistic in the light of later measurements.

On Mars, it was realized, astronauts would have to wear pressure suits as on the Moon, although a landing craft could employ a parachute to slow its descent. These data were important to the design of a future lander. No magnetic field was detected—a surprise to those who fancied that Mars has an iron core like the Earth and would generate a magnetic field with its Earthlike speed of rotation. The chemical composition of the atmosphere remained undetermined, but nitrogen and carbon dioxide were speculated.

When the *Mariner IV* photographs were shown at the White House in Washington, President Johnson remarked: "It may be . . . it may just be that life as we know it, with its humanity, is more unique than many have thought and we must remember this." The president was thinking in terms of nuclear disarmament. The disclosures of *Mariner IV* enhanced the conservationist tenet that there's no place like Earth, an observation that was to be reinforced three years later by the lunar orbit cruise of *Apollo VIII*.

MARINERS VI AND VII: NIX OLYMPICA

Late in 1964, the Soviets launched a Zond spacecraft to Mars with a capsule designed to enter the atmosphere, but communications failed before the spacecraft passed Mars, at a distance of 960 miles, in August 1965.

So far as Mars reconnaissance went, the United States enjoyed consistently better luck than the Soviets, mainly because American communication equipment was more reliable. In their Mars and Venus efforts, the Soviet failure record would have put NASA out of business; but the Russians pressed on doggedly.

Two more Mariner-class vehicles were lofted to Mars in 1969 by Atlas-Centaur rockets. *Mariner VI* was launched February 24 and passed within 2,120 miles of the Martian equator July 31, 1969. *Mariner VII*, launched March 27, flew by the southern hemisphere at a distance of 2,190 miles on August 5, 1969.

These were heavier vehicles than *Mariner IV*, weighing about one-half ton. Each carried two television cameras plus an array of radiometers and spectrometers.

The *Mariner VI* and *VII* photos confirmed the lunar character of the Martian surface. In some regions, craters averaged 5 to 175 kilometers (3.1 to 109 miles) across. In others, however, smoother lowlands appeared, analogous to the lunar maria.

Crossing the midlatitudes, *Mariner VI* returned a picture of a large crater, 500 kilometers (310 miles) in diameter, with high frost-coated rims. The experimenters called it Nix Olympica ("Snows of Olympus").

The marialike dark regions of Mars, which had been noted from Earth for centuries, now become more clearly defined in the 75 *Mariner VI* and the 126 *Mariner VII* photos. Their boundaries were irregular; their interiors were mottled. Volcanism could be assumed on Mars on the basis of the lunar analogy.

Passing over the south polar region, where it was winter, *Mariner VII* showed that the north edge of the ice cap was sharp but irregular. Large circular craters appeared at the boundary of the cap, one 130 kilometers (80.6 miles) in diameter. Within the cap itself there appeared to be a crater.

Most of the cap was obscured by a "hood" of haze or clouds. It seemed to have formed from ice particles and vapor transported from the volatilizing north polar cap, where it was summer. Earlier in 1960, Ronald A. Schorn and C. B. Farmer at the Jet Propulsion Laboratory and Stephen J. Little at the University of Texas confirmed previous reports of water vapor in the atmosphere of Mars. They detected it in an analysis of photographic plates made at the McDonald Observatory, University of Texas, in December 1968 and February and March 1969.[6]

The data from the *Mariner VII* infrared spectrometer and radiometer were not conclusive in identifying the composition of the cap. Frozen carbon dioxide (dry ice) was assumed as forming part, possibly the bulk, of the cap, because the temperature in the polar atmosphere at six kilometers altitude was low enough to condense it. However, temperatures above the freezing point of carbon dioxide were observed at the pole. Part of the cap was thus reasoned to be water ice.

Thickness of the cap could not be determined from the photos with any confidence, but it appeared to be at least several feet thick or more—not the thin crust of rime that some astronomers had speculated.

Crater photos from both spacecraft showed evidence of soil weathering and transport, probably by wind. Once the lunarlike features of Mars had been recognized, the experimenters searched for differences between the two bodies. The ice caps, the atmosphere, and the existence of water vapor were the most obvious nonlunar features. Although both bodies had craters, those on Mars now appeared more subdued. Their floors were flatter, and some appeared younger than lunar craters. Moreover, Mars was not entirely cratered. A bright region called Hellas was nearly devoid of craters. And there was another area, a very large one at the equator, of tumbled chaotic terrain that seemed to run for hundreds of kilometers. Nothing like it had been seen on the Moon.

It was evident now that erosion had been much more active on Mars than on the Moon. Because Mars is nearer the Asteroid Belt, experimenters reasoned that the Red Planet should have been bombarded much more heavily. If it had been, much of the evidence had been erased. For the first time since *Mariner IV*, scientists began to speculate about water erosion on Mars.

The occultation of radio beams by the Martian atmosphere indicated a surface pressure of five to seven millibars, a significant drop from the earlier data of *Mariner IV*. Early in the Mars investigation, scientific opinion favored nitrogen as the main constituent of the atmosphere. That idea was dispelled by the spectrometry data of *Mariners VI* and *VII*. They reported carbon dioxide, the gas that had been found to have constituted the bulk of the atmosphere of Venus. Spectrometer data also hinted at the presence of silicates on Mars, in the surface rocks and in tiny dust grains in the atmosphere. Dust was to play a dramatic role in the exploration of Mars.

The presence of a carbon dioxide atmosphere and polar caps composed principally of dry ice plus the hint of silicates indicated a planet that had been differentiated by volcanic processes. Carbon dioxide is exhaled from planetary interiors by volcanoes. That was the story on Earth, where the gas had been broken up by plant photosynthesis, bound up in the rocks, and absorbed in the oceans. There were no oceans on Mars or on Venus. Life was questionable. And they had carbon dioxide atmospheres.

The temperature regimes on Mars were not wholly inimical to life as we know it on Earth. At the equator, the *Mariner VI* radiometer reported daytime surface temperatures of 3.6 to 9.84 degrees C. (38.5 to 49.7 degrees F.). Nighttime temperatures went from 63 to 153 degrees below zero F.[7]

With the new data, scientists amended their view of Mars. The emergence of the planet from fantasy through several stages of illusion and reality is one of the great achievements of space science. Roughly, it recapitulated the European experience of the fifteenth and sixteenth centuries in ascertaining the geography of the Earth and the nature, particularly, of the Americas.

One important clue to Earthlike tectonic activity had been found—the smooth, bright region of Hellas. There the land form had been modified in a way never seen on the Moon. And although such terrestrial features as mountain ranges, basins, and stream-cut channels had not been recognized from the flyby photos,[8] Mars was displaying faint evidence of Earth's dynamic processes.

But it was not like Earth, and, after *Mariners VI* and *VII*, it was not as much like the Moon as many had thought. Mars was in some intermediate stage of development, if it could be considered to be developing at all. In 1969, that could not be determined.

The prospects for finding life on Mars had improved somewhat as a result of the 1969 reconnaissance. But although not now entirely negative, they remained rather dim. Summarizing them, Norman H. Horowitz, a biologist of the California Institute of Technology, told a news conference in Washington: "There's nothing new in the data that encourages the belief that Mars is a body of life. But the results don't exclude the possibility. We have seen no signs of the noble race of beings that built the canals or launched the satellites of Mars." [9] The last sentence is a reference to speculation by a Soviet astronomer that the Martian moons were artificial satellites of some long-vanished race.

Although water vapor had been detected, the atmosphere pressure was too low to allow liquid water on the surface. The only stable states of water on Mars were vapor and ice, Horowitz pointed out.[10] If life exists on Mars, he said, it must be in a form that can use water in those states. But no known terrestrial species could exist in conditions on Mars as the *Mariner IV, VI,* and *VII* flybys depicted them. Mars, the biologist admitted, was a cold desert.

Nevertheless, preparations for more detailed reconnaissance went forward. A new Mariner was prepared to go into orbit around Mars for long-term photographic observation of the surface. Beyond this, development commenced on the Viking orbiter and lander mission, initially scheduled for 1973 and then, under money pressure, postponed to 1975.

All was not discouraging on the life front, however. In the spring of 1971, Horowitz and two colleagues, Jerry S. Hubbard and James P. Hardy, reported the results of experiments indicating the probability of organic matter on Mars.[11] By simulating Martian conditions in the laboratory, they found that ultraviolet light with the intensity that the Mariners had measured in sunlight at Mars would produce the organic compounds formaldehyde, acetaldehyde, and glycolic acid. These products formed from the interaction of a 97 percent carbon dioxide atmosphere with carbon monoxide and water vapor—all ingredients of the Martian atmosphere.

In their 1968–1969 water vapor studies, Schorn, Farmer, and Little had suggested that liquid water, precipitated out of the atmosphere during the warm part of the Mars day, could seep into the ground before it evaporated and remain trapped there for months.[12]

Water was the key to life. The amount bound up in ice at the poles, or as permafrost in the soil, was a critical factor in justifying the expense of a landing mission instrumented to conduct life-detection experiments.

The transport of vapor through the atmosphere had been confirmed. Over each of the poles, a hood of clouds formed in the local autumn and winter. Just before the spring equinox, the hood disappeared, and the outlines of the cap sharpened. The northern cap grew as the southern cap waned. Vapor passed from pole to pole. As each cap diminished, astronomers had noticed a dark collar around it. The collar implied the release of liquid water at the edge of the polar cap because of its resemblance to moist ground. [13]

MARINER IX: OLYMPUS MONS

Several major questions that had been raised by nearly a century of telescopic observation from Earth remained unanswered by the Mariner flybys. Of the canals, there was no sign and no explanation. A wave of darkening that seemed to spread from the polar regions during the local spring remained unexplained. The region called Mare Acidalium changed color from winter shades of gray and brown to spring shades of dark gray and blue-gray, with "oases" of gray-green that some observers thought were vegetation. [14] In 1956, Gerard Kuiper reported that in the spring, dark marialike regions were a neutral gray with a touch of green near the equator. Equatorial regions seemed to remain dark all year. These changes in hues had been reported since the mid-seventeenth century, and the darkening wave consistently appeared to move toward lower latitudes from the polar regions as the ice caps diminished in spring and summer. [15]

The color of Mars is red to the naked eye, but it resolves in the telescopes into orange, yellow, and brown regions, especially in the northern hemisphere. Polarization studies have indicated the possibility of limonite, a hydrated iron oxide, as a principal soil component. [16] But the silicate readings from Mariner tended to cast doubt on that interpretation.

Thus, the old questions persisted as new ones arose with the reconnaissance of the flybys. Was the wave of darkening moisture? Vegetation? Or was it the wind removal of dust from a marialike basaltic surface? And—what made Mars appear red?

Two advanced Mariners were hoisted atop Atlas-Centaur rockets in the spring of 1971 for a look at Mars from orbit. Each weighed a metric ton and carried retro-rocket engines with 970 pounds of propellant to drop them into Mars orbit when they encountered the Red Planet. Each carried two television cameras, one with a 50-millimeter lens for wide angle large-scale photos and another with a 500-millimeter telephoto lens for closeup photos. Both vehicles were equipped with infrared radiometers to measure temperature, ultraviolet spectrometers to analyze the atmosphere, and infrared interferometer spectrometers to identify chemical constituents of the atmosphere and the surface. They were the most sophisticated and costly spacecraft NASA had attempted to launch to another planet.

Mariner VIII failed and fell into the Atlantic Ocean May 8, 1971, because of a malfunction in the second-stage Centaur rocket. But *Mariner IX* was launched beautifully May 30, 1971, on a trajectory so accurate that only one course correction was needed to put it into the slot for retrofire when it arrived at Mars November 13, 1971. The retro engine was fired for fifteen minutes, inserting the spacecraft into an elliptical orbit of 1,387 kilometers (862 miles) by 17,113 kilometers (10,610 miles) with an inclination of sixty-five degrees to the Martian equator. The periapsis, or low point, of the orbit was later raised to 1,653 kilometers (1,025 miles) to improve radio communication as the Earth-Mars geometry changed in 1972.

Meanwhile, the Russians were also launching to Mars. Their luck was no improvement, at first, on *Mariner VIII*. A vehicle identified as *Kosmos 419* was launched May 8, 1971, but the Mars payload failed to get out of Earth orbit. The Soviets then launched *Mars II* on May 19. It reached Mars and went into orbit around the planet (15,500 by 855.6 miles) November 27, fourteen days after *Mariner IX* entered Mars orbit. A third Soviet craft, *Mars III*, was launched May 28 and reached Mars December 2.

Both Soviet Mars vessels were considerably larger (10,250 pounds each) than *Mariner IX* and were more complex spacecraft. Each consisted of an orbital bus and a lander vehicle, which was estimated to weigh about a ton, including fuel for retro-rockets and parachute.

The *Mars II* descent vehicle reached the surface of Mars bearing the hammer-and-sickle coat of arms, but apparently little else; nothing further was heard from it. *Mars III* ejected a capsule that landed by parachute and retro-rockets in a featureless, shallow basin about 900 miles in diameter ringed by ancient, eroded hills. The Russians announced the landing as opening the way for the search for life on Mars, but if any life-detection equipment existed on the lander, its nature was not disclosed.

However, the lander did carry a television camera, instruments to measure atmosphere pressure and temperature, a mass spectrometer to identify the chemistry of the atmosphere and of the soil, a wind-speed meter, and a device to test soil mechanical properties. Unhappily, twenty seconds after the equipment was turned on and the television camera began to send a picture, communication ceased. Several theories were proposed to account for the disaster suffered by the first "live" vehicle to land on Mars. One suggested that the communications relay system on the orbital bus failed—that the lander kept broadcasting, but the orbiter was not relaying the signal to

Earth. Another is that the violent winds, which had kicked up a major dust storm at the time, simply toppled the lander. The *Mars II* and *III* orbiters continued relaying data and photographs of the dust storm and cloud tops.

Late in January 1972, Moscow Radio broadcast an opinion that conditions on Mars observed by the orbiters were compatible with a theory that life in the form of microorganisms and plants could exist.

Blinded by the dust storm, which concealed most of the Martian surface, *Mariner IX* also was confined to photographing cloud tops and peculiar black dots that seemed to stick up through a curtain of dust like rocks in the sea. The dust storm was the worst in memory. It seemed incredible that an atmosphere as thin as that of Mars could produce such a maelstrom.

The Mariner science team spent the first month of the *Mariner IX* orbit studying the dynamics of the Martian atmosphere. Winds appeared to be blowing more than 100 miles an hour. The storm was analogous to a global hurricane.

With an orbital period of 11.9 hours, *Mariner IX* circled Mars about twice a day. On its ninety-fifth orbit, late in December 1971, the spacecraft camera began to see parts of the surface. The storm was abating; the dust was settling. During the first week of January 1972, the cameras were programmed to commence mapping.

Gradually, the surface materialized, as though a dense fog was draining away. First appeared the highest elevations. The dark spots that had looked like islands in the sea resolved into the tops of massive, volcanic mountains, a truly startling discovery. The largest of them loomed up twenty degrees north of the equator. The huge crater of Nix Olympica that had been seen in 1969 turned out to be the top of the largest volcano ever seen. It was a volcanic caldera (collapsed vent), surrounded by smaller vents, atop a volcanic pile whose vast height became apparent only when the dust had settled. Nix Olympica was renamed Olympus Mons ("Mount Olympus"). On its vast slopes, there were residues of long lava tongues, like those creeping down the sides of Mauna Loa.

The pile of Olympus dwarfed the Hawaiian volcanic pile. Olympus could be classified as a "shield volcano," its shield-shaped slopes built up from successive lava flows, with a main crater, or caldera, so huge as to resemble a giant meteor crater on the Moon. The shield was calculated to be 600 kilometers (372 miles) across and from 23 to 29 kilometers (14 to 18 miles) high.

Mariner IX established Mars clearly as a volcanic planet—a far cry indeed from its lifeless appearance in the photos of *Mariner IV*. Nothing on Earth seemed to compare with Olympus, rising from the surrounding region in an initial 13,000-foot cliff. The vast pile was ringed about for 500 kilometers by arcuate ridges and troughs.

About 700 miles to the southeast of Olympus appeared a line of three more massive volcanoes, astride the equator. They form the bulk of the Tharsis Ridge and could be classified also as shield volcanoes. Each is about

400 kilometers (248 miles) across and 19 to 20 kilometers (11.7 to 12.4 miles) high.

More huge volcanoes were detected in photos of the region called Elysium. The largest, Elysium Mons, is about 250 kilometers (155 miles) across and 15 kilometers (9.3 miles) high. To the north of the Tharsis-Elysium regions, a low volcanic structure was discerned and called Alba Patera. The main volcanic ring was nearly 600 kilometers across, with a huge caldera near the center, but lava flows radiated as far as 800 kilometers (496 miles) from the crater.

In his studies of the volcanoes of Mars, Michael H. Carr, of the U.S. Geological Survey, noted that the larger and younger volcanoes were clustered in the northern hemisphere.[17] He estimated that Olympus Mons was about 200 million years old, the volcanoes of Tharsis Ridge were about 400 million years, and those in Elysium were between 1 and 2 billion years old.

Older volcanoes were seen in the southern hemisphere, where extensive cratering from meteorites indicated that they predated those in the less cratered regions of the northern hemisphere. One, called Tyrrhenum Patera, exhibited a 200-kilometer (124-mile) fracture ring around the central caldera. Volcanic features in the southern hemisphere appeared to be 3.5 billion years old from the density of impact craters. Carr concluded that volcanism has been a persistent feature of Mars for most of its history.

East of the Tharsis Ridge appeared another feature, a great plateau slashed by faults running in three directions. They formed a rift valley, Valles Marineris, stretching along the equator for 80 degrees of longitude—about 2,952 miles.

This split in the crust produced a system of canyon lands on equatorial Mars that makes the Grand Canyon of Arizona look like a ditch. Valles Marineris, in addition to being nearly 3,000 miles long, is 43 miles wide and 4 miles deep. Its analogue on Earth is the East African rift valley, running the length of Africa and forming the Dead Sea and the Jordan valley on the western rim of Asia.

The fault zones were evidence of massive rearrangement of the crust by internal upheaval. Great blocks were lifted up, thrust down, and tilted. "We think this indicates a very dynamic substratum under the Martian crust," said Harold Masursky, of the U.S. Geological Survey, chief of the photo geology experiment team. He said that photos of the fault zones showed that the crust had been broken many times, a clear indication of a "dynamic, geochemically active planet." Moreover, he added, the crispness of the edges of the volcanic piles and the lack of impact features indicated that the volcanoes were relatively young.

Along the great rift were subsidiary valleys, formed not only by faulting and by volcanic eruptions, but also by an erosion process. Experimenters experienced certain inhibitions about identifying them. They mused, they mulled it over, they argued, and finally they admitted their conclusion. They were caused by erosion by running water.

There had been rivers and streams on Mars. Powerful torrents of water had flowed and shaped the land. It had rained, the ice had melted, and the permafrost had gushed forth. All that had been exhibited in the photos of *Mariner IX*, for there were the unmistakable patterns of river valleys with headwaters and tributaries. They branched. They were braided by sediments. There were little islands or sand bars in these channels. One was traced for approximately sixty miles, with numerous, smaller branches. The photo-interpretation team was "hard put" to find a mechanism other than water that would produce such waterways.[18]

Here, at last, were the *canali* of Mars—not the visual figments of Schiaparelli and Lowell, but natural rivers and streams arising from running water in the tropic zones. The main channels emerged from slumped masses of debris on the northern edge of the rift valley. They ran northward, down into the deepest part of a large basin, which might have been a sea. Some of the channels were broad, like those made on Earth by Pleistocene floods that broke loose with the melting of the glaciers. Others on the plateau had cut their way into cratered lands. They twisted and wound and exhibited multiple tributaries that came together, making the stream bed wider and deeper in the downstream direction. Other channels appeared at the foot of craters, formed by networks of smaller ones.

Masursky noted that some channels seemed to be crisp and geologically recent; others were worn, eroded, and seemed older. The differences suggested more than one episode of water flow on Mars—cyclical flows, perhaps. And this meant that other geophysical parameters of Mars changed, too, such as the density of the atmosphere and the temperature regime. The channels thus implied not only past running water on Mars, but climatic oscillations.

With *Mariner IX*, a new Mars made its debut to the scientific community. It was a live, active planet, still evolving. On the Moon, the processes of planetary evolution had stopped 3 billion years ago. On Mars, they were still going on. Cirrus-type clouds hung over the great Martian volcanoes, an indication that gases were being vented from the depths of the planet. Spectra of the clouds showed they were composed of water ice crystals.

WATER, WATER . . .

Where had the water gone? *Mariner IX*'s ultraviolet spectrometer showed a cloud of atomic hydrogen around the planet extending out 12,400 miles. The hydrogen cloud is the product of the breakup of water vapor molecules by sunlight. The process also releases oxygen. Was it a clue to where surface water had gone?

Earth is similarly encapsulated in a cloud of hydrogen. Robert Jastrow, of the Goddard Space Flight Center, has explained that water is inhibited from escaping Earth by a cold trap that prevents vapor from accumulating above 6.2 miles altitude. There the temperature is so low that the atmosphere will hold only 1/1,000 of the vapor it can hold at sea level. Another factor is Earth's ozone layer, which prevents ultraviolet radiation (or most of it) from penetrating the atmosphere below 6.2 miles. Consequently, loss of water by photodissociation of water vapor in Earth's atmosphere does not appear significant.[19] It was difficult to believe that the hydrogen cloud around Mars accounted for the loss of running water. Other possibilities had to be considered.

During the winter of 1971–1972, as *Mariner IX* settled into the orbital reconnaissance of Mars, water vapor was detected over the south polar cap by the infrared interferometer spectrometer, an instrument usually referred to as ISIS to avoid its tongue-twisting label. It was summer in the southern hemisphere. The south polar cap, which had been observed as stretching at least 50 degrees of latitude (1,815 miles) by *Mariner VII* in 1969 had shrunk to 10 degrees (363 miles) when *Mariner IX* began photographing it in the austral summer of 1971–1972.

The water vapor detected over the south polar cap was not impressive, hardly 1/1,000 that in Earth's atmosphere, experimenters estimated. It was calculated at 20 precipitable microns; that is, if precipitated, it would cover the planet to a depth of 20 microns (or 20/1,000 of a millimeter). No water vapor was detected over the frozen north pole, where it would condense, presumably, as fast as it arrived.

With these observations, it was tempting to formulate a theory that water vapor was emitted from the volcanoes and precipitated at the poles during the local fall and winter. A small amount escaped the planet and was dissociated by solar ultraviolet to form the hydrogen cloud. An estimate that 100,000 gallons of water a day are lost from the entire atmosphere of Mars was suggested by investigators.[20]

THE ICE AGES

Evidence of climatic cycles, or oscillations, with alternating warm-wet and cold-dry periods, suggested a theory that Mars is now in an ice age and has been in and out of ice ages for much of its history.

The theory supposed that climatic conditions on Mars change every 25,000 years in the planet's precession cycle. As it rotates on its axis, Mars wobbles, causing its axis to precess, or change its position relative to the stars, as Earth does. Precession is the wobble of a spinning top, especially as it spins down. Polar flattening on Mars suggests that the planet rotated faster than it does now before it cooled from a molten state.

The Mars precession cycle runs 50,000 (Earth) years, so that the axial tilt is reversed, relative to the sun and stars, each 25,000 years. It is the linkage of this phenomenon with Mars' eccentric orbit that is cited as the probable cause of climate change.

At this epoch, Mars is closer to the sun during the southern hemisphere summer, as mentioned earlier. The effect is to cause most of the southern ice cap to vaporize, except for a residue of water ice. During the northern summer, Mars is farthest away from the sun. Consequently, the northern summer is relatively cool. The result is that while part of the northern ice cap melts, some of it remains frozen over the summer. The portion that would be expected to volatize first is the carbon dioxide, which vaporizes at temperatures that would keep water frozen as hard as rock.

It was considered possible that a permanent glacier of water ice exists at the north pole of Mars and never melts. Buried below the water ice may be a large reservoir of solid carbon dioxide 300 to 1,000 meters thick. This estimate was based on an interpretation of photos of the residual north polar cap taken on Mariner orbits 667 and 668 (see note 29).

According to the theory, the summer temperatures at the poles would tend to equalize as the axis precesses, and there would come a time when the water and carbon dioxide now impounded at the north pole would be released into the atmosphere. Complete vaporization of the ice would increase atmospheric density enough to hold water on the surface in a liquid state.[21] Then it would rain. The violent dust storms on Mars may be characteristic of its present orbit and axial attitude, because they seem to occur at the conjunction of the southern summer solstice and perihelion.[22]

Another theory proposes that changes in the orbit of Mars, influenced by the perturbation effects of mighty Jupiter and Saturn, are the cause of climatic change. A more elongated orbit, which would bring Mars closer to the sun, would warm the polar caps sufficiently to release a denser atmosphere and hydrosphere from the ice.[23]

However, flowing water might be accounted for by volcanism that would force red hot lava upward toward the surface and melt the permafrost—which is assumed to be extensive on the planet. Most Mariner scientists believe the amount of water stored on Mars, in the polar caps and as permafrost and vapor, is significant.[24]

One observation suggesting this is photographic evidence of widespread permafrost melting. The evidence is an interpretation of landscapes that resemble areas on Earth where such melting has occurred.

The "chaotic" terrain first seen in *Mariner VI* photos and later shown in more detail by *Mariner IX* looks like a type of landscape called thermokarst on Earth. It is produced by the melting of subsurface permafrost and the subsequent collapse of the overburden after the water has flowed out of the ground.

Among the first to suggest this interpretation of the Martian chaotic terrain were Carl Sagan and two colleagues, Owen B. Toon and Peter J. Gierasch.[25] Similarities between the Martian chaos country and Alaskan thermokarst country have been pointed out by Lawrence W. Gatto and Duwayne M. Anderson, of the U.S. Army Cold Regions Research Laboratory. They compared *Mariner IX* photos with those taken of Alaska by *Earth Resources Technology Satellite I*. The ERTS photos showed a thermokarst region consisting of pits, basins, valleys, and hummocks formed by surface collapse when the subsurface ice melted. These features are characteristic of the Martian counterpart.[26]

A rather small increase in the amount of heat absorbed by the poles on Mars would trigger a chain reaction, Sagan and his colleagues suggested.[27] The pressure would rise, improving the efficiency of atmospheric heat transport, which would add more heat to the poles. If the polar caps were entirely volatilized, the released gases might raise the atmospheric pressure on Mars to one bar—the sea level pressure on Earth. But even if the release of volatiles from the polar caps raised the pressure to only forty millibars (4 percent of Earth's sea level pressure), it would be enough to hold liquid water on the surface, according to Sagan and his associates.

In their view, atmospheric pressure had gone up and down with climate oscillation. They suggested that the present Martian climate might be modified artificially by darkening the poles so that less sunlight would be reflected and more heat absorbed there.[28]

These ideas reflected one view of *Mariner IX* data. A contrary one was expressed by Bruce C. Murray, then a planetologist at the California Institute of Technology. Murray published a paper with Michael C. Malin, a graduate student, rejecting the oscillation hypothesis on the grounds that the amount of solar heat each pole received during a Martian year was about the same.[29]

However, the paper concluded that a reservoir of permanent solid carbon dioxide did, indeed, exist in the north polar region, under a residual film of water ice. It probably amounted to two to five times the volume of carbon dioxide in the atmosphere, and it tended to stabilize the five-millibar average pressure of the atmosphere. Even if total vaporization did occur, they said, the increase in atmospheric pressure would reach only fifteen to thirty millibars.

Although a cyclical change in solar heating at the poles had been theorized in 1966 by Murray and Robert B. Leighton, Murray later found the hypothesis in error. He had concluded later that there was little possibility that an atmospheric pressure approaching Earth's ever had obtained or ever could obtain on Mars. If liquid water produced the erosion features investigators interpreted as river beds, it must have done so in some bygone epoch, according to the Murray-Malin paper. They ruled out the likelihood of intermittent or recurrent climate changes that the apparently different ages of the channels suggested.

In a more recent review of *Mariner IX* findings, Murray commented: "If the channels were created by rainfall, it would seem that one must postulate two miracles in series: one to create the earthlike atmosphere for a relatively brief epoch and another to destroy it." [30]

However, James B. Pollack, of NASA's Ames Research Center, argued that any process raising the atmosphere's carbon dioxide content would also raise its water vapor content, "which would effectively warm the Martian surface by the greenhouse effect." Thus, he concluded, "plausible mechanisms seem to be available for creating the climatic conditions needed for running water to be stable in the equatorial regions of the Martian surface." [31]

Sagan emerged as the leading proponent of the water-life hypothesis for Mars, and Murray emerged as the leading doubter. Sagan and George Mullen suggested that life could have evolved on Mars during a warm epoch about a billion years after its accretion. Then the organisms might have adapted to increasingly cold, arid conditions. [32]

However, the two scientists projected a warm Mars in the future. They cited the astrophysical theory that the luminosity of the sun has increased about 40 percent throughout geologic time and continues to increase. As this process goes on, the Earth will become hotter. About 4.5 billion years hence, according to Sagan and Mullen, a "runaway greenhouse effect" will make Earth as hot as Venus is now (about 800 degrees Fahrenheit on the surface). Atmospheric pressure on Earth then will rise to 300 times the present sea level pressure, and because all the water would have been vaporized, it would be 300 "bars of steam."

At the same time, Mars will warm up to about the present average for Earth. "If there are any organisms left on our planet in that remote epoch," the scientists mused, "they may wish to take advantage of this coincidence."

VENUS

The notion that the Earth can look forward to a Venusian future is singularly unattractive, for the reconnaissance of Venus has shown that life is much less likely there than on Mars—or on Jupiter, for that matter.

Since 1960, the United States and the Soviet Union have attempted to probe Venus as well as Mars at each opportunity—that is, when the alignment of the planets with Earth made it possible for probes to reach the planets on a minimum-energy trajectory and transmit data to Earth.

NASA began its reconnaissance of Venus with the launch of *Pioneer V* in 1960. The small spacecraft did not recieve enough push from its Atlas-Able launcher and went into solar orbit between the Earth and Venus, returning invaluable evidence of the existence of the hypothetical solar wind.

The USSR double-launched *Sputnik IV* and *Venera I* in February 1961. Sputnik failed to leave Earth orbit. *Venera I* passed Venus at 62,000 miles but did not return data.

The second American Venus probe, *Mariner II*, flew by Venus December 14, 1962, after a predecessor, *Mariner I*, veered off course at launch and was destroyed. Perhaps the major scientific contribution of the flight was the confirmation by *Mariner II*'s plasma detector of the solar wind. The instrument reported a steady stream of ionized gas flowing outward from the solar corona and breaking, like the surf of an ocean, against the boundary of the geomagnetic field. Earth's great magnetic umbrella extends sunward 40,000 miles. *Mariner II*'s instruments registered the shock wave where the solar wind strikes the field and is deflected around the Earth. The wind streams out on the antisolar side of the planet to form a long magnetic tail that stretches beyond the orbit of the Moon.

From its nearest approach of 21,598 miles, *Mariner II* completed three radiometer scans of the dark side of Venus, the terminator (day-night boundary), and the day side. From these data, a picture of an incredibly hostile planet emerged, with surface temperatures around 800 degrees Fahrenheit, as previously indicated by microwave observations from Earth. The cloud deck that hid the surface was estimated to be at least fifteen miles thick. No magnetic field was detected.

Like Mars, Venus has been the subject of several scenarios. In the early Roman pantheon, Venus was the goddess of plants. She did not acquire the love and beauty characteristics of the Greek Aphrodite until rough Roman ways were modified by Hellenic culture.

Because Venus, the brightest object in the sky after the sun and Moon, is both the morning and evening star, the ancients believed it was two stars. The Greeks called the morning star Phosphorus and the evening one, Hesperus. Four thousand years ago, Babylonians recorded the motions of Venus. Mayan astronomers based a calendar on Venus. Galileo observed that Venus exhibited phases, like the Moon—proof that it was orbiting the sun. Harassed by the Italian Inquisition, he wrote, cryptically, "the mother of loves imitates the forms of Cynthia [the Moon]."

Twice about every 130 years, Venus can be seen from Earth passing across the face of the sun. As I have related earlier, these transits enabled astronomers to compute the distance between the Earth and the sun (the astronomical unit) by means of trigonometry before the invention of radar. During the transit of 1761, the Russian astronomer Lomonosov observed a haze encircling the planet's disk. He concluded that it represented an atmosphere.

In 1890, after two years of observation, Schiaparelli reported that the planet's period of rotation was the same as its year, 225 (Earth) days. Lowell confirmed the observation. However, as *Mariner II* was heading toward Venus in 1962, the Jet Propulsion Laboratory scanned Venus by radar from the 210-foot antenna at Goldstone, California, and reported that the planet was rotating backwards with a period of 250 days plus or minus 50 days. The rotation period was pegged at 243 days five years later by tracking certain features of the planet previously seen by radar. The retrograde rotation of Venus has been cited as evidence for the scenario of the psychiatrist-cosmogonist Emanuel Velikovsky, circa 1950, that Venus began its career as a comet that was hurled by Jupiter into the inner solar system. Before settling down into its present benign nearly circular orbit as a well-behaved planet, the comet that became Venus grazed the Earth several times in the second and first millennia, B.C., causing a series of catastrophes, such as the flood of Noah and the plagues of Egypt; it also bumped into Mars, according to the scenario.

Another scenario was developed by a Swedish scientist who became a mystic, Emanuel Swedenborg, in the eighteenth century. He proclaimed that Venus was the habitat of two races of men, one good, the other bad. Mayan and Toltec priests observed Venus as a source of prophecy in all ranges, from good tidings to doom.

Venus has been regarded traditionally as a "sister" planet to Earth. It is the planet nearest Earth, at a distance of only 26 million miles when it is on the same side of the sun. At this position (inferior conjunction), however, Venus can be seen only as a silvery crescent. The full disk is visible when Venus is on the other side of the sun (superior conjunction). Its brightness, which has led many a contemporary spectator to report it as an unidentified flying object, is due to the high albedo (reflectivity) of the eternal cloud cover.

In size, Venus is nearly Earth's twin, with a mean diameter of 7,520 miles, only 400 miles less than Earth's. Its mass is 82 percent that of Earth, and its relative density about 91 percent Earth's. With those data, however, the similarities end. Since 1956, when the Naval Research Laboratory detected microwave emissions from Venus indicating a very hot surface, evidence has accumulated that the "sister" planet is a celestial hell, with a surface temperature hot enough to melt lead and a carbon dioxide atmosphere 100 times as dense as that of Earth.

Following *Venera I*, the Soviets launched four Venus probes in 1962. All of them failed to get out of Earth orbit. In 1964, at the next Venus launch opportunity, two Zond-class vehicles carrying entry capsules were boosted from Tyuratam spaceport March 27 and April 2. (Launch opportunities, or "windows," for Venus come about every nineteen months, when the planet is in range of a minimum energy flight. Mars launch windows come every two years.) The March launch resulted in the failure of the payload to leave Earth orbit and was designated *Kosmos XXVII*. The vehicle launched in April flew past Venus July 19, 1964, after communications failed.

The Russians fired two more Zonds at Venus, November 12 and 16, 1965. The first, designated *Venera II*, passed Venus at 14,880 miles February 27, 1966, and the second, *Venera III*, struck the surface of Venus March 1, 1966, near the center of the disk. This achievement was hailed in the Soviet press as man's first physical contact with another planet. Later, the Russians admitted that communications had failed on both vehicles before they reached Venus and that their progress had been tracked by radar. A third 1965 Venus shot was launched November 23, but it failed to leave Earth orbit and was recorded officially as *Kosmos XCVI*.

So far as planetary reconnaissance was concerned, the Zond program was conspicuously unrewarding. In its report on Soviet Space Programs, 1966–1970, the staff of the U.S. Senate Committee on Aeronautical and Space Sciences counted eighteen Zond payloads expended without the return of any planetary data.

The Soviets did not achieve significant data return from Venus until 1967, when advanced spacecraft, *Venera IV*, dropped an egg-shaped 845-pound capsule into the Venusian atmosphere on the dark side near the equator October 18, 1967. Only a meter in diameter, the capsule carried two thermometers, a barometer, a radio altimeter, an atmosphere density gauge, and eleven gas analyzers. During its entry and descent on a parachute, the capsule transmitted radio signals for ninety-six minutes; but the signals ceased before it reached the surface, or so it is supposed. For the temperature and pressure reports last received indicated that the probe was above the surface when communications cut off—or else on a very tall mountain. Temperature data ranged from 505 to 530 degrees Fahrenheit, and pressure ranged from fifteen to twenty atmospheres, indicating an altitude of up to fifteen miles. The probe reported the composition of the atmosphere as more than 90 percent carbon dioxide, 7 percent nitrogen, and 1 percent oxygen.

Two days after the launch of *Venera IV* (June 12, 1967), NASA's second Venus probe, *Mariner V*, was boosted off Cape Canaveral, on June 14, 1967. It flew by Venus at 2,544 miles on October 19, 1967, the day after *Venera IV* landed.

This quarter-ton flyby actually was the backup craft for the *Mariner IV* Mars flyby, refurbished for Venus. It carried an ultraviolet photometer to examine the properties of the Venusian atmosphere, a plasma detector, a magnetometer, and energetic-particle sensors. The path of *Mariner V* carried it part way around Venus so that it could pass a radio beam through the atmosphere.

The occultation experiment produced surprising results. So thick was the atmosphere, it "extinguished" the beam at lower altitudes; that is, it bent the signal to such an extent that it could not be received at Earth. Radio signals of three frequencies were directed through the atmosphere as *Mariner V* passed behind the planet. The experimenters found, however, that the bottom of the atmosphere could not be probed because: "at some limiting altitude, estimated to be 10 kilometers, the refractivity gradient of the dense CO_2 atmosphere is so high that a light ray or radio ray entering tangentially is bent into an inward spiral and cannot escape." [33]

The light-trap effect on Venus gave rise to an amusing speculation among several scientists. They imagined that light rays could be bent to such an extent by the thick atmosphere that an astronaut would see the back of his head in front of him. A whole array of "crazy house" visual distortions could be hypothecated. As later events showed, the speculation turned out to be a piece of whimsy.

Both *Mariner V* and *Venera IV* observed a standing shock wave at about 500 kilometers (310 miles) from the surface, where the solar wind broke upon an extended ionosphere. A similar effect of much greater intensity has been observed at the sunward boundary of Earth's magnetic field, where the shock wave forms at about 40,000 miles from the surface. Again, no magnetic field was sensed by *Mariner V*, and no trapped particles (as in Earth's magnetic field) were detected. However, both the solar wind detector and the magnetometer "observed clear and significant, though weak, 'signatures' of the planet." [34] The effects were attributed to the interaction of the solar wind and the ionosphere. Lack of a magnetic field was attributed to the planet's slow rotation, because it was assumed to have a metallic core like the Earth. [35]

The ultraviolet photometers on *Mariner V* and *Venera IV* saw a hydrogen envelope around Venus, presumably from photodissociation of water, as at Earth and Mars. *Venera IV* reported water vapor below the clouds of Venus at a concentration of 0.1 to 0.7 percent. In view of the high surface temperature, all water on Venus could be expected to be in a vapor state in the atmosphere.

The concentration of oxygen at 1 percent reported by *Venera IV* was surprising. Spectroscopic analysis from Earth indicated the abundance of oxygen at 0.001 percent. The thousandfold difference could not be explained. Jastrow noted that an oxygen content of 1 percent of the atmosphere on Venus would equal the total amount in Earth's atmosphere. [36]

Interpretation of *Mariner V* data yielded a higher surface temperature than *Venera IV* reported, supporting the conclusion that the Russian probe had not reached the surface when it ceased transmitting. Mariner data indicated a temperature of 700 degrees Kelvin (800.6 F.) and a pressure of sixty-five atmospheres.

The Soviets launched *Venera V* and *VI* in January 1969 for another shot at the surface of Venus. The data radioed back from both landers as they descended through the atmosphere gave the main constituents as 97 percent carbon dioxide (plus or minus 4 percent), 2 percent nitrogen, and 0.1 percent oxygen—a tenfold reduction in oxygen from *Venera IV*. Surface pressure was reported at 100 atmospheres and temperature at 500 degrees C., or 932 F. Neither lander survived on the surface.

Venus was a hard case to investigate. Although the Soviet landers were built to withstand loads of 450 gravities at atmosphere entry and temperatures exceeding 1,000 degrees F., the weird environment of Venus was simply chewing them up. Both American and Soviet scientists speculated that sulfuric acid was a constituent of the clouds, making Venus appear more hellish than ever.

It was not until December 15, 1970, that the Soviet Venus effort chalked up a clear landing triumph with the successful touchdown of *Venera VII*. The half-ton Russian lander came down on the night side and radioed data for twenty-three minutes—temperature 475 C. (887 F.), pressure ninety (plus or minus fifteen) atmospheres. Compared with a previous thirty-five-minute transmission during the descent, the transmission at the surface was so weak that the Russians had to use computer techniques to extract the message from interplanetary background noise. Either the capsule had tipped over on landing, throwing its antenna out of alignment, or the refractivity of the atmosphere was bending the signal so that only a fraction of it reached Earth. The Soviet press noted that while *Venera VII* was "talking" to Earth from Venus, the Soviet lunar roller Lunikhod was sending reports from the Moon.

The long and costly procession of Russian Venus probes continued in 1972. *Venera VIII* was launched March 27 and landed on the Venusian day side July 22. It transmitted for fifty minutes. Soil-analysis data showed concentrations of potassium, uranium, and thorium. The radiometer reported that contrary to expectation, nearly two-thirds of the sunlight observed at the cloud tops was reaching the ground. *Venera VIII* reported the atmosphere as 97 percent carbon dioxide, 2 percent nitrogen, and 0.1 percent oxygen. The measurements were now consistent with earlier Venera data, as were temperature indications at the surface.

The crowning achievements of the Russian Venus program came with the landings of *Veneras IX* and *X* October 22 and 25, 1975. Transmitting for fifty-three minutes, *Venera IX* sent a photograph of a dim landscape over which were strewn rocks and boulders, a view not unlike one on the Moon. Landing about 1,300 miles away, *Venera X*, which transmitted for sixty-five minutes, returned a photo of a mountain scene, showing a line of eroded hills.

The first photos of Venus dispelled the speculation that its surface had been planed by ferocious winds to a featureless desert. Commented Boris Nepaklonov, Venera program chief of topography: "We can surely now dismiss the old idea of Venus as a desert created by constant wind erosion, high pressures and temperatures." [37]

Even though *Venera VIII* had prepared them for surface lighting, Soviet scientists were surprised at the amount of sunlight the photos revealed at the surface. No wonder Venus is so hot, commented Professor Vasily Moroz, one of the Venera scientists. [38]

MARINER X

More restricted by budget than the Russians apparently were on planet reconnaissance, NASA designed a double shot to Venus and Mercury for the 1973 Venus launch opportunity. The success of *Mariner IX* at Mars had given the American space agency confidence in Mariner design. For the modest sum of $98 million, Congress was briefed, it was possible to survey two planets for the price of one, using the gravity-assist principle to boost a half-ton Mariner-class spacecraft flying by Venus on a trajectory to Mercury.

Launched by an Atlas-Centaur rocket November 3, 1973, *Mariner X* flew past Venus February 5, 1974, at an altitude of 3,000 miles. Venus bent the flight path so that the spacecraft passed Mercury March 29, 1974, at an altitude of 620 miles; it flew by it a second time September 22, 1974, and a third time March 16, 1975. The third passage brought the octagonal 1,108-pound spacecraft to within 193 miles of the surface of Mercury.

Mariner X carried two cameras with 1,500 millimeter telescope lenses, two magnetometers, an ultraviolet spectrometer, and a charged particle detector. It was powered by two solar panels. It could be accelerated or decelerated by a rocket engine and positioned for photography and other observations by nitrogen gas jets at the tips of the solar panels and on outriggers.

The gravity-assist operation required precision at launch and in course corrections. NASA published an estimate that a trajectory error of 1 mile at Venus would result in a miss of 1,000 miles at Mercury. The planned approach to within 620 miles of Mercury's surface was to provide maximum opportunity for pictures of the surface.

On the Venus pass, Mariner's ultraviolet spectrometer was deployed to search for deuterium, the heavy isotope of hydrogen, but none was seen. Instead, the instrument reported the presence of ordinary hydrogen, which appeared to be a major element in the clouds, and "an important amount" of atomic oxygen—about ten times more than observed at Mars. Helium also was seen "in fair abundance." [39]

Mariner X photos of Venus reveal with particular clarity the banded appearance of its heavy atmosphere, similar to but less marked than Jupiter's. "We're looking at the top of an enormously thick atmosphere," Bruce Murray told a press conference at Pasadena. "At the bottom, 50 miles or so below, the pressure is what you would experience in a submarine at 3 kilometers [two miles] depth in the ocean and the temperature is such that lead would melt. If you could survive all that, the gases are noxious, poisonous. There is no oxygen. In no way is Venus habitable. There are people who have speculated on possibly converting it into a habitable atmosphere, but that's something for our great-great-great-great grandchildren to worry about, I think. Not for us." [40]

On to Mercury fled *Mariner X*, its flight schedule astronomically precise. In Earth telescopes, the Mercurian surface resembled that of the Moon; but details were not clear, because Mercury, not much larger than the Moon, is much more distant and difficult to observe. Consequently, the surface of Mercury was largely terra incognita.

Mariner's television cameras began to photograph the planet at a distance of 3.3 million miles March 23, 1974. They continued to take pictures as the spacecraft swept actually to 431 miles of the surface March 29 and then pulled away from the planet. On this first pass, about 2,300 photos were radioed back to Earth.

The surface of Mercury turned out to be more lunar in appearance than expected. It was gouged and potholed by bombardment, displaying basins, craters, scarps, and ridges. There were plains resembling the lunar maria, and these were cratered to the same degree as their lunar counterpart, indicating a basalt fill after the early episodes of bombardment. [41] Moreover, a smooth, dark material resembling the lunar basalt filled the large craters. And wrinkled ridges like those on the Moon appeared on the Mercurian plains.

Irregular scarps ran for hundreds of miles across the surface, transecting plains and craters alike. Some of them rose a kilometer above their surroundings. It appeared that lava flooding had occurred extensively. Curiously, the flooded basins were distributed principally on one hemisphere, as on the Moon. The impression of the photo-geology team was that the formation of the basins and the largest craters dated back to the final stages of Mercury's accretion. [42]

The similarities of the surfaces of Mercury and the Moon are striking, especially in the light of their bulk composition differences. With a diameter of 3,008 miles, Mercury is one-third larger than the Moon but has a density approximating that of Earth. Indeed, its uncompressed density, as noted in an earlier chapter, is considered to be higher than that of Earth, making it the densest planet in the solar system. Compared with Mercury's 5.5 grams per cubic centimeter, the density of the Moon is 3.3. Yet both bodies lacking a "sensible" atmosphere, show the results of similar processes on their surfaces and a similar development.

Mercury has a solar day 176 Earth days long. The long solar day results from resonance between the sidereal day of fifty-nine Earth days and the planet's eighty-eight day year. Although Mercury rotates once every fifty-nine days with respect to the stars, it covers two-thirds of the way around the sun in that period. The solar day is thus lengthened to three times the sidereal day and twice the orbital period. Surface temperatures appear to range from 940 degrees Fahrenheit on the day side to 350 degrees below zero Fahrenheit on the night side.

Because of its density, Mercury is suspected to contain a massive iron core, which may comprise two-thirds or three-fourths of its mass. Even with its slow rotation, this concentration of iron should give it some magnetic field—and it does. Mariner's magnetometers detected a magnetic field of about one-thirtieth that of Earth.

No satellites of Mercury were seen by Mariner, confirming telescopic observations from Earth that there are none. The surface was covered with a regolith much like that of the Moon and with the same reflection characteristics.

As on the Moon, craters represented the predominant land form and came in all sizes, from small ones below the 1.5- to 2-kilometer resolution of the cameras to the 1,300-kilometer (806-mile) basin called Caloris. Heavily cratered regions resembled the lunar highlands. The Mercurian "maria" displayed a lack of craters similar to that of the lunar maria. It appeared that whatever bombarded these bodies hit them at about the same time and subsided at about the same time.

In general appearance, however, the surface of Mercury was "more bland" than that of the Moon; there was less contrast between adjacent units.[43]

The Caloris Basin was the most conspicuous feature *Mariner X* photographed. It was the counterpart of the Imbrium Basin on the Moon, and investigators surmised that it was formed by an impacting body some tens of kilometers in diameter.

Caloris was ringed by mountains rising to two kilometers above the basin floor. In the northeast part appeared a landscape of smooth hills or domes, resembling that of the Moon's Orientale Basin. The floor appeared to be smooth and relatively free of craters. This was observed in other basins, indicating a fill of volcanic lava.

The plains appeared to be younger than the heavily cratered uplands of Mercury, another indication of their similarity in origin to the lunar maria. It was the consensus of the *Mariner X* photo analysts that the plains materials "favor a volcanic origin" as opposed to the solidified melt of impact heating, although "we have no direct evidence of volcanism."[44]

On the other side of the planet, antipodal to the Caloris Basin, *Mariner X* photographed "peculiar terrain" consisting of hills and extensive linear features. The region, covering 500,000 square kilometers, suggested surface upheaval resulting from the shock wave transmitted through the planet by the impact that had created Caloris. Similar "peculiar terrain" has been observed on the far side of the Moon opposite Mare Imbrium and also Mare Orientale.[45]

With this first clear view of Mercury, planet scientists were closer than ever before to a synthesis of terrestrial planet evolution. Like the Moon and Mars, Mercury had undergone heavy bombardment, followed by widespread eruptions of red-hot liquid rock from the interior. Radar scans had detected craterlike structures in the equatorial regions of Venus.

The evidence of cataclysmic bombardment on the Moon four billion years ago was repeated on Mercury. It appeared to shoot down the theory that the heavy bombardment of the Moon was the final stage of its accretion from debris in Earth orbit.

Whatever had cratered the Moon also had cratered Mercury and Mars at the same time. And probably Earth and Venus, too, although the scars were mostly healed on Earth. And so it could be assumed that widespread cratering and basin formation dating back to the final stages of accretion may be common to all the terrestrial planets.[46]

The source of the projectiles had never been determined in lunar studies, and now the inspection of Mercury had only deepened the mystery.

From the reconnaissance of the Moon, Mars, and Mercury, a synthesis of planetary evolution showed that the terrestrial planets had similar early geologic histories, according to Paul D. Lowman, Jr., Goddard Space Flight Center.[47] There was an initial differentiation of materials to form a global crust. This was followed by bombardment 4 billion years ago, the source undetermined. Localized eruptions of magma from the interior then filled the larger basins.

Earth's development was similar, Lowman concluded. Its continents are the thickened, altered remnants of the original global sialic crust. Lowman thought that Earth's continued development has been a process of ocean formation.

The flyby and orbital reconnaissance of Mars, the flybys and probes of Venus, and the Mercury scans had revolutionized the new science of planetology in fifteen years. In 1975, the time for a bolder step had come. Vainly, the Russians had tried to land on Mars; curiously, they had failed there while succeeding, at least for brief periods, in getting data back from the surface of hostile Venus. Now it was NASA's turn to try for a Mars landing.

THE GREAT MARTIAN MICROBE HUNT

The general theory of biology now in vogue holds that life is a product of chemical evolution in a continuum that begins with the creation of the universe, the origin of the chemical elements in successive generations of stars, and the accretion and development of planets in the systems of main-sequence suns.

Under certain conditions, which may be found throughout the universe, common elements interact with energy to form organic molecules. These evolve into living systems, which are characterized basically by their ability to replicate, mutate, and reproduce the mutation, and by their power to modify the environment.

Thus, the general theory, which claims man's descent from the stars as a tenet, implies that life is not an accidental development confined to a single planet but may exist where conditions allow throughout the star-studded universe. This, of course, is the rationale for attempts to pick up radio signals that may be broadcast by some distant intelligence in the galaxy and for the rise of the science of exobiology. It was the reason for the quarantine imposed on astronauts returning from the early lunar landing missions and the basis for a controversy about the contamination risk of returning soil samples from Mars whether Viking finds evidence of life or not.

In this form, the general theory is a product of the present century. The concept of archebiosis (the rise of living material from nonliving material) is older. It was considered by Charles Darwin and by others in the nineteenth century.

In 1924, the Russian biologist Aleksander I. Oparin formulated a statement that life was a consequence of planet evolution and would arise wherever conditions made it possible from simple compounds of hydrogen, carbon, nitrogen, and oxygen.[48] The British geneticist J. B. S. Haldane advanced a similar theory in 1928. He proposed that organic compounds were formed by the action of ultraviolet light on atmospheric gases.

The materialistic approach of chemical evolution goes beyond Darwinism in challenging fundamentalist theological doctrine, but it does not account for the laws of nature science has revealed. It offers an accommodation in the struggle between science and religion, insofar as the general theory does not abolish the role of Creator, but enhances it with complexity. Thus, while the theory seeks to explain the *process* of creation, it does not account for the *creation* of the process.

What the theory offers science is a uniformitarian matrix for biological evolution in the solar system. As Lowman, one of the *Mariner IX* coexperimenters has observed: "The direct consequence of the general theory of biology is that life will evolve independently on countless planets which lie in the 'life zones' with respect to their stars and which experience the appropriate environmental history." [49]

Even before *Mariner IX*, which, as Carl Sagan pointed out, was the first reconnaissance that could have detected an Earthstyle civilization on Mars,[50] the Lowell hypothesis of advanced Martian life had been dismissed by all except science fiction writers. Only primitive life could be expected as the arid nature of the planet with its thin atmosphere became perceptible.

The rationale for a biological reconnaissance of Mars was the scientific necessity for testing the general theory of biology on another planet. That objective was cited in support of an unmanned expedition to Mars in a 1964 report of the Science Board of the National Academy of Sciences. Chairmen of the study group were Colin S. Pittendrigh, then of Princeton University, and Joshua Lederberg, of Stanford. "Implicit in the evolutionary treatment of life is the proposition that the first appearance of organisms was only a chapter in the natural history of planets as a whole," the report stated. The study assigned "the highest scientific priority in the nation's space program" to the exploration of Mars by unmanned spacecraft. It gave much needed support to NASA's Project Voyager, which was designed to land a reconnaissance vehicle on Mars during the 1971 or 1973 launch opportunities. Voyager was a big, costly enterprise, so heavy it would have required a Saturn class vehicle with a Centaur upper stage to launch it.

I have wondered if the scientists who wrote the academy report would have been as enthusiastic about the prospects of life on Mars if the results of *Mariner IV* had been available to them in 1964. Partly as a result of the dismal view of the Red Planet from *Mariner IV*, the Voyager project was dropped from the NASA budget in the 1968 fiscal year. It was replaced by a more modest project—Viking—which could be launched to Mars by a relatively economical (compared to Saturn) Titan-Centaur combination.

It is to NASA's credit that Viking survived the *Mariner VI* and *VII* flybys, for the story they told hardly added an optimistic note to the report of *Mariner IV*. Viking was well down the road in development when the sensational photographs of *Mariner IX* turned around the whole concept of Mars as another Moon and brought it into focus for the first time as an active, evolving planet with evidence of a past clement environment in which life might have arisen.

An extension of Mariner technology, Viking is a two-part vehicle consisting of an orbital module, or orbiter, weighing 5,125 pounds, and a landing module (lander), weighing 2,633 pounds. Together, the two stood ten feet high and measured thirty-two feet across with the orbiter's four solar panels extended. Total weight at launch was 7,758 pounds. Viking was the heaviest interplanetary payload launched by NASA, but it did not match in weight the five-ton Soviet probes fired to Mars and Venus. The difference did not reflect any deficit in weight-lifting capacity by the United States; it merely indicated the constraint of economy under which NASA was required to operate after Apollo. Compared with the lavish interplanetary launches by the USSR, NASA's planetary reconnaissance was a poor man's program; yet it had produced incredible results at relatively modest cost.

Nestled against the orbiter during the launch and the interplanetary cruise, the lander was to remain passive until it separated from the dual spacecraft in orbit around the planet and fired retro-rockets to enter the Martian atmosphere.

The main structure of the orbiter is an eight-foot octagonal ring on which were mounted sixteen bays containing electronic equipment. The orbiter carried two television cameras that could be controlled by radio from Earth and could resolve a surface area the size of a football field. It carried also an infrared spectrometer to survey atmospheric water vapor and an instrument to map temperatures at various latitudes and longitudinal zones of the planet. The orbiter was built by the Jet Propulsion Laboratory, Pasadena.

Attached to the orbiter frame was an uprated *Mariner IX* rocket engine capable of producing 300 pounds of thrust by burning monomethyl hydrazine and nitrogen tetroxide. Viking carried three times as much fuel as *Mariner IX*.

The propulsion system was designed to make four course-correction burns during the cruise. It would make one orbit-insertion burn of up to fifty minutes duration and twenty trim-maneuver burns to put the dual vehicle in an orbit of 930 by 20,200 miles with an inclination of 33.4 degrees to the Mars equator. The period of the orbit was to be 24.6 hours, the same as Mars' rotation.

During the 505-million-mile cruise, which would carry the two Vikings 180 degrees around the Sun in 305 to 360 days, the orbiter/lander was navigated by a crew of 700 men and women on duty around the clock at the Jet Propulsion Laboratory. In flight, the attitude of each spacecraft was stabilized by sensors on the orbiter bus that enabled the computer to align it with the Sun and with the star Canopus, as on previous Mariner flights. Attitude was controlled by gas jets on the solar panel tips. Two computers governed course maneuvers, orientation of the spacecraft for scientific observations, and the pointing of the high-gain antenna; controllers commanded the spacecraft through the computers.

Developed from lunar Surveyor technology, the lander measured ten feet across and seven feet tall from its three landing pads to the top of its disk-shaped S-band antenna. The vehicle was built by Martin-Marietta Aerospace, Denver. Its basic structure was a hexagonal box of aluminum-titanium, insulated with spun fiberglass and dacron cloth. Within the box was an automated chemical laboratory of great mechanical and electronic complexity where three basic biology experiments designed to detect evidence of microorganisms were to be carried out.

From the hexagonal structure sprouted three fifty-one-inch-long legs; a retractable boom ten feet long with a shovel and hoe at the end to dig, sort, and collect soil for analysis by the laboratory; a second boom, which carried instruments to measure atmospheric pressure and temperature; a seismometer, to measure Mars-quakes; and two facsimile cameras.

Protruding above the whole array was the disk antenna, which could be pointed at Earth or at the orbiter as it came into radio view of the lander each day.[51]

Lander electric power was to be provided, as on the Moon, by two SNAP-19 radioisotope thermoelectric generators, conveniently called RTGs. Each produced seventy watts of electricity from plutonium[238]. In addition, the lander carried four nickel-cadmium batteries, which could be recharged by the RTGs when power requirements were low.

The communications, propulsion, and electric power systems on the Viking orbiters and landers had been used before. They were products of a tested technology, and the Viking team had confidence in them. What was new was the biology laboratory, the heart of the whole mission. Prime contractor for the biology instrument was the TRW Systems Group, Redondo Beach, California. It was so complex that its effective functioning in the detection of microbes seemed to the layman to call for a miracle. As several Viking scientists observed at the prelaunch symposium, it might have been simpler and more effective to have equipped the lander with a remotely controlled microscope.

Soil for analysis was to be collected by the automatic shovel. It was designed to dig with a force of thirty pounds and lift with a force of five pounds. The hoe had a force of twenty pounds. Two pairs of magnets were mounted on the hoe to display the magnetic and adhesive properties of dirt clinging to it to a magnifying mirror that reflected into a camera. The later Surveyor spacecraft carried a similar device.

The digging was to be done under the direction of the lander's guidance computer. The shovel was to deliver about a handful of dirt to each of three inlets on top of the lander box. One batch would be analyzed by three biology experiments, another by a gas chromatograph mass spectrometer (conveniently called GCMS), and a third by an X-ray fluorescence spectrometer.

Each of the three biology experiments was designed to detect some characteristic activity of living organisms on the terrestrial model. The uniformitarian philosophy of the general theory of biology made it reasonable to assume that microorganisms on Mars would function in a similar way.

Each of the investigations incubated soil samples. Inside the biology instrument, heaters and thermolectric coolers maintained temperatures of 46 to 63 degrees F.

One investigation (the "pyrolytic" experiment) would seek to detect photosynthetic or chemical fixation of carbon dioxide or carbon monoxide by soil organisms in the following way. About .25 cubic centimeters of soil would be put in a test cell to incubate for five days. During that time, it would be exposed to the normal Martian atmosphere, to which radioactive carbon dioxide and carbon monoxide would have been added. The sample would then be irradiated by a xenon arc lamp, which simulates Martian sunlight. After five days, the container would be flushed with nitrogen to remove any free radioactive carbon[14]. Then the sample would be heated to 625 degrees centigrade to break down the cells of any organisms in the soil. The resulting vapor would then be passed through a carbon[14] detector. If the radioactive carbon was detected, its presence would signify that the sample did, indeed, contain organisms that ingested the carbon[14], retained it in their cells when the container was flushed with nitrogen, and released it only after being vaporized by the heater.

A second test, the "labelled release" experiment, was designed to register living cell activity involving the production and consumption of gases. Again, one-half cubic centimeter of dirt was to be placed in a container. It then would be moistened with a nutrient solution containing carbon[14]. The mix was to be allowed to incubate for a period of up to eleven days. During that time, any microorganisms present would be expected to ingest the nutrient and release gases containing carbon[14] as waste products. The test could be repeated three times.

A third experiment was designed to provide evidence of life in the form of an exchange of gases. It was based on the principle that living organisms alter their environment as they breathe, eat, and reproduce. For this test, the recipe called for one cubic centimeter of soil in a sealed container. A mixture of helium, krypton, and carbon dioxide was to be pumped into the container as an incubation atmosphere. Next, a nutrient solution of nineteen amino acids, vitamins, and salts would be introduced. The sample was to be incubated for twelve days, and the gases sampled every two to four days by the GCMS. The appearance of molecular hydrogen, nitrogen, oxygen, methane, or carbon dioxide would show that metabolism has taken place. After twelve days, another sample could be tested. The decision on whether or not evidence of life has been found would be made by the entire Viking biology team.

Supplementing the biology experiments was a further analysis of the soil by the GCMS seeking the presence of organic compounds. The X-ray fluorescence spectrometer was designed to analyze the inorganic chemistry of the soil. The experiment exposed a sample to X rays from a radioisotope source. This radiation causes elements in the soil to fluoresce in characteristic ways by which the spectrometer could identify them. Similar experiments that sensed the fluorescence of solar X rays were successfully conducted over broad areas of the Moon from orbit during Apollo.

The inorganic chemistry experiment was of intense interest to geologists who were anxious to pin down the composition of the soil. This had been determined by remote sensing on the Moon in another way by Surveyor spacecraft using an instrument that bombarded the soil by alpha particles instead of X rays.

The lander's weather station measured atmospheric pressure by changes in the electrical capacitance of a thin diaphragm stretched over a drum. Temperature was sensed by three thermocouples. Wind speed was indicated by the amount of wind cooling of an electrically heated cylinder of aluminum oxide. The device was claimed to be accurate to within 10 percent at wind speeds from 4½ to 340 miles an hour.

Geophysicists eagerly looked forward to reports from the seismometer that would provide clues to the planet's internal structure. Sensing ground motion through the lander, it contained a pendulum and a signal coil suspended between two magnets. Ground motion would cause the pendulum to displace the coil and create electric current proportional to the displacement.

Each lander carried an array of emblems, as did the Soviet counterparts, which betrayed either a blind faith in the future of space travel by Earthlings or in the contingency that other space-faring species might be around. The array included the U.S. flag, symbols of the American bicentennial, and a prize-winning insignia designed by Peter P. Purol, seventeen, a Baltimore high school student, depicting the sail of a Viking longship superimposed on the image of the lander on Mars.

At launch, the lander was encased in a "bioshield" consisting of a fiberglass dome and base that lent the vehicle the configuration of a flying saucer. The lander was sealed in the bioshield after being sterilized to prevent the importation of Earth microbes to Mars, where the biology experiments might detect them in lieu of native organisms. The upper part of the bioshield was jettisoned by explosive charges after Viking exited the Earth's atmosphere. The base was to be kicked off after the lander separated from the orbiter for landing.

At this stage, the lander was protected from the heat of entry into the atmosphere by a structure called an aeroshell. It consisted of a heat shield and twelve reaction control engines. At the proper point in the orbit around Mars, the engines would fire to reduce velocity and drop the lander out of orbit. It would enter the atmosphere at 151 miles altitude, later jettison the aeroshell, and come to a soft landing by deploying a parachute and firing a second set of retro-rockets attached to the lander frame. The descent would be controlled by a radar altimeter signaling the autopilot. At atmosphere entry, heating was expected to reach 2,700 degrees F. There the breath-holding part of the mission would start for the controllers.

Friction of the atmosphere was expected to slow down the lander from entry speed of 10,294 miles an hour to 670 miles an hour at 21,000 feet, where the aeroshell was to be cast off. At 19,000 feet, a mortar was to fire and deploy the 53-foot dacron polyester parachute, braking descent velocity to 138 miles an hour. At 4,000 feet, the three lander descent engines were to ignite and reduce the fall to 5.5 miles an hour. A landing shock of 8 feet a second was to be absorbed by the three landing legs with 12-inch circular footpads.

Both landers were targeted for the northern hemisphere of Mars and were constructed to operate for 120 days—through the northern hemisphere summer. *Viking I* was scheduled to arrive at Mars June 19, 1976, and land July 4 in a region called Chryse at 19.5 degrees north latitude and 34 degrees west longitude. Chryse lies at the lower end of Valles Marineris, the Martian Grand Canyon, and appeared in photos to be a drainage basin for several dried up rivers. It seemed plausible that life could have evolved there in view of the channel evidence of liquid water in the past, and the region was tropical enough to have daytime temperatures above freezing. Some moisture might still be present for short periods of time, if the atmospheric pressure was 6.1 millibars or above, experimenters calculated.

Refinement of the *Mariner IX* pressure data showed that there was a considerable range of pressures on Mars, from 2.8 millibars in the mountainous region of Tharsis to 9 millibars in the Hellas lowlands. About 65 degrees north latitude, pressure ranged from 7 to 10 millibars, indicating a trough some four to six kilometers below the average surface where pressure registered at 6.1 millibars.

The prime landing site for *Viking II* was a lowland named Cydonia in the region of Mare Acidalium at 44.3 degrees north and 10 degrees west. *Mariner IX* had indicated a surface pressure there of 7.8 millibars. Cydonia appeared to lie at the edge of the north polar hood, which is expected to contain water vapor during the northern summer. *Viking II* was scheduled to arrive at Mars August 7, 1976, and to land, after orbital inspection of the landing site, about September 9.

SATURDAY NIGHT ON MARS

As the countdown progressed at the Kennedy Space Center for *Viking A* (so-called before launch), ninety-four project scientists and observers assembled at the center auditorium for a two-day symposium entitled, "Earth and Mars: The Role of Life."

The meeting was called to order on the morning of August 7, 1975, by Gerald A. Soffen, of NASA's Langley Research Center, chairman of the science steering group. Nearby but off limits to all but launch crews stood the two Vikings, *A* and *B*, enshrouded and secured in the steel embrace of the Air Force Titan-3 Launch Complex. The members of the science group seemed to exude an aura of mild euphoria at the imminence of the long-awaited landing mission and some anxiety about the launch. The launcher for each four-ton Viking was the hefty Titan 3-E military rocket with a Centaur upper stage. Although the Titan had been used to boost military satellites and the Centaur had been flown as an upper stage of the Atlas to launch

Mariner IX, the combination of the two was new. It had worked only once before, to launch a heavy West German solar observatory called *Helios* the previous December 10.

Titan 3-E is a mighty machine. It consists of a two-stage Titan liquid-fuel rocket of the type used in Gemini, flanked by two, solid rocket strap-ons. At launch, the solid rockets put out a combined thrust of 2.4 million pounds. At altitude, the two stages of the Titan core rocket ignite in sequence, adding 621,000 pounds of thrust to the boost. Then the Centaur's hydrogen engines flash on for 126 seconds and add 30,000 pounds of thrust to establish the payload in orbit.

In the Viking launches, the critical time came at thirty minutes after lift-off, when the Centaur engines were programmed to ignite for a second time and burn for 320 seconds to lift Viking out of Earth orbit on the trans-Mars trajectory.

The "Earth and Mars" symposium has some historical importance inasmuch as it exhibited the Viking team's knowledge, speculation, and expectations about Mars on the eve of the launch.

It was opened with a review by H. D. Holland, of Harvard University, of the ways that the development of life had altered the chemistry of Earth, notably by adding oxygen, a waste product of photosynthesis, to the atmosphere.

Without life, Earth would have ended up with a carbon dioxide atmosphere, he said, like that of Mars or Venus. The observation suggested that the apparent lack of oxygen on Mars was evidence against the development of life there.

Carl Sagan argued that the existence of the channels implied a past epoch, or several of them, of higher atmospheric pressure and, probably, of higher temperature. *Mariner IX* photos had shown ten large channels that coursed for hundreds of kilometers and at least 2,000 small ones. The larger channels had substantial tributary systems.

Moreover, Sagan continued, the fact that they were concentrated along the equatorial Mariner Valley and did not appear at higher latitudes reinforced the hypothesis of water erosion. Only in this region did daytime temperatures rise above the freezing point of water.

The larger channels, Sagan estimated, were hundreds of millions of years old; but the smaller ones, he said, "for all we know were made a week ago Tuesday." The channels visible in the *Mariner IX* photos thus indicated cycles of climatic change, Sagan said.

Some of the experimenters had been excited by engineering telemetry that had been received from the Soviet *Mars VI* lander before communications died as it descended toward the surface of Mars in 1974. The telemetry reported the operation of the vehicle's mass spectrometer atmosphere pump. It showed a very high percentage of an inert gas, probably argon, in the atmosphere—perhaps 25 percent. Viking scientists and consultants were allowed to check these data in Moscow. They did so, because the indication pointed to a different atmosphere composition and density, perhaps, than Viking engineers had calculated for landing maneuvers. The Viking team would have to resolve the problem before the first lander was committed for touchdown.

A high abundance of argon in the Martian atmosphere was a factor to reckon with, not only because it would affect descent navigation but also because it implied a denser atmosphere in the past. The concentration of argon, an inert gas, in Earth's atmosphere amounts to only 1 percent. A high argon ratio on Mars could be interpreted as the residue of a past atmosphere of much higher density than the five-millibar average at present.

In Sagan's view, the argon question "powerfully connects" with the question of more clement environmental conditions in the past, when life might have started on Mars. If Viking confirmed an argon concentration of several tens of percent, Sagan said, the case for a dense primitive atmosphere would be strengthened.

If the atmosphere had been denser in the past, as the argon clue and channels indicated, where did it go? There seemed to be a consensus that it was not lost to space. Sagan's speculation that one of several astronomical effects could be responsible for climatic oscillations was not seriously challenged. Nor was his hypothesis that the planet was in an ice age, with enough carbon dioxide frozen in the polar caps to bring atmospheric density up to one bar (Earth's sea-level atmosphere density) if the caps were vaporized by a warming of the planet. A discussion evoked the possibility that wind erosion could have sculpted the tropical river valleys and arroyos, but that speculation aroused no enthusiasm.

It was clear that the state of knowledge about Mars on the eve of the Viking launches was more speculative than factual and that most of the optimism that life might be found had been derived from *Mariner IX*. If Viking worked, it would increase the knowledge of Mars several orders of magnitude. If life was discovered, the prospects of a manned expedition were likely to increase by orders of magnitude also.

Joshua Lederberg, a member of the Viking biology team who had been an adviser on Mars reconnaissance for more than a decade, offered a comment about the channel speculation. He recalled the effort of *Apollo XV* to ascertain the origin of the Hadley Rille on the Moon. "So we mounted an expedition to go there and among other things find out what caused that rille," he said. "Whether it was caused by flowing fluid, collapse or tectonics. So— *Veni, Vidi, Vici* and we still argue whether it is flowing fluid, collapse or tectonics." Sagan added: "They didn't go down into that rille. They just stuck their toe in it."

Lederberg was critical of the design of the life detection experiments. They purported to test for Mars organisms under Earth conditions of temperature and humidity. Of course, he admitted, something had to be rigged up that would detect life on Earth so that it could be tested. But would it detect anything on Mars? Lederberg thought that the experiments would provide a "novel experience" for any Mars organisms—a much warmer, more moist, and more nutritious environment than the Red Planet could offer. The question was: If Mars organisms were geared for Martian conditions, would they even survive the stress of terrestrial conditions in the Viking laboratory?

"I can see all kinds of possibilities where life might be flourishing on Mars and it will be the cameras rather than the life detection experiments that are likely to pick it up," Lederberg said. A questioner asked Lederberg what he expected to see in the slow-scan camera photos, "excluding an elephant walking by." Lederberg replied:

> Well, Carl [Sagan] is more optimistic about that elephant walking by at the scan speed of the camera.
>
> I just had in mind that if you are thinking about solar energy as driving the system, you have light capturing devices as part of the organisms living there, so you'll see them when you take your pictures. Looking out the window is the best means of detecting life on Earth in our immediate vicinity, present company excepted, so it's not such an improbable event. The color may be helpful, too.
>
> I'll say something about size. I am, of course, very fond of microorganisms, but Mars may be a very special place at the present time and with things like the flux of ultraviolet and the problems of obtaining moisture, very small organisms may have a very difficult time of it on Mars.
>
> So, it would hardly astonish me to find that if there is life on Mars it would be a little more like the desert that you fly over, where you see scattered shrubs of some size as the adaptation to that kind of aridity on a very different scale.
>
> I don't think we could exclude having sessile [dwarfed] vegetable forms of life of macroscopic dimensions. You're facing the problem of putting together moisture and sunlight. You need some extended dimensions to do that with any efficacy, so that's another argument for having a root and a leaf connected.

Another biology team member, Norman Horowitz, of the California Institute of Technology, said: "In the most hostile regions of the Earth, the microorganisms are the last survivors." Sagan commented: "As we've heard, and I think there's no gainsaying it, it is perfectly possible that there are large, visible plants on the planet."

Called upon to give a personalized summary of the symposium, Holland reminded his colleagues that "we still know very little about the amount of water." Estimates of water in solid and vapor states had ranged from a puddle to an ocean in the equivalent liquid state. He said he had been impressed by the "flap" the Soviet argon hint had created. So far as evidence for biology was concerned, he suggested that the channel arguments must be regarded as inconclusive. Nor would Viking settle the question of whether they were cut by flowing water.

From his viewpoint as a geologist, Holland said, it would be "nice to have some inorganic chemical data" that would show the composition of the surface rocks. As to the question of life, Holland referred to Sagan. "Carl," he said, "used to tell this story, I don't know whether he still does, of the astronauts who came back from the first manned mission to Mars and as they stepped out of the space capsule were asked, 'Well, is there life on Mars?' And the answer was, 'Yes, there is, but only on Saturday nights.' Is there life on Mars? We obviously don't know and the fear that everyone has, of course, is that Saturday night never came to Mars."

Battery trouble in the *Viking A* orbiter delayed its scheduled launch August 11, and *Viking B* was launched first, on August 20, 1975, to become designated as *Viking I*. Eventually launched September 9, 1975, *Viking A* became *Viking II*. Battery trouble in its lander was reported during the early phase of the flight. An attempt to recharge the *Viking II* lander batteries from its RTGs failed, and a backup recharging system had to be used.

In spite of the launch delay, *Viking I* remained targeted for a landing at Chryse July 4, 1976. On January 1, it was 185 days from its goal, and its telemetry sang merry electronic tunes in the receivers at JPL that all was well.

During the second week of June, as the orbiter cameras on *Viking I* were turned on the ocher ball of Mars, the experimenters began to assemble at JPL. And there they waited with the expectation and impatience of explorers throughout history for the landing of their vessel on a new world.

CHRYSE PLANITIA

Viking I landed in Chryse Planitia, the Golden Plains of Mars, July 20, 1976, on the seventh anniversary of the first manned landing on the Moon. The radio signals reporting the landing were received at the Jet Propulsion Laboratory, Pasadena, at 5:12:07 A.M. Pacific Daylight Time (12:12:07 Greenwich Mean Time). They confirmed that the 1320-pound automated laboratory * had settled down on its three legs in perfect order on the firm soil of the Martian plain.

Chryse Planitia is a mare-like basin, 1000 miles across, in the northern hemisphere. The landfall was pegged at 22.4 degrees north latitude and 48.0 degrees west longitude, about 2860 miles east of the great volcano, Olympus Mons.

Amazingly sharp and detailed, the first photographs from the lander revealed a desert landscape, strewn with rocks of fist to football sizes. It stretched to the horizon about 1.8 miles away where a broken line of hills,

* Earth weight.

seemingly the rim of an eroded impact crater, was silhouetted against an incredibly bright sky.

Although it appeared to be as flat and stark as a Dali landscape, this scene also seemed surprisingly Earthlike. The similarity enhanced a sense of wonder that it actually was a scene on the planet Mars, a distant spark that could be seen in the evening skies of Chicago or Denver twinkling redly in the Constellation of Leo.

Strewn all over the field of view, as though by a careless giant, the rocks exhibited familiar and fantastic shapes. Some were the products of erosion processes new to Earth scientists, although some of the shapes were analogs of weirdly eroded boulders in the dry valleys of Antarctica. One boulder near the lander looked like a battered automobile muffler, another like a wooden shoe. Most were sharply faceted; some were smoothly rounded. Streakings of sand indicated a prevailing, northeasterly wind. The bright sky was a startling contrast to the space-black sky of Moon photos and it enhanced the terrestrial aspect of the scene.

The lander had come down gently (at eight feet a second) on the Golden Plains on a summer afternoon. It was 4:13 P.M. Mars local time there when the signals reached Earth. The sun was going down and an evening chill gripped the rock-strewn land. There was no sign of life in the desert scene; no bushes, no shrubs, no lichens. The land was empty and desolate except for the three-legged, insectile, and semi-intelligent machine that had just arrived on a journey of 440 million miles from Earth.

The calendar for *Viking I* was reckoned in Mars solar days, or Sols. Sol 0 was July 20. On Sol 1, July 21, one of the lander's two facsimile cameras photographed the landscape in color, using red, blue, and green filters. An amazing color photo appeared on television monitors at JPL. Now the landscape appeared to be a strong, brick red, dotted with blue-gray boulders, and beyond the horizon loomed an incredible blue sky, faintly streaked with pink. The sky was incredible because it appeared so Earthlike.

But the blue sky soon turned out to be only an illusion, created by overly hasty color calibration. It was not blue—it was pink, deriving that color from the dust in the atmosphere. Particles of the rust-red Mars soil, carried aloft by the winds, absorbed the blue and scattered red light. The pink sky was the only unearthly feature of Mars, reddening toward the horizon at sunset and dawn.

The pink sky introduced a disquieting touch of strangeness into the otherwise terrestrial scene. A number of observers were disappointed at losing the blue, as though something truly wonderful was being taken away. Perhaps that illusory blue sky assuaged an inchoate longing in modern society for another Earth.

Yet, the landscape in rich color was so similar to that of a desert in Arizona or New Mexico that, as a writer for the *Los Angeles Times* remarked, one half expected to see a highway sign warning: No Services Next 80 Miles.

Meanwhile, *Viking II*, the twin of the first arrival, was rapidly approaching Mars. On Sol 1, it was less than 3 million miles out and on Sol 7, July 27, its orbiter engine burned for 25 seconds to correct its approach. The second Viking was due to go into orbit around Mars August 7, preparatory to a landing September 4 at 46 degrees north latitude, where lie the dark plains of Acidalia under the polar hood. The hood is a veil of supposed water vapor that enshrouds the higher latitudes in late fall and winter. However, the northern site appeared to have more moisture in the atmosphere than the *Viking I* landfall in the Golden Plains; but it was riskier because it was out of view of Earth-based radar. Photos by the *Viking I* orbiter and, later, by the *Viking II* orbiter would provide the only data to the flight team for landing site selection.

On the surface, the *Viking I* lander commenced its life detection and soil analysis experiments on Sol 8, July 28. This was a new departure in human exploration, one in which an electromechanical surrogate took over the functions of human hands and brain. The onset of the life search marked a new climax in the mission—its final one.

Like the launch from the Kennedy Space Center in 1975, the landing of *Viking I* had been delayed. NASA intended to bring the lander down on the evening of July 4, to symbolize 200 years of achievement on the bicentennial birthday of the United States. This landing date looked feasible when *Viking I* arrived at Mars June 19, 1976. The two-stage vessel was inserted into an oval orbit of 930 by 31,400 miles around the red planet by the firing of its rocket engine for 37 minutes, 49 seconds. On June 21, the orbit was changed by another engine firing to reduce the apoapsis (high point) to 22,000 miles. The second maneuver synchronized *Viking's* period of revolution to 24.6 hours, the same as the period of Mars's rotation, so that the cameras could observe the Chryse region at the same time every day.

The July 4 landing site lay near the center of the great basin at 19.5 degrees north latitude and 34 degrees west longitude. This A-1 site had been selected from *Mariner IX* photos made in 1971. It was near large channels, presumably ancient river beds, running from the highlands into the old mare basin that may have been a sea. Now, it was assumed, the basin floor was covered with sediments, deposited by torrents of water and mud that appeared to have cascaded down from the highlands in a bygone era of a wet Mars. Geologists were aching to study the sediments, and biologists believed they contained microbial life—if not visible plants.

Although the two cameras on the orbiter's scan platform did not provide much better surface resolution that that of *Mariner*, the photos they radioed to Earth were detailed enough to reveal a rough landscape at the A-1 landing site. Heavy fluvial erosion had left the ground a succession of mounds and troughs.

Toward the end of June, the flight team at JPL began to get cold feet about a July 4 landing at the A-1 site. At that point in the mission, the priority objective was to get the lander down without hitting a boulder or falling into a hole.

Orbiter cameras showed smoother terrain to the northwest. On July 2, project directors decided to move the landing site about 310 miles to the west-northwest. They announced that landing would be made July 17. The second site was a channeled lowland like the first, but appeared to be much smoother in the orbital photos. However, the flight team was not entirely satisfied. James S. Martin, Jr., of the Langley Research Center, the Viking Project Manager, and his associates called for a radar study of the site. Fortunately, it was in the view of the 1000-foot radio telescope at Arecibo, Puerto Rico, a powerful instrument operated by Cornell University.

Echoes of the radio waves that the huge antenna beamed at Mars bounced back to Arecibo and revealed surface roughness at the alternate site that the orbiter cameras did not see. Farther to the northwest, however, smoother terrain appeared and the radar scan confirmed it. The third site lay at 47.5 degrees west—about 460 miles from the A-1 landfall. It seemed to be a relatively level landscape between two regions of fluvial erosion marked by ridges and gullies; it was unmarred by rivers of mud, sand, and water that had flowed out of the highlands on the rim of the Chryse Basin. Although near an area of channel deposits, the site resembled lunar mare terrain. Even though it was not a region of ancient stream flow, the biology experimenters conceded that the likelihood of finding evidence of life there was reasonably high since the site lay at a low point in the basin where the atmosphere was dense enough to hold a substantial amount of water vapor during the heat of a summer's day.

The site selection process was an agonizing one. The scientific teams, concerned with their investigations in geology, seismology, chemistry, and meteorology, as well as biology, had to make compromises in their surmises and expectations. Although the third site was not as promising in terms of biology and was, perhaps, geologically less interesting than the earlier ones, it offered a more reasonable chance of getting the lander down without an accident, and that had to be the first priority. Radar studies by Arecibo and by the smaller dish (210 feet) at Goldstone, California, showed that Mars was five times as rough as Moon.

On July 14, the orbit of *Viking I* was adjusted for the landing July 20. Touchdown was computed to occur at 5:11:49.8 A.M. Pacific Daylight Time—Earth received time. As landing preparations went forward, a multichannel radiometer aboard the orbiter mapped surface temperatures below.

It returned data showing that temperatures at the south pole, where it was winter, fell below the freezing point of carbon dioxide at the average pressure (6.1 millibars) of the Mars atmosphere. This meant that carbon dioxide was precipitating—snowing—at the pole; presumably that process accounted for the polar cap.

Of critical importance to the expectation of finding life on Mars was the amount of water vapor in the atmosphere. As mentioned earlier, it was first detected about a decade ago by Earth-based telescopic observations. Compared with Earth, the amount was tiny, an average of about 10 microns—one hundredth of a millimeter—if all of it rained out over the surface of the planet. Earth's atmosphere contains several thousand times more water.

The Mars Atmosphere Water Detector team leader, C. Barney Farmer of JPL, reported that observations by the infrared grating spectrometer on the orbiter showed 20 to 30 microns of water vapor at midday over a cold region called Hellas in the southern hemisphere, where it was winter. Water vapor readings at the northern hemisphere landing sites ranged only from 7 to 9 microns. However, they were limited by the geometry of the orbiter's flight path to times of the day when the temperature was low. Farmer pointed out that the amount of water vapor at any particular locale could change drastically with 100-degree fluctuations in temperature during the day.

The moisture cycle was visualized in this way: In the late afternoon, as the sun goes down, moisture in the air freezes out and forms a thin layer of ice on the ground—about the thickness of a sheet of tissue paper. When the sun rises, the ice vaporizes and rises into the cold air where it condenses into a morning fog. As the sun warms the ground and the air is heated, the fog dissipates. The maximum amount of water would be expected to be present in the atmosphere at noon or shortly thereafter. Then, as the afternoon progresses and sun begins to sink, the vapor once more condenses as a low fog. Farmer speculated that as the vapor mixes with dust on the ground, it might go through a liquid phase so that small amounts of water might then be available to microorganisms before it finally freezes.

A "SUPER-NOMINAL" LANDING

In the small hours of Tuesday morning, July 20, several hundred news media and JPL employees converged on the Von Karman auditorium of the Laboratory to observe the first American attempt to land a reconnaissance vehicle on Mars. Nestled in the foothills of the San Gabriel Mountains at Pasadena, the Jet Propulsion Laboratory is a space age landmark. On this historic morning, the geometrical complex of highrise and horizontal buildings, containing laboratories, shops, and offices, was brilliantly lighted. The glow could be seen for miles along Interstate 210, the Foothill Freeway.

At 1:51 A.M. July 20, the flight team received a signal from *Viking* that the lander was detached from the orbiter by the detonation of small explosives, following a "Go" signal from JPL that was transmitted 45 minutes earlier.

Springs pushed the lander away from the orbiter. Attitude control thrusters on the lander then put it into position for the 22-minute de-orbit burn. Seven minutes after separation, the thrusters fired and changed the flight path of the Viking lander from one around Mars to one that would intersect the surface of the planet at the planned landfall. The orbiter meanwhile continued on its rounds, photographing the surface. It would serve as a communications satellite to relay photos and scientific data from the Golden Plains to Earth when the lander was on the ground.

When the descending lander reached an altitude of 806,490 feet, the entry sequence was started and the radar altimeter was turned on. A controller monitoring the radio signals from the altimeter called out the numbers. At 595,000 feet, the lander was coming in at 15,000 feet (2.8 miles) a second; at 500,000 feet, the rate of descent had risen to 15,350 feet a second, and at 400,000 feet to 15,400 feet a second. A voice announced: "Two points on the altitude-time curve are right on the nominal." All was well. The sighs of relief could be heard from the control room over the public address system.

At 314,000 feet, the descent rate was 15,480 feet a second. A pitch-down program, meanwhile, aligned the squat vehicle so that it would experience lift when it hit the sensible atmosphere at 100,000 feet or 19 miles. Lift would reduce the heating on the aeroshell which served as a heat shield.

When the lander hit the top of the sensible atmosphere, an accelerometer on board registered 0.05 gravities. Gravitational forces built up quickly as the thicker atmosphere slowed the vessel's plunge. There was a minute of radio blackout as the heat of friction generated an ionized sheath of gas around the vehicle that radio waves could not penetrate. This was a familiar phenomenon during the reentry of manned spacecraft into Earth's atmosphere where the blackout lasted longer.

At 100,000 feet, the descent rate fell to 10,900 feet a second and the "G" force rose to 6.8 gravities. The lander passed through "Max Q"—the region of maximum dynamic pressure in the high atmosphere—without any damage. The landing on Mars was analogous to a landing on Earth rather than to one on the Moon. The "G" forces peaked at 8.4 gravities—higher than expected—before they began to level off. At 88,000 feet, the rate of descent was 6000 feet a second. At 74,000 feet, the rate fell to 2372 feet a second.

Controllers noted with satisfaction that the temperature of the aeroshell protecting the lander was cooling now. At 65,000 feet, the vehicle was dropping at 1800 feet a second. Controllers now held their breath, waiting for the signal that a mortar had fired to deploy the parachute. The parachute came out exactly on time and, simultaneously, the aeroshell was jettisoned. The lander swung under the 'chute, but was quickly stabilized by attitude control jets.

The parachute was cast off and the terminal descent rocket engine ignited at 4921 feet. The rate of descent slowed very quickly, to 188 feet a second at 2600 feet; 140 feet a second at 366 feet; 73 feet a second below that.

"Green for touchdown," called a voice from the control room. The babble of voices in the auditorium ceased. "Eight feet a second. Touchdown! Touchdown! We have touchdown!"

Cheering broke out in the control center, was picked up in the crowded auditorium, and spread throughout the campus, misty in a pearly dawn. "Roger, down!" cried a voice in the control room. "Looking good." A torrent of voices came over the public address and television loudspeakers. "Fantastic!" "Fabulous!" "Beautiful!" "It was nominal!" "No. It was Super-Nominal!" The United States was on Mars, safe and sound. Project Manager Martin, Pickering, the retired JPL Director, and Administrator Fletcher shook hands with each other and all around. "Thank you, gentlemen, for an excellent job," said Fletcher. It seemed to some of us like the understatement of the year. But then, most of the members of the flight team were a little stunned at what they had wrought: A flawless landing on Mars the first time. A newsman asked Martin to describe the landing in non-technical terms. He said: "Everything worked just fine, like it was supposed to." In the space business, where Murphy's law that anything that can fail probably will holds sway, that landing was nothing less than a miracle. But it happened. We all saw it; and so history will record it.

Because Mars was at that time 19 light minutes (212 million miles) from Earth, the lander actually had been squatting on ground at Chryse Planitia during those hectic moments when we were all following the process of its descent. And while the control team was gasping and sweating, the busy little machine was industriously photographing its footpad and the surrounding landscape under the direction of its computer.

The flight team had calculated that it would receive the touchdown signals at 5:11:49.8 Pacific Daylight Time, but the signal actually was received at 5:12:07 PDT. It was 17 seconds later than expected, the only deviation from the "super-nominal" landing. The lander made physical contact with the Mars surface 19 minutes earlier, at 4:53 A.M. PDT. In terms of Mars local time, based on a 24.6 hour day, it was late afternoon but the light was still good. The camera presented the viewers at JPL with a magnificent panorama of Mars landscape in the late afternoon of a summer day. It was a desert scene of marvelous contrast and immaculate detail, covering 300 degrees of azimuth. Nothing comparable to this photo had ever been received before from another planet. It had the picture quality of a photo taken on Earth with the same camera. Compared to those murky pictures transmitted by *Mariner IV* eleven years ago, the first surface photos of Mars were picture postcards. They illustrated revolutionary advances in interplanetary photographic technique in little more than a decade.

In the panoramic photo, the lander soil sampler housing looms in the immediate foreground. The surface is fairly dark and the littered rocks exhibit both light and dark faces. Some are quite sharp as though recently cleaved or fractured; others are wind eroded or sand blasted. There is a scattered profusion of them. Since the lander cameras stand only 4 feet 3 inches above the ground, and because Mars is smaller than Earth, the horizon is closer to the camera than it would appear to a photographer of medium height shooting a desert scene on Earth.

On the left of the panoramic photo appears a bright prominence. Possibly it is the rim of old craters, three of which could now be detected on the horizon. A variety of rock shapes show up clearly in the foreground, indicating unusual erosion processes. The sky is bright, probably from the light scattering property of dust in the atmosphere. The brightness makes it appear similar to the sky of Earth. There is an illusion that this scene could be on Earth. Such an illusion was never generated by photos of the landscape of the Moon and its black sky.

The next event after the landing photos had been exhibited on the television monitors was the ceremonial news conference. NASA officials and Viking project scientists arranged themselves on the stage of the Von Karman auditorium and, in the euphoria that gripped them, ideas and feelings surfaced that had been long repressed.

Noel W. Hinners, the youthful associate administrator for space science, shed bureaucratic restraint and embraced the audience with enthusiasm. "I'm almost speechless," he confessed, eyes moist. "Really, I can't think about science right now. My heart is beating fast and I had tears in my eyes this morning for the first time, I guess, since I got married. It's really an emotional experience. It's mind-boggling what has happened; that we're going out and we're going to go farther."

Administrator Fletcher issued the customary congratulations. "It really surprised me how perfectly everything worked," he said.

President Ford, who had seen the Mars photos on television in the White House, praised the team with enthusiasm. If history said little else about his administration, it would have to record that the first successful landing on Mars had occurred then.

When the official utterances were fulfilled, a correspondent asked Fletcher: What should America do next about Mars? It was one of those simplistic yet hard policy questions bureaucrats talk around. Of all the NASA administrators since the ebullient Webb, Fletcher had exhibited the most caution in discussing such matters. But in the euphoria of the moment, the bureaucratic tabus and inhibitions fell away, and Fletcher responded surprisingly:

"Well, obviously, we are not going to do like the first Vikings and leave it to somebody else to exploit. There's no question but that we, the Americans, will go back and visit Mars, and I think we'll do some of it with persons. I think the only question is what timetable it will be on. And I think we have various ideas of what that timetable should be in NASA. And as time goes on, our ideas improve."

For the moment, caution had been swept away by the Viking landing on the magic morning of July 20, 1976. But beyond the confines of JPL, there was no doubt that the old skepticism about the social value of space exploration persisted. In a letter on the editorial page of the *Chicago Sun-Times*, a reader commented: "For the city dweller breathing poisoned air, for the cancer patient in want of a cure or for the unemployed longing for a respectable and steady job, the televised shots of a Martian landscape may hold little meaning."

One must wonder: How much meaning did the voyages of Columbus and Magellan hold for the Iberian peasant?

THE NEW MARS

In the brief period of the descent from orbit, the Viking lander instruments resolved questions about Mars that had puzzled scientists for centuries. Alfred O. C. Nier of the University of Minnesota reported that the upper atmosphere mass spectrometer saw nitrogen and argon as well as carbon dioxide in the Mars atmosphere. The argon content was small—about 1½ percent. It was nothing to worry about so far as the organic chemistry experiment was concerned, for that amount, although half again as much as the 1 percent argon in Earth's atmosphere, would not affect the operation of the gas chromatograph mass spectrometer.

The discovery of nitrogen, perceived for the first time, was exciting. The data indicated on a concentration of 3 percent. Thus, for the first time, the composition of the Mars atmosphere became fully known: 95 percent carbon dioxide, 2 to 3 percent nitrogen, 1 to 2 percent argon, and 0.1 to 0.4 percent oxygen.

The amount of hitherto undetected nitrogen was good news to biologists for they would have been hard pressed to account for life on Mars without it. Nitrogen is a basic element in proteins and is present in all terrestrial living material. However, it becomes available to living organisms only through fixation or conversion into compounds with other elements. On Earth, nitrogen is extracted from the atmosphere and fixed by soil bacteria. What fixation process might exist on Mars? Michael B. McElroy of Harvard University suggested that nitrogen could be fixed in the atmosphere by ionization and thus made available to living organisms in the form of nitrous oxide. He surmised that historically the amount of nitrogen available on Mars to biology was large enough so that there was no reason to exclude the evolution of life on that account.

Atmosphere pressure at the landing site was registered at 7.7 millibars, or nearly eight-tenths of 1 percent of Earth's sea level pressure. Men would need at least light weight space suits and breathing gear to roam the Golden Plains. The pressure indicated that the landing site lay 2.9 kilometers below the mean surface of Mars—the 6.1 millibar level, Alvin Seiff of the Ames Research Center calculated. It was about as cool as an antarctic dry valley on a late autumn day. The temperature at the time of landing in the afternoon was 241 degrees Kelvin, or −30 C. (−22 F.).

The automatic weather station on the lander had not been idle and it transmitted data for the first weather report from Mars. It was recited by Seymour L. Hess of Florida State University as follows on July 21: "Light winds from the east in the late afternoon changing to light winds from the southeast after midnight. Maximum wind was 15 miles per hour. Temperatures ranged from −122 F. just after dawn to −22 F., but this was not the maximum. Pressure was steady at 7.7 millibars."

THE SKY IS PINK

On July 21, or Sol 1, the lander presented its operators 200 million miles away with the first color pictures of the Golden Plains landfall. The red soil confirmed what mankind has known since the stone age—that Mars is colored red. But in the first photo transmission, the sky was colored blue, a lovely, light blue. Everyone was pleased about that; here was another planet with a homey blue sky. It was beautiful. When one looked closely at the hard copies of the color photo, the blue sky was streaked with pink.

The blue sky lasted hardly a day. James A. Pollock of Ames explained that it was only an illusion, caused by erroneous color calibration in the photographic process. In reality, said Pollock, the sky of Mars was pink, deriving that tint from the red dust particles suspended in the atmosphere. The particles derived their color from a light coating of iron oxide—rust.

Later color photos showing the color chart on the lander and the U.S. flag with bright red stripes confirmed that the sky was pink; that the ground was a rusty, orange-red, and that some of the boulders that were not oxidized were a bluish gray.

No one had ever dared predict a pink sky at Mars. Not even science fiction dared it. In this instance, truth was stranger than science fiction.

Inevitably, problems began to crop up; Murphy's law began to work in the new environment. The seismometer became stuck. Its quake-sensor, a pendulum and signal coil suspended between two magnets, had been secured or "caged" by three pins to protect it against the landing jar. Ground motions transmitted through the lander structure would cause the pendulum to swing and thus displace the coil between the magnets. This would generate an electrical current proportional to the amount of motion. The pins, however, prevented the pendulum and coil from moving. After the landing, small motors on the instrument were commanded to pull out the pins and "uncage" the quake sensor. Two of the pin-puller motors extracted their pins, but the third did not. It was surmised that an electrical connection had failed and that current was not reaching the motor. There was a second seismometer on *Viking II*, now rapidly nearing Mars, but the seismologists wanted two instruments at some distance apart to locate the epicenter of Mars quakes.

Another problem appeared in the all-important soil sample collector. During a test, its 10-foot boom jammed. Analysis showed that the jamming was caused by a pin that had not fallen to the surface, as it was supposed to do, when a shroud covering the sterilized collector head was ejected. Perhaps, Martin reasoned, the boom had not been extended far enough the first time to allow the pin to drop out. The team signaled the computer to extend the boom farther than on the first test. The pin dropped out.

On Sol 8—July 28—the soil sampler was commanded to fill the hoppers of the biology experiment, the GCMS organic chemistry experiment, and the X-ray fluorescence spectrometer that would do the inorganic chemistry experiment.

Sensors in these instruments reported that the biology experiment had received seven cubic centimeters of Mars dirt that was distributed mechanically to the pyrolytic release experiment chamber, the labelled release experiment chamber, and the gas exchange chamber. Another load of Mars soil had been deposited in the X-ray fluorescence spectrometer, its sensor said. But from the vital organic chemistry analysis instrument—the GCMS—there was no indication of a soil deposit.

RESULTS—AND AMBIGUITIES

The progress of the lander experiments was related at JPL in daily briefings, a process that caused the search for life by the semi-intelligent robot to unfold in installments, like an interplanetary soap opera. For the scientists, the experience of trying to interpret, for the laymen of the press, incomplete and often ambiguous data as received day by day must have been uncomfortable, if not nightmarish.

Accustomed to working in secluded laboratories, the scientists found themselves functioning in a fishbowl, their every speculation, premise, and hope on display. Never before had a scientific investigation of this magnitude been so publicly prosecuted. As Norman H. Horowitz of the biology group expressed it: "What we're trying to do is normal science in an abnormal environment." He meant the environment of the fishbowl, not of Mars. "I want to emphasize," he added, "that if this were normal science, we wouldn't even be here. We would be working in our labs for three more months. You wouldn't even know what was going on until we came out to tell you the answer. Having to work in a fishbowl like this—none of us is used to it."

Assuming that the CCMS had missed receiving its soil load from the surface sampler, the controllers made a second attempt to dump soil into the instrument. The collector head dutifully dug a second trench in the red soil, took a bite of it in its jaws and began to elevate. But as the boom began to retract, it jammed again. Once more the engineers launched an analysis to see what was wrong with it.

The first instrument to yield results was the X-ray fluorescence spectrometer, which made the inorganic chemistry analysis. Priestley Toulminn III of the U.S. Geological Survey reported that the main constituents were iron (14 percent!), calcium, silicon, titanium, and aluminum. Benton C. Clark of Martin Marietta Aerospace, Denver, another inorganic chemistry investigator, disclosed that such trace elements as vanadium, molybdenum, rubidium, strontium, and zirconium seemed to be missing. That was curious because they are present in Earth and in lunar soil.

Was the lack of trace elements an indication that the Mars surface was relatively primitive and considerably less differentiated than the surface of the Earth? And could such an indication be inferred from a thimbleful of dirt from a planet with a land area greater than the land area of Earth?

On August 1, or Sol 12 by the Viking calendar, the gas exchange experiment registered an unexpected surge of oxygen in the test cell. The rapid emission of the gas was astonishing. About 1 cubic centimeter of soil in the chamber had been moistened by an injection of water vapor and allowed to "incubate" in an atmosphere of helium, krypton, and carbon dioxide. In theory, if the water vapor stimulated metabolic activity in microorganisms, the resulting data would show the emission of hydrogen, nitrogen, methane, and oxygen as by-products.

The oxygen emission could be the result of a biological process, said Harold Klein, the team leader, but it could also be the product of a nonbiological reaction of something in the soil with the injected water. Photosynthesis was ruled out because there was no light source in the test cell. "We believe we have at least preliminary evidence of a very active surface material," Klein said. "It may mimic biological activity."

If nothing else was demonstrated, the gas exchange test had pointed a way toward a quick process of extracting oxygen from the red soil of Mars. Someday, when men arrived, that might be an important contribution to their life support systems. But at this moment, the reaction was confusing. A team of experts was recruited to see if the oxygen emission could be duplicated by some inorganic process.

Advancing the search for life a halting step further, data from the labelled release experiment came in. Its soil sample had been doped with a nutrient containing carbon[14] as a radioactive tracer. If microbes were present and consumed the "chicken soup," as the team referred to the nutrient, they would cause the emission of gas containing the carbon[14] tracer. It seemed to be a straightforward way of getting evidence that something was living in the dirt, but the results were not straightforward at all.

Five days after the incubation period began, a fairly high level of radioactive gas was detected in the chamber. Eureka! Life? No, not quite, although Klein admitted that: "It looks at first indication very much like biological activity." If, indeed, the oxygen produced in the gas exchange test and the radioactive carbon dioxide that appeared in the labelled release test were products of living things, Klein conceded, "microbial life is more intense and developed than on Earth."

Perhaps it was hungrier and thirstier and reacted more vehemently to food and water from Earth. If so, it could be dangerous to Earth. But such speculations were premature. While there was no way to rule out the oxygen and labelled gas reactions as biological, there was also no way to rule them in. "It is possible that we are seeing oxidation of one or more of the radioactive materials used in the experiment by a nonbiological process," Klein said, commenting on the labelled release data.

As work progressed, the biology team began to favor a nonbiological reaction for these effects, even though no one professed to be able to classify it.

Mysterious Mars! It exhibited a species of chemistry no one seemed to understand. Carefully, and with great deliberation, the team avoided the "Occam's razor" (simpler) explanation that biological processes were at work. The chemists and the biologists wanted clearer signs of life before they would admit its presence; they wanted chemical data that would tell them in no uncertain terms that "here there be tygers." Gilbert V. Levin of Biospherics, Inc., a team member, characterized the oxygen emission in the gas exchange test as something between a biological and a nonbiological response.

In both the gas exchange and labelled release tests, the early data became even more ambiguous with time because they levelled off too quickly to suggest growth, a principal characteristic of life. In the labelled release cell, there was no increase in the gas that would show that growth was occurring, Levin said. He summarized the views of his colleagues: "We must try every other possibility to explain the response we are seeing before absolutely being driven to the conclusion that we can explain it only by living reactions."

So far, the gas exchange test had been run only with water vapor. The next step was to add 2 cubic centimeters of a nutrient soup containing 19 amino acids, vitamins, other organic compounds, and salts. This was done and on August 6 Vance I. Oyama of Ames, a biology investigator, announced: "We are waiting with bated breath for the results to fall."

Meanwhile, a second shot of soup was injected into the labelled release test chamber. The elixir was a dilute, aqueous solution of formate, glycine, lactate, alanine, and glycolic acid, laced with carbon 14 as the tracer.

This time, there was no sudden, big emission of oxygen from the gas exchange test. Whatever had produced it when the water vapor was injected was no longer working. Perhaps the oxidant had been used up. Observers settled down to watch for a more orderly emission of gases that would indicate life processes going on at a familiar level.

The second shot of nutrient into the labelled release test cell produced another burst of radioactive gas, however. The radioactivity in the nutrient reappeared in the gas emission at a level of 1200 counts per minute in just eight minutes. Then the count rate dropped 30 percent. That was confusing. The biological reaction the initial surge suggested should have continued to emit the radioactive gas or to increase it. Apparently, if metabolism was occurring, it was not accompanied by growth—and that was puzzling.

For twelve days, nothing had been heard from the third biology experiment—the pyrolytic release test. In this one, carbon metabolism, mainly by photosynthesis, was to be stimulated by artificial light.

After a quarter of a cubic centimeter of soil was deposited in the test cell, radioactive carbon monoxide and carbon dioxide were injected into it and the "sun"—a xenon lamp—was turned on. Norman Horowitz explained that the lamp simulated the sunlight that reaches the surface of Mars, except for some of the ultraviolet wavelengths that were screened out in the test cell by a quartz window. Horowitz said that the shorter wavelengths could produce a false positive in the experiment because organic compounds are synthesized by the short, ultraviolet wavelengths acting on carbon monoxide, water vapor, and silicates.

On August 7, Horowitz announced that the team had completed the first of three runs on the pyrolytic release experiment. After five days, the "sun" was turned off. If microorganisms were present and had learned how to do photosynthesis, they would have extracted the carbon[14] from the atmosphere and converted it into compounds for growth. The next step was to vaporize the organic compounds and determine whether any radioactive gas was released.

The sample was first heated and purged of its atmosphere by an injection of helium to get rid of nonbiological carbon[14]. Then the sample was cooked at 700 degrees C. to break down organic compounds and free any radioactive carbon that had been fixed or assimilated.

The metabolized carbon would come off in oxidized form as radioactive carbon dioxide. Its detection by a radiation counter could be considered evidence that a biological process had been at work.

Had any such gas appeared? It had, Horowitz reported. It was detected by the counter, which showed a peak rate of 573 counts a minute. Background radiation from the radioisotope electric generators had to be taken into account. It amounted to 477 counts a minute.

When this was subtracted from the total, it left a net of 96 counts a minute. That was a signature of the carbon[14] that had been fixed in an organic compound and released when the compound was cooked. The count was comparable to that from a test run of soil from a dry valley in Antarctica—the nearest Earthly analog of the cold, tropical desert where *Viking I* squatted on Mars. The antarctic sample had yielded 106 counts of radioactivity.

Was this proof positive of biology? No, said Horowitz. "I want to emphasize that we have not discovered life on Mars; we have not! The data point we have is conceivably of biological origin but the biological explanation is only one of a number of alternative explanations that have to be excluded. We hope by the end of this mission to have excluded all but one."

If no carbon assimilation process had taken place, Horowitz said, the experiment would have seen only 15 counts per minute in the data. The peak of 96 counts showed that some conversion process had operated. Was it biological? It could have been a photo-catalytic process peculiar to the soil and environment of Mars, the scientist speculated.

To be sure, a control experiment would have to be run in which the sample would be sterilized before the radioactive gases were added. If a carbon assimilation effect were again demonstrated, the likelihood that it represented living organisms would drop toward zero. Beyond the control, the whole experiment had to be repeated.

"In biology," said Horowitz, "it's a cardinal rule that you don't believe it until it happens twice."

Klein was asked at a news conference: Is what you see biological activity?

"It could be," admitted the team leader. "But we've done only half the experiment. I am very tantalized." Later, when the control test was run on a heat-sterilized sample, no evidence of carbon assimilation was seen.

On the morning of August 7, *Viking II* arrived at Mars and was inserted into a 27.6 hour orbit around the red planet with a 39-minute braking burn of its main engine. It was the third time that the United States had put a spacecraft into orbit around another planet, noted A. Thomas Young, the mission director, with pride, and all had gone well. *Viking II* was in position to drop its lander on the forty-sixth parallel of the northern hemisphere and it began a photo reconnaissance of the region as it swung to within 941.8 miles of the surface.

The next day, the soil sampler was freed of the paralysis that had mysteriously caused it to be stuck for days with a soil sample in its jaws. The engineers radioed instructions to it to complete the delivery of the sample to the gas chromatograph mass spectrometer so that the organic chemistry analysis could proceed. Organically, the soil was barren.

THE ULTIMATE ANSWER

On August 10, 1976, on the twenty-first day after *Viking I* had landed on the Golden Plains, members of the scientific team assembled in the Von Karman auditorium of JPL to review the results of the search for life thus far. A year had passed since these investigators and others had discussed the prospects of that search at a pre-launch symposium in Florida. Then the Viking team faced the uncertainties of launch, of the 400-million-mile journey part way around the sun to Mars, and of the landing. Now the scientists faced the uncertainties of discoveries they did not understand. The raw question of was there life on Mars had been refined to another: Were the reactions they were seeing in the test cells of the biology experiment the products of biological or of nonbiological chemistry? It was a more complex question; it implied the possibility that on the surface of Mars there existed a stage of chemical evolution that was neither life nor non-life, a stage through which the Earth had passed eons ago; it implied, also, a peculiar kind of soil chemistry on Mars that chemists had not encountered anywhere on Earth.

Harold Klein, the biology leader, reviewed the results of the first round of biology experiments. What experimenters had seen were real data, not false signals from quirks in the instruments or electronics, he said.

"We believe that none of the inferences we are drawing from the data are attributable to instrument malfunctions or anomalies," he said. "We believe that Mars is really talking to us and is telling us something. The question is whether Mars is talking with a forked tongue or giving us the straight dope."

At best, the message of Mars was oracular; it could be interpreted in several ways. On Earth, the data might have been interpreted as biological activity, of a sort, but on Mars, as Norman Horowitz suggested, one had to consider a "Martian explanation." It was possible that Mars has some unique, chemical capabilities that give the kind of results scientists have not yet observed in terrestrial samples, Horowitz said.

As an example, he cited the photosynthesis (pyrolytic release) experiment in which ultraviolet had been filtered out of the light from the xenon arc lamp to exclude the possibility it would react with the soil sample and create organic compounds. Perhaps these compounds were created in the highly reactive soil of Mars by longer wavelengths that have no such effects on Earth. That had to be investigated, he said, along with other, nonbiological, carbon fixing reactions.

There was a long way to go to resolve the question of life, Horowitz said, adding candidly: "Nobody wants to be wrong in public on a question as important as that of life on Mars."

Leslie E. Orgel, an investigator from the Salk Institute, San Diego, commented: "Six months ago, we were talking about the potential dangers of bringing back a sample of Martian soil. And I said, somewhat rashly, that if someone would bring back a sample, I would be happy to eat it. I must say that in the light of what *Viking I* has found, I will withdraw that offer."

Orgel did not mean to imply that he believed Viking had found biota, but simply that the oxidation proclivity the soil had exhibited would make it likely to burn the mouth. "We're seeing some fancy chemistry," he added, "but it's not yet out of the range of what you can get with inorganic materials." The experiments had produced biological systems, but the organic chemistry analysis had failed to confirm them.

Joshua Lederberg characterized the stage scientists had reached in the search for life on Mars as "puzzling, difficult, tendentious." "What is plain," he said, "is that Mars is seething with chemical activity, to a surprising degree. The question now is whether that chemical activity is strictly non-organic and whether one can account for all of the observations in ways that are not bizarre by non-organic hypotheses.

"We're not able to decide whether we're looking at a primitive inorganic process—you may think of it as being an early stage of the chemical evolution of a planet—or whether it has been incorporated in cells and become a part of an evolutionary system."

The senior scientist added that even if new results suggested enzymes with a high degree of biological specificity instead of simple soil complexes, "we would still not have reached the fundamental criteria of what we mean by living organisms."

"For that," said Lederberg, "we have to see growth. We have to see reproduction. We have to see the possibility of evolution and diversification."

He was asked: When will we know the ultimate answer to the question of whether there is life on Mars?

He answered: "We may not be able to answer that question on the basis of the Viking mission. In fact, I think that's the likeliest outcome—that with the completion of the remaining experiments we'll be roughly in the position we are now—of having a set of very exciting and very provocative data and not too likely to have been able to make a categorical conclusion about it."

Not all of Lederberg's colleagues agreed with that outlook, but it was clear now that the search for life on Mars had only begun with Viking.

For Viking was a machine. And machines can only reconnoiter. On September 3, 1976, *Viking II* landed on the rock-strewn plains of a subpolar region called Utopia, nearly half way around Mars from *Viking I*. As on the Moon, reconnaissance would be followed by exploration. And exploration was man's role. And man's fate.

NOTES

CHAPTER I   VINLAND

1. The history of the Norse voyages to Vinland is related in sagas, or prose narratives that were written down a century later on vellum from oral accounts. None of the Icelandic sagas were transcribed until the beginning of the twelfth century, when Ari Thorgilsson (also known as Ari, the Learned) began to record them. See R. A. Skelton, *The Vinland Map, The Vinland Map and the Tartar Relation* (New Haven, Conn.: Yale University Press, 1965).

However, the first written reference to Vinland appears to have been in Adam of Bremen's "Descriptio Insularum Aquilonis," which was composed about 1070. Adam of Bremen said that he got his information about Vinland from Sven Estridsson, the well-informed king of Denmark, who died in 1076.

The earliest Icelandic reference is only a passing one in the "Islendingabok" ("Icelandic Book"), by Ari the Learned circa 1124. About this period, according to Skelton, an Icelandic geographical text referred to the discovery of Vinland by Leif Ericsson (often spelled Eiriksson) and to two other lands in the western Ocean, Helluland and Markland. The text was prefixed to an itinerary of the Holy Land written by Abbot Nicolaus Bergsson of Tvera, according to Skelton.

Two principal sagas tell different versions of the Vinland period. One is the "Vinland History of the Flat Island Book" ("Flatcyjarbok"), so-called because it was owned by a family living on Flat Island in Broad Firth on the northwest coast of Iceland. It is commonly called also the "Tale of the Greenlanders."

The second main source is the "Saga of Eric the Red," which is derived from two texts. One of them is the "Hauk's Book" ("Hauksbok"), written by or at the direction of Hauk Erlendsson, a "law man" of Iceland in 1294. Hauk was a direct descendant of Thorfinn Karlsefni, who led one of the Vinland expeditions. The other text is a collection of sagas compiled in the fifteenth century. In addition, there is a codex compiled in the last two decades of the fourteenth century that includes the "Saga of Eric the Red," the "Tale of the Greenlanders," and the "Saga of Olaf Tryggvason," the Norse king who spread Christianity from Norway to Iceland and Greenland. All of these documents are preserved in the Royal Library in Copenhagen.

For the most part, I have relied on translations published by Gwyn Jones of University College, Cardiff, in his *North Atlantic Saga* (New York: Oxford University Press, 1964), and in J. Franklin Jameson, ed., *Original Narratives of Early American History* (New York: Scribner, 1906).

According to recent comparisons of the "Saga of Eric the Red" and the "Tale of the Greenlanders" by Jones and by Samuel Eliot Morison, *The European Discovery of America, the Northern Voyages* (New York: Oxford University Press, 1971), the "Tale of the Greenlanders" is the older of the two versions. I have used it as the main framework of the narrative. From a nonscholarly, journalistic point of view, it seems to me to be more coherent than the "Saga of Eric the Red."

Skelton points out that the "Saga" represents an Icelandic version of the Vinland story and the "Tale," a Greenlandic version. This may explain, to some extent, the discrepancies between the two.

The "Tale" tells of six voyages concerning Vinland—those of: Bjarni Herjolfsson, who sights the coast of eastern Canada when he is blown off course while en route to Greenland; Leif, who follows up Bjarni's sighting and builds a base in Vinland; his brother Thorvald, who is killed on a follow-up expedition; another brother, Thorstein, who seeks Thorvald's body but never reaches Vinland; Karlsefni, who attempts to colonize the new land; and, finally, Leif's half sister, Freydis, and her husband, Thorvard.

In the "Saga," these six voyages are condensed into three. Bjarni Herjolfsson is not mentioned. His accidental discovery is made by Leif; Thorstein attempts a follow-up but is storm-tossed at sea and does not reach the coast; and Karlsefni's expedition includes Thorvald, Freydis, and others.

I have elected to follow the sequences and events in the "Tale of the Greenlanders," adding some material from the "Saga of Eric the Red" where it seems relevant.

In the Icelandic version Karlsefni, not Leif, is the main hero, an emphasis explainable by the fact that the compiler was Karlsefni's descendant Hauk. Leif's sighting of America is summarized in only one paragraph, and no indication is given that he ever established a base there. Only Karlsefni's multiship expedition is credited with any attempt to explore and settle the new lands. The naming of Helluland, Markland, and Vinland is attributed to Karlsefni, not to Leif.

If the Greenlandic version, which attributes the discovery and naming of the lands to Bjarni and Leif, is the older, as it appears to be, the "Saga" may then be regarded as a version heavily edited by Hauk Erlendsson and his scribes to glorify Karlsefni.

2. Jones, *op. cit.* Norse sailors of the eleventh century did not know the compass nor how to determine longitude at sea. They found their way across the Atlantic Ocean by latitude sailing, using sun and stars. To find latitude, they used a shadow board, or gnomon (as the classical Greeks did), to measure the length of the sun's shadow at noon or a notched pole, a forerunner of the mariner's cross-staff, to find the height of the sun (or north star) above the horizon.

To sail from Norway to Greenland (Gwyn Jones), the ship's master departing from Bergen sailed about thirty miles up the coast to a landmark called Stad. It was on the same degree of latitude as the landfall he expected to make in Greenland. After passing the Faeroe Islands, he would reach the longitude of Iceland to the south of the island in about seven days, assuming fair weather and a following wind. In another seven days, he should sight the east coast of Greenland, about eighty miles north of Cape Farewell. Then he had to head south and west to reach the settlements on the west coast, either by rounding the cape or threading through Prins Christian Sund.

If he wanted to go to Vinland, he could turn southwest for the east coast of Canada, Jones adds, until he reached the southern part of Baffin Island. Heading south, he would pass the inlet of Frobisher Bay and the entrance to Hudson Bay. He would sight the forests of Labrador, and then he might look for the long, white beaches or Furdustrandir and keel-shaped Cape Porcupine—the Kjalarnes, Jones says, of the sagas.

Southward, according to this reconstructed itinerary, he would sail past Battle Harbor to Belle Isle, then to the northernmost tip of Newfoundland and Cape Bauld.

From there, he would steer his vessel into Epaves Bay, and he would see the Norse settlement near the stream now called Black Duck Brook.

3. The most famous Viking ship known to this century is a longship unearthed at Gokstad, Norway and preserved at Oslo. The vessel was built about the middle of the ninth century, according to a model displayed at the Smithsonian Museum of History and Technology, Washington, D.C. The ship was seventy-nine feet long with a beam of sixteen and one-half feet and measured six feet four inches from the keel bottom to the gunwale amidships.

The keel was a single oak timber fifty-seven feet nine inches long. The ship was clinker-built (the external planks overlapped like clapboarding on a frame house) of sixteen planks with calculated differences in thickness. These were joined by round-headed iron rivets held inside by iron plates. Caulking was done with tarred animal hair or wool.

According to Gwyn Jones, the hull of this vessel was held in shape by nineteen frames and crossbeams. A pine deck was laid over these, and the space below was used for storage. Although this long, slender vessel drew only three and one-half feet of water, it could cross the Atlantic Ocean. The Gokstad ship presumably was not the largest of its type, but it was a foot and one-half longer than Columbus' flagship, the *Santa Maria*, although not as wide. The *Santa Maria* had a twenty-six-inch beam and a capacity of 106 tons (Smithsonian).

4. Farley Mowat, *West Viking: The Ancient Norse in Greenland and North America* (Boston: Little, Brown, 1965). A number of differing chronologies for the voyages have been proposed by experts. Morison puts Bjarni Herjolfsson's accidental discoveries in 986, Leif's voyage to Vinland in 1001–1002, Thorvald's expedition in 1004–1005, and Karlsefni's starting in 1009.

The "Tale of the Greenlanders" indicates 985 for Bjarni's discovery, 1003–1004 for Leif's voyage to Vinland, 1005–1007 for Thorvald's expedition, 1007 for Thorstein's abortive voyage, 1009–1012 for the Karlsefni expedition, and 1012–1013 for Freydis' expedition.

The "Saga of Eric the Red" indicates that Leif's accidental discovery of Vinland was made on his return voyage from Norway in 1000, that Thorstein's voyage was made in 1001, and that Karlsefni's took place 1003–1006.

Still another chronology is proposed by Farley Mowat. Although he gives 985 as the probable year of Bjarni's discovery, Mowat has Leif going to Vinland in 995–996, Thorstein's voyage in 999, and the Karlsefni expedition in 1004–1007.

There are several historical markers that confirm some of the dates. According to Ari the Learned, Eric the Red led his first contingent of colonists to Greenland fifteen or sixteen winters before Christianity came to Iceland. Christianity became the legal religion of Iceland in 1000 or 1001, so the year when Eric established the Greenland colony was 985 or 986. The same year, Bjarni Herjolfsson arrived in Iceland seeking his father, who had gone off with Eric. Bjarni's voyage to Greenland via the east coast of Canada was thus 985 or 986.

The year 1000 was the latest that Leif Ericsson could have visited the court of King Olaf Tryggvason, for Olaf was killed later that year in the Battle of Svold.

It seems reasonable to me that Leif heard about Bjarni's discoveries in Norway rather than in Greenland. Consequently, Leif's expedition to Vinland would have taken place after 1000, either in 1001 or, more likely, in 1002. The earliest he would have returned, then, is the summer of 1003. Thorvald's voyage, in that case, would not have started before the summer of 1004. The passage of seasons described in the "Tale of the Greenlanders" shows that Thorvald and his men spent two winters in Vinland and then moved on north, toward or to Hamilton Inlet, where Thorvard was fatally wounded by a Skraeling arrow in the summer of 1006. The survivors of the expedition then returned to Vinland and spent their third winter there, sailing back to

Greenland in the spring of 1007. Thorstein, after an abortive attempt to recover his brother's body, died that winter, leaving Gudrid widowed.

Karlsefni arrived from Iceland the following summer, married Gudrid later that year, and the following summer (1009) set out for Vinland. After three winters, the expedition returned in the spring of 1012. Freydis' bloody excursion to Vinland took place after that.

Like so many uncertainties in history and science, this chronology must be qualified by a plus or minus factor; but I do not think it should be more than one year.

5. *Ibid.*
6. *Ibid.*
7. *Ibid.*
8. "Saga of Eric the Red."
9. Jones, *op. cit.*
10. "Tale of the Greenlanders."
11. *Ibid.*
12. *Ibid.*
13. Morison, *op. cit.*
14. "Tale of the Greenlanders."
15. *Ibid.*
16. Morison, *op. cit.*
17. Suggested by William Hovgaard, *Voyages of the Norsemen to America* (New York: American Scandinavian Foundation, 1914).
18. "Tale of the Greenlanders."
19. "Saga of Eric the Red."
20. *Ibid.*
21. "Tale of the Greenlanders."
22. *Ibid.*
23. Helge Ingstad, *Westward to Vinland* (London: Jonathan Cape, 1966). Geographical locations of Vinland range from Newfoundland to Cape Cod. Morison locates Helluland on Baffin Island and Markland in Labrador. An important clue to the location of Markland is the Furdustrand, the forty-mile beach (Morison says thirty miles) behind which grows a spruce forest. The description of Leif's landfall in the "Tale of the Greenlanders" suggests Belle Isle, just off the northern tip of Newfoundland Island. Belle Isle might also have been Karlsefni's Straumsey in the "Saga of Eric the Red."

Morison also suggests that the cape described in the "Saga" could have been Cape Bauld, Newfoundland, and that Leifsbudir was on the northern tip of Newfoundland Island, near the present hamlet of L'Anse-au-Meadow ("Bay of the Meadow.").

In 1964, a Norwegian explorer and archaeologist, Helge Ingstad, former governor of Spitsbergen, identified as Norse a dwelling site on the north coast of Newfoundland five miles west-southwest of Cape Bauld. The site is near L'Anse-au-Meadow on a terraced beach, 100 yards from Epaves Bay on the east side of Sacred Bay.

Excavations made by Dr. Ingstad, his wife Anne Stine, and an international group of scientists (*National Geographic*, Vol. 126, No. 5, November 1964) uncovered the foundations of turf houses and a smithy. Anne Stine found that one big house measured seventy by fifty-five feet. It had five or six rooms, several fireplaces, and a floor of packed sand or clay. Lumps of iron slag were found in several houses. In nearby peaty areas, Ingstad and others found deposits of bog iron, which they believed the Norse worked. They found the stone anvil and charcoal in the smithy. Attempts to determine the age of the relics by radiocarbon dating have yielded one reading of A.D. 860 plus or minus ninety years and another of 1060 plus or minus seventy years. Aside from pieces of worked iron, one of the most significant finds at L'Anse-au-

Meadow was a soapstone spindle whorl, a device Norse women used as a flywheel to spin a wooden shaft that twisted raw wool into yarn.

In 1914, William Hovgaard, then Professor of Naval Design and Construction at the Massachusetts Institute of Technology, published *The Voyages of the Norsemen to America*, which identified Bjarni Herjolfsson's three landfalls as northeastern Newfoundland, eastern Labrador near Hamilton Inlet, and Resolution Island off the southeast coast of Baffin Island. He placed Helluland in Baffin Land, Markland in Nova Scotia, and Vinland on the Cape Cod peninsula, with Kjalarnes on Cape Cod.

Cape Cod is a rather popular choice for Vinland. One plus factor is that grapes are more likely to have been growing there a thousand years ago than in Newfoundland. Nevertheless, the only substantial archaeological evidence of Norse habitation in North America has been found in Helge Ingstad's dig at L'Anse-au-Meadow. Whether it was occupied by Leif, Karlsefni, or another Norse party cannot be determined from this evidence, but the conclusion stands that it was Norse.

24. *Ibid.*
25. Gwyn Jones, *History of the Vikings* (New York: Oxford University Press, 1968).
26. "Tale of the Greenlanders."
27. *Ibid.*
28. *Ibid.*
29. Jameson, *op. cit.*

CHAPTER II   THE PASSAGE

1. *Geography of Claudius Ptolemy*, ed., trans., Edward Luther Stevenson (New York Public Library, 1932).
2. J. H. Parry, *The Age of Reconnaissance* (Cleveland and New York: World, 1963).
3. *Ibid.*
4. Samuel Eliot Morison, *Admiral of the Ocean Sea: A Life of Christopher Columbus* (Boston: Little, Brown, 1942).
5. *Ibid.*
6. Smithsonian Institute Museum of History and Technology, Washington, D.C.
7. Martin Waldseemuller (1470–1522) was a German cosmographer of Saint Die, Lorraine. He sketched the New World in two maps, which were published in 1507 along with a treatise, "Cosmographiae Introductio, and Vespucci's account of his voyages. He also prepared a new edition of Ptolemy that was published in 1513.
8. Morison, *op. cit.*
9. *Ibid.*
10. Longitude could not be determined with any degree of certainty until the last quarter of the eighteenth century, when clocks of sufficient reliability at sea were developed. Each fifteen degrees of longitude represents a difference of one hour in time. The difference in time between a clock set at Greenwich, England, at noon and one set on the high seas would indicate the longitude of the ship's position. In the early sixteenth century, it was easy to conclude, as did King Charles' secretary, Maximilian of Transylvania, that: "Though it was not quite sure whether the city of Malacca was within the confines of the Spaniards or the Portuguese because, as yet, nothing of the longitude had been clearly proved, yet it was quite plain that the Great Gulf [Magnus Sinus] and the people of Sinae lay within the Spanish boundary . . . this, too, was held to be most certain, that the islands which they call the Moluccas . . . lay within the Spanish western division." Charles E. Nowell, ed., *Magellan's*

Voyage Around the World, Three Contemporary Accounts (Evanston, Ill.: Northwestern University Press, 1962).

11. *Ibid.*

12. Magellan displayed a planisphere, or flat map of the world, made by Jorge Reinel, a Portuguese map maker living in Seville. It showed the Moluccas on the equator due west of Panama in the Spanish zone.

13. Charles McKew Parr, *So Noble a Captain: the Life and Times of Magellan* (New York: Crowell, 1953).

14. *Ibid.*

15. The office of Holy Roman Emperor was created in 800 A.D. when Charlemagne was crowned Imperator Augustus Romanorum by Pope Leo III as successor to the Caesars of the old Roman Empire. Successors to Charlemagne were elected by princes called electors. These were the king of Bohemia; the duke of Saxony; the duke of the Rhenish Palatinate; the margrave of Brandenburg; and the archbishops of Trier, Mainz, and Cologne. Parr says that Jakob Fugger invested 350,000 florins (about $15 million, circa 1950) in bribes to five of the seven electors on behalf of Charles I. There was no way the Spanish treasury could repay this debt short of a commercial windfall. That made Magellan's voyage of great importance not only to the king but also to the Fugger interests.

16. Parr, *op. cit.*

17. According to Parr, the spices in the hold of the *Victoria* brought 45,000 ducats ($675,000)—enough to pay all expedition costs and provide a profit.

18. The Eleven Thousand Virgins refers to the legend of Saint Ursula, who took 10,999 young virgins besides herself on a three-year cruise to escape the trial of marriage. The cruise ended at Cologne, where Attila the Hun was attacking the city and massacred the lot.

19. Nowell, *op. cit.*

20. The name of the Archipelago of Saint Lazarus was changed to the Philippine Islands by Ruy Lopez de Villalobos, who led an expedition there from Mexico to Mindanao in 1542.

21. Samar, to the north of Leyte, lies in 125 degrees east longitude at 11 degrees north latitude. If the line of demarcation is considered to have run at 46 degrees 30 minutes west of Greenwich, the Armada de Maluco sailed 188 degrees 30 minutes from it to reach Samar—an equatorial distance of 11,310 nautical miles. Considering Magellan's zigzag course from the Canary Islands, the distance covered was considerably greater than that.

22. Nowell, *op. cit.*

23. "The Voyage of Magellan," Journal of Antonio Pigafetta, trans. from the French version by Paula Spurlin Paige from the edition in the William L. Clements Library, University of Michigan. (Englewood Cliffs, N.J.: Prentice-Hall, 1969).

24. *The World Encompassed: Sir Francis Drake*, March of America Facsimile Series no. 11.

CHAPTER III   TERRA AUSTRALIS

1. When the planet Venus passes across the face of the sun, its time of transit as measured from two widely separated points on Earth provides a means of determining the parallax of the sun. When that is known, the distance from the Earth to the sun can be calculated by trigonometry. This distance, called the astronomical unit (AU), is a yardstick for the solar system.

In ancient times, Hipparchus and Ptolemy calculated the distance from the Earth to the moon by parallax, but the determination of solar parallax was much more difficult. Halley's proposal that it could be determined by observing the transit of Venus across the face of the sun offered a mathematical method that could be applied in the eighteenth century, but it was not without its difficulty.

In his "Treatise on Spherical Astronomy" (1908), Sir Robert Ball, professor of astronomy and geometry at the University of Cambridge, England, pointed out that one problem is that Venus does not orbit the sun in the ecliptic plane. Because the Venusian orbit is inclined 3 degrees 23 minutes and 35 seconds to the ecliptic, the planet passes above or below the sun most of the time when both have the same geocentric longitude. On occasions when a transit does occur, Venus is seen as a black disc on the brilliant face of the sun at its first internal contact. This is the point where the planet first appears to be entirely within the solar disc. In four hours, Venus reaches the second internal contact, the position on the other side of the disc, where the leading edge of the planet contacts the trailing edge of the solar disc. The task of each observer is to measure the time of the transit from first to second internal contacts. For each, the time will be different. The difference is the basis on which Halley determined the solar parallax.

Ball said: "The determination of the distance of the sun from the Earth is of unique importance in astronomy. When it has been found, the dimensions of the sun are easily ascertained; so are the distances of the planets and of their satellites; and the sizes and even the masses of these bodies are also deduced." He pointed out, too, that distances to the stars can be determined only with reference to the sun's distance, the base line for sidereal measurements. Thus, Cook's astronomy mission in 1768–1769 was a step not only in the exploration of the Earth but of the universe.

On the basis of the 1769 transit and also an earlier transit in 1761 solar parallax was determined as 9 seconds of arc. This value was amended during the nineteenth century to 8.5776 seconds in 1834, to 8.95 in 1870, to 8.848 in 1882, and set at 8.80 at a Paris conference in 1901.

In 1944, solar parallax was determined to be 8.79 seconds. This was later refined to 8.7942 from radar observations of Venus in 1961 yielding an average distance of 92,956,000 miles between the Earth and the sun. This is the astronomical unit.

2. *Proceedings of the Royal Society of London*, Vol. 62, No. 387.

3. James Cook, "Voyage Toward the South Pole and Around the World" (London, 1775).

4. Charles Wilkes, "Narrative of the U.S. Exploring Expedition, 1838–4?" (Philadelphia, 1845).

5. It was essential to navigation by compass to know how far the magnetic poles were offset from the geographic poles, or how much "true" north or "true" south varied from magnetic north or magnetic south. Besides the geographic south pole, which is the southern tip of the Earth's axis of rotation, and the south magnetic pole, there is a third pole in Antarctica. It is called the Pole of Inaccessibility. It is the point on the antarctic continental ice cap most distant from the coasts.

6. L. P. Kirwan, *A History of Polar Exploration* (New York: Norton, 1959).

7. *Ibid*.

8. Edward C. Thiel, C. Bentley, N. Ostenso, Albert P. Crary, "Structure of West Antarctica," *Science*, Vol. 131 (January 15, 1960).

9. Campbell Craddock, "Antarctic Geology and Gondwanaland," *Science and Public Affairs*, Vol 2, No. 10 (December 1970).

10. Eduard Suess, *Face of the Earth*, Vol. I. (Oxford: Clarendon Press, 1904.)

11. Alfred Lothar Wegener, *Origin of the Continents and Oceans*, 3rd ed. (New York: Dutton, 1926).

12. Craddock, *op. cit.*

13. Alexander L. Du Toit, *Our Wandering Continents* (New York: Hafner, 1937).
14. Richard S. Lewis, *A Continent for Science* (New York: Viking Press, 1965).
15. Donald L. Turcotte and E. Ronald Oxburgh, "Continental Drift," *Physics Today* (April 1969).
16. *Ibid.*
17. Harry H. Hess, Mid-Ocean Ridges and Tectonics of the Sea Floor. "Submarine Geology and Geophysics," *Colston Papers*, Vol. 17, London: Butterworths, 1965.
18. Maurice and John Ewing, *Bulletin of the Geological Society of America* (1959).
19. Robert S. Dietz and J. C. Holden, *Journal of Geophysics Research*, Vol. 75 (page 4939) (1970).
20. This configuration does not consider classical Gondwanaland (Africa, Antarctica, Australia, India, Madagascar, and South America) as a southern hemisphere unit, as separate from North America and Eurasia, the northern hemisphere unit called Laurasia. Drift theory shifts about, just as the continents are believed to have done.
21. P. M. Hurley, "Confirmation of Continental Drift," *Scientific American* (April 1968).
22. A. Cox, G. B. Dalrymple, and R. R. Doell, "Reversals of the Earth's Magnetic Field," *Scientific American* (February 1967).
23. *Ibid.*
24. Personal interview, December 4, 1974.
25. David H. Elliot, Edwin Harris Colbert, William J. Breed, James A. Jensen, and John S. Powell, "Triassic Tetrapods from Antarctica: Evidence for Continental Drift," *Science*, Vol. 169 (September 18, 1970).
26. Personal interview, October 15, 1974.
27. Edwin Harris Colbert, *Wandering Lands and Animals* (New York: Dutton, 1973).
28. *Ibid.*, Introduction by Laurence M. Gould.
29. In addition to Kitching, of the University of Witwatersrand, South Africa, members of the McGregor Glacier party were John Ruben, University of California, Berkeley, and Thomas Rich, Columbia University, New York. Like Colbert's group, Kitching and his colleagues were part of a geological expedition headed by Elliot.

CHAPTER IV   THE ENTERPRISE OF THE MOON

1. The Space Age pioneer Krafft A. Ehricke, chief scientific advisor on advanced programs to North American Rockwell Company's Space Division, called it "the extraterrestrial imperative" in a lecture published by the *Bulletin of the Atomic Scientists*, Vol. 27 (November 1971).
2. U.S. Senate Committee on Aeronautical and Space Sciences, *Soviet Space Programs, 1962–65*, 1966. 89th Congress, second session.
3. Y. I. Perelman, *Ziolkovsky* (Moscow, 1932).
4. Melvin Kransberg and Carrol W. Pursell, Jr., *Technology in Western Civilization*, Vol. II, "The Challenge of Space." New York: Oxford University Press, 1967.
5. Eugene M. Emme, *The History of Rocket Technology* (Detroit: Wayne State University Press, 1964); G. Edward Pendray, "Pioneer Rocket Development in the United States." In 1960, the National Aeronautics and Space Administration announced the award of $1 million to Mrs. Esther Goddard, the inventor's widow, and the Guggenheim Foundation, for government rights to Goddard's patents, "which cover basic inventions in the field of rockets, guided missiles and space exploration." The award was made on behalf of the U.S. Army, Navy, and Air Force, and NASA.

6. Milton Lehman, *This High Man, The Life of Robert Goddard* (New York: Farrar, Straus & Giroux, 1963).

7. Walter R. Dornberger, "The German V-2," in Emme, *op. cit.* Former General Walter R. Dornberger, who commanded the force that developed the V-2 in Germany, made this comment: "Technical data [regarding Goddard's work] could not be found." Almost 90 percent of Goddard's patents were not available, and the Germans never saw them. This is particularly true regarding the use of jet rudders, film cooling, stabilization, and control. Dornberger added that any group of interested and skilled people facing the same technical problems the developers of the V-2 faced would have reached the same solutions. These remarks are reprinted in Emme from a paper Dornberger presented at the annual meeting of the American Association for the Advancement of Science, Philadelphia, 1962.

8. Wernher Von Braun, Letter of February 13, 1975, to Cadet T. J. Conneran, U.S.C.C., West Point, N.Y.

9. Nicholas Daniloff, *The Kremlin and the Cosmos* (New York: Knopf, 1972).

10. Willy Ley, *Rockets, Missiles and Men in Space* (New York: Viking Press, 1968).

11. Lehman, *op. cit.*

12. Ley, *op. cit.*

13. Gregory A. Tokaty, "Soviet Rocket Technology," as reprinted in Emme, *op. cit.* Originally presented as a paper September 22, 1961, to the British Interplanetary Society in London and subsequently published in the magazine *Spaceflight*, Vol. 5, No. 2 (March 1963).

14. *Ibid.*

15. Leonid Vladimirov, *The Russian Space Bluff* (New York: Dial Press, 1973).

16. In 1950, Von Braun was asked by the Army Ordnance Corps to examine the Goddard patents and prepare an opinion as to whether and to what extent the V-2 rocket and postwar rockets developed from its designs infringed on Goddard patents. His opinion was solicited in connection with the Goddard Estate patent-infringement suit against the government. Von Braun recalled (in his letter of February 13, 1975, to Cadet T. J. Conneran, U.S.C.C.) that his report "certificated that there were indeed infringements all over the place." He said they included jet vanes for rocket flight path control, turbopumps to feed the liquid propellants from the low pressure tanks to the high pressure combustion chamber and the use of gyroscopes for flight path control.

17. Tokaty, *op. cit.*

18. R. S. Lewis, *Appointment on the Moon* (New York: Viking Press, 1969).

19. The German V-2 offensive against England began September 9, 1944, and continued intermittently until March 27, 1945, when the last rocket to fall on England struck Orpington, Kent. British government casualty summaries showed that the V-2s killed 2,754 persons and injured 6,523. The V-1 buzz bombs killed 6,184 and injured 17,181. Aircraft bombing killed 51,509 and injured 62,423.

20. U.S. Senate Committee on Armed Services, Preparedness Investigating Subcommittee, *Inquiry into Satellite and Missile Programs*, 85th Congress, first session, November 1957–January 1958.

21. Dieter Huzel, *Peenemunde to Canaveral* (Englewood Cliffs, N.J.: Prentice-Hall, 1955).

22. Tokaty, *op. cit.*

23. *Ibid.*

24. *Inquiry into Satellite and Missile Programs, op. cit.*

25. Tokaty, *op. cit.*

26. *Ibid.*

27. *Ibid.*

28. U.S. Senate Special Committee on Atomic Energy, *Hearings, Atomic Energy,* 79th Congress, first session, 1945, Part I.
29. Emme, *op. cit.*
30. Vernon Van Dyke, *The Pride and the Power* (Urbana: University of Illinois Press, 1964). Also Emme, *Aeronautics and Astronautics, a Chronology of Science and Technology in the Exploration of Space 1915–1960* (Washington, D.C.: NASA, 1961).
31. Van Dyke, *op. cit.* Reference to Lloyd V. Berkner lecture, "Science and the World of Tomorrow," Industrial College of the Armed Forces, January 19, 1962.
32. *Newsweek* (October 21, 1957).
33. *Report of the Special Committee for the IGY* (National Academy of Sciences, 1954).
34. Daniloff, *op. cit.*
35. Daniloff, *op. cit.* Reference to C. C. Furnas, "Birth Pangs of the First Satellite," *Research Trends,* Cornell Aeronautical Laboratory, Inc. (spring 1970).
36. Lewis, *op. cit.*
37. U.S. House of Representatives Committee on Science and Astronautics, *Review of the Soviet Space Program,* 90th Congress, first session, 1967. Prepared by Charles S. Sheldon, Science Policy Research Division, Legislative Ref. Sv., Library of Congress.
38. U.S. Senate Committee on Armed Services, Preparedness Investigating Subcommittee, *U.S. Guided Missile Program,* 86th Congress, 1st session, 1959. Prepared by Charles H. Donnelly, senior specialist in national defense, Legislative Ref. Sv., Library of Congress.
39. Evgeny Riabchikov, *Russians in Space,* (Moscow: Novosti Press Agency Publishing House; Garden City, N.Y.: Doubleday, 1971).
40. Lewis, *op. cit.*
41. Jerome B. Wiesner, *Where Science and Politics Meet* (New York: McGraw-Hill, 1965).
42. *Ibid.*
43. The X-15 was a rocket airplane, launched from a bomber at high altitude. It was developed jointly by the air force and NACA to explore the problems and potential of rocket aircraft. The vehicle was an advanced version of the X-1, on which research was begun in 1944 by NACA and the army air force. The ultimate aim of the X-15 program was to determine if such a vehicle could be accelerated to orbital velocity (five miles a second). In a decade of research and testing, the craft never got out of the atmosphere. Flight data the experimentation provided were useful in developing Mercury, Gemini, and Apollo spacecraft and in the Space Shuttle.
44. L. S. Swenson, Jr.; J. M. Grimwood; and C. C. Alexander, *This New Ocean: A History of Project Mercury* (Washington, D.C.: NASA, 1966).
45. *Ibid.*
46. Riabchikov, *op. cit.*
47. Lewis, *op. cit.*
48. Swenson *et al., op. cit.*
49. *Report of the Space Science Board* (National Academy of Sciences, 1961).
50. Helen Fuller, *Year of Trial: Kennedy's Crucial Decision* (New York: Harcourt Brace Jovanovich, 1962).
51. John M. Logsdon, *The Decision to Go to the Moon* (Cambridge, Mass.: Massachusetts Institute of Technology Press, 1970).
52. *Ibid.*
53. *Ibid.*
54. Van Dyke, *op. cit.*

CHAPTER V   GENESIS

1. Frank B. Gibney and George J. Feldman, *The Reluctant Spacefarers* (New York: New American Library, 1965).
2. Gherman S. Titov, *An Autobiography* (New York: Crosscurrents Press, 1962).
3. *Ibid.*
4. Vostok reentry into the atmosphere began about 18,000 kilometers from the touchdown point and lasted an hour. The retroengine was fired at 8,000 kilometers, and the spherical vessel reached the Earth's surface in thirty minutes or less. To transfer the vessel to a descent trajectory, orbital velocity was reduced by about 100 meters a second. The ship reentered at only slightly less than orbital velocity at an altitude of 90 to 100 kilometers. The high temperature phase lasted fifteen minutes, until the plunge was decelerated by brake flaps and a steel strip parachute. Titov was ejected from the cabin at an altitude of 7 kilometers and parachuted to the ground at a rate of 5 to 8 meters a second. The Vostok parachute system was activated at 4 kilometers altitude, and the main parachute deployed at 3 kilometers. The ship landed at 10 meters a second. (U.S. Senate Committee on Aeronautical and Space Sciences, *Soviet Space Programs, 1962–65*, 1966, p. 198.) 92nd Congress, first session.
5. Sir Bernard Lovell, "The Great Competition in Space," *Foreign Affairs*, Vol. 51, No. 1 (October 1972).
6. *Soviet Space Programs, 1962–65, op. cit.*
7. *Ibid.*
8. *New York Times*, August 14, 1962, p. 14.
9. U.S. House of Representatives Committee on Science and Astronautics, *Hearings, NASA Authorization, Fiscal Year 1964*, pp. 547–548. 88th Congress, first session.
10. *Soviet Space Programs, 1962–65, op. cit.*, p. 179.
11. *Ibid.*
12. *Soviet Space Programs, 1962–65, op. cit.* Report of Leon H. Herman, Library of Congress specialist in Soviet economics.
13. Robert E. Marshak, *Bulletin of the Atomic Scientists*, Vol. 18, No. 4. (April 1963).
14. *Hearings, NASA Authorization, Fiscal Year 1964, op. cit.*, p. 5.
15. *Ibid.*
16. *Public Papers of the Presidents of the United States, 1963* (Washington, D.C.: U.S. Government Printing Office, 1964), p. 277.
17. *Ibid.*
18. *Soviet Space Programs, 1962–65, op. cit.* Report of Roscoe Drummond, *Christian Science Monitor*, May 15, 1963.
19. Webb, Speech at Hartford, Conn., May 15, 1963.
20. *Congressional Record*, November 6, 1963, p. 20140. *New York Times*, October 27, 1963.
21. *Washington Post* and *New York Times*, November 7, 1963.
22. *Soviet Space Programs, 1962–65, op. cit.*
23. *Congressional Record* (daily ed.), August 9, 1963, p. 13903.
24. U.S. House of Representatives Independent Offices Committee, *Appropriation Hearings, Fiscal 1964*, p. 88. 88th Congress, first session.
25. *Soviet Space Programs, 1962–65, op. cit.*, p. 107.
26. U.S. Senate Committee on Aeronautical and Space Sciences, *Hearings*, 88th Congress, first session, 1963, pp. 3, 28.
27. Lyndon B. Johnson, Address dedicating the Douglas Aircraft Space Systems Center, California, November 14, 1963.
28. *Public Papers of the Presidents of the United States, 1963, op. cit.*, p. 887.
29. G. Harry Stine, "Big Boosters of the USSR," *Analog Science Fiction-Science Fact* (September 1969); I. N. Bubnov and Nikolai L. Kamanin, *Manned Space Stations*

(Military Publishing House of the USSR, Ministry of Defense), translation by U.S. Department of Commerce Clearinghouse for Federal Scientific and Technical Information, January 1967.

30. According to accounts in *Pravda* and *Krasnaya-zvezda* (March 22 and 27, 1965), Leonov began preparing for egress from the ship soon after it reached orbit. He breathed pure oxygen for more than an hour to get rid of nitrogen in body tissues. When cabin and airlock pressures were equalized, the hatch between the cabin and airlock was opened, and Leonov squeezed in. He then pressurized his suit and tested it for leaks. Belyayev closed the cabin hatch and reduced the airlock pressure to nearly zero before opening the outside hatch. Rechecking Leonov's spacesuit and life-support system, Belyayev then gave Leonov a "go" to climb outside.

31. Excerpts from the *Voskhod II* Press Conference, Soviet Space Programs, Appendix 16, p. 557.

32. *Soviet Space Programs, 1962–65, op. cit.*, p. 118.

33. *Washington Post*, March 19, 1965, p. A-15.

34. *Soviet Space Programs, 1962–65, op. cit.*, p. 211.

CHAPTER VI   VICTORY AND RETREAT

1. Interview with Christopher C. Kraft, Jr., July 18, 1975.

2. Interview with Robert R. Gilruth, June 21, 1975.

3. As early as March 1968, academician Leonid Sedov, a spokesman for Soviet space policy, was quoted as saying that the rocket required for the manned lunar landing already existed. Russian preparations for such a venture included the construction of tracking stations in Egypt, Mali, Guinea in West Africa, and Cuba. The 11,000-ton tracking ship *Kosmonaut Vladimir Komarov*, with a complement of 240 men, was stationed that year in Havana harbor.

4. U.S. Senate Committee on Aeronautical and Space Sciences, *Soviet Space Programs, 1966–70*, 92nd Congress, first session. Charles S. Sheldon, *The Soviet Manned Lunar Landing Program.*

5. *Ibid.*

6. Interview with Michael Collins, director, National Aeronautics and Space Museum, Washington, D.C., December 15, 1975.

7. Michael Collins, *Carrying the Fire* (New York: Ballantine Books, 1974).

8. For a detailed account, see Richard S. Lewis, *Appointment on the Moon* (New York: Viking Press, 1969), and *The Voyages of Apollo* (New York: Quadrangle, 1974).

9. Apollo Historical Summary, NASA, February 1971.

10. *Ibid.*

11. Space Task Group Report to the President, *The Post Apollo Space Program: Directions for the Future* (September 1969).

12. NASA Release 72-4, Washington, D.C.

13. Estimate by the Office of the Directorate of Space Headquarters, USAF, presented August 26, 1975, at the American Astronautical Society's twenty-first annual meeting, Denver, Colorado.

14. Charles W. Mathews, Keynote address, AIAA Advanced Space Transportation Meeting, February 4–6, 1970.

15. Luther Carter, *Science*, Vol. 165 (September 5, 1969).

16. *New York Times*, September 16, 1969, p. 1.

17. For details of this and other Apollo lunar missions, see Lewis, *The Voyages of Apollo.*

18. Two types of nuclear-powered propulsion were in development: the NERVA (Nuclear Energy for Rocket Vehicle Application), which was the project of NASA, and the Atomic Energy Commission's nuclear reactor, which heated hydrogen gas as a propellant. An electric engine, the "ion drive" of science fiction, had been developed, but it lacked an adequate source of electric power to accelerate nuclear particles as a propellant. For interplanetary missions, the ion engine required a nuclear-electric generator. A pair of electron bombardment ion engines were tested on a spacecraft called *SERT II* (Space Electric Rocket Test), which was launched from the Western Test Range at Vandenberg Air Force Base, California, February 3, 1970. The engines develop 0.006 pounds of thrust by expelling mercury vapor ions at velocities of 50,000 miles an hour. The test was inconclusive, although one of the engines operated for 2,011 hours. Both were powered by solar cells producing 1,471 watts.
19. *New York Times,* July 20, 1970.
20. Interview with Thomas O. Paine, Sept. 18, 1975.
21. U.S. Senate Committee on Aeronautical and Space Sciences, *Soviet Space Programs, 1971.* (92nd Congress, second session.
22. *Ibid.*
23. *Ibid.*

CHAPTER VII   DÉTENTE

1. Interview with Robert R. Gilruth, July 18, 1975.
2. Thomas O. Paine, "Man's Future in Space," the 1972 Tizard Memorial Lecture, London, Westminster School, March 14, 1972.
3. *Ibid.*
4. U.S. Senate Committee on Aeronautical and Space Sciences, *Soviet Space Programs, 1962–65,* (1966.) Joseph G. Whelan, *Soviet Attitudes Toward International Space Cooperation.* 89th Congress, second session.
5. *Ibid.*
6. Dale D. Myers, associate administrator for manned space flight, NASA. Statement to U.S. House of Representatives Committee on Science and Astronautics, Manned Space Flight Subcommittee, February 27, 1973. 93rd Congress, first session.
7. NASA briefing, Apollo Applications Program, January 26, 1967.
8. Paine, *op. cit.*
9. NASA Technical Memorandum X-64814, of October 1974, indicated that air pressure built up under the shield during powered flight through the atmosphere as the result of certain structural anomalies and raised the forward end. High-velocity air then rammed under the shield and tore it outward from its mountings on the Workshop. Aerodynamic drag of the partially lifted shield caused the vehicle to roll, and the metal began to wrap around solar wing number 2. The wing tiedowns were broken, and the wing started to deploy, causing the shield then to unwind and wrap itself around solar wing number 1. The shield then ripped apart from top to bottom at a longitudinal joint adjacent to wing 1, pulling a portion of the joint assembly over the wing to clamp it firmly against the hull as the remainder of the shield section blew away.

Wing 2, which was partially deployed at the start of this cataclysmic process, could not extend fully because of the rush of air against it. But when Skylab left the atmosphere and was injected into orbit, the wing swung outward with such force that it broke its ninety-degree stops and tore free at the hinge link. The memorandum makes it clear that all available data point to a design failure in an auxiliary tunnel structure associated with the shield.

10. Change of Shift Briefing, Johnson Space Center, May 26, 1973.

11. J. R. Hordinsky, NASA, "Evaluation of Life in Skylab from a Medical Viewpoint," Paper presented to the American Astronautical Society Annual Meeting, August 20–24, 1974.

12. *New York Times*, December 27, 1974.

13. *New York Times*, April 12, 1975.

14. From the *Report on the Liquidation of ELDO Programs*, submitted on the occasion of the entry into force, de facto, of the Convention of the European Space Agency, May 29, 1975.

15. R. Aubiniere, secretary-general, ELDO, "Tenth Anniversary of the Establishment of ELDO," *ESRO/ELDO Bulletin*, No. 24 (March 1974).

16. *Europa II Summary of Principal Conclusions of the General Report of the Project Review Commission*, ELDO, 1972.

17. *Ibid.*

18. Spacelab is designed in three configurations, or modules, to serve different needs. One is a pressurized cylinder 7 meters (22.75 feet) long and 4 meters (13 feet) in diameter. It would be carried aloft as a workshop and laboratory for about four experimenters, who would be housed during off-duty hours in the Orbiter cabin. Access between the Orbiter cabin and the Spacelab module is provided by a tunnel. A second configuration is a 13½-foot-long pressurized cylinder attached to an open instrument platform or pallet. Instruments such as telescopes, cameras, spectrometers, and radiometers would be mounted on the pallet and operated and monitored from the small workshop. A third configuration is the open pallet only, which could be 15 meters (48.75 feet) long. A large space telescope could be emplaced on it, or a series of instruments, all of which could be monitored within the Orbiter cabin. The pallet would be available in segments, each 3 meters long, and these would be carried as needed up to a maximum of five.

19. The docking module was a cylindrical airlock with docking mechanisms on both ends. It was ten feet four inches long and four feet eight inches in diameter. It weighed 4,436 pounds. The airlock was constructed of welded five-eighths-inch aluminum. On the Apollo end, it tapered to form a tunnel and bulkhead, and the docking mechanism was the standard probe and drogue hardware developed for docking Apollo with the lunar module. On the forward end, with which Soyuz docked, it carried a bulkhead and docking assembly matching one attached to Soyuz. The docking assemblies on the Apollo and Soyuz sides were operated in both active and passive modes. During the initial docking, the Apollo system was active. It extended a guide with three petal-shaped guide plates, three capture latches, and six hydraulic shock absorbers. Following capture, the Apollo guide ring was retracted by an electric cable drive to pull the structural rings on the Apollo and Soyuz docking mechanisms tightly together and compress their rubber seals to form an air-tight linkage. Eight structural latches were engaged to lock the vehicles. Apollo and Soyuz were then hard docked. This system could be adapted to virtually any manned space vehicle, such as the Shuttle and the Salyut space station. At launch, the docking module was housed in an adapter at the forward end of the S4B stage behind the Apollo CSM—in the position where the lunar module was carried. Upon separating the CSM from the S4B in orbit, the command module pilot performed a transposition-and-docking maneuver to extract the docking module from its housing (in the spacecraft-LM adapter), following the same procedure used in extracting the LM during lunar missions. The CSM then continued in orbital flight with the docking module affixed to the nose of the command module and its international docking mechanism pointing forward.

20. Christopher S. Wren, *New York Times*, May 12, 1975.
21. *Aviation Week & Space Technology* (June 2, 1975).
22. United Press International, May 17, 1975. (*New York Times*, May 18, 1975.)
23. In one of the five experiments, Apollo maneuvered to blot out the Sun for Soyuz so that the Russians could photograph the solar corona. The idea of creating an artificial eclipse had been proposed by the USSR Institute of Terrestrial Magnetism. A second joint experiment measured the amount of neutral oxygen and nitrogen atoms at the flight altitude. This was calculated by determining the absorption of certain wavelengths in a light beam emitted by Apollo and reflected back to a spectrometer on the American vessel by a mirror on Soyuz. A third joint experiment sought to determine the degree of microbe exchange between the two crews during their visits to each other's ships. Two other joint experiments examined the effects of radiation and zero gravity on the biological rhythms of fungi and the advantages of making metal alloys in an electric furnace and of growing crystals in zero gravity.
24. United Press International, July 29, 1975. (*Chicago Sun-Times*, July 30, 1975.)
25. Kurt Waldheim, *Astronautics and Aeronautics*, Vol. 13, No. 9 (September 1975).

CHAPTER VIII   THE SEARCH FOR CREATION

1. Harrison H. Schmitt, "Evolution of the Moon, the 1974 Model," *Proceedings of the Soviet-American Conference on the Cosmochemistry of the Moon and Planets*, Moscow (June 4–8, 1974).
2. Sidney W. Fox, "The Apollo Program and Amino Acids," *Science and Public Affairs, the Bulletin of the Atomic Scientists*, Vol. 29, No. 10 (December 1973).
3. Schmitt, *op. cit.*
4. John S. Lewis, "Origin of Planets and Satellites," *Technology Review* (October, November 1973).
5. *Ibid.*
6. *Ibid.*
7. For a detailed account of this event, see Richard S. Lewis, *Appointment on the Moon* (New York: Viking Press, 1969).
8. Farouk El Baz, "Crater Characteristics: Analysis of Apollo 8 Photographs and Visual Observations," *Apollo 8 Report*, NASA, 1969.
9. G. J. Wasserburg *et al.*, "Lunar Chronology and Evolution," Third Lunar Science Conference, January 10–13, 1972.
10. "Report of the Lunar Sample Preliminary Examination Team," Apollo 14 Preliminary Science Report, June 1, 1971.
11. Schmitt, *op. cit.*
12. "The Heat Flow Experiment," Apollo 15 Preliminary Science Report.
13. Schmitt, *op. cit.*
14. *Ibid.*
15. *Ibid.*
16. Don L. Anderson, "Constraints on Structure and Composition of the Deep Interior," Summary Session, Lunar Science Conference, March 21, 1975.
17. Schmitt, *op. cit.*
18. Anderson, *op. cit.*
19. A detailed discussion of capture theory is presented in Richard S. Lewis, *The Voyages of Apollo* (New York: Quadrangle, 1974).
20. W. M. Kaula, "Mechanical Processes Affecting Differentiation of Proto-Lunar

Material," *Proceedings of the Soviet-American Conference on the Cosmochemistry of the Moon and Planets*, Moscow (June 4–8, 1974).

21. S. Fred Singer, "Origin of the Moon and its Consequences," Paper presented at the 51st Annual Meeting, American Geophysical Union, April 24, 1970.

22. Brian Mason and William G. Melson, *The Lunar Rocks* (New York: Wiley, 1970).

23. "Post-Apollo Lunar Science," Report of a study by the Lunar Science Institute, July 1972.

24. (New York: Pergamon, 1975).

25. Ernst Stuhlinger, "Skylab Results; Review and Outlook," Marshall Space Flight Center.

26. *Ibid.*

27. *Ibid.*

28. E. Hildner, "Solar Corona as Seen from Skylab," Paper presented to the AIAA/AGU Conference on Scientific Experiments of Skylab, Huntsville, Alabama, October 30–November 1, 1974.

29. *Ibid.*

30. Stuhlinger, *op. cit.*

31. William C. Snoddy and G. Allen Gary, "Skylab Observations of Comet Kohoutek" (Paper presented to the AIAA/AGU Conference on Scientific Experiments of Skylab, *op. cit.*

32. Stuhlinger, *op. cit.*

33. *Ibid.*

34. *Ibid.*

35. Thomas Gold, *Science*, Vol. 165 (September 26, 1969).

36. "Post-Apollo Lunar Science," *op. cit.*

37. Eugene N. Parker, "The Sun," *Scientific American*, Vol. 233, No. 3 (September 1975).

38. R. K. Ulrich, "Solar Neutrinos and Variations in Solar Luminosity," *Science*, Vol. 190 (November 14, 1975).

39. Harrison H. Schmitt, "The Progeny of Skylab," Paper presented to the AIAA/AGU Conference on Scientific Experiments of Skylab, *op. cit.*

CHAPTER IX   THE LIQUID PLANET

1. *Outer Planets Exploration, 1972–85* (National Academy of Sciences-National Research Council, November 1971).

2. The gravitational assist principle had been worked out quite early in the space program. One of America's most advanced early planners of space exploration, Homer J. Stewart, of the California Institute of Technology, had proposed a scheme using the gravitational fields of Jupiter and Saturn to make course and velocity changes in a passing spacecraft that would accelerate it to any of the outer planets or out of the solar system entirely. This game of "interplanetary billiards," as Stewart dubbed it, enabled NASA to make a reconnaissance of the outer planets without resorting to mammoth boosters and exotic propulsion systems.

Wernher Von Braun explained at a Washington press conference on March 31, 1970: "You are stealing some energy out of the gravitational field of Jupiter and this is equivalent to a very powerful chemical booster, way out in the planets, that will hurl your spacecraft to other planets. You can use the Jupiter boost to drive it out to Saturn and then the same thing with Saturn once more and drive it all the way out to Pluto."

By approaching Jupiter earlier or later, the slingshot effect of Jovian gravity would swing the spacecraft to Uranus, and Uranus' gravity would hurl it out to Neptune. There were other options that included a flyby of Pluto—the strangest of the outer planets because it more nearly is the size and density of the Earth. Indeed, in these respects, Pluto seems to be a twin of Earth, although it is 3.7 billion miles from the sun.

In the magazine *Astronautics and Aeronautics* for June 1969, James E. Long, of the Jet Propulsion Laboratory, proposed two Grand Tour missions. One would swing by Jupiter, Saturn, and Pluto and the other by Jupiter, Uranus, and Neptune.

Long visualized a 1,200-pound spacecraft on the order of the Space Science Board's TOPS that would be lifted by a Titan 3C booster with a Centaur second stage. The voyage to Pluto could be made in seven or eight years, using the gravitational assist of Jupiter and Saturn. A direct flight to Pluto would take forty-one years.

"So," Von Braun told the press conference, "the intriguing part of the Grand Tour is not only that you have all the planets lined up and you can visit them in a kind of interplanetary bowling contest, but the fact that you can use, during this particular opportunity, the boost of Jupiter to reach all of the outer planets. That means that you can do with a much smaller rocket. In fact, a thing like the Titan 3C, using this trick, would hurl about the same type of spacecraft to Neptune and Pluto that would otherwise require a vehicle the size of a Saturn 5 plus a Centaur stage on top of it to do all this without Jupiter's help. That is why we are so excited about the Grand Tour."

3. U.S. House of Representatives Committee on Science and Astronautics, *1969 NASA Authorization Hearings*, February 7 and 8, 1968, No. 3, Pt. 1. 90th Congress, second session.

4. "Pioneer Odyssey: Encounter with a Giant," NASA, 1974.

5. Ideas about Jupiter's internal composition have varied. In 1943, a University of Virginia astrophysicist, Rupert Wildt, estimated that 18 percent was ice and 43 percent a metallic, rocky core. In 1948, W. H. Ramsey suggested that the planet could be made entirely of hydrogen, which became solid under a pressure of 800,000 atmospheres. The model favored at the time the Pioneers were launched was suggested in 1968 by Fred L. Whipple, director of the Smithsonian Astrophysical Observatory. It considered that Jupiter consisted of 80 percent hydrogen and the rest, helium plus several Earth masses of heavy materials such as silicates and metals. A similar model, which became the predominant one at the end of 1974, proposed that most of the hydrogen was in a liquid-metallic phase and that there was rocky core of several Earth masses.

6. Fred L. Whipple, *Earth, Moon and Planets*, 3rd ed. (Cambridge, Mass.: Harvard University Press, 1968).

7. *Ibid.*

8. "U.S. Space Science Program," Report to COSPAR, sixth meeting, Warsaw, June 1963.

9. Whipple, *op. cit.*

10. H. C. Urey, *The Planets, Science in Space*, ed. Lloyd V. Berkner and Hugh Odishaw (New York: McGraw Hill, 1961).

11. "Astronomy Missions Board Position Paper," NASA, July 1969.

12. The polarimeter function of the imaging photopolarimeter was to measure the brightness and the polarization of light reflected by Jupiter's atmosphere to provide clues to its structure and the height of the great clouds. The polarimeter also measured the light reflected by space dust while the Pioneers were enroute to Jupiter.

In a nonpolarized state, light waves vibrate in all directions—up and down, sideways, etc.—perpendicular to their line of travel or propagation. Certain materials (such as those used in polaroid sunglasses) pass the light rays that are vibrating only in one direction, thus polarizing the light beam. The polarizing effect is produced also by anything that reflects or refracts (bends) light.

The polarization of light by a planetary atmosphere provides clues to its structure and composition. Detailed polarization measurements of the atmosphere of Venus from Earth indicated the height of the clouds and the size and shape of cloud particles when coupled with laboratory model experiments.

Ground-based polarization measurements of the Jovian atmosphere were inconclusive because of certain observational limitations. The Pioneers provided the opportunity to make closeup measurements of the linear polarization of sunlight by Jupiter's atmosphere as a means of probing its structure and cloud heights. The imaging photopolarimeter was the instrument designed to do that job, as well as to make telephotos of the planet in color.

13. James A. Van Allen, Interview, *Bulletin of the Atomic Scientists*, Vol. 29, No. 10 (December 1973).

14. John Wolfe, NASA Press Conference, April 1, 1974.

15. *Ibid.*

16. David L. Coffeen, "Optical Measurements of the Jupiter Atmosphere," *Journal of Geophysical Research*, Vol. 79, No. 25 (September 1, 1974).

17. It has been theorized that the Great Red Spot derives its color from organic molecules that have formed in the atmosphere of Jupiter from chemical reactions that are believed to have started the evolution of life on Earth. At least the basic chemistry of organic evolution seems to be possible in the atmosphere of Jupiter. Scientists have speculated that the key to the development of organic molecules is the survivability of their precursors—amino acids, for example. This requires a relatively stable region of the atmosphere—not one that is in constant, violent turnover. There may be regions of the Jovian atmosphere where conditions are stable enough and favorable enough for the chemistry of life to proceed. Research scientists at Ames have pointed out that building blocks of life—methane, ammonia, acetylene, and ethane—are present on Jupiter. Organic chemists see the colors in the Red Spot and in the clouds as organic molecules. The relative quietness and apparent stability of the polar regions may provide the environment for life on Jupiter. It would be a life form that floats in that fantastic atmosphere.

CHAPTER X   VIKING

1. Percival Lowell, *Mars As an Abode of Life* (New York: Macmillan, 1908).

2. W. A. Webb, "On the Rejection of the Martian Canal Hypothesis," *Scientific Monthly* (July 1957).

3. E. M. Antoniadi, *Popular Astronomy*, Vol. 21, No. 416 (1913).

4. Webb, *op. cit.*

5. Samuel Glasstone, *The Book of Mars* (Washington, D.C.: NASA, 1968).

6. Ronald A. Schorn, C. B. Farmer, and Stephen J. Little, "Preliminary Results of 1968–69 Water Vapor Studies," NASA Report, 1969.

7. A. Kliore *et al.*, Mariner VI and VII Radio Occultation, *Science*, Vol. 166 (December 12, 1969).

8. R. B. Leighton *et al.*, Mariner VI Television Pictures," *Science*, Vol. 165 (August 15, 1969).

9. Norman H. Horowitz, "Progress Report on Mariner," NASA News Conference, Washington, D.C., September 11, 1969.

10. *Ibid.*

11. *Proceedings*, National Academy of Sciences (March 1971).

12. Sohorn, Farmer, and Little, *op. cit.*
13. Glasstone, *op. cit.*
14. *Ibid.*
15. *Ibid.*
16. U.S. Senate Committee on Aeronautical and Space Sciences, *Soviet Space Programs, 1971.* 92nd Congress, second session.
17. Michael H. Carr, "The Volcanoes of Mars," *Scientific American,* Vol. 234, No. 1 (January 1976); *Journal of Geophysical Research,* Vol. 78, No. 20 (July 10, 1973).
18. Mariner 9 News Conference, Washington, D.C., NASA, February 2, 1972.
19. Robert Jastrow, "The Planet Venus," *Science,* Vol. 160 (June 28, 1968).
20. Charles A. Barth, Mariner 9 News Conference, *op. cit.*
21. Bradford Smith, Mariner 9 News Conference, *op. cit.*
22. Conway Leovy, Mariner 9 News Conference, *op. cit.*
23. Smith, *op. cit.*
24. Harold Masursky and Robert Steinbacher, Mariner 9 News Conference, *op. cit.*
25. Carl Sagan, Owen B. Toon, and Peter J. Gierasch, "Climatic Change on Mars," *Science,* Vol. 181 (September 14, 1973).
26. Lawrence W. Gatto and Duwayne M. Anderson, "Alaskan Thermokarst and Possible Martian Analog," *Science,* Vol. 188 (April 18, 1975).
27. Sagan, Toon, and Gierasch, *op. cit.*
28. Ibid.
29. Bruce C. Murray and Michael C. Malin, "Polar Volatiles on Mars," *Science,* Vol. 182 (November 2, 1973).
30. Bruce C. Murray, "Mercury," *Scientific American,* Vol. 233, No. 3 (September 1975).
31. James B. Pollack, "Mars," *Scientific American,* Vol. 233, No. 3 (September 1975).
32. Carl Sagan and G. Mullen, "Earth and Mars," *Science,* Vol. 177 (July 7, 1972).
33. Conway Snyder, "Mariner V Flight Past Venus," *Science,* Vol. 158 (December 29, 1967).
34. James A. Van Allen, "Venus," *Science,* Vol. 158 (December 29, 1967).
35. *Ibid.*
36. Jastrow, *op. cit.*
37. Associated Press, Moscow, October 26, 1975.
38. *Ibid.*
39. Lyle Broadfoot, Mariner 10 Venus Encounter News Conference, Pasadena, Jet Propulsion Laboratory, February 7, 1974.
40. Bruce C. Murray, Mariner 10 Venus Encounter News Conference, *op. cit.*
41. Bruce C. Murray *et al.,* "Mariner 10 Pictures of Mercury," *Science,* Vol. 184 (April 26, 1974).
42. *Ibid.*
43. Bruce C. Murray *et al.,* "Television Observations of Mercury by Mariner 10," *Proceedings of the Soviet-American Conference on the Cosmochemistry of the Moon and Planets,* Moscow (June 4–8, 1974).
44. *Ibid.*
45. Donald E. Gault, *New York Times,* September 24, 1974.
46. Murray *et al., Science, op. cit.*
47. Paul D. Lowman, Jr., "Crustal Evolution of the Moon, Mercury and Mars. Implications for the Origin of Continents," Goddard Space Flight Center Report, 1974.
48. Glasstone, *op. cit.*
49. P. A. Straat, G. V. Levin, and Paul D. Lowman, Jr., "Mariner 9: Prelude to the First Field Test of a General Theory of Biology," Goddard Space Flight Center, November 1974.

50. Viking Pre-Launch Symposium, Kennedy Space Center, August 8, 1975.

51. In the facsimile camera, a nodding mirror reflects the light from a small part of an object to a diode sensor, and the image is built up line by line so that the picture is accumulated slowly. There are twelve diodes in the focal plane of each camera. One acquires a black-white picture; three have filters transmitting blue, green, and red light; three more have filters that pass light in the near infrared wave lengths; and four are located to get precise focus for high-resolution black-white pictures. A twelfth diode has reduced sensitivity so that it can photograph the sun. Although the cameras were designed for very high resolution of still objects, their line-by-line operation made them unsuitable to record motion, except as a streak. The design reflected a conclusion that if there was any life on Mars, it was not the kind that might be seen moving. The photos could be transmitted directly back to Earth or to the orbiter for relay in real time or by delayed transmission from a tape recording.

INDEX

Advanced Research Projects Agency,
    See ARPA
Age of Discovery
    and international rivalry, 40
    politics in, 320–321
    power of bankers in, 42–43
    related to Norse explorations, 3–4
    related to Space Age, *xiii*
    search for passage to Indies in, 29–30, 37–38
Age of Innocence, 117–121
Agena rocket, 186–187, 188–190
Agnew, Spiro T., 214
Aldrin, Edwin F. (Buzz), Jr., 191–192,
    217–218, 297, 314
Ambartsumyan, V. N., 132
America, discoveries of, 3, 7, 10–11, 16,
    35–36
Amundsen, Roald, 78, 82–85, 112
Anders, William A., 192–193, 194, 205, 209,
    296
Anderson, Don L., 306
Anderson, Duwayne M., 369
Anderson, John D., 334, 343
Anderson, Vernon H., 91
Animals, in space flight tests, 145, 146, 147, 148
Antarctic ice cap, 88–89, 94, 314–316
Antarctic Ocean, exploration of, 71, 77
Antarctica
    airplane reconnaissance of, 89
    animal fossils found in, 105
    bases on, 90
    climatic changes in, 86
    coal found in, 86, 87
    and continental drift theory, 78, 80, 93–96
    crossing of, 89, 90, 91–92
    depth of ice on, 91–92
    description of, 80
    development of, 90
    expeditions to, 73–78, 85–107

fossils found in, 85–86, 87, 94–95, 104, 105
geological structure of, 80, 92–93
Antoniadi, E. M., 355
Apollo, 144, 172, 197–198
    See also Apollo program; ASTP
Apollo Application Program, 238, 240
Apollo program, 192–193, 195, 199, 200–202,
    204–208, 210–211, 216–220, 226–233,
    287, 297, 299–300, 302–306
    compared with Mercury and Gemini, 196
    cost of, 213, 352
    cutbacks in, 220, 221
    debate over, 174–180
    findings of, 296–297, 300–309
    fire on *Apollo I*, 196–197, 201, 220, 238
    Highland missions of, 231–233
    risks of, 195, 202–204, 220
    Skylab and, *see* Skylab
Apollo-Soyuz Test Project, *see* ASTP
Argon, in Martian atmosphere, 353, 388, 389,
    398
Armstrong, Neil A., 188–189, 190, 208,
    209–210, 217–218, 223, 297, 314
Army Ballistic Missile Agency, 134, 138, 139,
    173
ARPA, 139, 141, 328
Artukhin, Yuri, 259–260
Asteroid Belt, planetary exploration and, 320,
    322, 328, 331, 333, 335, 340, 342, 360
ASTP, 234–237, 238, 269–284
    crews of, 267
    docking of, 273–274
    exchange of medallion halves on, 280
    political results of, 283–284
    preparations for, 258–261, 266–269
    problem in Apollo during, 274, 281–283
    purpose of, 269
Astronauts
    as heroes, 213

Astronauts (cont.)
  mass media and, 178–179
  repairs in space by, 248–249, 250, 252–253
  selection of, 146
  selection for lunar landing, 208, 209–210
  See also under individual names of
Atlas, 127, 129–130, 138, 143, 145, 322, 338, 358, 376
Aurora VII, 168–169
Australia, 67, 70

Baikonour Cosmodrome, 127–128, 148, 200, 222, 223, 230, 258, 268–269, 274
Baillie, Ralph, 100–101
Balboa, Vasco Núñez de, 38
Banks, Joseph, 67
Barbosa, Diogo, 43, 44, 46
Barbosa, Duarte, 53, 54, 56, 61, 63
Barnard, E. E., 324
Barrett, Peter J., 100, 101
Bean, Alan L., 217, 218, 253–254, 255, 300
Beardmore, William, 82
Beardmore Glacier, 82, 83, 84, 85, 96
Behaim, Martin, 37, 38, 50, 55
Bellinghausen, Fabian Gottlieb von, 75, 77
Belyayev, Pavel A., 182–183
Bentley, Charles R., 91
Beregovoy, Georgiy T., 207
Berkner, Lloyd V., 133, 140, 141, 152, 179–180
Berry, Dr. Charles A., 193
Blagonravov, Anatoly A., 125, 204, 236
Bland, William M., Jr., 143
Blue Streak missile, 262, 263
Borgia family, 39
Borman, Frank, 187–188, 192–193, 194, 205, 206, 209, 211, 223, 296
Bowers, Henry R., 84, 85
Brand, Vance DeVoe, 267, 271, 272, 277, 278, 279–280, 282, 283
Brazil, 37, 39, 50
Breed, William J., 101
Brown, Harrison, 152
Bruce, Dr. W. S., 81
Bubnov, I. N., 180
Buckley, Oliver, 137
Buglia, James J., 143
Bumper–WAC, 128–129
Burke, Bernard F., 326
Burroughs, Edgar Rice, 356
Bush, Vannevar, 127
Bykovsky, Valery Fyodorovich, 171–172
Byrd, Richard E., 89, 106

Cabot, John, 37, 43
Canada, Norse discoveries of, 3–4, 24
Canals, Martian, see Martian canals
Cape Canaveral, 128–129, 135, 143, 149, 163, 167, 338
Cape of the Eleven Thousand Virgins, 54, 58, 66
Capture theory of moon origins, 290–291, 293, 306, 307
Carpenter, Malcolm Scott, 146, 168–169

Carr, Gerald P., 254, 255, 256
Carr, Michael H., 365
Cartagena, Juan de, 45, 56, 47, 50, 52, 54
Carvalho, Juan Lopez, 60, 63
Casa de Contratacion, 320–321
Cebu, 60–63
Cernan, Eugene A., 189, 191, 208, 232–233, 305
Chaffee, Roger B., 196
Challenger (lunar module), 78, 233, 305
Charles I (king of Spain), 29, 44, 45, 46
Choate, Joseph H., 79, 80
Chryse Planitia, 316, 386, 390–393, 396
Clark, Benton C., 401
Climate
  of Antarctica, 92
  fluctuations of, 86–87, 88–89
  on Mars, 353, 361, 367–370
  Norse explorations and, 6
  See also Temperature
Coalsack Bluff, fossils from, 103, 106–107
Coca, Antonio de, 45, 50, 52, 53
Colbert, Edwin Harris, 101–105
Cold War, space exploration and, 112, 153–157, 162, 175, 234–237
  See also Moon race; Space race
Collins, Michael, 189–190, 206, 208
Columbus, Christopher, 3, 7, 25, 29, 31–37, 39, 41, 68, 111, 174, 320, 321
Comet Kohoutek, 254–255, 259, 310, 311–312
Communications with spacecraft, 144–145, 160, 166, 168, 196, 230, 269–279, 357, 358, 363–364
  See also Mission Control
Concepcion, 45, 52, 55, 56, 63
Congress, space program and, 140–141, 176–178, 197, 321
Congreve, William, 113
Conrad, Charles (Pete), Jr., 186, 190–191, 208, 217–218, 244, 246, 247–249, 250, 251, 300
Continental drift theory, 87, 93–98, 100–107
Cook, James, xiii, 67–73, 79, 112
Cooper, Leroy Gordon, Jr., 146, 156, 169–170, 183, 186
Corona, Skylab data on, 310–311
Cosmic rays, 322, 332, 342
Cosmonauts, 146–148
  See also under names of
Cost(s)
  of ASTP, 237
  of Explorer I, 215
  and international space exploration, 235, 262
  and Jupiter exploration, 322
  of launching, Shuttle and, 240
  of Luna and Apollo lunar missions compared, 225, 229
  of Mars landing, 216
  of outer planet exploration, 318–320, 376
  of Rover, 228
  of space transportation system, 215
  of Viking program, 352
Crary, Albert P., 91

Cunningham, Walter, 201–202
Cydonia, 316, 386

da Gama, Vasco, 36, 39
Darwin, Charles, 287, 380
Davis, Raymond, Jr., 315–316
de Gaulle, Charles, 223
de Haro, Cristobal, 42–43
de Haro, Diego, 42, 43, 44–47, 50
Del Cano, 63–65
Demin, Lev, 260
Détente, space programs and, 221, 234–237, 283
Dietz, Robert S., 97
Distant Early Warning (DEW), 112–113, 126
Dobrynin, Anatoly F., 162, 271
Docking, 188–189, 202, 230, 236–237, 260, 273–274
Donnelly, Charles H., 133
Dorbrovolski, Georgiy, 230
Dornberger, Walter R., 116, 121, 124
Douglas, James H., 138
Drake, Francis, xiii, 65–66, 67, 69, 111–112
Dryden, Hugh, L., 141, 236
DuBridge, Lee A., 214
Duke, Charles M., 231, 232, 304
d'Urville, Jules Sebastian Cesar Dumont, 75, 77, 78
Du Toit, Alexander L., 94–96
Dyna-Soar, 138, 139

Earth
    circumference of, 25, 31–32, 40
    climatic oscillation of, 86–87, 88
    compared with Jupiter, 325
    compared with Mars, 356–357
    compared with Moon, 307
    compared with Venus, 372
    completion of reconnaissance of, 111
    crust of, 96
    distance from sun, 68
    evolution of, 291–292, 294–295
    magnetic field of, 95–96
    magnetic poles of, 99–100
    magnetic shield of, 99–100
    motivation for exploration of, 85
    in Ptolemaic system, 25
    "runaway greenhouse effect" and, 370–371
    as seen from Moon, 160, 182, 194, 297, 309
    as seen from Skylab, 253
Earth Resources Experiment Package, see EREP
East Indies, route to, 28–57
Eaton, Cyrus S., 160
Eisele, Donn F., 201
Eisenhower, Dwight D., 129–130, 131, 132, 134, 137, 139, 141, 150, 321
ELDO, 261–263, 264
Elliot, David H., 101, 102–103, 106–107
Emanuel I (king of Portugal), 29, 40–41, 42–43, 44, 46
Emme, Eugene M., 115

Endeavor, 228–229, 302
Eratosthenes, 31–32
EREP, 312–314
Eric the Red, 7–8, 9, 12–13, 18–20
Ericsson, Leif, 3, 5, 8, 10, 12–16, 17, 18, 23, 24, 26, 33, 37, 84
Ericsson, Thorstein, 5, 8, 10, 15, 17–18
Ericsson, Thorvald, 5, 8, 10, 16–17
Ericsdottir, Freydis, 5, 8, 10, 19, 20, 21, 23–24
Esnault-Pelterie, Robert, 119
Espinosa, Gonzalo Gomes de, 45–46, 50, 53, 63, 64
ESRO, 263–265
ESTEC, 264, 265
Europa rockets, 262–263, 324
European Launcher Development Organization, see ELDO
European Space Research Organization, see ESRO
Evans, Edgar, 84–85
EVAs, 190, 191–192, 297
    on Apollo flights, 218, 227, 229, 232
    on Skylab, 252–253, 255
Ewing, John, 97
Ewing, W. Maurice, 96, 97
Exploration
    in eighteenth century, 67
    motivations for, xiv, 4, 29, 40, 73–76, 85, 111–112
    role of financiers in, 42–44
    as scientific enterprise, 212–213
    secrecy of, see Secrecy
Explorer I, 135–136
Extravehicular activity, see EVAs

Faget, Maxime A., 142, 143
Falcon (lunar module), 170–171, 228
Faleiro, 43, 44, 45
Farmer, C. Barney, 359, 361, 394
Feldman, George J., 155, 156
Feoktistov, Konstantin P., 182
Ferdinand and Isabella (king and queen of Spain), 29, 33, 35, 39, 41, 171
Ferrar, Hartley T., 95
Filchner, Dr. Wilhelm, 89
Filipchenko, Anatoly V., 222, 260
Fillius R. Walker, 332
Fletcher, James C., 271, 349, 396, 397
"Flux tube," 348–349
Fonseca, Juan Rodriguez de, 43–47, 50
Ford, Gerald, 275–276, 281, 283, 397
Forrestal, James E., 128
Fossils, in Antarctica, 85–86, 87, 94–95, 100–107
Foster, John V., 350
Fox, Sidney W., 287
Fra Mauro Formation, 226–229, 301–302
France
    explorations by, 69, 75, 81
    space travel and, 119, 262
Frank, M. P. "Pete," 269
Franklin, Kenneth L., 326

Franzgrote, Ernest, 294
Freedom VII, 149–150
Friendship VII, 164–168
Fuchs, Sir Vivian, 90
Fugger, Jakob, *see* House of de Haro
Fuller, Helen, 152
Fulton, James G., 323
Furneaux, Tobias, 71, 72

Gagarin, Yuri Alekseyevich, 148, 150, 151, 152, 155, 156, 160, 162, 171, 269
Galilei, Galileo, 25, 288, 289, 324
Ganymede, 324, 345
Garland, Benjamin A., 142–143
Garriott, Owen K., 251
Gatto, Lawrence W., 369
Gauss, Johann Karl Friedrich, 75
Gehrels, Thomas, 334, 346
Gemini program, 144, 173, 174–180, 184–192, 196, 223
Germany
   Antarctica exploration by, 80, 89
   rocket research in, 112, 118, 121–124
   space research by, 262, 263, 265
Gibney, Frank B., 155, 156
Gibson, Edward G., 254, 255, 256
Gierasch, Peter J., 369
Gilruth, Robert R., 142, 144, 163, 203–204, 210, 235
Ginnungagap, 37–38, 77, 82
GIRD, 117, 118, 120
Glass deposits on Moon, 305, 314–315
Glenn, John Herschel, Jr., 146, 159, 162–168, 169
Glennan, 148, 156
Glossopteris fossil, 86, 87, 95, 100
Glushko, Valentin Petrovich, 126
Goddard, Robert H., 114–117, 118, 119, 122, 123, 124
Gold, Thomas, 314–315
Golden Hind, 65–66, 67
Golden Plains of Mars, *see* Chryse Planitia
Gomes, Estevan, 43, 54, 56–57, 58
Gondwanaland, 93–96
Gorbatko, Viktor, 222
Gordon, Richard F., Jr., 190–191, 217, 218
Gottlieb, Peter, 295
Gould, Laurence, M., 106
Great Britain
   Antarctica exploration by, 74, 77, 79–83
   astronomical explorations and 68–70
   ELDO and, 262
   explorations by, 65–66, 67, 69
Great Red Spot of Jupiter, 325, 326, 345, 346, 349
Grechko, Georgiy, 260
Greenhouse effect, 370
Greenland, 3, 4, 5, 6, 8–10, 12–13, 24
Grimolfsson, Bjarni, 19, 20, 21
Grissom, Virgil I. (Gus), 146, 158–159, 183–184, 196

Group for Study of Reactive Propulsion, *see* GIRD
Gubarev, Aleksiy, 260
Guggenheims, 115, 119–120

Haise, Fred, Jr., 219
Hale, George, 355
Hale, William, 113, 123
Hall, Asaph, 354
Halley, Edmund, 68
Handler, Philip, 326
Hansen, Helmer, 84
Heberlig, Jack C., 143
Helluland, 13, 15, 20
Henry the Navigator, 28, 30–31
Herjolfsson, Bjarni, 10–11, 12, 13
Heroic Age of polar exploration, 74–89
Hess, Harry H., 97, 323
Hess, Seymour L., 399
Hillary, Sir Edmund, 90
Hinners, Noel W., 397
Hirsch, Andre, 119
Hohmann, Walter, 119
Holland, H. D., 387, 389–390
Holmes, Arthur, 96
Hooke, Robert, 325
Horowitz, Norman H., 361, 389, 401, 403–404, 405
House of de Haro, 42, 43–44
House of Representatives, 155, 158, 183
Huzel, Dieter, 124

ICBMs, 112–113, 121–126, 127–130, 137–138, 143
Iceland, settling of, 3, 4, 5–6, 9, 11
Imaging photopolarimeter, *see* IPP
Imbrium Basin, 226, 302
Indian Ocean, 26, 27, 28, 29–30, 33, 34, 35, 37, 38, 50, 97
Infrared spectrometers and radiometers, 333–334, 359–360, 394
   See also ISIS
Intercontinental ballistic missile, *see* ICBMs
International Geophysical Year (IGY), 90–93, 131, 212–213
Io, 324, 342, 345, 348–349, 350
IPP, 334, 339–340, 345, 346
Irwin, James B., 228–229, 302, 303
Isabella, *see* Ferdinand and Isabella
Isayev, Alaksei M., 126

Jastrow, Robert, 367
Jensen, James A., 101
Jet Propulsion Laboratory, 128, 135, 141, 294, 295, 372, 390, 394, 405
John II (king of Portugal), 29, 31, 37, 39, 41
Johnson, Lyndon B., 150, 152–153, 158, 177, 180, 203, 204, 235, 321, 358
Johnston, David, 100
Judge, Darrell L., 333, 345
June, Harold, 89

Jupiter, 316 010, 324–328, 333–334, 342–350
    See also Jupiter exploration; Pioneers
Jupiter exploration, 320, 322–324, 328, 330,
    335–336
    See also Pioneers

Kaminin, Nikolai L., 147, 180, 183
Kapitsa, Peter L., 132
Karlsefni, Gudrid, 5, 7, 9, 15, 18, 19
Karlsefni, Thorfinn, 5, 18–21, 23, 33
Karth, Joseph E., 323
Kaula, W. M., 307
Keldysh, Mstislav V., 125, 171, 178, 211, 235,
    236–237
Kennedy, John F., 137, 148–157, 161–162,
    174–180, 221, 235, 321, 322
Kennedy Space Center, 199, 204, 219, 269,
    270–271, 386
Kerr, Robert S., 153
Kerwin, Dr. Joseph P., 243, 246, 247–249, 250
Khrunov, Yevgeny, 207
Khrushchev, Nikita, 148, 152, 162, 177–178,
    235
Killian, James R., 137
Kinard, William H., 333
Kinzler, Jack, 246
Kishkin, M. S., 125
Kissinger, Henry, 235
Kistiakowski, George B., 141
Kitching, James W., 107
Klein, Harold, 401, 402, 404, 405
Klimuk, Pyotr, 259, 260–261
Kohoutek, see Comet Kohoutek
Komarov, Vladimir, 182
Korolev, Sergei Pavlovich, 118, 121, 126, 128,
    134, 147
Kosmos, 223, 363, 373
Kowal, Charles, 317
Kraft, Christopher Columbus, Jr., 144, 163,
    203–204, 206, 245, 254
KREEP, 290, 302
Kristensen, Leonard, 77
Kubasov, Valeriy Nikolaevich, 222, 267, 260,
    270, 271, 275, 277–278, 279, 280
Kummersdorf test center, 121, 122

Laika, 133–134
Land, Edwin F., 141
Lang, Fritz, 110
Langemak, Georgi, 121
Larsen, C. A., 77, 80, 94
Laser reflector experiments, 298, 300
Lazarev, Vasily G., 259, 260
Lebedev, Valentin, 259
Lederberg, Joshua, 152, 351, 381, 388–389,
    406
Lee, Chester M., 260
Leighton, Robert B., 369–370
Leonov, Alexei Arkhipovich, 182–183, 184,
    267, 269, 271–272, 273, 274, 275, 276,
    277–279, 280
Lewis, John S., 292

Levin, Gilbert V., 402
Ley, Willy, 118, 119
Liberty Bell VII, 158–159
Life
    chemical evolution theory of, 380
    on other planets, 331
    See also Life on Mars; Life on Venus
Life on Mars, 351–353, 354, 355–356,
    357–358, 361–362, 363, 370, 380, 381,
    386–390, 393–394, 398, 400–406
Life on Venus, 372, 377
Lindbergh, Charles A., 115
Little Climatic Optimum, 6, 9, 15
Lousma, Jack R., 251, 252–253
Lovell, Sir Bernard, 161, 178
Lovell, James A., Jr., 187–188, 191, 192–193,
    194, 205, 206, 209, 219, 220, 223, 296
Low, George M., 150, 210, 236–237, 268
Lowell, Percival, 354, 355
Lowman, Paul D., Jr., 379, 380
Luna program, 142, 223–225, 226, 293, 294,
    301, 304
Lunar crust, 290, 299, 301, 303–306, 307
Lunar findings, 287–309, 314–316
Lunar landings
    by Apollo XI, 209–211
    after Apollo XI, 217–219, 226–229
    cost of, 150
    crew selection for, 208–209
    cutbacks in space program and, 212
    and earth-orbit rendezvous, 171
    Kennedy and, 153–154, 155–157, 161–162
    necessity of, 308–309
    Oklahoma conference on, 156–157
    political effect of, 211
    political pressures for, 152–154
    public opinion poll on, 178
Lunar Module, 195, 201, 202, 207–208
Lunar rock and soil samples, 223–224, 232, 236,
    284, 290, 294, 299, 300–303, 305–306, 308
Lunar Roving Vehicle (LRV), 302
Lunney, Glynn, 268
Lunokhod, 224 225, 226, 228, 375
Lystrosaurus fossil, 103, 104, 105, 106, 107

MA-VII, 168–170, 183
McDivitt, James A., 184–186, 208
McDonald, Frank B., 332
McElroy, Michael B., 398
McElroy, Neil H., 134–135
McNamara, Robert S., 153
Mactan, 61–63, 73
Magellan, Ferdinand, xii, 26, 29, 38–39,
    40–47, 50–63, 65, 73, 111, 321
Magnetic field
    distance and, 342
    of Jupiter, 326–327, 336, 341, 342, 343, 347
    of Mars, 358
Magnetic poles, shifts in, 75–76, 82, 86, 95–96,
    98–100
    See also North magnetic pole; South
    magnetic pole

Makarov, Oleg G., 259, 260
Malin, Michael C., 369
Manned Spacecraft Center, 157–158, 196
Mariner missions, 216, 357–358, 359–381, 386–387
Marius, Simon, 324
Mars
　age of, 356
　atmospheric pressure on, 398–399
　attempted landings on, 379
　canals of, see Martian canals
　chaotic terrain of, 369
　climatic cycles on, 316, 367–370
　color changes on, 362
　compared with Earth, 356–357
　compared with Moon, 357–358
　as evolving planet, 366–368
　life on, see life on Mars
　in literature, 353–356
　manned flights to, 214–217, 358, 401–402
　sky of, 391, 399
　telescopic observations of, 354–356
　temperatures on, 393, 399
　water on, 351
　See also Mariner missions; Mars exploration
Mars exploration
　critics of, 398
　future plans for, 397
　postponement of, 220, 221, 238
　purpose of, 316, 351–353
　tests necessary prior to, 219
　U.S. vs. Soviet, 358–359
Mars flights, 353, 357, 363–364, 387–388
Marshak, Robert E., 176
Martian canals, 354–356, 357, 362, 366, 370, 387
Martin, James S., Jr., 393, 396
Mason, Brian, 307
Masursky, Harold, 365
Mathews, Charles W., 215–216
Mattingly, Thomas K., 231
Medaris, John B., 134, 135
Media
　and Jupiter mission, 336–337
　and Mars mission, 394, 397–398, 400
　and Moon program, 178–179
Medical findings of Skylab, 257–258
Meinesz, F. A. Venning, 96
Melson, William G., 307
Mendoza, Luis de, 45, 50, 52, 53
Mercury (planet), 310, 377–379
Mercury (space ship), see Project Mercury
Mercury-Atlas VI, 162–168
Mercury-Redstone IV, 158–159, 184
Mesquita, Alvaro, 50, 52, 53, 54–55, 56
Meteors, spaceships and, 118–119, 244–249
Microorganisms
　on Mars, 389, see also life on Mars
　on Moon, 299
Miller, George P., 183
Miller, Paul M., 295

Missile gap, 126, 127–130, 140–141
Mission Control, 164, 201, 202, 205, 208, 211, 212, 213, 219–220, 244–249
Mission Control, ASTP
　Houston, 271, 273, 275, 278–279
　Moscow, 270, 277, 278, 280
Mitchell, Edgar Dean, 226–228, 301–302
Modularized equipment transporter, see MET
Moluccas, 29, 33, 39–40, 44, 58, 61, 63–64
Moon
　basaltic events on, 306
　chemical differentiation of, 306
　compared with Earth, 287–288
　compared with Mars, 357–358
　compared with Mercury, 377–379
　evolution of, 288–289, 294–925, 302
　explorations of, 217–222
　far side of, 293, 299
　gravitational attraction on, 295
　heat flow out of, 303
　"hot" and "cold," 295–296
　laser reflector experiments on, 298
　magnetic field of, 300–301
　microbes and viruses on, 227–228
　molten core of, 304
　as observation platform, 233
　origin of, 290–291, 293, 306–308, 344
　photographs on, 223
　as planet, 287
　reconnaissance vehicles to, 193
　seismic sounding of, 227, 297–298, 299
　similarities with Earth, 287–288
　Soviet exploration of, 222–226
　surface of, 193–194
　See also Apollo program; Moon race; and entries under Lunar
Moon quakes, 298–299
Moon race
　and Apollo program, 199–200, 201–202, 209–210
　and circumlunar flights, 200–201
　cost of, 176
　debate over, 174–180
　Gemini program and, 180–186
　Leonov's space walk and, 183
　politics of, 112–113
　Saturn program and, 172–174
　Vostok flights and, 170–172, 182–183
　and Zond program, 207
　See also Lunar landing; Space race
Moon shots, 141–142, 328–329
Moons
　of Jupiter, 324, 327, 341, 344
　of Mars, 353–354, 361
　of Mercury, 378
Morison, Samuel Eliot, 31, 32, 33, 35
Mosher, Charles A., 322–323
Mueller, George E., Jr., 204, 238
Mullen, George, 370
Murray, Bruce C., 369–370, 377
Mutiny, on Magellan's voyage, 47, 50, 52–53, 56–57

NASA
and Apollo flights, 195, 199–202
cutbacks in, 220–221, 321
expansion of, 157–158
and fire on *Apollo I*, 196–197
and Gagarin flight, 148
and Glenn mission, 162–168
and joint manned flights, 235–237
and lunar landing, 152–154, 156
Mercury project, 146
and orbital moon flights, 162–168
organization of, 141–146, 148–149
and Pioneer program, 142, 328–335
and planetary exploration, 320–324
program of manned space flight, 142–146,
152–154
recruitment of astronauts, by, 146
research centers of, 157
and Saturn, 172–174
selection of lunar landing sites by, 295
and Skylab, 238, 240–244, 249
and Soyuz launch failure, 260
and Spacelab-Shuttle partnership with Europe, 261–266
on space shuttles, 215–216
and Venus reconnaissance, 371, 373–375
National Academy of Sciences, 131, 157
Space Science Board of, 151–152, 176, 291,
317–318, 319, 320, 323–324
National Aeronautics and Space Administration, *see* NASA
National Science Foundation, 94, 97, 101–105,
131, 151, 353
Naugle, John E., 323
Nepaklonov, Boris, 376
Nesmeyanov, Alexander N., 131
New Zealand, 67, 68–69, 70, 72
Newfoundland Island, 3, 4, 5, 6, 15, 37
Newton, Sir Isaac, 113, 119
Nier, Alfred O. C., 398
Nikolayev, Andrian Gregoryevich, 170–171,
223
Nitrogen, in Martian atmosphere, 308
Nixon, Richard M., space policy of, 137, 212,
217, 218–219, 234, 235, 261, 297, 321
Nordenskjöld, Dr. Otto, 80, 81
Norse voyages, *xiii, xiv,* 3–24, 30, 33, 37–38,
85, 111, 222
North pole, 82–83
Norway, Greenland colonists and, 5, 11

OAMS thrusters, 184, 188–189, 191
Oberth, Hermann, 118–119
Oceanographic exploration, 96–99, 111
Oceanus Procellarum, 217, 288, 300
Occulation experiments, 341–342, 358, 374
Olaf Tryggvason (king of Norway), 5, 12, 20
Orbiter, 193, 265–266, 295
Orbiting Solar Observatory, 254, 255, 310–311
Orgel, Leslie E., 405–406

Oxygen tanks, 143, 219–200
Oyama, Vance I., 403

Pacific Ocean, exploration of, 31, 56–61, 66, 72
Paine, Thomas O., 214, 218–219, 221–222,
235, 236, 240, 261, 262
Parker, Eugene N., 316
Parr, Charles McKew, 42, 45
Patagonian giants, 52, 55, 58
Patseyev, Viktor, 230
Patterson, James H., 294
Peenemunde group, 123–124, 125
Pendray, G. Edward, 115
Perelman, Y. I., 118
Perry, Robert L., 127
Peterson, Norman V., 171
Petrone, Rocco, 245
Pettit, Edison, 355
Philippines, 57, 58–59
Philipps, Samuel C., 197, 199–200, 203–204
Pickering, William H., 128, 354, 396
Pigafetta, Anthony, journal of, 50–66
Pinzón, Vicente Yanez, 35, 37
Pioneer F, 319, 320, 322, 329–335
See also Pioneer X
Pioneer G, 319, 320, 322, 329–330, 335–338,
340
See also Pioneer XI
Pioneer program, 134, 135, 136, 139, 142, 319,
322, 328–329, 371
See also Pioneer F, G, X, XI
Pioneer X
scientific results of, 342–350
voyage of, 338–342
See also Pioneer F
Pioneer XI, voyage of, 347–350
See also Pioneer G
Pittendrigh, Colin S., 381
Planets
density of, 292–293
evolution of, 379
exploration plans for, 320–324
See also under names of
Plate tectonics theory, 87, 96–98
Pogo effect, 199, 200, 201
Pogue, William R., 254, 255, 256
Politics
and *Apollo VIII* flight, 203–204
and choice of first astronaut on moon,
209–210
and debate over Moon race, 174–180
and exploration, 320–323
and Leonov's space walk, 183
and Mars landing plans, 216–217
Pollack, James B., 370, 399
Polo, Marco, 25, 28, 30, 32, 33
Popovich, Pavel Romanovich, 170–171, 259–
260
Portuguese explorations, 28–29, 30–31, 33, 35,
37, 38, 39, 40, 41, 46, 47
Powell, John S., 101
Powers, John A. "Shorty," 156

President's Science Advisory Committee, 137, 141, 160
Priestly, Raymond, 87, 95
Project Mercury, 139, 142–152 158–160, 162–170, 174
Project Orbiter, 131–132
Ptolemaic geography, 25, 26, 27, 28, 31, 37, 58, 66, 67
Purol, Peter P., 385

Quarantine procedure, 228, 299, 302, 380
Quesada, Gaspar de, 45, 52–53

Radiation field of Jupiter, 320, 327, 328, 341–342, 343, 345, 347, 348, 349–350
Ranger program, 142, 193, 293–294, 296
Real, Gaspar de Corte, 37
Redstone rockets, 129, 144, 149
Rendezvous in space, 170–171, 186, 187–190, 222–223
Retrofire, 160, 168, 181
Riabchikov, Eugeny, 147
Ritland, O. J., 157
Rocket research, 113–121
   See also ICBM
Rocks
   from Antarctic Ocean, 77
   of Antarctica, 92–93
   magnetic orientation of, 95, 98–99
   of Mars, 390–391, 396–397
   See also Lunar rock and soil samples
Rogallo, Francis M., 181
Rogers, William P., 235
Roosa, Stuart A., 226–227, 228, 302
Rosmer, Claus, 324
Ross, James Clark, 75, 76–77, 78, 79
Ross Shelf, 76–77, 81–82, 91, 92, 95
Rover, 228–229, 232, 302
Rukavishnikov, Nikolai N., 230, 260
Rynin, Nikolai A., 118, 119

"Saga of Eric the Red," 4ff, 15–16, 19–21
Sagan, Carl, 331, 351, 369, 374, 381, 387, 389, 390
Salyut program, 229–230, 258–261
San Antonio, 45, 57, 50, 52, 55, 56–57, 58
San Martin, Andres de, 56–57
Sänger, Eugen, 119
Santa Maria, 35, 36, 50, 54
Santiago, 45, 53–54
Sarafanov, Gennady, 260
Saturn rocket, 141, 156, 171–173, 192, 196, 198–199, 201, 205, 208, 243, 266
Saturn Workshop program, see Skylab
Schiaparelli, Giovanni V., 354–356, 372
Schirra, Walter M., Jr., 146, 167, 169, 183, 186–188, 201–202
Schmitt, Harrison H. (Jack), 232, 233, 287, 289, 305, 306, 316
Schneider, William C., 243, 245, 249
Schorn, Ronald A., 359, 361
Schroeter, Johannes, 354

Schweickart, Russell L., 208, 249
Scott, David, R., 188–189, 190, 208, 228–229, 302, 303
Scott, Robert Falcon, 79–85, 86, 90, 95, 112
Seamans, Robert C., Jr., 214
Secchi, Pierre Angelo, 354
Secrecy, space programs and, 69, 116, 118, 122, 127–129, 147, 223, 268–269
Sedov, Leonid I., 132, 180
Seiff, Alvin, 399
Seismic sounding, 91–92, 227, 297–298, 299, 300, 302, 303–306
Serov, Ivan A., 125
Serrano, Francisco, 40, 44, 45, 46, 53, 54–55, 61, 63
Sevastyanov, Vitaliy, 223, 260–263
Shackleton, Ernest Henry, 81–82, 83, 84, 86, 89, 90, 95
Shatalov, Vladamir A., 207, 222–223, 230
Sheldon, Charles S., 204, 207
Shepard, Alan B., Jr., 146, 149–150, 152, 156, 159, 165, 167–168, 226–228, 301–302
Shonin, Georgiy, 222
Shuttle, see Orbiter; Space shuttle
Simpson, John A., 332, 336–337, 343
Singer, S. Fred, 307
Sjogren, William L., 295
Skraelings, 4, 18–19, 20
Skylab, 218–219, 234, 238–244, 250–258
   and Comet Kohoutek, 311–312
   compared with Salyut, 259
   as "dry" workshop, 242–244
   and EREP, 312–314
   instrumentation of, 309–310
   launching of, 243–244
   medical findings of, 257–258
   observations of Sun by, 309–311, 316
   shield problem with, 244–250
   as "wet" workshop, 240–242
Slayton, Donald K. (Deke), 146, 205, 210, 267, 271, 274, 275, 276, 277, 278, 280, 282, 283
Slipher, V. M., 355
Smith, William, 74, 343
SNAP power supply, 323, 335
Soberman, Robert K., 333
Society for Space Travel, see VfR
Soften, Gerald A., 386
Soil samples, Martian, 375, 383, 400, 401–407
   See also Lunar rock and soil samples
Solar system
   biological evolution in, 380
   evolution of, xiii–xiv, 25, 291–293, 314–315, 327
Solar wind, 193, 310, 316, 340, 342, 348, 371
Solis, Juan Diaz de, 38, 50
South magnetic pole, 75, 76, 82
South Pole, expeditions to, 79–85
Soviet space program, 117–118, 120–121
   and first crew transfer, 207
   and first manned orbital flight, 159–161
   and Gagarin's flight, 150
   and group flights, 170–172, 182

Soviet space program (*cont.*)
  and launching of *Sputnik I*, 132–134
  and manned space craft, 143–144, 146–148
  and Mars missions, 353, 357, 363–364
  and Moon shots, 141–142
  and planetary exploration, 322, 323
  and preparations for ASTP, 258–261
  and rocket research, 113, 120–121, 122, 124–126
  Salyut, 229–230
  and satellites, 131
  spending on, 176
  and Venus reconnaissance, 371, 372–373, 375–376
  and Vostok flights, 170–172, 182, 183
  and Zond program, 200–201, 203, 358
Soyuz program, 207, 222–223, 229–231, 235, 259–260, 261
  See also ASTP
Space lab, 262, 264–265, 266
Space race
  after ASTP, 283
  and birth of NASA, 140–146
  Explorer I and, 134–136
  and Jupiter exploration, 323
  and manned space flight, 138–140
  and missile gap, 126, 127–130
  and planetary exploration, 322–323
  satellites and, 130–134
  Sputnik and, 136–138
  and Titov's flight, 159–161
  See also Moon race
Space rescue, 236, 251
Space shuttle, 214–216, 221, 234, 238, 240, 261, 265–266
Space stations, 207, 216, 222
  See also Salyut; Skylab; Spacelab
Space suits, 169–170, 183–185
Space tug, 215, 221, 262
Space walks, 182–183, 184, 185, 189
Spain, exploration by, 31, 37, 38, 39, 41–44
Spice trade, exploration and, 28, 29, 30
Sputniks, 133–134, 136–138, 140–141, 147–148, 150, 155, 162, 371
Stafford, Thomas P., 186–188, 189, 208, 267, 271ff
Stalin, J., 120–121, 124–126
Stalin, V. I., 125
Stechkin, Boris Sergeivich, 120
Stewart, Homer J., 128
Strait of Patagonia, 54–56, 65
Stuhlinger, 313–314
Sun, 68, 309–311, 314–316, 375, 376
Surveyor program, 193, 294, 295, 299
Swedenborg, Emanuel, 372
Swift, Jonathan, 353–354
Swigert, John L., 219

"Tale of the Greenlanders," 4ff, 15–16, 19–21, 23–24
Tasman, Abel, 68–69
Taylor, Stuart Ross, 308–309

Teller, Edward, 138
Temperature
  and Greenhouse effect, 370
  on Mars, 360, 399
  of Venus, 372ff
Tereshkova, Valentina, 171–172
Terra Australis, 50, 56, 55–74, 77
Terra Nova, 79, 83, 86, 87, 88
Thiel, Edward C., 92
Thomas, Albert, 158
Thomson, William, 356
Thor-Able rocket, 142
Thor missile, 130
Thorbjorn, 7, 9–10, 19
Thorvald, 7, 10, 20, 21
Thorvaldsson, Eric, *see* Eric the Red
Thorvard, 20, 23, 24
Thrinaxodon, 105, 107
Tierra del Fuego, 56, 65, 66, 69
Tikhonravov, Mikhail K., 117, 122, 126
Titan ICBMs, 124, 127, 130, 138, 182, 183–184, 317, 386–387
Titov, Gherman Stepanovich, 148, 159–161, 165, 169
Tokaty, Gregory A., 120, 122, 124–125, 126
Toon, Owen B., 369
TOPS, 318, 319, 320
Toulminn, Priestley, III, 401
Tranquility Base, 210, 211, 314–315
Trinidad, 36, 45, 52, 53, 55, 56, 63, 64
Truly, Richard H., 271
Truman, Harry, 125, 137, 148
Trumpler, R. J., 355
Tsander, Friedrich Arturovich, 117–118, 120
Tukhachevsky, Mikhail, 121
Tupolev, Andrei, 121
Turkevich, Anthony, 294

Ulrich, R. K., 316
Unipeds, 21, 52
United States
  antarctic exploration by, 74–75, 89, 90
  rocket research in, 114–117, 129–130
  See also United States space program
United States space program
  and competition with Soviet Union, 112–113
  critics of, 213
  and development of transatlantic rocket, 124
  and *Explorer I*, 134–136
  and Gagarin flight, 148–149
  and manned space flight, 138–140, 142–146, 168–170
  and moon shots, 142
  politics and, 158
  in post-lunar period, 214–217, 234–237
  and satellites 130–132, 134
  spending for, 176
  and Sputniks, 133
Urey, Harold C., 152, 179, 296, 327–328

V-2 rocket, 112, 115–117, 122–124, 125, 127
Valier, Max, 119

Van Allen, James A., 152, 322–323, 335–337, 343
Van Allen radiation zone, 136, 193
Vanguard project, 132, 135, 136, 141
Velikovsky, Emanuel, 372
Veneras, 371, 373, 374, 375–376
Venus, 25, 68, 69, 147, 283, 356, 370–377
Verne, Jules, 113
Vespucci, Amerigo, 3, 37, 38, 43
VfR, 118, 119, 120, 121–124
Victoria, 45, 50ff, 63, 64–65
Vietnam war, space program and, 212, 336
Viking project, 132, 225, 351–353, 381–384, 386–387, 390, 391, 400, 404, 406
    See also Viking lander
Viking lander, 382–383, 385–386, 392, 394–406
Vinland, discovery of, 3, 4, 13–15, 16–17, 20, 21, 23–24, 85
Vladimirov, Leonid, 120–121
Volcanoes
    on Jupiter, 326
    on Mars, 359, 364–365
    on Moon, 232, 233, 296
Volkov, Vladislav, 222, 230
Volynov, Boris, 207
Von Braun, Wernher, 116–117, 119, 121, 124–125, 127, 129, 131–132, 135–136, 139, 141, 152, 156, 173, 203–204, 214, 238
Von Karman, Theodore, 127, 128
Voskhods, 172, 182–183, 184, 267
Vostoks, 143–144, 147–148, 159–161, 165, 170–172

Waldheim, Kurt, 284
Wallis, Samuel, 68, 69
Warwick, James W., 349
Water
    and Mars, 351, 359, 360, 361–362, 366–367, 393–394
    and Moon, 287, 290
    and Venus, 374
Waterman, Alan T., 131

Webb, James E., 148–149, 153, 156, 157–158, 176–177, 178, 204, 210, 214, 322
Weddell, James, 75, 76, 77
Weddell Sea, 75, 80, 81
Wegener, Alfred Lothar, 93–94
Weightlessness, 159, 255, 258, 269, 302, 313–314
Weitz, Paul, J., 244, 246, 247, 248, 250
Welles, Orson, 355
Wells, H. G., 113, 330, 355
Welsh, Edward C., 183
Whelan, Joseph G., 112
Whipple, Fred L., 326, 327
White, Edward H., II, 184–186, 196
Wiesner, Jerome B., 137, 151
Wilkes, Charles, 74–75, 76, 77, 78
Wilkins, Sir Hubert, 89
Williams, Walter C., 163
Wilson, Charles, 131
Wilson, Dr. Edward A., 84, 85, 86, 95
Wolfe, John, 342–343, 347
Wolff, Lester L., 323
Women
    as astronauts, 171–172
    Viking, 7, 21
Worden, Alfred M., 228, 302
Wright, Charles Seymour, 87
Wyld, James, 116

Yegorov, Boris B., 182
Yeliseyev, Aleksey, 207, 222–223, 230
York, Herbert F., 141
Young, A. Thomas, 404
Young, John W., 183–184, 189–190, 208, 231, 232, 304

Zhukovsky, Nikolai E., 120
Ziegler, Ronald L., 217
Ziolkovsky, Konstantin Eduardovich, 113–114, 117, 118, 119, 275
Zond program, 200–201, 203, 204, 205, 223–224, 373
"Zot" gun, 185, 190